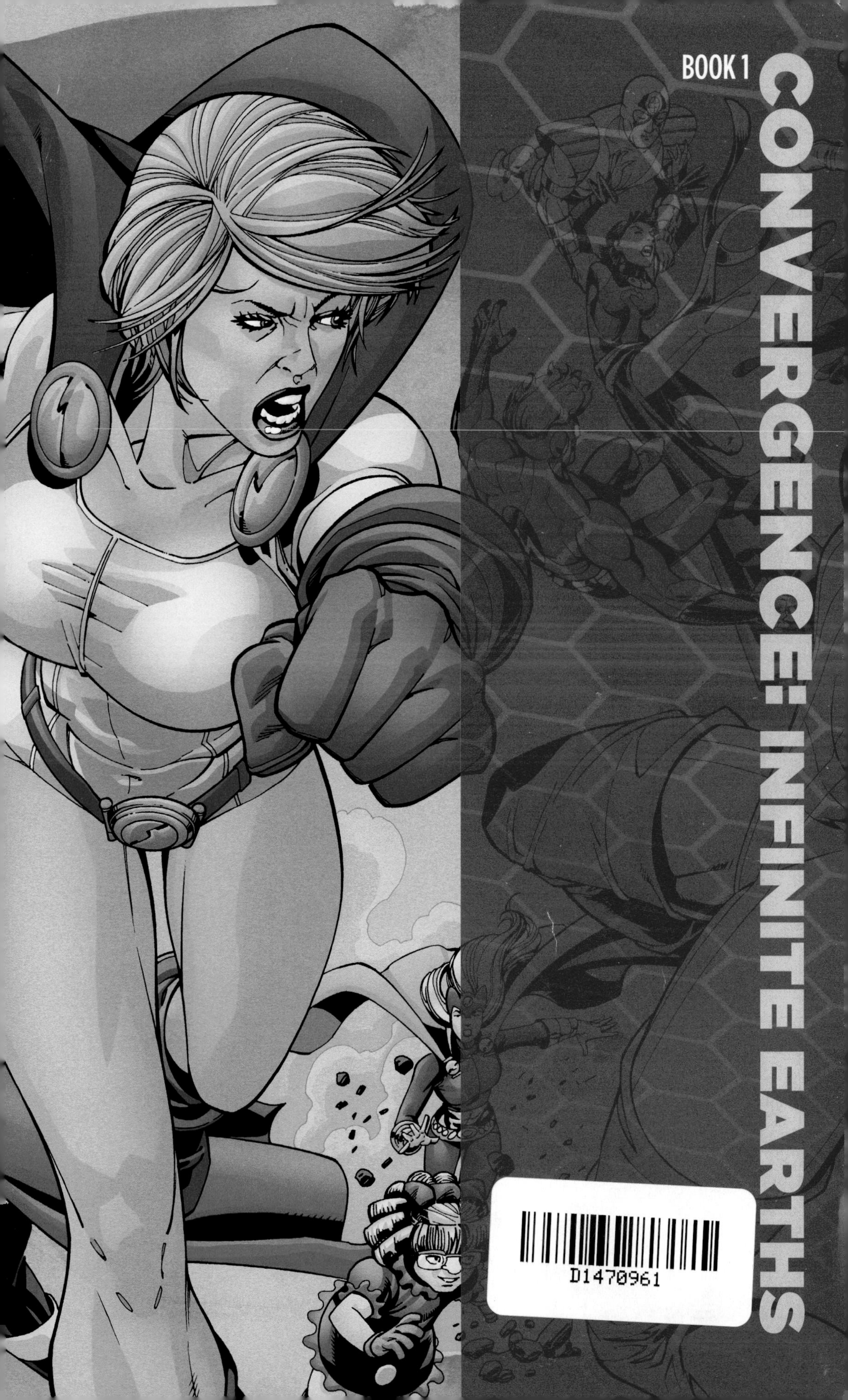
BOOK 1
CONVERGENCE: INFINITE EARTHS

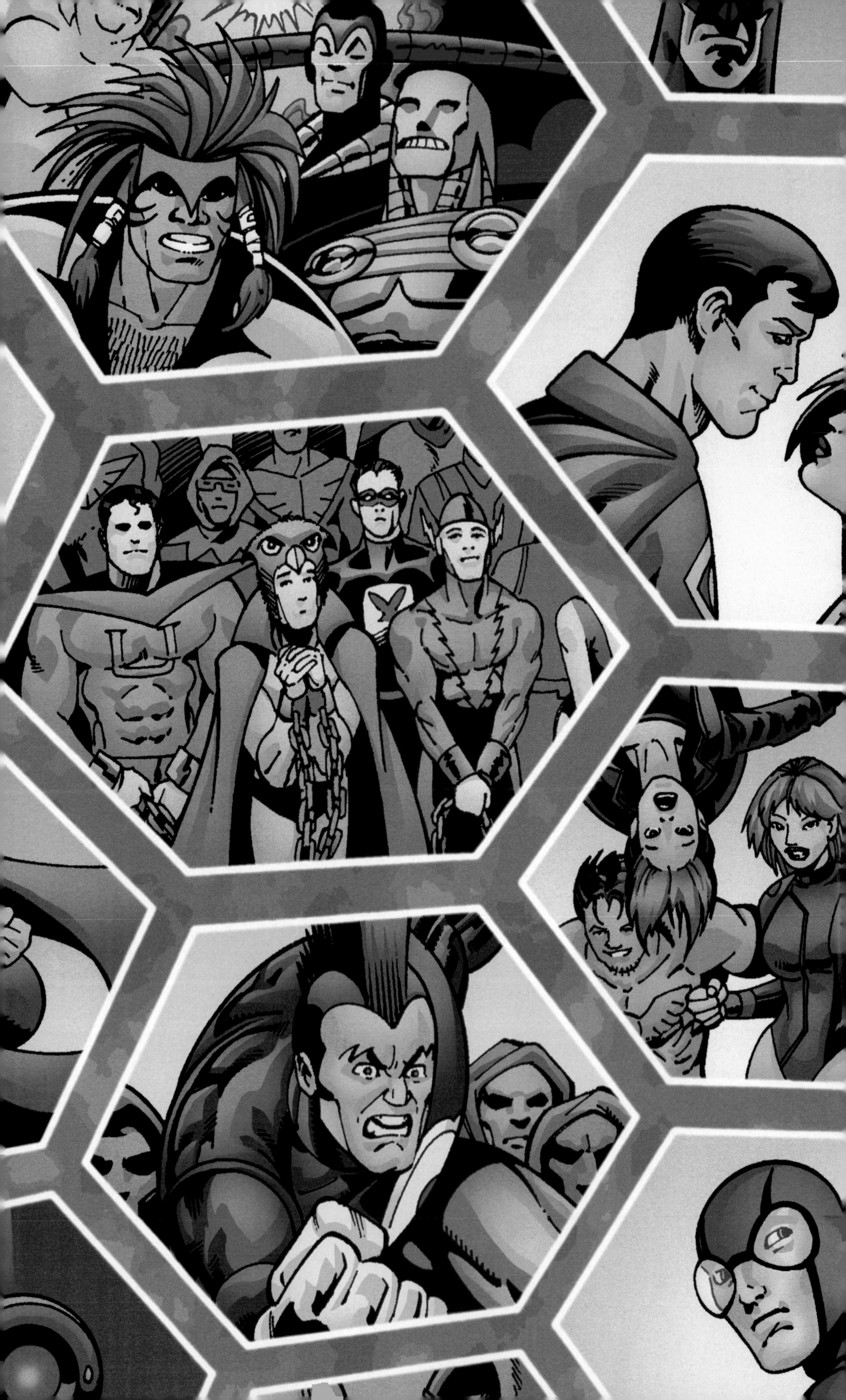

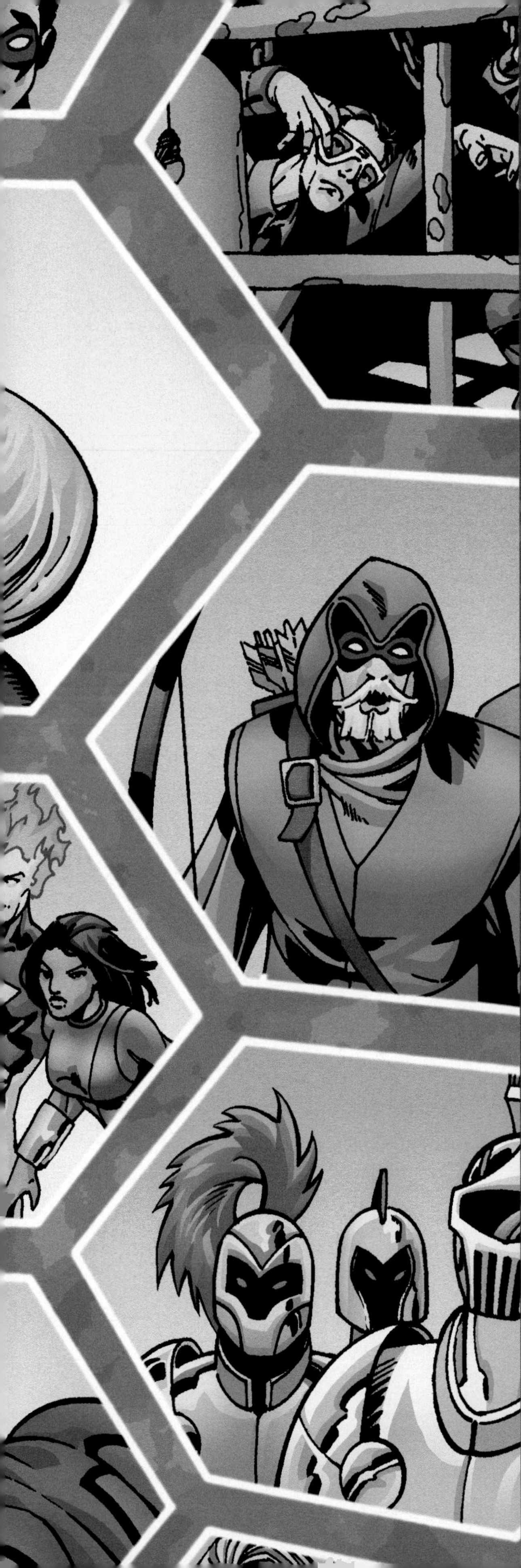

BOOK 1

CONVERGENCE: INFINITE EARTHS

COLLECTION COVER ARTIST
DAN PANOSIAN

SUPERMAN CREATED BY
JERRY SIEGEL & JOE SHUSTER
BY SPECIAL ARRANGEMENT WITH THE JERRY SIEGEL FAMILY

BATMAN CREATED BY
BOB KANE

INFINITY INC. CREATED BY
ROY THOMAS, JERRY ORDWAY AND MIKE MACHLAN

MARIE JAVINS Editor – Original Series
BRITTANY HOLZHERR MICHAEL KRAIGER Assistant Editors – Original Series
JEB WOODARD Group Editor – Collected Editions
LIZ ERICKSON Editor
DAMIAN RYLAND Publication Design

BOB HARRAS Senior VP – Editor-in-Chief, DC Comics

DIANE NELSON President
DAN DIDIO and JIM LEE Co-Publishers
GEOFF JOHNS Chief Creative Officer
AMIT DESAI Senior VP – Marketing & Global Franchise Management
NAIRI GARDINER Senior VP – Finance
SAM ADES VP – Digital Marketing
BOBBIE CHASE VP –Talent Development
MARK CHIARELLO Senior VP – Art, Design & Collected Editions
JOHN CUNNINGHAM VP – Content Strategy
ANNE DEPIES VP – Strategy Planning & Reporting
DON FALLETTI VP – Manufacturing Operations
LAWRENCE GANEM VP – Editorial Administration & Talent Relations
ALISON GILL Senior VP – Manufacturing & Operations
HANK KANALZ Senior VP – Editorial Strategy & Administration
JAY KOGAN VP – Legal Affairs
DEREK MADDALENA Senior VP – Sales & Business Development
JACK MAHAN VP – Business Affairs
DAN MIRON VP – Sales Planning & Trade Development
NICK NAPOLITANO VP – Manufacturing Administration
CAROL ROEDER VP – Marketing
EDDIE SCANNELL VP – Mass Account & Digital Sales
COURTNEY SIMMONS Senior VP – Publicity & Communications
JIM (SKI) SOKOLOWSKI VP – Comic Book Specialty & Newsstand Sales
SANDY YI Senior VP – Global Franchise Management

CONVERGENCE: INFINITE EARTHS BOOK 1

Originally published in single magazine form in CONVERGENCE ACTION COMICS 1-2, CONVERGENCE DETECTIVE COMICS 1-2, CONVERGENCE JUSTICE SOCIETY OF AMERICA 1-2, CONVERGENCE INFINITY INC. 1-2, CONVERGENCE WORLD'S FINEST 1-2 © 2015 DC Comics. All Rights Reserved. All characters, their distinctive likenesses and related elements featured in this publication are trademarks of DC Comics. The stories, characters and incidents featured in this publication are entirely fictional. DC Comics does not read or accept unsolicited ideas, stories or artwork.

DC Comics, 4000 Warner Blvd., Burbank, CA 91522
A Warner Bros. Entertainment Company.
Printed by RR Donnelley, Salem, VA, USA. 9/25/15. First Printing.
ISBN: 978-1-4012-5837-5

Library of Congress Cataloging-in-Publication Data

Ordway, Jerry.
Convergence: Infinite Earths book one / Jerry Ordway, Ben Caldwell, Paul Levitz.
pages cm
ISBN 978-1-4012-5837-5
1. Graphic novels. I. Caldwell, Ben, 1973- II. Levitz, Paul. III. Title.
PN6728.C676O73 2015
741.5'973—dc23
2015011796

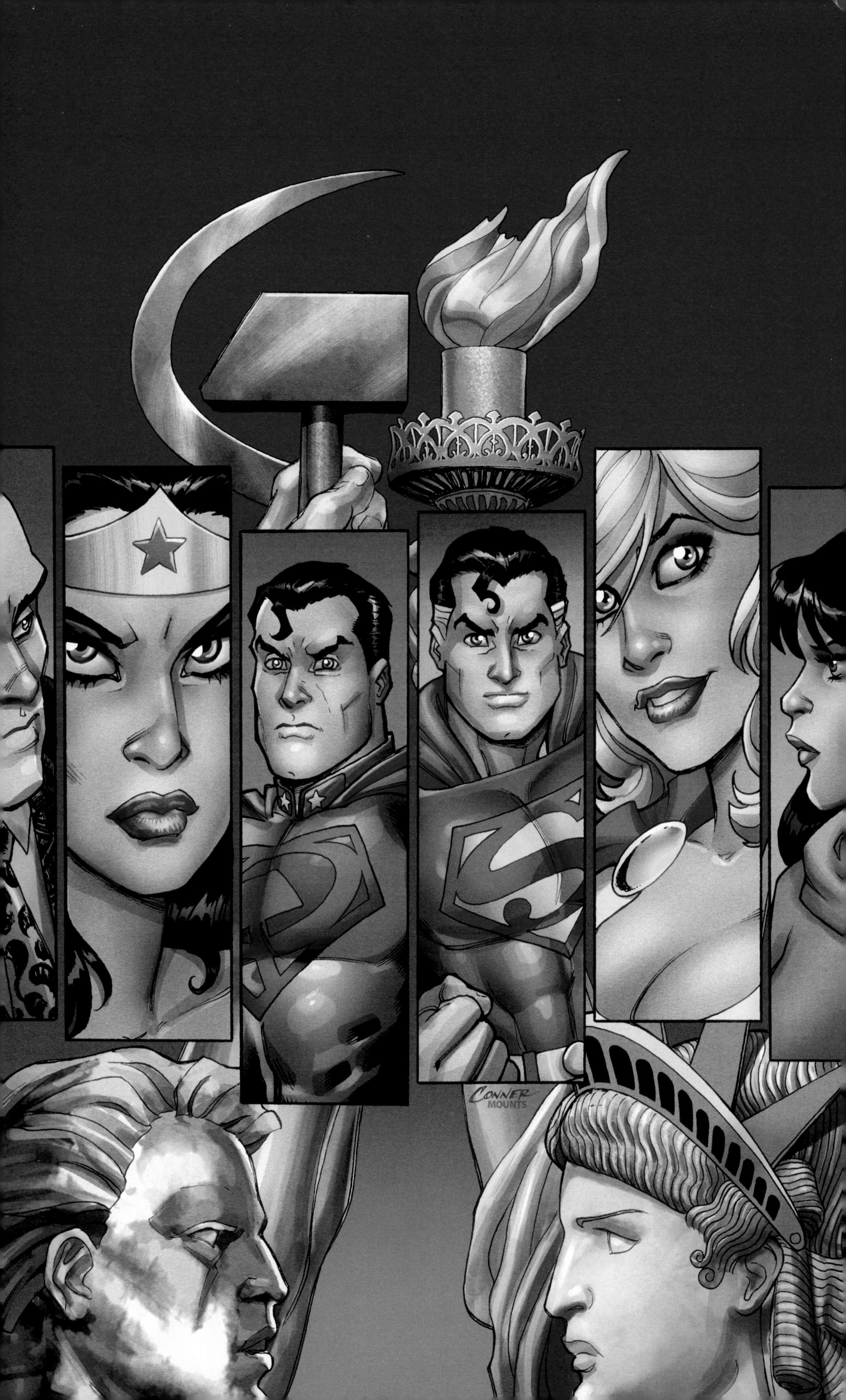
CONNER
MOUNTS

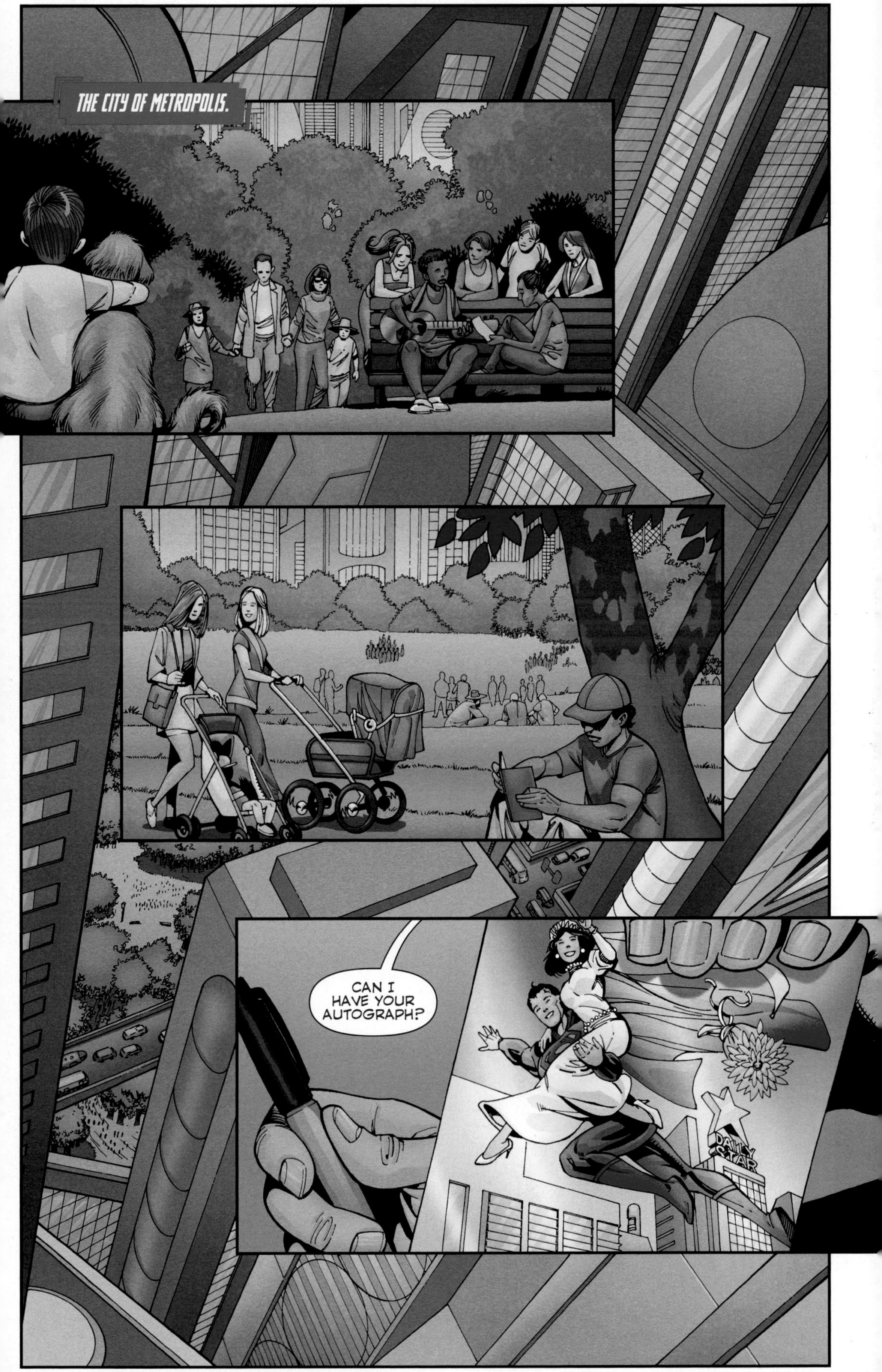
THE CITY OF METROPOLIS.
CAN I HAVE YOUR AUTOGRAPH?
DAILY STAR

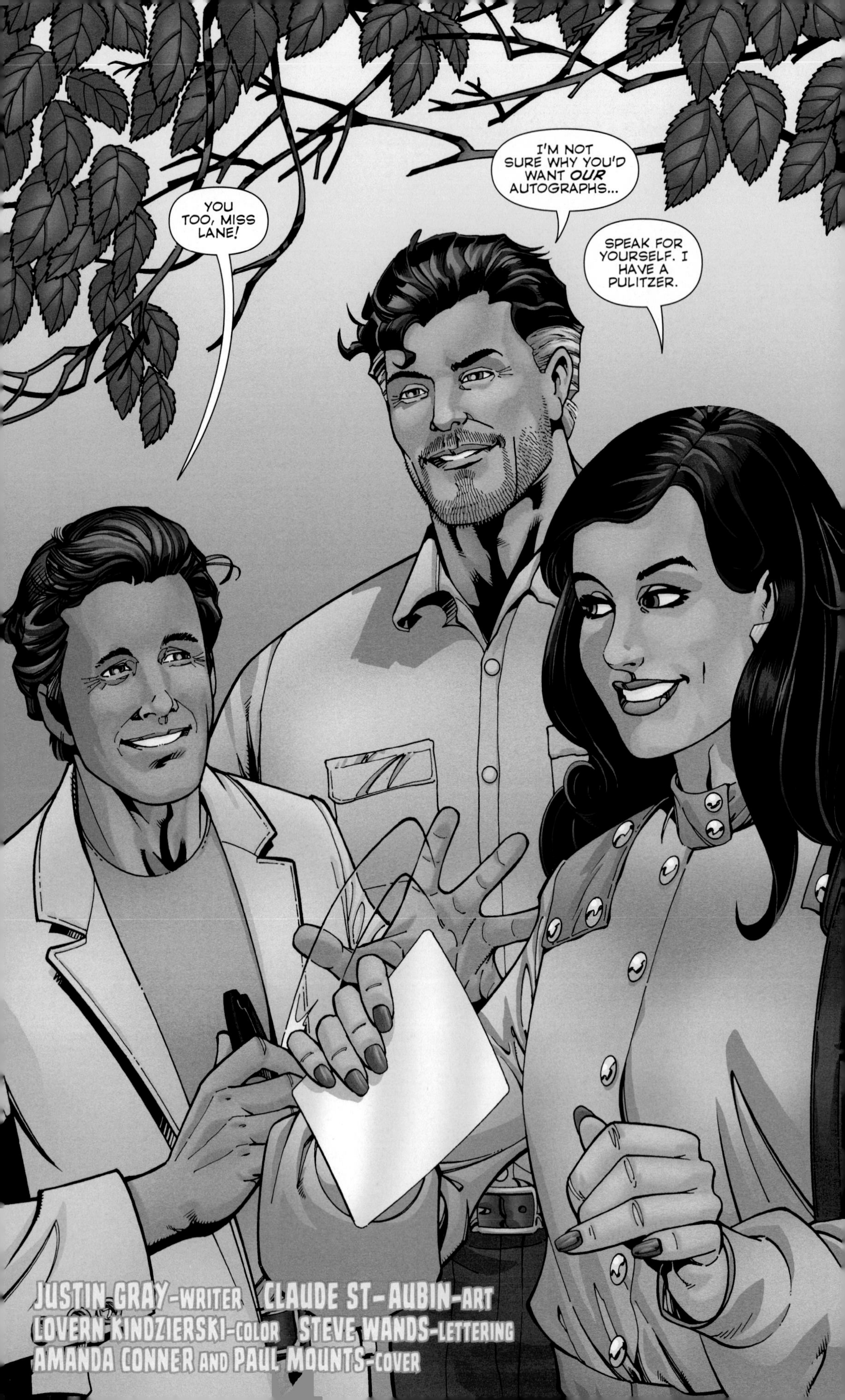
YOU TOO, MISS LANE!
I'M NOT SURE WHY YOU'D WANT OUR AUTOGRAPHS...
SPEAK FOR YOURSELF. I HAVE A PULITZER.
JUSTIN GRAY-WRITER CLAUDE ST-AUBIN-ART
LOVERN KINDZIERSKI-COLOR STEVE WANDS-LETTERING
AMANDA CONNER AND PAUL MOUNTS-COVER

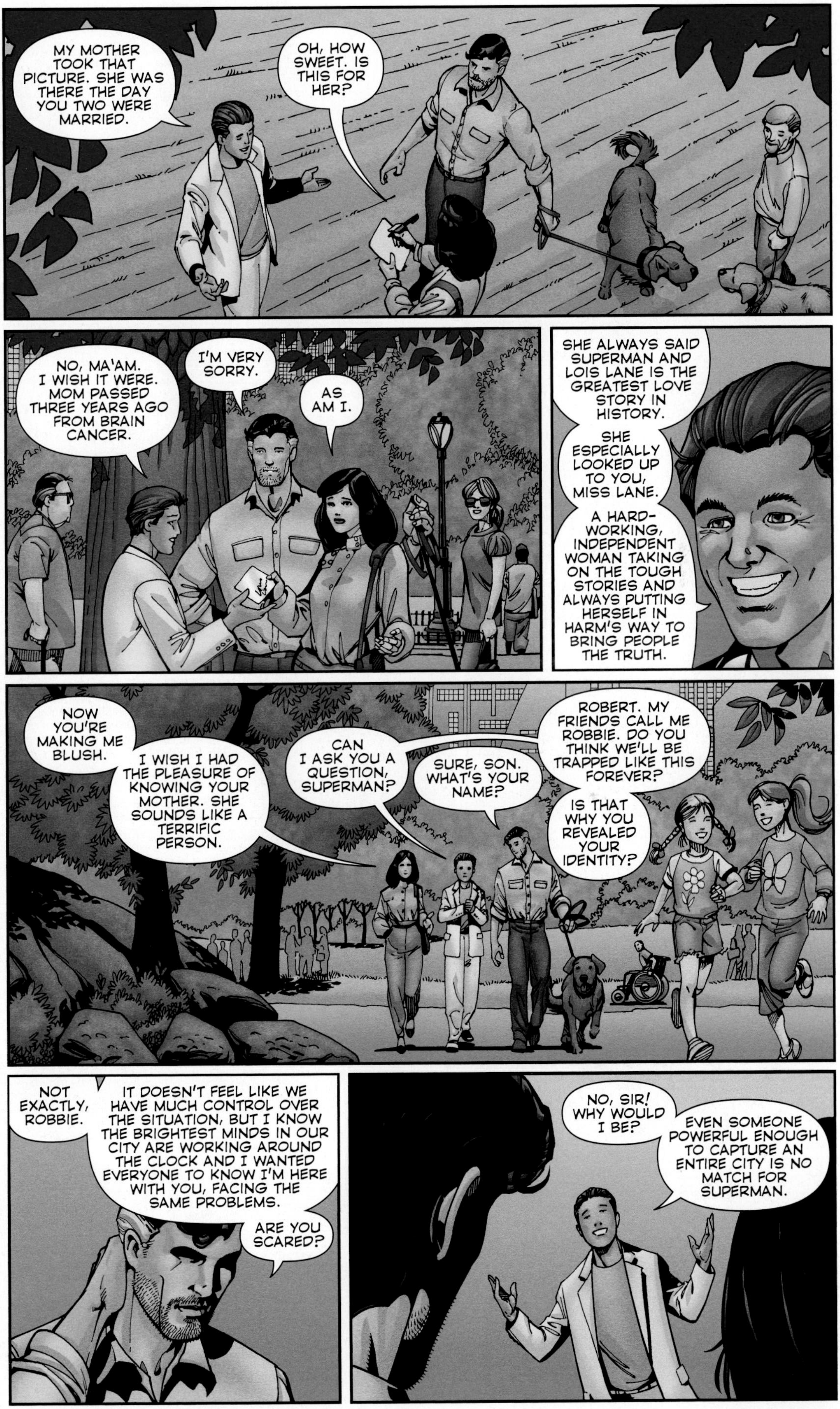

MY MOTHER TOOK THAT PICTURE. SHE WAS THERE THE DAY YOU TWO WERE MARRIED.
OH, HOW SWEET. IS THIS FOR HER?
NO, MA'AM. I WISH IT WERE. MOM PASSED THREE YEARS AGO FROM BRAIN CANCER.
I'M VERY SORRY.
AS AM I.
SHE ALWAYS SAID SUPERMAN AND LOIS LANE IS THE GREATEST LOVE STORY IN HISTORY.
SHE ESPECIALLY LOOKED UP TO YOU, MISS LANE.
A HARD-WORKING, INDEPENDENT WOMAN TAKING ON THE TOUGH STORIES AND ALWAYS PUTTING HERSELF IN HARM'S WAY TO BRING PEOPLE THE TRUTH.
NOW YOU'RE MAKING ME BLUSH.
I WISH I HAD THE PLEASURE OF KNOWING YOUR MOTHER. SHE SOUNDS LIKE A TERRIFIC PERSON.
CAN I ASK YOU A QUESTION, SUPERMAN?
SURE, SON. WHAT'S YOUR NAME?
ROBERT. MY FRIENDS CALL ME ROBBIE. DO YOU THINK WE'LL BE TRAPPED LIKE THIS FOREVER?
IS THAT WHY YOU REVEALED YOUR IDENTITY?
NOT EXACTLY, ROBBIE.
IT DOESN'T FEEL LIKE WE HAVE MUCH CONTROL OVER THE SITUATION, BUT I KNOW THE BRIGHTEST MINDS IN OUR CITY ARE WORKING AROUND THE CLOCK AND I WANTED EVERYONE TO KNOW I'M HERE WITH YOU, FACING THE SAME PROBLEMS.
ARE YOU SCARED?
NO, SIR! WHY WOULD I BE?
EVEN SOMEONE POWERFUL ENOUGH TO CAPTURE AN ENTIRE CITY IS NO MATCH FOR SUPERMAN.

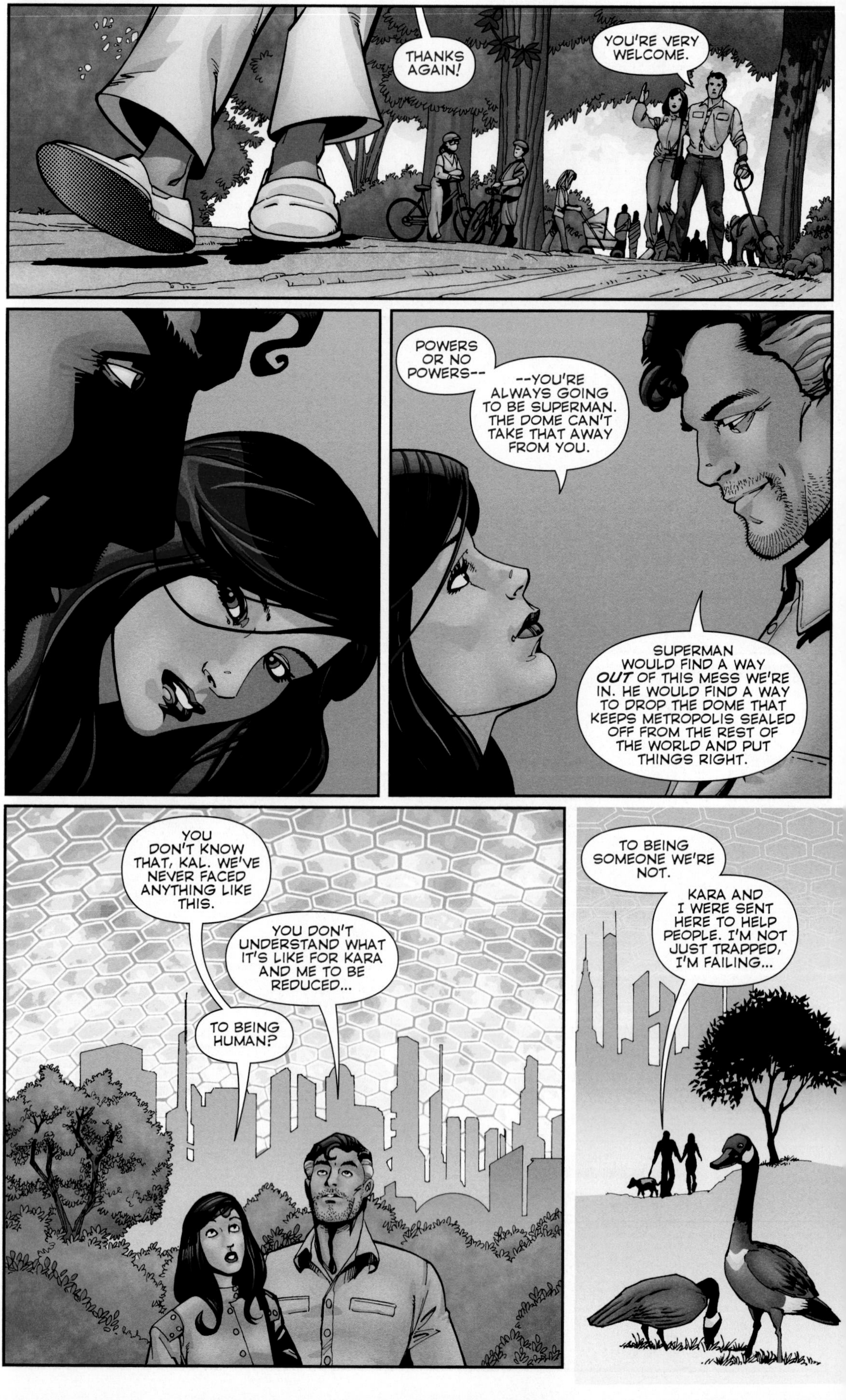
THANKS AGAIN!
YOU'RE VERY WELCOME.
POWERS OR NO POWERS--
--YOU'RE ALWAYS GOING TO BE SUPERMAN. THE DOME CAN'T TAKE THAT AWAY FROM YOU.
SUPERMAN WOULD FIND A WAY *OUT* OF THIS MESS WE'RE IN. HE WOULD FIND A WAY TO DROP THE DOME THAT KEEPS METROPOLIS SEALED OFF FROM THE REST OF THE WORLD AND PUT THINGS RIGHT.
YOU DON'T KNOW THAT, KAL. WE'VE NEVER FACED ANYTHING LIKE THIS.
YOU DON'T UNDERSTAND WHAT IT'S LIKE FOR KARA AND ME TO BE REDUCED...
TO BEING HUMAN?
TO BEING SOMEONE WE'RE NOT.
KARA AND I WERE SENT HERE TO HELP PEOPLE. I'M NOT JUST TRAPPED, I'M FAILING...

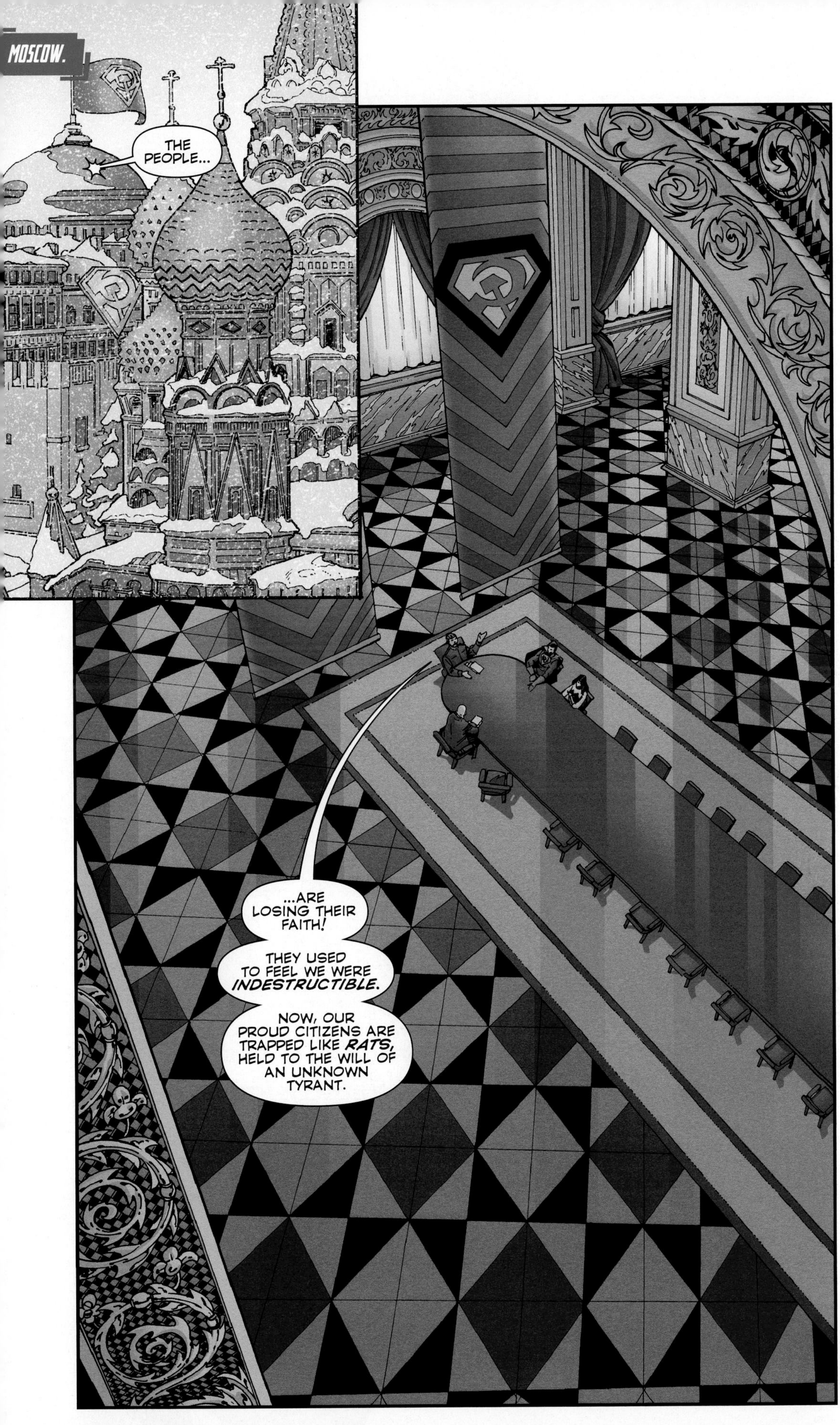
MOSCOW.
THE PEOPLE...
...ARE LOSING THEIR FAITH!
THEY USED TO FEEL WE WERE INDESTRUCTIBLE.
NOW, OUR PROUD CITIZENS ARE TRAPPED LIKE RATS, HELD TO THE WILL OF AN UNKNOWN TYRANT.

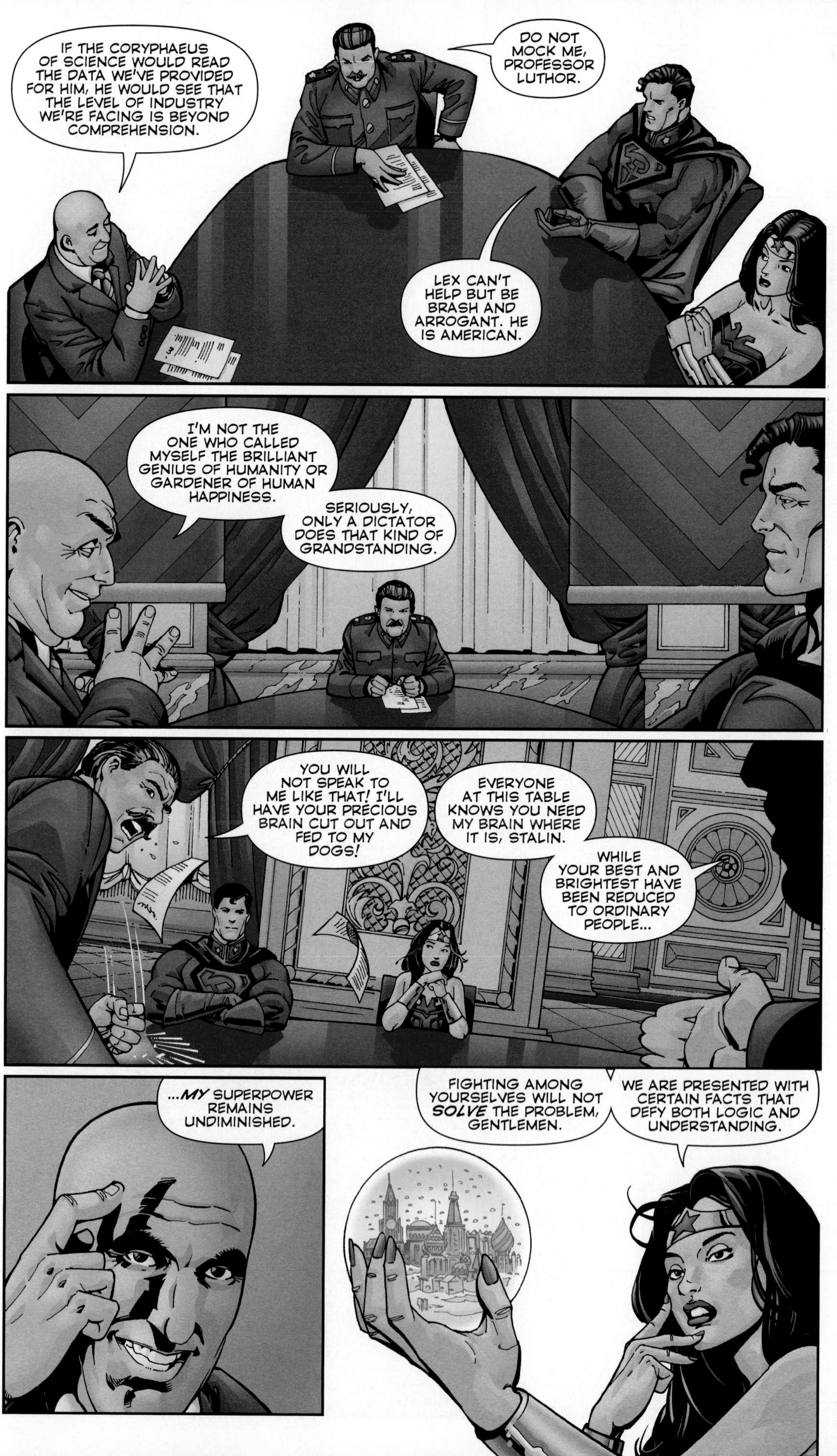
IF THE CORYPHAEUS OF SCIENCE WOULD READ THE DATA WE'VE PROVIDED FOR HIM, HE WOULD SEE THAT THE LEVEL OF INDUSTRY WE'RE FACING IS BEYOND COMPREHENSION.
DO NOT MOCK ME, PROFESSOR LUTHOR.
LEX CAN'T HELP BUT BE BRASH AND ARROGANT. HE IS AMERICAN.
I'M NOT THE ONE WHO CALLED MYSELF THE BRILLIANT GENIUS OF HUMANITY OR GARDENER OF HUMAN HAPPINESS.
SERIOUSLY, ONLY A DICTATOR DOES THAT KIND OF GRANDSTANDING.
YOU WILL NOT SPEAK TO ME LIKE THAT! I'LL HAVE YOUR PRECIOUS BRAIN CUT OUT AND FED TO MY DOGS!
EVERYONE AT THIS TABLE KNOWS YOU NEED MY BRAIN WHERE IT IS, STALIN.
WHILE YOUR BEST AND BRIGHTEST HAVE BEEN REDUCED TO ORDINARY PEOPLE...
...*MY* SUPERPOWER REMAINS UNDIMINISHED.
FIGHTING AMONG YOURSELVES WILL NOT *SOLVE* THE PROBLEM, GENTLEMEN.
WE ARE PRESENTED WITH CERTAIN FACTS THAT DEFY BOTH LOGIC AND UNDERSTANDING.

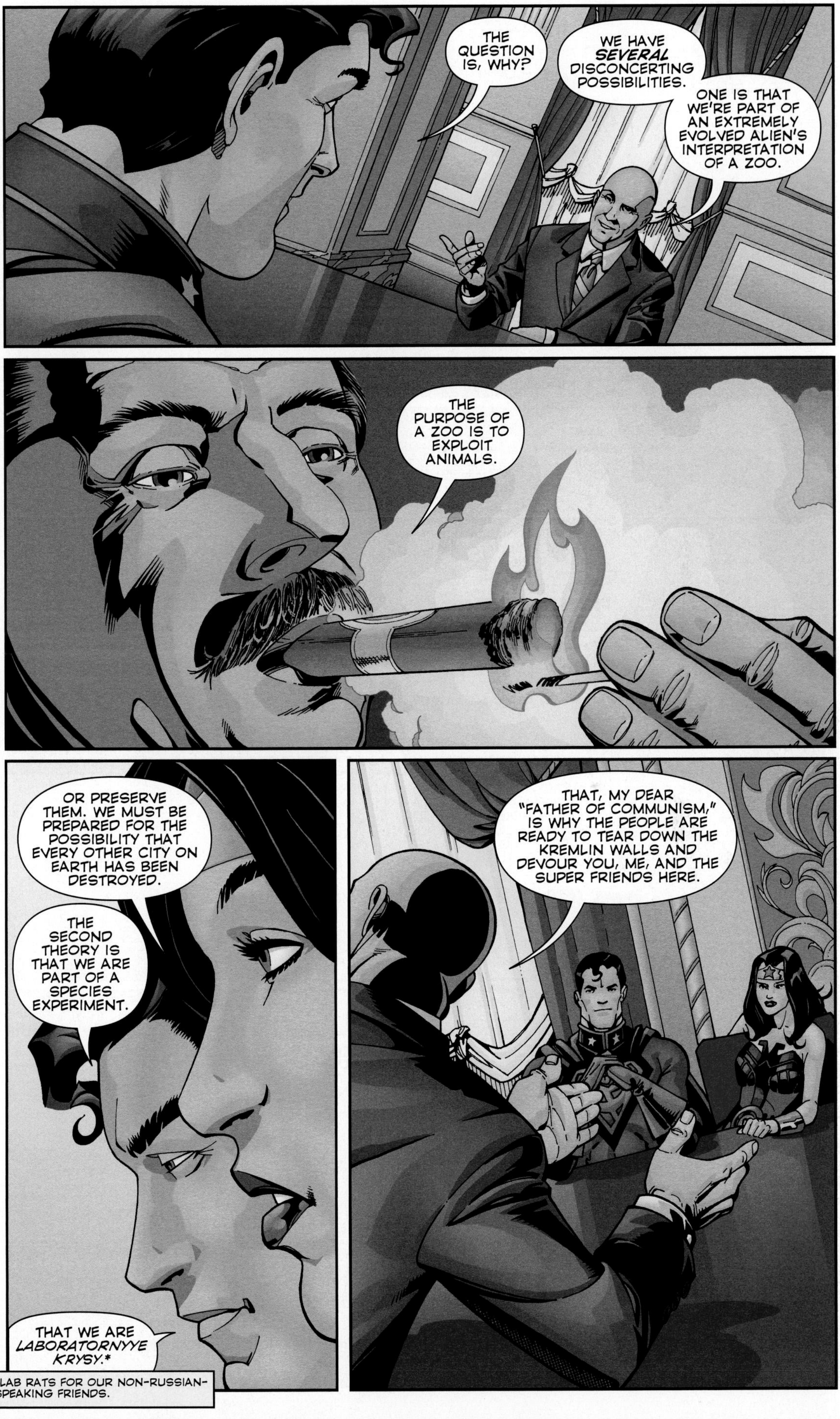
THE QUESTION IS, WHY?
WE HAVE *SEVERAL* DISCONCERTING POSSIBILITIES.
ONE IS THAT WE'RE PART OF AN EXTREMELY EVOLVED ALIEN'S INTERPRETATION OF A ZOO.
THE PURPOSE OF A ZOO IS TO EXPLOIT ANIMALS.
OR PRESERVE THEM. WE MUST BE PREPARED FOR THE POSSIBILITY THAT EVERY OTHER CITY ON EARTH HAS BEEN DESTROYED.
THE SECOND THEORY IS THAT WE ARE PART OF A SPECIES EXPERIMENT.
THAT WE ARE *LABORATORNYYE KRYSY.**
*LAB RATS FOR OUR NON-RUSSIAN-SPEAKING FRIENDS.
THAT, MY DEAR "FATHER OF COMMUNISM," IS WHY THE PEOPLE ARE READY TO TEAR DOWN THE KREMLIN WALLS AND DEVOUR YOU, ME, AND THE SUPER FRIENDS HERE.

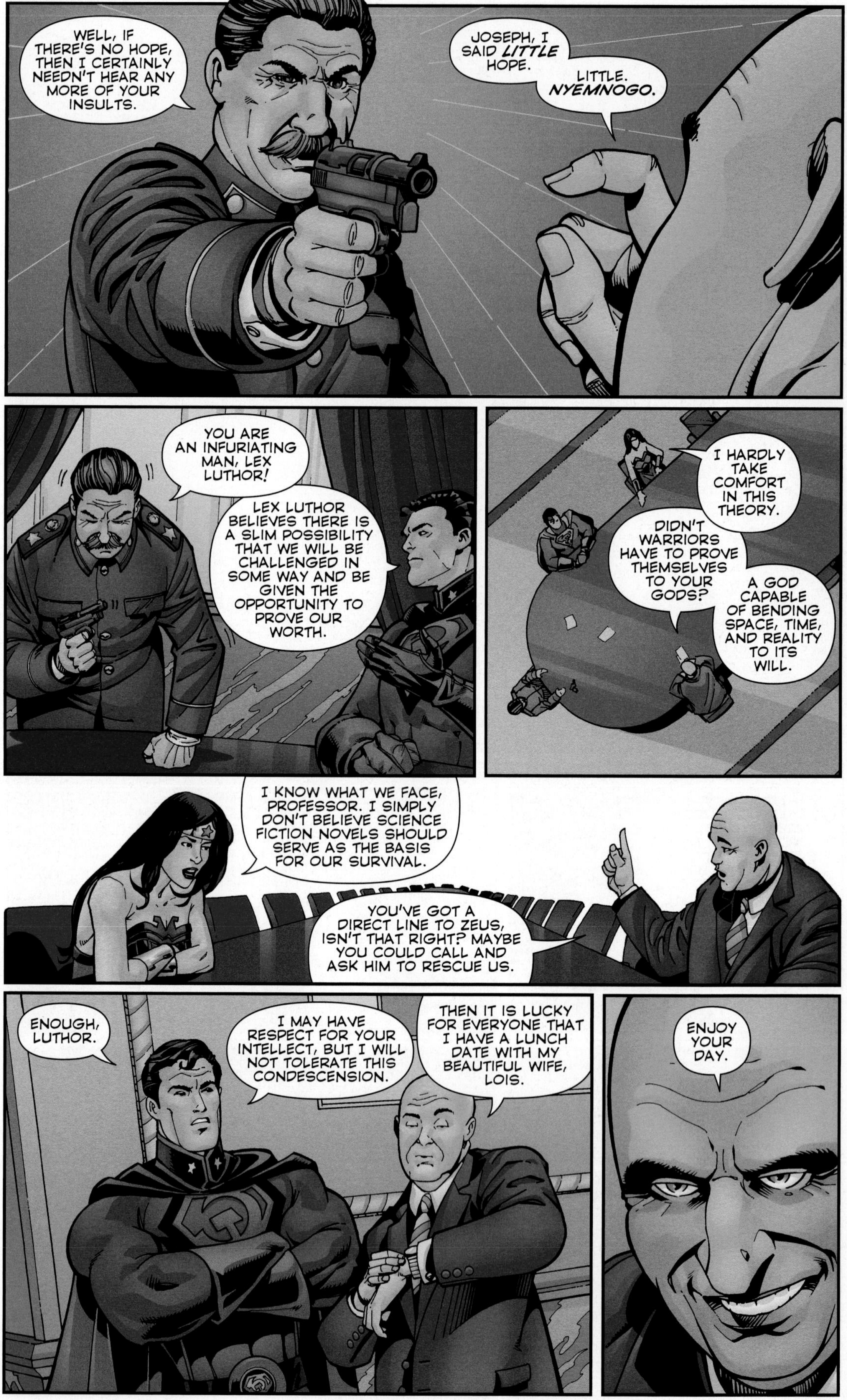
WELL, IF THERE'S NO HOPE, THEN I CERTAINLY NEEDN'T HEAR ANY MORE OF YOUR INSULTS.
JOSEPH, I SAID *LITTLE* HOPE.
LITTLE. *NYEMNOGO.*
YOU ARE AN INFURIATING MAN, LEX LUTHOR!
LEX LUTHOR BELIEVES THERE IS A SLIM POSSIBILITY THAT WE WILL BE CHALLENGED IN SOME WAY AND BE GIVEN THE OPPORTUNITY TO PROVE OUR WORTH.
I HARDLY TAKE COMFORT IN THIS THEORY.
DIDN'T WARRIORS HAVE TO PROVE THEMSELVES TO YOUR GODS?
A GOD CAPABLE OF BENDING SPACE, TIME, AND REALITY TO ITS WILL.
I KNOW WHAT WE FACE, PROFESSOR. I SIMPLY DON'T BELIEVE SCIENCE FICTION NOVELS SHOULD SERVE AS THE BASIS FOR OUR SURVIVAL.
YOU'VE GOT A DIRECT LINE TO ZEUS, ISN'T THAT RIGHT? MAYBE YOU COULD CALL AND ASK HIM TO RESCUE US.
ENOUGH, LUTHOR.
I MAY HAVE RESPECT FOR YOUR INTELLECT, BUT I WILL NOT TOLERATE THIS CONDESCENSION.
THEN IT IS LUCKY FOR EVERYONE THAT I HAVE A LUNCH DATE WITH MY BEAUTIFUL WIFE, LOIS.
ENJOY YOUR DAY.

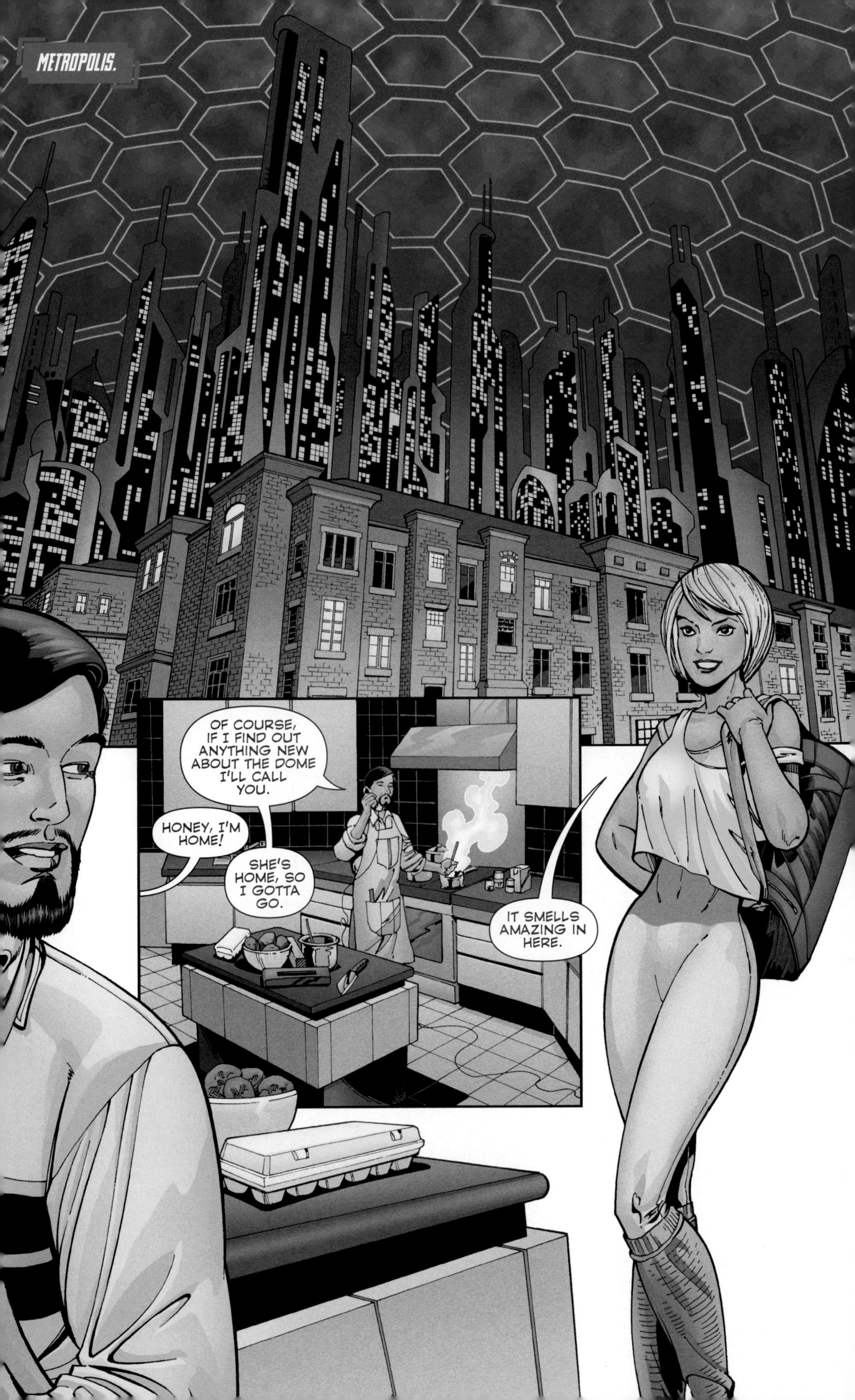
METROPOLIS.
HONEY, I'M HOME!
OF COURSE, IF I FIND OUT ANYTHING NEW ABOUT THE DOME I'LL CALL YOU.
SHE'S HOME, SO I GOTTA GO.
IT SMELLS AMAZING IN HERE.

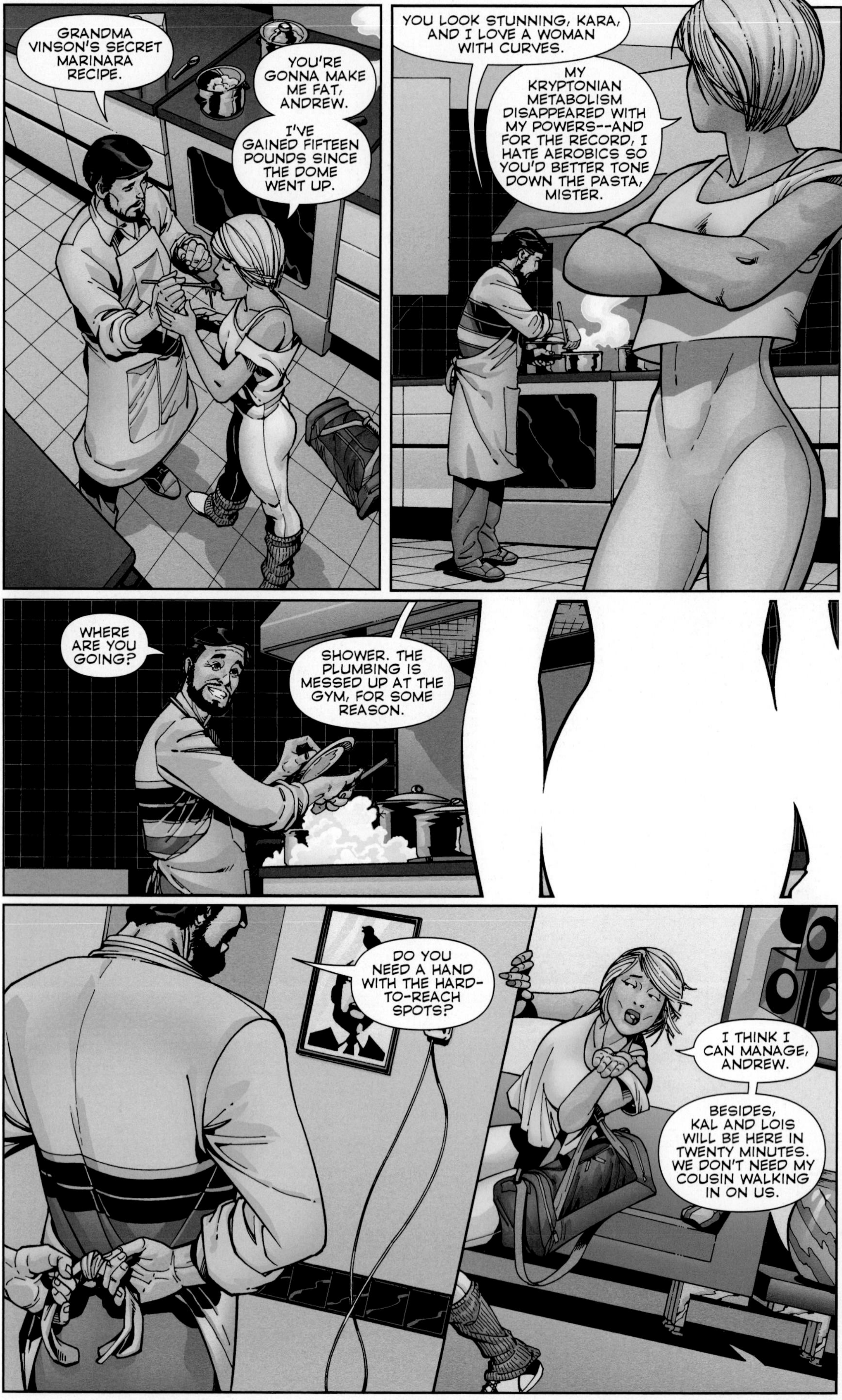
GRANDMA VINSON'S SECRET MARINARA RECIPE.
YOU'RE GONNA MAKE ME FAT, ANDREW.
I'VE GAINED FIFTEEN POUNDS SINCE THE DOME WENT UP.
YOU LOOK STUNNING, KARA, AND I LOVE A WOMAN WITH CURVES.
MY KRYPTONIAN METABAOLISM DISAPPEARED WITH MY POWERS--AND FOR THE RECORD, I HATE AEROBICS SO YOU'D BETTER TONE DOWN THE PASTA, MISTER.
WHERE ARE YOU GOING?
SHOWER. THE PLUMBING IS MESSED UP AT THE GYM, FOR SOME REASON.
DO YOU NEED A HAND WITH THE HARD-TO-REACH SPOTS?
I THINK I CAN MANAGE, ANDREW.
BESIDES, KAL AND LOIS WILL BE HERE IN TWENTY MINUTES. WE DON'T NEED MY COUSIN WALKING IN ON US.

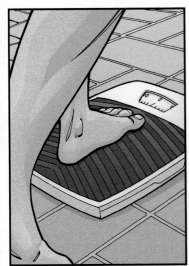

Ugh!

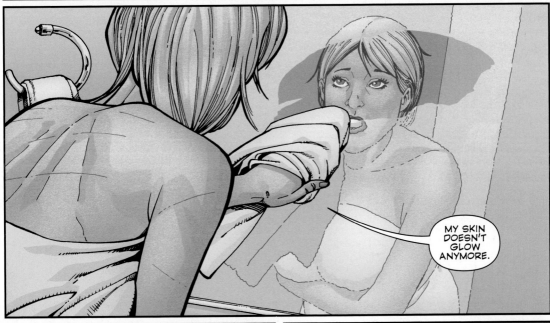

MY SKIN
DOESN'T
GLOW
ANYMORE.

I HAVE
BAGS UNDER
MY EYES. I
GET TIRED.

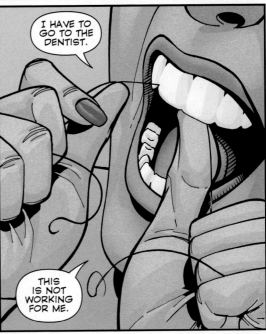

I HAVE TO
GO TO THE
DENTIST.

THIS
IS NOT
WORKING
FOR ME.

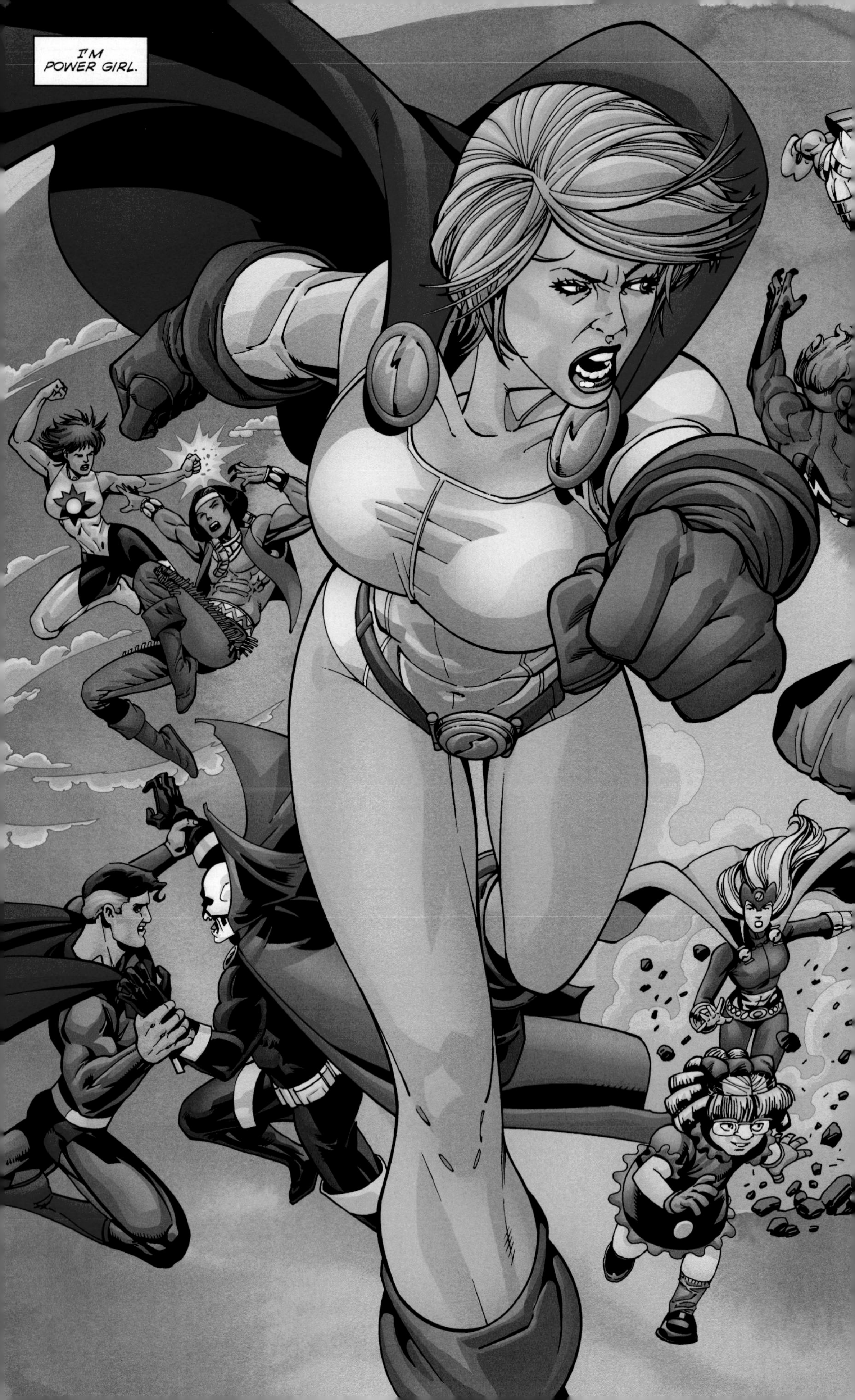
I'M POWER GIRL.

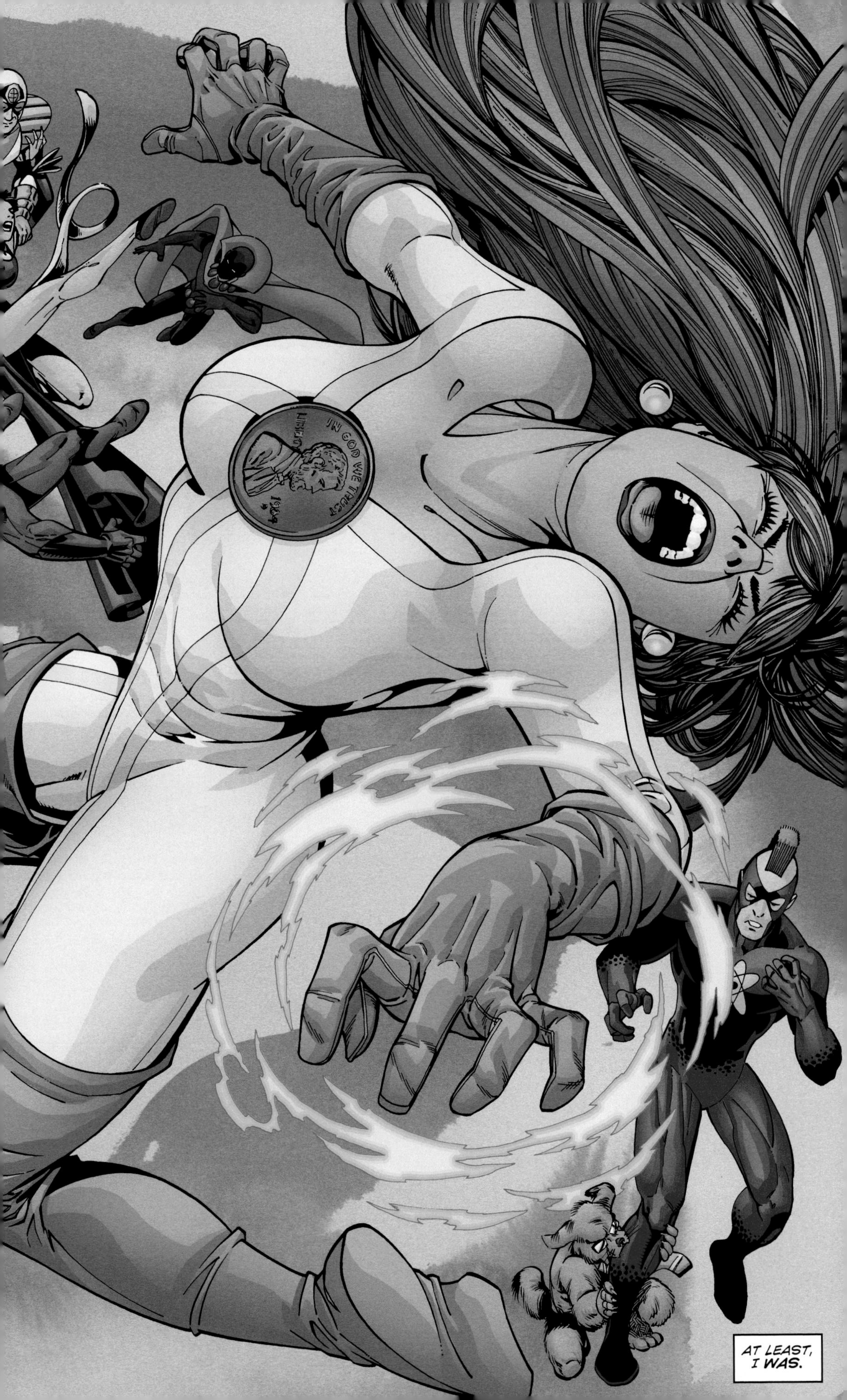
IN GOD WE TRUST
LIBERTY
AT LEAST, I WAS.

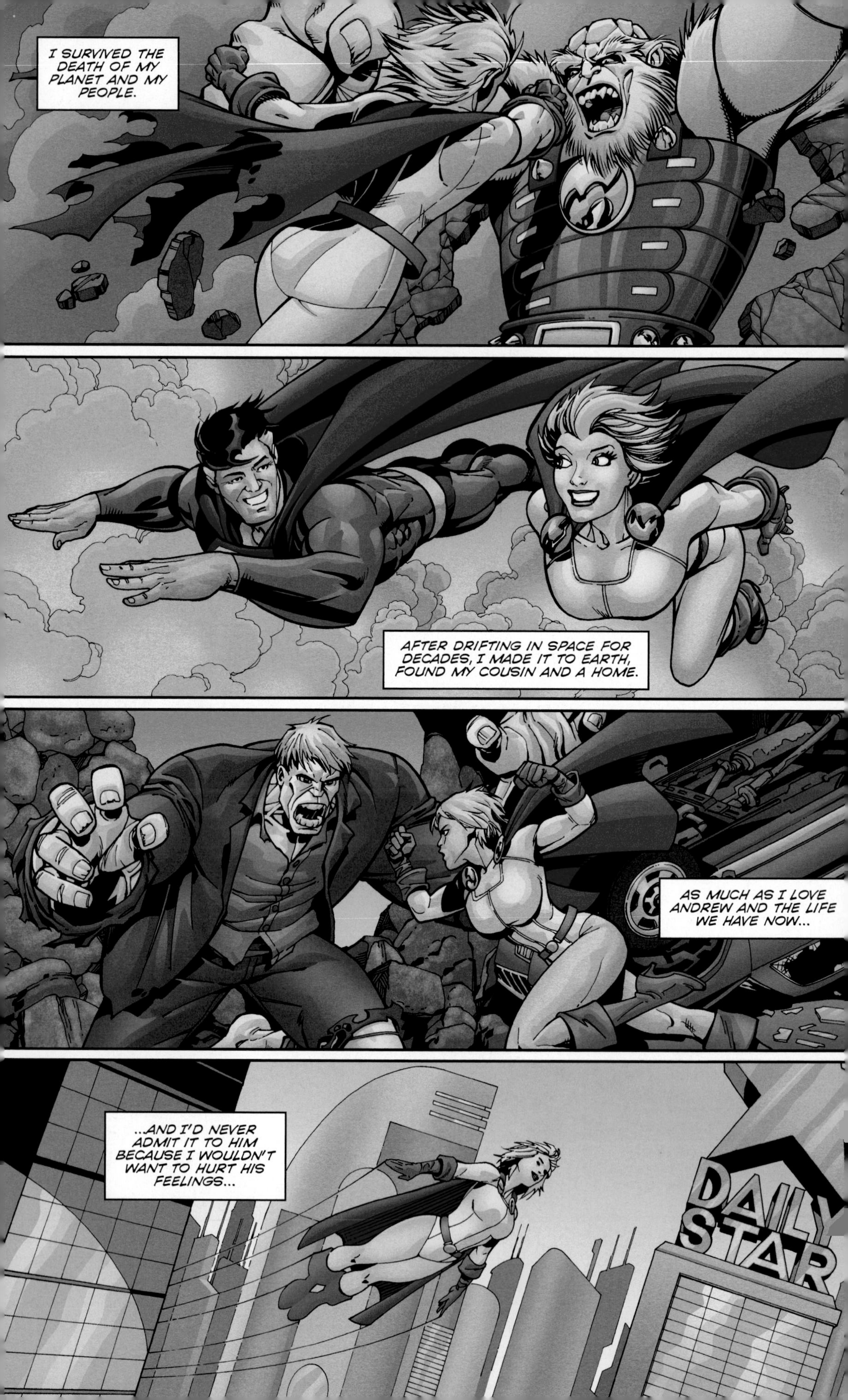
I SURVIVED THE DEATH OF MY PLANET AND MY PEOPLE.
AFTER DRIFTING IN SPACE FOR DECADES, I MADE IT TO EARTH, FOUND MY COUSIN AND A HOME.
AS MUCH AS I LOVE ANDREW AND THE LIFE WE HAVE NOW...
...AND I'D NEVER ADMIT IT TO HIM BECAUSE I WOULDN'T WANT TO HURT HIS FEELINGS...
DAILY STAR

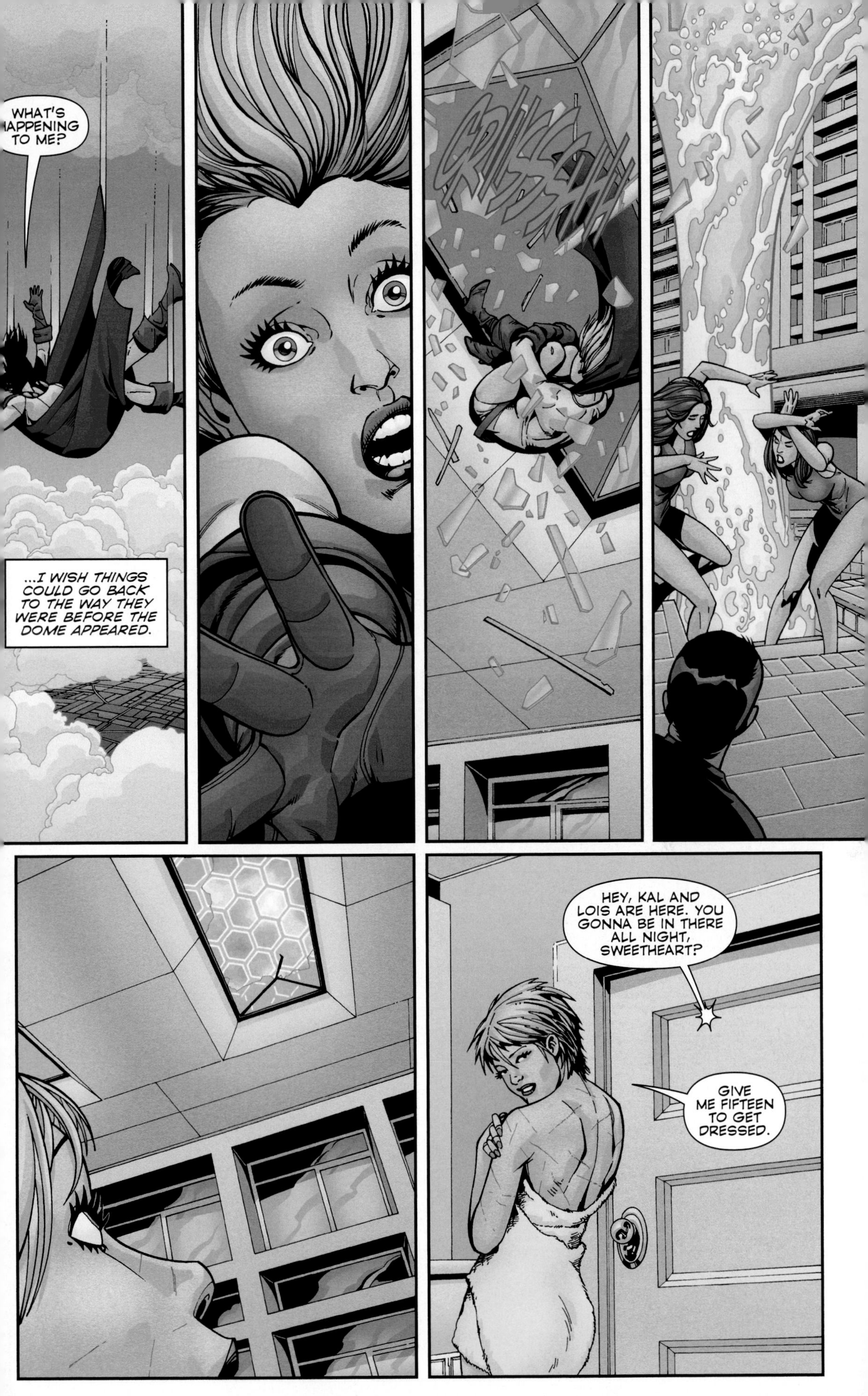
WHAT'S HAPPENING TO ME?
...I WISH THINGS COULD GO BACK TO THE WAY THEY WERE BEFORE THE DOME APPEARED.
CRSSHH
HEY, KAL AND LOIS ARE HERE. YOU GONNA BE IN THERE ALL NIGHT, SWEETHEART?
GIVE ME FIFTEEN TO GET DRESSED.

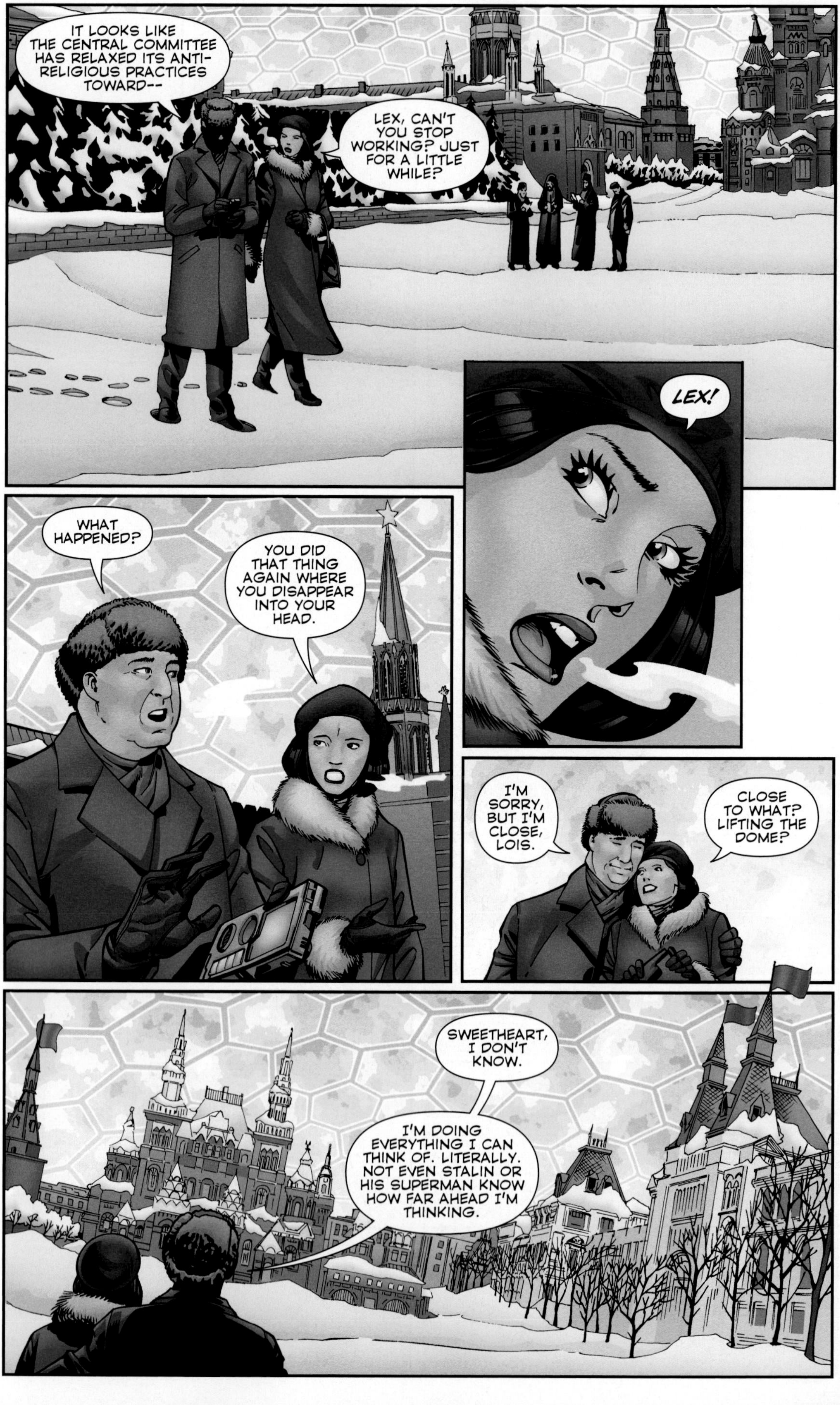
IT LOOKS LIKE THE CENTRAL COMMITTEE HAS RELAXED ITS ANTI-RELIGIOUS PRACTICES TOWARD--
LEX, CAN'T YOU STOP WORKING? JUST FOR A LITTLE WHILE?
LEX!
WHAT HAPPENED?
YOU DID THAT THING AGAIN WHERE YOU DISAPPEAR INTO YOUR HEAD.
I'M SORRY, BUT I'M CLOSE, LOIS.
CLOSE TO WHAT? LIFTING THE DOME?
SWEETHEART, I DON'T KNOW.
I'M DOING EVERYTHING I CAN THINK OF. LITERALLY. NOT EVEN STALIN OR HIS SUPERMAN KNOW HOW FAR AHEAD I'M THINKING.

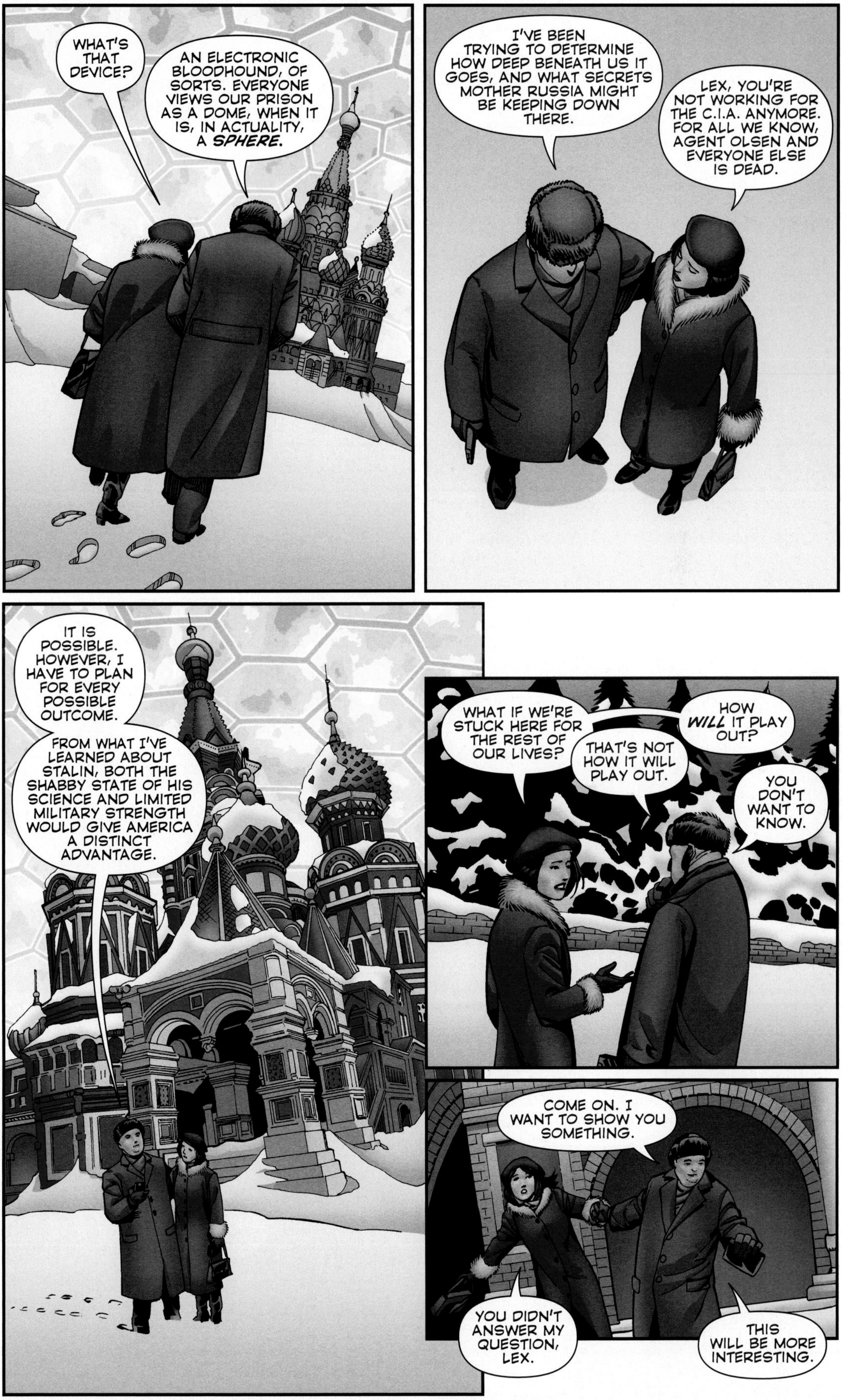
WHAT'S THAT DEVICE?
AN ELECTRONIC BLOODHOUND, OF SORTS. EVERYONE VIEWS OUR PRISON AS A DOME, WHEN IT IS, IN ACTUALITY, A SPHERE.
I'VE BEEN TRYING TO DETERMINE HOW DEEP BENEATH US IT GOES, AND WHAT SECRETS MOTHER RUSSIA MIGHT BE KEEPING DOWN THERE.
LEX, YOU'RE NOT WORKING FOR THE C.I.A. ANYMORE. FOR ALL WE KNOW, AGENT OLSEN AND EVERYONE ELSE IS DEAD.
IT IS POSSIBLE. HOWEVER, I HAVE TO PLAN FOR EVERY POSSIBLE OUTCOME.
FROM WHAT I'VE LEARNED ABOUT STALIN, BOTH THE SHABBY STATE OF HIS SCIENCE AND LIMITED MILITARY STRENGTH WOULD GIVE AMERICA A DISTINCT ADVANTAGE.
WHAT IF WE'RE STUCK HERE FOR THE REST OF OUR LIVES?
THAT'S NOT HOW IT WILL PLAY OUT.
HOW WILL IT PLAY OUT?
YOU DON'T WANT TO KNOW.
COME ON. I WANT TO SHOW YOU SOMETHING.
YOU DIDN'T ANSWER MY QUESTION, LEX.
THIS WILL BE MORE INTERESTING.

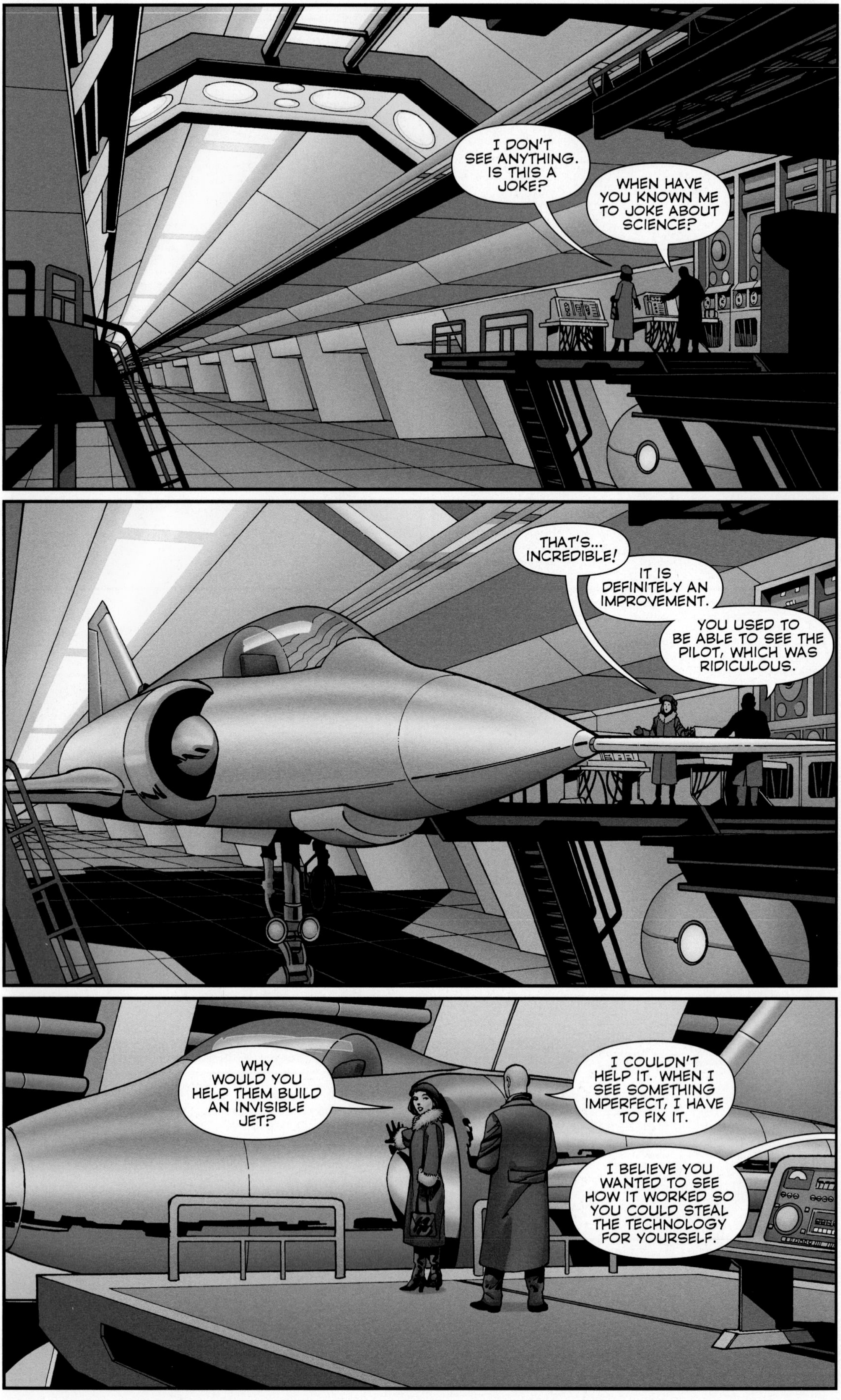
I DON'T SEE ANYTHING. IS THIS A JOKE?
WHEN HAVE YOU KNOWN ME TO JOKE ABOUT SCIENCE?
THAT'S... INCREDIBLE!
IT IS DEFINITELY AN IMPROVEMENT.
YOU USED TO BE ABLE TO SEE THE PILOT, WHICH WAS RIDICULOUS.
WHY WOULD YOU HELP THEM BUILD AN INVISIBLE JET?
I COULDN'T HELP IT. WHEN I SEE SOMETHING IMPERFECT, I HAVE TO FIX IT.
I BELIEVE YOU WANTED TO SEE HOW IT WORKED SO YOU COULD STEAL THE TECHNOLOGY FOR YOURSELF.

WHAT A HEINOUS ACCUSATION.
YOU HAVE TO STOP ANTAGONIZING STALIN.
LEX, YOU DIDN'T!
HE'S A DICTATOR AND A TERRIFIED OLD MAN WHO SHOULD WORRY MORE ABOUT HIS SON, PYOTR.
THAT BOY WANTS HIS FATHER'S JOB IN THE WORST WAY. ANYONE CAN SEE IT.
I CAME HERE TO WARN YOU THAT TODAY WAS THE LAST TIME STALIN IS GOING TO TOLERATE YOUR DISRESPECT.
I WILL NOT BE ABLE TO HELP YOU AGAIN.

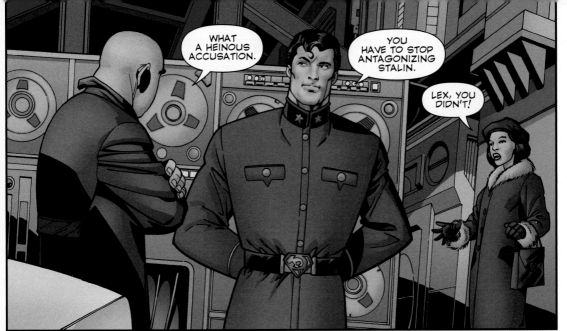

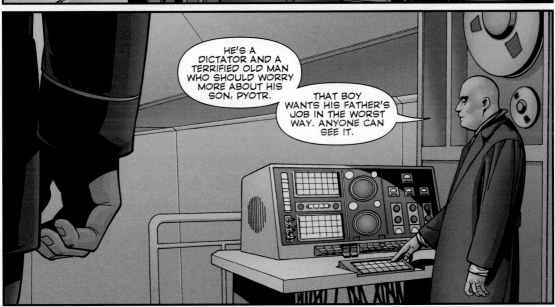

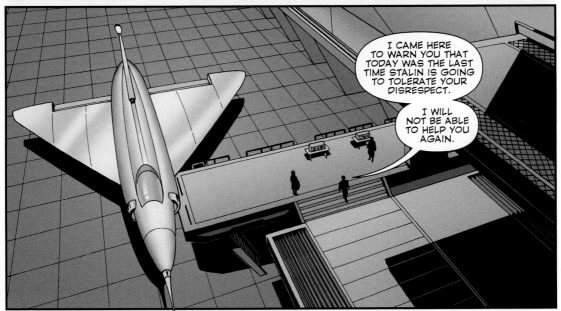

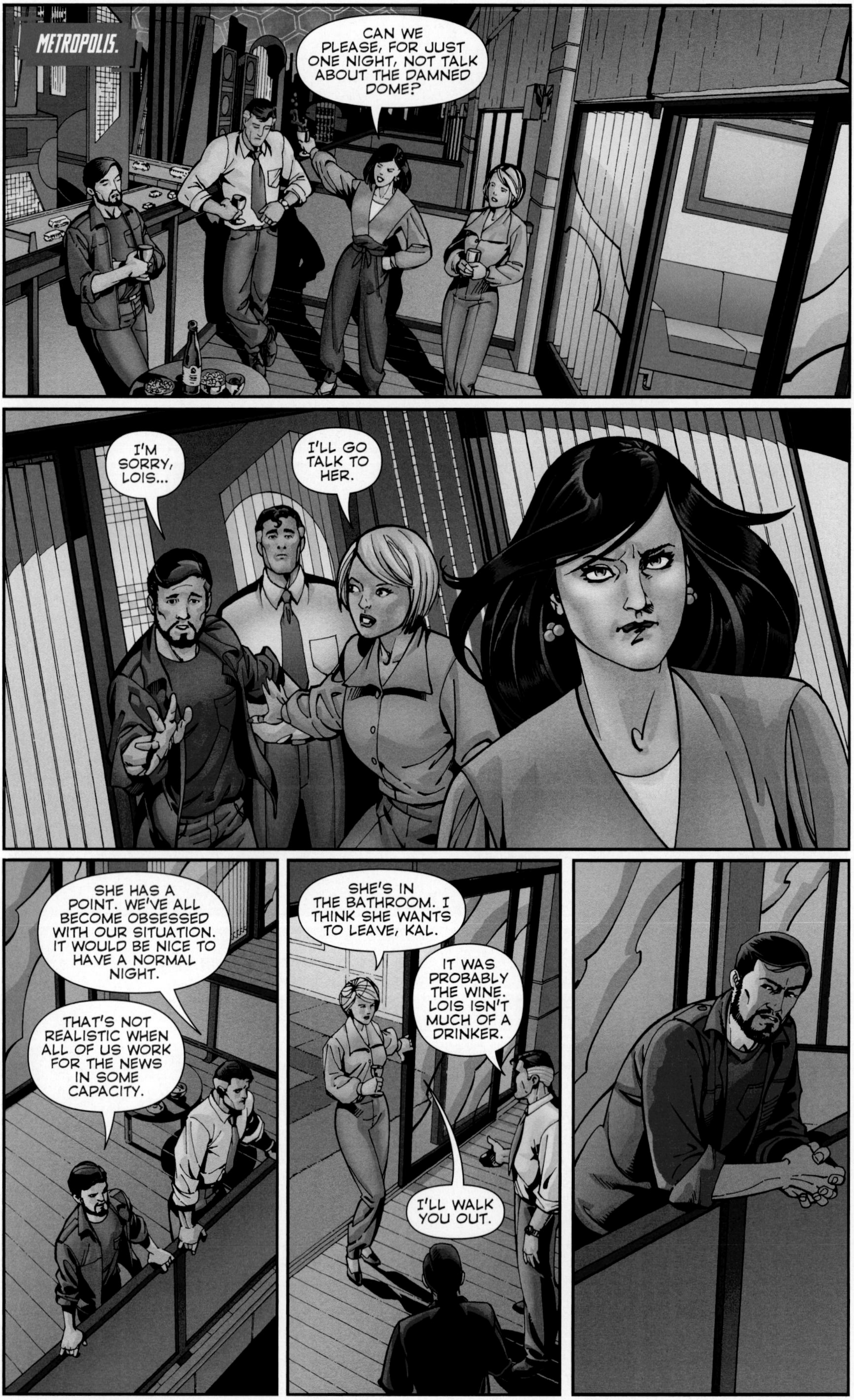
METROPOLIS.
CAN WE PLEASE, FOR JUST ONE NIGHT, NOT TALK ABOUT THE DAMNED DOME?
I'M SORRY, LOIS...
I'LL GO TALK TO HER.
SHE HAS A POINT. WE'VE ALL BECOME OBSESSED WITH OUR SITUATION. IT WOULD BE NICE TO HAVE A NORMAL NIGHT.
THAT'S NOT REALISTIC WHEN ALL OF US WORK FOR THE NEWS IN SOME CAPACITY.
SHE'S IN THE BATHROOM. I THINK SHE WANTS TO LEAVE, KAL.
IT WAS PROBABLY THE WINE. LOIS ISN'T MUCH OF A DRINKER.
I'LL WALK YOU OUT.

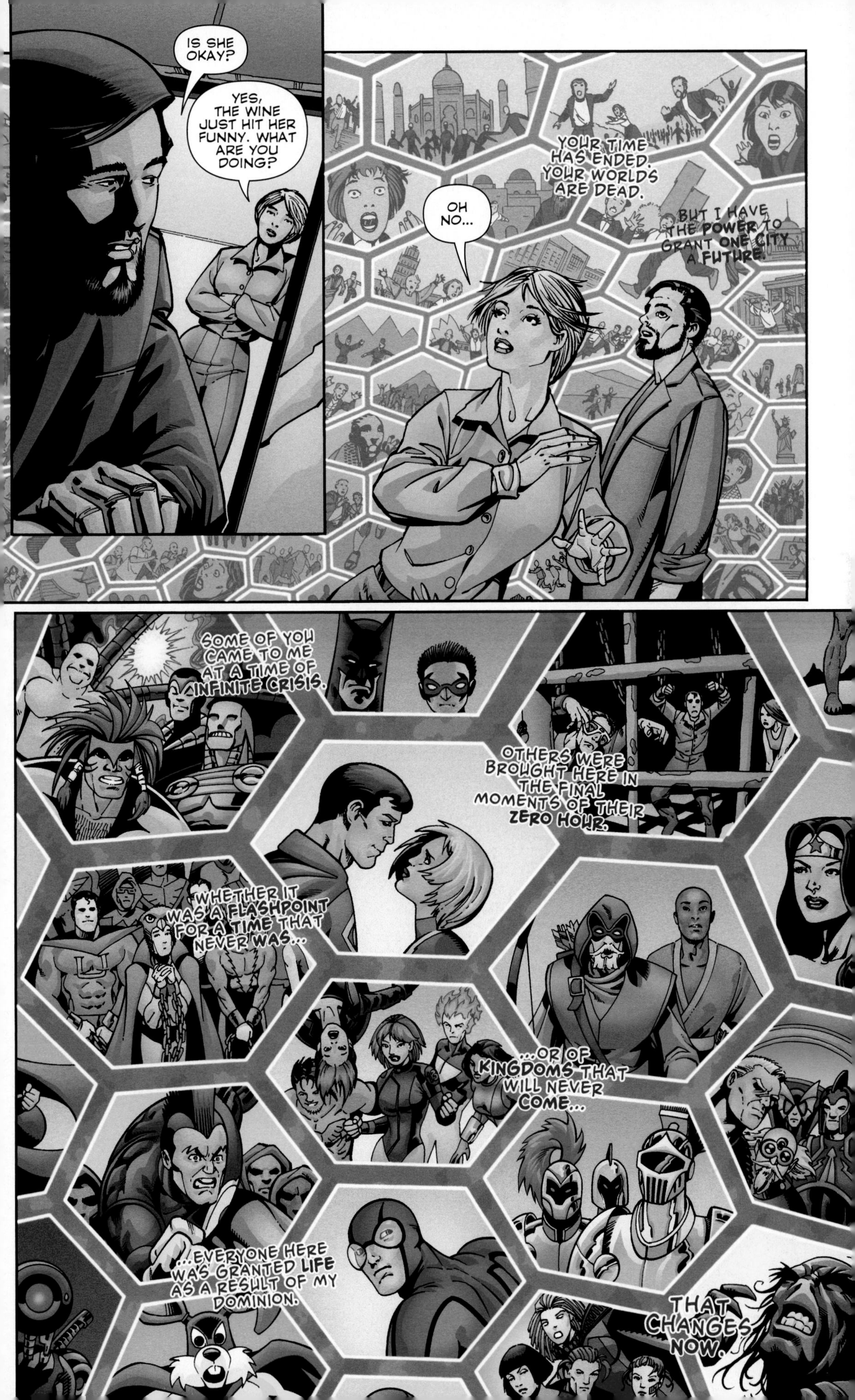
IS SHE OKAY?
YES, THE WINE JUST HIT HER FUNNY. WHAT ARE YOU DOING?
YOUR TIME HAS ENDED. YOUR WORLDS ARE DEAD.
OH NO...
BUT I HAVE THE POWER TO GRANT ONE CITY A FUTURE.
SOME OF YOU CAME TO ME AT A TIME OF INFINITE CRISIS.
OTHERS WERE BROUGHT HERE IN THE FINAL MOMENTS OF THEIR ZERO HOUR.
WHETHER IT WAS A FLASHPOINT FOR A TIME THAT NEVER WAS...
...OR OF KINGDOMS THAT WILL NEVER COME...
...EVERYONE HERE WAS GRANTED LIFE AS A RESULT OF MY DOMINION.
THAT CHANGES NOW.

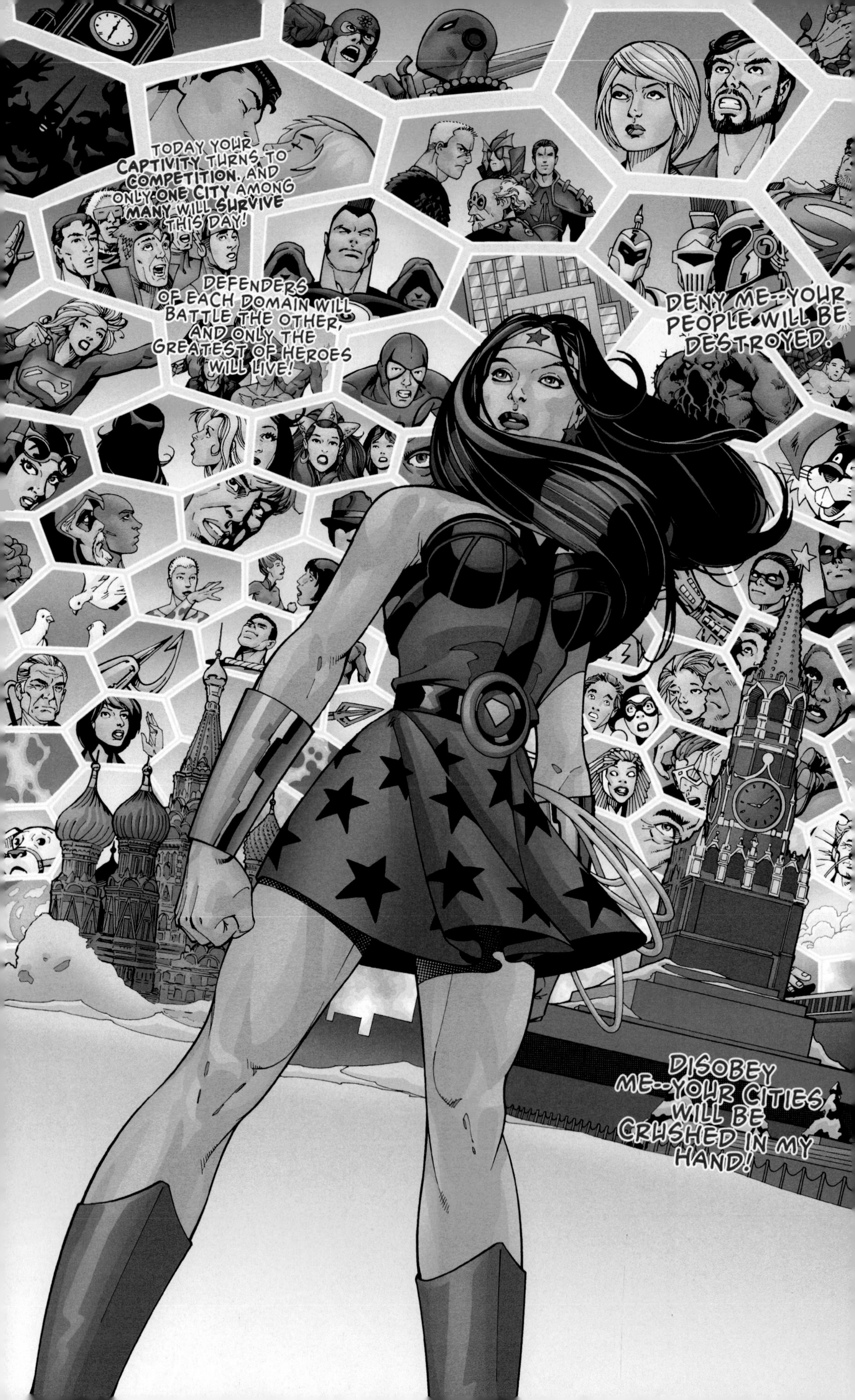
TODAY YOUR CAPTIVITY TURNS TO COMPETITION, AND ONLY ONE CITY AMONG MANY WILL SURVIVE THIS DAY!
DEFENDERS OF EACH DOMAIN WILL BATTLE THE OTHER, AND ONLY THE GREATEST OF HEROES WILL LIVE!
DENY ME--YOUR PEOPLE WILL BE DESTROYED.
DISOBEY ME--YOUR CITIES WILL BE CRUSHED IN MY HAND!

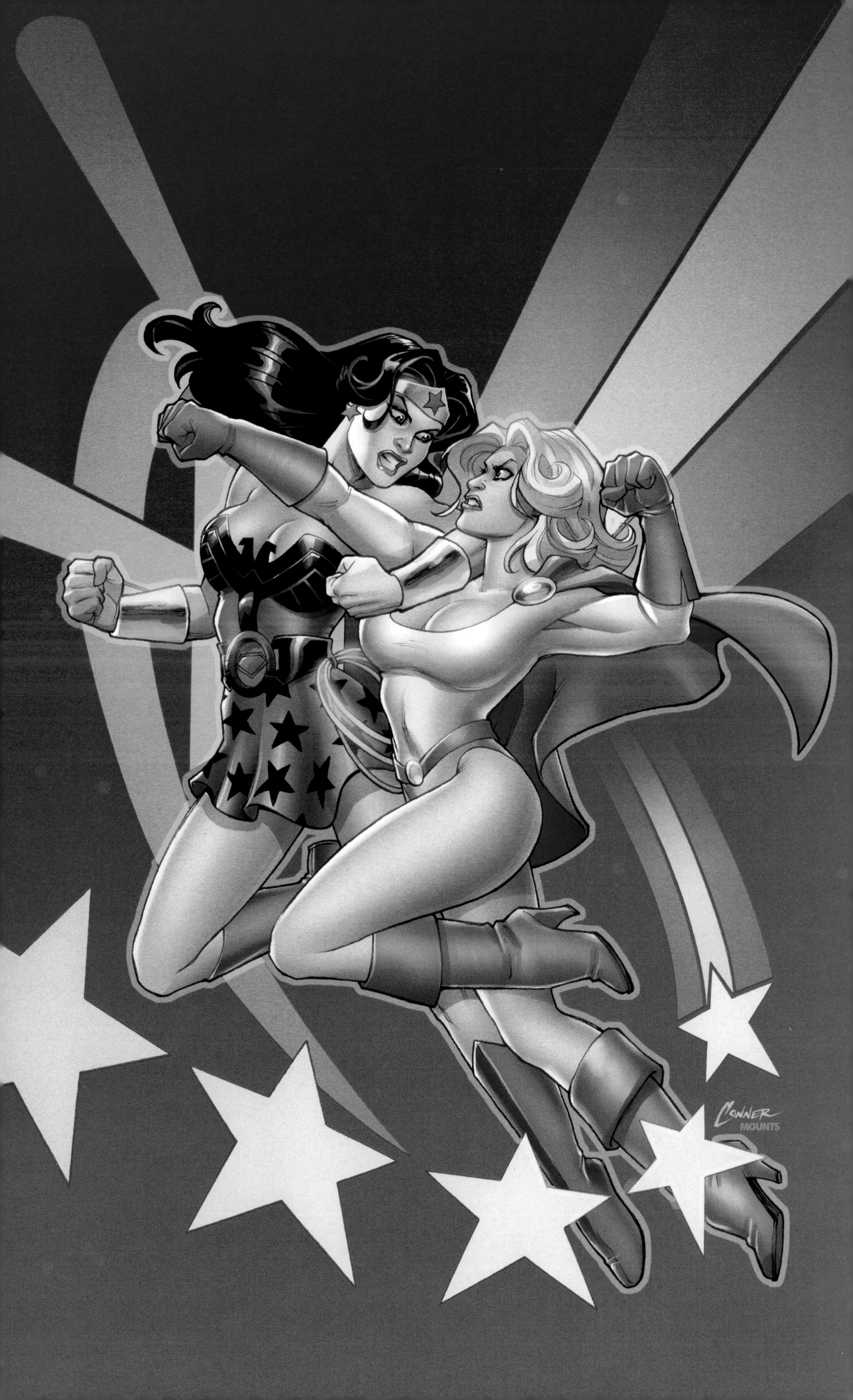

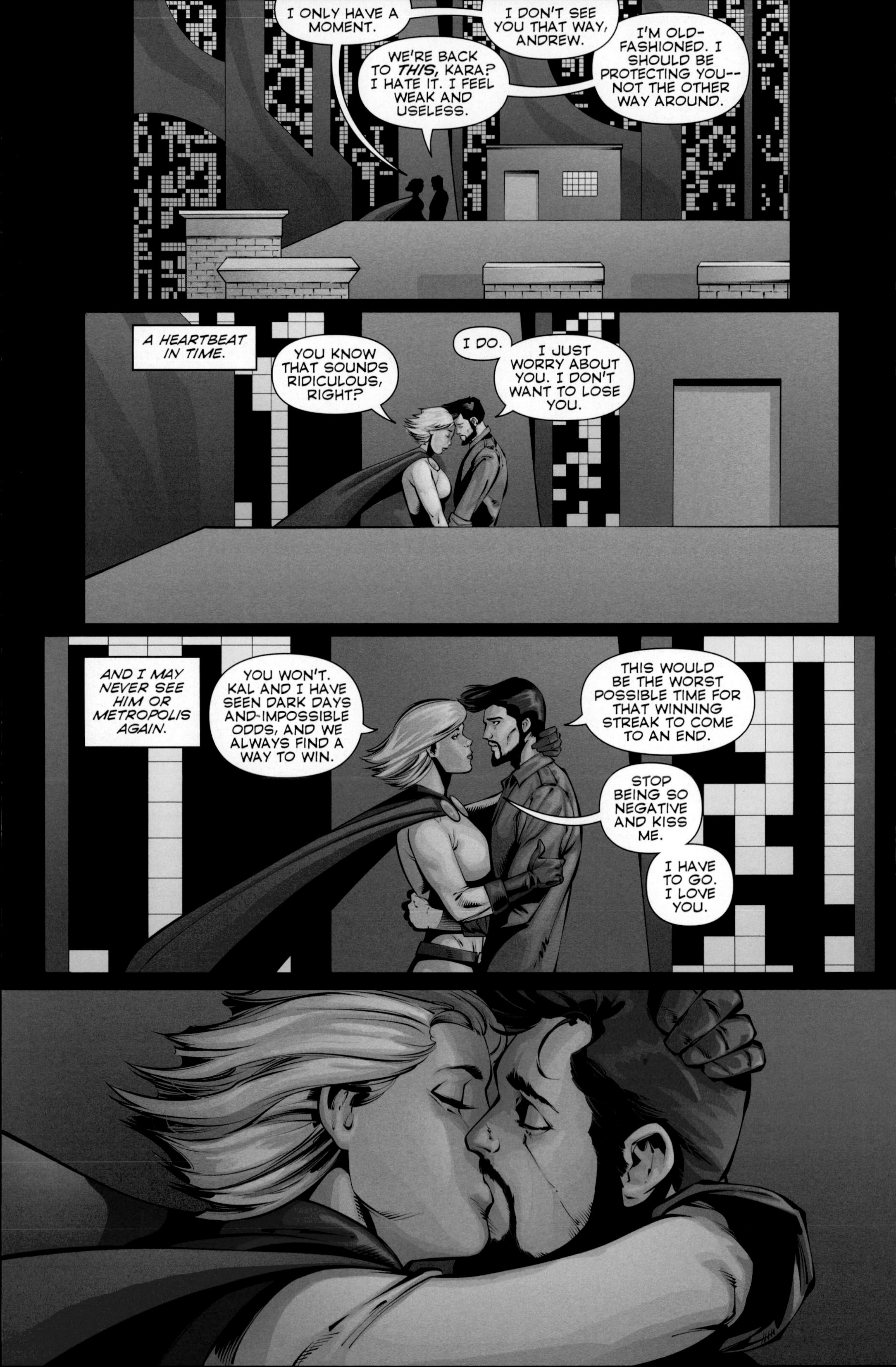
I ONLY HAVE A MOMENT.
WE'RE BACK TO *THIS*, KARA? I HATE IT. I FEEL WEAK AND USELESS.
I DON'T SEE YOU THAT WAY, ANDREW.
I'M OLD-FASHIONED. I SHOULD BE PROTECTING YOU-- NOT THE OTHER WAY AROUND.
A HEARTBEAT IN TIME.
YOU KNOW THAT SOUNDS RIDICULOUS, RIGHT?
I DO.
I JUST WORRY ABOUT YOU. I DON'T WANT TO LOSE YOU.
AND I MAY NEVER SEE HIM OR METROPOLIS AGAIN.
YOU WON'T. KAL AND I HAVE SEEN DARK DAYS AND IMPOSSIBLE ODDS, AND WE ALWAYS FIND A WAY TO WIN.
THIS WOULD BE THE WORST POSSIBLE TIME FOR THAT WINNING STREAK TO COME TO AN END.
STOP BEING SO NEGATIVE AND KISS ME.
I HAVE TO GO. I LOVE YOU.

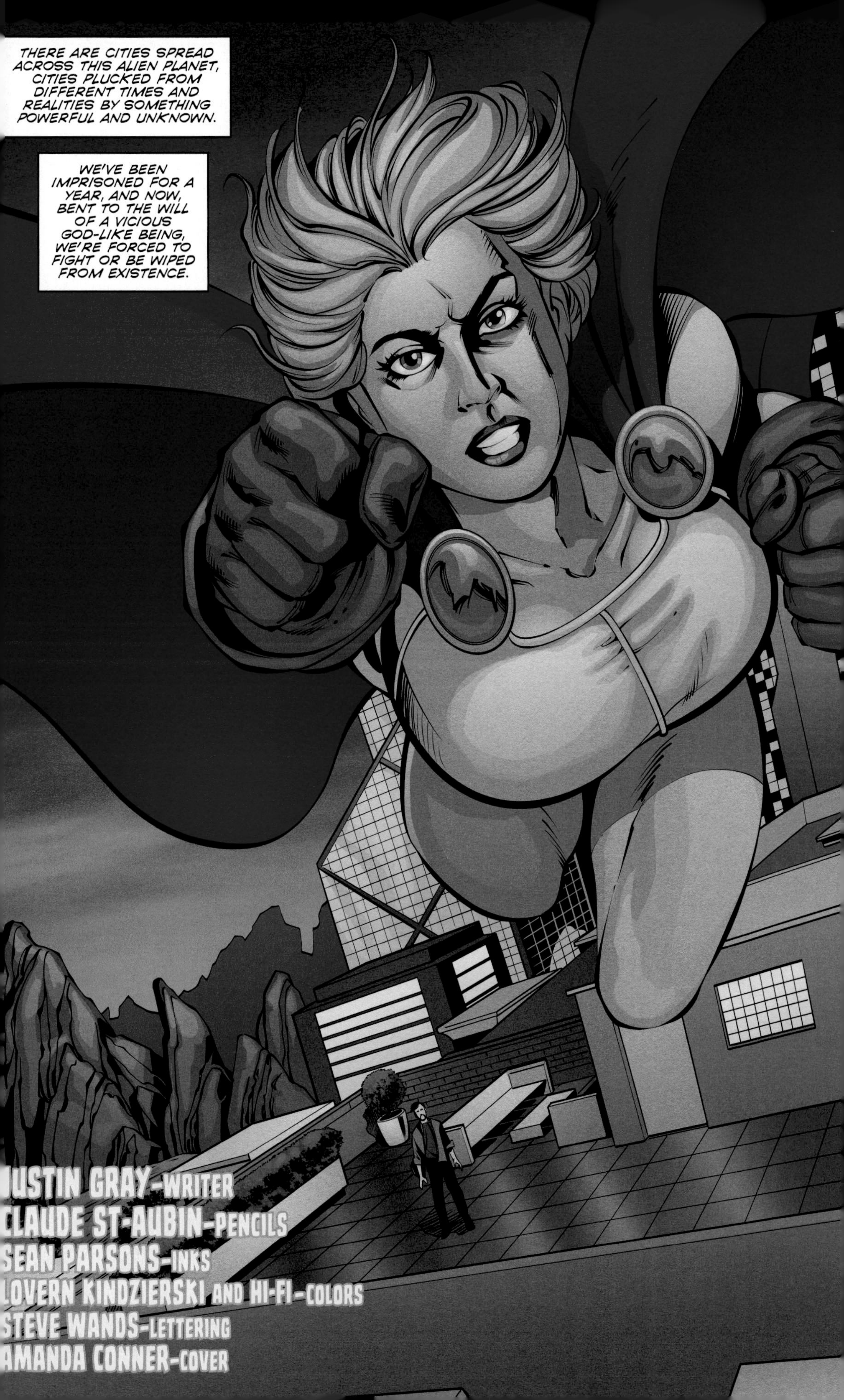

THERE ARE CITIES SPREAD ACROSS THIS ALIEN PLANET, CITIES PLUCKED FROM DIFFERENT TIMES AND REALITIES BY SOMETHING POWERFUL AND UNKNOWN.
WE'VE BEEN IMPRISONED FOR A YEAR, AND NOW, BENT TO THE WILL OF A VICIOUS GOD-LIKE BEING, WE'RE FORCED TO FIGHT OR BE WIPED FROM EXISTENCE.
USTIN GRAY-WRITER
CLAUDE ST-AUBIN-PENCILS
SEAN PARSONS-INKS
LOVERN KINDZIERSKI AND HI-FI-COLORS
STEVE WANDS-LETTERING
AMANDA CONNER-COVER

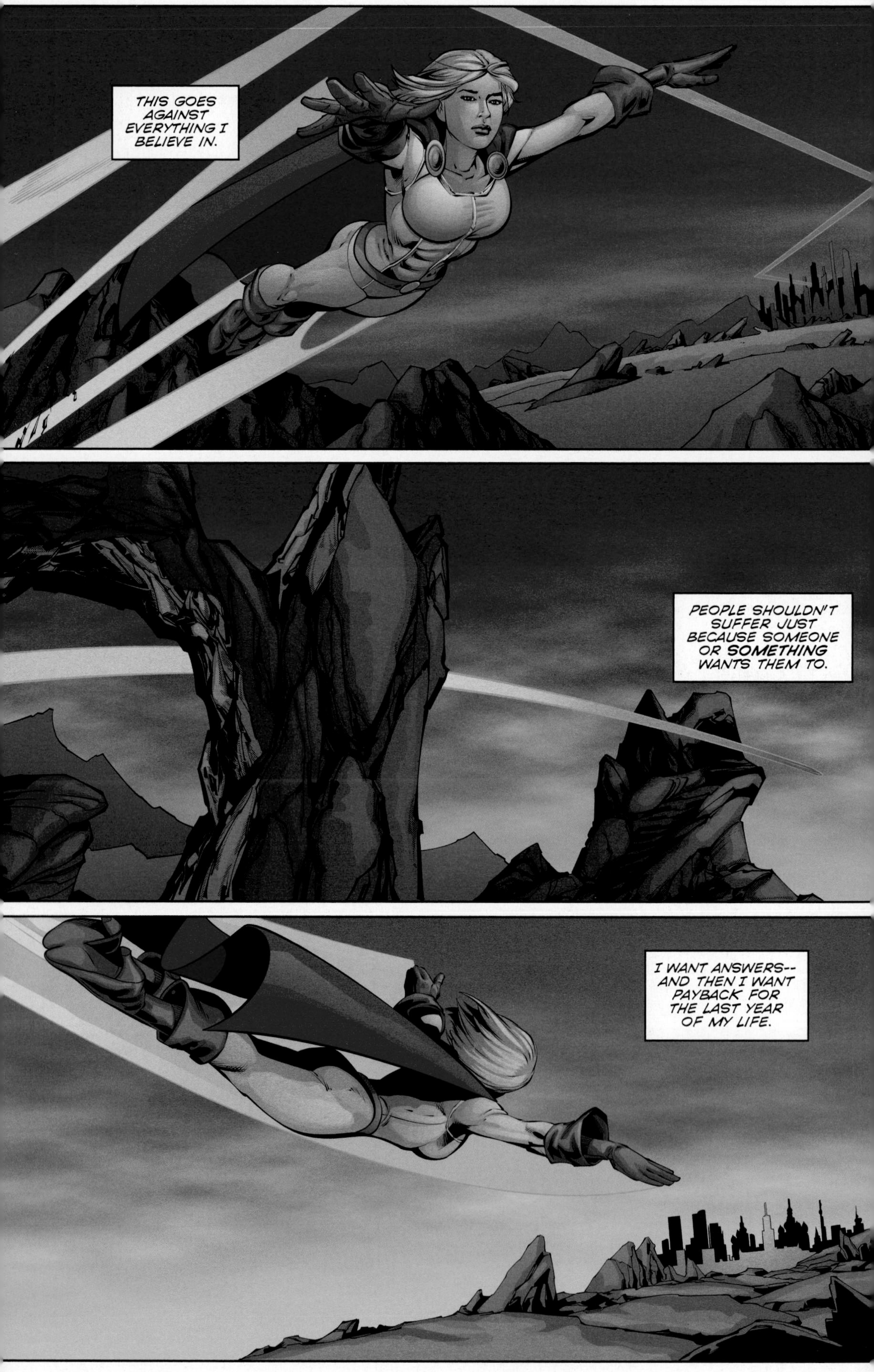
THIS GOES AGAINST EVERYTHING I BELIEVE IN.
PEOPLE SHOULDN'T SUFFER JUST BECAUSE SOMEONE OR **SOMETHING** WANTS THEM TO.
I WANT ANSWERS-- AND THEN I WANT PAYBACK FOR THE LAST YEAR OF MY LIFE.

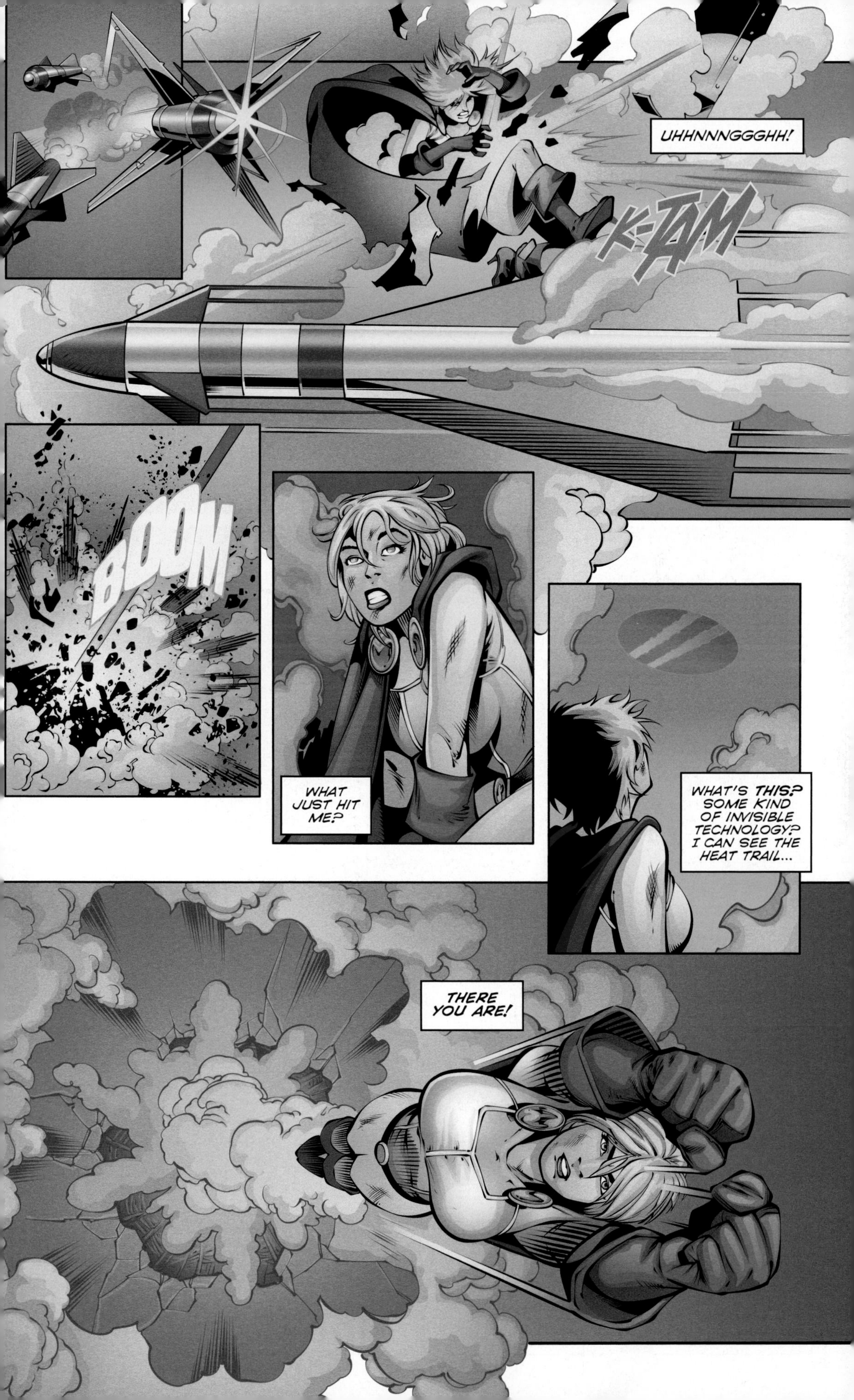
UHHNNNGGGHH!
K-TAM
BOOM
WHAT JUST HIT ME?
WHAT'S THIS? SOME KIND OF INVISIBLE TECHNOLOGY? I CAN SEE THE HEAT TRAIL...
THERE YOU ARE!

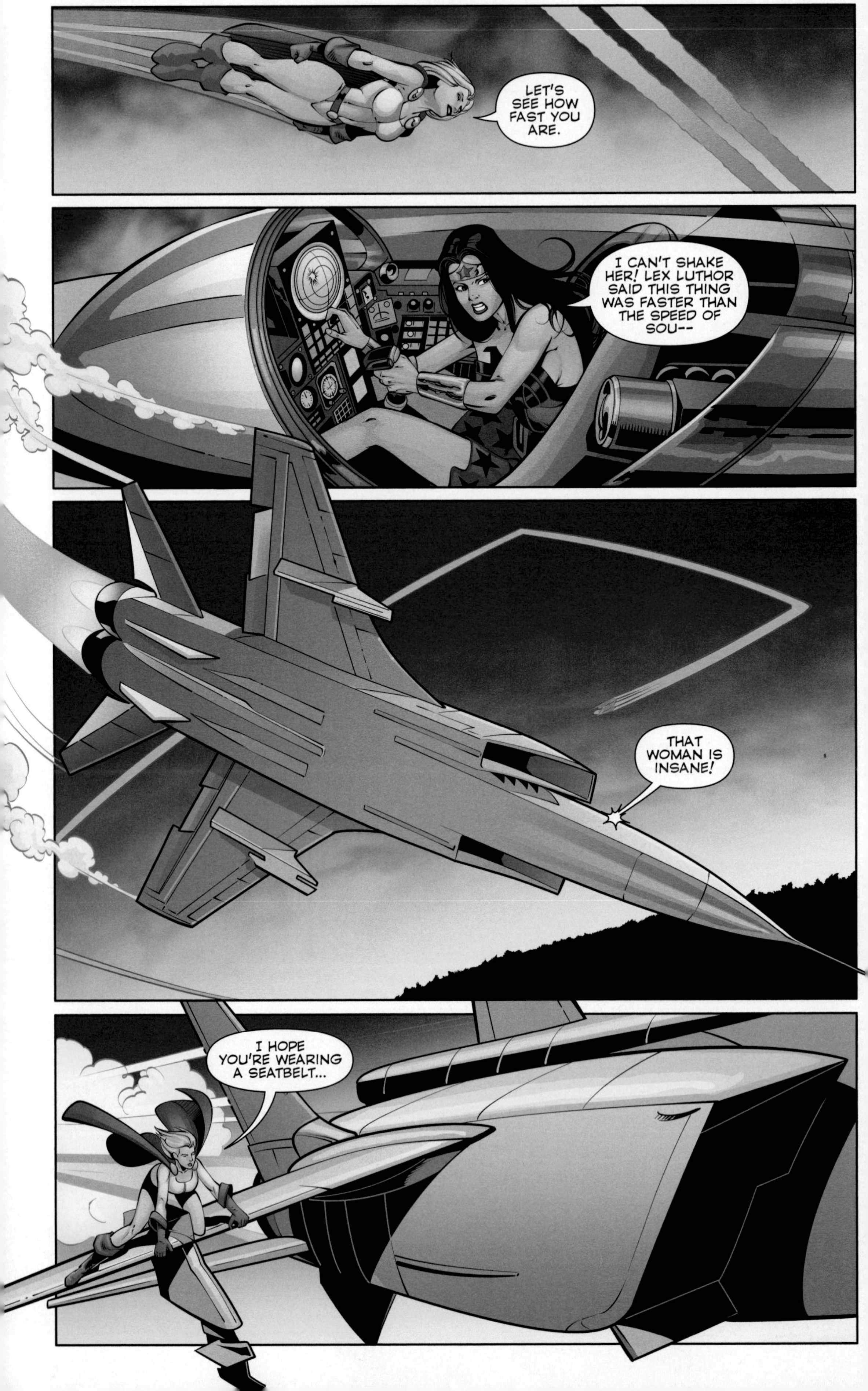
LET'S SEE HOW FAST YOU ARE.
I CAN'T SHAKE HER! LEX LUTHOR SAID THIS THING WAS FASTER THAN THE SPEED OF SOU--
THAT WOMAN IS INSANE!
I HOPE YOU'RE WEARING A SEATBELT...

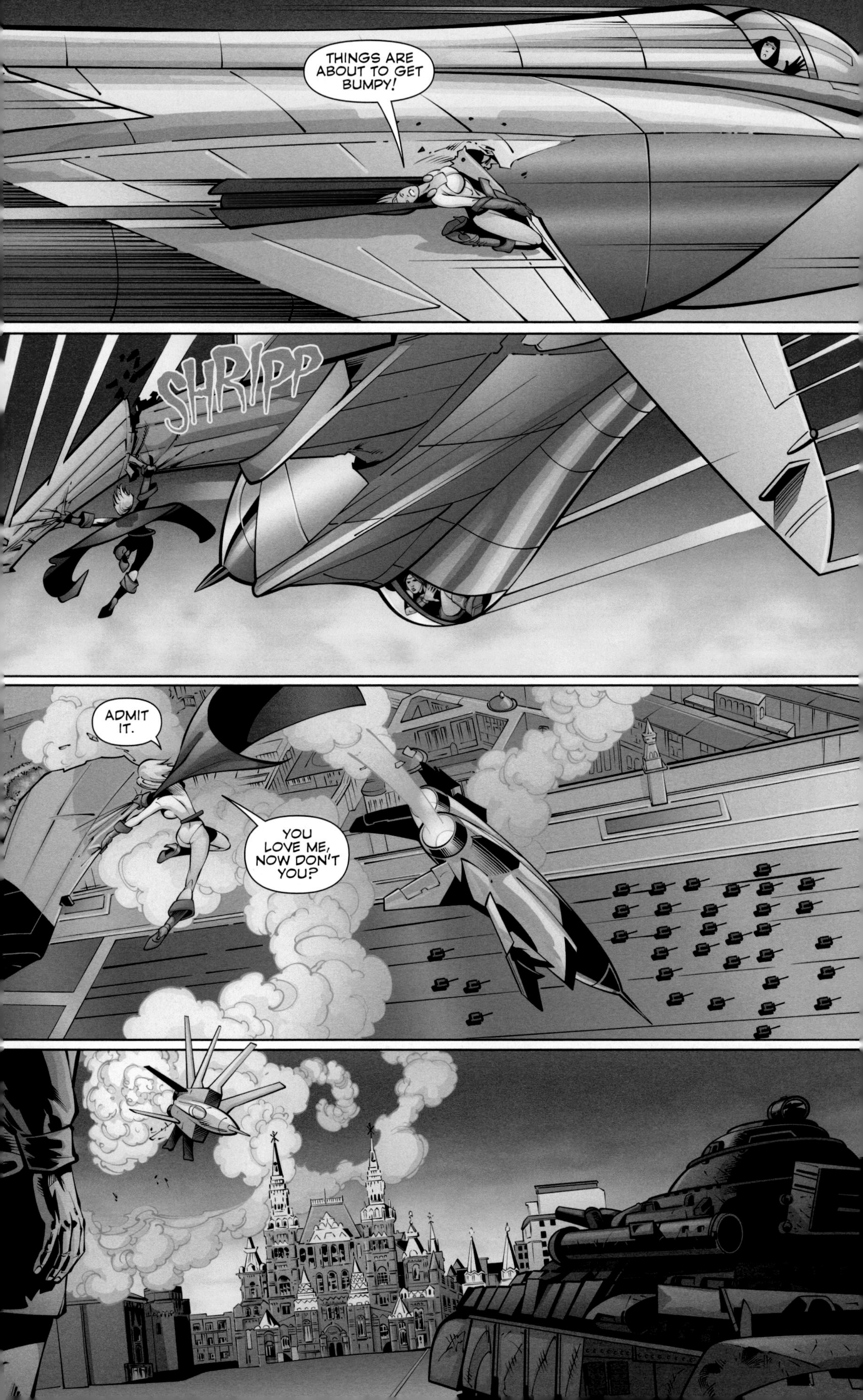
THINGS ARE ABOUT TO GET BUMPY!
SHRIPP
ADMIT IT.
YOU LOVE ME, NOW DON'T YOU?

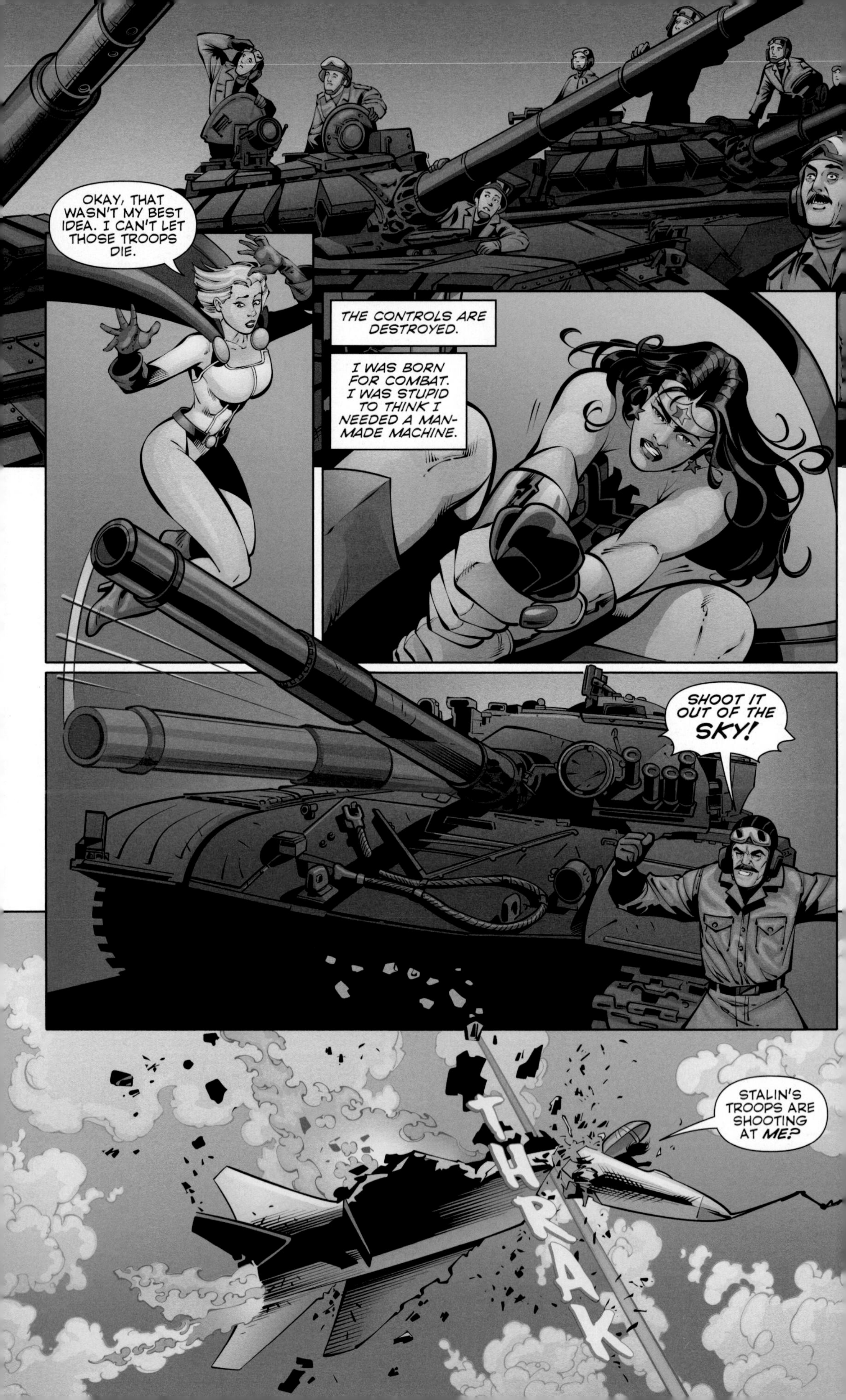
OKAY, THAT WASN'T MY BEST IDEA. I CAN'T LET THOSE TROOPS DIE.
THE CONTROLS ARE DESTROYED.
I WAS BORN FOR COMBAT. I WAS STUPID TO THINK I NEEDED A MAN-MADE MACHINE.
SHOOT IT OUT OF THE SKY!
THRAK
STALIN'S TROOPS ARE SHOOTING AT ME?

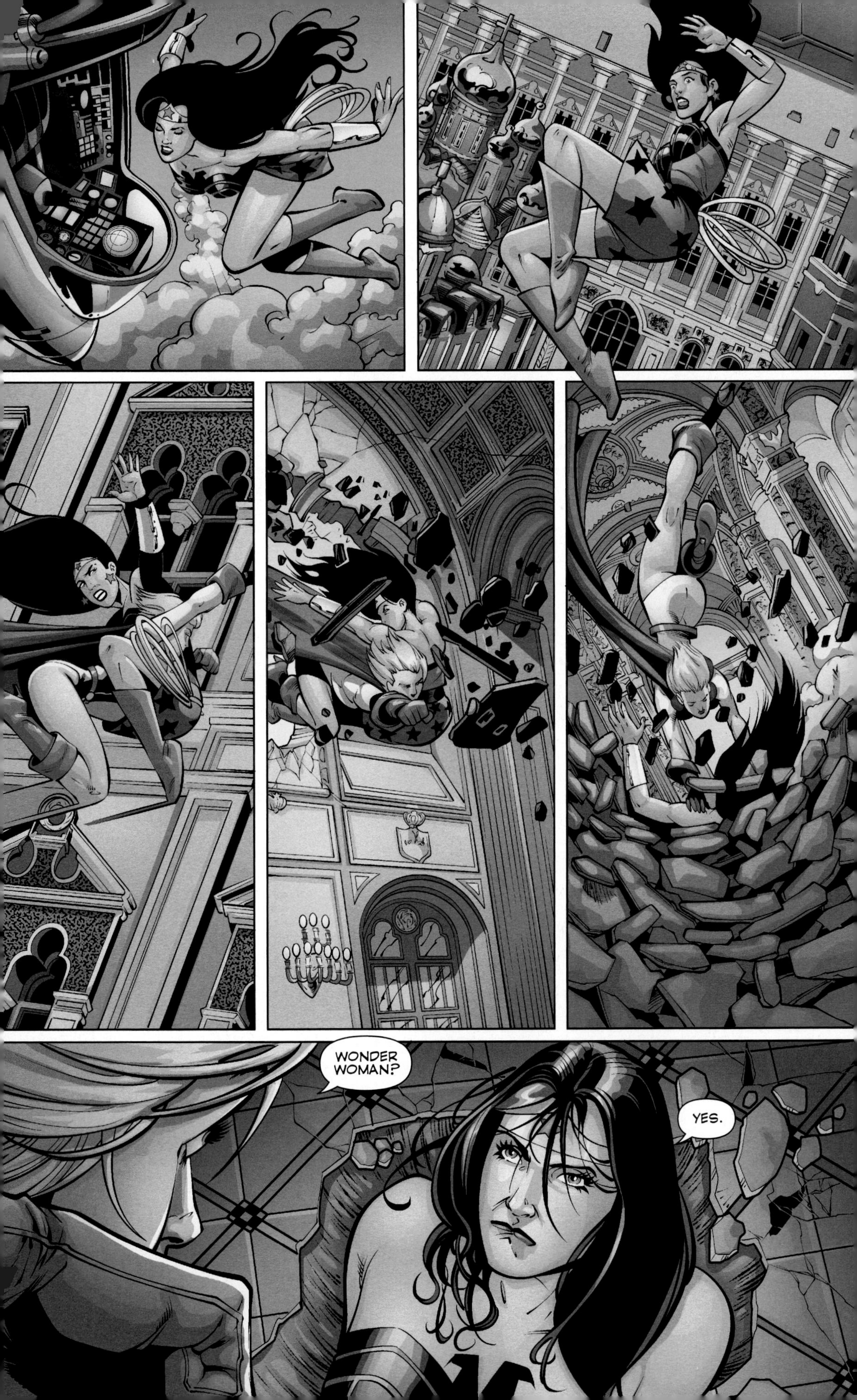
WONDER WOMAN?
YES.

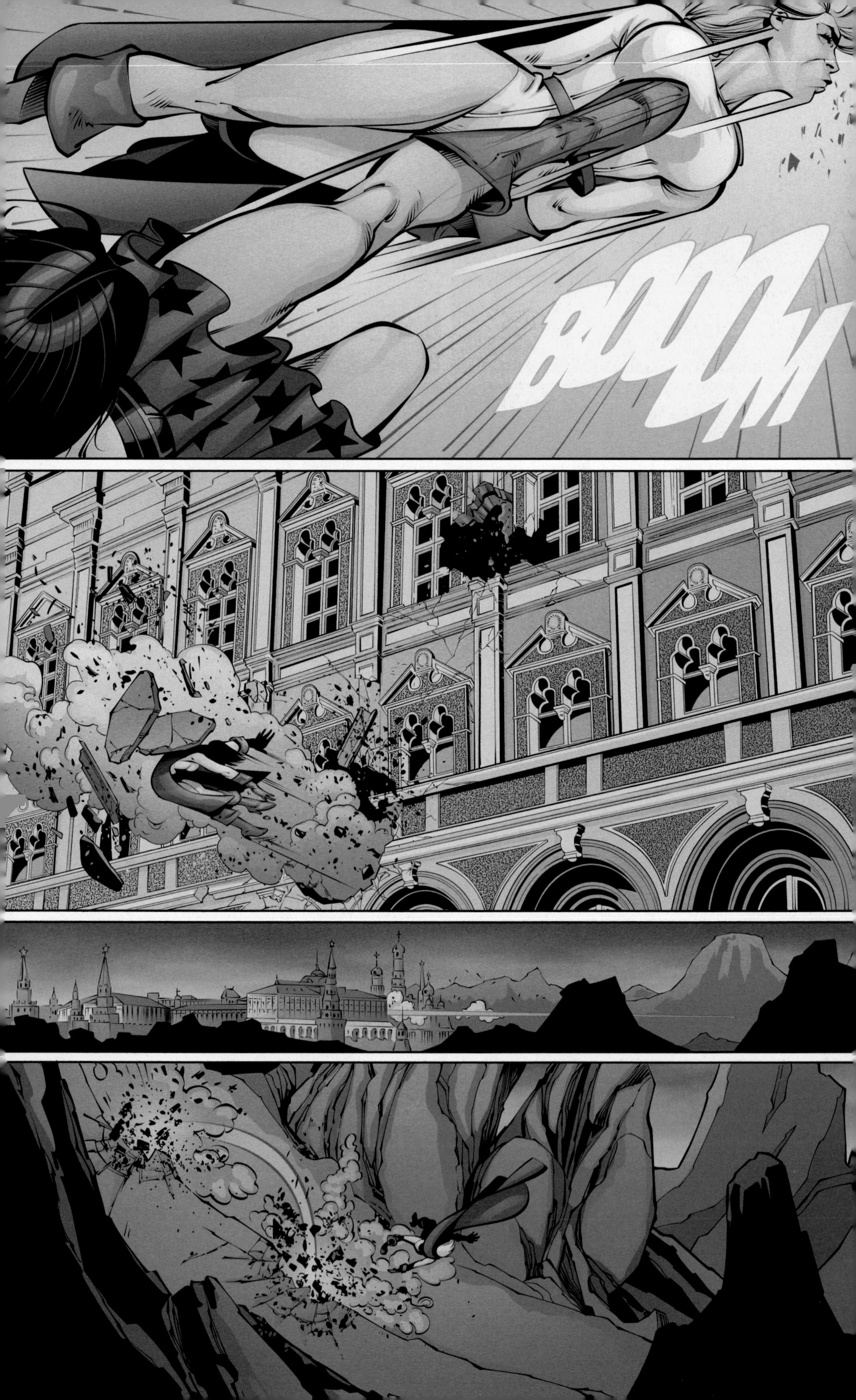
BOOOM

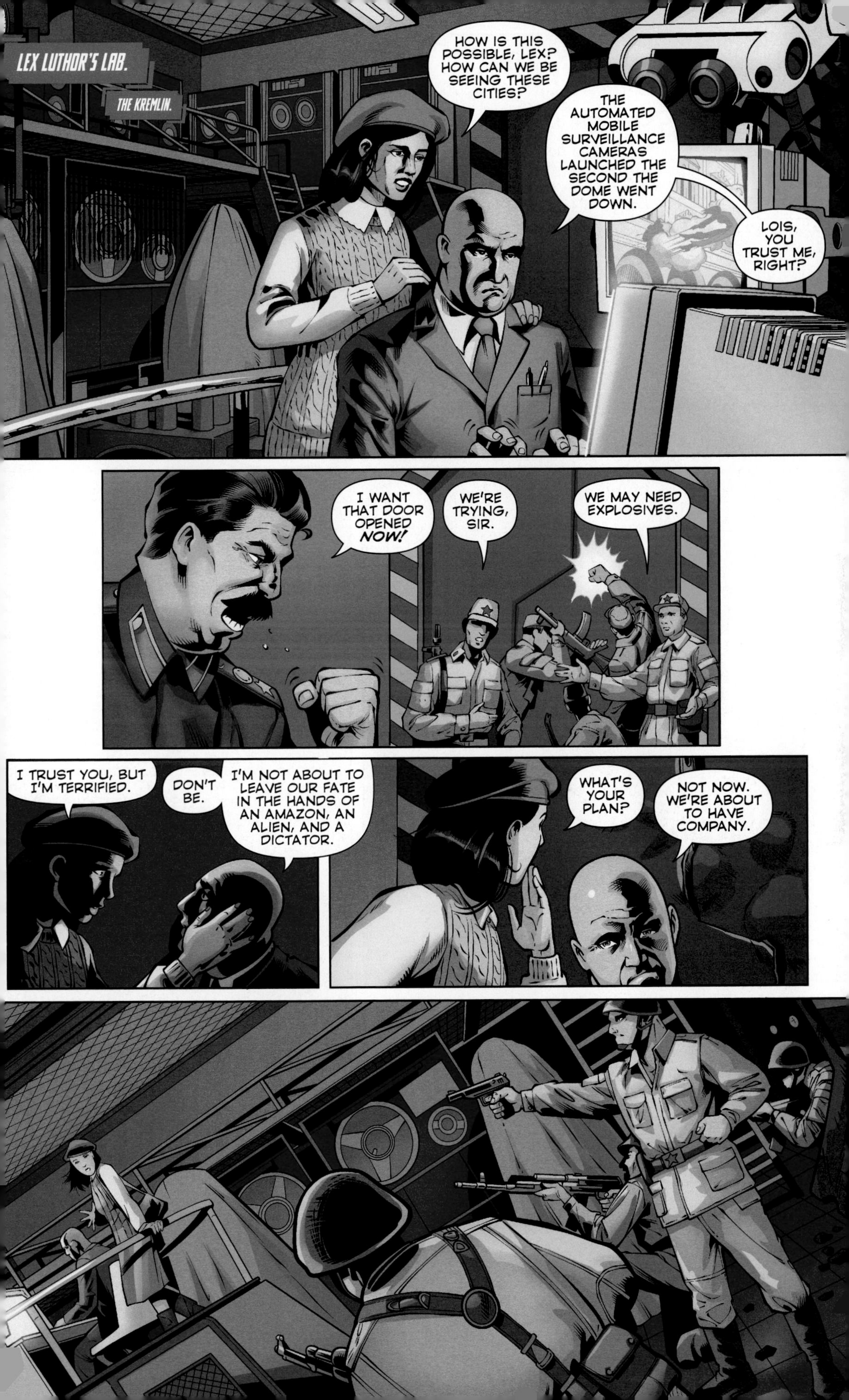
LEX LUTHOR'S LAB.
THE KREMLIN.
HOW IS THIS POSSIBLE, LEX? HOW CAN WE BE SEEING THESE CITIES?
THE AUTOMATED MOBILE SURVEILLANCE CAMERAS LAUNCHED THE SECOND THE DOME WENT DOWN.
LOIS, YOU TRUST ME, RIGHT?
I WANT THAT DOOR OPENED *NOW!*
WE'RE TRYING, SIR.
WE MAY NEED EXPLOSIVES.
I TRUST YOU, BUT I'M TERRIFIED.
DON'T BE.
I'M NOT ABOUT TO LEAVE OUR FATE IN THE HANDS OF AN AMAZON, AN ALIEN, AND A DICTATOR.
WHAT'S YOUR PLAN?
NOT NOW. WE'RE ABOUT TO HAVE COMPANY.

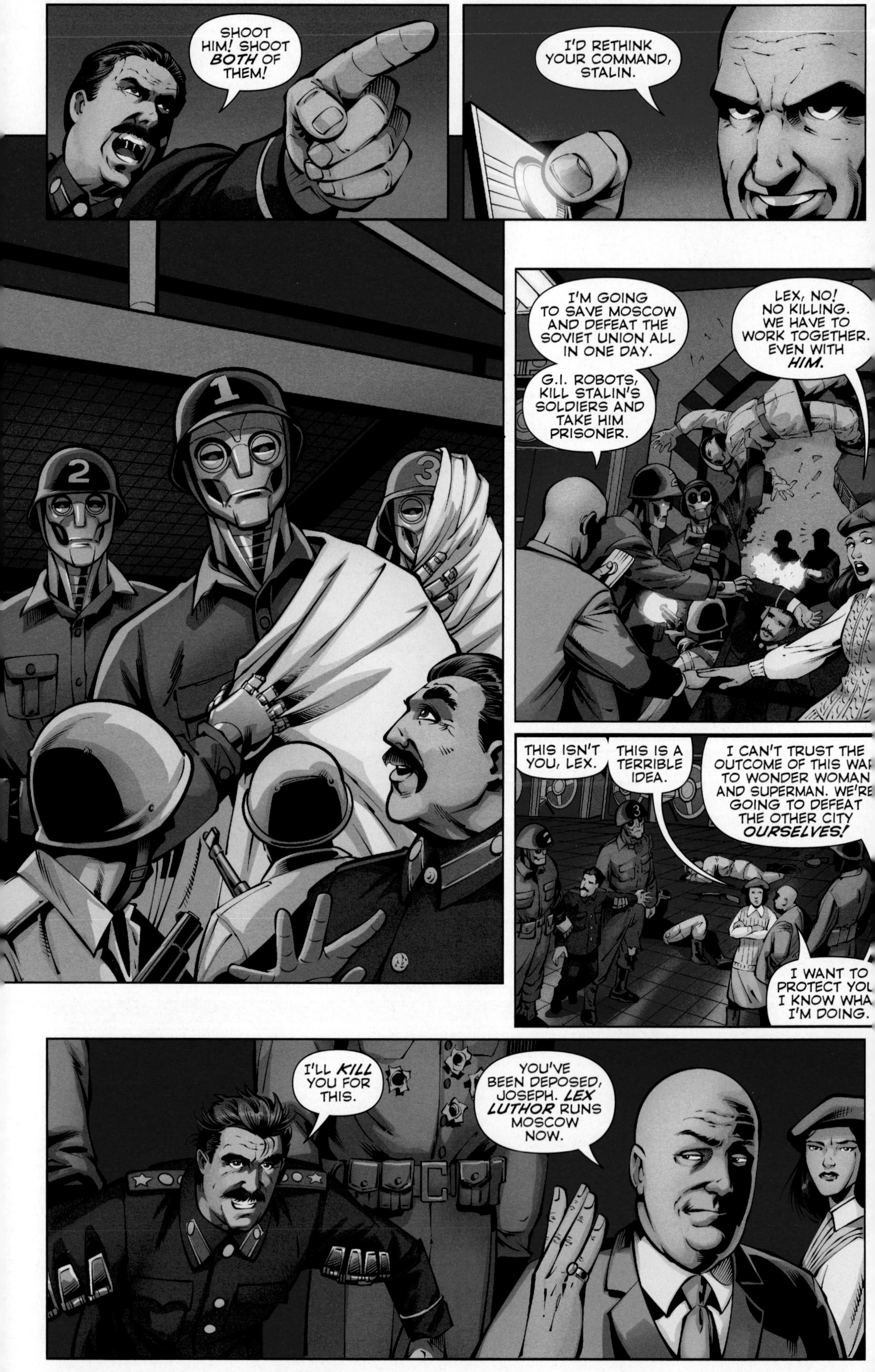
SHOOT HIM! SHOOT *BOTH* OF THEM!
I'D RETHINK YOUR COMMAND, STALIN.
I'M GOING TO SAVE MOSCOW AND DEFEAT THE SOVIET UNION ALL IN ONE DAY.
G.I. ROBOTS, KILL STALIN'S SOLDIERS AND TAKE HIM PRISONER.
LEX, NO! NO KILLING. WE HAVE TO WORK TOGETHER. EVEN WITH *HIM*.
THIS ISN'T YOU, LEX.
THIS IS A TERRIBLE IDEA.
I CAN'T TRUST THE OUTCOME OF THIS WAR TO WONDER WOMAN AND SUPERMAN. WE'RE GOING TO DEFEAT THE OTHER CITY *OURSELVES!*
I WANT TO PROTECT YOU. I KNOW WHAT I'M DOING.
I'LL *KILL* YOU FOR THIS.
YOU'VE BEEN DEPOSED, JOSEPH. *LEX LUTHOR* RUNS MOSCOW NOW.

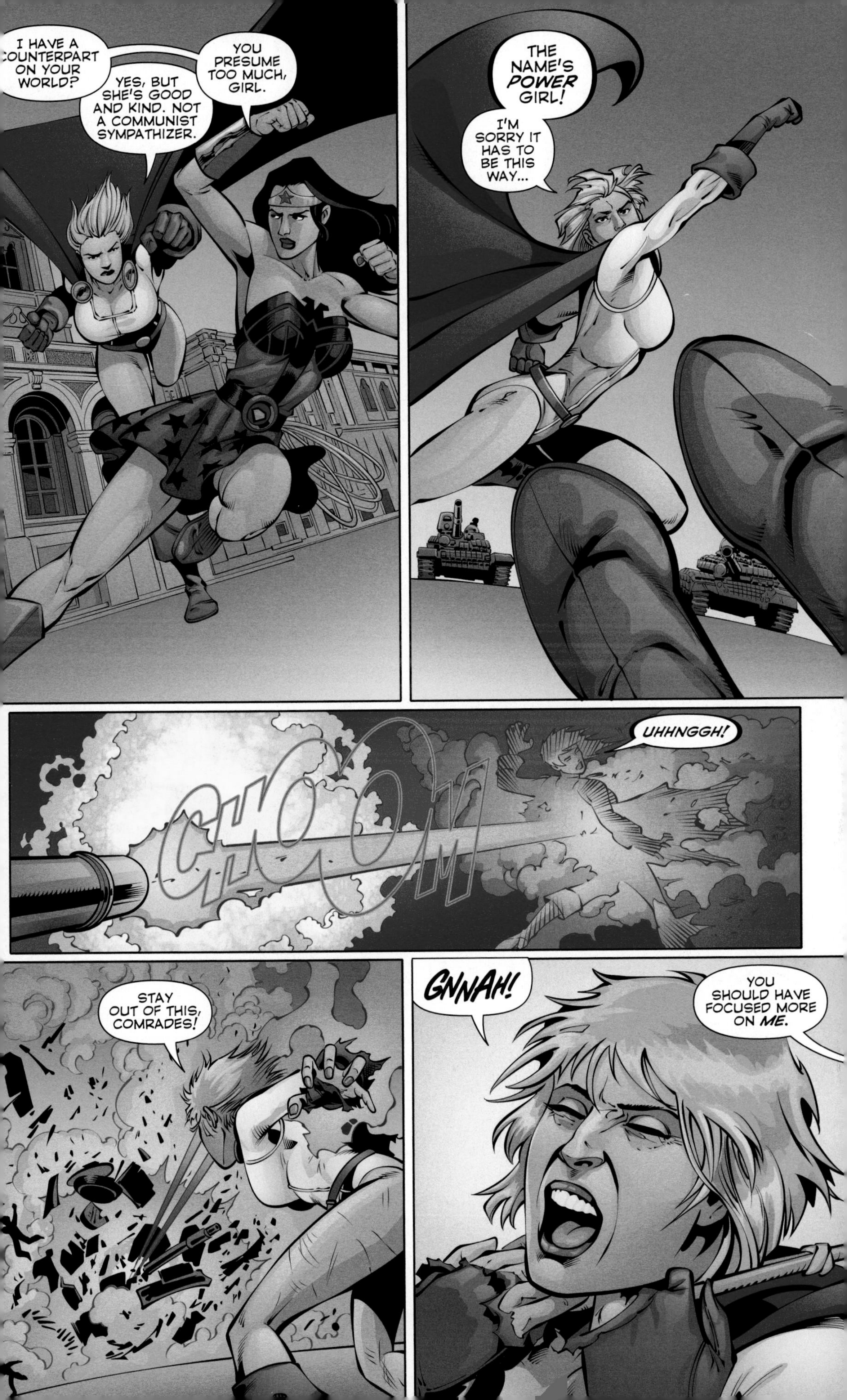
I HAVE A COUNTERPART ON YOUR WORLD?
YOU PRESUME TOO MUCH, GIRL.
YES, BUT SHE'S GOOD AND KIND. NOT A COMMUNIST SYMPATHIZER.
THE NAME'S POWER GIRL!
I'M SORRY IT HAS TO BE THIS WAY...
UHHNGGH!
CHOOM
STAY OUT OF THIS, COMRADES!
GNNAH!
YOU SHOULD HAVE FOCUSED MORE ON ME.

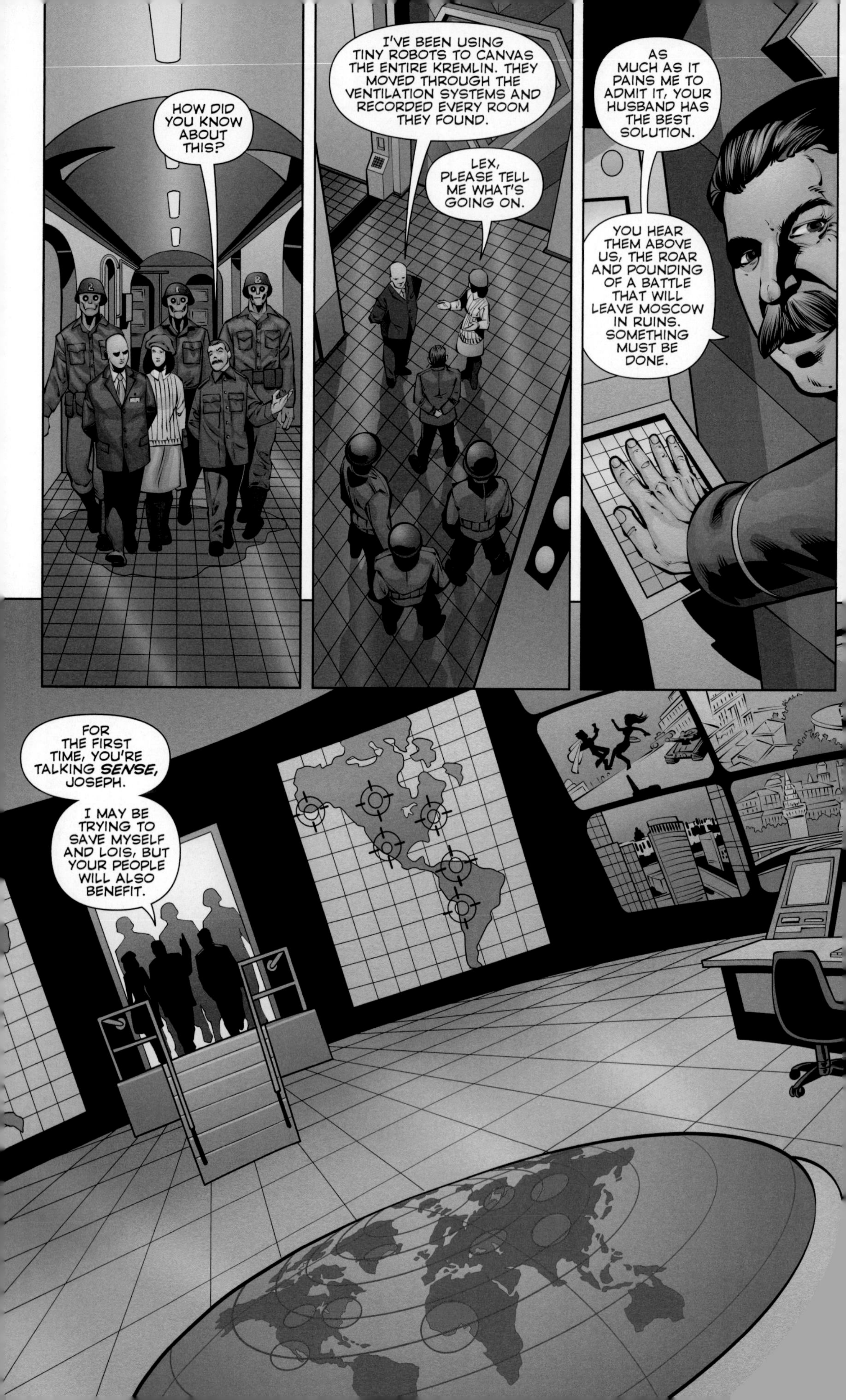
HOW DID YOU KNOW ABOUT THIS?
I'VE BEEN USING TINY ROBOTS TO CANVAS THE ENTIRE KREMLIN. THEY MOVED THROUGH THE VENTILATION SYSTEMS AND RECORDED EVERY ROOM THEY FOUND.
LEX, PLEASE TELL ME WHAT'S GOING ON.
AS MUCH AS IT PAINS ME TO ADMIT IT, YOUR HUSBAND HAS THE BEST SOLUTION.
YOU HEAR THEM ABOVE US, THE ROAR AND POUNDING OF A BATTLE THAT WILL LEAVE MOSCOW IN RUINS. SOMETHING MUST BE DONE.
FOR THE FIRST TIME, YOU'RE TALKING *SENSE,* JOSEPH.
I MAY BE TRYING TO SAVE MYSELF AND LOIS, BUT YOUR PEOPLE WILL ALSO BENEFIT.

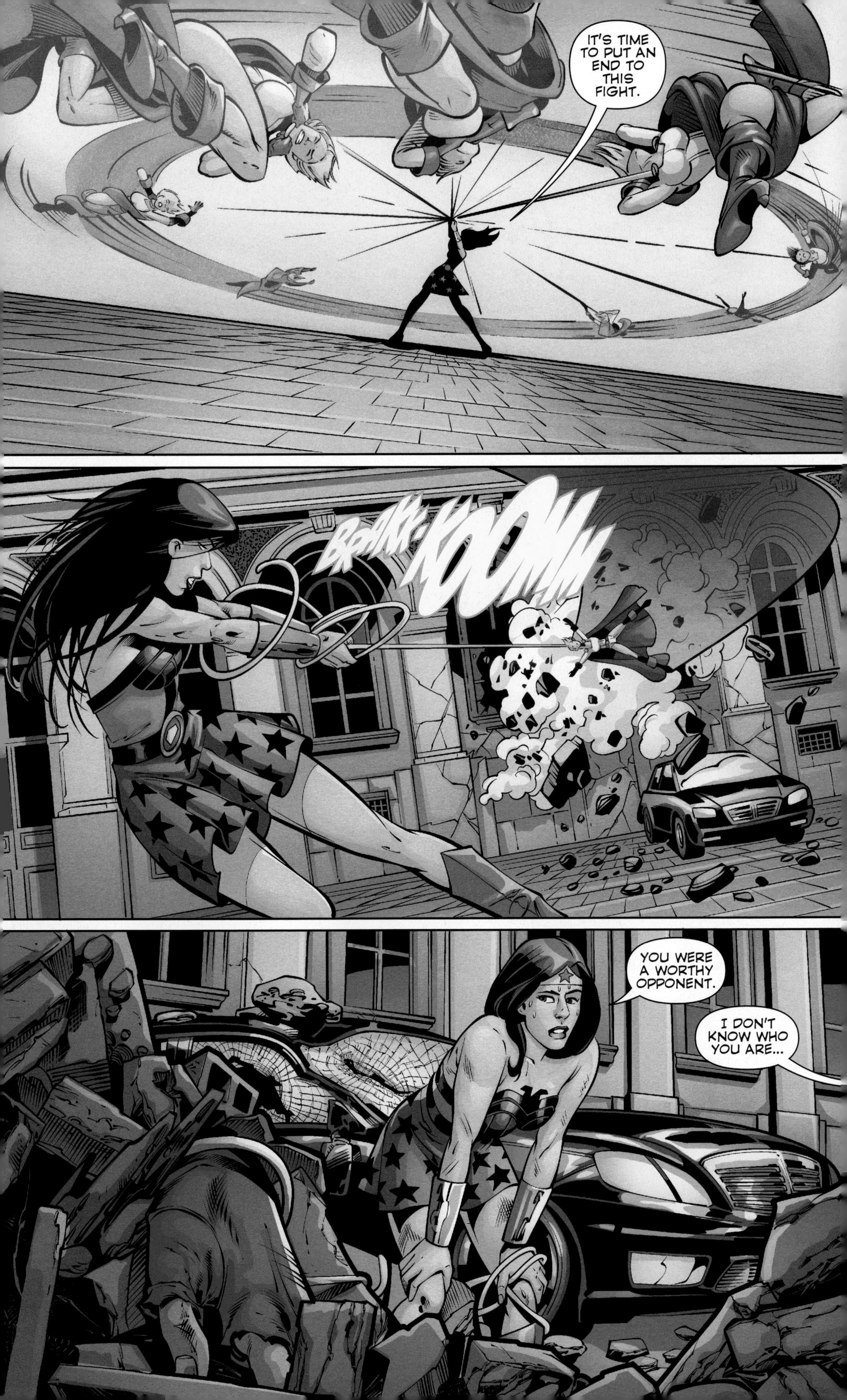
IT'S TIME TO PUT AN END TO THIS FIGHT.
BRAKK-KOOMM
YOU WERE A WORTHY OPPONENT.
I DON'T KNOW WHO YOU ARE...

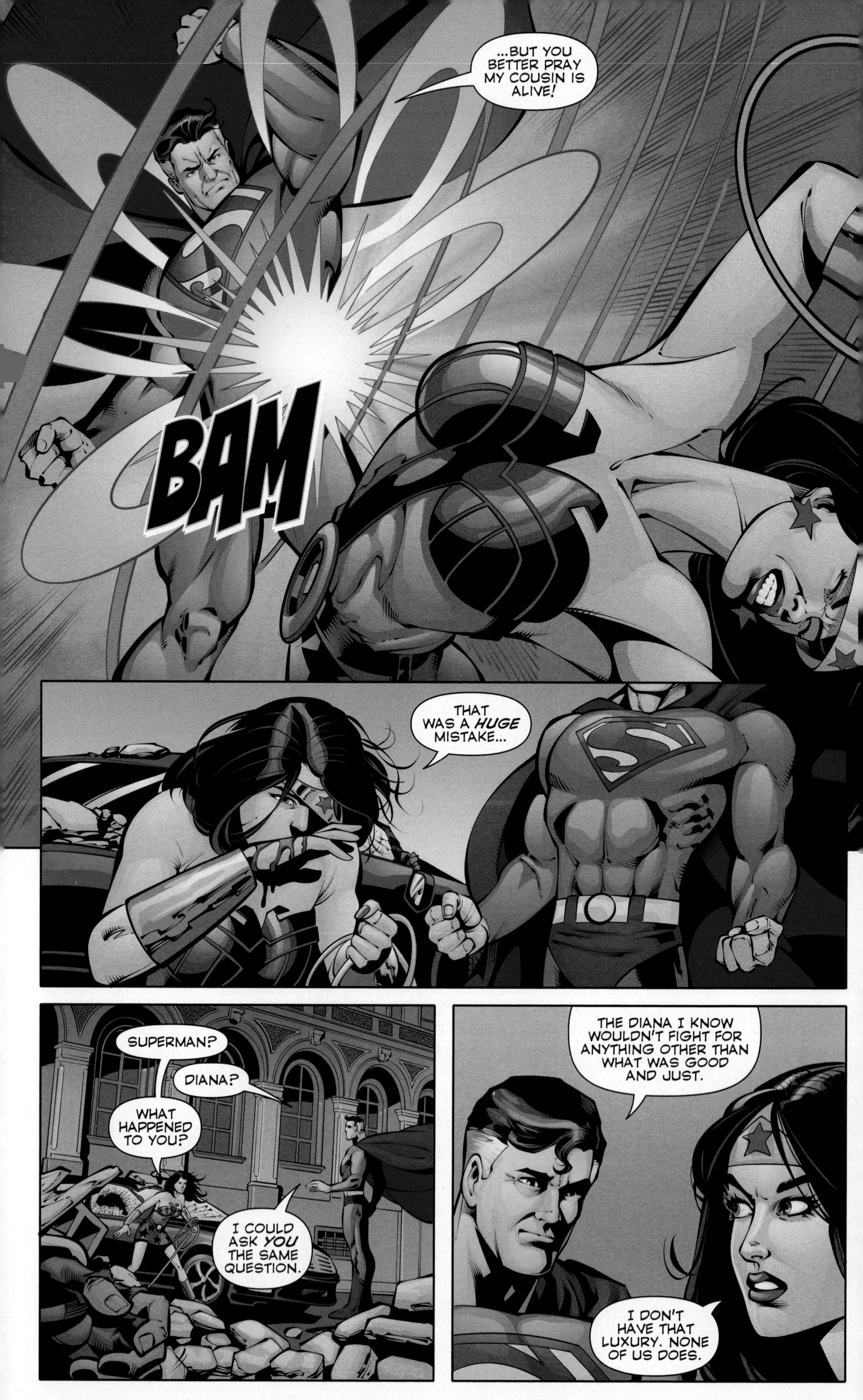
...BUT YOU BETTER PRAY MY COUSIN IS ALIVE!
BAM
THAT WAS A *HUGE* MISTAKE...
SUPERMAN?
DIANA?
WHAT HAPPENED TO YOU?
I COULD ASK *YOU* THE SAME QUESTION.
THE DIANA I KNOW WOULDN'T FIGHT FOR ANYTHING OTHER THAN WHAT WAS GOOD AND JUST.
I DON'T HAVE THAT LUXURY. NONE OF US DOES.

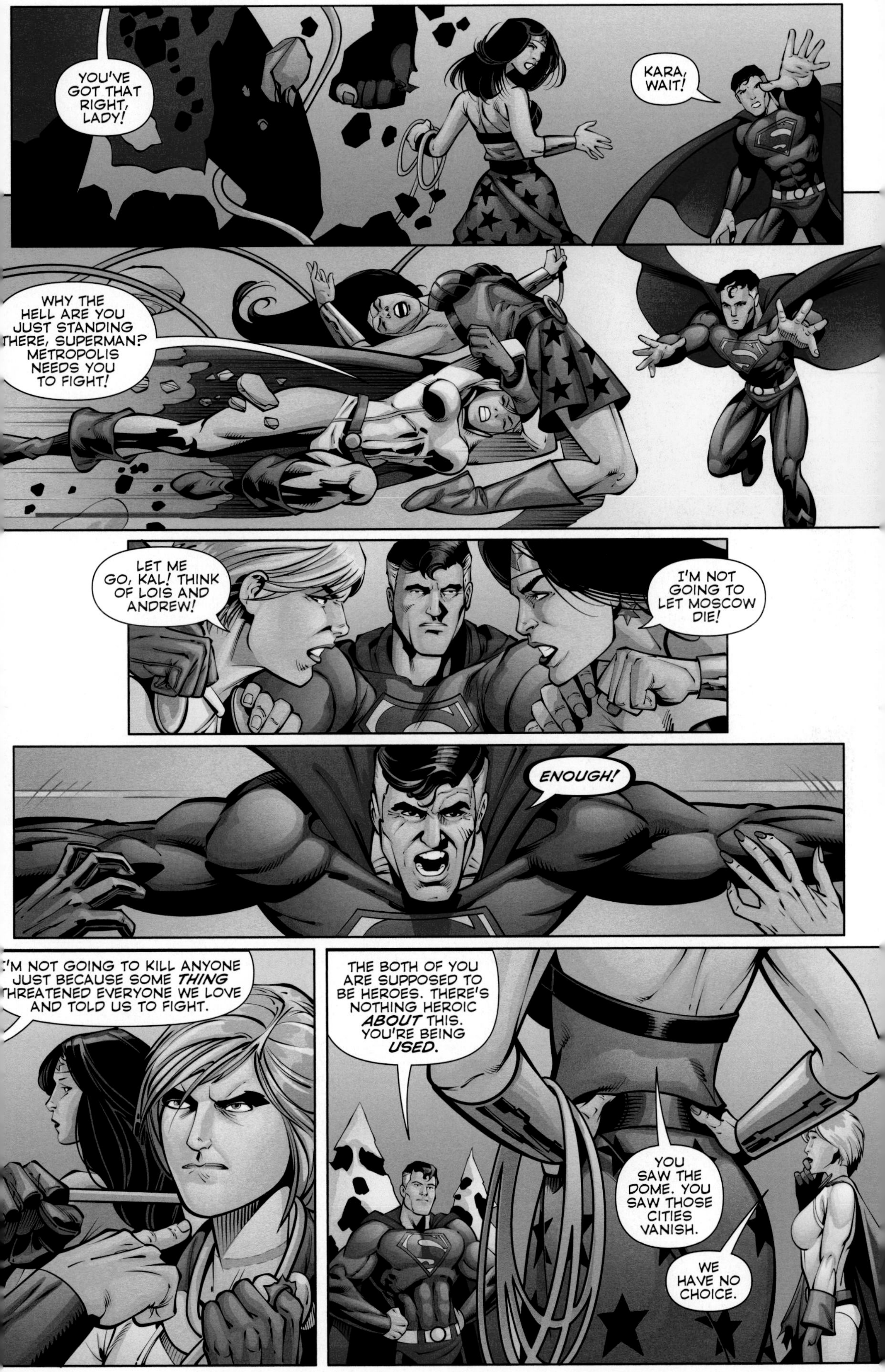
YOU'VE GOT THAT RIGHT, LADY!
KARA, WAIT!
WHY THE HELL ARE YOU JUST STANDING THERE, SUPERMAN? METROPOLIS NEEDS YOU TO FIGHT!
LET ME GO, KAL! THINK OF LOIS AND ANDREW!
I'M NOT GOING TO LET MOSCOW DIE!
ENOUGH!
I'M NOT GOING TO KILL ANYONE JUST BECAUSE SOME THING THREATENED EVERYONE WE LOVE AND TOLD US TO FIGHT.
THE BOTH OF YOU ARE SUPPOSED TO BE HEROES. THERE'S NOTHING HEROIC ABOUT THIS. YOU'RE BEING USED.
YOU SAW THE DOME. YOU SAW THOSE CITIES VANISH.
WE HAVE NO CHOICE.

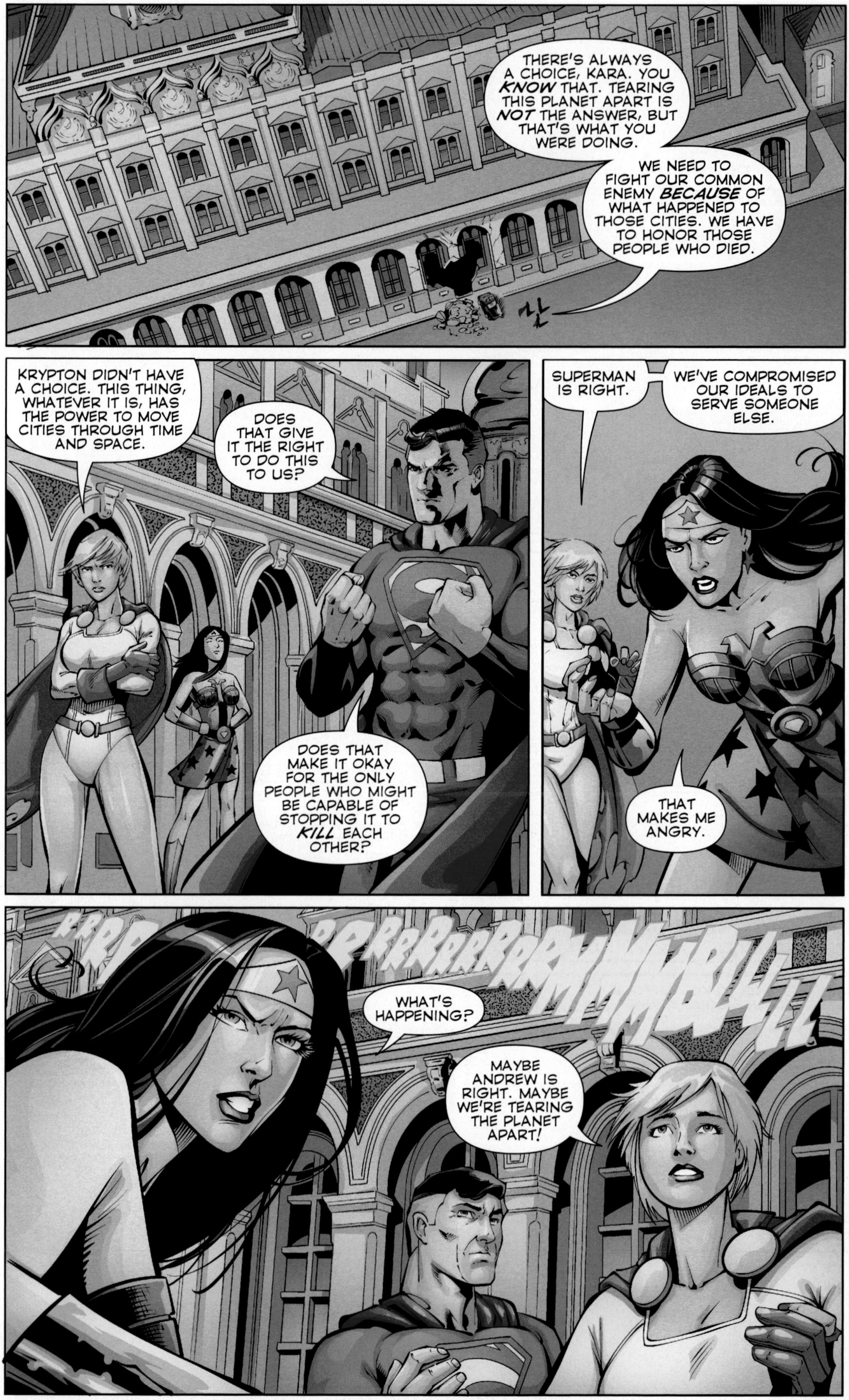
THERE'S ALWAYS A CHOICE, KARA. YOU KNOW THAT. TEARING THIS PLANET APART IS NOT THE ANSWER, BUT THAT'S WHAT YOU WERE DOING.
WE NEED TO FIGHT OUR COMMON ENEMY BECAUSE OF WHAT HAPPENED TO THOSE CITIES. WE HAVE TO HONOR THOSE PEOPLE WHO DIED.
KRYPTON DIDN'T HAVE A CHOICE. THIS THING, WHATEVER IT IS, HAS THE POWER TO MOVE CITIES THROUGH TIME AND SPACE.
DOES THAT GIVE IT THE RIGHT TO DO THIS TO US?
DOES THAT MAKE IT OKAY FOR THE ONLY PEOPLE WHO MIGHT BE CAPABLE OF STOPPING IT TO KILL EACH OTHER?
SUPERMAN IS RIGHT.
WE'VE COMPROMISED OUR IDEALS TO SERVE SOMEONE ELSE.
THAT MAKES ME ANGRY.
WHAT'S HAPPENING?
MAYBE ANDREW IS RIGHT. MAYBE WE'RE TEARING THE PLANET APART!

CRRRRRRRRRRRRRRMMMBLLLLLLL

WHY IS THE ROOM SHAKING?

I DON'T KNOW, BUT WE NEED TO ACT QUICKLY.

LEX, *PLEASE*. I'M BEGGING YOU NOT TO DO THIS. THIS IS *INSANITY*.

THIS MAKES *SENSE*. WE MUST DO EVERYTHING IN OUR POWER TO SAVE MOSCOW.

SO YOU'RE GOING TO KILL AN *ENTIRE CITY* FULL OF *INNOCENT PEOPLE?* IS THIS THE KIND OF MAN I MARRIED?

I'M DOING THIS FOR *YOU!*

I'M TRYING TO SAVE *YOUR* LIFE!

IS IT ABOUT *ME? TRULY?*

YES.

THEN I DON'T WANT IT.

I'M SORRY. *WHAT?*

I CAN'T LIVE WITH THAT.

I CAN'T BE RESPONSIBLE FOR WHAT YOU'RE ABOUT TO DO.

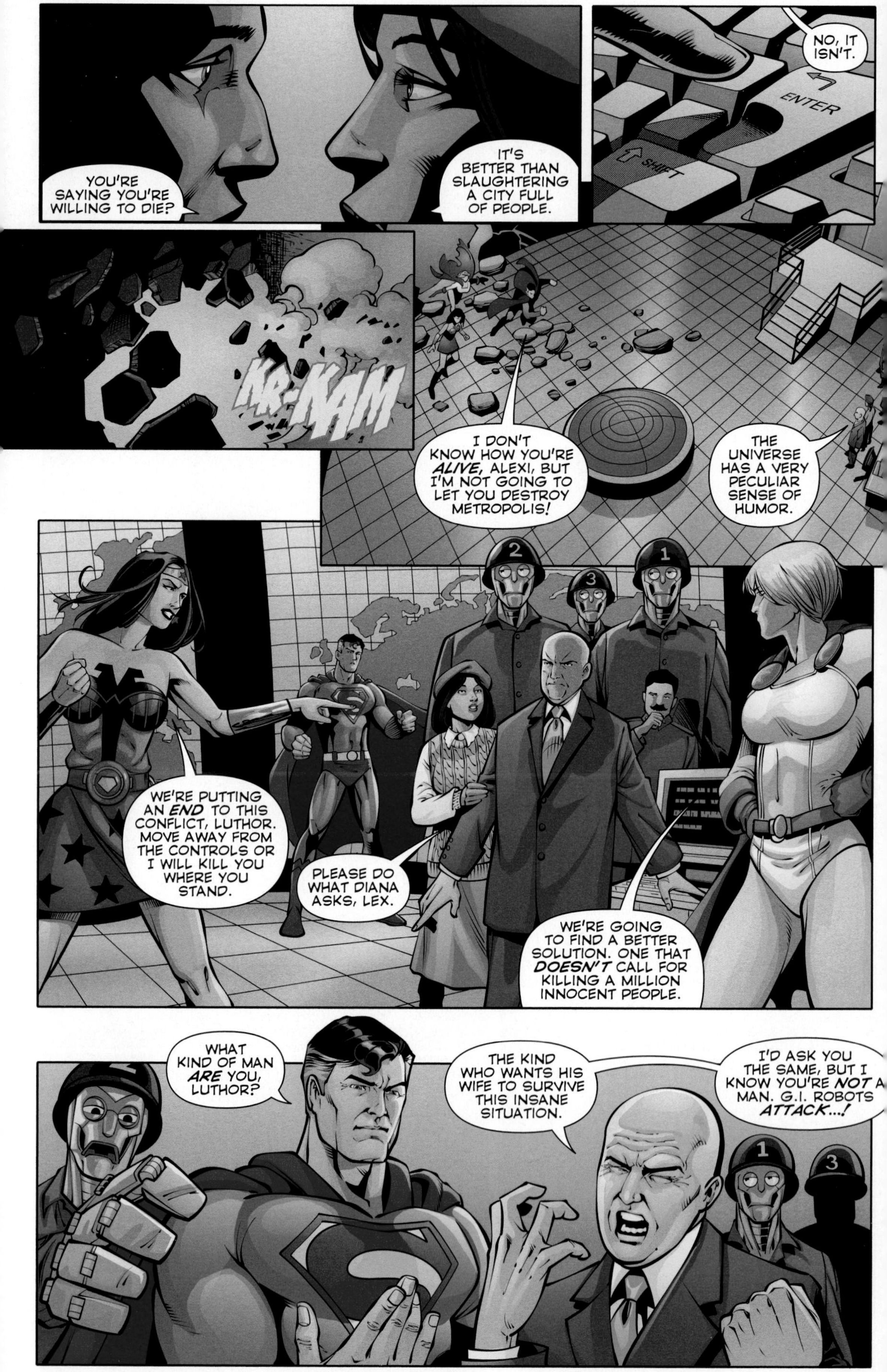
YOU'RE SAYING YOU'RE WILLING TO DIE?
IT'S BETTER THAN SLAUGHTERING A CITY FULL OF PEOPLE.
NO, IT ISN'T.
ENTER
SHIFT
KR-KAM
I DON'T KNOW HOW YOU'RE ALIVE, ALEXI, BUT I'M NOT GOING TO LET YOU DESTROY METROPOLIS!
THE UNIVERSE HAS A VERY PECULIAR SENSE OF HUMOR.
WE'RE PUTTING AN END TO THIS CONFLICT, LUTHOR. MOVE AWAY FROM THE CONTROLS OR I WILL KILL YOU WHERE YOU STAND.
PLEASE DO WHAT DIANA ASKS, LEX.
WE'RE GOING TO FIND A BETTER SOLUTION. ONE THAT DOESN'T CALL FOR KILLING A MILLION INNOCENT PEOPLE.
WHAT KIND OF MAN ARE YOU, LUTHOR?
THE KIND WHO WANTS HIS WIFE TO SURVIVE THIS INSANE SITUATION.
I'D ASK YOU THE SAME, BUT I KNOW YOU'RE NOT A MAN. G.I. ROBOTS ATTACK...!

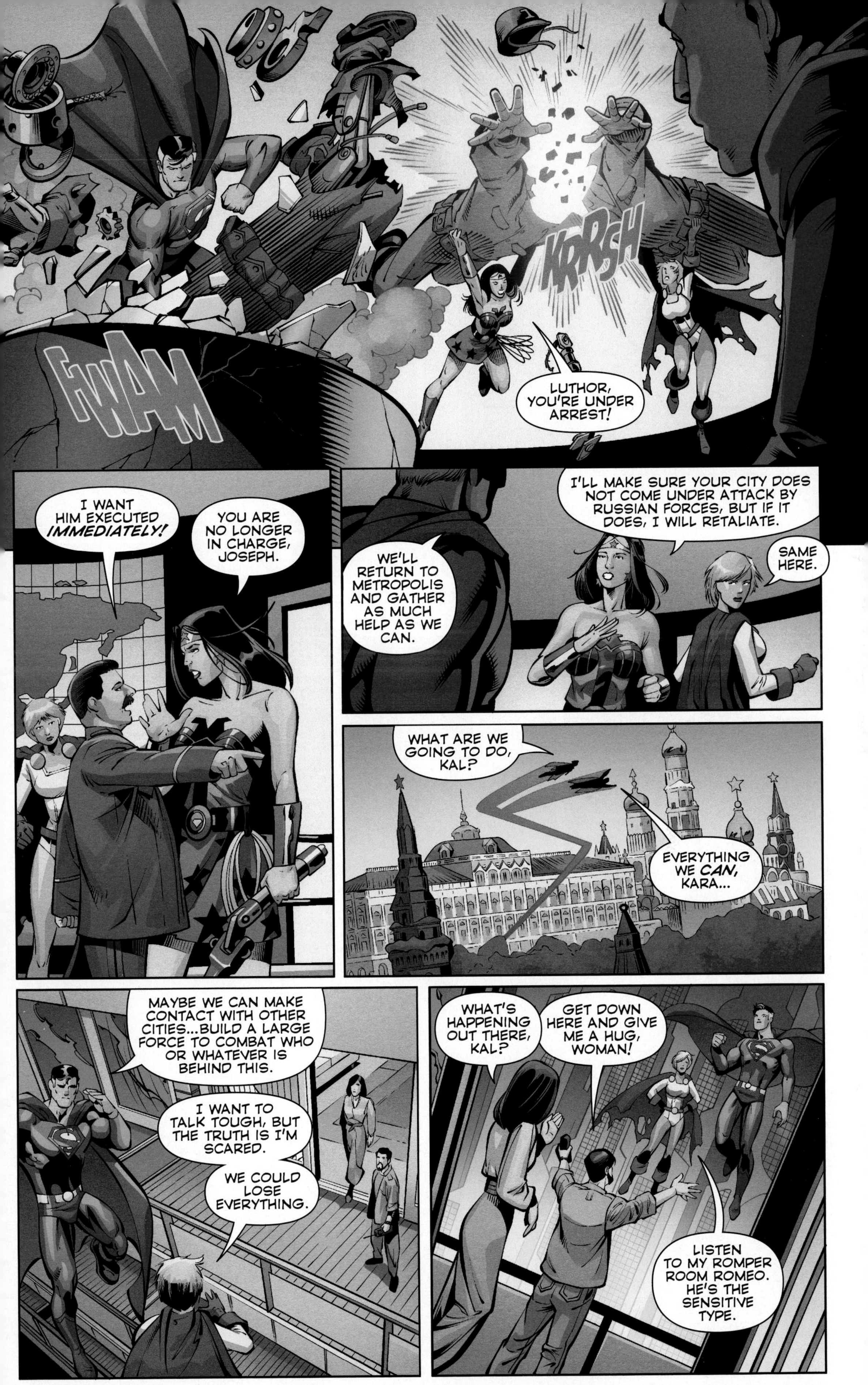

KRRSH
FWAM
LUTHOR, YOU'RE UNDER ARREST!
I WANT HIM EXECUTED IMMEDIATELY!
YOU ARE NO LONGER IN CHARGE, JOSEPH.
I'LL MAKE SURE YOUR CITY DOES NOT COME UNDER ATTACK BY RUSSIAN FORCES, BUT IF IT DOES, I WILL RETALIATE.
WE'LL RETURN TO METROPOLIS AND GATHER AS MUCH HELP AS WE CAN.
SAME HERE.
WHAT ARE WE GOING TO DO, KAL?
EVERYTHING WE CAN, KARA...
MAYBE WE CAN MAKE CONTACT WITH OTHER CITIES...BUILD A LARGE FORCE TO COMBAT WHO OR WHATEVER IS BEHIND THIS.
I WANT TO TALK TOUGH, BUT THE TRUTH IS I'M SCARED.
WE COULD LOSE EVERYTHING.
WHAT'S HAPPENING OUT THERE, KAL?
GET DOWN HERE AND GIVE ME A HUG, WOMAN!
LISTEN TO MY ROMPER ROOM ROMEO. HE'S THE SENSITIVE TYPE.

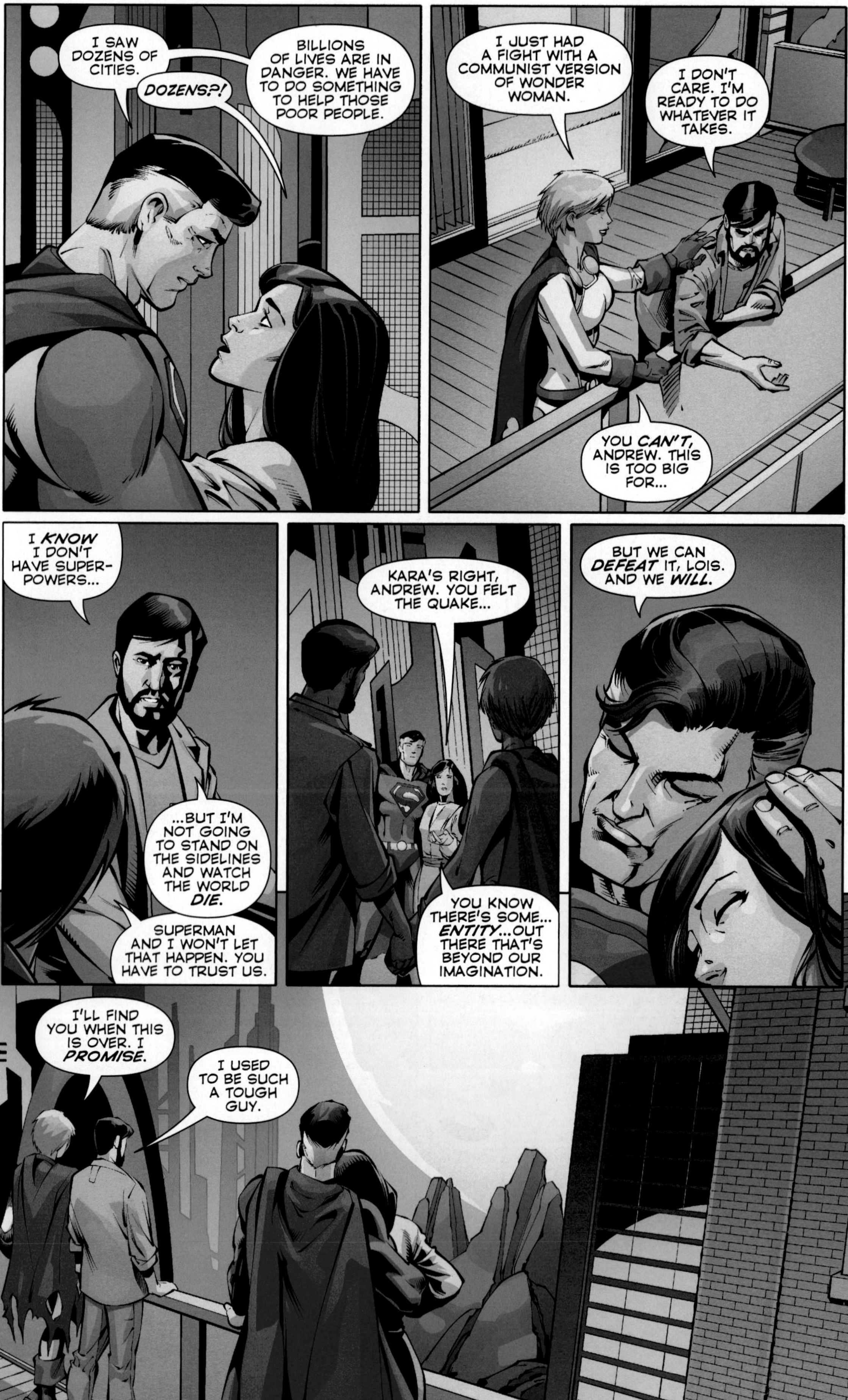

I SAW DOZENS OF CITIES.
DOZENS?!
BILLIONS OF LIVES ARE IN DANGER. WE HAVE TO DO SOMETHING TO HELP THOSE POOR PEOPLE.
I JUST HAD A FIGHT WITH A COMMUNIST VERSION OF WONDER WOMAN.
I DON'T CARE. I'M READY TO DO WHATEVER IT TAKES.
YOU CAN'T, ANDREW. THIS IS TOO BIG FOR...
I KNOW I DON'T HAVE SUPER-POWERS...
...BUT I'M NOT GOING TO STAND ON THE SIDELINES AND WATCH THE WORLD DIE.
SUPERMAN AND I WON'T LET THAT HAPPEN. YOU HAVE TO TRUST US.
KARA'S RIGHT, ANDREW. YOU FELT THE QUAKE...
YOU KNOW THERE'S SOME... ENTITY...OUT THERE THAT'S BEYOND OUR IMAGINATION.
BUT WE CAN DEFEAT IT, LOIS. AND WE WILL.
I'LL FIND YOU WHEN THIS IS OVER. I PROMISE.
I USED TO BE SUCH A TOUGH GUY.

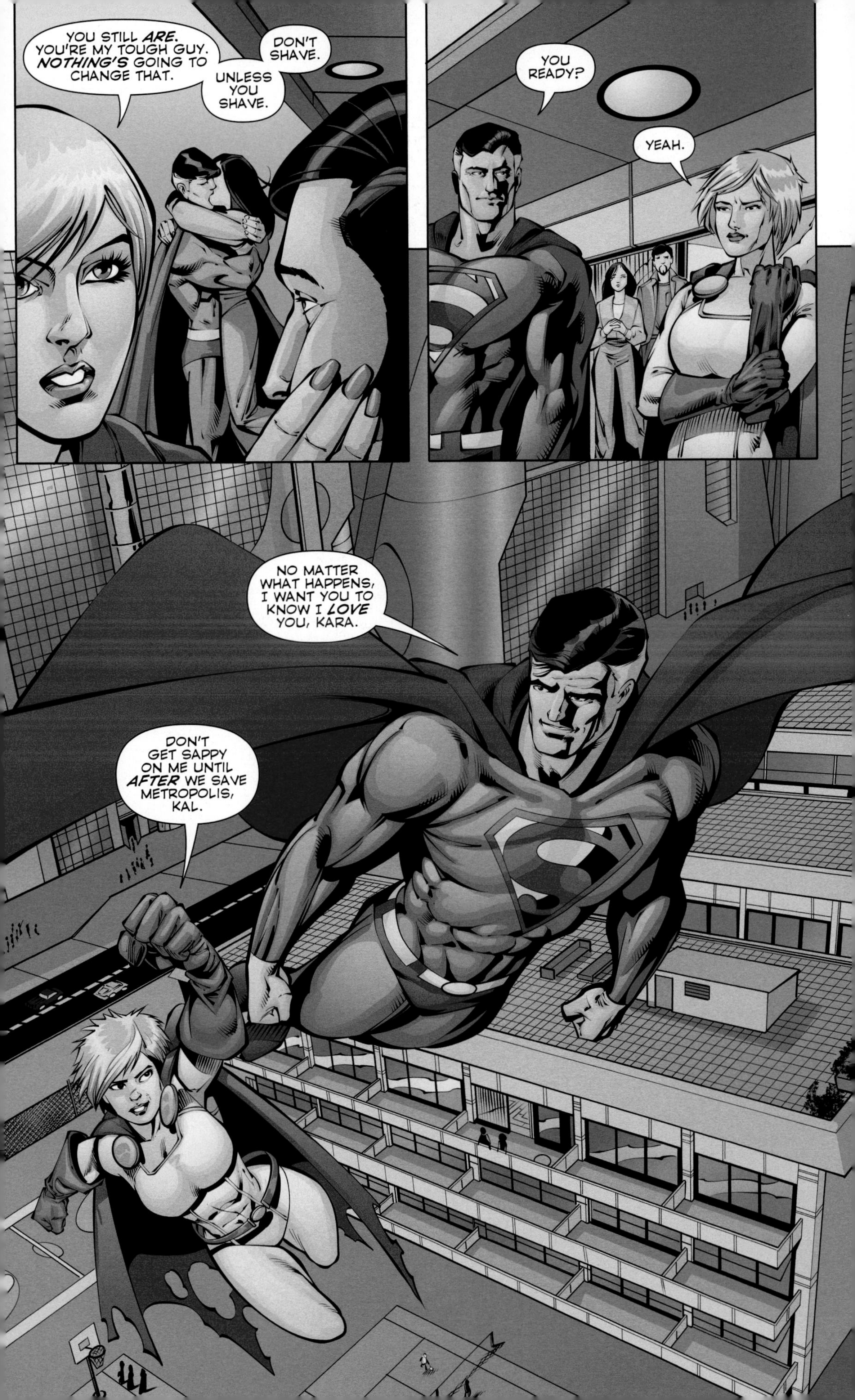
YOU STILL ARE. YOU'RE MY TOUGH GUY. NOTHING'S GOING TO CHANGE THAT.
DON'T SHAVE.
UNLESS YOU SHAVE.
YOU READY?
YEAH.
NO MATTER WHAT HAPPENS, I WANT YOU TO KNOW I LOVE YOU, KARA.
DON'T GET SAPPY ON ME UNTIL AFTER WE SAVE METROPOLIS, KAL.

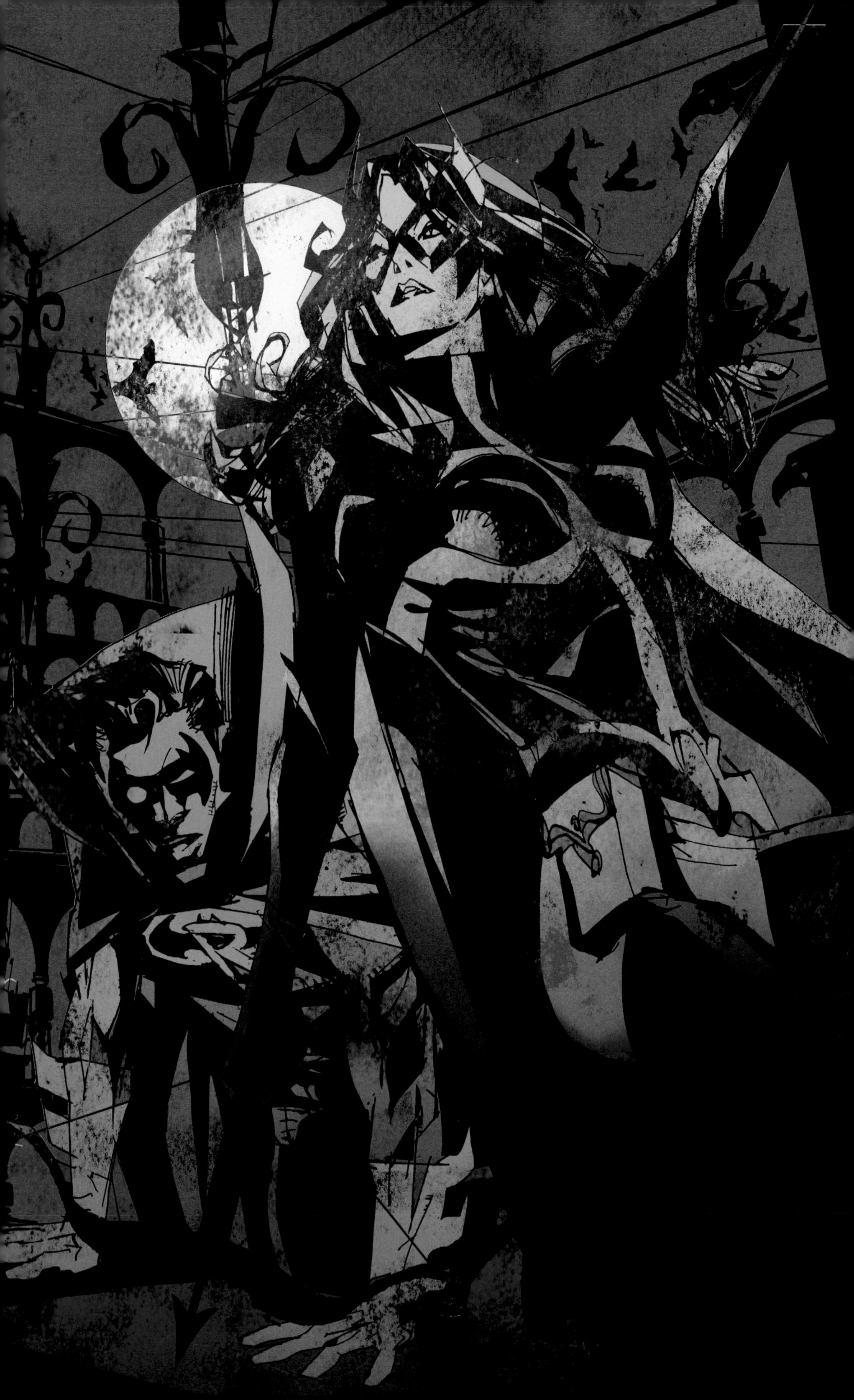

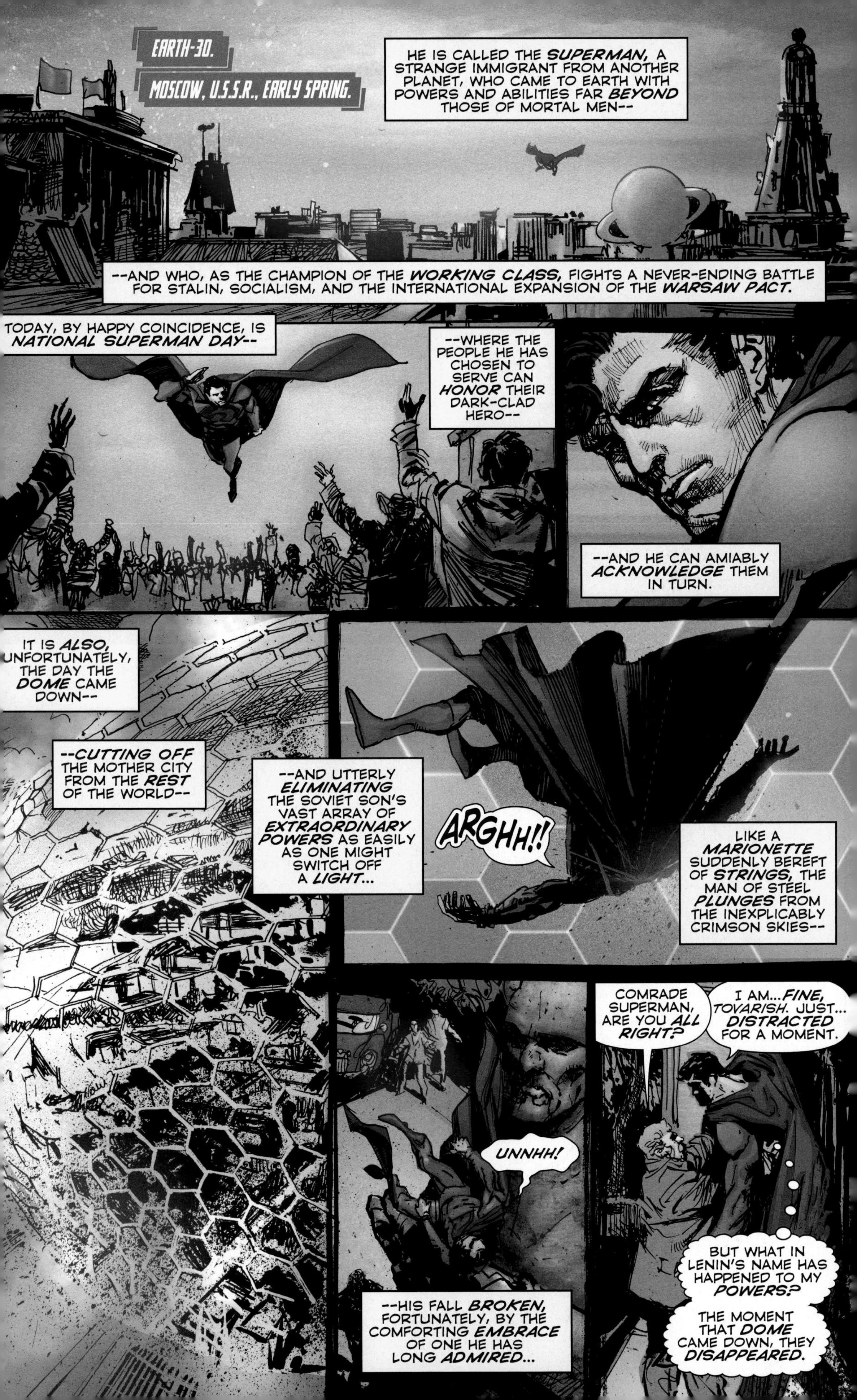

EARTH-30.
MOSCOW, U.S.S.R., EARLY SPRING.
HE IS CALLED THE SUPERMAN, A STRANGE IMMIGRANT FROM ANOTHER PLANET, WHO CAME TO EARTH WITH POWERS AND ABILITIES FAR BEYOND THOSE OF MORTAL MEN--
--AND WHO, AS THE CHAMPION OF THE WORKING CLASS, FIGHTS A NEVER-ENDING BATTLE FOR STALIN, SOCIALISM, AND THE INTERNATIONAL EXPANSION OF THE WARSAW PACT.
TODAY, BY HAPPY COINCIDENCE, IS NATIONAL SUPERMAN DAY--
--WHERE THE PEOPLE HE HAS CHOSEN TO SERVE CAN HONOR THEIR DARK-CLAD HERO--
--AND HE CAN AMIABLY ACKNOWLEDGE THEM IN TURN.
IT IS ALSO, UNFORTUNATELY, THE DAY THE DOME CAME DOWN--
--CUTTING OFF THE MOTHER CITY FROM THE REST OF THE WORLD--
--AND UTTERLY ELIMINATING THE SOVIET SON'S VAST ARRAY OF EXTRAORDINARY POWERS AS EASILY AS ONE MIGHT SWITCH OFF A LIGHT...
ARGHH!!
LIKE A MARIONETTE SUDDENLY BEREFT OF STRINGS, THE MAN OF STEEL PLUNGES FROM THE INEXPLICABLY CRIMSON SKIES--
UNNHH!
--HIS FALL BROKEN, FORTUNATELY, BY THE COMFORTING EMBRACE OF ONE HE HAS LONG ADMIRED...
COMRADE SUPERMAN, ARE YOU ALL RIGHT?
I AM...FINE, TOVARISH. JUST... DISTRACTED FOR A MOMENT.
BUT WHAT IN LENIN'S NAME HAS HAPPENED TO MY POWERS?
THE MOMENT THAT DOME CAME DOWN, THEY DISAPPEARED.

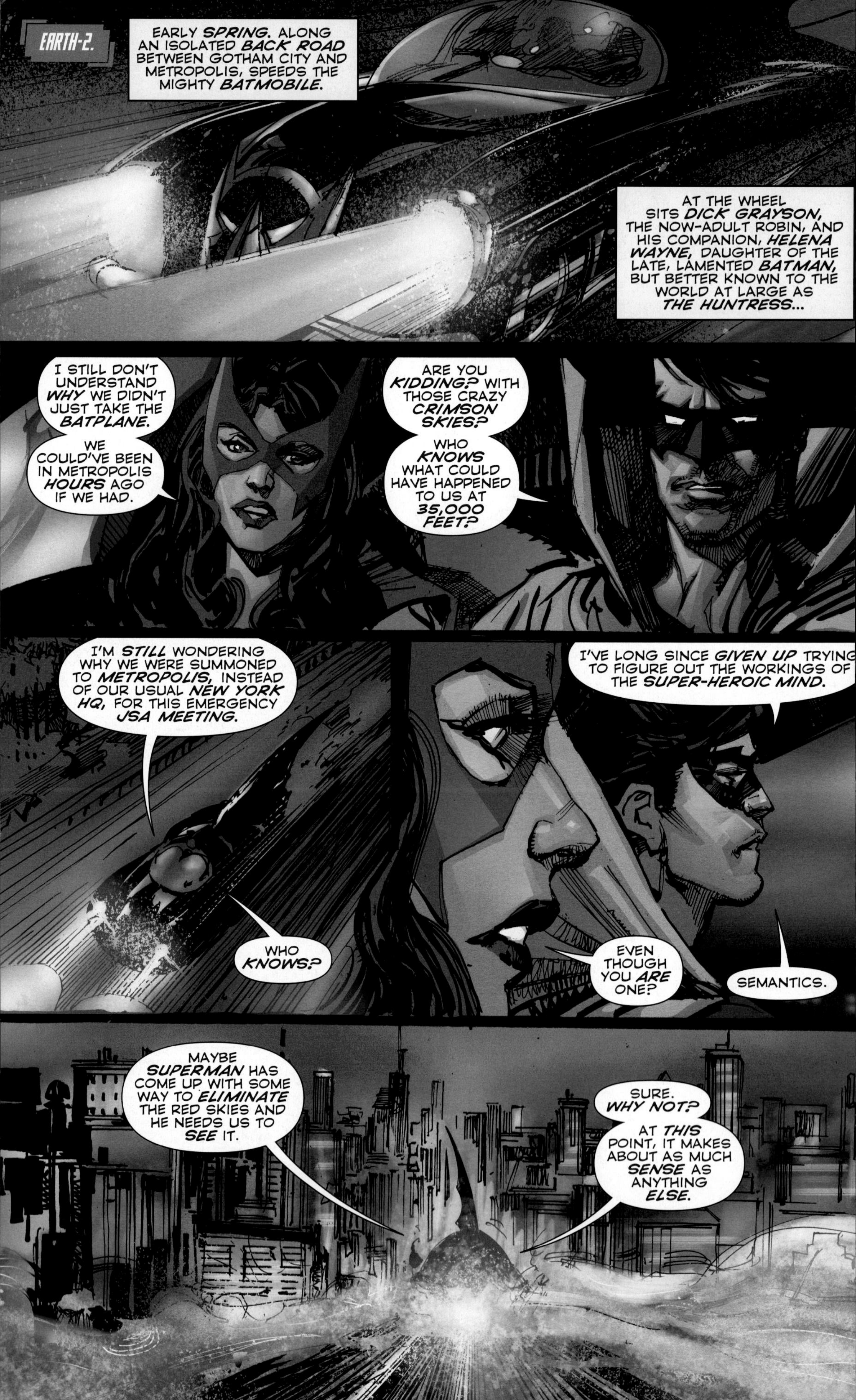
EARTH-2.
EARLY SPRING. ALONG AN ISOLATED BACK ROAD BETWEEN GOTHAM CITY AND METROPOLIS, SPEEDS THE MIGHTY BATMOBILE.
AT THE WHEEL SITS DICK GRAYSON, THE NOW-ADULT ROBIN, AND HIS COMPANION, HELENA WAYNE, DAUGHTER OF THE LATE, LAMENTED BATMAN, BUT BETTER KNOWN TO THE WORLD AT LARGE AS THE HUNTRESS...
I STILL DON'T UNDERSTAND WHY WE DIDN'T JUST TAKE THE BATPLANE.
WE COULD'VE BEEN IN METROPOLIS HOURS AGO IF WE HAD.
ARE YOU KIDDING? WITH THOSE CRAZY CRIMSON SKIES?
WHO KNOWS WHAT COULD HAVE HAPPENED TO US AT 35,000 FEET?
I'M STILL WONDERING WHY WE WERE SUMMONED TO METROPOLIS, INSTEAD OF OUR USUAL NEW YORK HQ, FOR THIS EMERGENCY JSA MEETING.
WHO KNOWS?
I'VE LONG SINCE GIVEN UP TRYING TO FIGURE OUT THE WORKINGS OF THE SUPER-HEROIC MIND.
EVEN THOUGH YOU ARE ONE?
SEMANTICS.
MAYBE SUPERMAN HAS COME UP WITH SOME WAY TO ELIMINATE THE RED SKIES AND HE NEEDS US TO SEE IT.
SURE. WHY NOT?
AT THIS POINT, IT MAKES ABOUT AS MUCH SENSE AS ANYTHING ELSE.

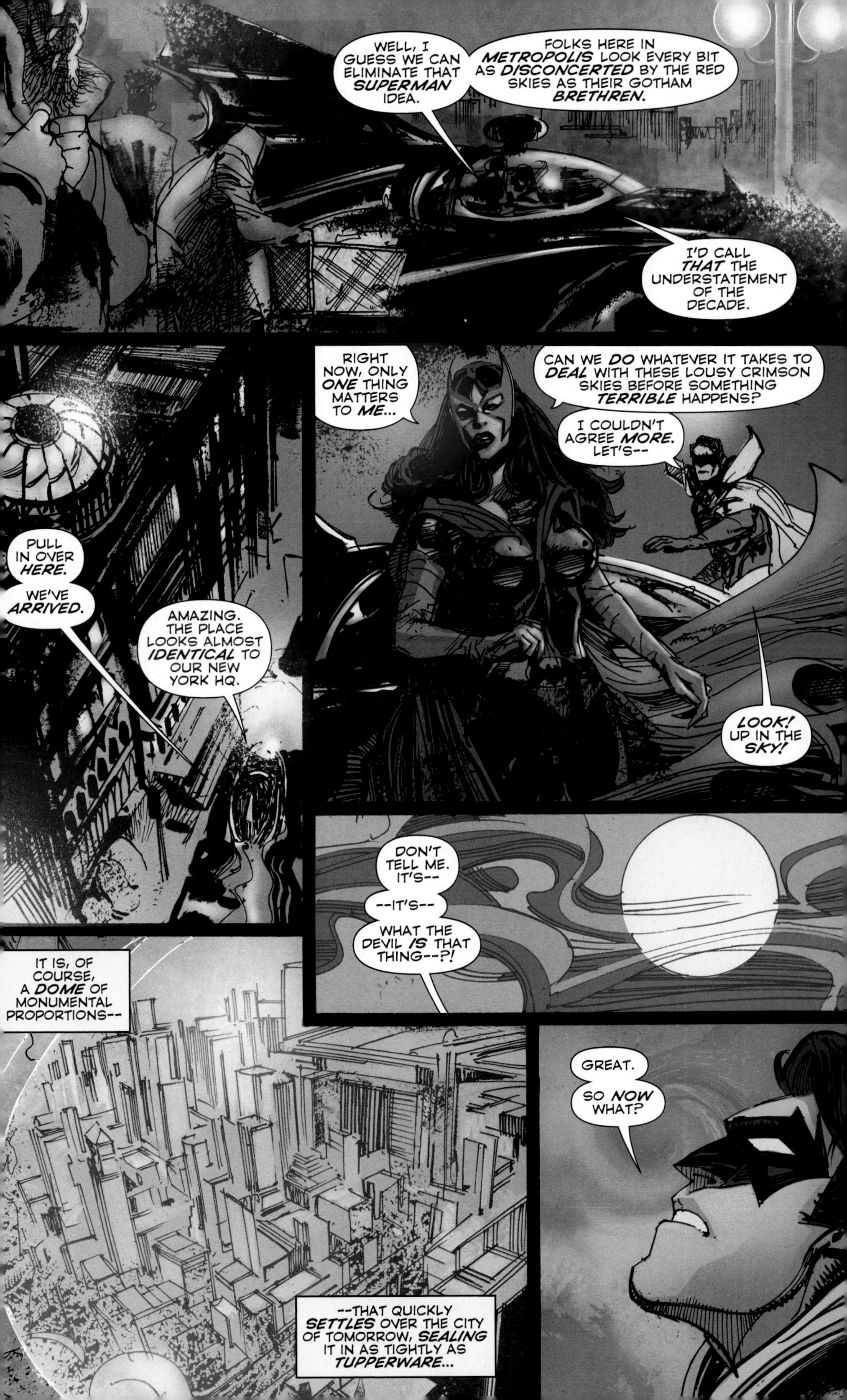
FOLKS HERE IN METROPOLIS LOOK EVERY BIT AS DISCONCERTED BY THE RED SKIES AS THEIR GOTHAM BRETHREN.
WELL, I GUESS WE CAN ELIMINATE THAT SUPERMAN IDEA.
I'D CALL THAT THE UNDERSTATEMENT OF THE DECADE.
PULL IN OVER HERE.
WE'VE ARRIVED.
AMAZING. THE PLACE LOOKS ALMOST IDENTICAL TO OUR NEW YORK HQ.
RIGHT NOW, ONLY ONE THING MATTERS TO ME...
CAN WE DO WHATEVER IT TAKES TO DEAL WITH THESE LOUSY CRIMSON SKIES BEFORE SOMETHING TERRIBLE HAPPENS?
I COULDN'T AGREE MORE. LET'S--
LOOK! UP IN THE SKY!
DON'T TELL ME. IT'S--
--IT'S--
WHAT THE DEVIL IS THAT THING--?!
IT IS, OF COURSE, A DOME OF MONUMENTAL PROPORTIONS--
--THAT QUICKLY SETTLES OVER THE CITY OF TOMORROW, SEALING IT IN AS TIGHTLY AS TUPPERWARE...
GREAT.
SO NOW WHAT?

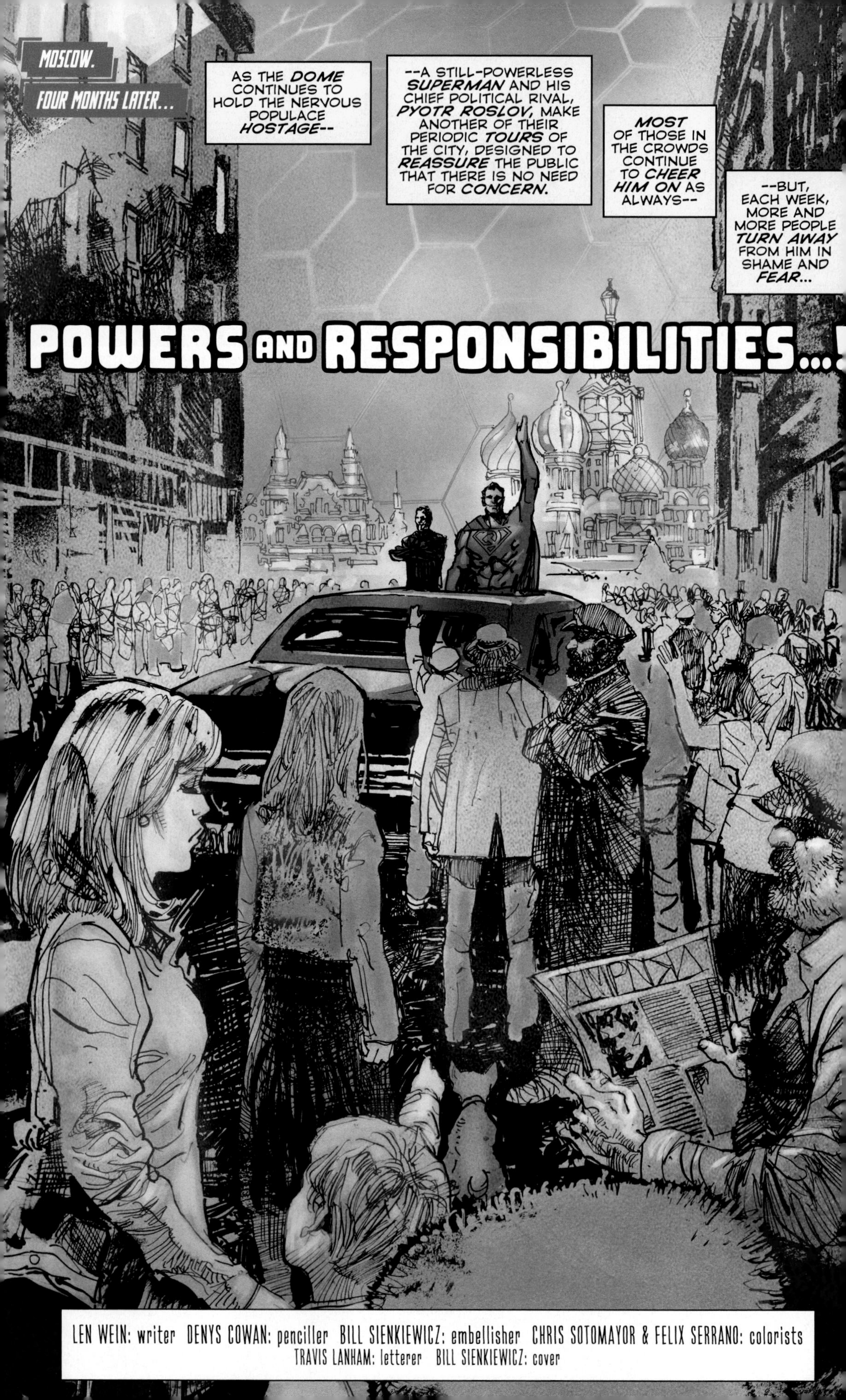
MOSCOW.
FOUR MONTHS LATER...
AS THE DOME CONTINUES TO HOLD THE NERVOUS POPULACE HOSTAGE--
--A STILL-POWERLESS SUPERMAN AND HIS CHIEF POLITICAL RIVAL, PYOTR ROSLOV, MAKE ANOTHER OF THEIR PERIODIC TOURS OF THE CITY, DESIGNED TO REASSURE THE PUBLIC THAT THERE IS NO NEED FOR CONCERN.
MOST OF THOSE IN THE CROWDS CONTINUE TO CHEER HIM ON AS ALWAYS--
--BUT, EACH WEEK, MORE AND MORE PEOPLE TURN AWAY FROM HIM IN SHAME AND FEAR...
POWERS AND RESPONSIBILITIES...!
LEN WEIN: writer DENYS COWAN: penciller BILL SIENKIEWICZ: embellisher CHRIS SOTOMAYOR & FELIX SERRANO: colorists
TRAVIS LANHAM: letterer BILL SIENKIEWICZ: cover

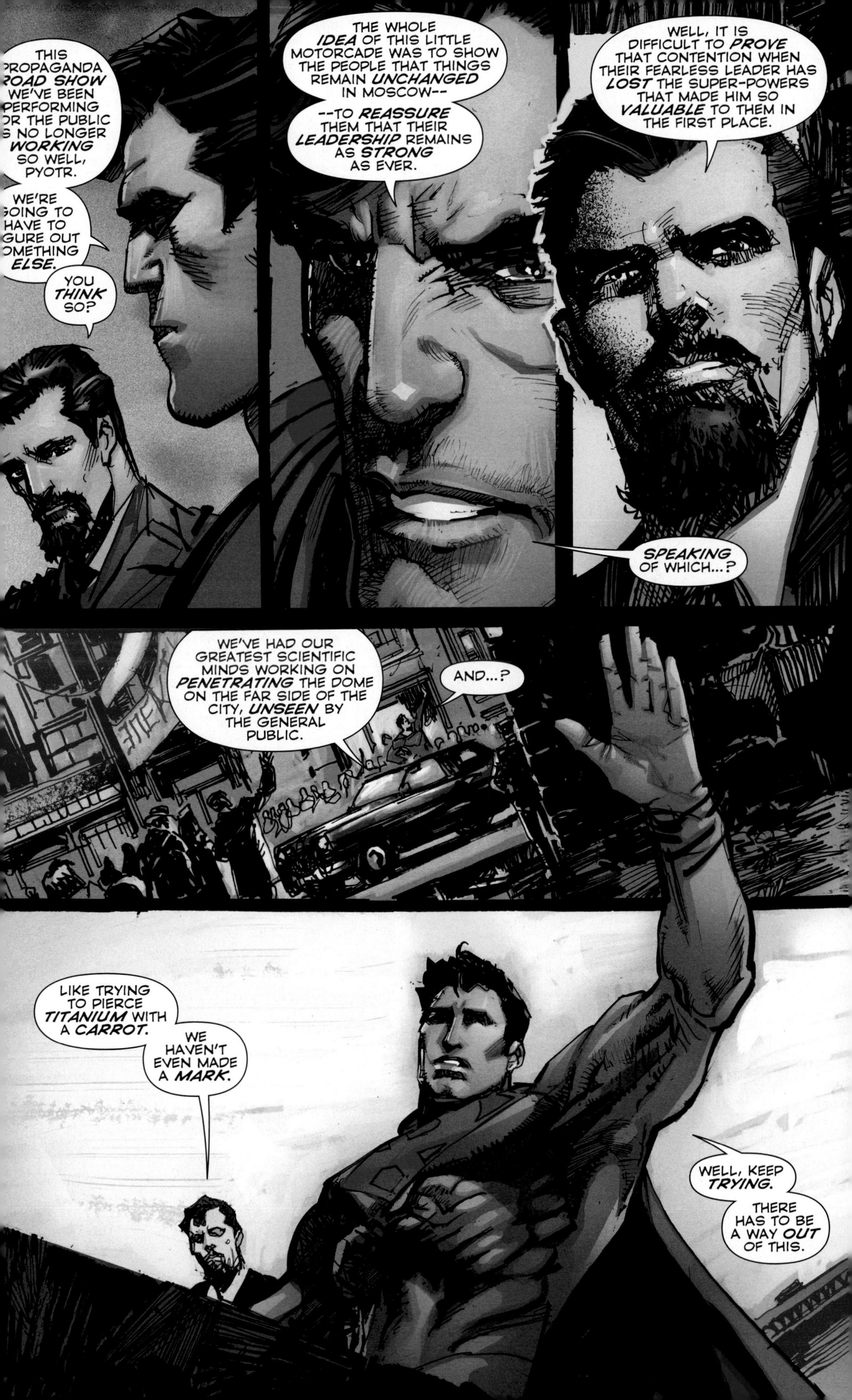
THIS PROPAGANDA ROAD SHOW WE'VE BEEN PERFORMING FOR THE PUBLIC IS NO LONGER WORKING SO WELL, PYOTR.
WE'RE GOING TO HAVE TO FIGURE OUT SOMETHING ELSE.
YOU THINK SO?
THE WHOLE IDEA OF THIS LITTLE MOTORCADE WAS TO SHOW THE PEOPLE THAT THINGS REMAIN UNCHANGED IN MOSCOW--
--TO REASSURE THEM THAT THEIR LEADERSHIP REMAINS AS STRONG AS EVER.
WELL, IT IS DIFFICULT TO PROVE THAT CONTENTION WHEN THEIR FEARLESS LEADER HAS LOST THE SUPER-POWERS THAT MADE HIM SO VALUABLE TO THEM IN THE FIRST PLACE.
SPEAKING OF WHICH...?
WE'VE HAD OUR GREATEST SCIENTIFIC MINDS WORKING ON PENETRATING THE DOME ON THE FAR SIDE OF THE CITY, UNSEEN BY THE GENERAL PUBLIC.
AND...?
LIKE TRYING TO PIERCE TITANIUM WITH A CARROT.
WE HAVEN'T EVEN MADE A MARK.
WELL, KEEP TRYING.
THERE HAS TO BE A WAY OUT OF THIS.

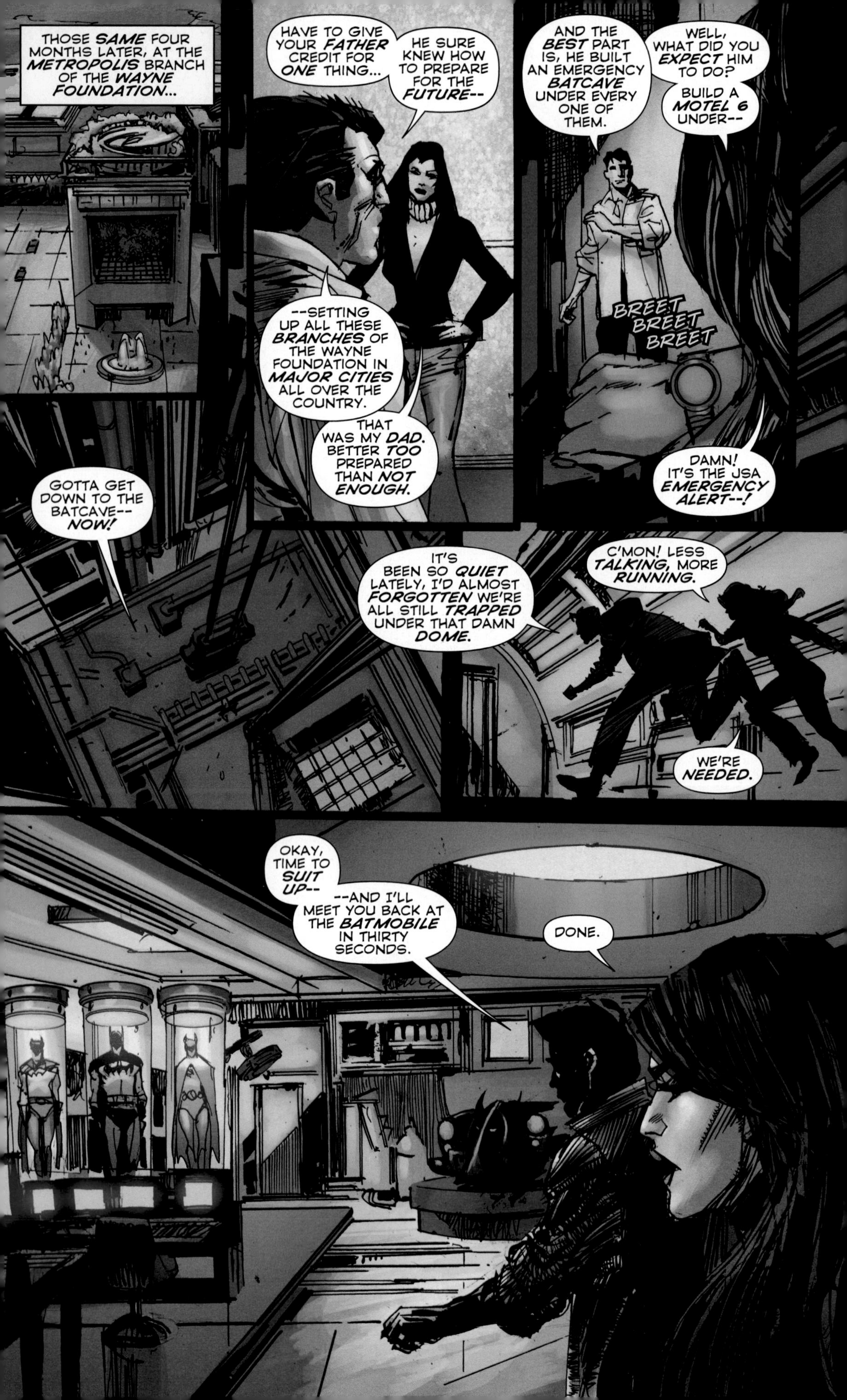
THOSE SAME FOUR MONTHS LATER, AT THE METROPOLIS BRANCH OF THE WAYNE FOUNDATION...
HAVE TO GIVE YOUR FATHER CREDIT FOR ONE THING...
HE SURE KNEW HOW TO PREPARE FOR THE FUTURE--
--SETTING UP ALL THESE BRANCHES OF THE WAYNE FOUNDATION IN MAJOR CITIES ALL OVER THE COUNTRY.
THAT WAS MY DAD. BETTER TOO PREPARED THAN NOT ENOUGH.
AND THE BEST PART IS, HE BUILT AN EMERGENCY BATCAVE UNDER EVERY ONE OF THEM.
WELL, WHAT DID YOU EXPECT HIM TO DO?
BUILD A MOTEL 6 UNDER--
BREET BREET BREET
DAMN! IT'S THE JSA EMERGENCY ALERT--!
GOTTA GET DOWN TO THE BATCAVE-- NOW!
IT'S BEEN SO QUIET LATELY, I'D ALMOST FORGOTTEN WE'RE ALL STILL TRAPPED UNDER THAT DAMN DOME.
C'MON! LESS TALKING, MORE RUNNING.
WE'RE NEEDED.
OKAY, TIME TO SUIT UP--
--AND I'LL MEET YOU BACK AT THE BATMOBILE IN THIRTY SECONDS.
DONE.

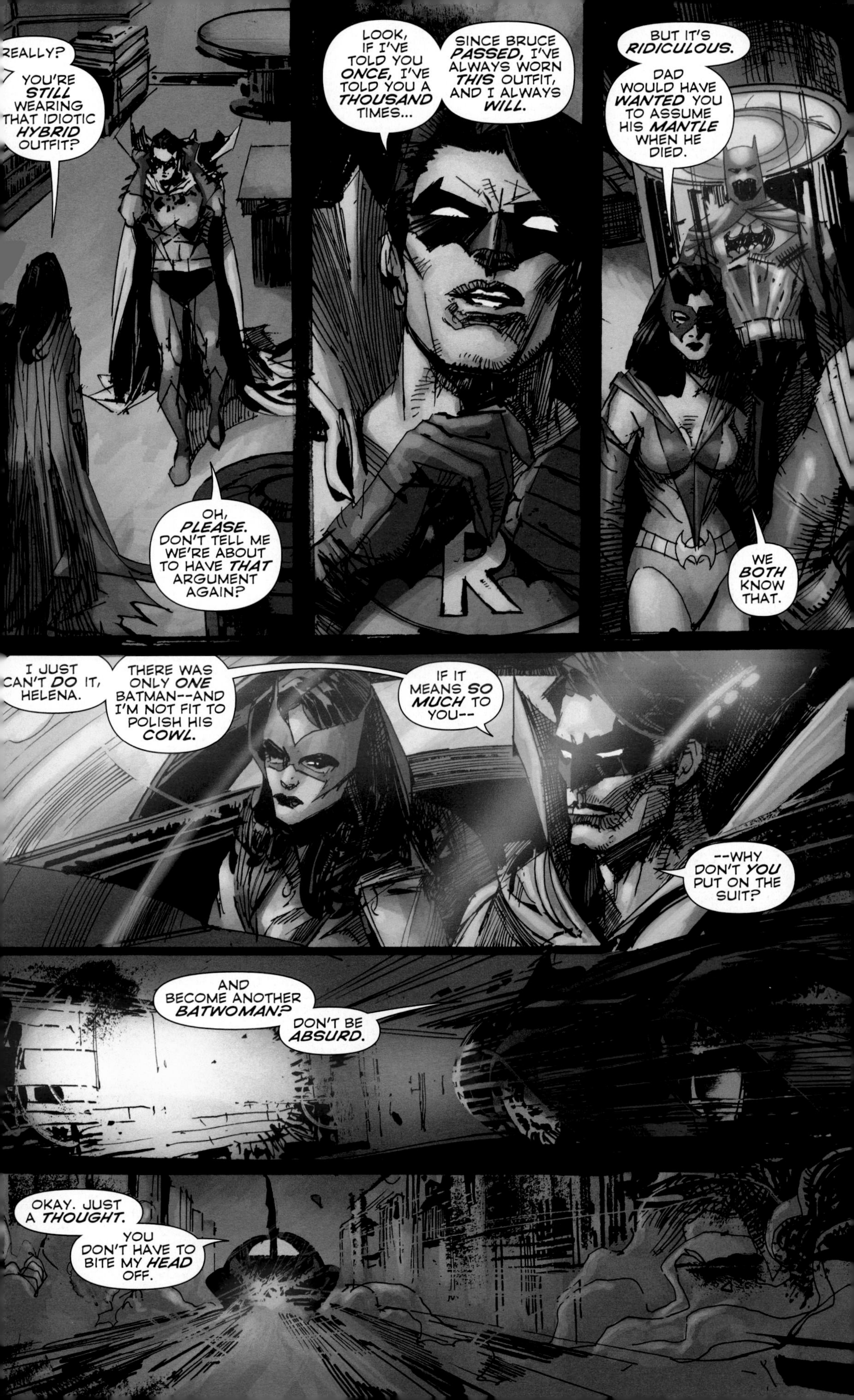
REALLY?
YOU'RE STILL WEARING THAT IDIOTIC HYBRID OUTFIT?
OH, PLEASE. DON'T TELL ME WE'RE ABOUT TO HAVE THAT ARGUMENT AGAIN?
LOOK, IF I'VE TOLD YOU ONCE, I'VE TOLD YOU A THOUSAND TIMES...
SINCE BRUCE PASSED, I'VE ALWAYS WORN THIS OUTFIT, AND I ALWAYS WILL.
BUT IT'S RIDICULOUS.
DAD WOULD HAVE WANTED YOU TO ASSUME HIS MANTLE WHEN HE DIED.
WE BOTH KNOW THAT.
I JUST CAN'T DO IT, HELENA.
THERE WAS ONLY ONE BATMAN--AND I'M NOT FIT TO POLISH HIS COWL.
IF IT MEANS SO MUCH TO YOU--
--WHY DON'T YOU PUT ON THE SUIT?
AND BECOME ANOTHER BATWOMAN?
DON'T BE ABSURD.
OKAY. JUST A THOUGHT.
YOU DON'T HAVE TO BITE MY HEAD OFF.

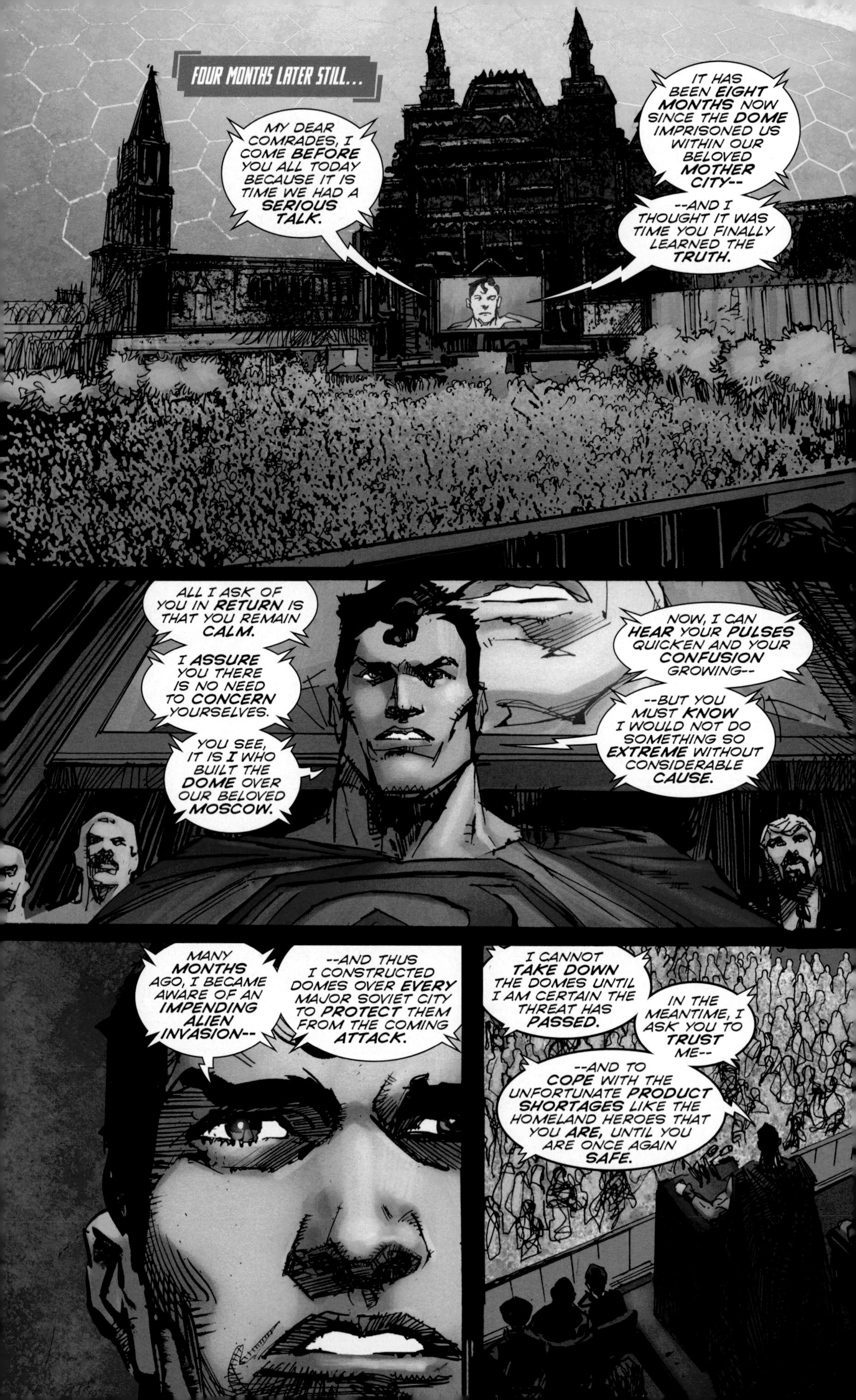
FOUR MONTHS LATER STILL...
MY DEAR COMRADES, I COME BEFORE YOU ALL TODAY BECAUSE IT IS TIME WE HAD A SERIOUS TALK.
IT HAS BEEN EIGHT MONTHS NOW SINCE THE DOME IMPRISONED US WITHIN OUR BELOVED MOTHER CITY--
--AND I THOUGHT IT WAS TIME YOU FINALLY LEARNED THE TRUTH.
ALL I ASK OF YOU IN RETURN IS THAT YOU REMAIN CALM.
I ASSURE YOU THERE IS NO NEED TO CONCERN YOURSELVES.
YOU SEE, IT IS I WHO BUILT THE DOME OVER OUR BELOVED MOSCOW.
NOW, I CAN HEAR YOUR PULSES QUICKEN AND YOUR CONFUSION GROWING--
--BUT YOU MUST KNOW I WOULD NOT DO SOMETHING SO EXTREME WITHOUT CONSIDERABLE CAUSE.
MANY MONTHS AGO, I BECAME AWARE OF AN IMPENDING ALIEN INVASION--
--AND THUS I CONSTRUCTED DOMES OVER EVERY MAJOR SOVIET CITY TO PROTECT THEM FROM THE COMING ATTACK.
I CANNOT TAKE DOWN THE DOMES UNTIL I AM CERTAIN THE THREAT HAS PASSED.
IN THE MEANTIME, I ASK YOU TO TRUST ME--
--AND TO COPE WITH THE UNFORTUNATE PRODUCT SHORTAGES LIKE THE HOMELAND HEROES THAT YOU ARE, UNTIL YOU ARE ONCE AGAIN SAFE.

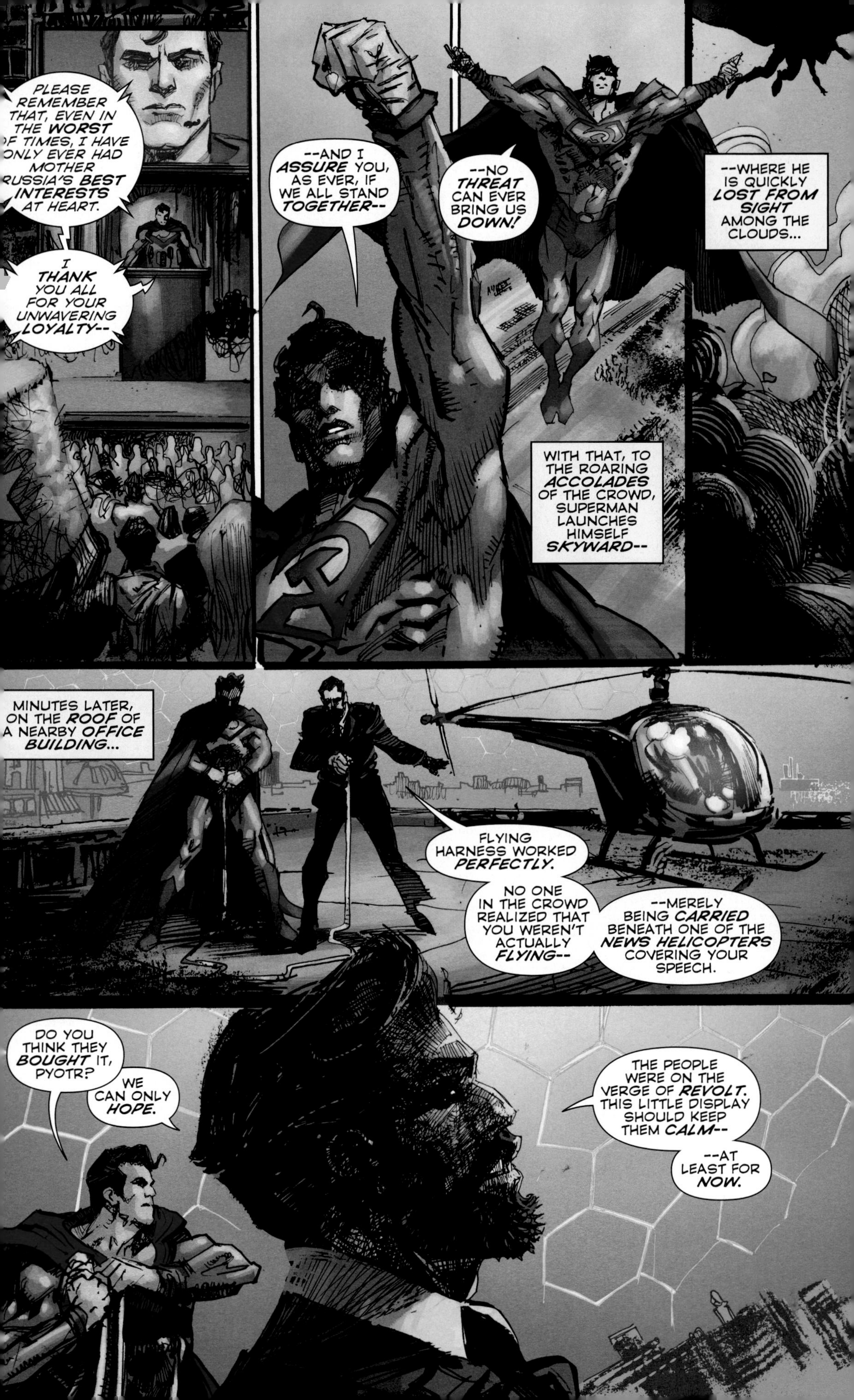
PLEASE REMEMBER THAT, EVEN IN THE WORST OF TIMES, I HAVE ONLY EVER HAD MOTHER RUSSIA'S BEST INTERESTS AT HEART.
I THANK YOU ALL FOR YOUR UNWAVERING LOYALTY--
--AND I ASSURE YOU, AS EVER, IF WE ALL STAND TOGETHER--
--NO THREAT CAN EVER BRING US DOWN!
WITH THAT, TO THE ROARING ACCOLADES OF THE CROWD, SUPERMAN LAUNCHES HIMSELF SKYWARD--
--WHERE HE IS QUICKLY LOST FROM SIGHT AMONG THE CLOUDS...
MINUTES LATER, ON THE ROOF OF A NEARBY OFFICE BUILDING...
FLYING HARNESS WORKED PERFECTLY.
NO ONE IN THE CROWD REALIZED THAT YOU WEREN'T ACTUALLY FLYING--
--MERELY BEING CARRIED BENEATH ONE OF THE NEWS HELICOPTERS COVERING YOUR SPEECH.
DO YOU THINK THEY BOUGHT IT, PYOTR?
WE CAN ONLY HOPE.
THE PEOPLE WERE ON THE VERGE OF REVOLT. THIS LITTLE DISPLAY SHOULD KEEP THEM CALM--
--AT LEAST FOR NOW.

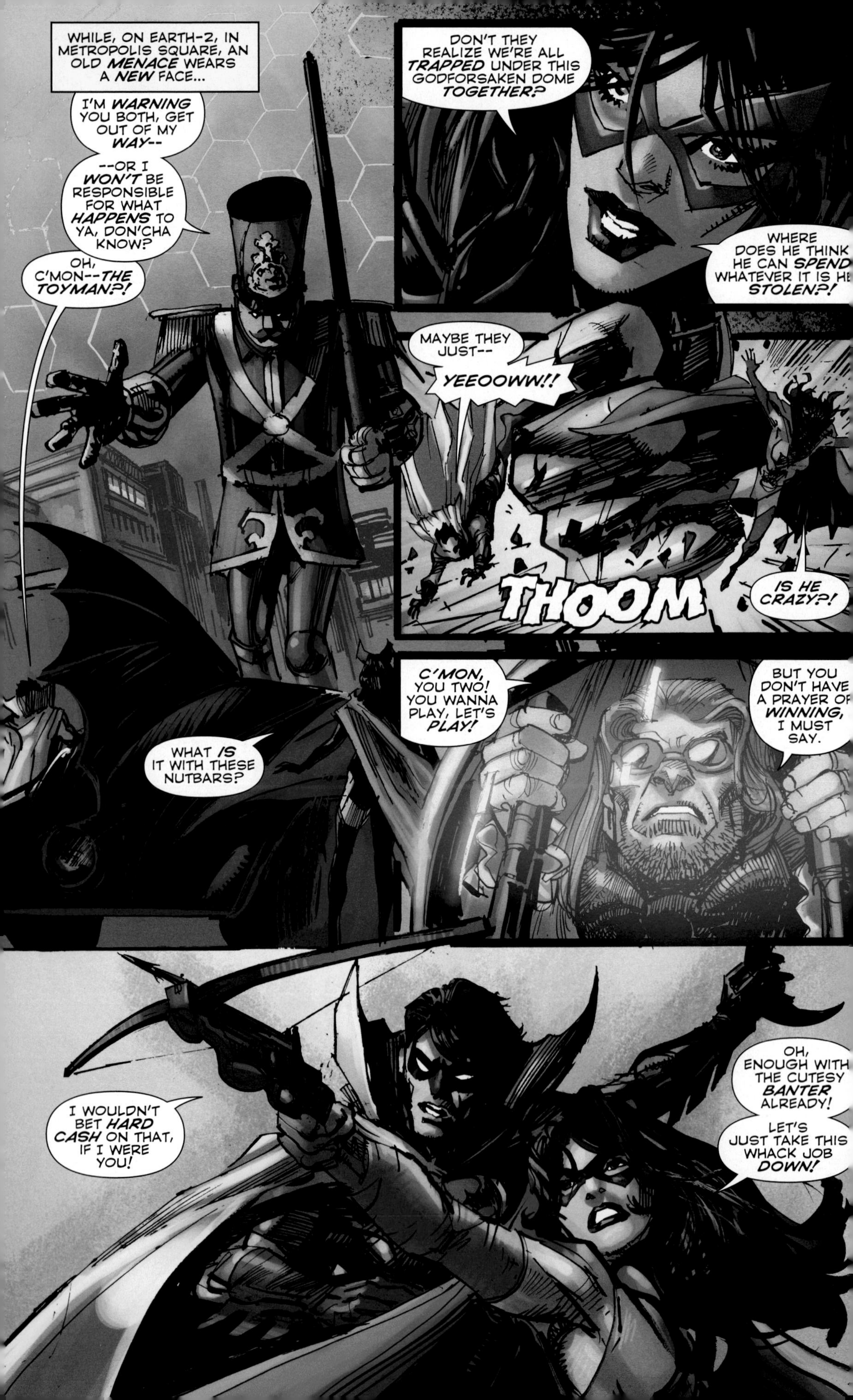

WHILE, ON EARTH-2, IN METROPOLIS SQUARE, AN OLD MENACE WEARS A NEW FACE...
I'M WARNING YOU BOTH, GET OUT OF MY WAY--
--OR I WON'T BE RESPONSIBLE FOR WHAT HAPPENS TO YA, DON'CHA KNOW?
OH, C'MON--THE TOYMAN?!
WHAT IS IT WITH THESE NUTBARS?
DON'T THEY REALIZE WE'RE ALL TRAPPED UNDER THIS GODFORSAKEN DOME TOGETHER?
WHERE DOES HE THINK HE CAN SPEND WHATEVER IT IS HE STOLEN?!
MAYBE THEY JUST--
YEEOOWW!!
THOOM
IS HE CRAZY?!
C'MON, YOU TWO! YOU WANNA PLAY, LET'S PLAY!
BUT YOU DON'T HAVE A PRAYER OF WINNING, I MUST SAY.
I WOULDN'T BET HARD CASH ON THAT, IF I WERE YOU!
OH, ENOUGH WITH THE CUTESY BANTER ALREADY!
LET'S JUST TAKE THIS WHACK JOB DOWN!

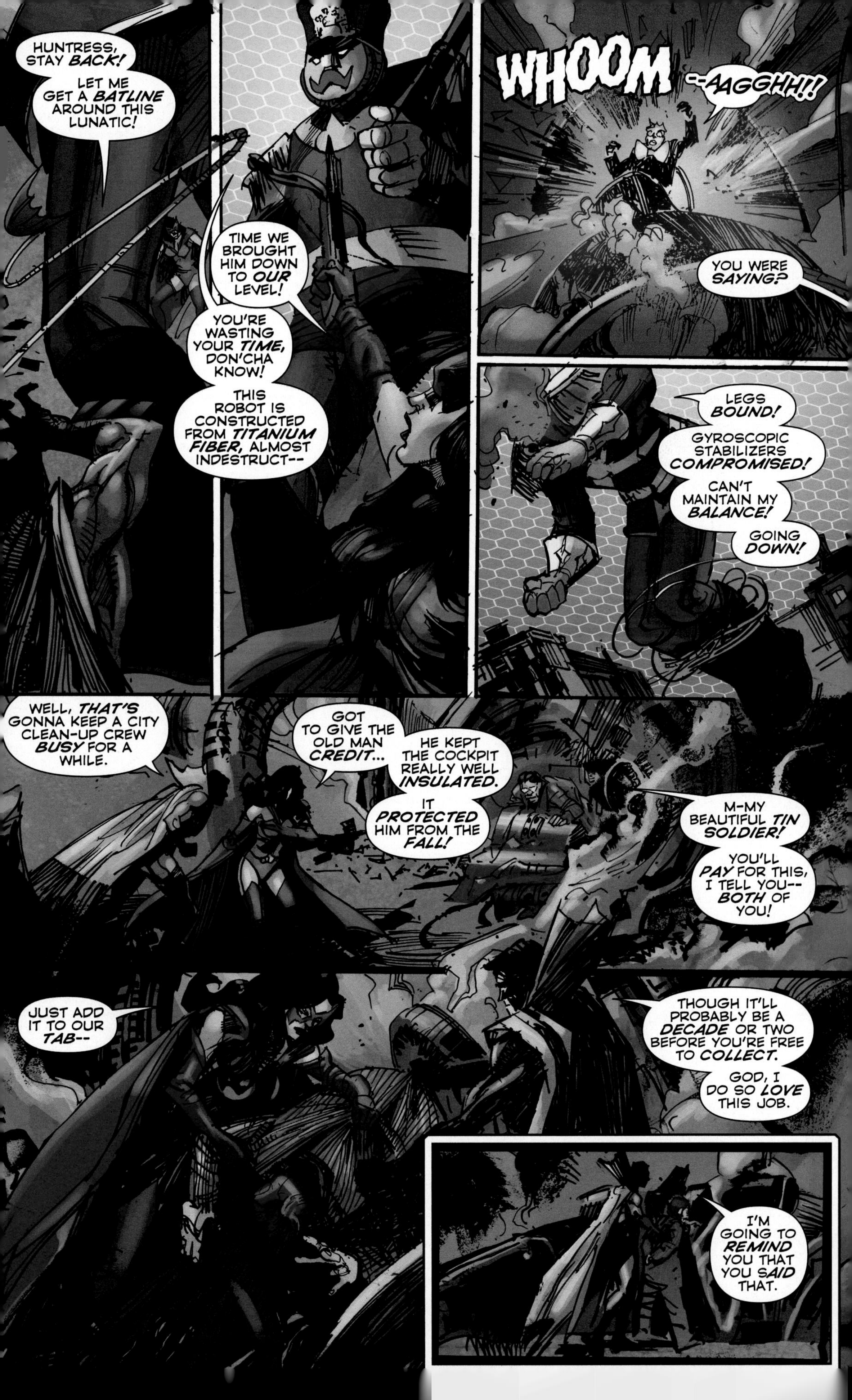
HUNTRESS, STAY BACK!
LET ME GET A BATLINE AROUND THIS LUNATIC!
TIME WE BROUGHT HIM DOWN TO OUR LEVEL!
YOU'RE WASTING YOUR TIME, DON'CHA KNOW!
THIS ROBOT IS CONSTRUCTED FROM TITANIUM FIBER, ALMOST INDESTRUCT--
WHOOM
--AAGGHH!!
YOU WERE SAYING?
LEGS BOUND!
GYROSCOPIC STABILIZERS COMPROMISED!
CAN'T MAINTAIN MY BALANCE!
GOING DOWN!
WELL, THAT'S GONNA KEEP A CITY CLEAN-UP CREW BUSY FOR A WHILE.
GOT TO GIVE THE OLD MAN CREDIT...
HE KEPT THE COCKPIT REALLY WELL INSULATED.
IT PROTECTED HIM FROM THE FALL!
M-MY BEAUTIFUL TIN SOLDIER!
YOU'LL PAY FOR THIS, I TELL YOU-- BOTH OF YOU!
JUST ADD IT TO OUR TAB--
THOUGH IT'LL PROBABLY BE A DECADE OR TWO BEFORE YOU'RE FREE TO COLLECT.
GOD, I DO SO LOVE THIS JOB.
I'M GOING TO REMIND YOU THAT YOU SAID THAT.

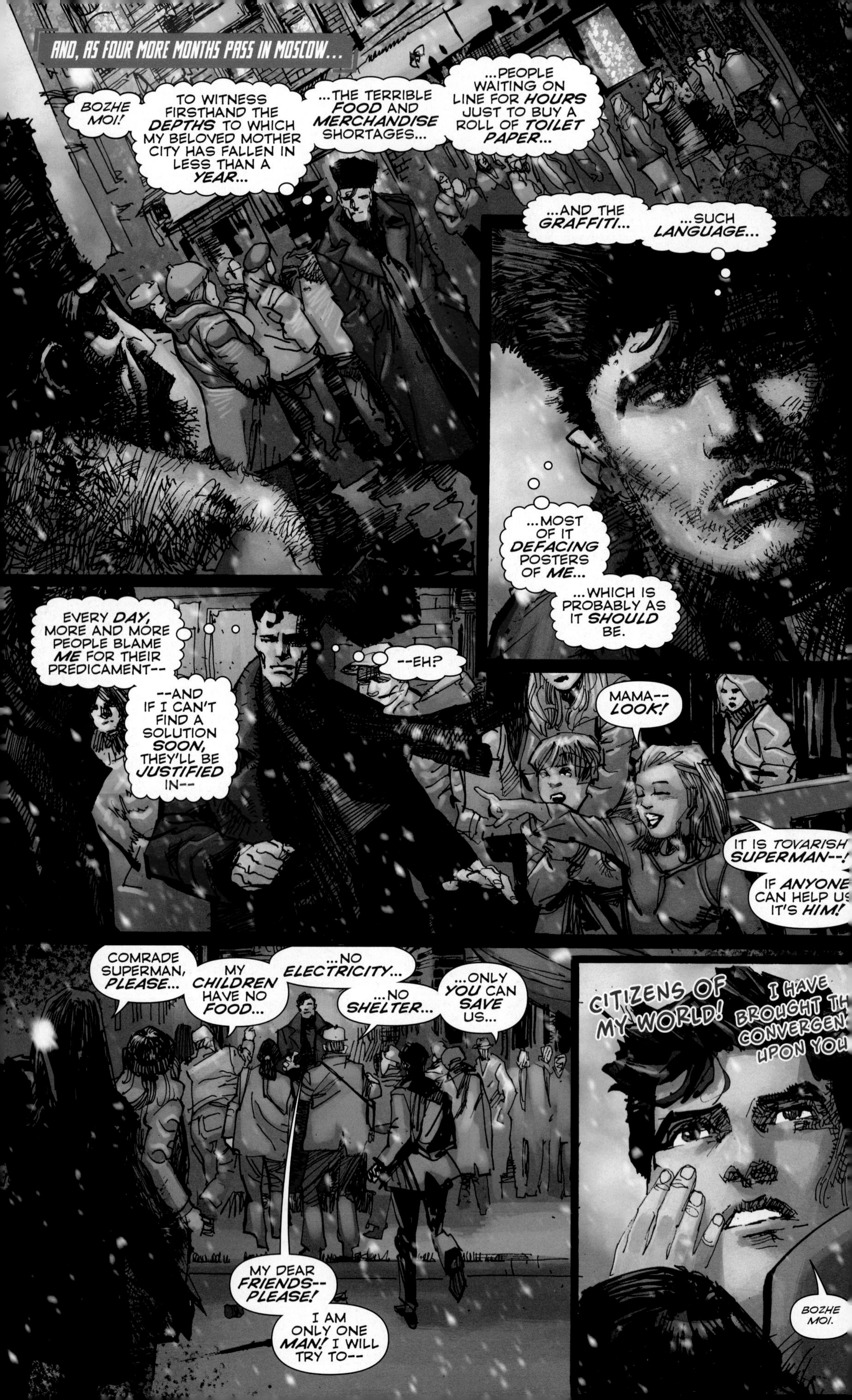
AND, AS FOUR MORE MONTHS PASS IN MOSCOW...
BOZHE MOI!
TO WITNESS FIRSTHAND THE DEPTHS TO WHICH MY BELOVED MOTHER CITY HAS FALLEN IN LESS THAN A YEAR...
...THE TERRIBLE FOOD AND MERCHANDISE SHORTAGES...
...PEOPLE WAITING ON LINE FOR HOURS JUST TO BUY A ROLL OF TOILET PAPER...
...AND THE GRAFFITI...
...SUCH LANGUAGE...
...MOST OF IT DEFACING POSTERS OF ME...
...WHICH IS PROBABLY AS IT SHOULD BE.
EVERY DAY, MORE AND MORE PEOPLE BLAME ME FOR THEIR PREDICAMENT--
--AND IF I CAN'T FIND A SOLUTION SOON, THEY'LL BE JUSTIFIED IN--
--EH?
MAMA--LOOK!
IT IS TOVARISH SUPERMAN--!
IF ANYONE CAN HELP US IT'S HIM!
COMRADE SUPERMAN, PLEASE...
MY CHILDREN HAVE NO FOOD...
...NO ELECTRICITY...
...NO SHELTER...
...ONLY YOU CAN SAVE US...
MY DEAR FRIENDS--PLEASE!
I AM ONLY ONE MAN! I WILL TRY TO--
CITIZENS OF MY WORLD!
I HAVE BROUGHT TH CONVERGEN UPON YOU
BOZHE MOI.

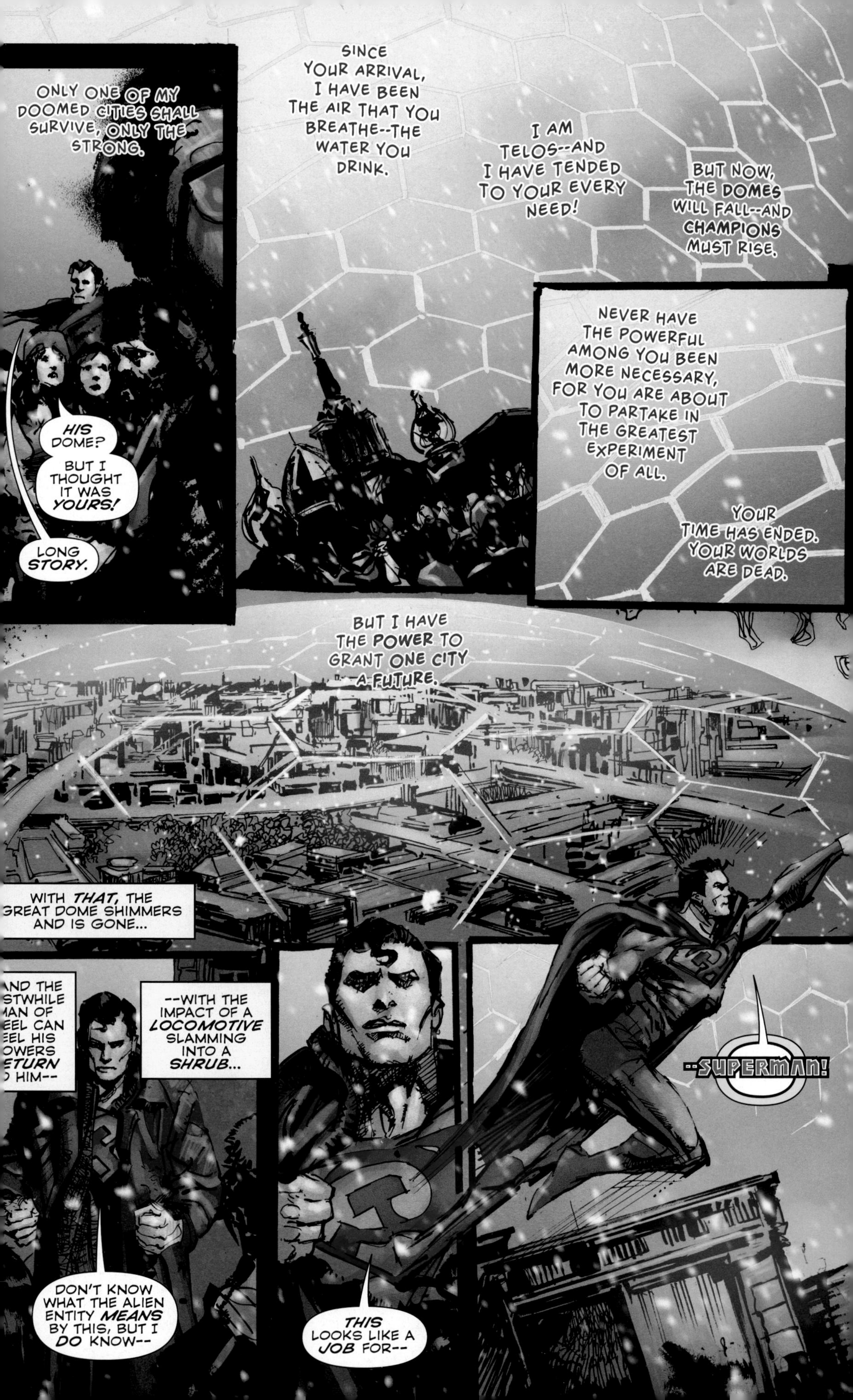

ONLY ONE OF MY DOOMED CITIES SHALL SURVIVE, ONLY THE STRONG.
SINCE YOUR ARRIVAL, I HAVE BEEN THE AIR THAT YOU BREATHE--THE WATER YOU DRINK.
I AM TELOS--AND I HAVE TENDED TO YOUR EVERY NEED!
BUT NOW, THE DOMES WILL FALL--AND CHAMPIONS MUST RISE.
HIS DOME? BUT I THOUGHT IT WAS YOURS!
LONG STORY.
NEVER HAVE THE POWERFUL AMONG YOU BEEN MORE NECESSARY, FOR YOU ARE ABOUT TO PARTAKE IN THE GREATEST EXPERIMENT OF ALL.
YOUR TIME HAS ENDED. YOUR WORLDS ARE DEAD.
BUT I HAVE THE POWER TO GRANT ONE CITY A FUTURE.
WITH THAT, THE GREAT DOME SHIMMERS AND IS GONE...
--WITH THE IMPACT OF A LOCOMOTIVE SLAMMING INTO A SHRUB...
DON'T KNOW WHAT THE ALIEN ENTITY MEANS BY THIS, BUT I DO KNOW--
THIS LOOKS LIKE A JOB FOR--
--SUPERMAN!

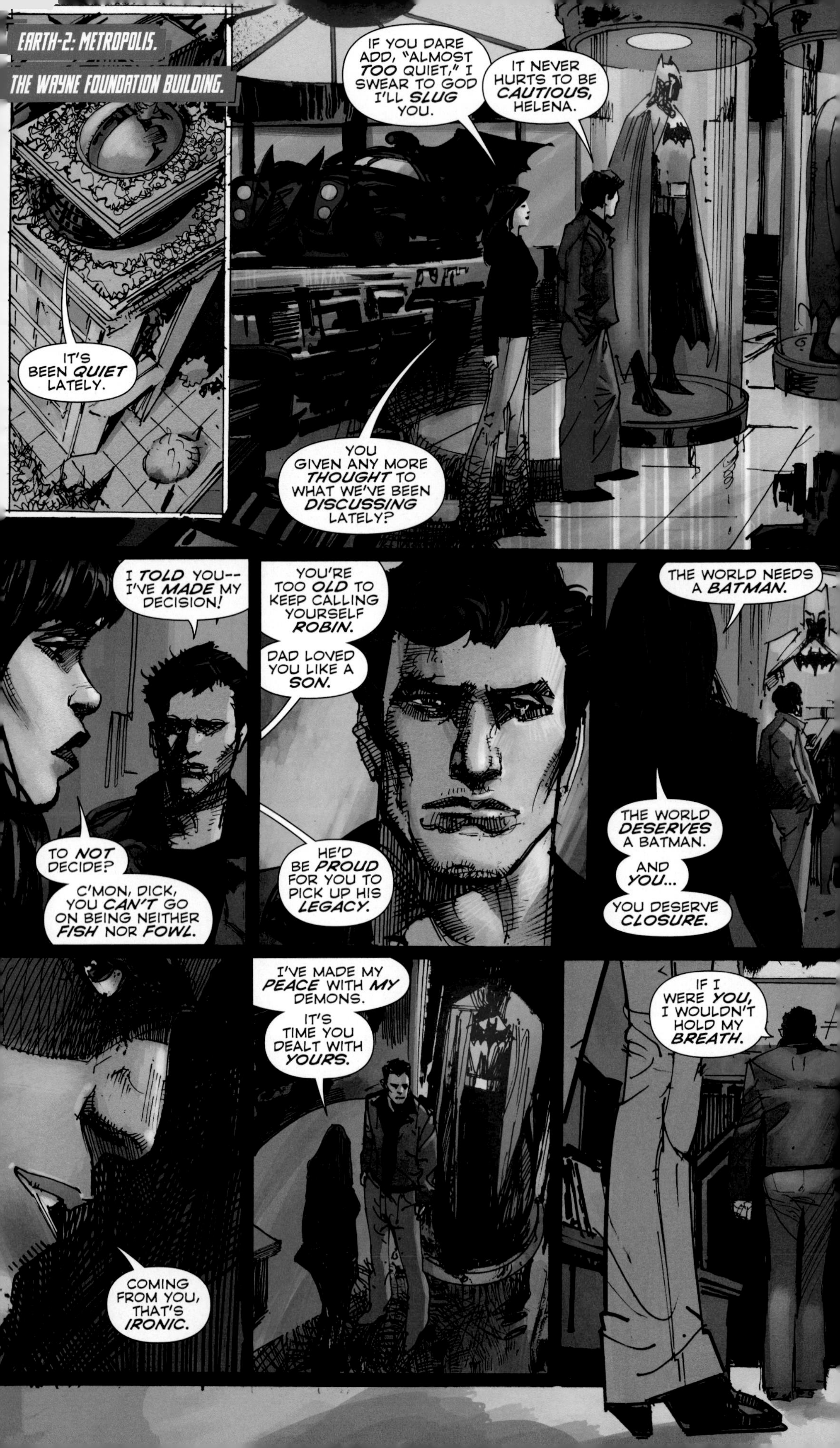
EARTH-2: METROPOLIS.
THE WAYNE FOUNDATION BUILDING.
IT'S BEEN QUIET LATELY.
IF YOU DARE ADD, "ALMOST TOO QUIET," I SWEAR TO GOD I'LL SLUG YOU.
IT NEVER HURTS TO BE CAUTIOUS, HELENA.
YOU GIVEN ANY MORE THOUGHT TO WHAT WE'VE BEEN DISCUSSING LATELY?
I TOLD YOU-- I'VE MADE MY DECISION!
TO NOT DECIDE?
C'MON, DICK, YOU CAN'T GO ON BEING NEITHER FISH NOR FOWL.
YOU'RE TOO OLD TO KEEP CALLING YOURSELF ROBIN.
DAD LOVED YOU LIKE A SON.
HE'D BE PROUD FOR YOU TO PICK UP HIS LEGACY.
THE WORLD NEEDS A BATMAN.
THE WORLD DESERVES A BATMAN.
AND YOU...
YOU DESERVE CLOSURE.
COMING FROM YOU, THAT'S IRONIC.
I'VE MADE MY PEACE WITH MY DEMONS.
IT'S TIME YOU DEALT WITH YOURS.
IF I WERE YOU, I WOULDN'T HOLD MY BREATH.

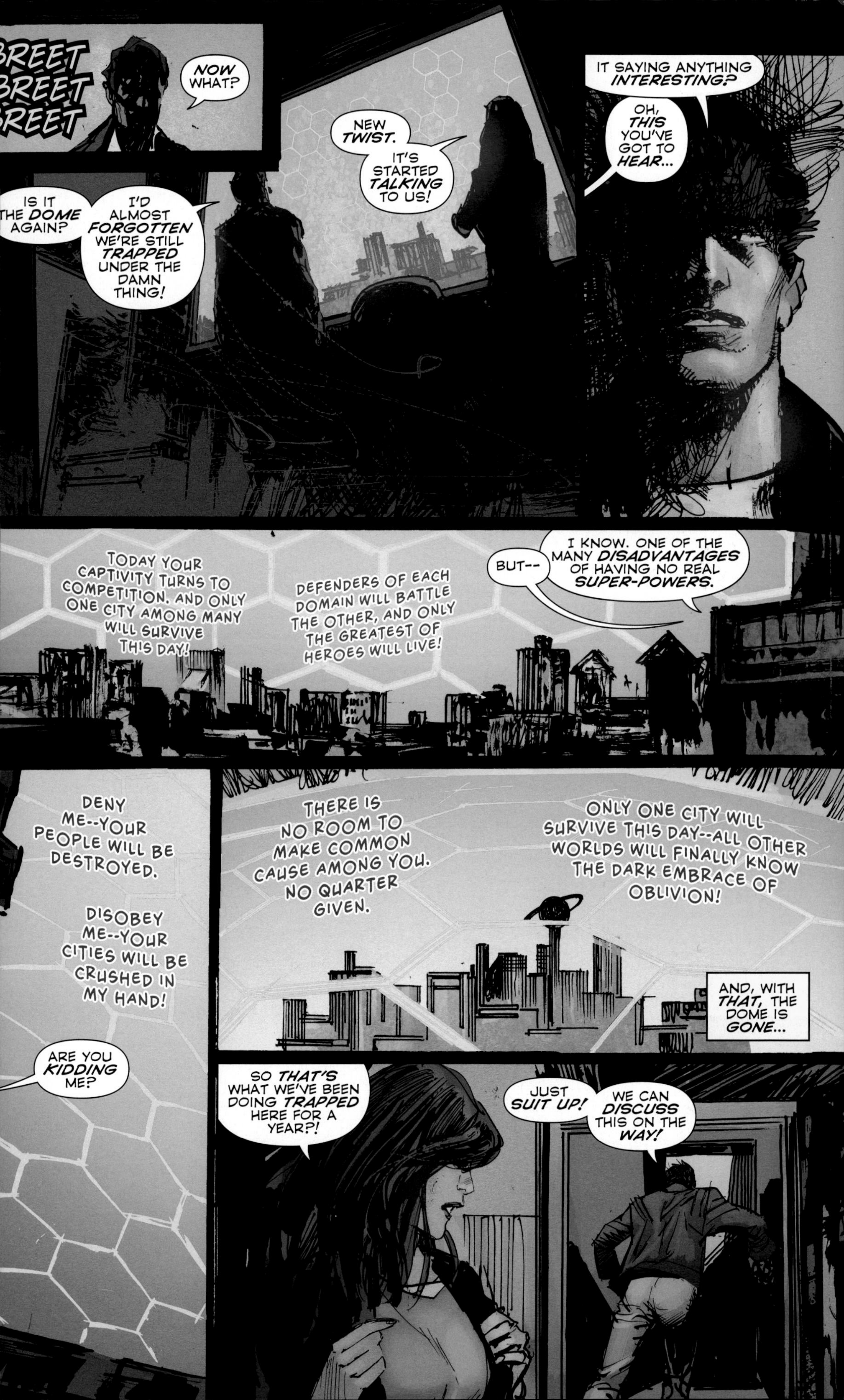
BREET BREET BREET
NOW WHAT?
NEW TWIST.
IT'S STARTED TALKING TO US!
IT SAYING ANYTHING INTERESTING?
OH, THIS YOU'VE GOT TO HEAR...
IS IT THE DOME AGAIN?
I'D ALMOST FORGOTTEN WE'RE STILL TRAPPED UNDER THE DAMN THING!
TODAY YOUR CAPTIVITY TURNS TO COMPETITION. AND ONLY ONE CITY AMONG MANY WILL SURVIVE THIS DAY!
DEFENDERS OF EACH DOMAIN WILL BATTLE THE OTHER, AND ONLY THE GREATEST OF HEROES WILL LIVE!
BUT--
I KNOW. ONE OF THE MANY DISADVANTAGES OF HAVING NO REAL SUPER-POWERS.
DENY ME--YOUR PEOPLE WILL BE DESTROYED.
DISOBEY ME--YOUR CITIES WILL BE CRUSHED IN MY HAND!
THERE IS NO ROOM TO MAKE COMMON CAUSE AMONG YOU. NO QUARTER GIVEN.
ONLY ONE CITY WILL SURVIVE THIS DAY--ALL OTHER WORLDS WILL FINALLY KNOW THE DARK EMBRACE OF OBLIVION!
AND, WITH THAT, THE DOME IS GONE...
ARE YOU KIDDING ME?
SO THAT'S WHAT WE'VE BEEN DOING TRAPPED HERE FOR A YEAR?!
JUST SUIT UP!
WE CAN DISCUSS THIS ON THE WAY!

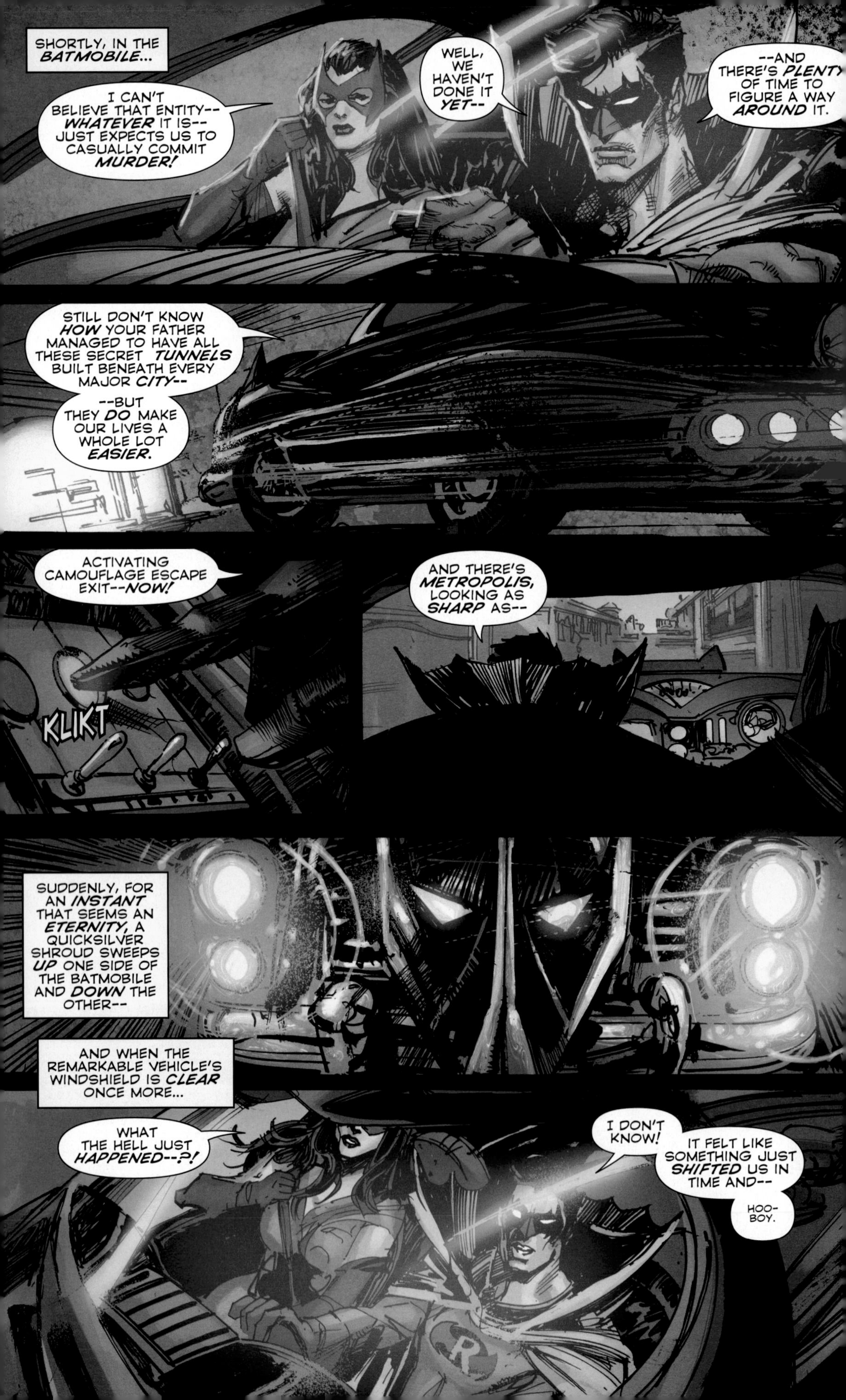
SHORTLY, IN THE BATMOBILE...
I CAN'T BELIEVE THAT ENTITY-- WHATEVER IT IS-- JUST EXPECTS US TO CASUALLY COMMIT MURDER!
WELL, WE HAVEN'T DONE IT YET--
--AND THERE'S PLENTY OF TIME TO FIGURE A WAY AROUND IT.
STILL DON'T KNOW HOW YOUR FATHER MANAGED TO HAVE ALL THESE SECRET TUNNELS BUILT BENEATH EVERY MAJOR CITY--
--BUT THEY DO MAKE OUR LIVES A WHOLE LOT EASIER.
ACTIVATING CAMOUFLAGE ESCAPE EXIT--NOW!
KLIKT
AND THERE'S METROPOLIS, LOOKING AS SHARP AS--
SUDDENLY, FOR AN INSTANT THAT SEEMS AN ETERNITY, A QUICKSILVER SHROUD SWEEPS UP ONE SIDE OF THE BATMOBILE AND DOWN THE OTHER--
AND WHEN THE REMARKABLE VEHICLE'S WINDSHIELD IS CLEAR ONCE MORE...
WHAT THE HELL JUST HAPPENED--?!
I DON'T KNOW!
IT FELT LIKE SOMETHING JUST SHIFTED US IN TIME AND--
HOO-BOY.

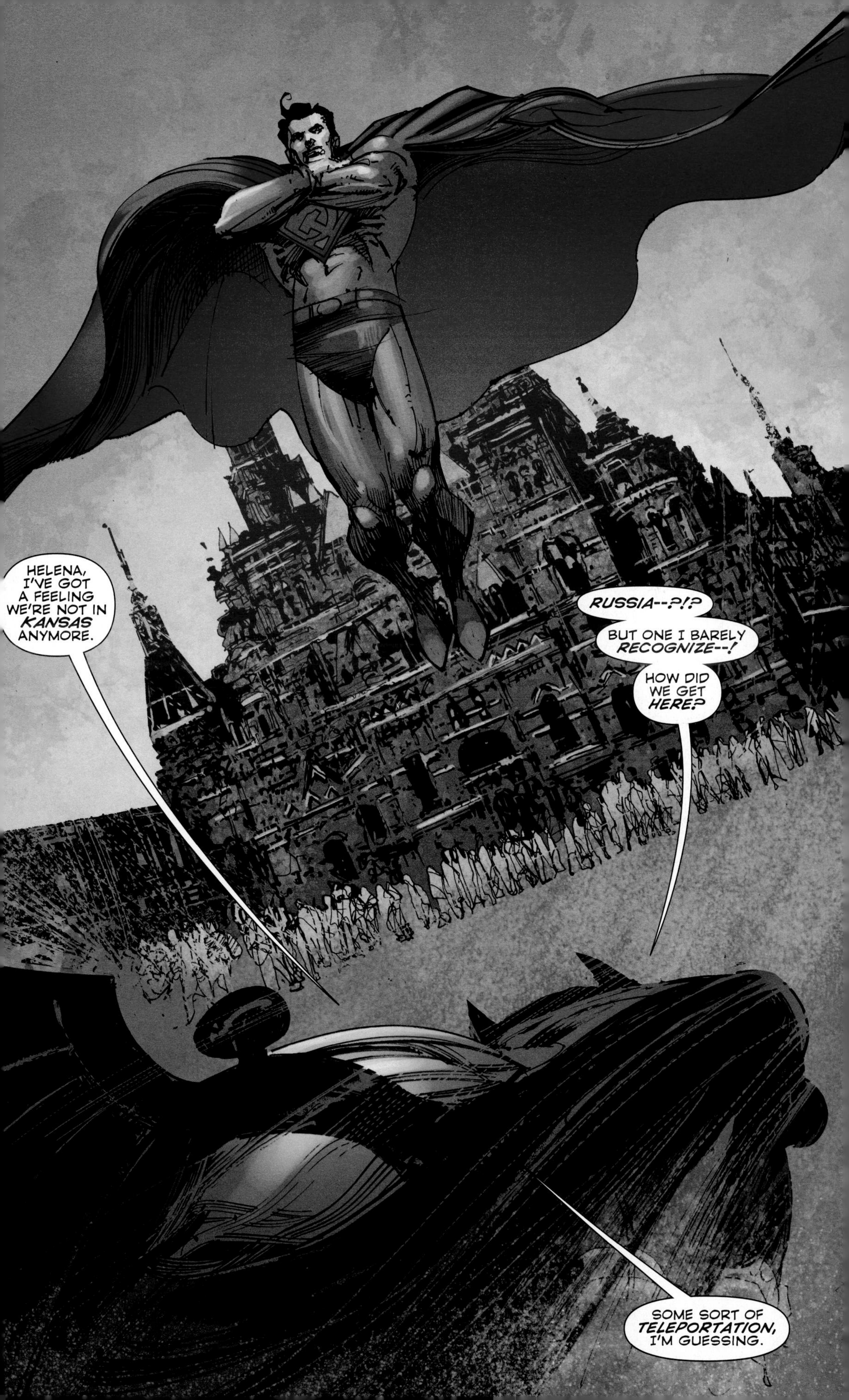

HELENA, I'VE GOT A FEELING WE'RE NOT IN KANSAS ANYMORE.
RUSSIA--?!?
BUT ONE I BARELY RECOGNIZE--!
HOW DID WE GET HERE?
SOME SORT OF TELEPORTATION, I'M GUESSING.

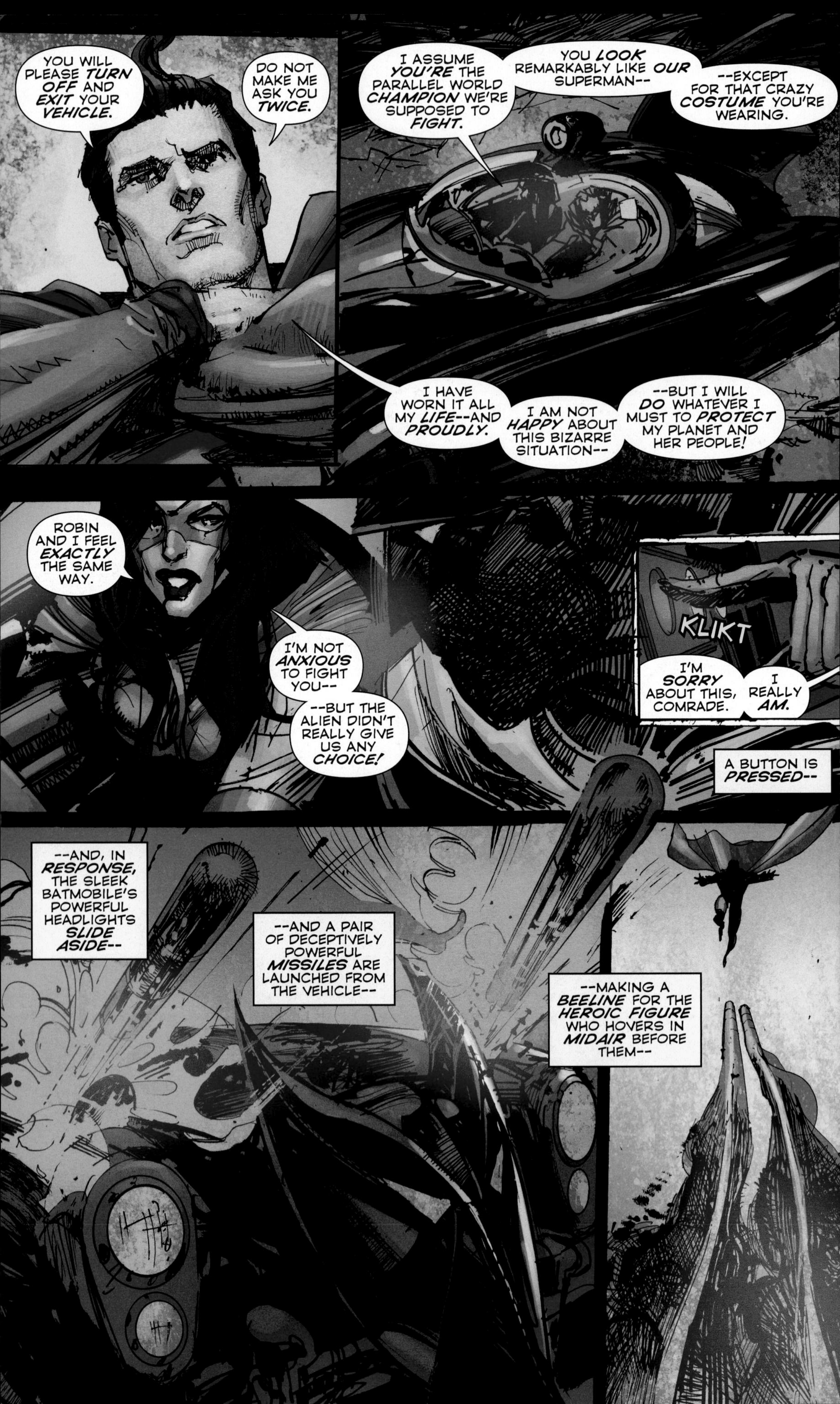

YOU WILL PLEASE TURN OFF AND EXIT YOUR VEHICLE.
DO NOT MAKE ME ASK YOU TWICE.
I ASSUME YOU'RE THE PARALLEL WORLD CHAMPION WE'RE SUPPOSED TO FIGHT.
YOU LOOK REMARKABLY LIKE OUR SUPERMAN--
--EXCEPT FOR THAT CRAZY COSTUME YOU'RE WEARING.
I HAVE WORN IT ALL MY LIFE--AND PROUDLY.
I AM NOT HAPPY ABOUT THIS BIZARRE SITUATION--
--BUT I WILL DO WHATEVER I MUST TO PROTECT MY PLANET AND HER PEOPLE!
ROBIN AND I FEEL EXACTLY THE SAME WAY.
I'M NOT ANXIOUS TO FIGHT YOU--
--BUT THE ALIEN DIDN'T REALLY GIVE US ANY CHOICE!
KLIKT
I'M SORRY ABOUT THIS, COMRADE.
I REALLY AM.
A BUTTON IS PRESSED--
--AND, IN RESPONSE, THE SLEEK BATMOBILE'S POWERFUL HEADLIGHTS SLIDE ASIDE--
--AND A PAIR OF DECEPTIVELY POWERFUL MISSILES ARE LAUNCHED FROM THE VEHICLE--
--MAKING A BEELINE FOR THE HEROIC FIGURE WHO HOVERS IN MIDAIR BEFORE THEM--

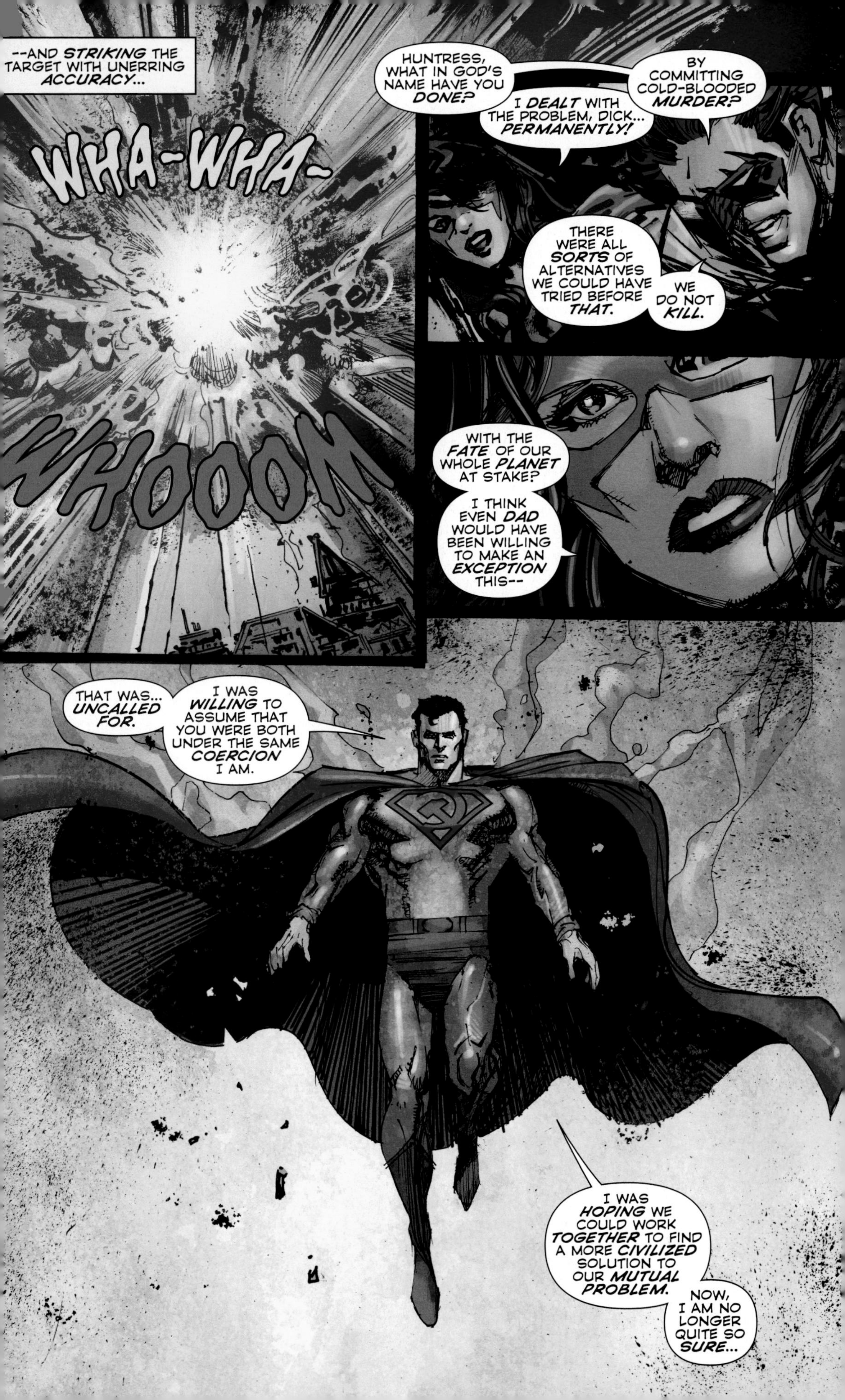
--AND STRIKING THE TARGET WITH UNERRING ACCURACY...
WHA-WHA-
WHOOOM
HUNTRESS, WHAT IN GOD'S NAME HAVE YOU DONE?
I DEALT WITH THE PROBLEM, DICK... PERMANENTLY!
BY COMMITTING COLD-BLOODED MURDER?
THERE WERE ALL SORTS OF ALTERNATIVES WE COULD HAVE TRIED BEFORE THAT.
WE DO NOT KILL.
WITH THE FATE OF OUR WHOLE PLANET AT STAKE?
I THINK EVEN DAD WOULD HAVE BEEN WILLING TO MAKE AN EXCEPTION THIS--
THAT WAS... UNCALLED FOR.
I WAS WILLING TO ASSUME THAT YOU WERE BOTH UNDER THE SAME COERCION I AM.
I WAS HOPING WE COULD WORK TOGETHER TO FIND A MORE CIVILIZED SOLUTION TO OUR MUTUAL PROBLEM.
NOW, I AM NO LONGER QUITE SO SURE...

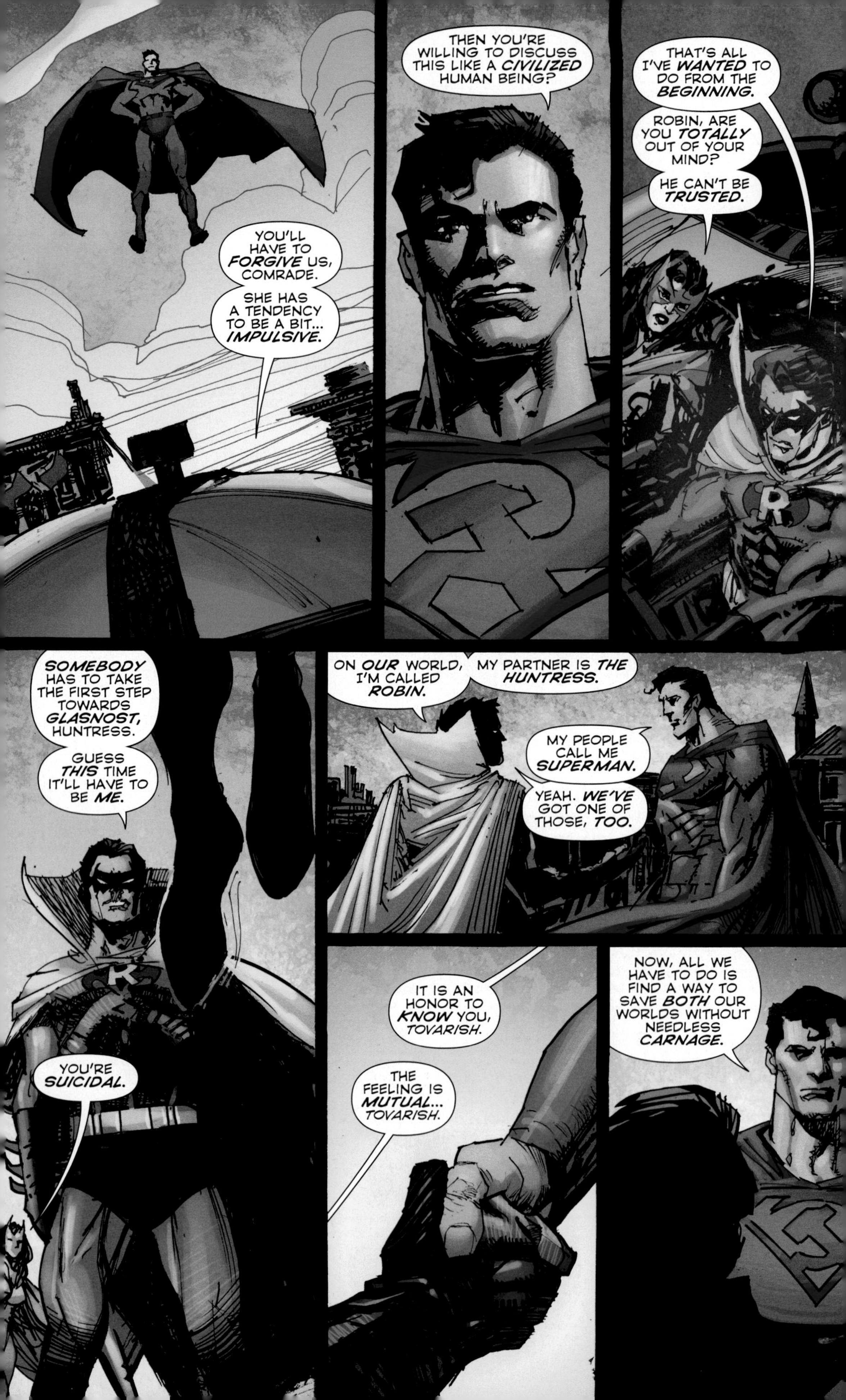
YOU'LL HAVE TO FORGIVE US, COMRADE.
SHE HAS A TENDENCY TO BE A BIT... IMPULSIVE.
THEN YOU'RE WILLING TO DISCUSS THIS LIKE A CIVILIZED HUMAN BEING?
THAT'S ALL I'VE WANTED TO DO FROM THE BEGINNING.
ROBIN, ARE YOU TOTALLY OUT OF YOUR MIND?
HE CAN'T BE TRUSTED.
SOMEBODY HAS TO TAKE THE FIRST STEP TOWARDS GLASNOST, HUNTRESS.
GUESS THIS TIME IT'LL HAVE TO BE ME.
YOU'RE SUICIDAL.
ON OUR WORLD, I'M CALLED ROBIN.
MY PARTNER IS THE HUNTRESS.
MY PEOPLE CALL ME SUPERMAN.
YEAH. WE'VE GOT ONE OF THOSE, TOO.
IT IS AN HONOR TO KNOW YOU, TOVARISH.
THE FEELING IS MUTUAL... TOVARISH.
NOW, ALL WE HAVE TO DO IS FIND A WAY TO SAVE BOTH OUR WORLDS WITHOUT NEEDLESS CARNAGE.

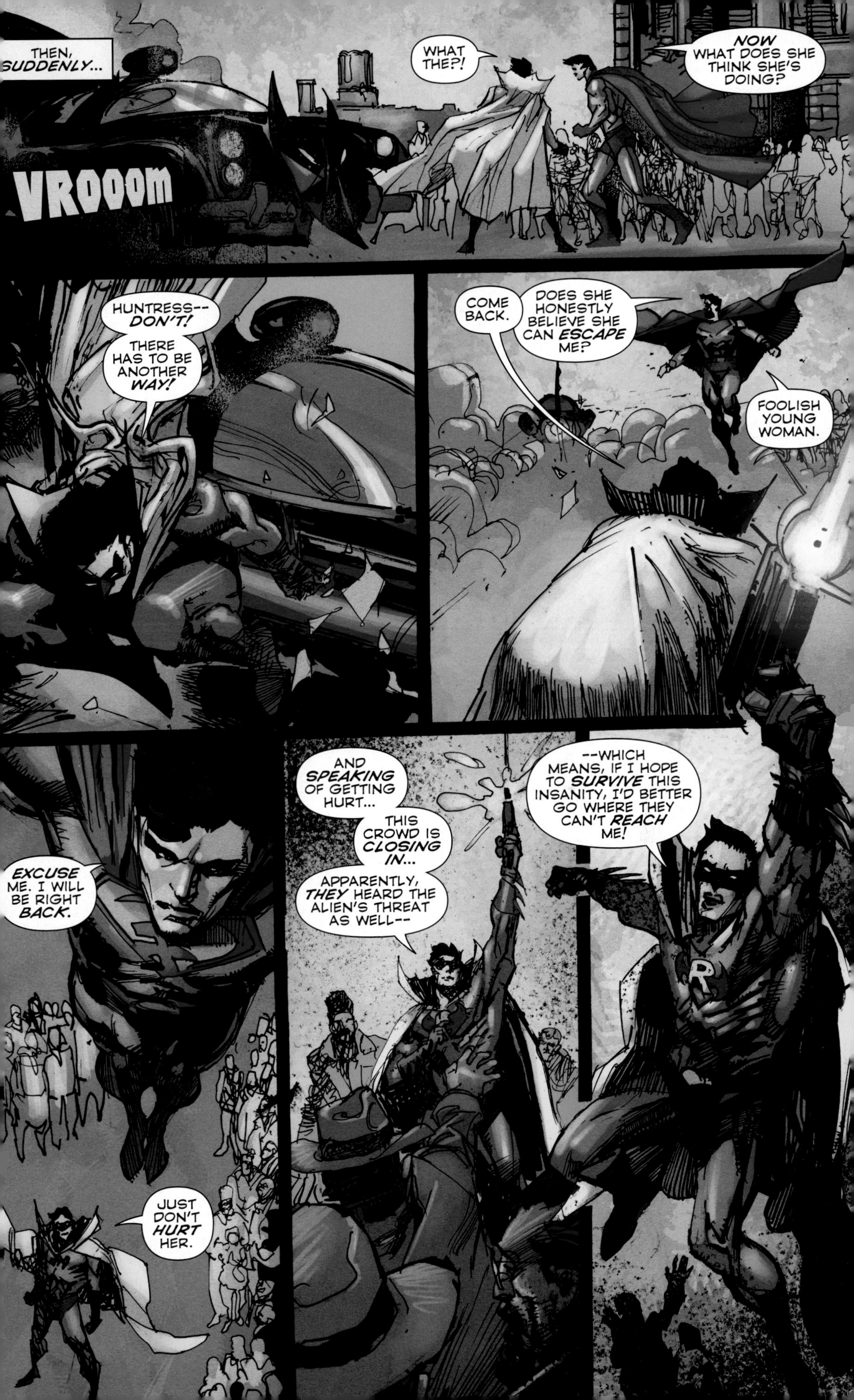

THEN, SUDDENLY...
VROOOM
WHAT THE?!
NOW WHAT DOES SHE THINK SHE'S DOING?
HUNTRESS-- DON'T!
THERE HAS TO BE ANOTHER WAY!
COME BACK.
DOES SHE HONESTLY BELIEVE SHE CAN ESCAPE ME?
FOOLISH YOUNG WOMAN.
EXCUSE ME. I WILL BE RIGHT BACK.
JUST DON'T HURT HER.
AND SPEAKING OF GETTING HURT...
THIS CROWD IS CLOSING IN...
APPARENTLY, THEY HEARD THE ALIEN'S THREAT AS WELL--
--WHICH MEANS, IF I HOPE TO SURVIVE THIS INSANITY, I'D BETTER GO WHERE THEY CAN'T REACH ME!

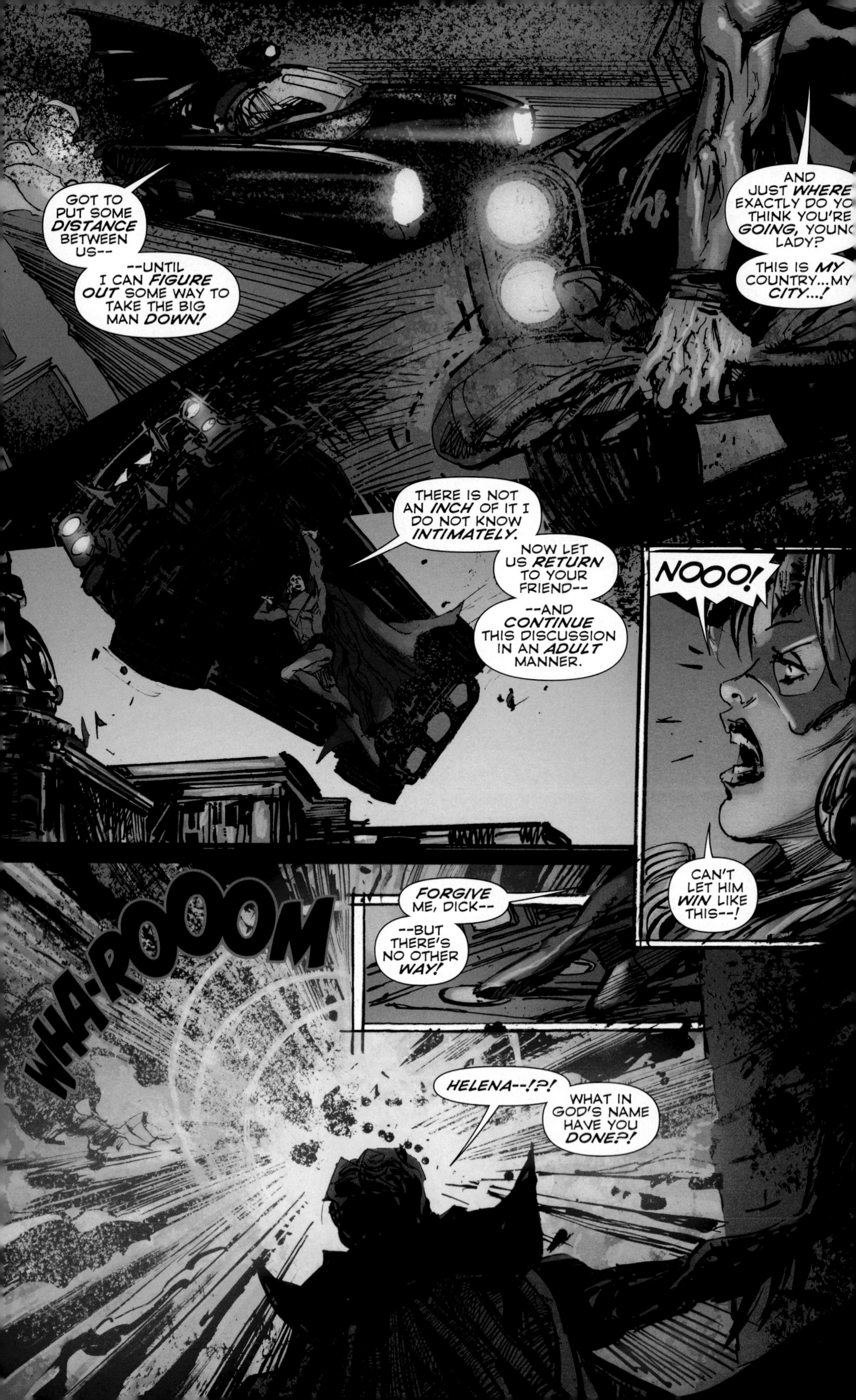

GOT TO PUT SOME DISTANCE BETWEEN US--
--UNTIL I CAN FIGURE OUT SOME WAY TO TAKE THE BIG MAN DOWN!
AND JUST WHERE EXACTLY DO YO THINK YOU'RE GOING, YOUNG LADY?
THIS IS MY COUNTRY...MY CITY...!
THERE IS NOT AN INCH OF IT I DO NOT KNOW INTIMATELY.
NOW LET US RETURN TO YOUR FRIEND--
--AND CONTINUE THIS DISCUSSION IN AN ADULT MANNER.
NOOO!
CAN'T LET HIM WIN LIKE THIS--!
FORGIVE ME, DICK--
--BUT THERE'S NO OTHER WAY!
WHA-ROOOOM
HELENA--!?!
WHAT IN GOD'S NAME HAVE YOU DONE?!

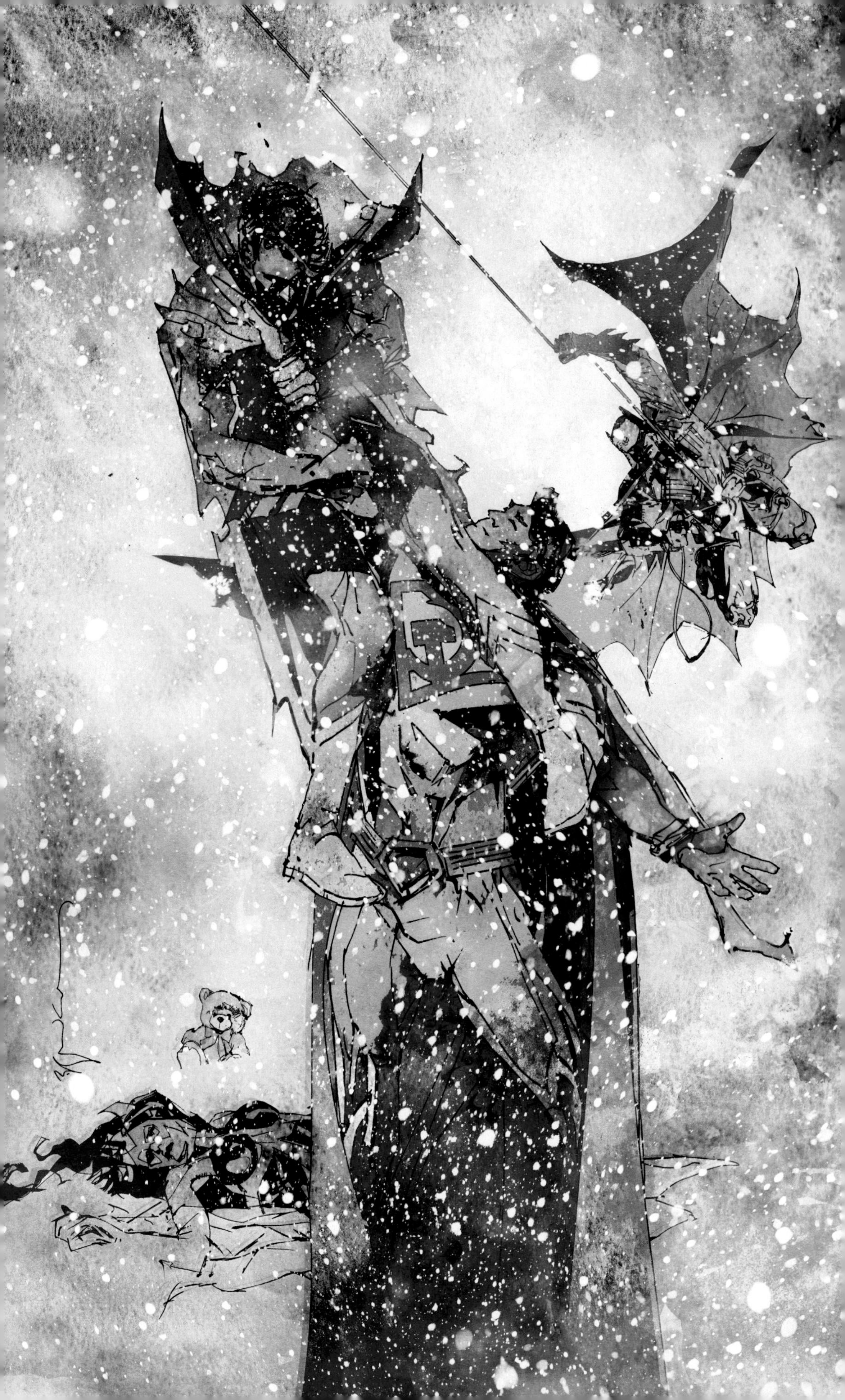

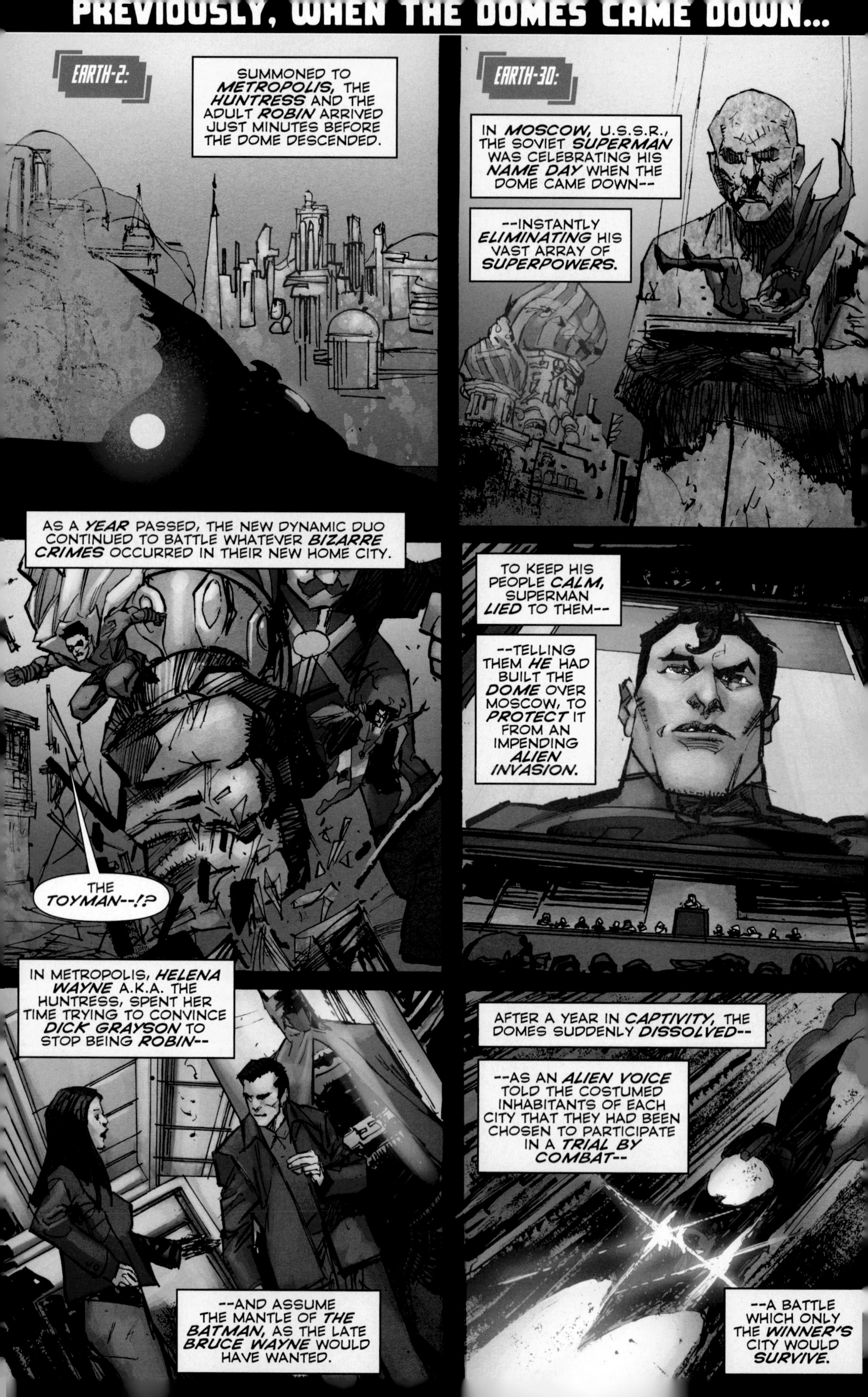
PREVIOUSLY, WHEN THE DOMES CAME DOWN...
EARTH-2:
SUMMONED TO METROPOLIS, THE HUNTRESS AND THE ADULT ROBIN ARRIVED JUST MINUTES BEFORE THE DOME DESCENDED.
EARTH-30:
IN MOSCOW, U.S.S.R., THE SOVIET SUPERMAN WAS CELEBRATING HIS NAME DAY WHEN THE DOME CAME DOWN--
--INSTANTLY ELIMINATING HIS VAST ARRAY OF SUPERPOWERS.
AS A YEAR PASSED, THE NEW DYNAMIC DUO CONTINUED TO BATTLE WHATEVER BIZARRE CRIMES OCCURRED IN THEIR NEW HOME CITY.
THE TOYMAN--!?
TO KEEP HIS PEOPLE CALM, SUPERMAN LIED TO THEM--
--TELLING THEM HE HAD BUILT THE DOME OVER MOSCOW, TO PROTECT IT FROM AN IMPENDING ALIEN INVASION.
IN METROPOLIS, HELENA WAYNE A.K.A. THE HUNTRESS, SPENT HER TIME TRYING TO CONVINCE DICK GRAYSON TO STOP BEING ROBIN--
--AND ASSUME THE MANTLE OF THE BATMAN, AS THE LATE BRUCE WAYNE WOULD HAVE WANTED.
AFTER A YEAR IN CAPTIVITY, THE DOMES SUDDENLY DISSOLVED--
--AS AN ALIEN VOICE TOLD THE COSTUMED INHABITANTS OF EACH CITY THAT THEY HAD BEEN CHOSEN TO PARTICIPATE IN A TRIAL BY COMBAT--
--A BATTLE WHICH ONLY THE WINNER'S CITY WOULD SURVIVE.

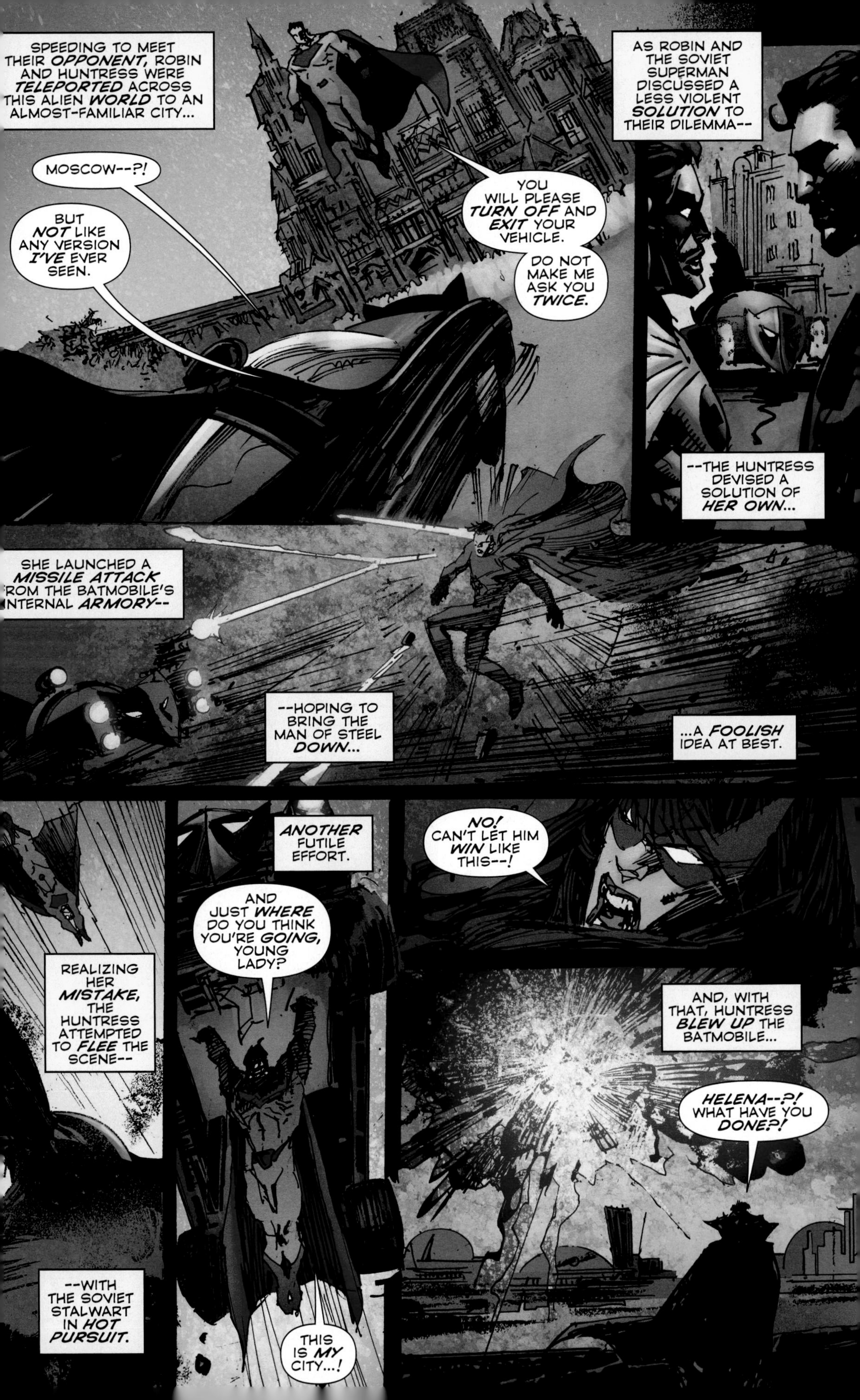
SPEEDING TO MEET THEIR OPPONENT, ROBIN AND HUNTRESS WERE TELEPORTED ACROSS THIS ALIEN WORLD TO AN ALMOST-FAMILIAR CITY...
MOSCOW--?!
BUT NOT LIKE ANY VERSION I'VE EVER SEEN.
YOU WILL PLEASE TURN OFF AND EXIT YOUR VEHICLE.
DO NOT MAKE ME ASK YOU TWICE.
AS ROBIN AND THE SOVIET SUPERMAN DISCUSSED A LESS VIOLENT SOLUTION TO THEIR DILEMMA--
--THE HUNTRESS DEVISED A SOLUTION OF HER OWN...
SHE LAUNCHED A MISSILE ATTACK FROM THE BATMOBILE'S INTERNAL ARMORY--
--HOPING TO BRING THE MAN OF STEEL DOWN...
...A FOOLISH IDEA AT BEST.
REALIZING HER MISTAKE, THE HUNTRESS ATTEMPTED TO FLEE THE SCENE--
--WITH THE SOVIET STALWART IN HOT PURSUIT.
ANOTHER FUTILE EFFORT.
AND JUST WHERE DO YOU THINK YOU'RE GOING, YOUNG LADY?
THIS IS MY CITY...!
NO! CAN'T LET HIM WIN LIKE THIS--!
AND, WITH THAT, HUNTRESS BLEW UP THE BATMOBILE...
HELENA--?! WHAT HAVE YOU DONE?!

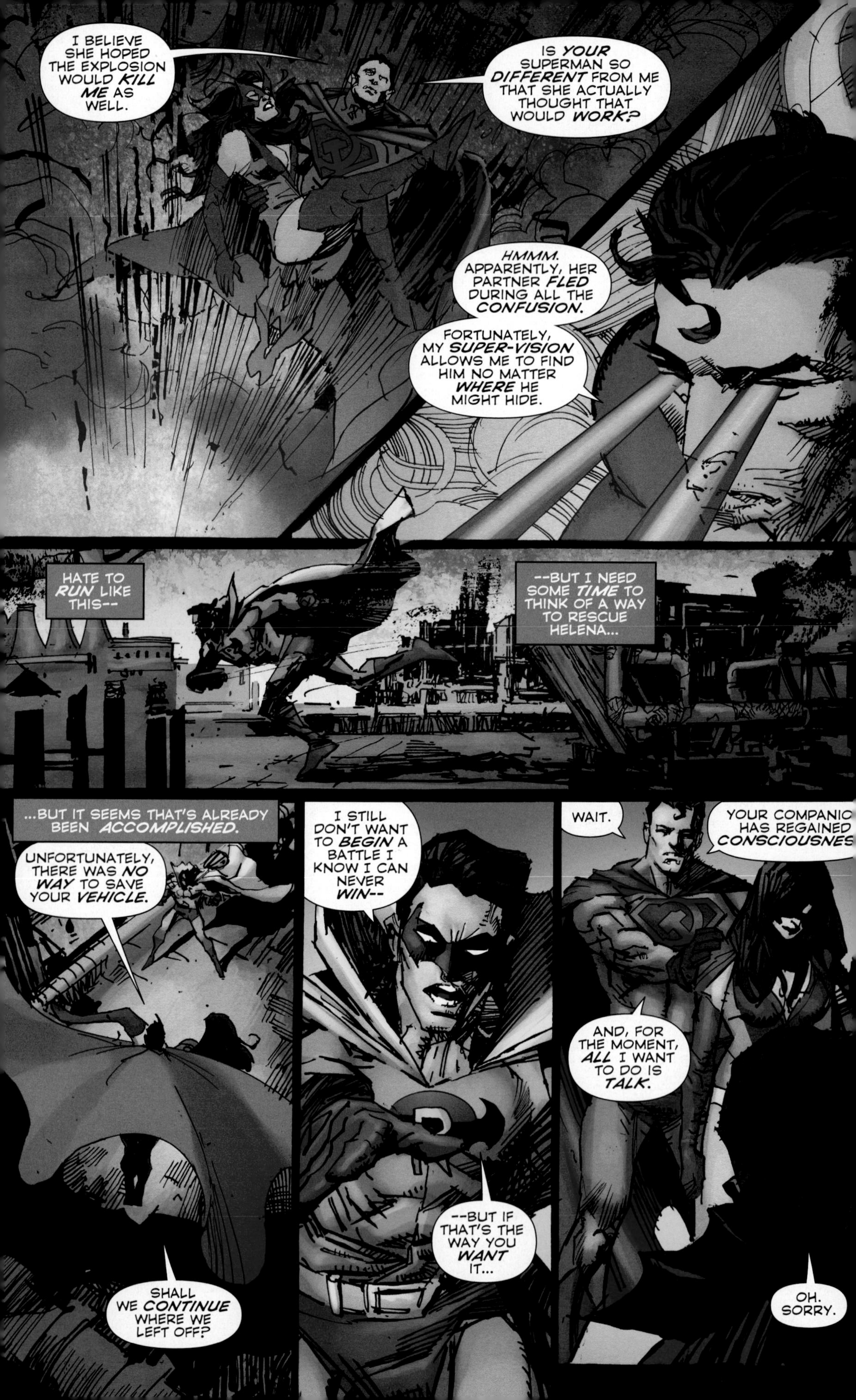
I BELIEVE SHE HOPED THE EXPLOSION WOULD KILL ME AS WELL.
IS YOUR SUPERMAN SO DIFFERENT FROM ME THAT SHE ACTUALLY THOUGHT THAT WOULD WORK?
HMMM. APPARENTLY, HER PARTNER FLED DURING ALL THE CONFUSION.
FORTUNATELY, MY SUPER-VISION ALLOWS ME TO FIND HIM NO MATTER WHERE HE MIGHT HIDE.
HATE TO RUN LIKE THIS--
--BUT I NEED SOME TIME TO THINK OF A WAY TO RESCUE HELENA...
...BUT IT SEEMS THAT'S ALREADY BEEN ACCOMPLISHED.
UNFORTUNATELY, THERE WAS NO WAY TO SAVE YOUR VEHICLE.
SHALL WE CONTINUE WHERE WE LEFT OFF?
I STILL DON'T WANT TO BEGIN A BATTLE I KNOW I CAN NEVER WIN--
--BUT IF THAT'S THE WAY YOU WANT IT...
WAIT.
AND, FOR THE MOMENT, ALL I WANT TO DO IS TALK.
OH. SORRY.

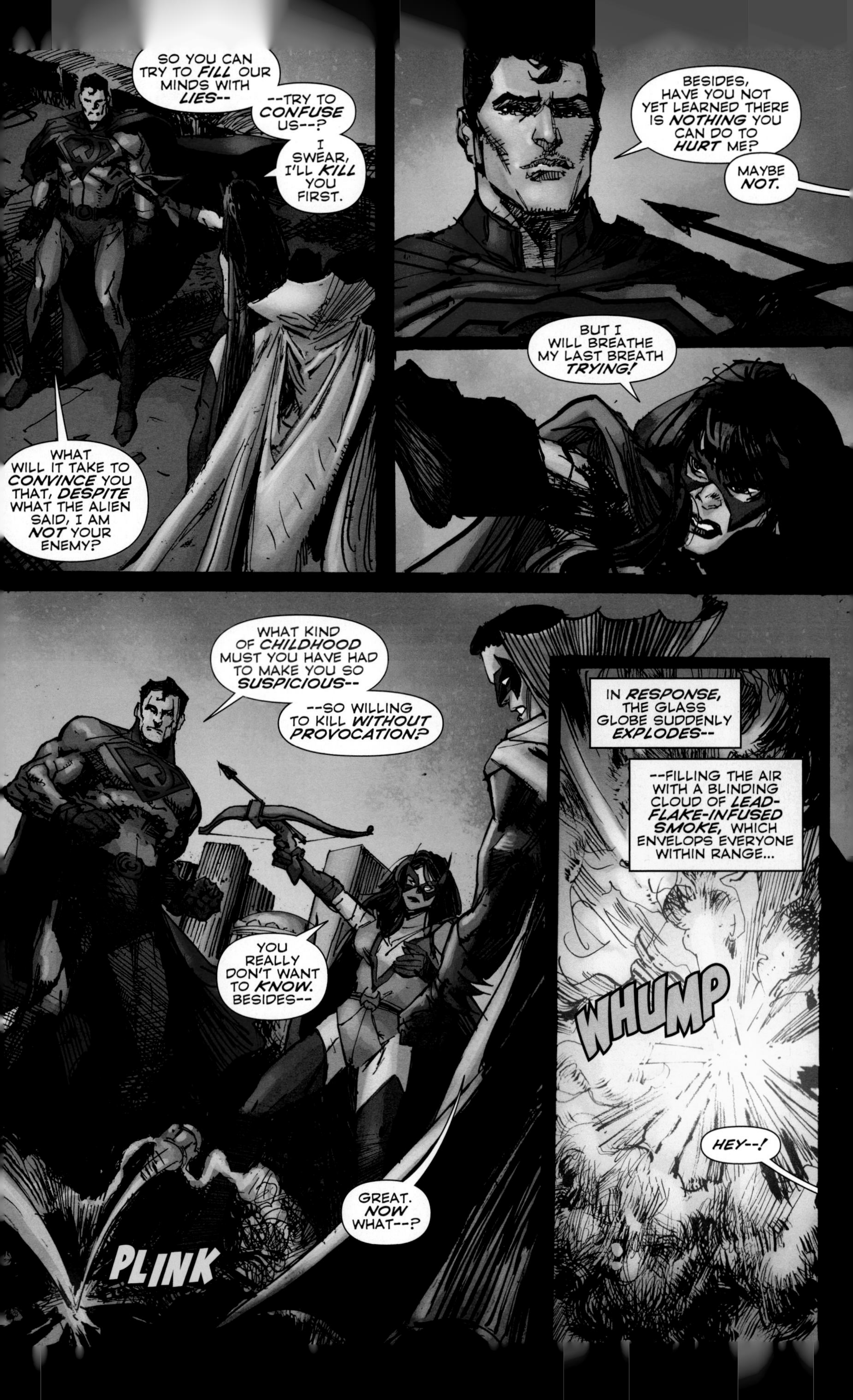
SO YOU CAN TRY TO FILL OUR MINDS WITH LIES--
--TRY TO CONFUSE US--?
I SWEAR, I'LL KILL YOU FIRST.
WHAT WILL IT TAKE TO CONVINCE YOU THAT, DESPITE WHAT THE ALIEN SAID, I AM NOT YOUR ENEMY?
BESIDES, HAVE YOU NOT YET LEARNED THERE IS NOTHING YOU CAN DO TO HURT ME?
MAYBE NOT.
BUT I WILL BREATHE MY LAST BREATH TRYING!
WHAT KIND OF CHILDHOOD MUST YOU HAVE HAD TO MAKE YOU SO SUSPICIOUS--
--SO WILLING TO KILL WITHOUT PROVOCATION?
YOU REALLY DON'T WANT TO KNOW. BESIDES--
GREAT. NOW WHAT--?
PLINK
IN RESPONSE, THE GLASS GLOBE SUDDENLY EXPLODES--
--FILLING THE AIR WITH A BLINDING CLOUD OF LEAD-FLAKE-INFUSED SMOKE, WHICH ENVELOPS EVERYONE WITHIN RANGE...
WHUMP
HEY--!

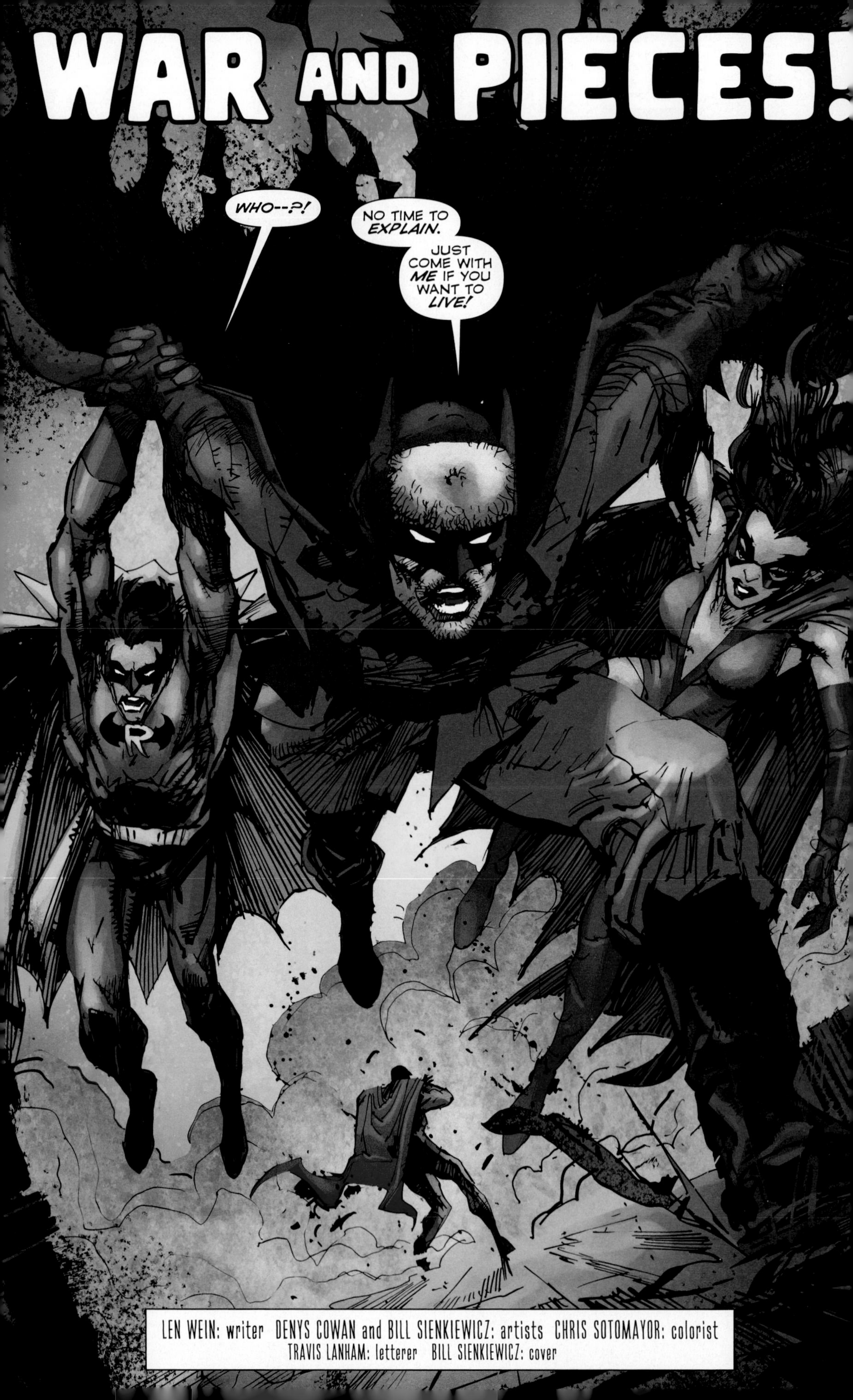
WAR AND PIECES!
WHO--?!
NO TIME TO EXPLAIN.
JUST COME WITH ME IF YOU WANT TO LIVE!
LEN WEIN: writer DENYS COWAN and BILL SIENKIEWICZ: artists CHRIS SOTOMAYOR: colorist
TRAVIS LANHAM: letterer BILL SIENKIEWICZ: cover

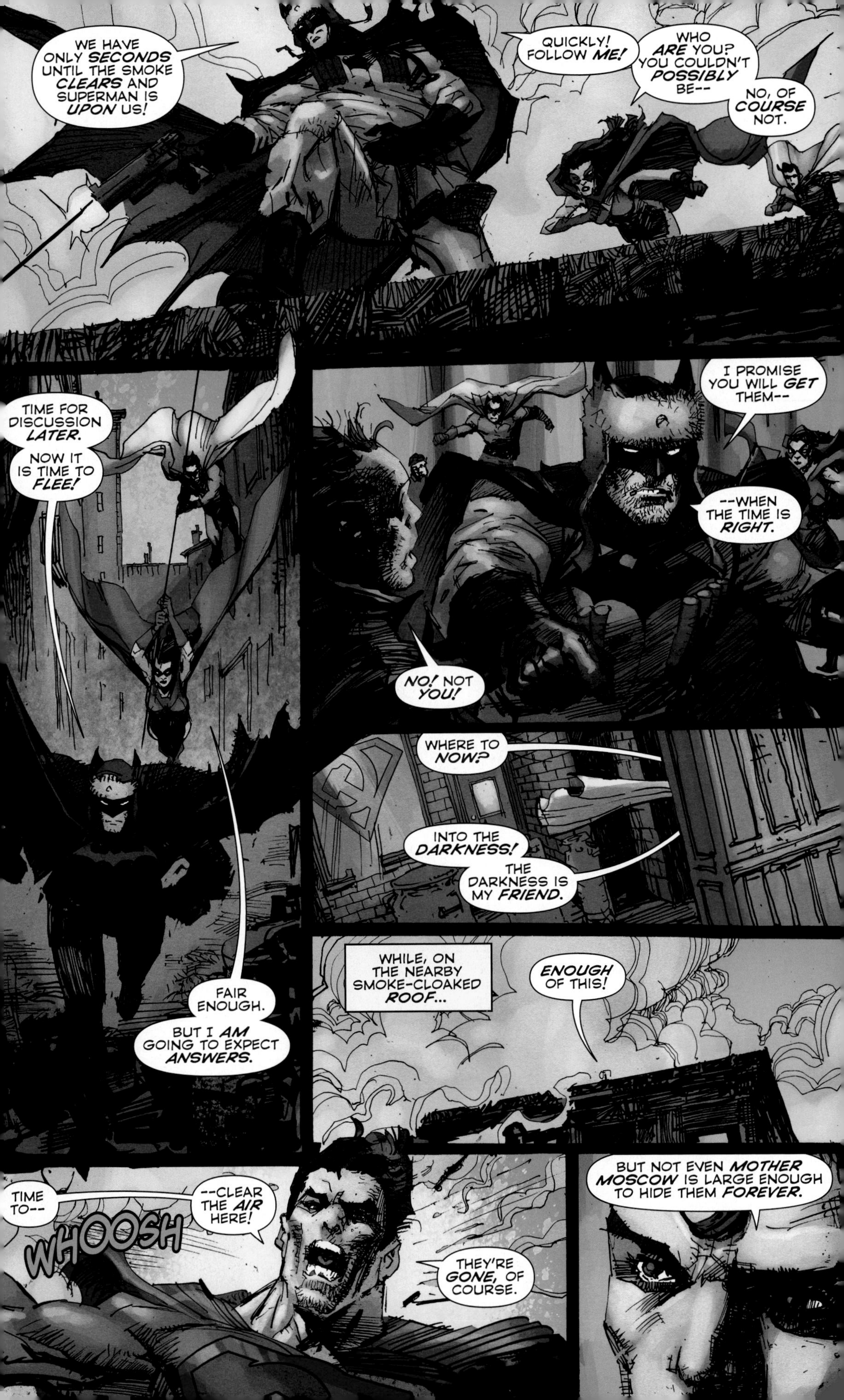
WE HAVE ONLY SECONDS UNTIL THE SMOKE CLEARS AND SUPERMAN IS UPON US!
QUICKLY! FOLLOW ME!
WHO ARE YOU? YOU COULDN'T POSSIBLY BE--
NO, OF COURSE NOT.
TIME FOR DISCUSSION LATER.
NOW IT IS TIME TO FLEE!
FAIR ENOUGH.
BUT I AM GOING TO EXPECT ANSWERS.
I PROMISE YOU WILL GET THEM--
--WHEN THE TIME IS RIGHT.
NO! NOT YOU!
WHERE TO NOW?
INTO THE DARKNESS!
THE DARKNESS IS MY FRIEND.
WHILE, ON THE NEARBY SMOKE-CLOAKED ROOF...
ENOUGH OF THIS!
TIME TO--
--CLEAR THE AIR HERE!
WHOOSH
THEY'RE GONE, OF COURSE.
BUT NOT EVEN MOTHER MOSCOW IS LARGE ENOUGH TO HIDE THEM FOREVER.

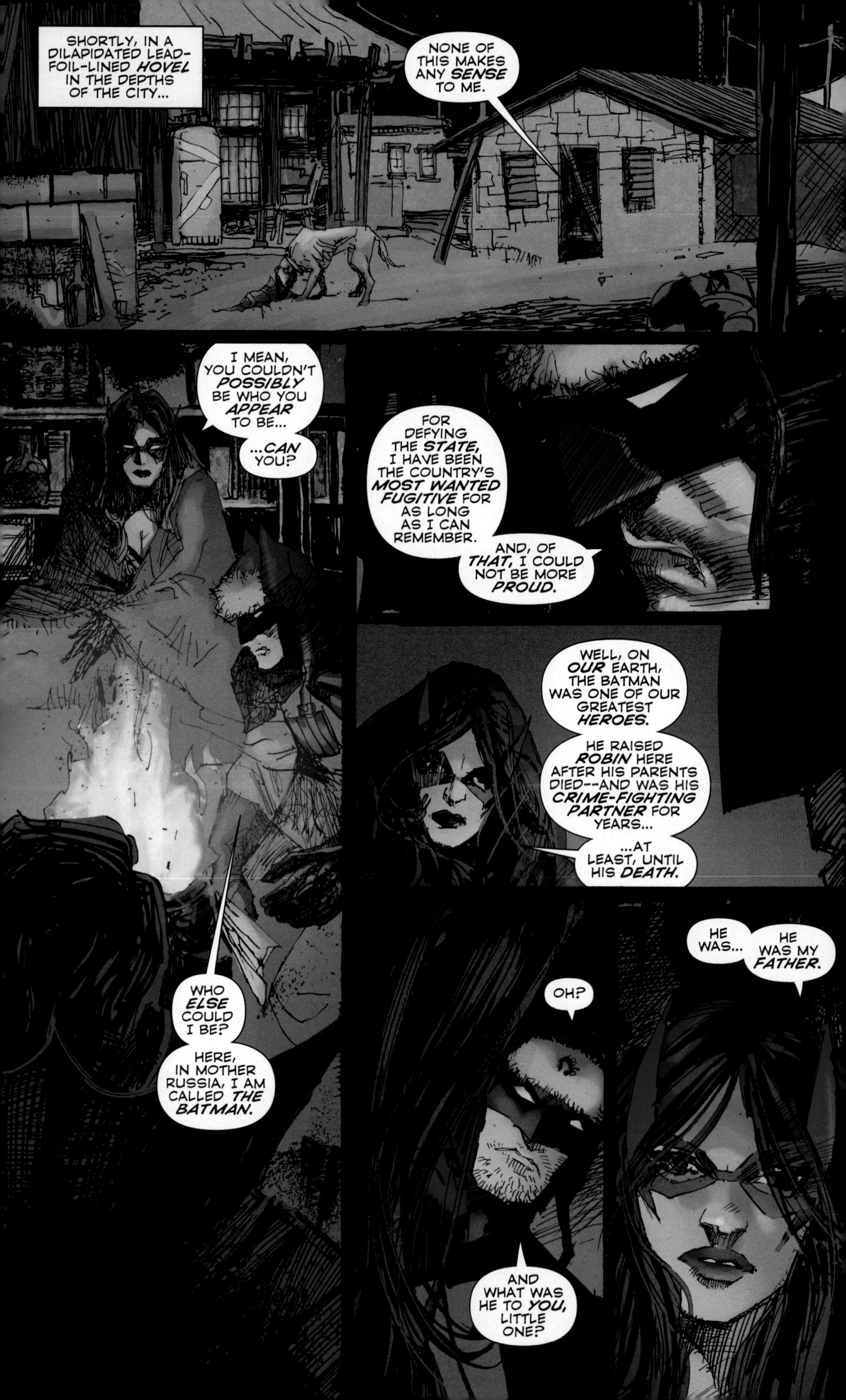
SHORTLY, IN A DILAPIDATED LEAD-FOIL-LINED HOVEL IN THE DEPTHS OF THE CITY...
NONE OF THIS MAKES ANY SENSE TO ME.
I MEAN, YOU COULDN'T POSSIBLY BE WHO YOU APPEAR TO BE...
...CAN YOU?
WHO ELSE COULD I BE?
HERE, IN MOTHER RUSSIA, I AM CALLED THE BATMAN.
FOR DEFYING THE STATE, I HAVE BEEN THE COUNTRY'S MOST WANTED FUGITIVE FOR AS LONG AS I CAN REMEMBER.
AND, OF THAT, I COULD NOT BE MORE PROUD.
WELL, ON OUR EARTH, THE BATMAN WAS ONE OF OUR GREATEST HEROES.
HE RAISED ROBIN HERE AFTER HIS PARENTS DIED--AND WAS HIS CRIME-FIGHTING PARTNER FOR YEARS...
...AT LEAST, UNTIL HIS DEATH.
OH?
AND WHAT WAS HE TO YOU, LITTLE ONE?
HE WAS...
HE WAS MY FATHER.

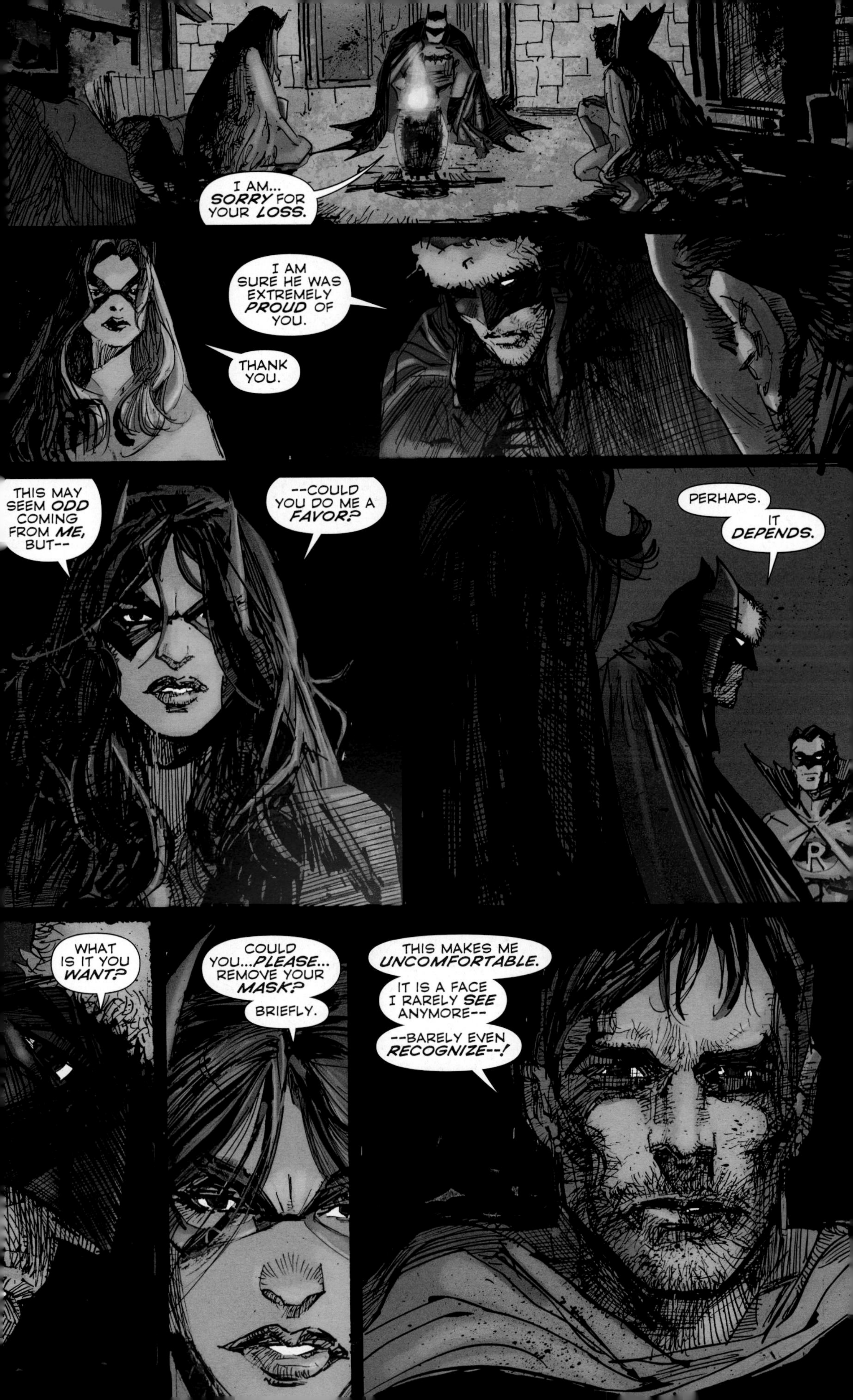
I AM... SORRY FOR YOUR LOSS.
I AM SURE HE WAS EXTREMELY PROUD OF YOU.
THANK YOU.
THIS MAY SEEM ODD COMING FROM ME, BUT--
--COULD YOU DO ME A FAVOR?
PERHAPS. IT DEPENDS.
WHAT IS IT YOU WANT?
COULD YOU...PLEASE... REMOVE YOUR MASK?
BRIEFLY.
THIS MAKES ME UNCOMFORTABLE.
IT IS A FACE I RARELY SEE ANYMORE--
--BARELY EVEN RECOGNIZE--!

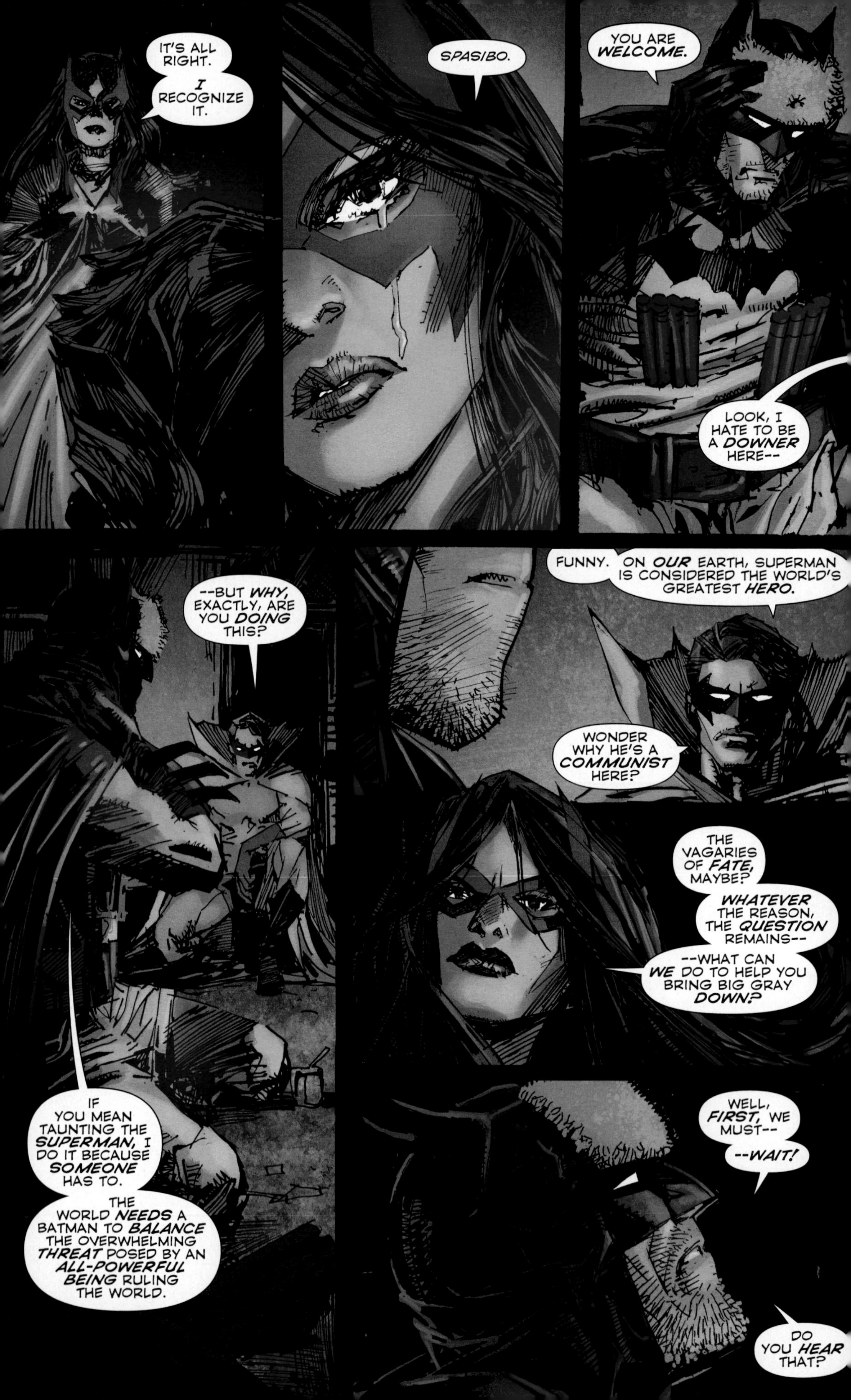
IT'S ALL RIGHT. I RECOGNIZE IT.
SPASIBO.
YOU ARE WELCOME.
LOOK, I HATE TO BE A DOWNER HERE--
--BUT WHY, EXACTLY, ARE YOU DOING THIS?
IF YOU MEAN TAUNTING THE SUPERMAN, I DO IT BECAUSE SOMEONE HAS TO.
THE WORLD NEEDS A BATMAN TO BALANCE THE OVERWHELMING THREAT POSED BY AN ALL-POWERFUL BEING RULING THE WORLD.
FUNNY.
ON OUR EARTH, SUPERMAN IS CONSIDERED THE WORLD'S GREATEST HERO.
WONDER WHY HE'S A COMMUNIST HERE?
THE VAGARIES OF FATE, MAYBE?
WHATEVER THE REASON, THE QUESTION REMAINS--
--WHAT CAN WE DO TO HELP YOU BRING BIG GRAY DOWN?
WELL, FIRST, WE MUST--
--WAIT!
DO YOU HEAR THAT?

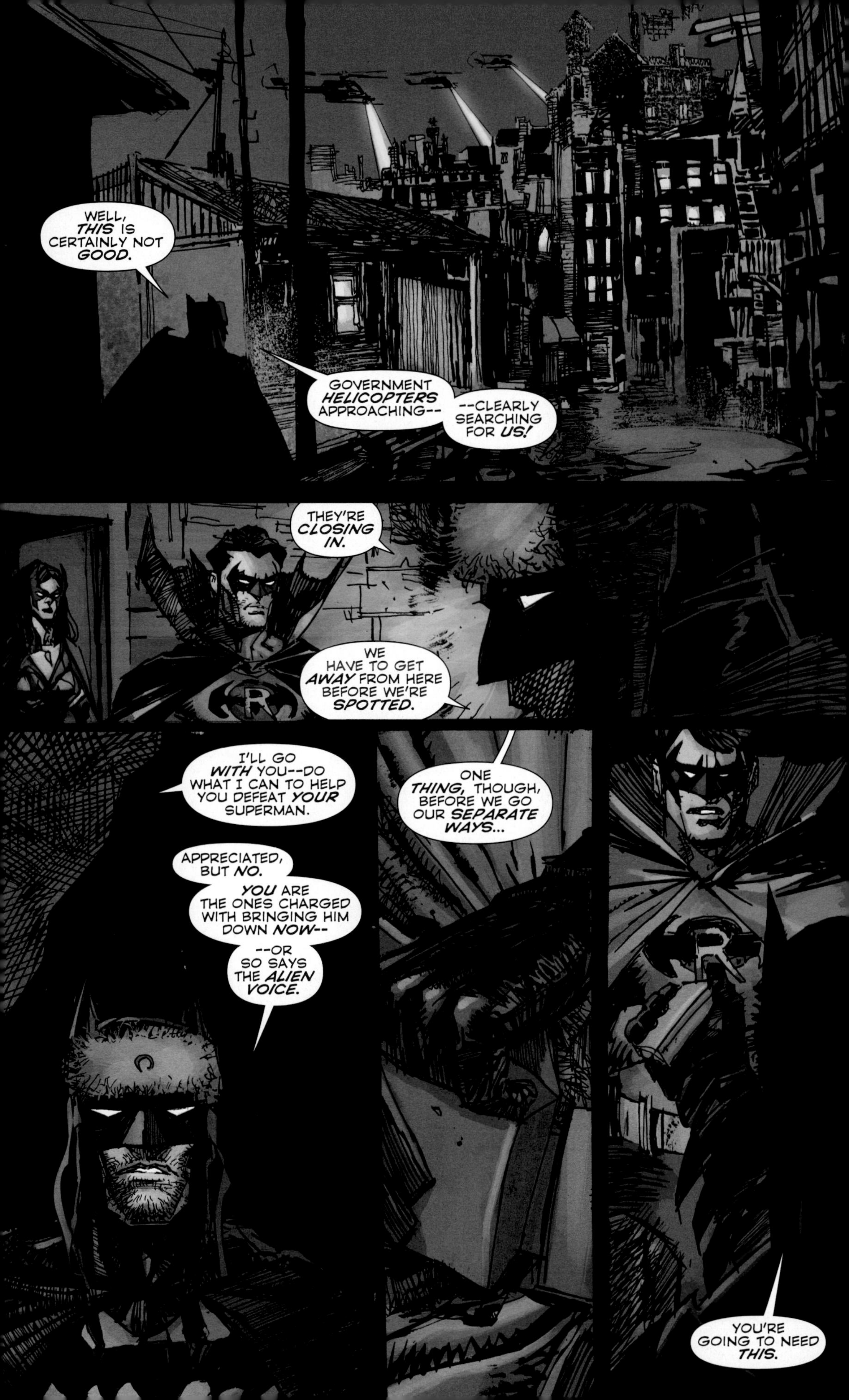
WELL, THIS IS CERTAINLY NOT GOOD.
GOVERNMENT HELICOPTERS APPROACHING--
--CLEARLY SEARCHING FOR US!
THEY'RE CLOSING IN.
WE HAVE TO GET AWAY FROM HERE BEFORE WE'RE SPOTTED.
I'LL GO WITH YOU--DO WHAT I CAN TO HELP YOU DEFEAT YOUR SUPERMAN.
APPRECIATED, BUT NO.
YOU ARE THE ONES CHARGED WITH BRINGING HIM DOWN NOW--
--OR SO SAYS THE ALIEN VOICE.
ONE THING, THOUGH, BEFORE WE GO OUR SEPARATE WAYS...
YOU'RE GOING TO NEED THIS.

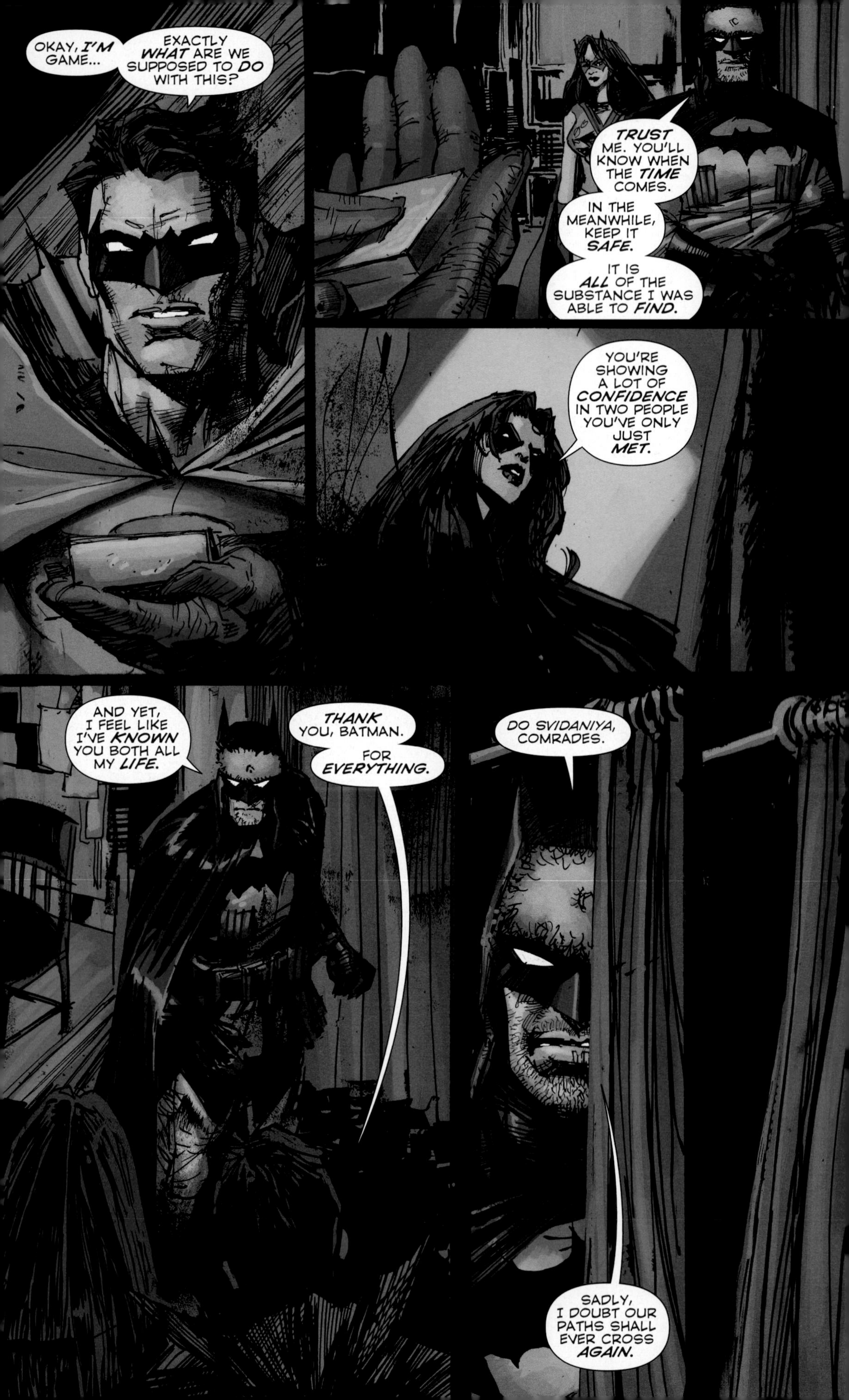
OKAY, I'M GAME...
EXACTLY WHAT ARE WE SUPPOSED TO DO WITH THIS?
TRUST ME. YOU'LL KNOW WHEN THE TIME COMES.
IN THE MEANWHILE, KEEP IT SAFE.
IT IS ALL OF THE SUBSTANCE I WAS ABLE TO FIND.
YOU'RE SHOWING A LOT OF CONFIDENCE IN TWO PEOPLE YOU'VE ONLY JUST MET.
AND YET, I FEEL LIKE I'VE KNOWN YOU BOTH ALL MY LIFE.
THANK YOU, BATMAN.
FOR EVERYTHING.
DO SVIDANIYA, COMRADES.
SADLY, I DOUBT OUR PATHS SHALL EVER CROSS AGAIN.

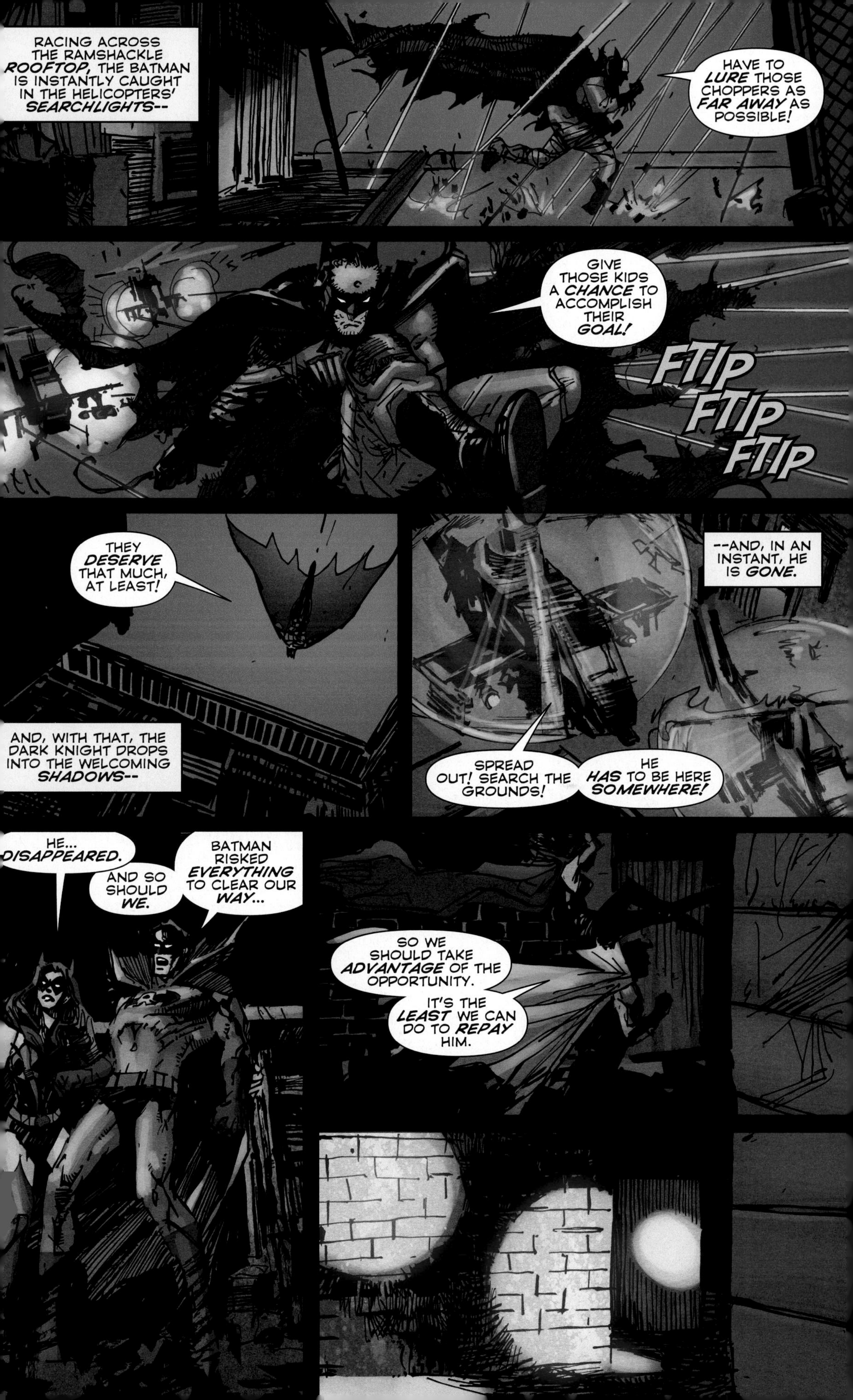
RACING ACROSS THE RAMSHACKLE ROOFTOP, THE BATMAN IS INSTANTLY CAUGHT IN THE HELICOPTERS' SEARCHLIGHTS--
HAVE TO LURE THOSE CHOPPERS AS FAR AWAY AS POSSIBLE!
GIVE THOSE KIDS A CHANCE TO ACCOMPLISH THEIR GOAL!
FTIP FTIP FTIP
THEY DESERVE THAT MUCH, AT LEAST!
AND, WITH THAT, THE DARK KNIGHT DROPS INTO THE WELCOMING SHADOWS--
--AND, IN AN INSTANT, HE IS GONE.
SPREAD OUT! SEARCH THE GROUNDS!
HE HAS TO BE HERE SOMEWHERE!
HE... DISAPPEARED.
AND SO SHOULD WE.
BATMAN RISKED EVERYTHING TO CLEAR OUR WAY...
SO WE SHOULD TAKE ADVANTAGE OF THE OPPORTUNITY.
IT'S THE LEAST WE CAN DO TO REPAY HIM.

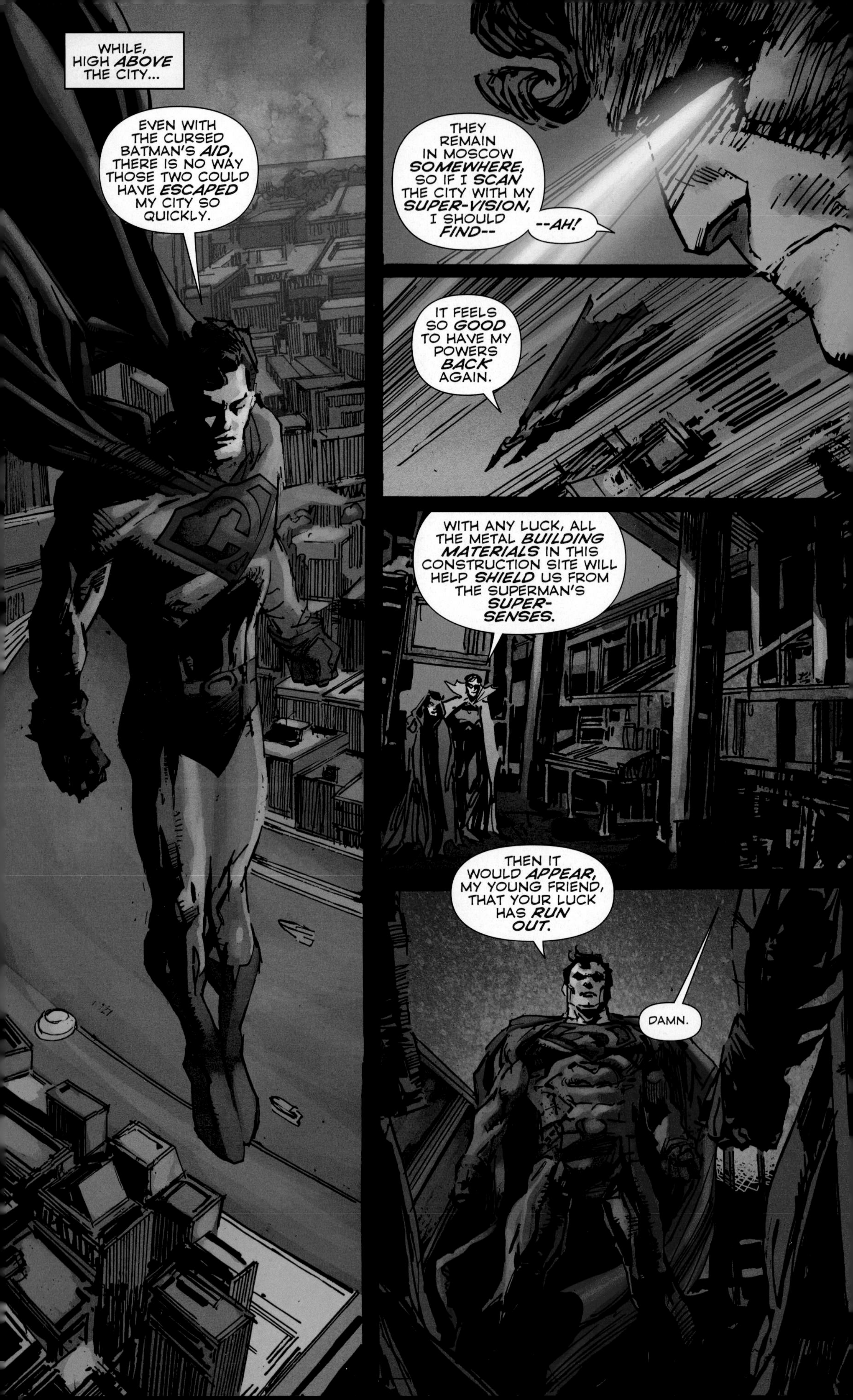
WHILE, HIGH ABOVE THE CITY...
EVEN WITH THE CURSED BATMAN'S AID, THERE IS NO WAY THOSE TWO COULD HAVE ESCAPED MY CITY SO QUICKLY.
THEY REMAIN IN MOSCOW SOMEWHERE, SO IF I SCAN THE CITY WITH MY SUPER-VISION, I SHOULD FIND--
--AH!
IT FEELS SO GOOD TO HAVE MY POWERS BACK AGAIN.
WITH ANY LUCK, ALL THE METAL BUILDING MATERIALS IN THIS CONSTRUCTION SITE WILL HELP SHIELD US FROM THE SUPERMAN'S SUPER-SENSES.
THEN IT WOULD APPEAR, MY YOUNG FRIEND, THAT YOUR LUCK HAS RUN OUT.
DAMN.

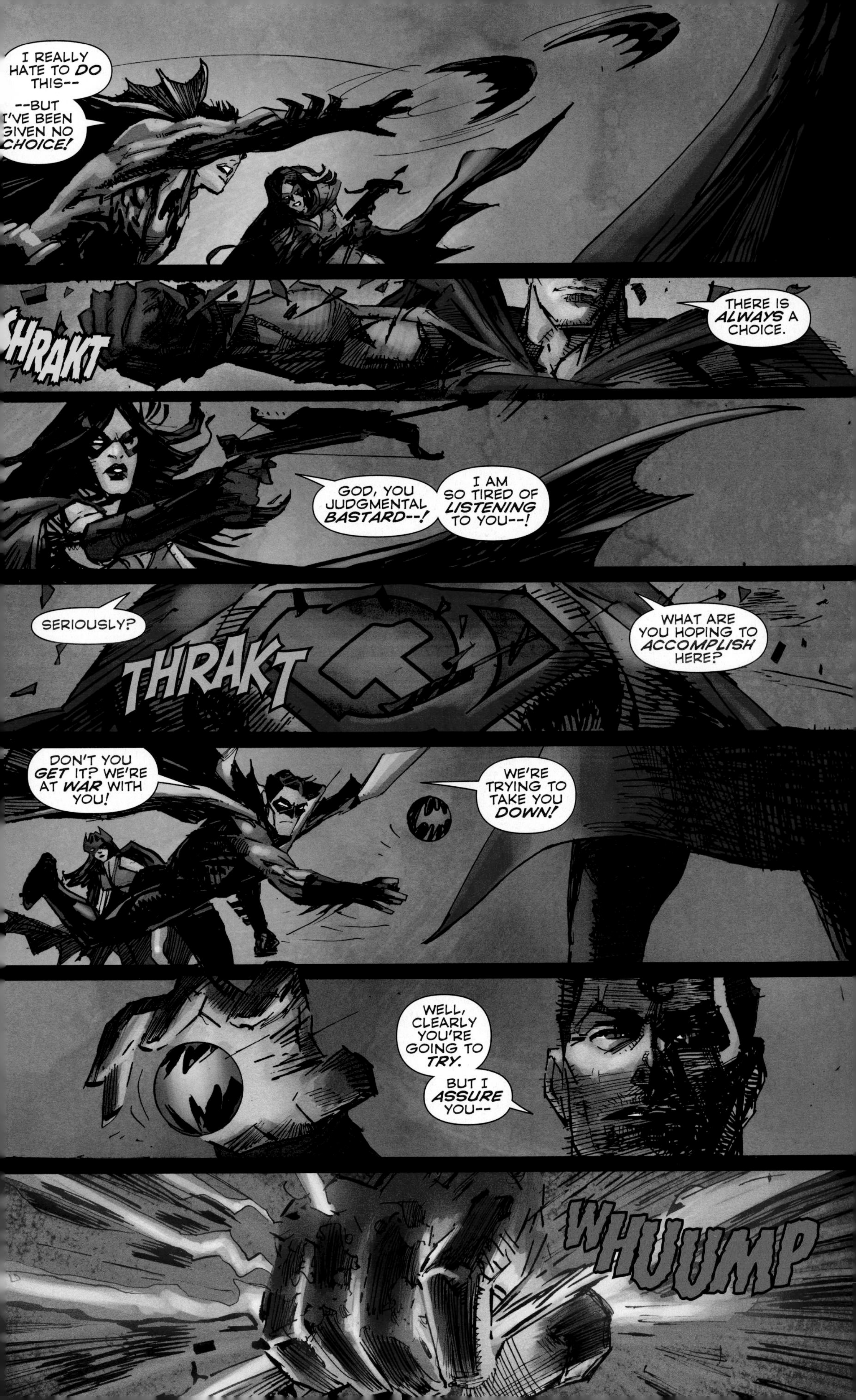

I REALLY HATE TO DO THIS--
--BUT I'VE BEEN GIVEN NO CHOICE!
THRAKT
THERE IS ALWAYS A CHOICE.
GOD, YOU JUDGMENTAL BASTARD--!
I AM SO TIRED OF LISTENING TO YOU--!
SERIOUSLY?
THRAKT
WHAT ARE YOU HOPING TO ACCOMPLISH HERE?
DON'T YOU GET IT? WE'RE AT WAR WITH YOU!
WE'RE TRYING TO TAKE YOU DOWN!
WELL, CLEARLY YOU'RE GOING TO TRY.
BUT I ASSURE YOU--
WHUUMP

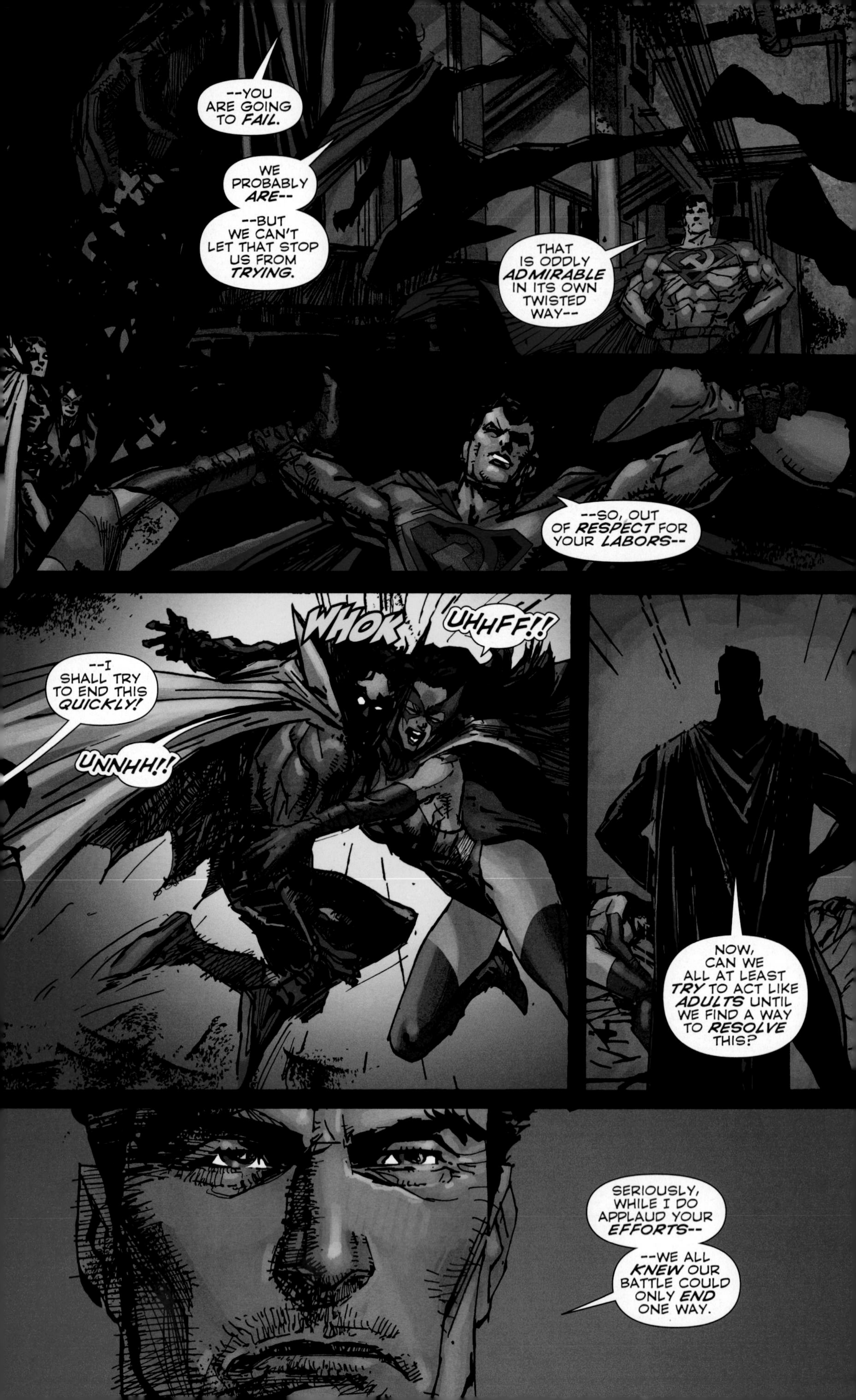
--YOU ARE GOING TO *FAIL*.
WE PROBABLY *ARE*--
--BUT WE CAN'T LET THAT STOP US FROM *TRYING*.
THAT IS ODDLY *ADMIRABLE* IN ITS OWN TWISTED WAY--
--SO, OUT OF *RESPECT* FOR YOUR *LABORS*--
WHOK
UHHFF!!
--I SHALL TRY TO END THIS *QUICKLY!*
UNNHH!!
NOW, CAN WE ALL AT LEAST *TRY* TO ACT LIKE *ADULTS* UNTIL WE FIND A WAY TO *RESOLVE* THIS?
SERIOUSLY, WHILE I DO APPLAUD YOUR *EFFORTS*--
--WE ALL *KNEW* OUR BATTLE COULD ONLY *END* ONE WAY.

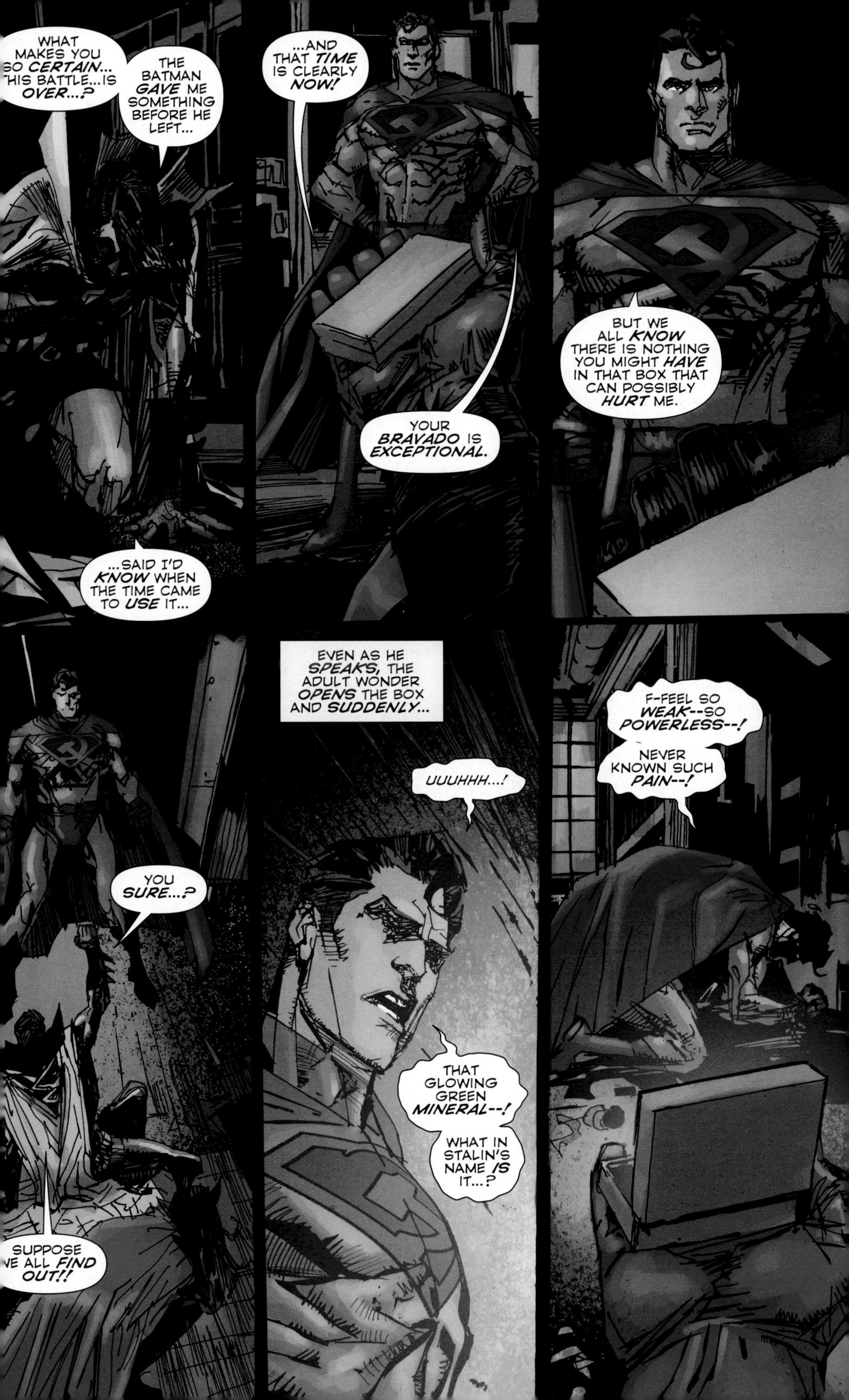
WHAT MAKES YOU SO CERTAIN... THIS BATTLE...IS OVER...?
THE BATMAN GAVE ME SOMETHING BEFORE HE LEFT...
...SAID I'D KNOW WHEN THE TIME CAME TO USE IT...
...AND THAT TIME IS CLEARLY NOW!
YOUR BRAVADO IS EXCEPTIONAL.
BUT WE ALL KNOW THERE IS NOTHING YOU MIGHT HAVE IN THAT BOX THAT CAN POSSIBLY HURT ME.
YOU SURE...?
SUPPOSE WE ALL FIND OUT!!
EVEN AS HE SPEAKS, THE ADULT WONDER OPENS THE BOX AND SUDDENLY...
UUUHHH...!
THAT GLOWING GREEN MINERAL--!
WHAT IN STALIN'S NAME IS IT...?
F-FEEL SO WEAK--SO POWERLESS--!
NEVER KNOWN SUCH PAIN--!

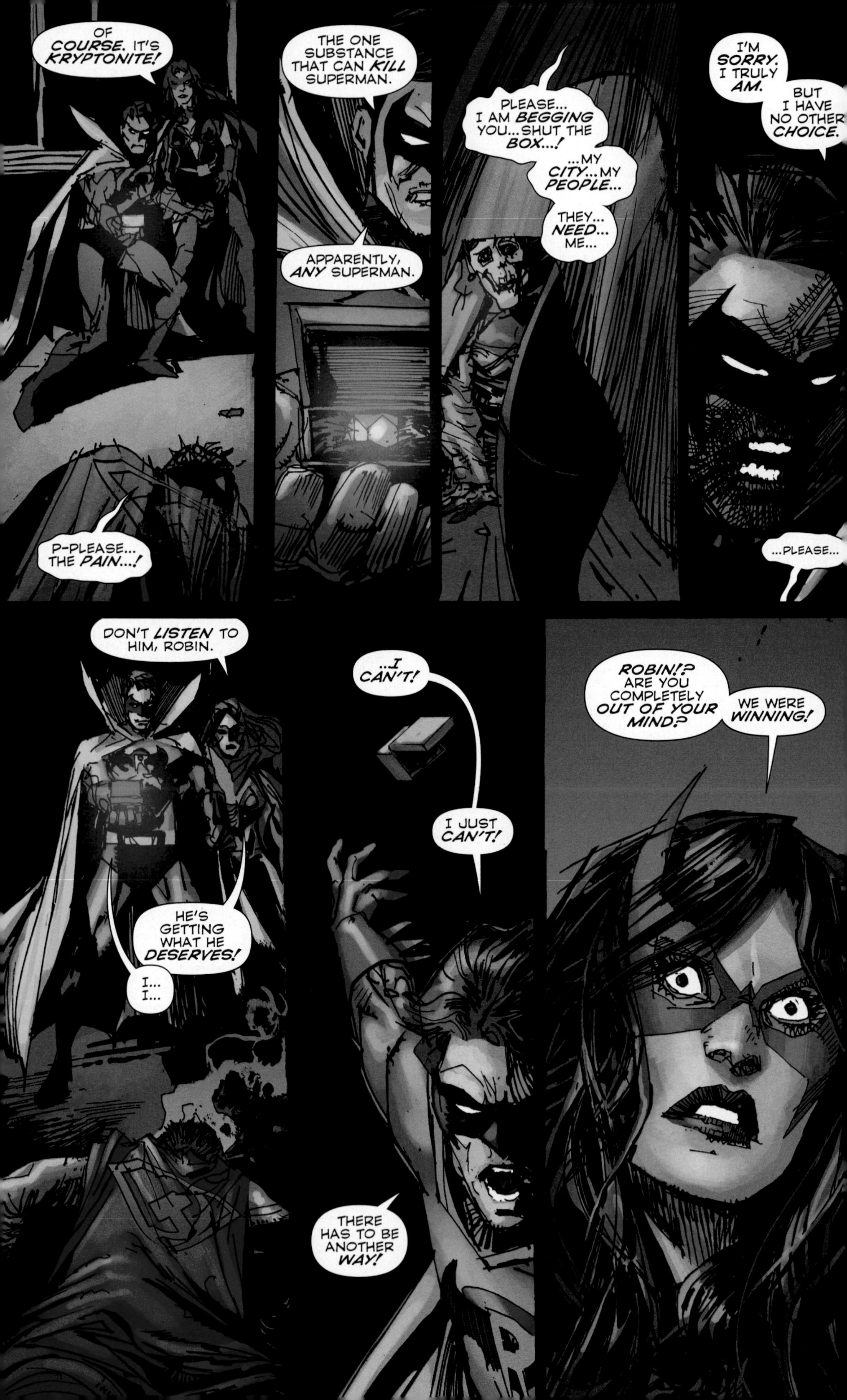
OF COURSE. IT'S KRYPTONITE!
P-PLEASE... THE PAIN...!
THE ONE SUBSTANCE THAT CAN KILL SUPERMAN.
APPARENTLY, ANY SUPERMAN.
PLEASE... I AM BEGGING YOU...SHUT THE BOX...!
...MY CITY...MY PEOPLE...
THEY... NEED... ME...
I'M SORRY. I TRULY AM.
BUT I HAVE NO OTHER CHOICE.
...PLEASE...
DON'T LISTEN TO HIM, ROBIN.
HE'S GETTING WHAT HE DESERVES!
I... I...
...I CAN'T!
I JUST CAN'T!
THERE HAS TO BE ANOTHER WAY!
ROBIN!? ARE YOU COMPLETELY OUT OF YOUR MIND?
WE WERE WINNING!

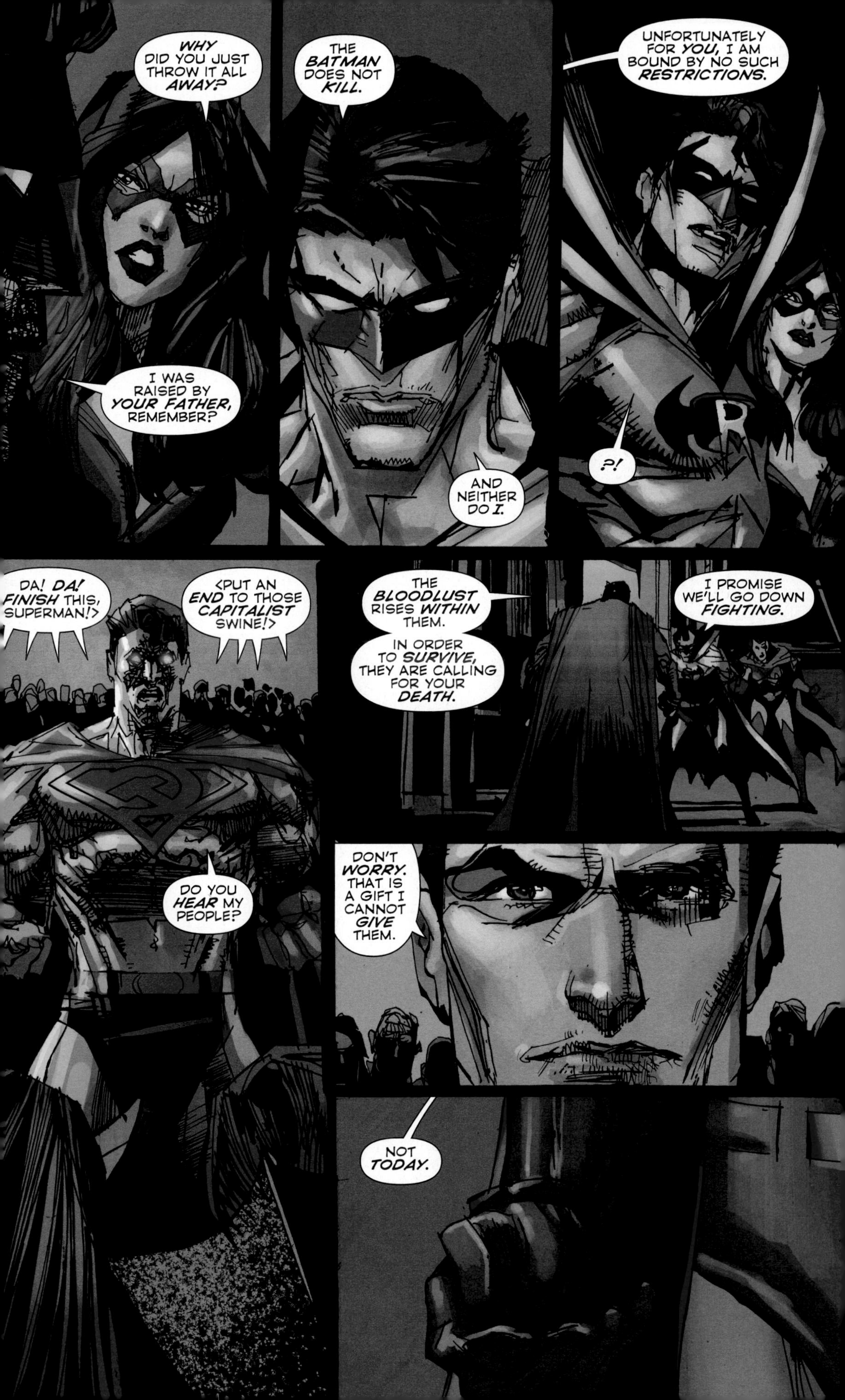
WHY DID YOU JUST THROW IT ALL AWAY?
I WAS RAISED BY YOUR FATHER, REMEMBER?
THE BATMAN DOES NOT KILL.
AND NEITHER DO I.
UNFORTUNATELY FOR YOU, I AM BOUND BY NO SUCH RESTRICTIONS.
?!
DA! DA! FINISH THIS, SUPERMAN!>
<PUT AN END TO THOSE CAPITALIST SWINE!>
DO YOU HEAR MY PEOPLE?
THE BLOODLUST RISES WITHIN THEM.
IN ORDER TO SURVIVE, THEY ARE CALLING FOR YOUR DEATH.
I PROMISE WE'LL GO DOWN FIGHTING.
DON'T WORRY. THAT IS A GIFT I CANNOT GIVE THEM.
NOT TODAY.

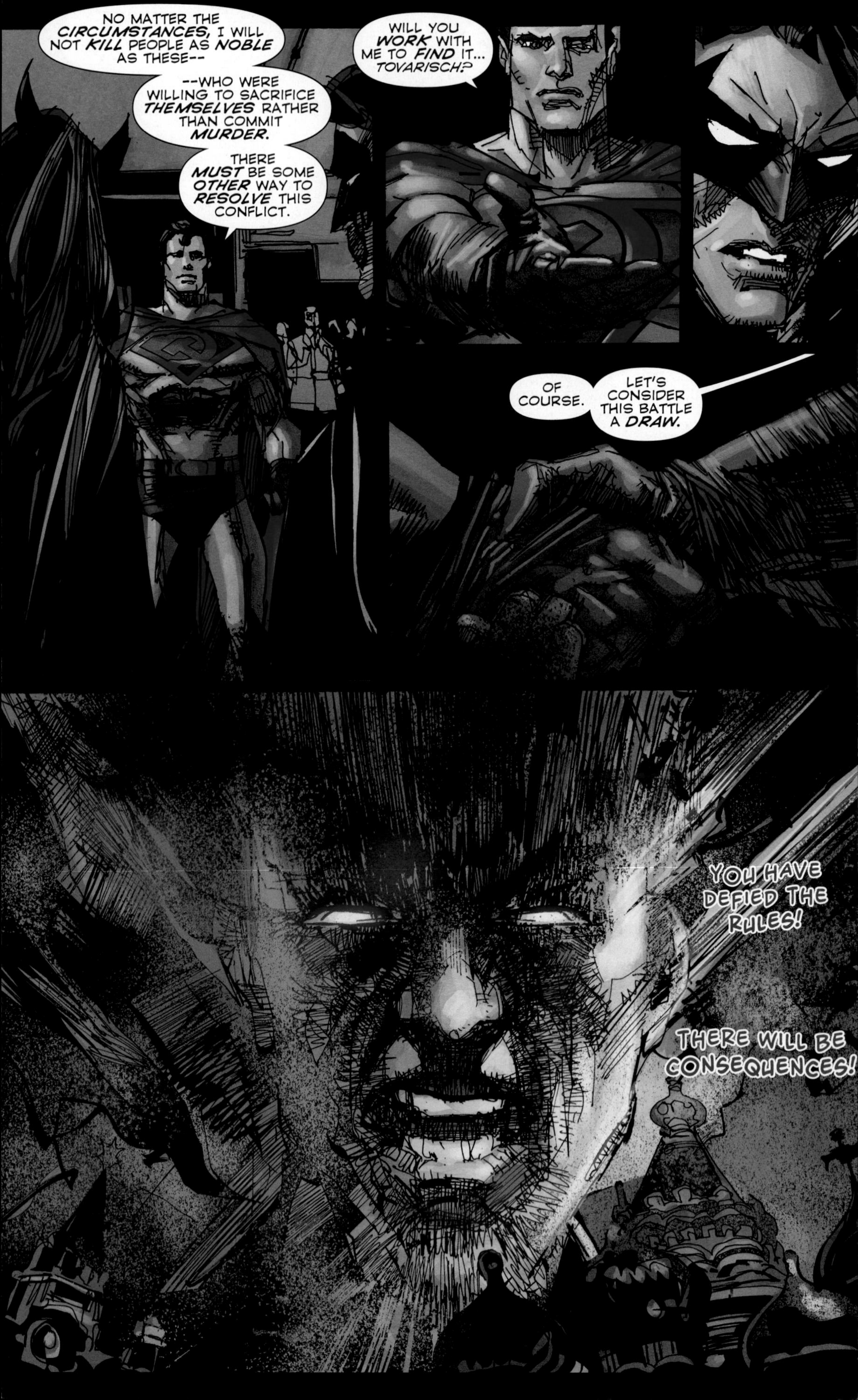
NO MATTER THE CIRCUMSTANCES, I WILL NOT KILL PEOPLE AS NOBLE AS THESE--
--WHO WERE WILLING TO SACRIFICE THEMSELVES RATHER THAN COMMIT MURDER.
THERE MUST BE SOME OTHER WAY TO RESOLVE THIS CONFLICT.
WILL YOU WORK WITH ME TO FIND IT... TOVARISCH?
OF COURSE.
LET'S CONSIDER THIS BATTLE A DRAW.
YOU HAVE DEFIED THE RULES!
THERE WILL BE CONSEQUENCES!

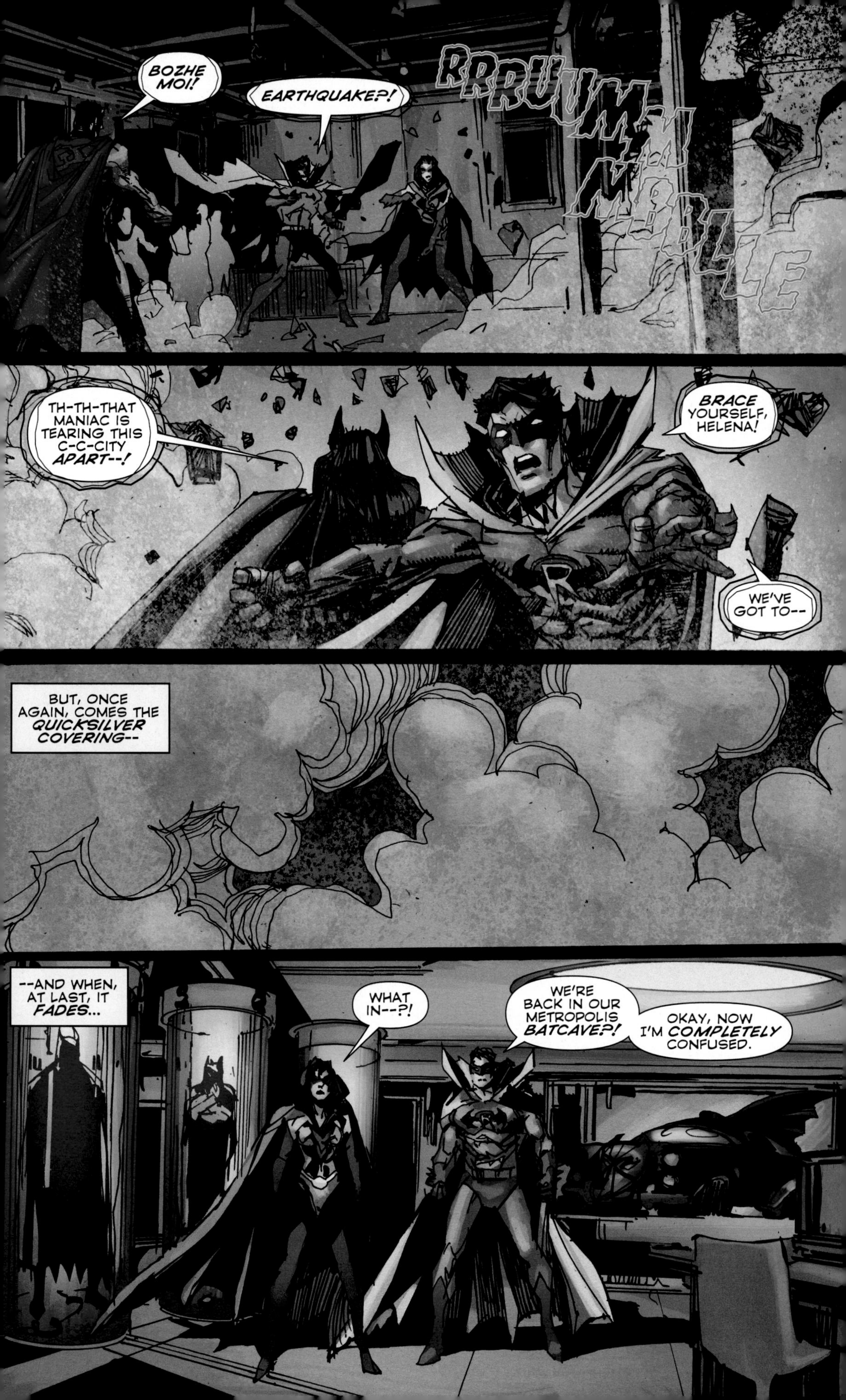
BOZHE MOI!
EARTHQUAKE?!
RRRUUMMMBLLLE
TH-TH-THAT MANIAC IS TEARING THIS C-C-CITY APART--!
BRACE YOURSELF, HELENA!
WE'VE GOT TO--
BUT, ONCE AGAIN, COMES THE QUICKSILVER COVERING--
--AND WHEN, AT LAST, IT FADES...
WHAT IN--?!
WE'RE BACK IN OUR METROPOLIS BATCAVE?!
OKAY, NOW I'M COMPLETELY CONFUSED.

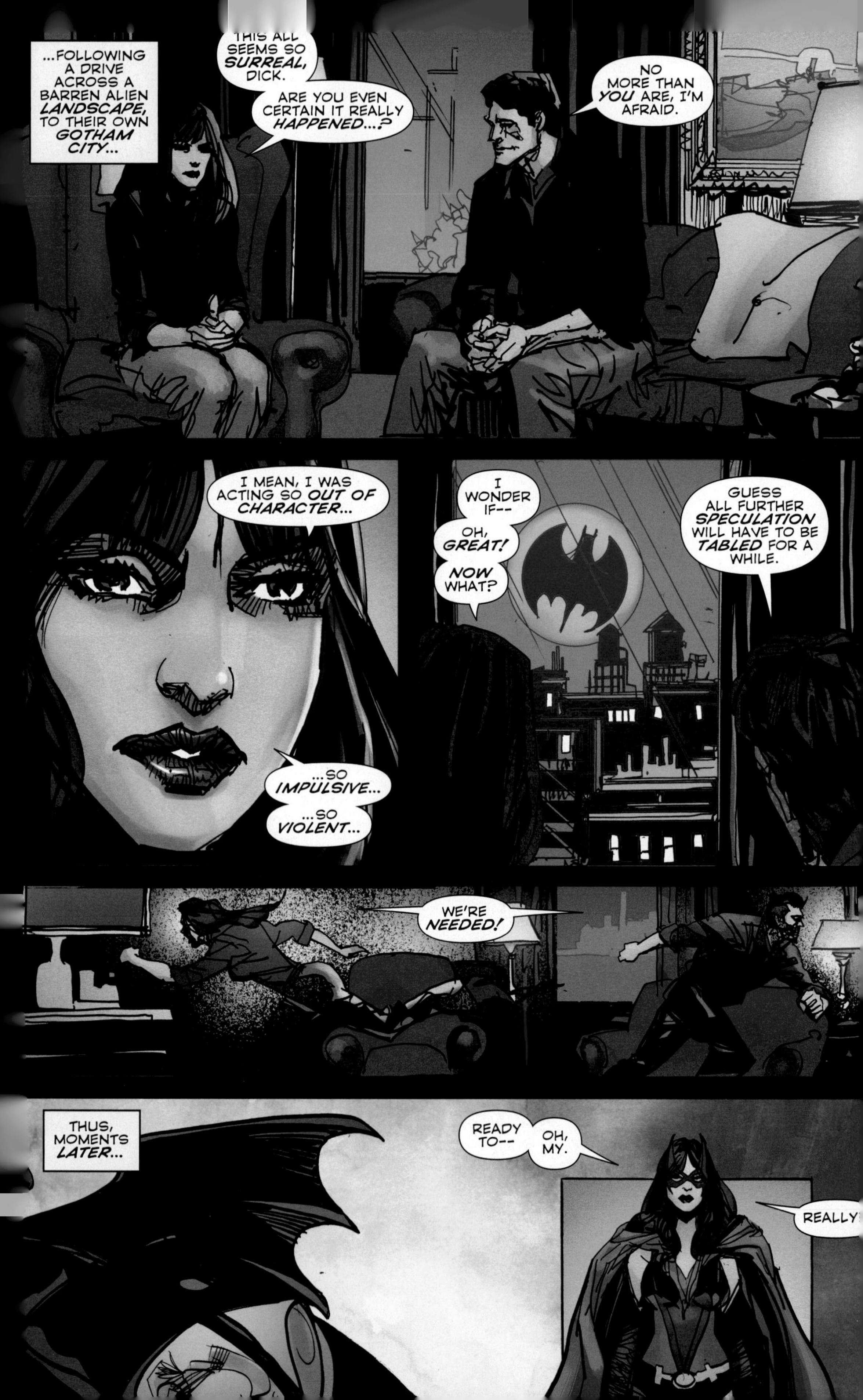
...FOLLOWING A DRIVE ACROSS A BARREN ALIEN LANDSCAPE, TO THEIR OWN GOTHAM CITY...
THIS ALL SEEMS SO SURREAL, DICK.
ARE YOU EVEN CERTAIN IT REALLY HAPPENED...?
NO MORE THAN YOU ARE, I'M AFRAID.
I MEAN, I WAS ACTING SO OUT OF CHARACTER...
...SO IMPULSIVE...
...SO VIOLENT...
I WONDER IF--
OH, GREAT!
NOW WHAT?
GUESS ALL FURTHER SPECULATION WILL HAVE TO BE TABLED FOR A WHILE.
WE'RE NEEDED!
THUS, MOMENTS LATER...
READY TO--
OH, MY.
REALLY

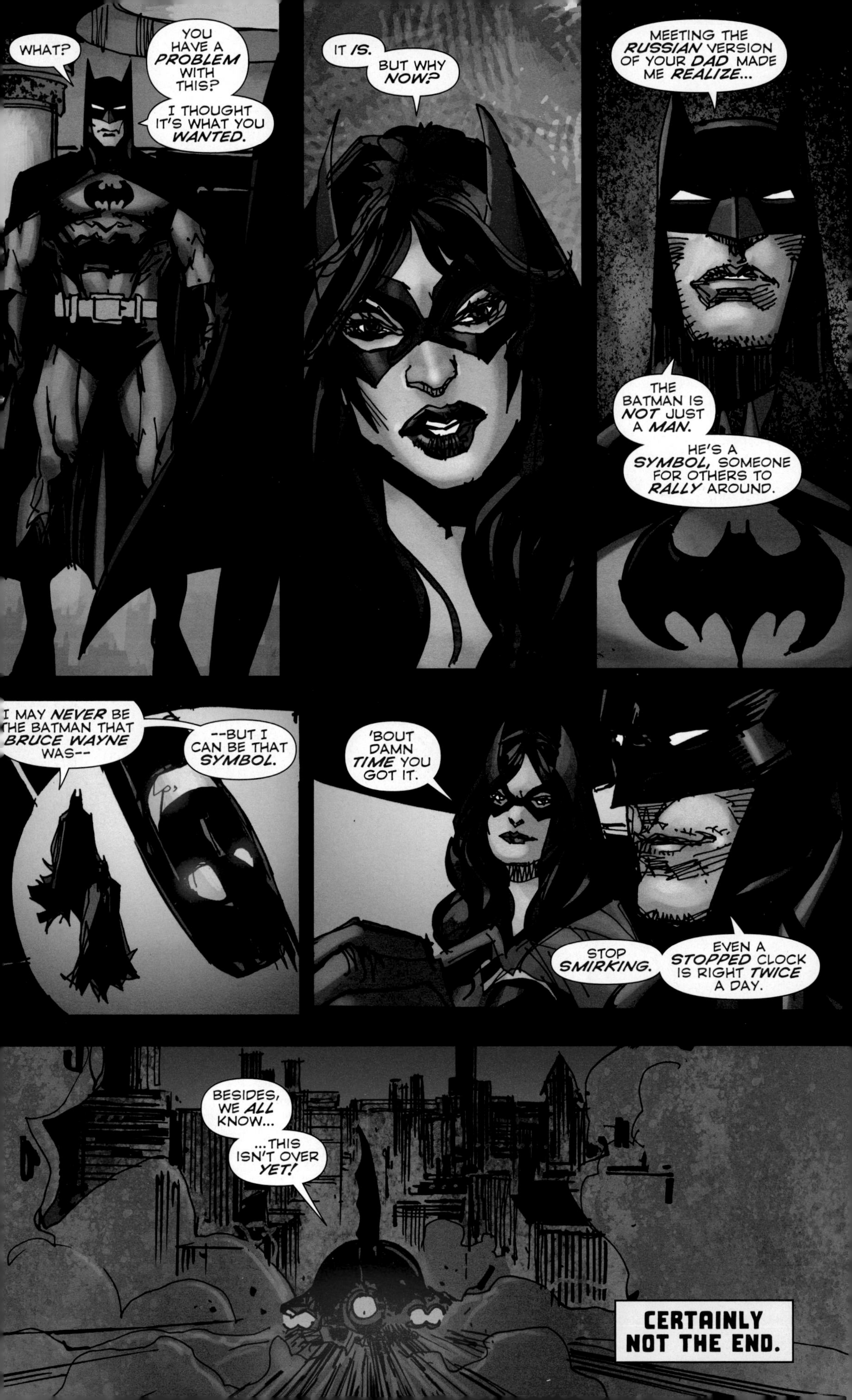

WHAT?
YOU HAVE A *PROBLEM* WITH THIS?
I THOUGHT IT'S WHAT YOU *WANTED.*
IT *IS.*
BUT WHY *NOW?*
MEETING THE *RUSSIAN* VERSION OF YOUR *DAD* MADE ME *REALIZE...*
THE BATMAN IS *NOT* JUST A *MAN.*
HE'S A *SYMBOL,* SOMEONE FOR OTHERS TO *RALLY* AROUND.
I MAY *NEVER* BE THE BATMAN THAT *BRUCE WAYNE* WAS--
--BUT I CAN BE THAT *SYMBOL.*
'BOUT DAMN *TIME* YOU GOT IT.
STOP *SMIRKING.*
EVEN A *STOPPED* CLOCK IS RIGHT *TWICE* A DAY.
BESIDES, WE *ALL* KNOW...
...THIS ISN'T OVER *YET!*
CERTAINLY NOT THE END.

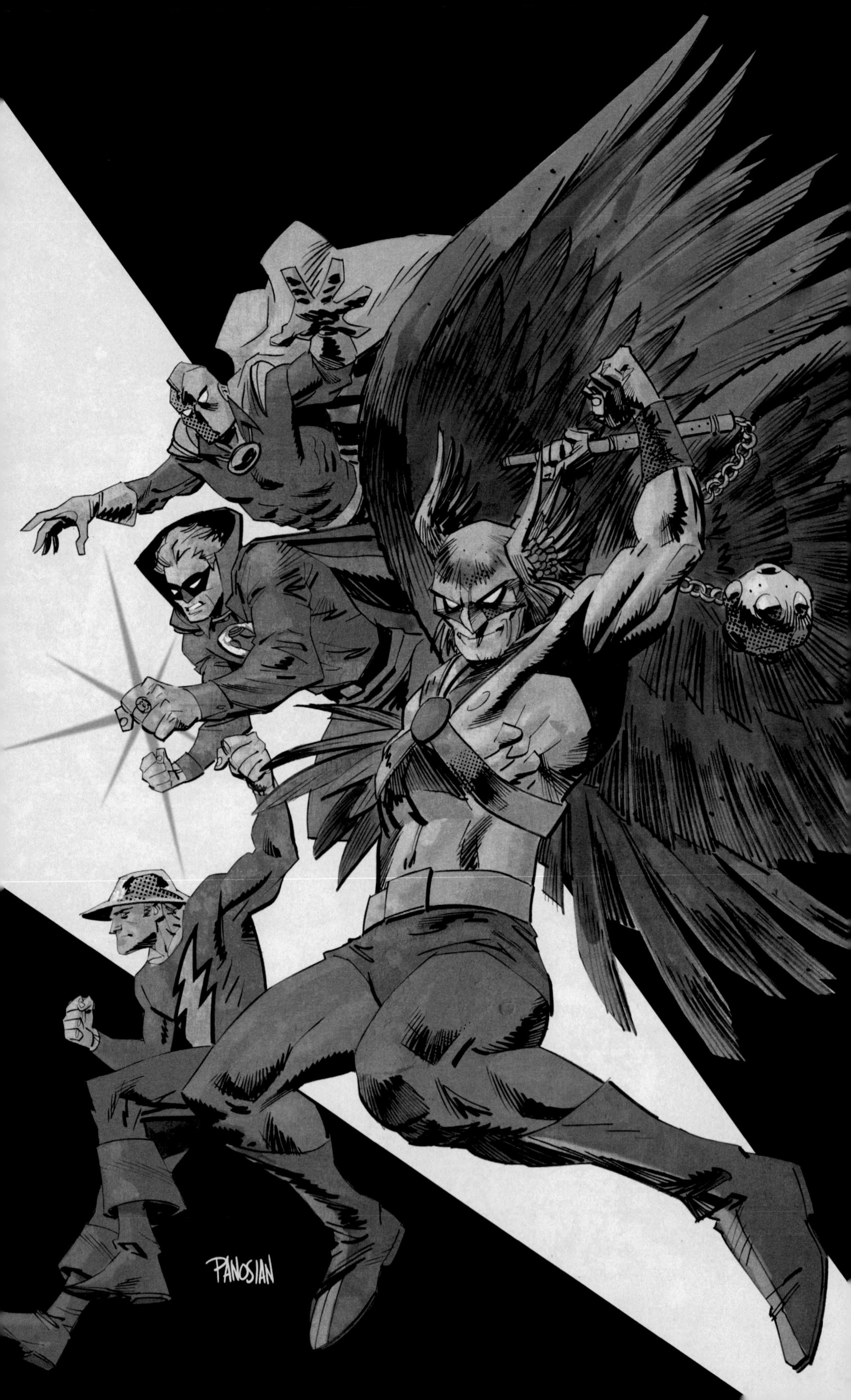
PANOSIAN

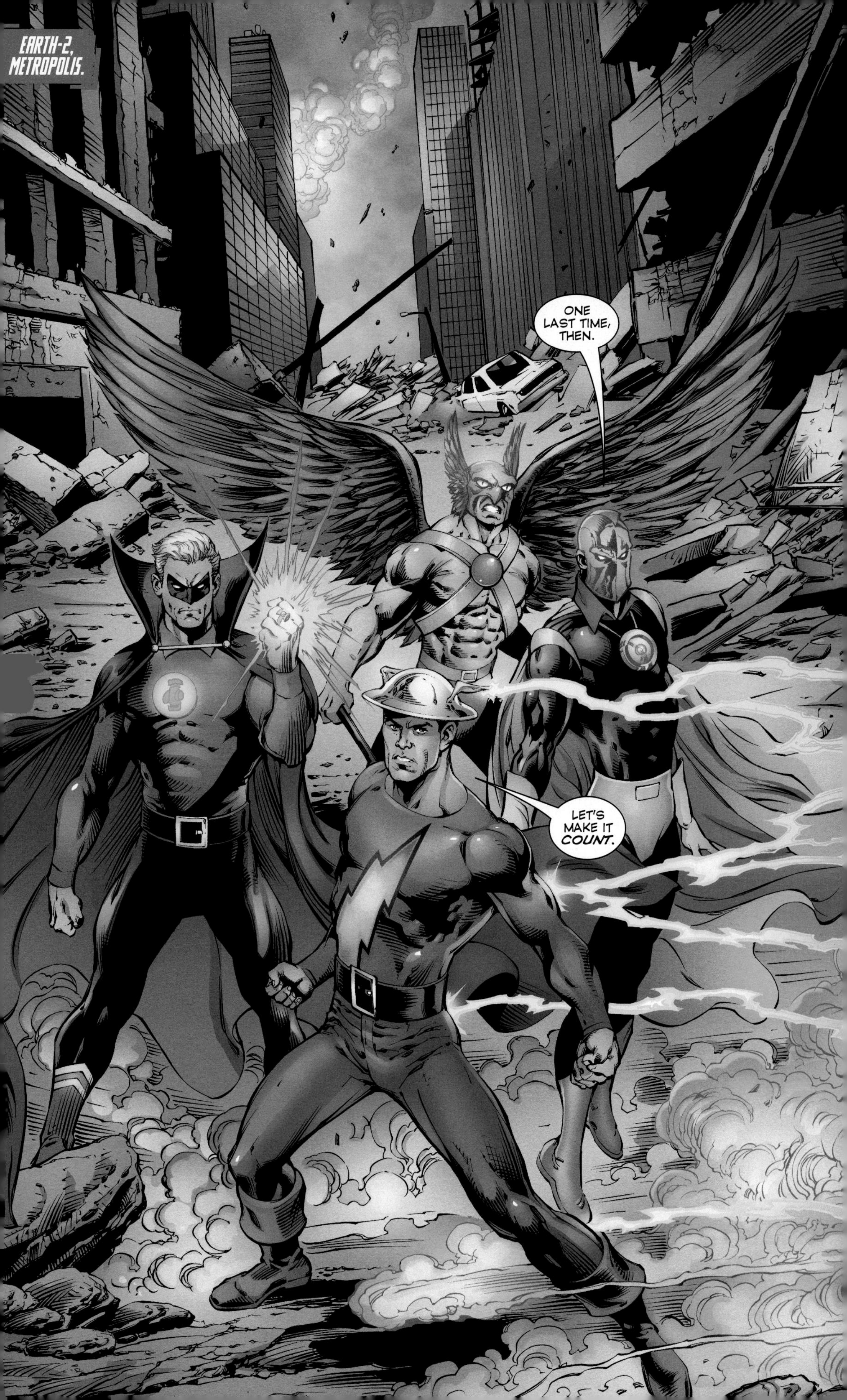
EARTH-2, METROPOLIS.
ONE LAST TIME, THEN.
LET'S MAKE IT COUNT.

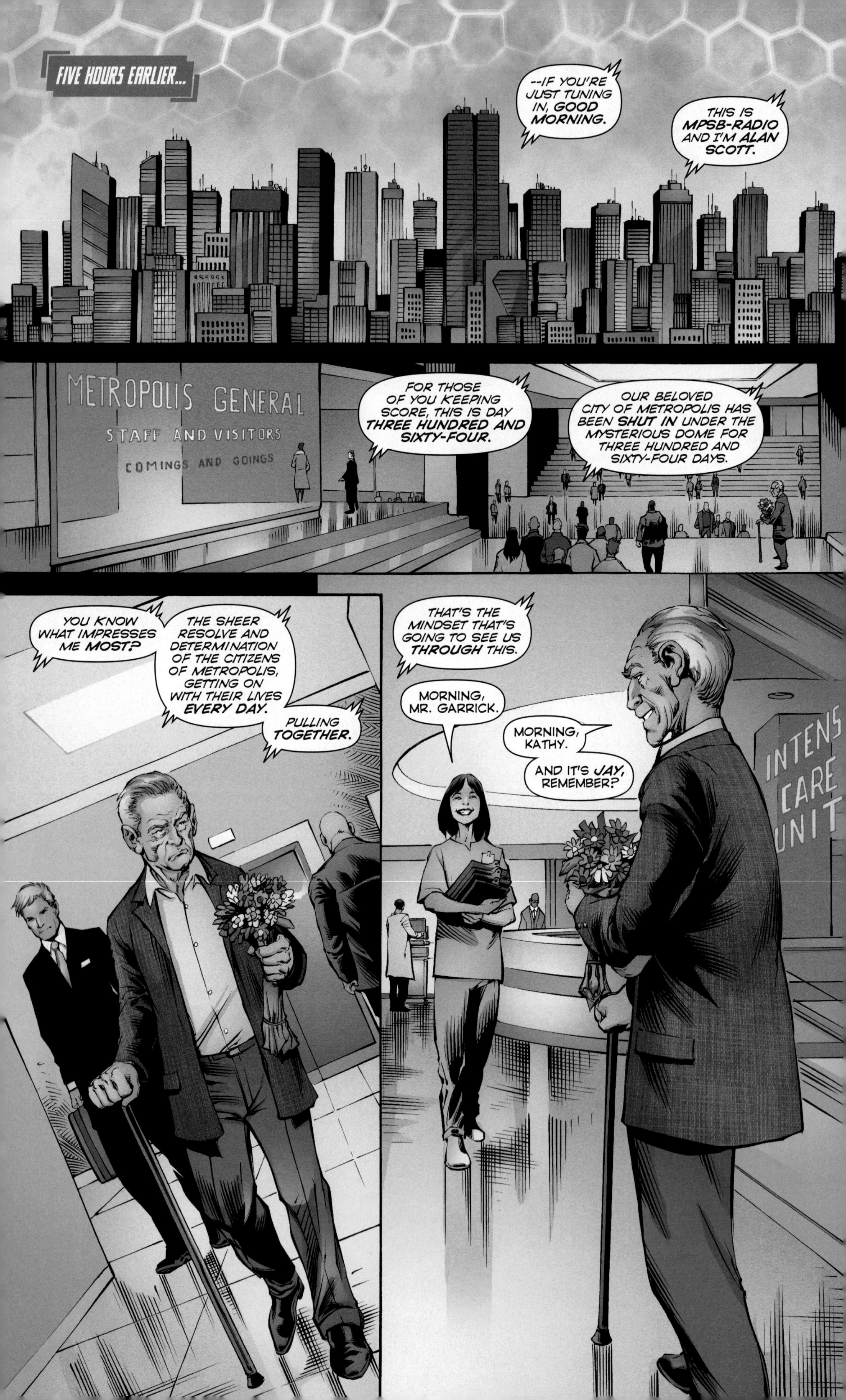
FIVE HOURS EARLIER...
--IF YOU'RE JUST TUNING IN, GOOD MORNING.
THIS IS MPSB-RADIO AND I'M ALAN SCOTT.
METROPOLIS GENERAL
STAFF AND VISITORS
COMINGS AND GOINGS
FOR THOSE OF YOU KEEPING SCORE, THIS IS DAY THREE HUNDRED AND SIXTY-FOUR.
OUR BELOVED CITY OF METROPOLIS HAS BEEN SHUT IN UNDER THE MYSTERIOUS DOME FOR THREE HUNDRED AND SIXTY-FOUR DAYS.
YOU KNOW WHAT IMPRESSES ME MOST?
THE SHEER RESOLVE AND DETERMINATION OF THE CITIZENS OF METROPOLIS, GETTING ON WITH THEIR LIVES EVERY DAY.
PULLING TOGETHER.
THAT'S THE MINDSET THAT'S GOING TO SEE US THROUGH THIS.
MORNING, MR. GARRICK.
MORNING, KATHY.
AND IT'S JAY, REMEMBER?
INTENS CARE UNIT

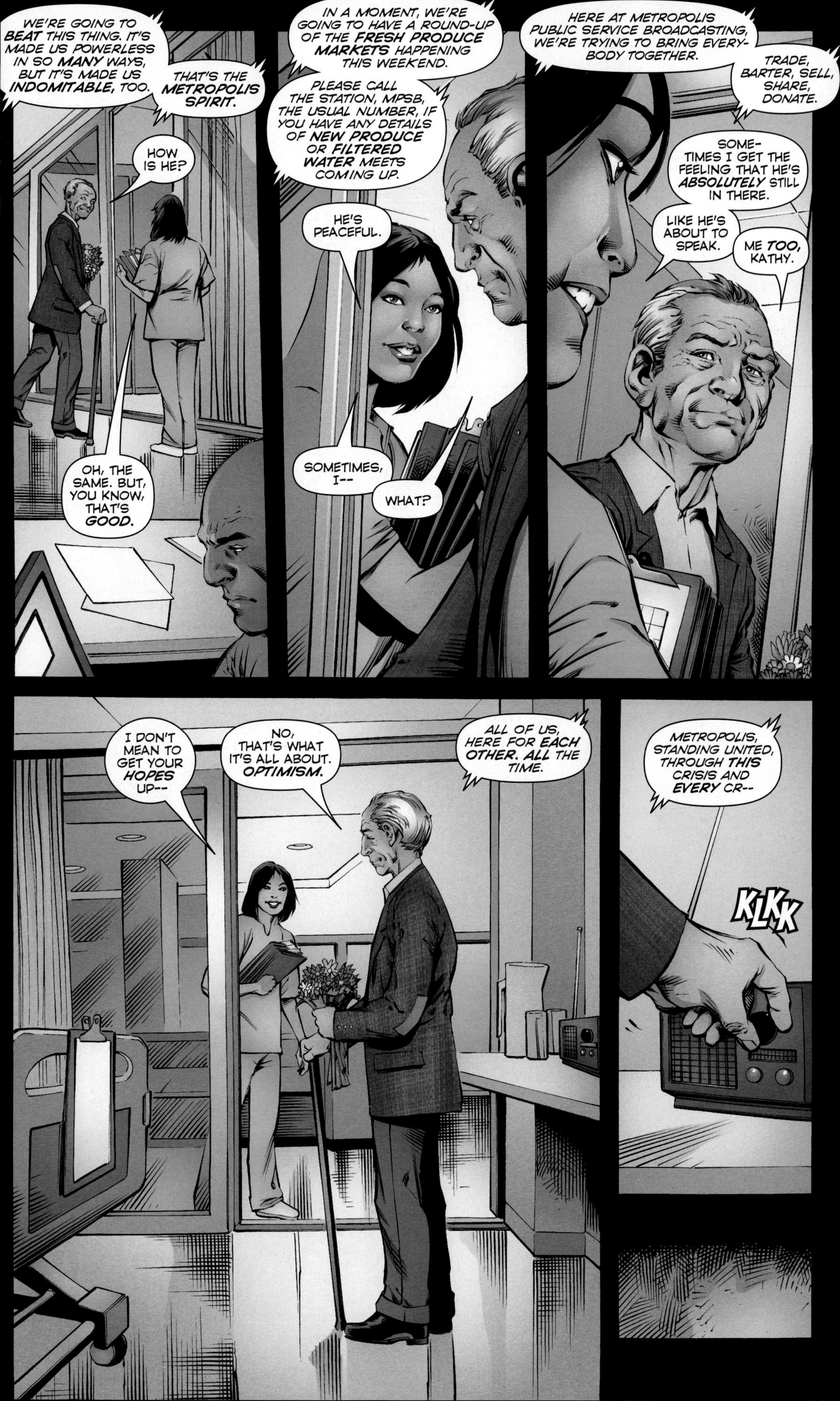
WE'RE GOING TO BEAT THIS THING. IT'S MADE US POWERLESS IN SO MANY WAYS, BUT IT'S MADE US INDOMITABLE, TOO.
THAT'S THE METROPOLIS SPIRIT.
HOW IS HE?
OH, THE SAME. BUT, YOU KNOW, THAT'S GOOD.
IN A MOMENT, WE'RE GOING TO HAVE A ROUND-UP OF THE FRESH PRODUCE MARKETS HAPPENING THIS WEEKEND.
PLEASE CALL THE STATION, MPSB, THE USUAL NUMBER, IF YOU HAVE ANY DETAILS OF NEW PRODUCE OR FILTERED WATER MEETS COMING UP.
HE'S PEACEFUL.
SOMETIMES, I--
WHAT?
HERE AT METROPOLIS PUBLIC SERVICE BROADCASTING, WE'RE TRYING TO BRING EVERY-BODY TOGETHER.
TRADE, BARTER, SELL, SHARE, DONATE.
SOME-TIMES I GET THE FEELING THAT HE'S ABSOLUTELY STILL IN THERE.
LIKE HE'S ABOUT TO SPEAK.
ME TOO, KATHY.
I DON'T MEAN TO GET YOUR HOPES UP--
NO, THAT'S WHAT IT'S ALL ABOUT. OPTIMISM.
ALL OF US, HERE FOR EACH OTHER. ALL THE TIME.
METROPOLIS, STANDING UNITED, THROUGH THIS CRISIS AND EVERY CR--
KLIKK

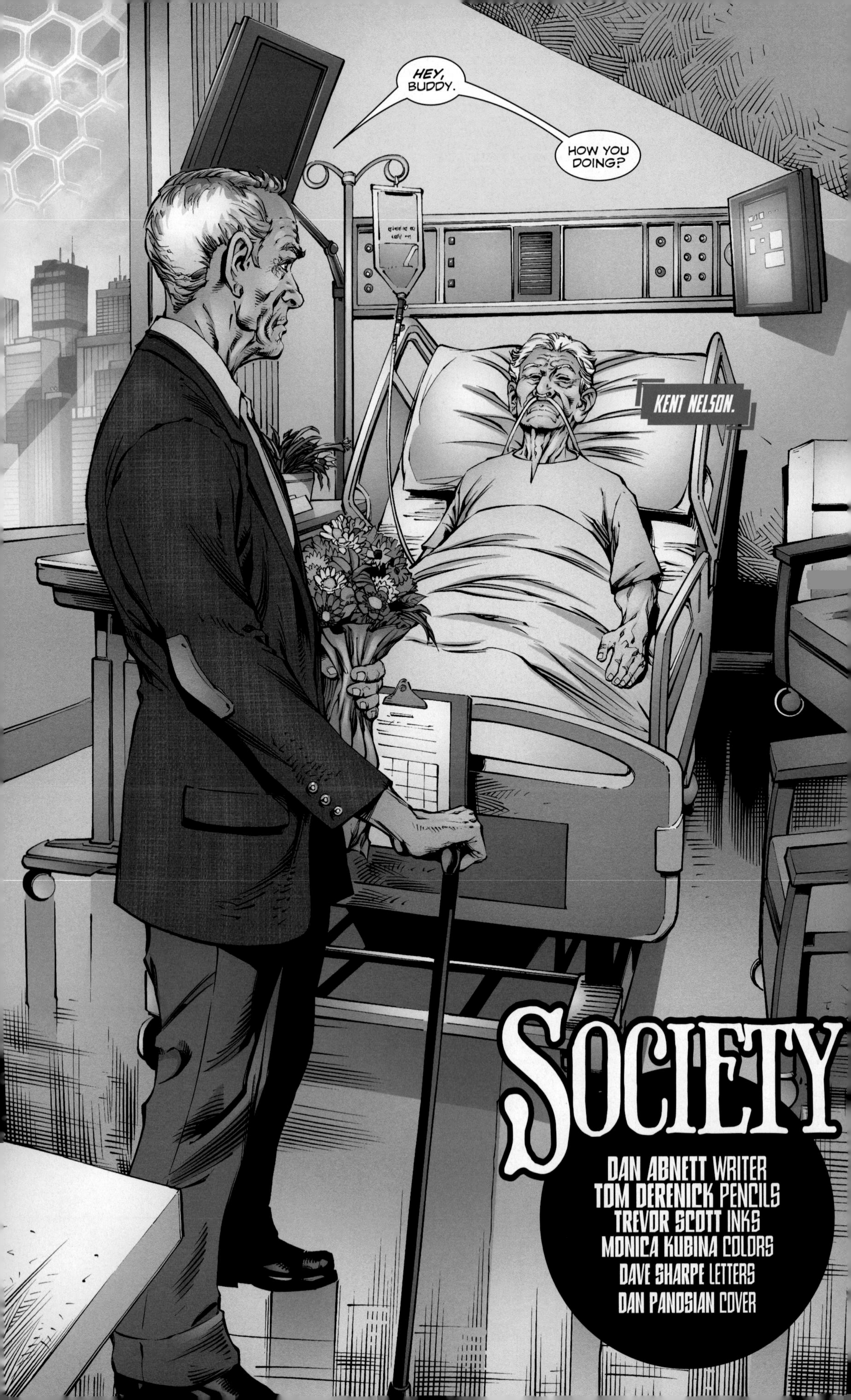
HEY, BUDDY.
HOW YOU DOING?
KENT NELSON.
SOCIETY
DAN ABNETT WRITER
TOM DERENICK PENCILS
TREVOR SCOTT INKS
MONICA KUBINA COLORS
DAVE SHARPE LETTERS
DAN PANOSIAN COVER

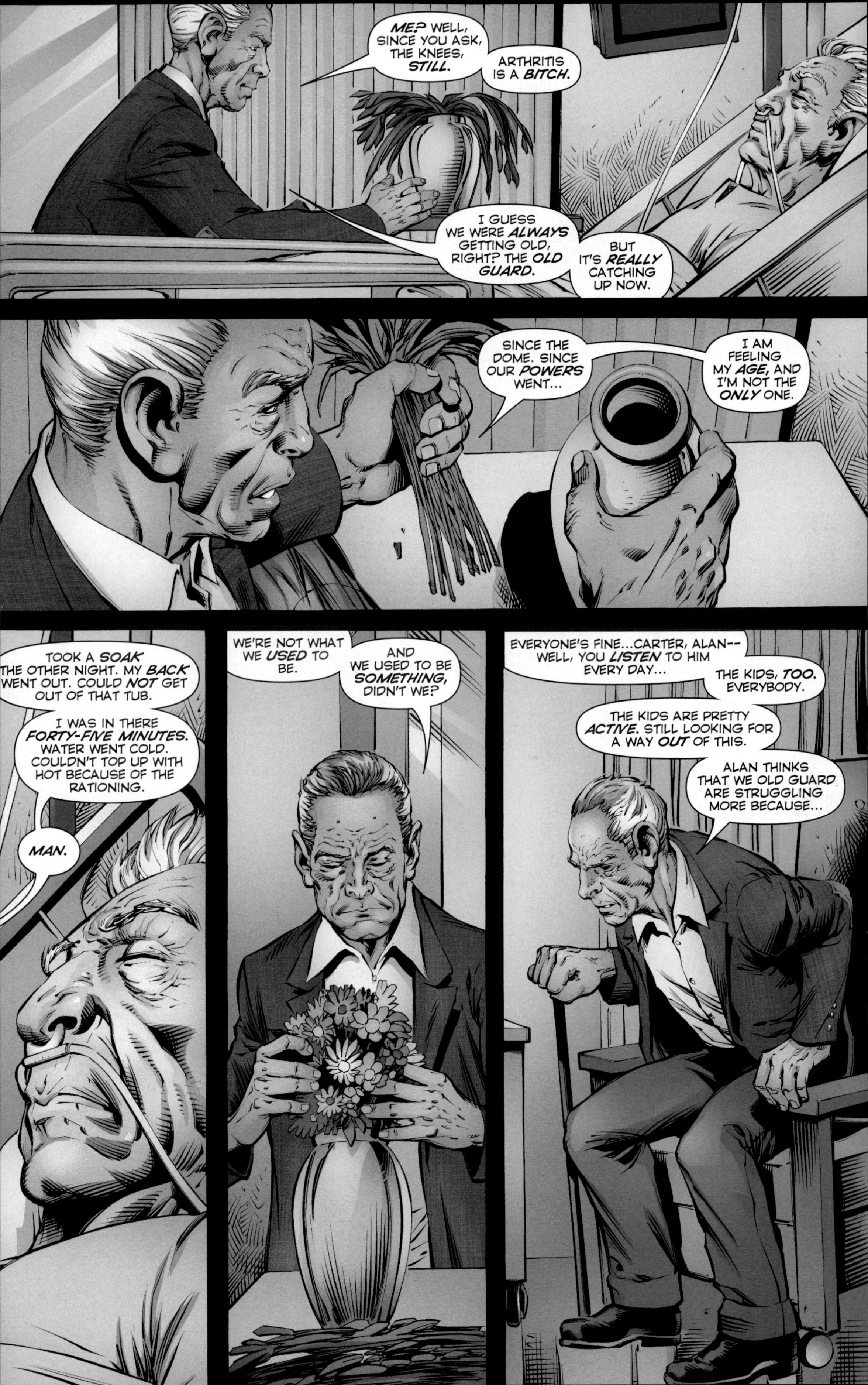

ME? WELL, SINCE YOU ASK, THE KNEES, STILL.
ARTHRITIS IS A BITCH.
I GUESS WE WERE ALWAYS GETTING OLD, RIGHT? THE OLD GUARD.
BUT IT'S REALLY CATCHING UP NOW.
SINCE THE DOME. SINCE OUR POWERS WENT...
I AM FEELING MY AGE, AND I'M NOT THE ONLY ONE.
TOOK A SOAK THE OTHER NIGHT. MY BACK WENT OUT. COULD NOT GET OUT OF THAT TUB.
I WAS IN THERE FORTY-FIVE MINUTES. WATER WENT COLD. COULDN'T TOP UP WITH HOT BECAUSE OF THE RATIONING.
MAN.
WE'RE NOT WHAT WE USED TO BE.
AND WE USED TO BE SOMETHING, DIDN'T WE?
EVERYONE'S FINE...CARTER, ALAN-- WELL, YOU LISTEN TO HIM EVERY DAY...
THE KIDS, TOO. EVERYBODY.
THE KIDS ARE PRETTY ACTIVE. STILL LOOKING FOR A WAY OUT OF THIS.
ALAN THINKS THAT WE OLD GUARD ARE STRUGGLING MORE BECAUSE...

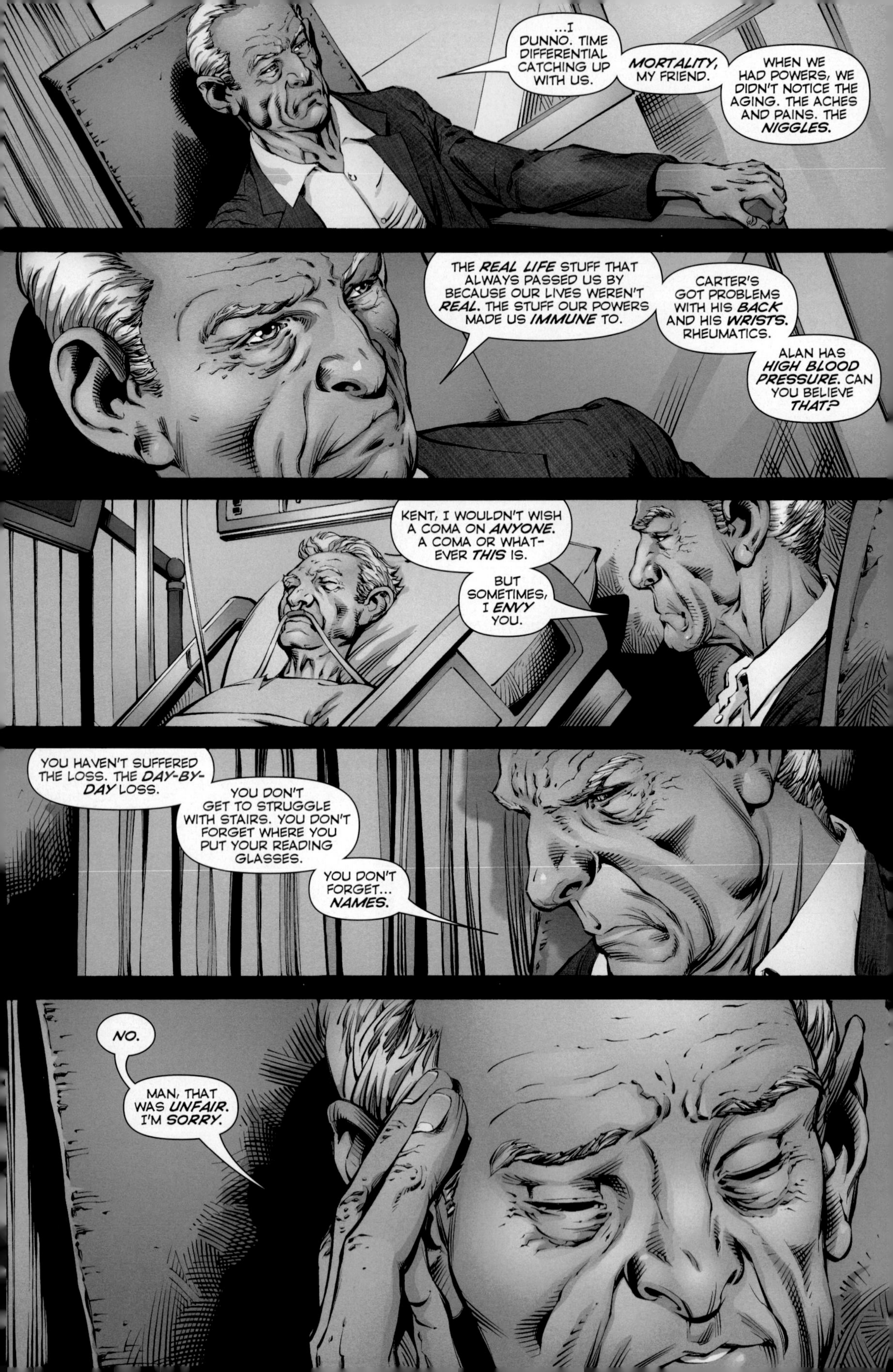

...I DUNNO. TIME DIFFERENTIAL CATCHING UP WITH US.
MORTALITY, MY FRIEND.
WHEN WE HAD POWERS, WE DIDN'T NOTICE THE AGING. THE ACHES AND PAINS. THE NIGGLES.
THE REAL LIFE STUFF THAT ALWAYS PASSED US BY BECAUSE OUR LIVES WEREN'T REAL. THE STUFF OUR POWERS MADE US IMMUNE TO.
CARTER'S GOT PROBLEMS WITH HIS BACK AND HIS WRISTS. RHEUMATICS.
ALAN HAS HIGH BLOOD PRESSURE. CAN YOU BELIEVE THAT?
KENT, I WOULDN'T WISH A COMA ON ANYONE. A COMA OR WHATEVER THIS IS.
BUT SOMETIMES, I ENVY YOU.
YOU HAVEN'T SUFFERED THE LOSS. THE DAY-BY-DAY LOSS.
YOU DON'T GET TO STRUGGLE WITH STAIRS. YOU DON'T FORGET WHERE YOU PUT YOUR READING GLASSES.
YOU DON'T FORGET... NAMES.
NO.
MAN, THAT WAS UNFAIR. I'M SORRY.

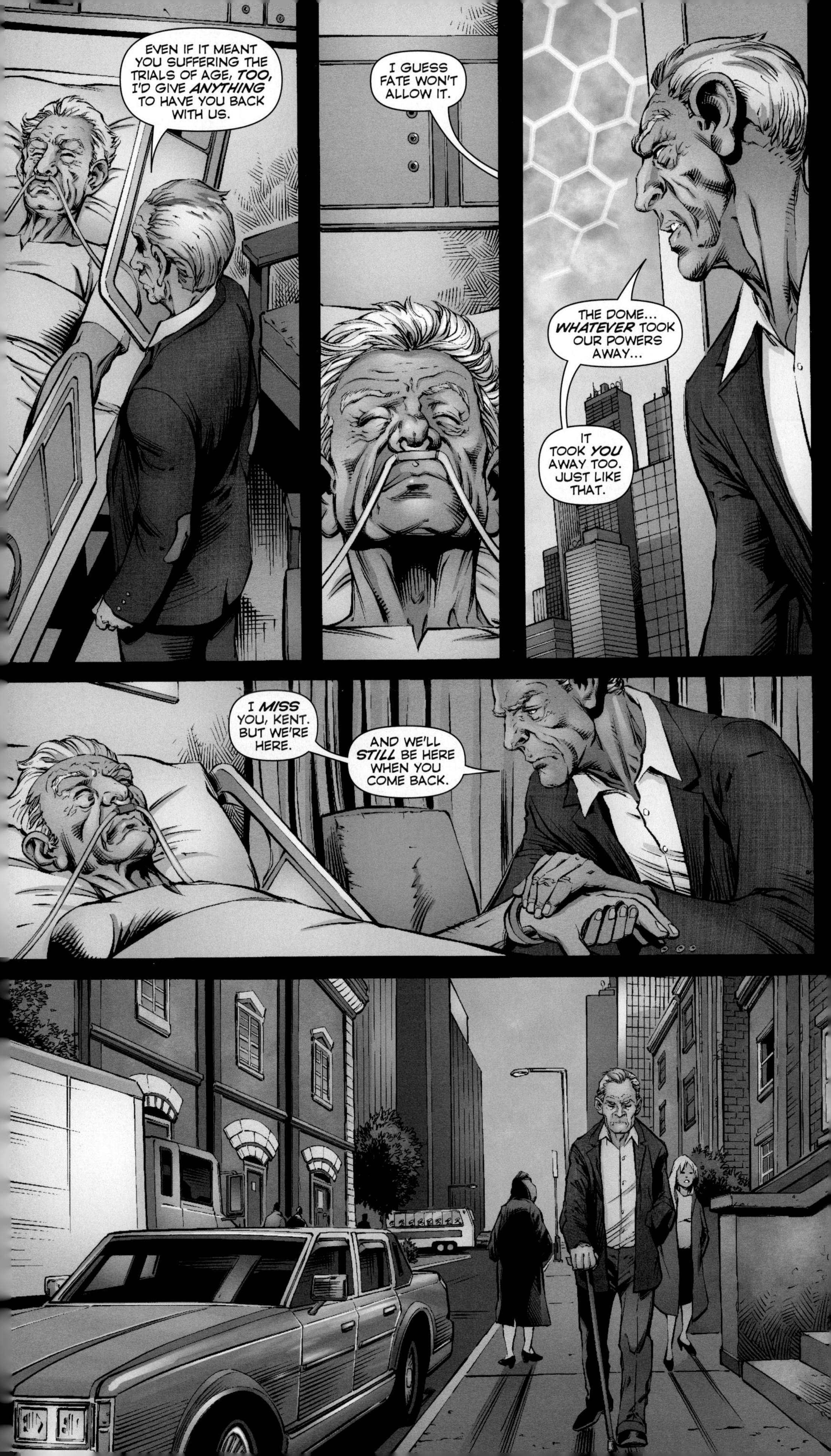
EVEN IF IT MEANT YOU SUFFERING THE TRIALS OF AGE, TOO, I'D GIVE ANYTHING TO HAVE YOU BACK WITH US.
I GUESS FATE WON'T ALLOW IT.
THE DOME... WHATEVER TOOK OUR POWERS AWAY...
IT TOOK YOU AWAY TOO. JUST LIKE THAT.
I MISS YOU, KENT. BUT WE'RE HERE.
AND WE'LL STILL BE HERE WHEN YOU COME BACK.

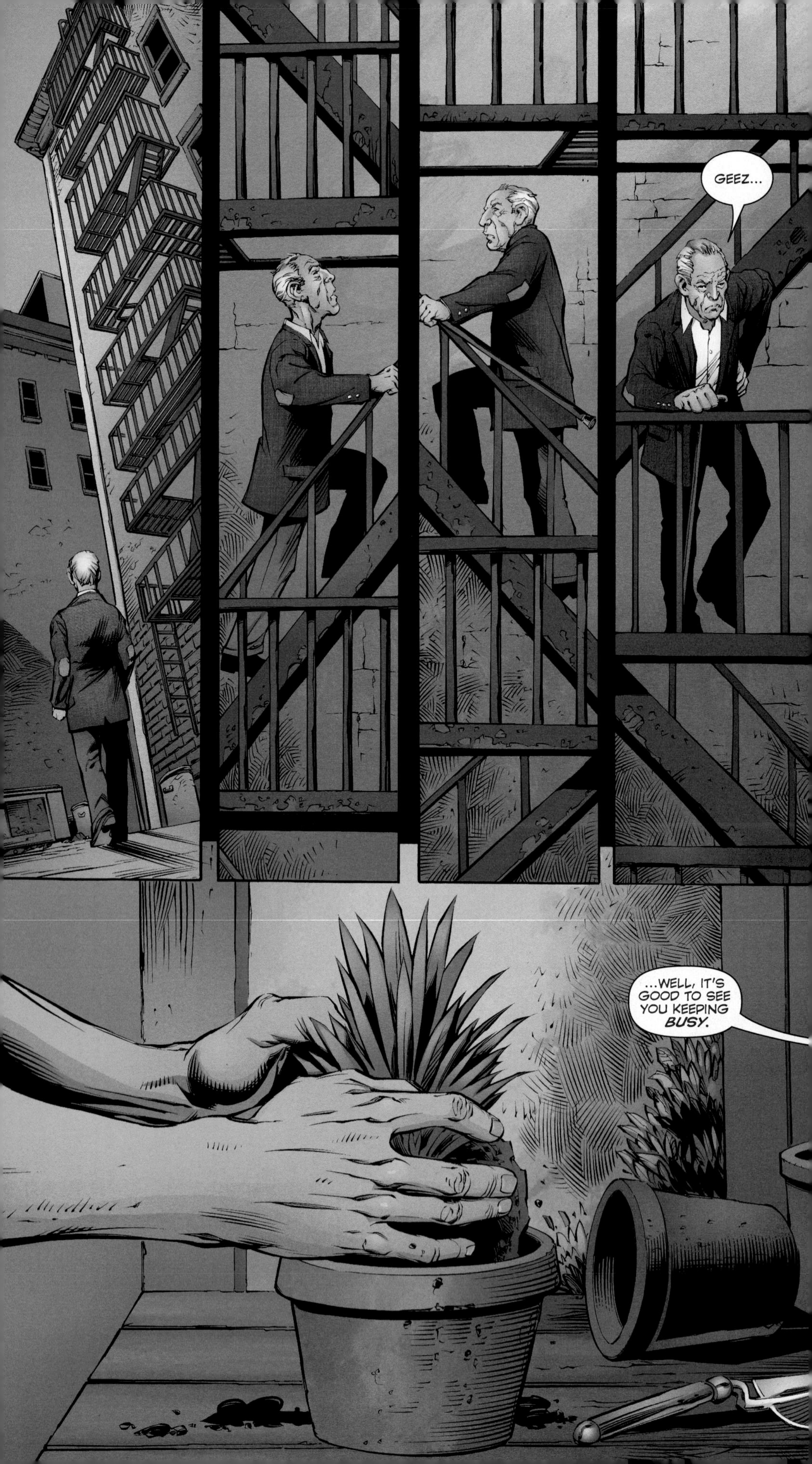
GEEZ...
...WELL, IT'S GOOD TO SEE YOU KEEPING BUSY.

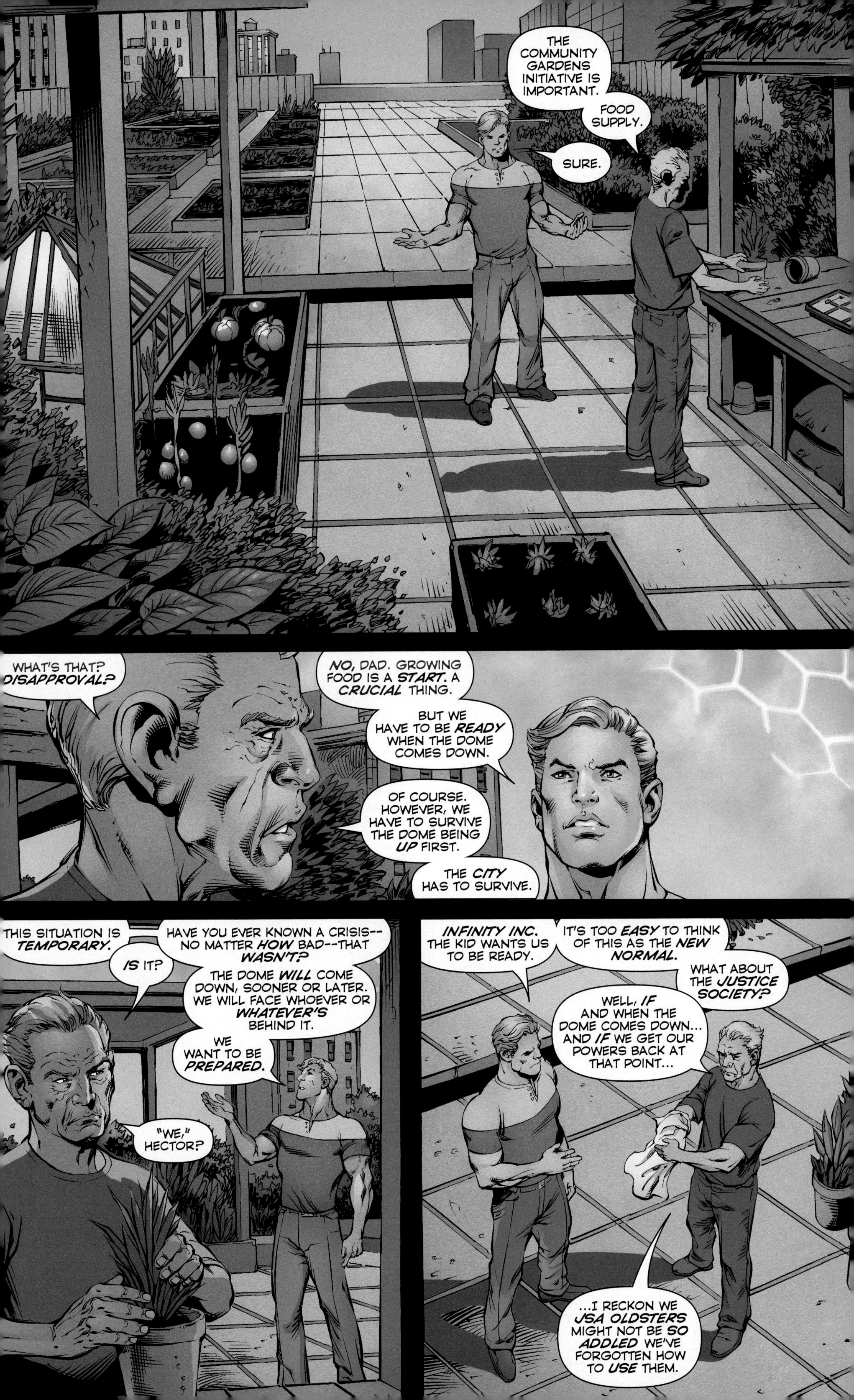
THE COMMUNITY GARDENS INITIATIVE IS IMPORTANT.
FOOD SUPPLY.
SURE.
WHAT'S THAT? DISAPPROVAL?
NO, DAD. GROWING FOOD IS A START. A CRUCIAL THING.
BUT WE HAVE TO BE READY WHEN THE DOME COMES DOWN.
OF COURSE. HOWEVER, WE HAVE TO SURVIVE THE DOME BEING UP FIRST.
THE CITY HAS TO SURVIVE.
THIS SITUATION IS TEMPORARY.
IS IT?
HAVE YOU EVER KNOWN A CRISIS--NO MATTER HOW BAD--THAT WASN'T?
THE DOME WILL COME DOWN, SOONER OR LATER. WE WILL FACE WHOEVER OR WHATEVER'S BEHIND IT.
WE WANT TO BE PREPARED.
"WE," HECTOR?
INFINITY INC. THE KID WANTS US TO BE READY.
IT'S TOO EASY TO THINK OF THIS AS THE NEW NORMAL.
WHAT ABOUT THE JUSTICE SOCIETY?
WELL, IF AND WHEN THE DOME COMES DOWN... AND IF WE GET OUR POWERS BACK AT THAT POINT...
...I RECKON WE JSA OLDSTERS MIGHT NOT BE SO ADDLED WE'VE FORGOTTEN HOW TO USE THEM.

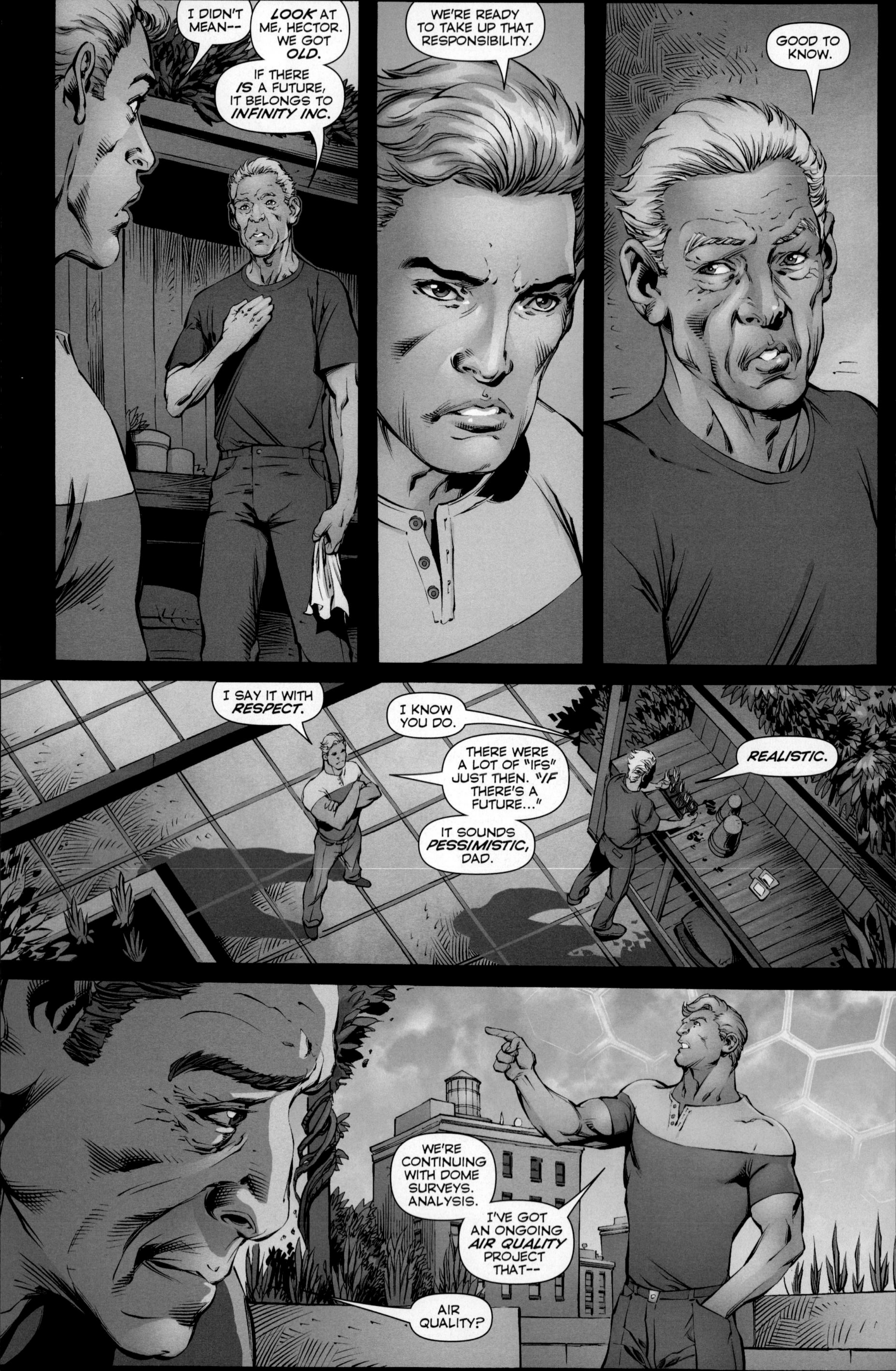
I DIDN'T MEAN--
LOOK AT ME, HECTOR. WE GOT OLD.
IF THERE IS A FUTURE, IT BELONGS TO INFINITY INC.
WE'RE READY TO TAKE UP THAT RESPONSIBILITY.
GOOD TO KNOW.
I SAY IT WITH RESPECT.
I KNOW YOU DO.
THERE WERE A LOT OF "IFS" JUST THEN. "IF THERE'S A FUTURE..."
IT SOUNDS PESSIMISTIC, DAD.
REALISTIC.
WE'RE CONTINUING WITH DOME SURVEYS. ANALYSIS.
I'VE GOT AN ONGOING AIR QUALITY PROJECT THAT--
AIR QUALITY?

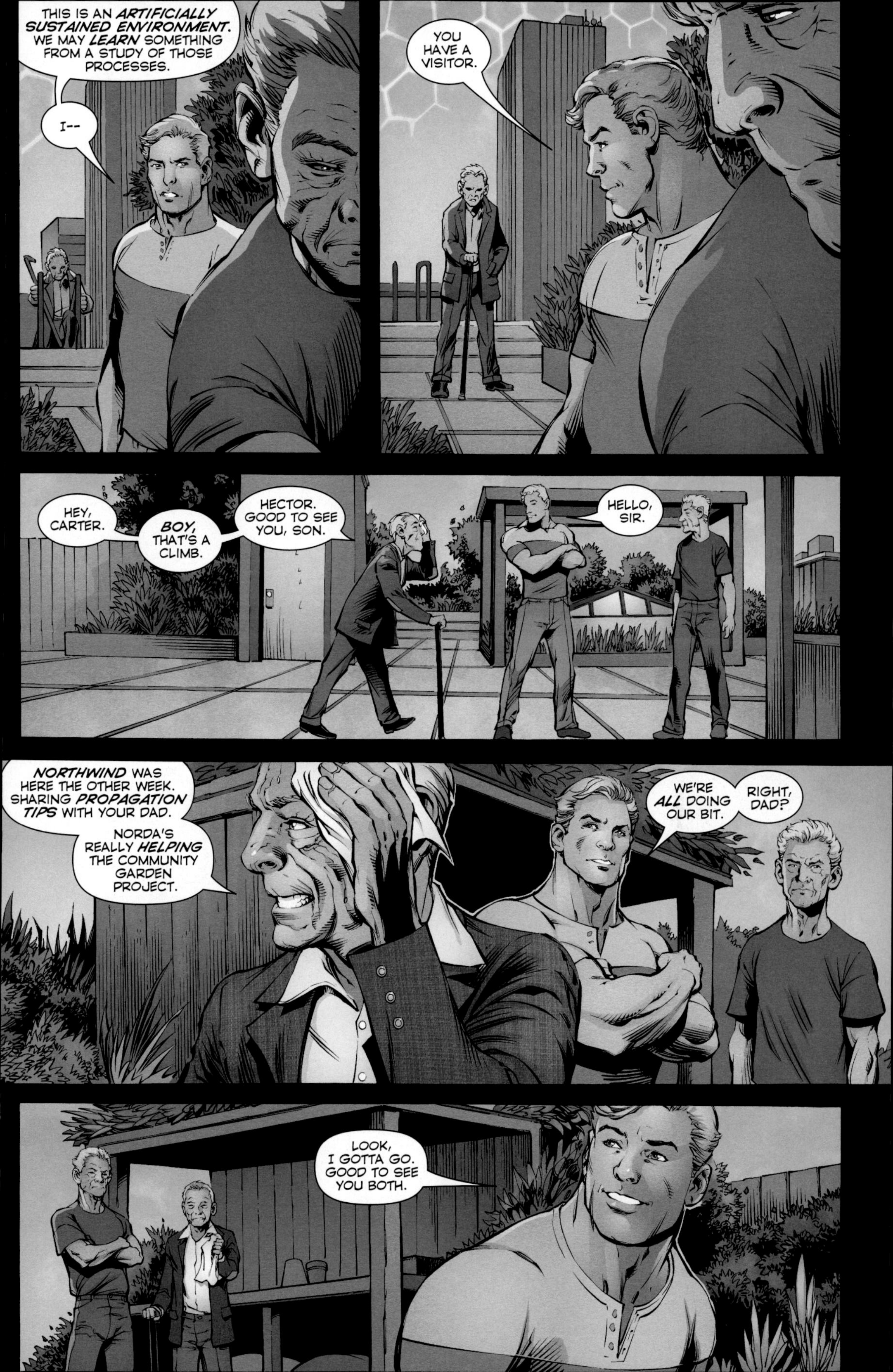
THIS IS AN *ARTIFICIALLY SUSTAINED ENVIRONMENT*. WE MAY *LEARN* SOMETHING FROM A STUDY OF THOSE PROCESSES.
I--
YOU HAVE A VISITOR.
HEY, CARTER.
BOY, THAT'S A CLIMB.
HECTOR. GOOD TO SEE YOU, SON.
HELLO, SIR.
NORTHWIND WAS HERE THE OTHER WEEK. SHARING *PROPAGATION TIPS* WITH YOUR DAD.
NORDA'S REALLY *HELPING* THE COMMUNITY GARDEN PROJECT.
WE'RE *ALL* DOING OUR BIT.
RIGHT, DAD?
LOOK, I GOTTA GO. GOOD TO SEE YOU BOTH.

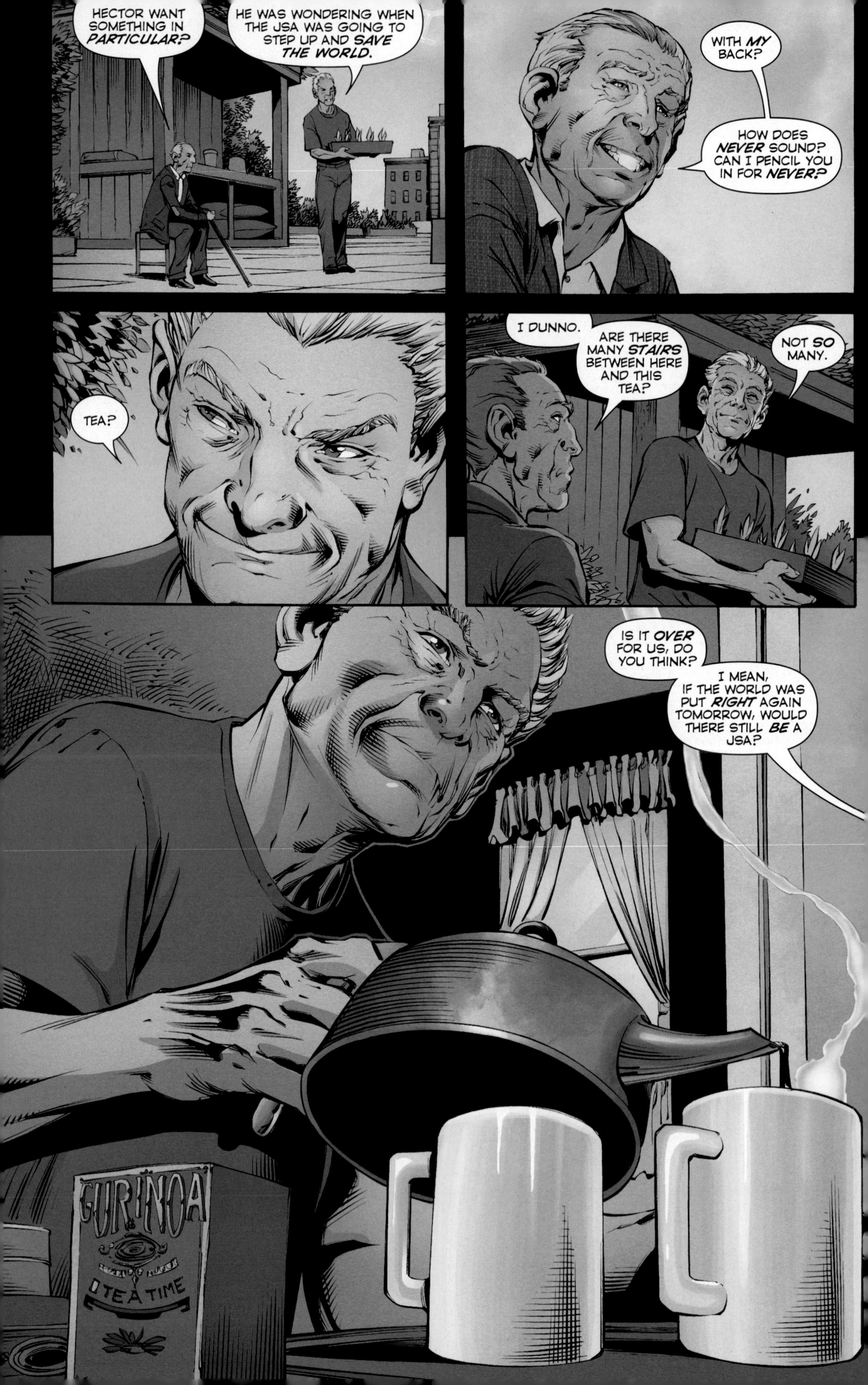
HECTOR WANT SOMETHING IN *PARTICULAR?*
HE WAS WONDERING WHEN THE JSA WAS GOING TO STEP UP AND *SAVE THE WORLD.*
WITH *MY* BACK?
HOW DOES *NEVER* SOUND? CAN I PENCIL YOU IN FOR *NEVER?*
TEA?
I DUNNO.
ARE THERE MANY *STAIRS* BETWEEN HERE AND THIS TEA?
NOT *SO* MANY.
IS IT *OVER* FOR US, DO YOU THINK?
I MEAN, IF THE WORLD WAS PUT *RIGHT* AGAIN TOMORROW, WOULD THERE STILL *BE* A JSA?
GURINOA
TEA TIME

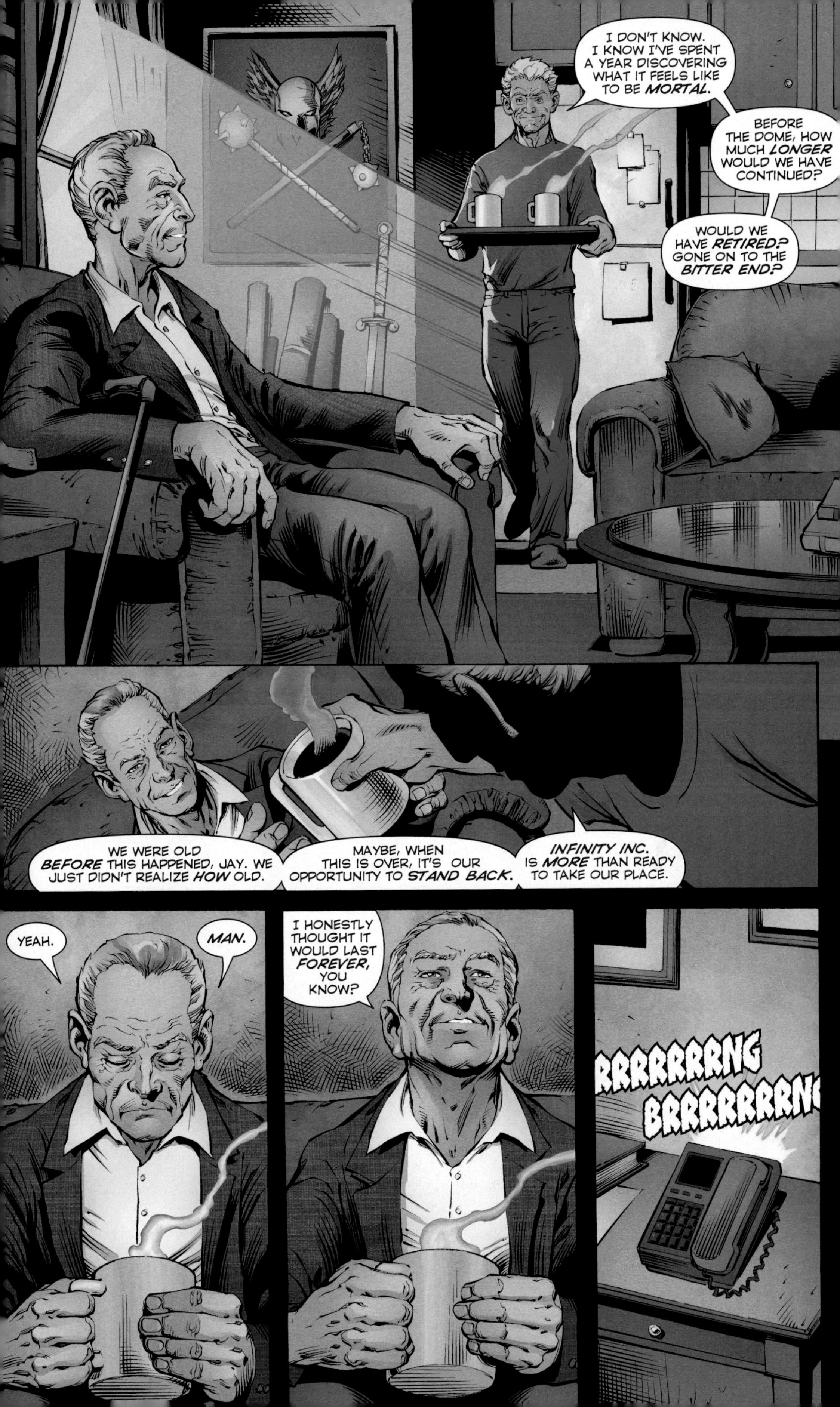
I DON'T KNOW. I KNOW I'VE SPENT A YEAR DISCOVERING WHAT IT FEELS LIKE TO BE MORTAL.
BEFORE THE DOME, HOW MUCH LONGER WOULD WE HAVE CONTINUED?
WOULD WE HAVE RETIRED? GONE ON TO THE BITTER END?
WE WERE OLD BEFORE THIS HAPPENED, JAY. WE JUST DIDN'T REALIZE HOW OLD.
MAYBE, WHEN THIS IS OVER, IT'S OUR OPPORTUNITY TO STAND BACK.
INFINITY INC. IS MORE THAN READY TO TAKE OUR PLACE.
YEAH.
MAN.
I HONESTLY THOUGHT IT WOULD LAST FOREVER, YOU KNOW?
BRRRRRRNG
BRRRRRRRNG

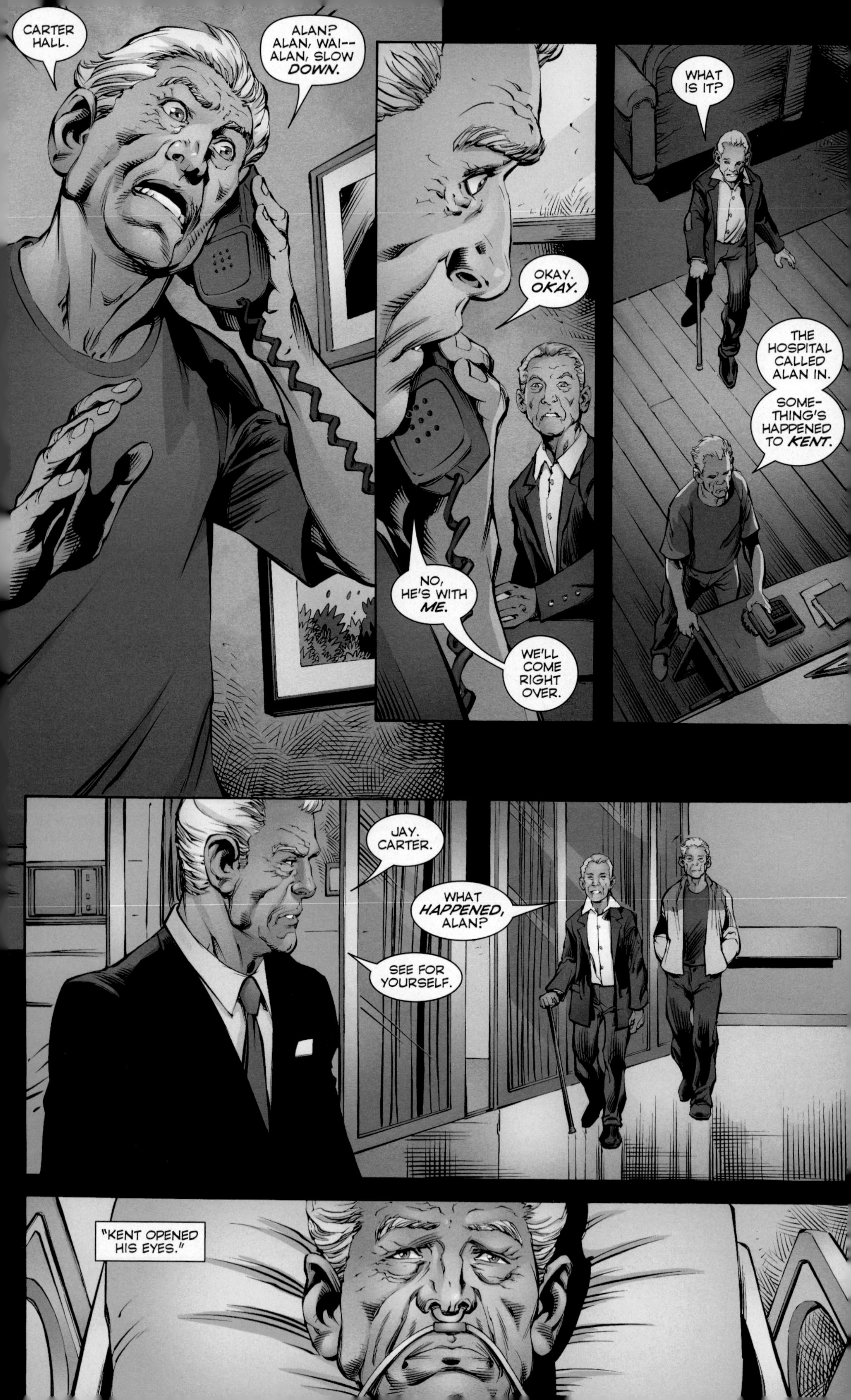
CARTER HALL.
ALAN? ALAN, WAI-- ALAN, SLOW DOWN.
OKAY. OKAY.
NO, HE'S WITH ME.
WE'LL COME RIGHT OVER.
WHAT IS IT?
THE HOSPITAL CALLED ALAN IN.
SOME-THING'S HAPPENED TO KENT.
JAY. CARTER.
WHAT HAPPENED, ALAN?
SEE FOR YOURSELF.
"KENT OPENED HIS EYES."

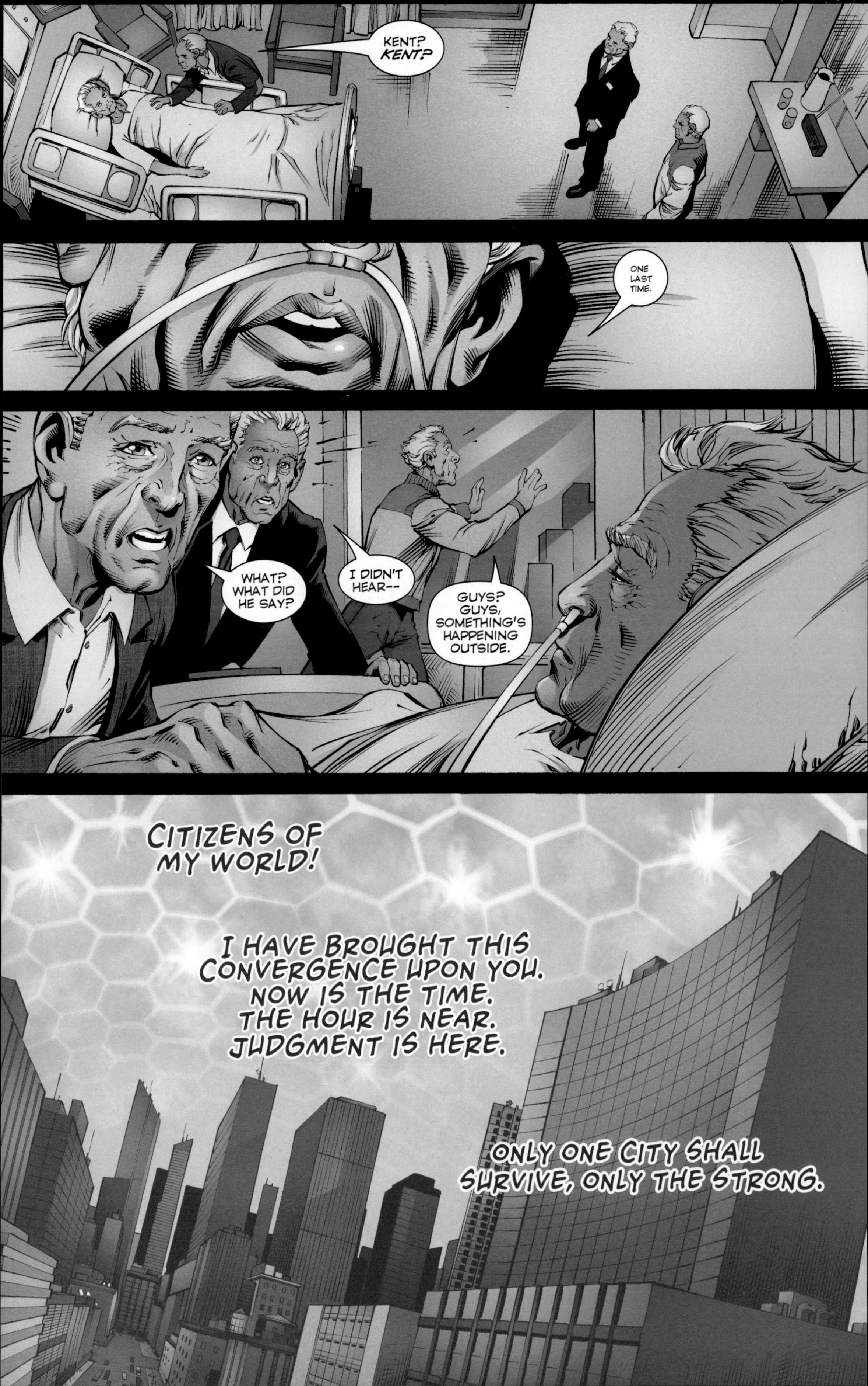
KENT? *KENT?*
ONE LAST TIME.
WHAT? WHAT DID HE SAY?
I DIDN'T HEAR--
GUYS? GUYS, SOMETHING'S HAPPENING OUTSIDE.
CITIZENS OF MY WORLD!
I HAVE BROUGHT THIS CONVERGENCE UPON YOU. NOW IS THE TIME. THE HOUR IS NEAR. JUDGMENT IS HERE.
ONLY ONE CITY SHALL SURVIVE, ONLY THE STRONG.

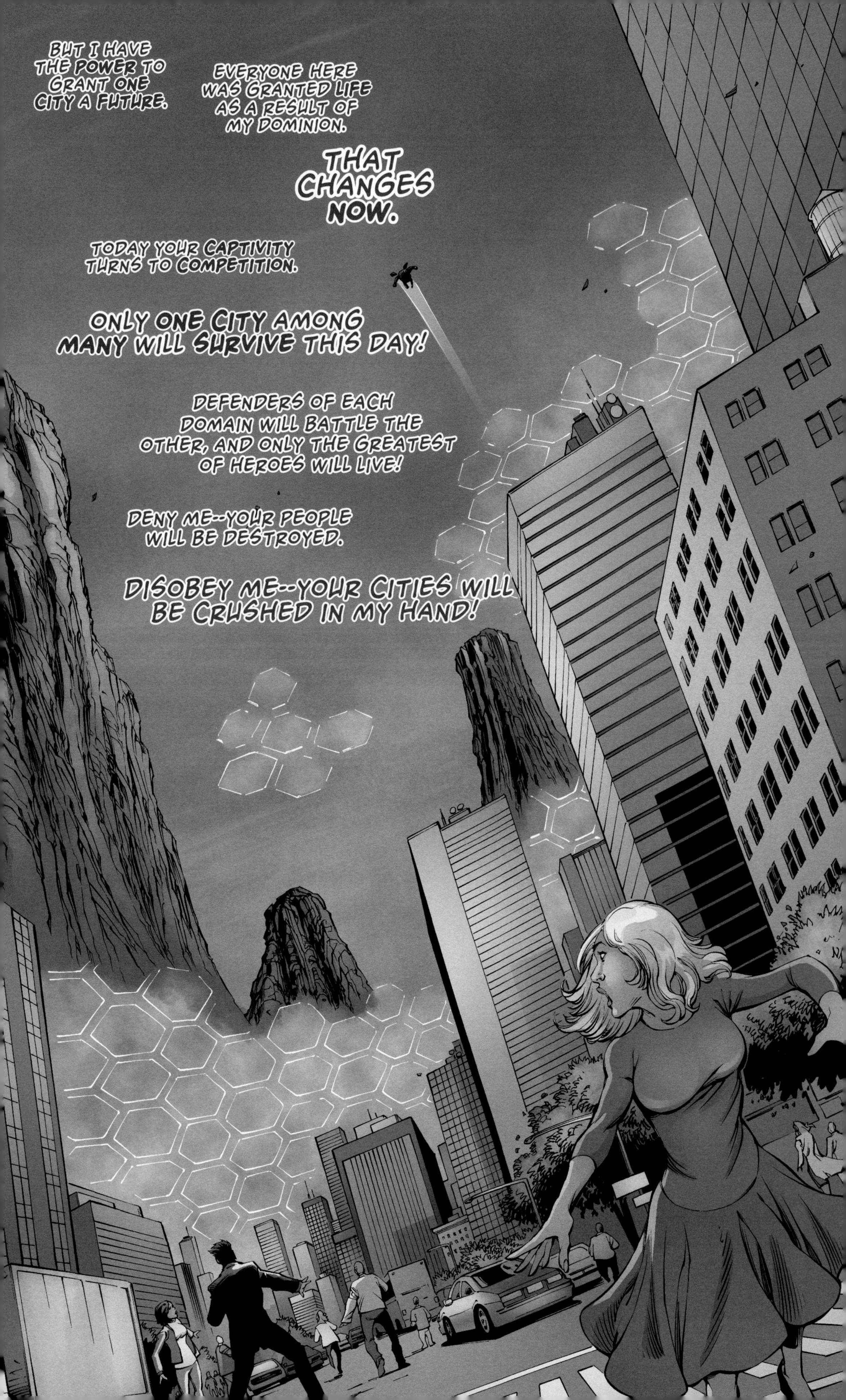
BUT I HAVE THE POWER TO GRANT ONE CITY A FUTURE.
EVERYONE HERE WAS GRANTED LIFE AS A RESULT OF MY DOMINION.
THAT CHANGES NOW.
TODAY YOUR CAPTIVITY TURNS TO COMPETITION.
ONLY ONE CITY AMONG MANY WILL SURVIVE THIS DAY!
DEFENDERS OF EACH DOMAIN WILL BATTLE THE OTHER, AND ONLY THE GREATEST OF HEROES WILL LIVE!
DENY ME--YOUR PEOPLE WILL BE DESTROYED.
DISOBEY ME--YOUR CITIES WILL BE CRUSHED IN MY HAND!

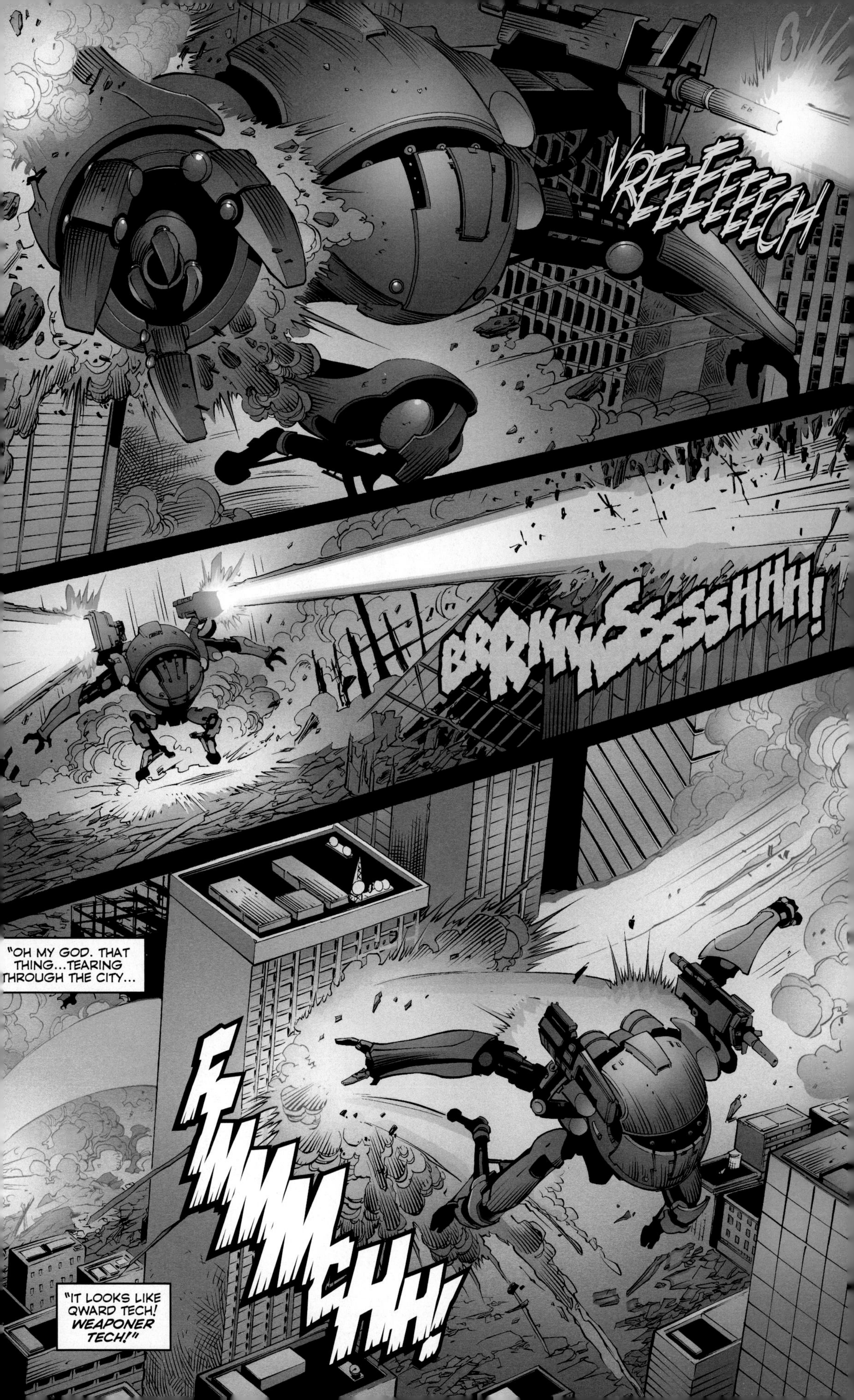
VREEEEEEEECH
BRRKKKSSSSSHHH!
"OH MY GOD. THAT THING...TEARING THROUGH THE CITY...
FMMMCHH!
"IT LOOKS LIKE QWARD TECH! WEAPONER TECH!"

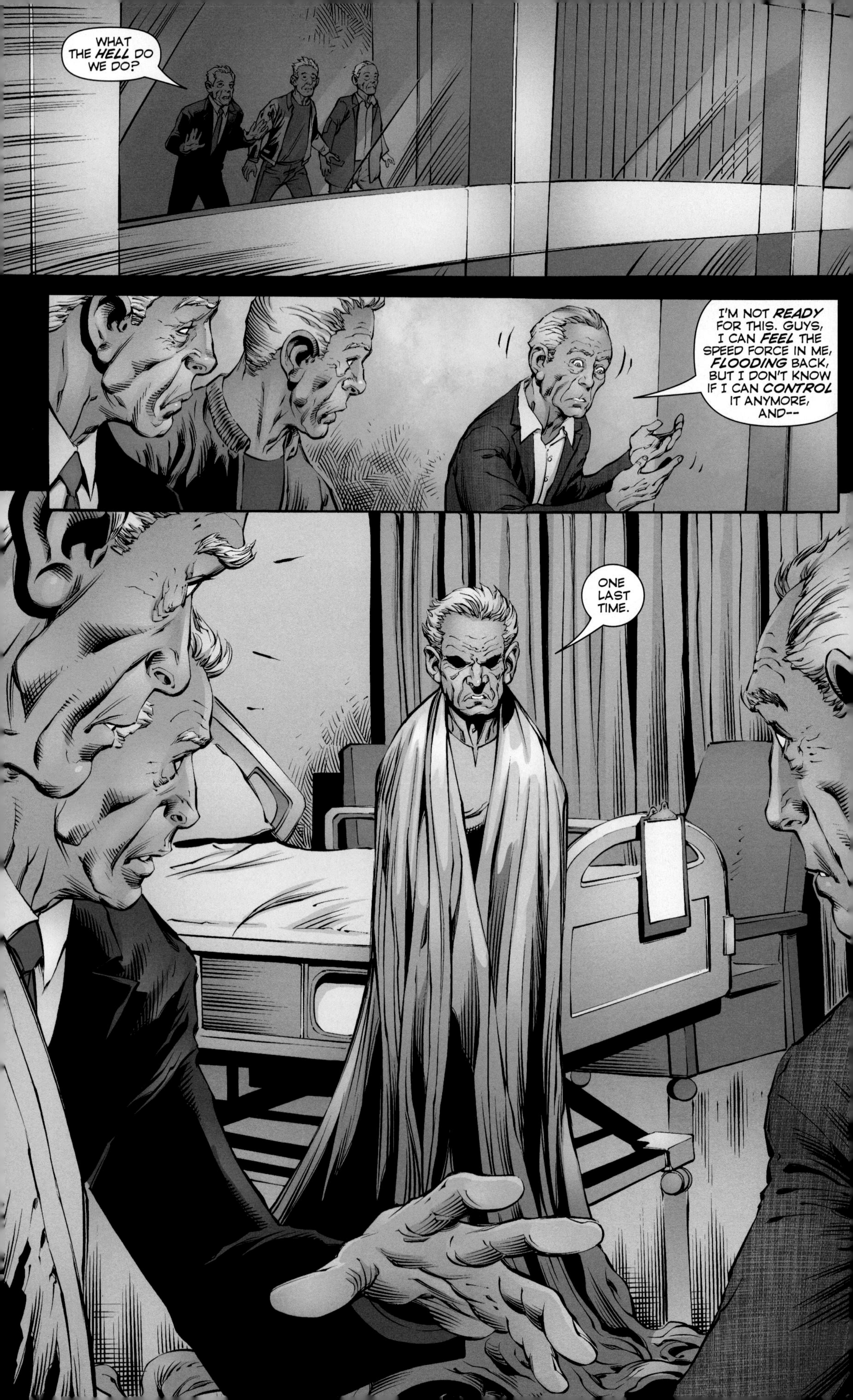
WHAT THE HELL DO WE DO?
I'M NOT READY FOR THIS. GUYS, I CAN FEEL THE SPEED FORCE IN ME, FLOODING BACK, BUT I DON'T KNOW IF I CAN CONTROL IT ANYMORE, AND--
ONE LAST TIME.

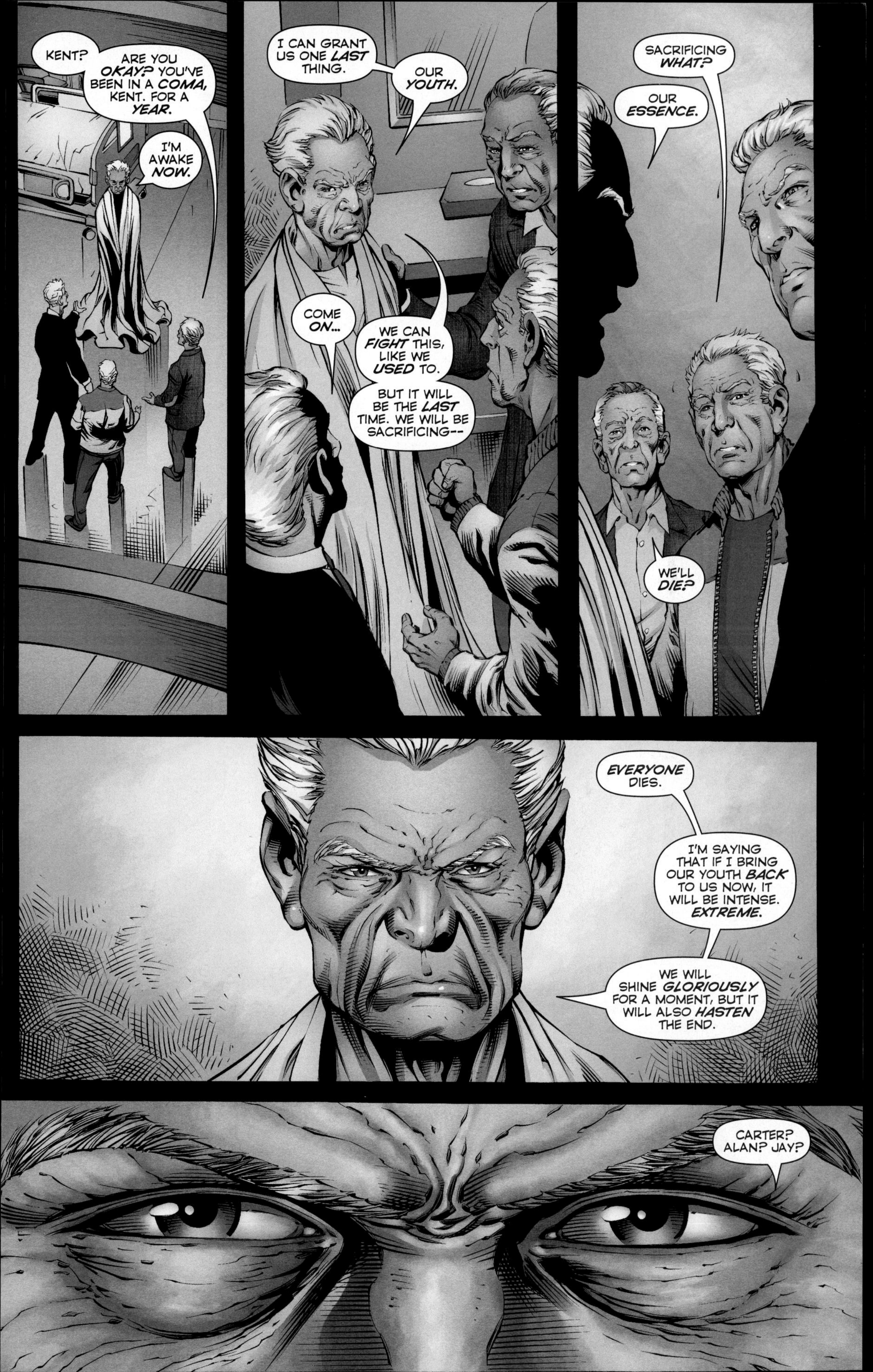
KENT?
ARE YOU OKAY? YOU'VE BEEN IN A COMA, KENT. FOR A YEAR.
I'M AWAKE NOW.
I CAN GRANT US ONE LAST THING.
OUR YOUTH.
COME ON...
WE CAN FIGHT THIS, LIKE WE USED TO.
BUT IT WILL BE THE LAST TIME. WE WILL BE SACRIFICING--
SACRIFICING WHAT?
OUR ESSENCE.
WE'LL DIE?
EVERYONE DIES.
I'M SAYING THAT IF I BRING OUR YOUTH BACK TO US NOW, IT WILL BE INTENSE. EXTREME.
WE WILL SHINE GLORIOUSLY FOR A MOMENT, BUT IT WILL ALSO HASTEN THE END.
CARTER? ALAN? JAY?

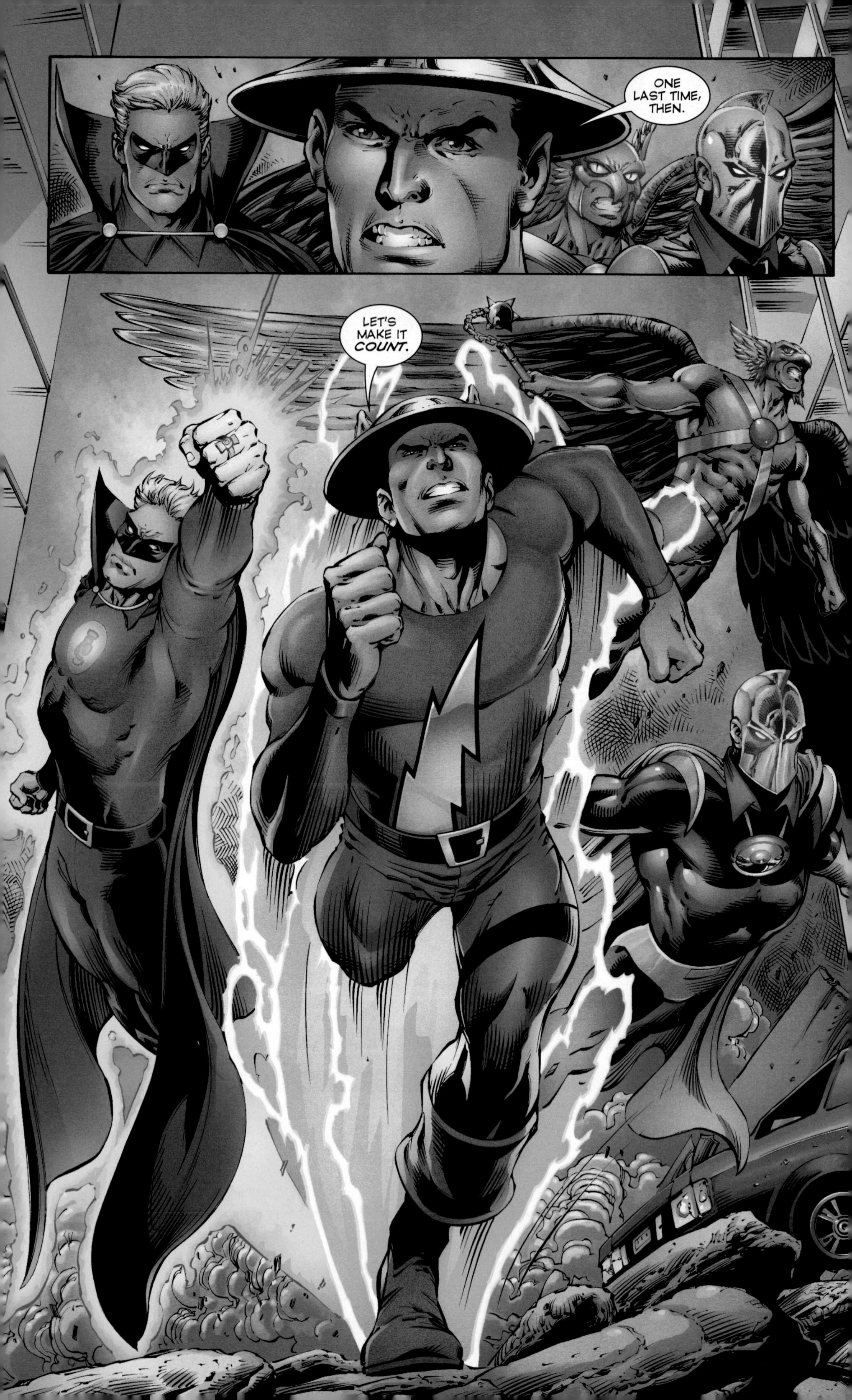
ONE LAST TIME, THEN.
LET'S MAKE IT COUNT.

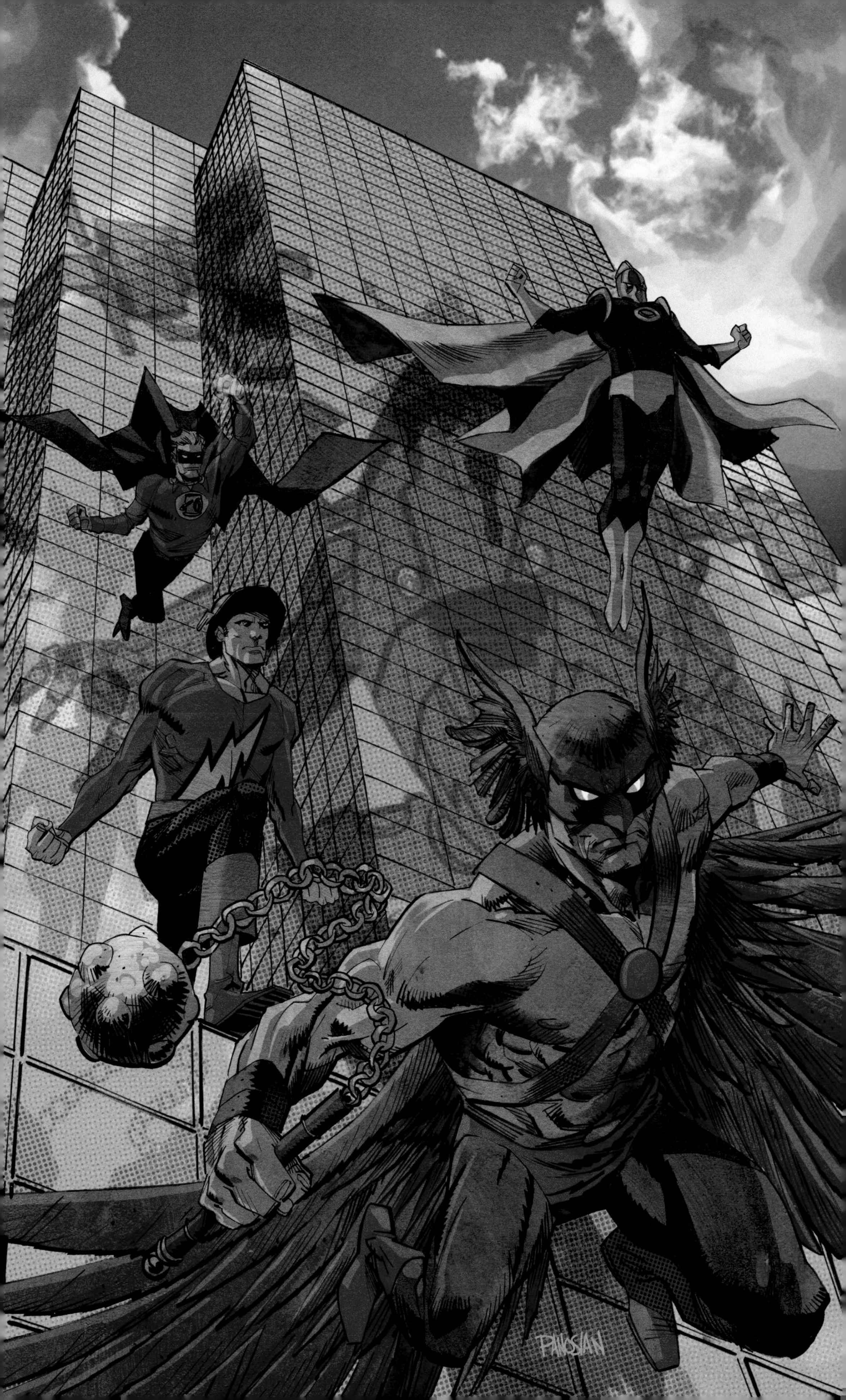
PANOSIAN

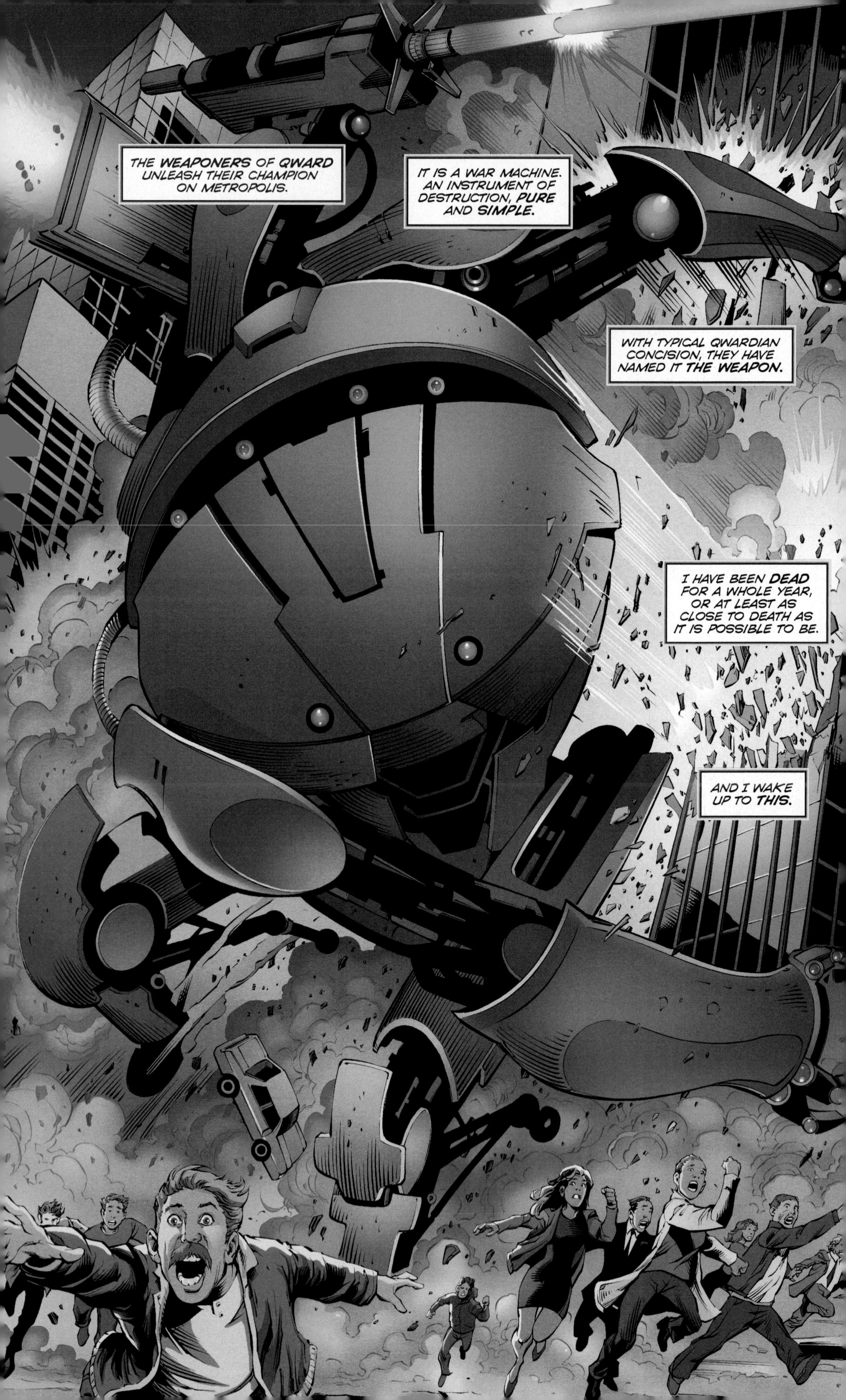
THE WEAPONERS OF QWARD UNLEASH THEIR CHAMPION ON METROPOLIS.
IT IS A WAR MACHINE. AN INSTRUMENT OF DESTRUCTION, PURE AND SIMPLE.
WITH TYPICAL QWARDIAN CONCISION, THEY HAVE NAMED IT THE WEAPON.
I HAVE BEEN DEAD FOR A WHOLE YEAR, OR AT LEAST AS CLOSE TO DEATH AS IT IS POSSIBLE TO BE.
AND I WAKE UP TO THIS.

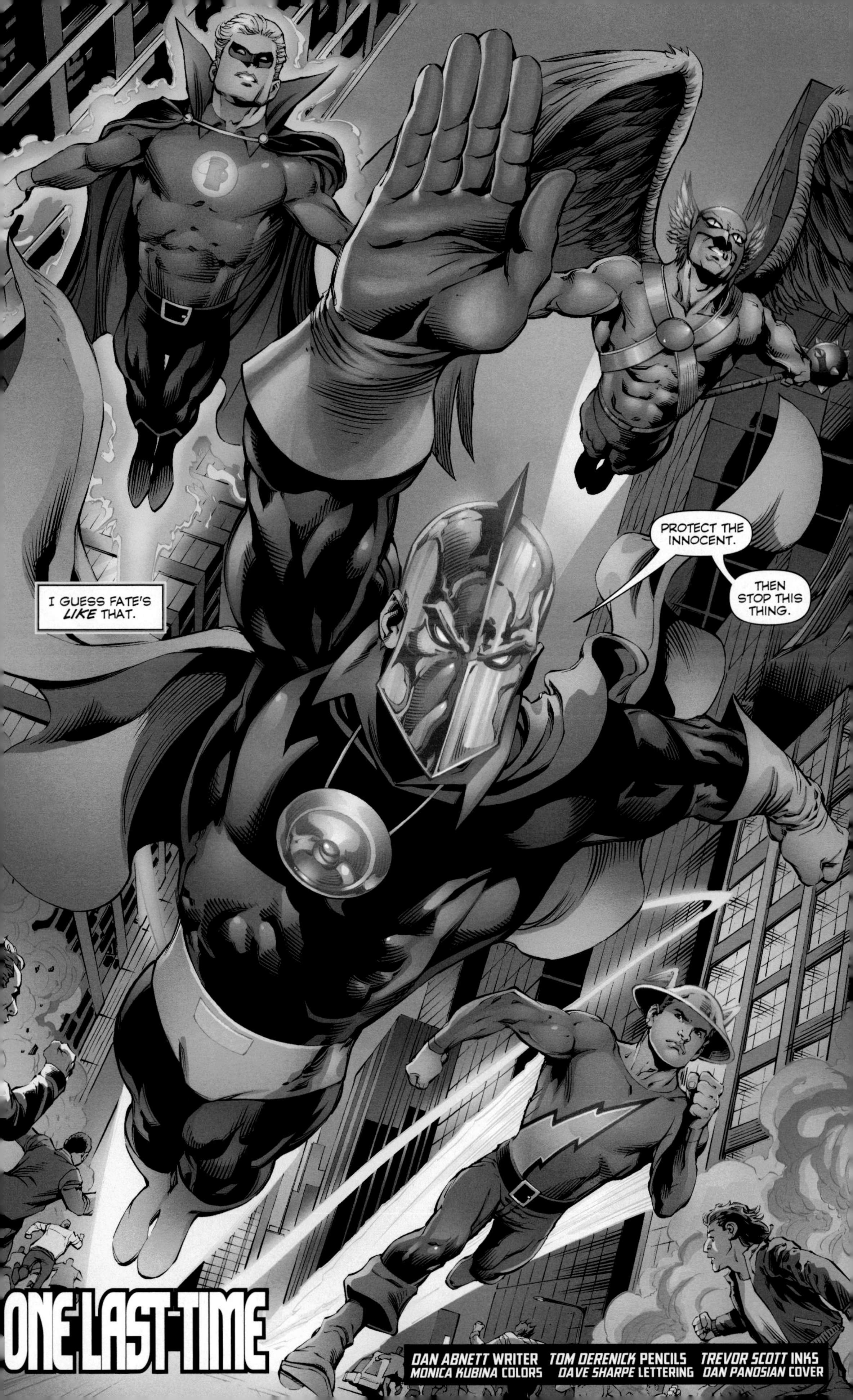

I GUESS FATE'S *LIKE* THAT.
PROTECT THE INNOCENT.
THEN STOP THIS THING.
ONE LAST TIME
DAN ABNETT WRITER TOM DERENICK PENCILS TREVOR SCOTT INKS
MONICA KUBINA COLORS DAVE SHARPE LETTERING DAN PANOSIAN COVER

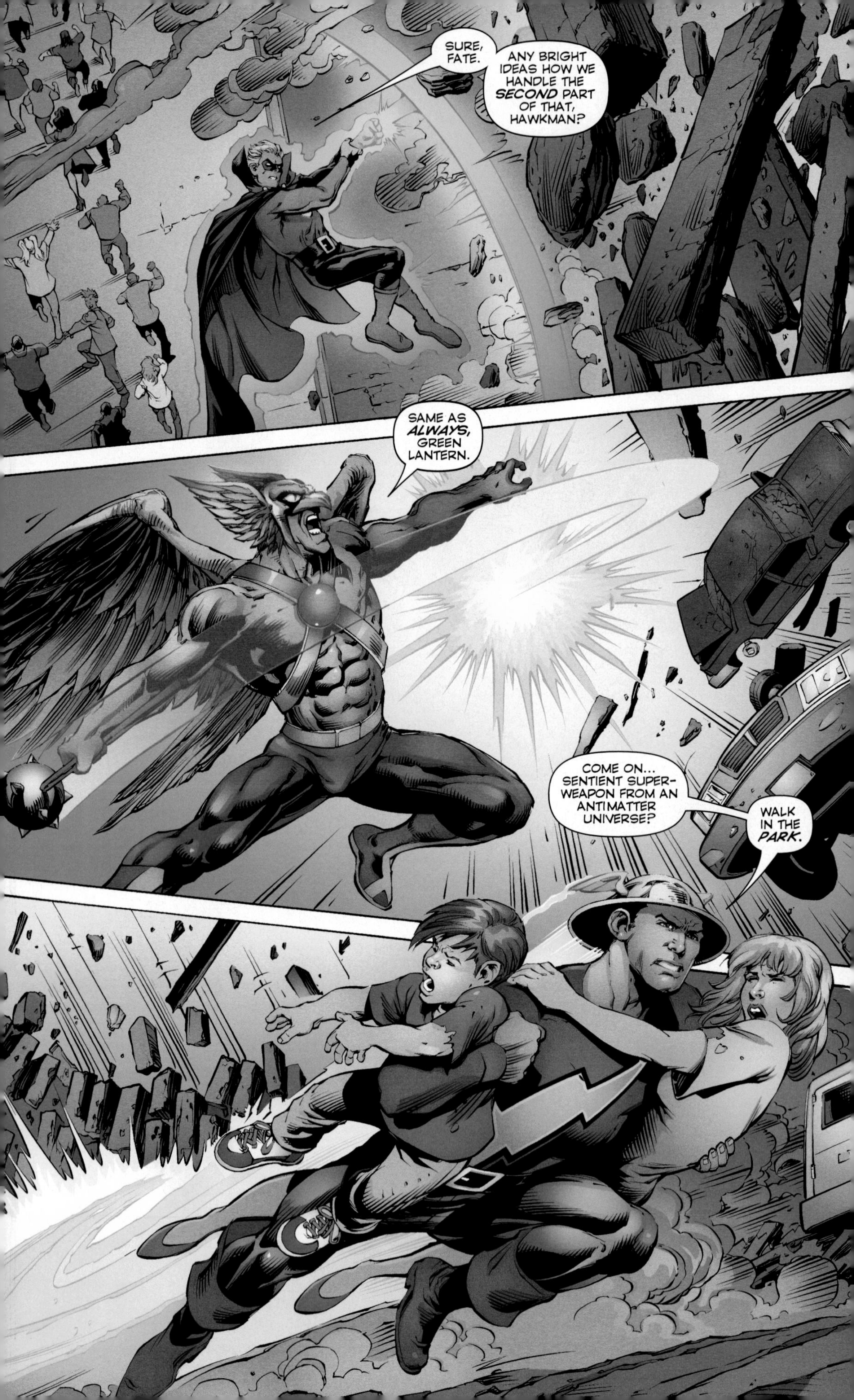
SURE, FATE.
ANY BRIGHT IDEAS HOW WE HANDLE THE SECOND PART OF THAT, HAWKMAN?
SAME AS ALWAYS, GREEN LANTERN.
COME ON... SENTIENT SUPER-WEAPON FROM AN ANTIMATTER UNIVERSE?
WALK IN THE PARK.

JAY SOUNDS *LIKE* HIS OLD SELF, BUT THIS *IS* NEW TO US.

WE GOT OLD. OUR POWERS WENT AWAY.

NONE OF US ARE CONFIDENT WE'RE STILL THE HEROES WE USED TO BE.

BUT METROPOLIS IS *COUNTING* ON US.

YOU'RE CLEAR. RUN AND FIND COVER.

WHOLESALE PROPERTY DAMAGE!

IT'S NOT TARGETING *US.* IT'S DISMANTLING THE *CITY.*

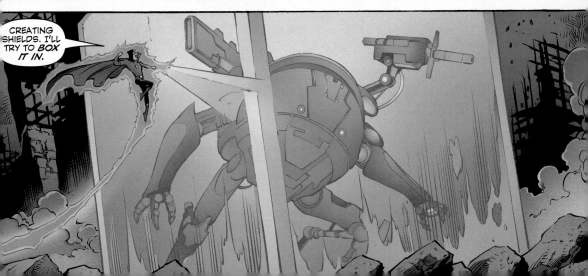

CREATING SHIELDS. I'LL TRY TO *BOX* IT IN.

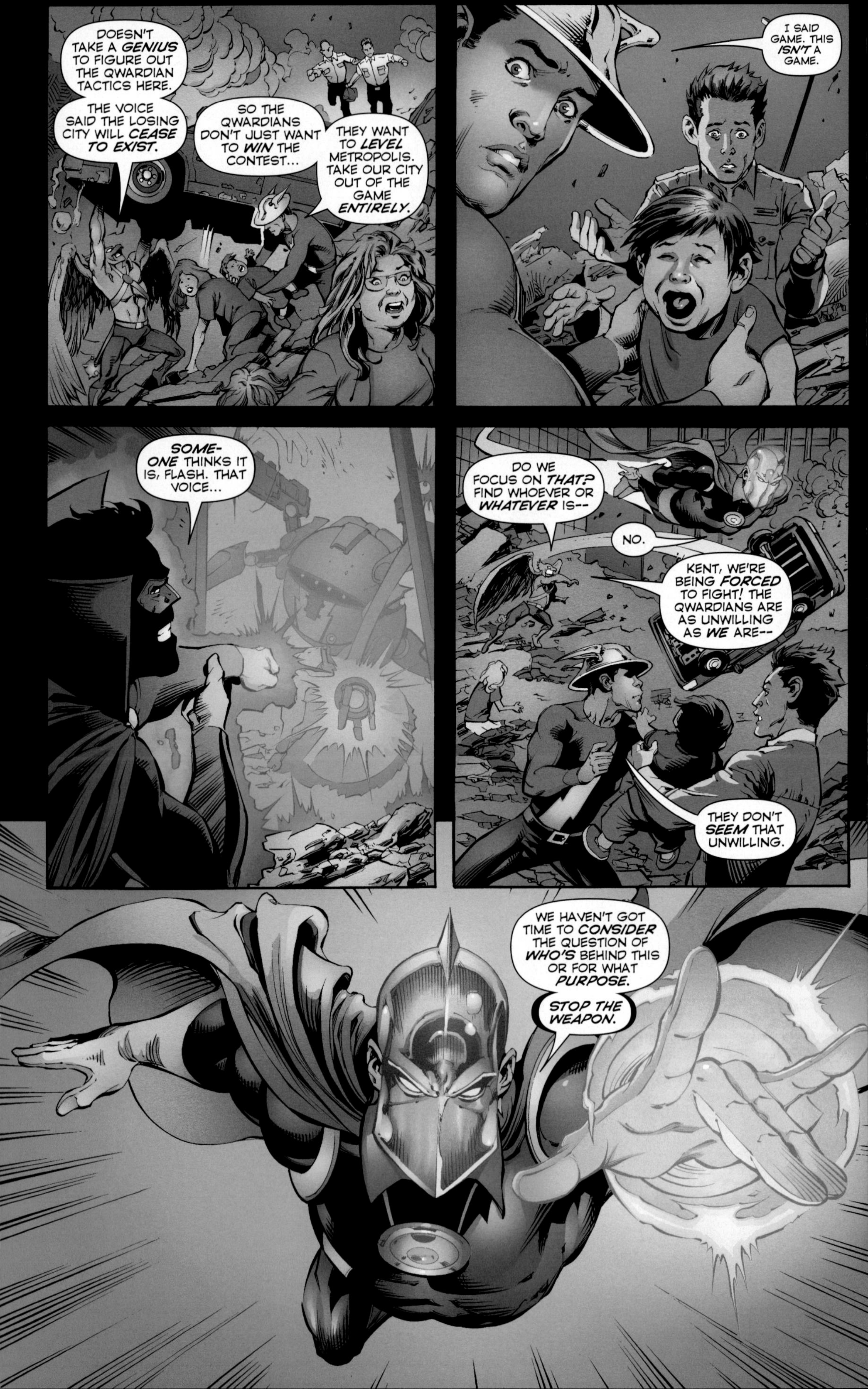

DOESN'T TAKE A *GENIUS* TO FIGURE OUT THE QWARDIAN TACTICS HERE.
THE VOICE SAID THE LOSING CITY WILL *CEASE TO EXIST*.
SO THE QWARDIANS DON'T JUST WANT TO *WIN* THE CONTEST...
THEY WANT TO *LEVEL* METROPOLIS. TAKE OUR CITY OUT OF THE GAME *ENTIRELY*.
I SAID GAME. THIS *ISN'T* A GAME.
SOME-ONE THINKS IT IS, FLASH. THAT VOICE...
DO WE FOCUS ON *THAT?* FIND WHOEVER OR *WHATEVER* IS--
NO.
KENT, WE'RE BEING *FORCED* TO FIGHT! THE QWARDIANS ARE AS UNWILLING AS *WE* ARE--
THEY DON'T *SEEM* THAT UNWILLING.
WE HAVEN'T GOT TIME TO *CONSIDER* THE QUESTION OF *WHO'S* BEHIND THIS OR FOR WHAT *PURPOSE*.
STOP THE WEAPON.

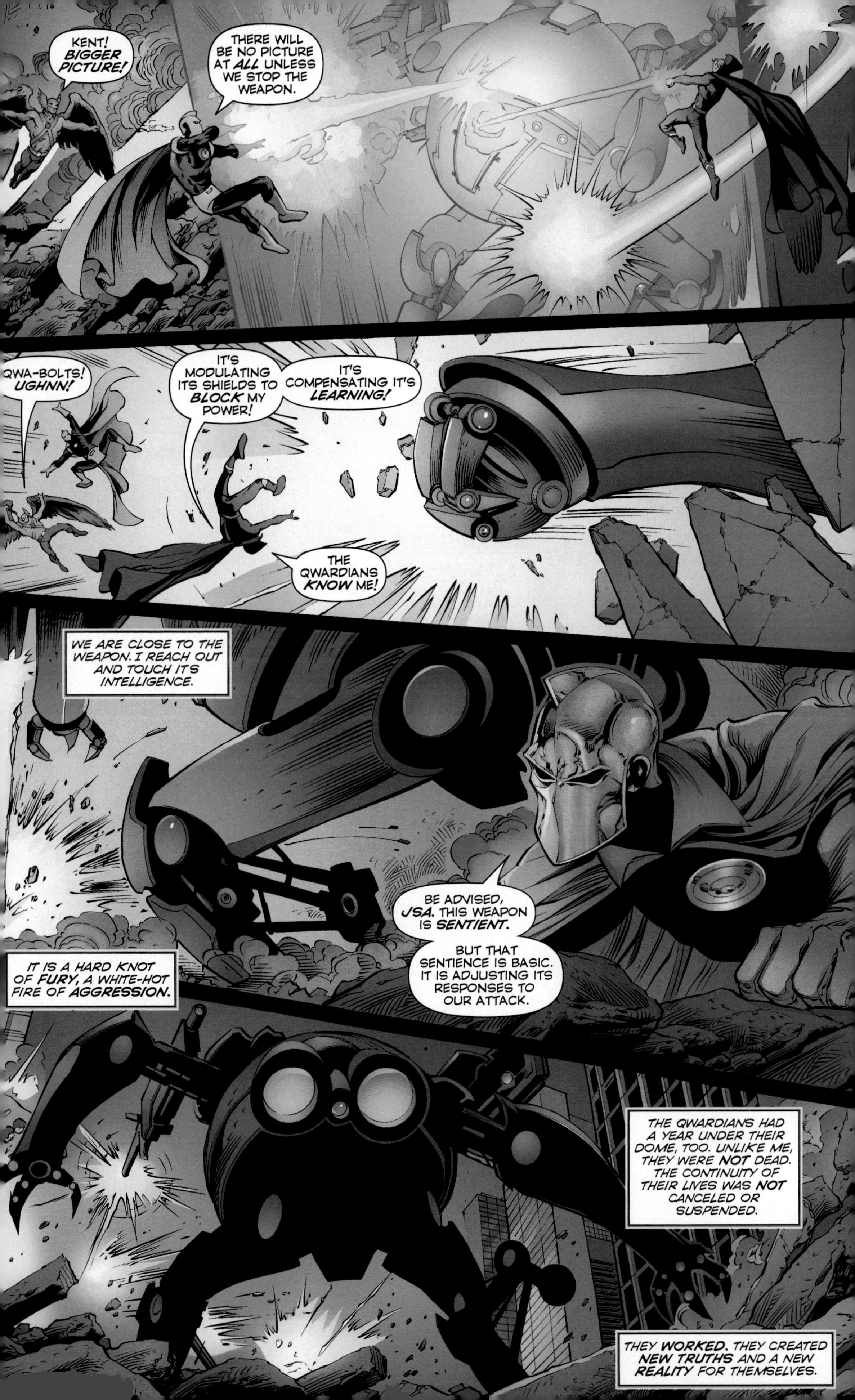
KENT! BIGGER PICTURE!
THERE WILL BE NO PICTURE AT ALL UNLESS WE STOP THE WEAPON.
QWA-BOLTS! UGHNN!
IT'S MODULATING ITS SHIELDS TO BLOCK MY POWER!
IT'S COMPENSATING IT'S LEARNING!
THE QWARDIANS KNOW ME!
WE ARE CLOSE TO THE WEAPON. I REACH OUT AND TOUCH ITS INTELLIGENCE.
BE ADVISED, JSA. THIS WEAPON IS SENTIENT.
BUT THAT SENTIENCE IS BASIC. IT IS ADJUSTING ITS RESPONSES TO OUR ATTACK.
IT IS A HARD KNOT OF FURY, A WHITE-HOT FIRE OF AGGRESSION.
THE QWARDIANS HAD A YEAR UNDER THEIR DOME, TOO. UNLIKE ME, THEY WERE NOT DEAD. THE CONTINUITY OF THEIR LIVES WAS NOT CANCELED OR SUSPENDED.
THEY WORKED. THEY CREATED NEW TRUTHS AND A NEW REALITY FOR THEMSELVES.

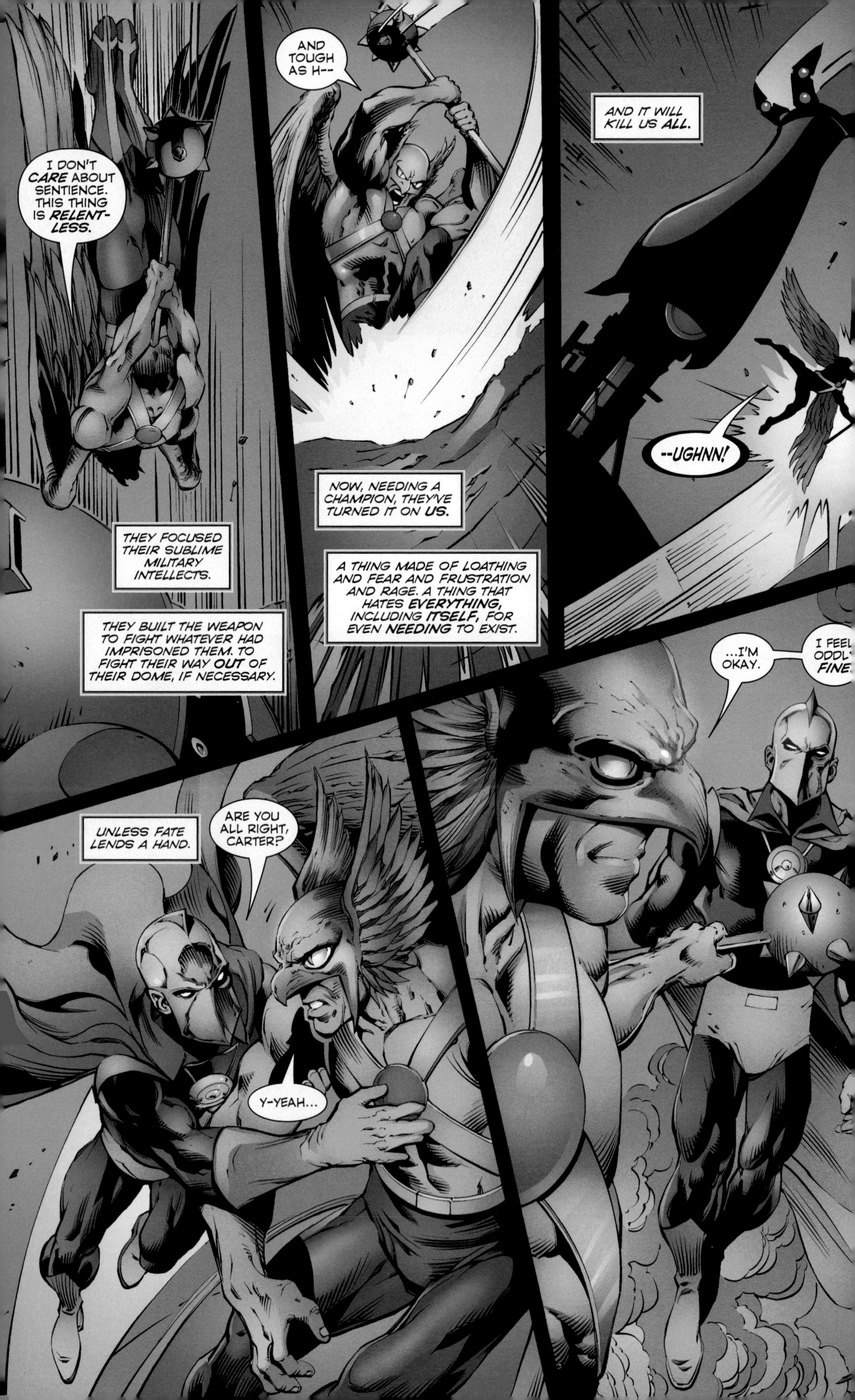
I DON'T CARE ABOUT SENTIENCE. THIS THING IS RELENTLESS.
AND TOUGH AS H--
AND IT WILL KILL US ALL.
--UGHNN!
NOW, NEEDING A CHAMPION, THEY'VE TURNED IT ON US.
THEY FOCUSED THEIR SUBLIME MILITARY INTELLECTS.
A THING MADE OF LOATHING AND FEAR AND FRUSTRATION AND RAGE. A THING THAT HATES EVERYTHING, INCLUDING ITSELF, FOR EVEN NEEDING TO EXIST.
THEY BUILT THE WEAPON TO FIGHT WHATEVER HAD IMPRISONED THEM. TO FIGHT THEIR WAY OUT OF THEIR DOME, IF NECESSARY.
UNLESS FATE LENDS A HAND.
ARE YOU ALL RIGHT, CARTER?
Y-YEAH...
...I'M OKAY.

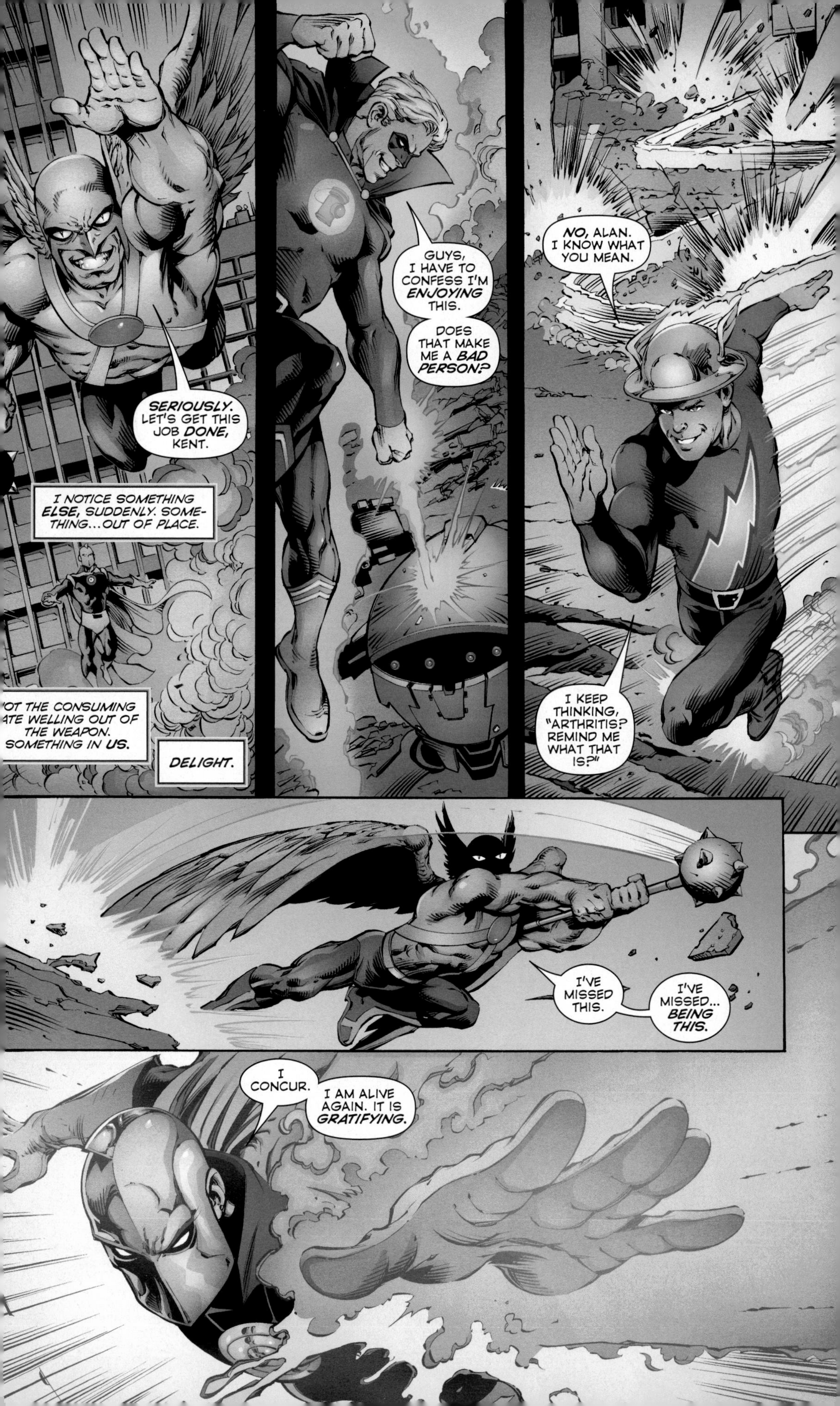

SERIOUSLY. LET'S GET THIS JOB DONE, KENT.
I NOTICE SOMETHING ELSE, SUDDENLY. SOMETHING...OUT OF PLACE.
NOT THE CONSUMING HATE WELLING OUT OF THE WEAPON. SOMETHING IN US.
DELIGHT.
GUYS, I HAVE TO CONFESS I'M ENJOYING THIS.
DOES THAT MAKE ME A BAD PERSON?
NO, ALAN. I KNOW WHAT YOU MEAN.
I KEEP THINKING, "ARTHRITIS? REMIND ME WHAT THAT IS?"
I'VE MISSED THIS.
I'VE MISSED... BEING THIS.
I CONCUR.
I AM ALIVE AGAIN. IT IS GRATIFYING.

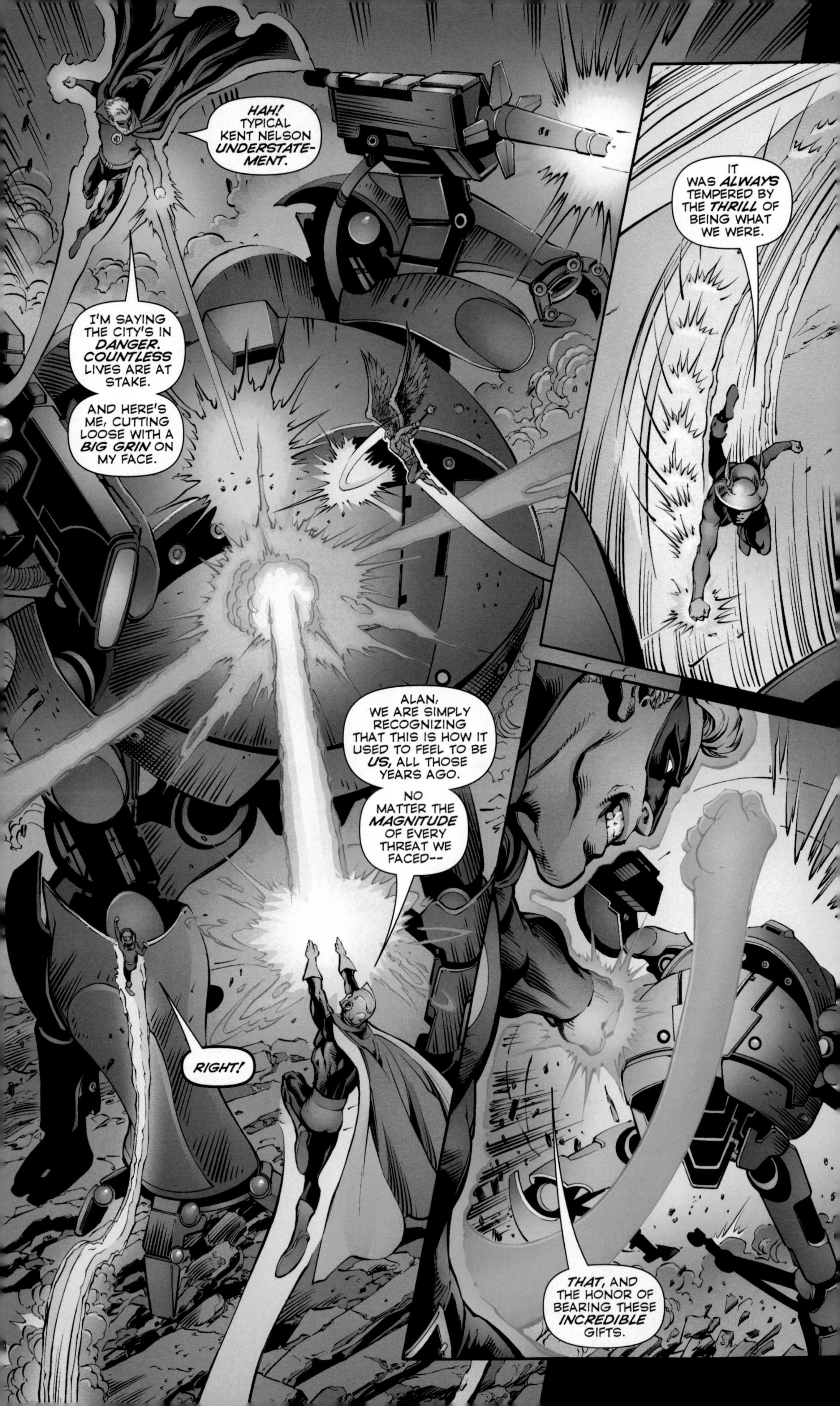
HAH! TYPICAL KENT NELSON UNDERSTATEMENT.
I'M SAYING THE CITY'S IN DANGER. COUNTLESS LIVES ARE AT STAKE.
AND HERE'S ME, CUTTING LOOSE WITH A BIG GRIN ON MY FACE.
IT WAS ALWAYS TEMPERED BY THE THRILL OF BEING WHAT WE WERE.
ALAN, WE ARE SIMPLY RECOGNIZING THAT THIS IS HOW IT USED TO FEEL TO BE US, ALL THOSE YEARS AGO.
NO MATTER THE MAGNITUDE OF EVERY THREAT WE FACED--
RIGHT!
THAT, AND THE HONOR OF BEARING THESE INCREDIBLE GIFTS.

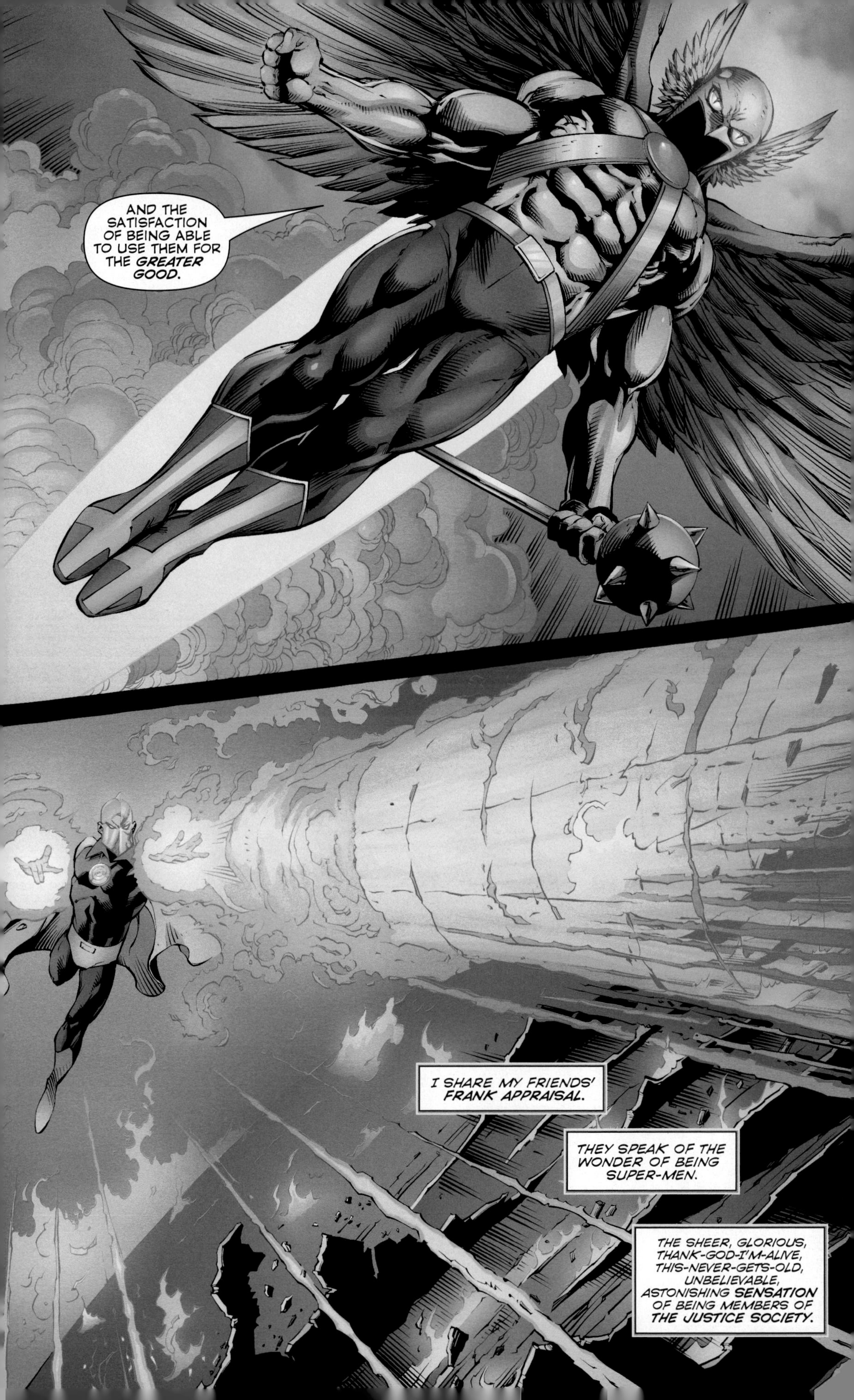
AND THE SATISFACTION OF BEING ABLE TO USE THEM FOR THE GREATER GOOD.
I SHARE MY FRIENDS' FRANK APPRAISAL.
THEY SPEAK OF THE WONDER OF BEING SUPER-MEN.
THE SHEER, GLORIOUS, THANK-GOD-I'M-ALIVE, THIS-NEVER-GETS-OLD, UNBELIEVABLE, ASTONISHING SENSATION OF BEING MEMBERS OF THE JUSTICE SOCIETY.

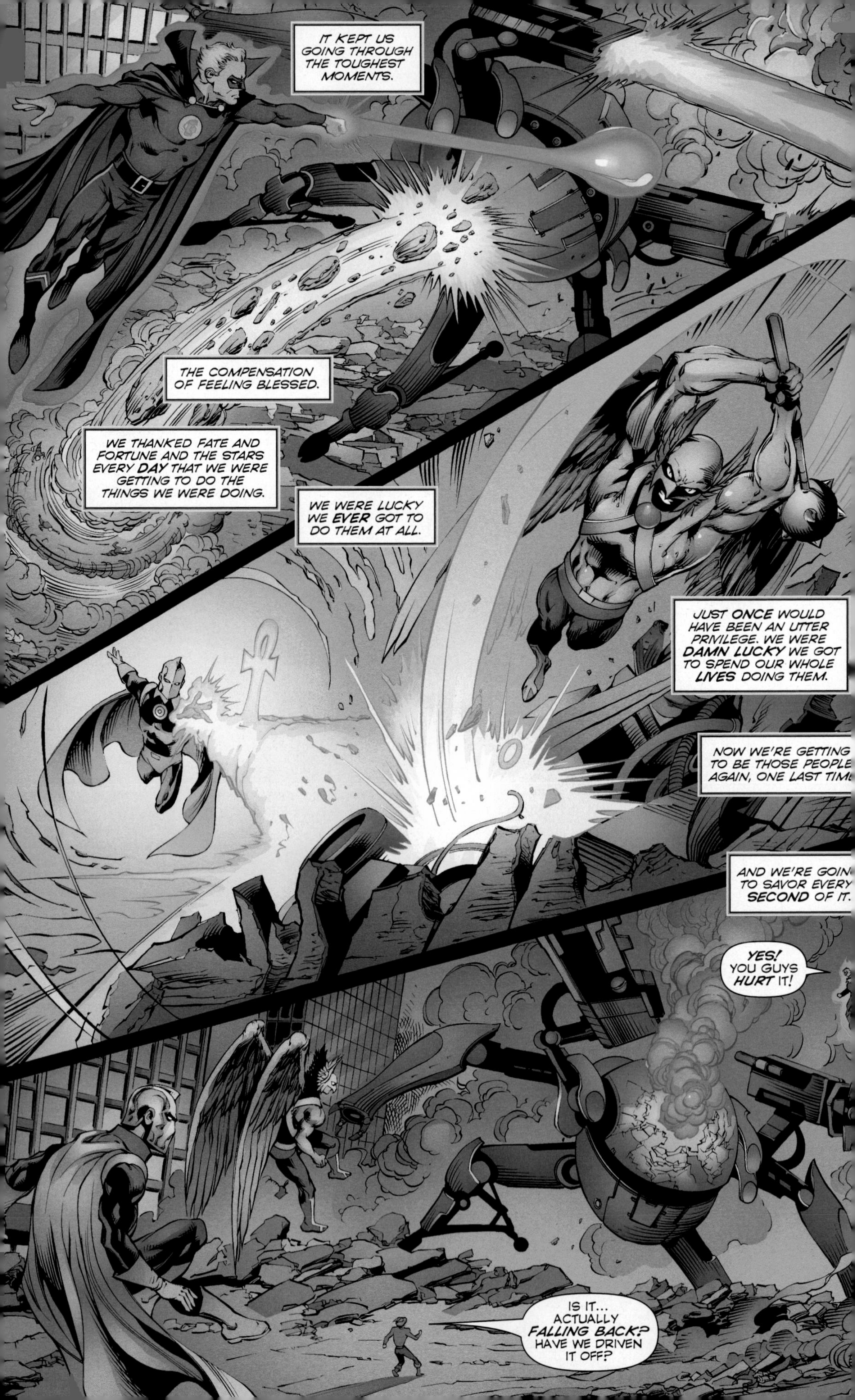
IT KEPT US GOING THROUGH THE TOUGHEST MOMENTS.
THE COMPENSATION OF FEELING BLESSED.
WE THANKED FATE AND FORTUNE AND THE STARS EVERY DAY THAT WE WERE GETTING TO DO THE THINGS WE WERE DOING.
WE WERE LUCKY WE EVER GOT TO DO THEM AT ALL.
JUST ONCE WOULD HAVE BEEN AN UTTER PRIVILEGE. WE WERE DAMN LUCKY WE GOT TO SPEND OUR WHOLE LIVES DOING THEM.
NOW WE'RE GETTING TO BE THOSE PEOPLE AGAIN, ONE LAST TIME
AND WE'RE GOING TO SAVOR EVERY SECOND OF IT.
YES! YOU GUYS HURT IT!
IS IT... ACTUALLY FALLING BACK? HAVE WE DRIVEN IT OFF?

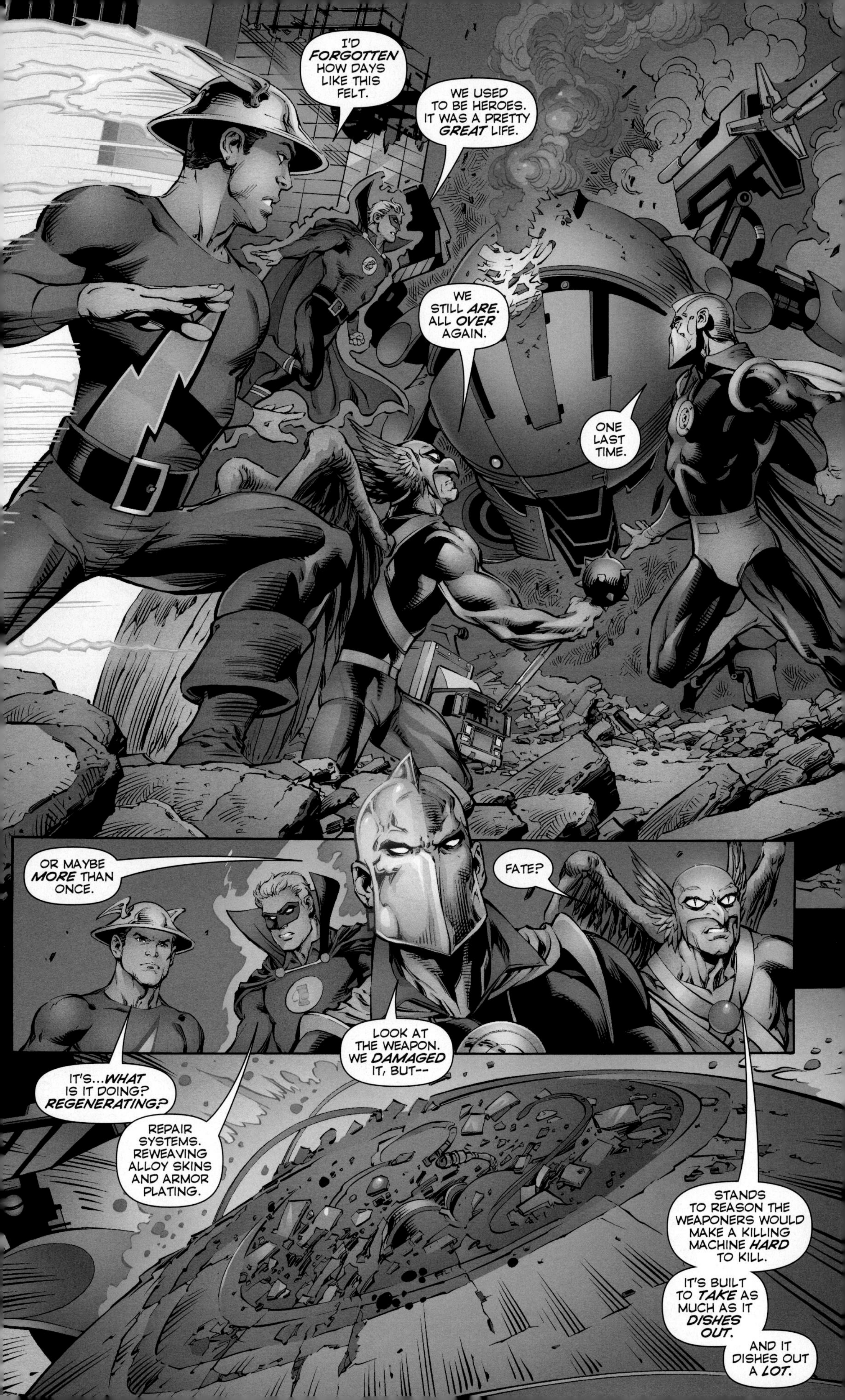

I'D FORGOTTEN HOW DAYS LIKE THIS FELT.
WE USED TO BE HEROES. IT WAS A PRETTY GREAT LIFE.
WE STILL ARE. ALL OVER AGAIN.
ONE LAST TIME.
OR MAYBE MORE THAN ONCE.
FATE?
LOOK AT THE WEAPON. WE DAMAGED IT, BUT--
IT'S...WHAT IS IT DOING? REGENERATING?
REPAIR SYSTEMS. REWEAVING ALLOY SKINS AND ARMOR PLATING.
STANDS TO REASON THE WEAPONERS WOULD MAKE A KILLING MACHINE HARD TO KILL.
IT'S BUILT TO TAKE AS MUCH AS IT DISHES OUT.
AND IT DISHES OUT A LOT.

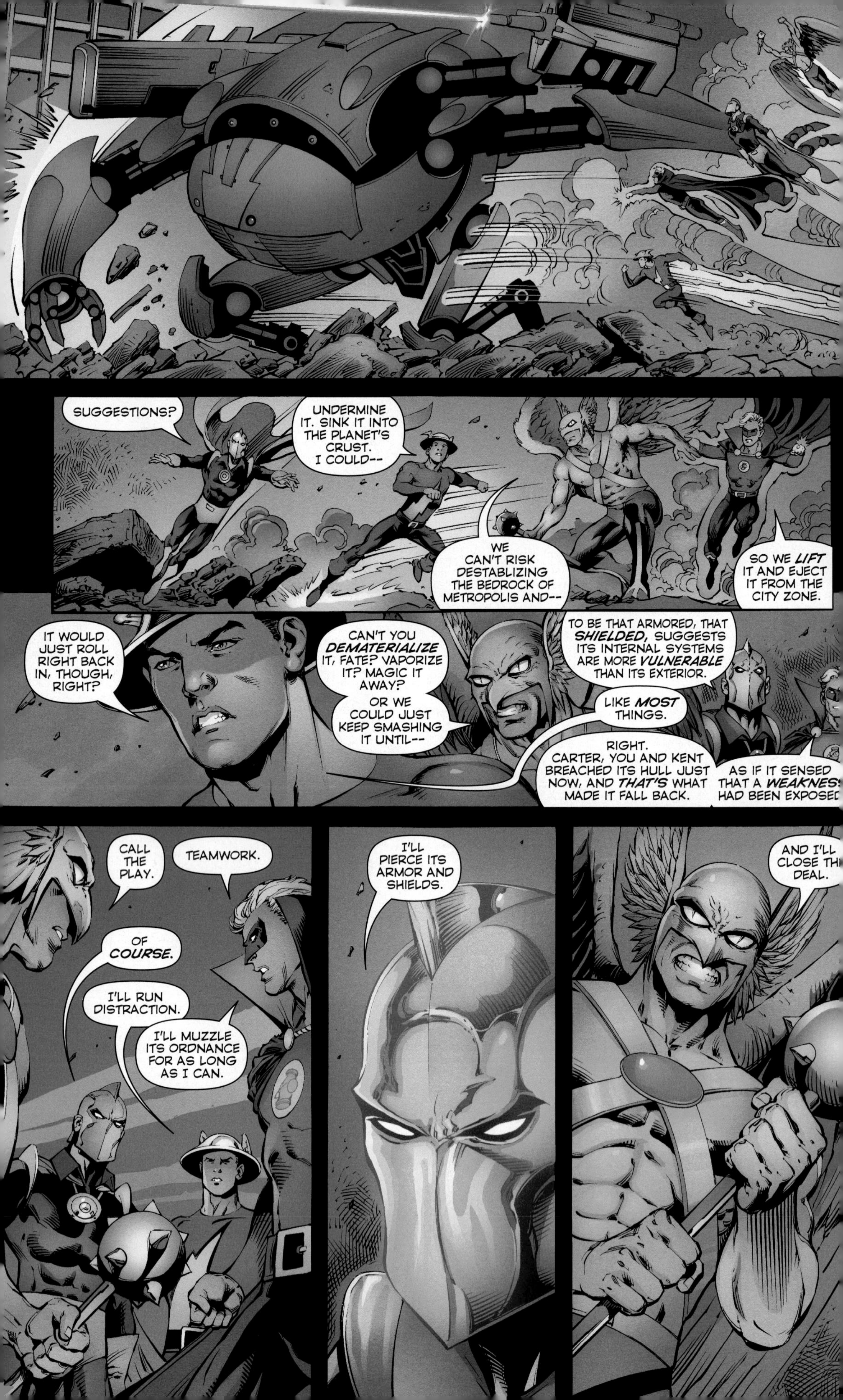
SUGGESTIONS?
UNDERMINE IT. SINK IT INTO THE PLANET'S CRUST. I COULD--
WE CAN'T RISK DESTABLIZING THE BEDROCK OF METROPOLIS AND--
SO WE LIFT IT AND EJECT IT FROM THE CITY ZONE.
IT WOULD JUST ROLL RIGHT BACK IN, THOUGH, RIGHT?
CAN'T YOU DEMATERIALIZE IT, FATE? VAPORIZE IT? MAGIC IT AWAY?
OR WE COULD JUST KEEP SMASHING IT UNTIL--
TO BE THAT ARMORED, THAT SHIELDED, SUGGESTS ITS INTERNAL SYSTEMS ARE MORE VULNERABLE THAN ITS EXTERIOR.
LIKE MOST THINGS.
RIGHT. CARTER, YOU AND KENT BREACHED ITS HULL JUST NOW, AND THAT'S WHAT MADE IT FALL BACK.
AS IF IT SENSED THAT A WEAKNES HAD BEEN EXPOSED
CALL THE PLAY.
TEAMWORK.
OF COURSE.
I'LL RUN DISTRACTION.
I'LL MUZZLE ITS ORDNANCE FOR AS LONG AS I CAN.
I'LL PIERCE ITS ARMOR AND SHIELDS.
AND I'LL CLOSE TH DEAL.

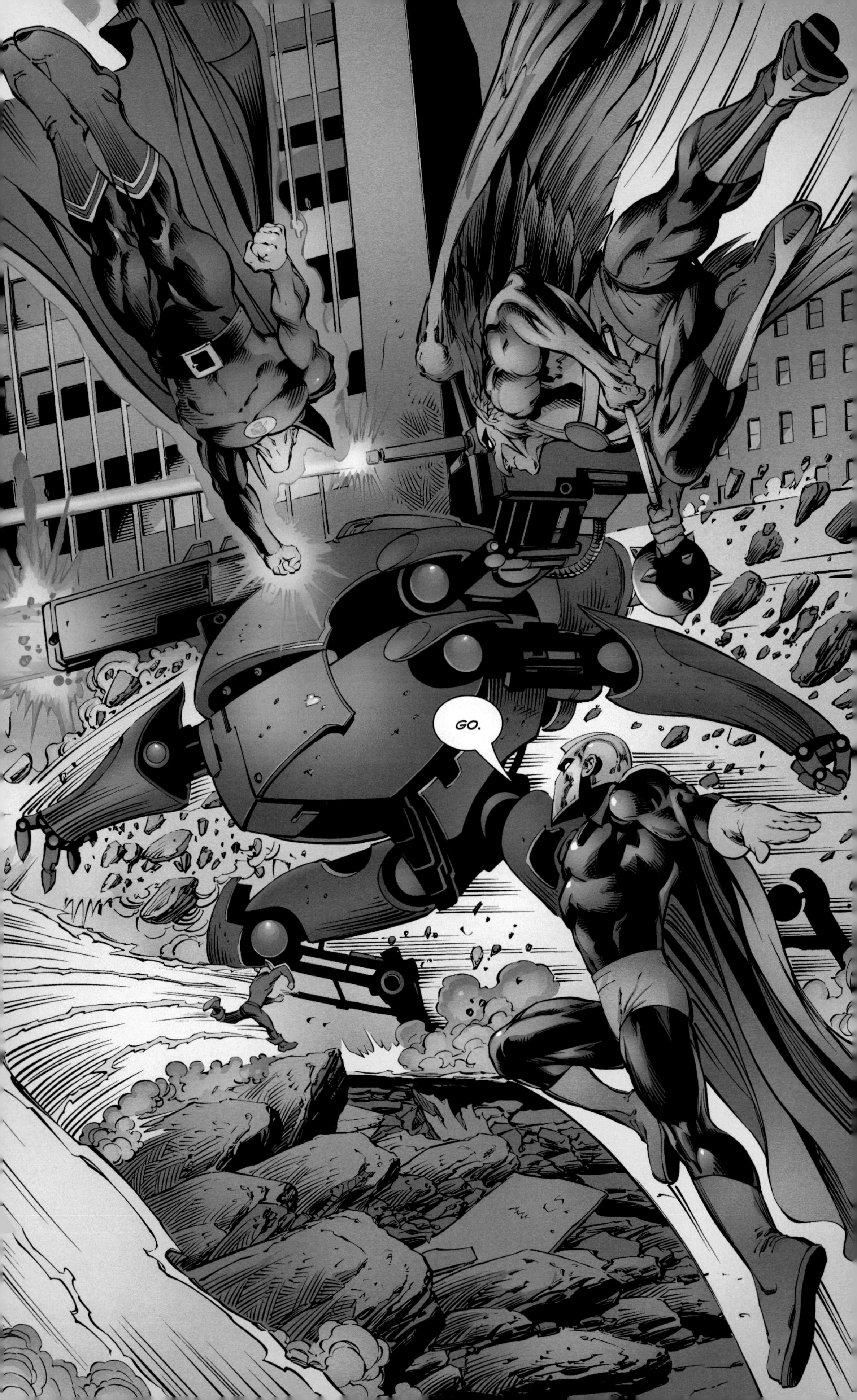
GO.

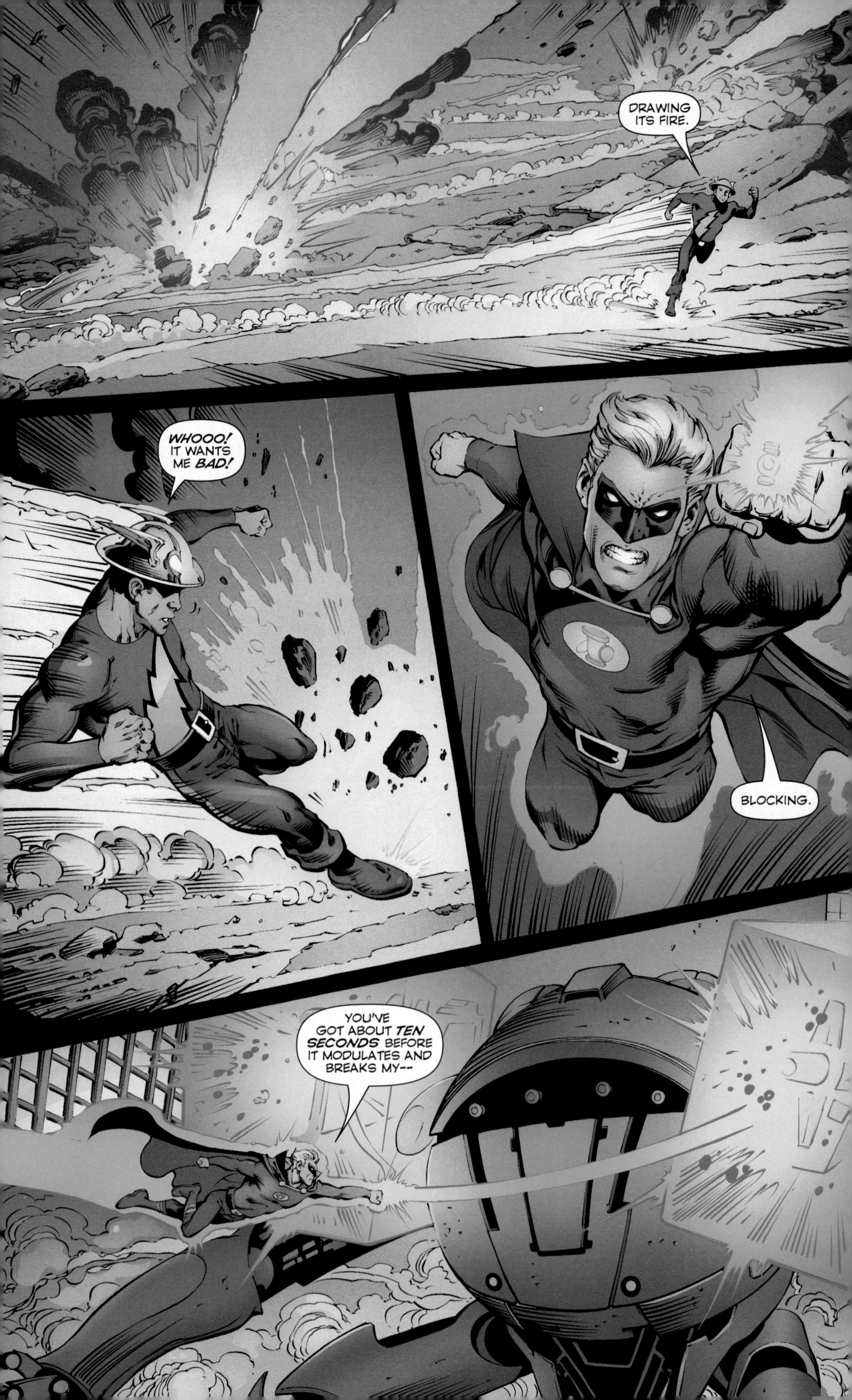
DRAWING ITS FIRE.
WHOOO! IT WANTS ME BAD!
BLOCKING.
YOU'VE GOT ABOUT TEN SECONDS BEFORE IT MODULATES AND BREAKS MY--

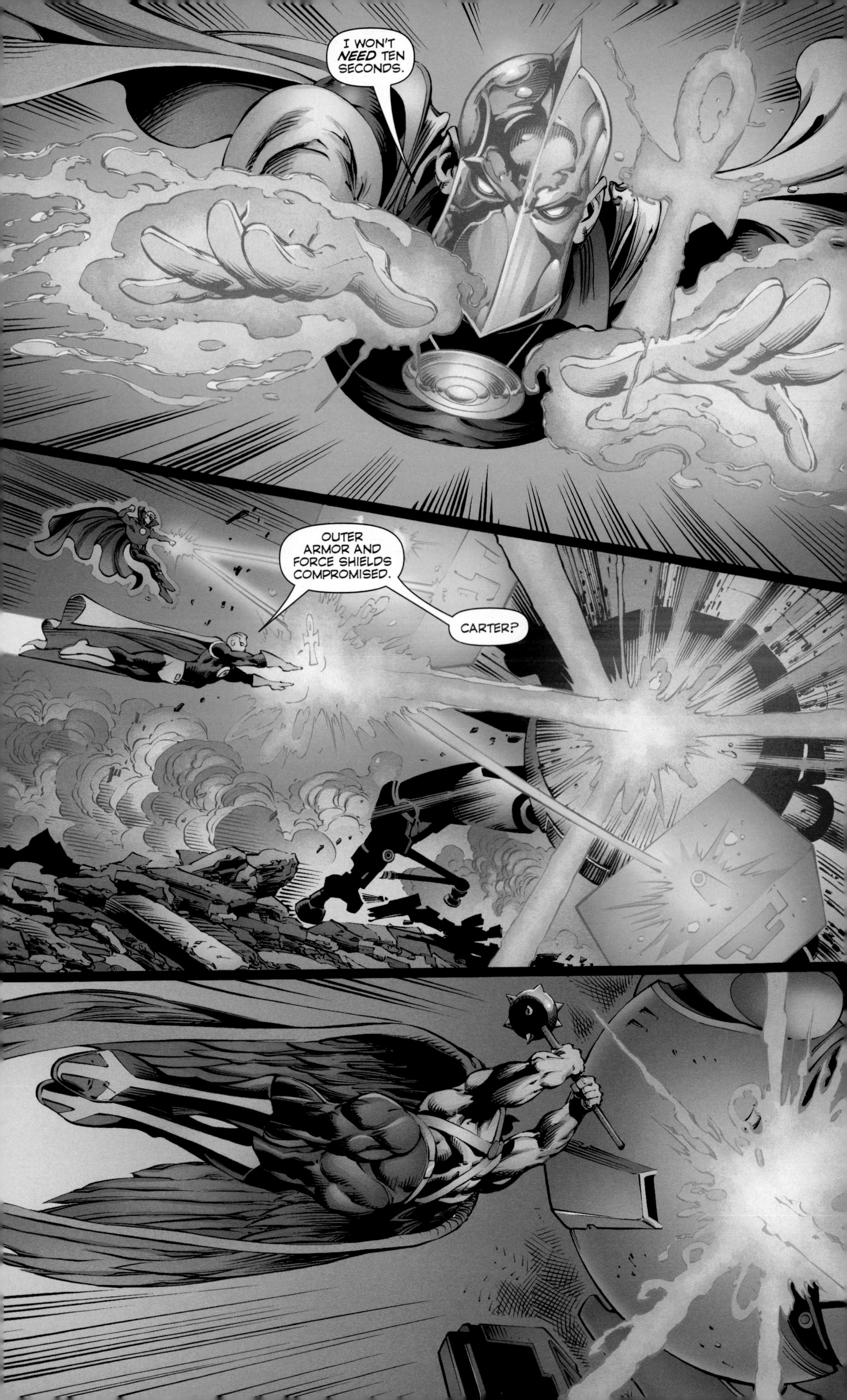
I WON'T *NEED* TEN SECONDS.
OUTER ARMOR AND FORCE SHIELDS COMPROMISED.
CARTER?

WE FOLLOW CARTER'S ASSAULT.

WE HIT IT TOGETHER.

WE HIT IT SO HARD THAT FOR A MOMENT IT FEELS LIKE AN EARTHQUAKE IS ROCKING THE CITY.

RRRRRRRRRRRMMMMMLBBBLLLL

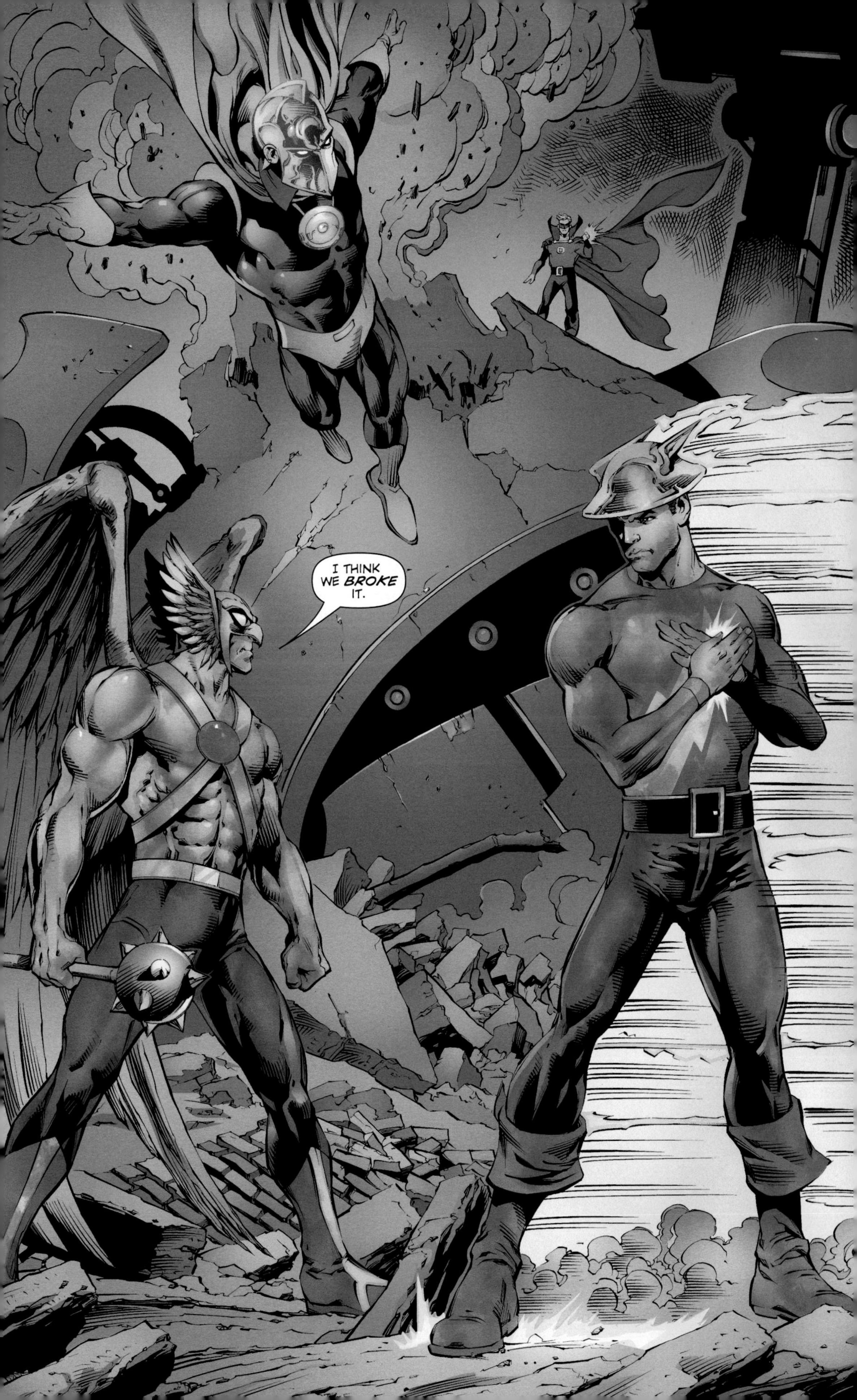
I THINK WE BROKE IT.

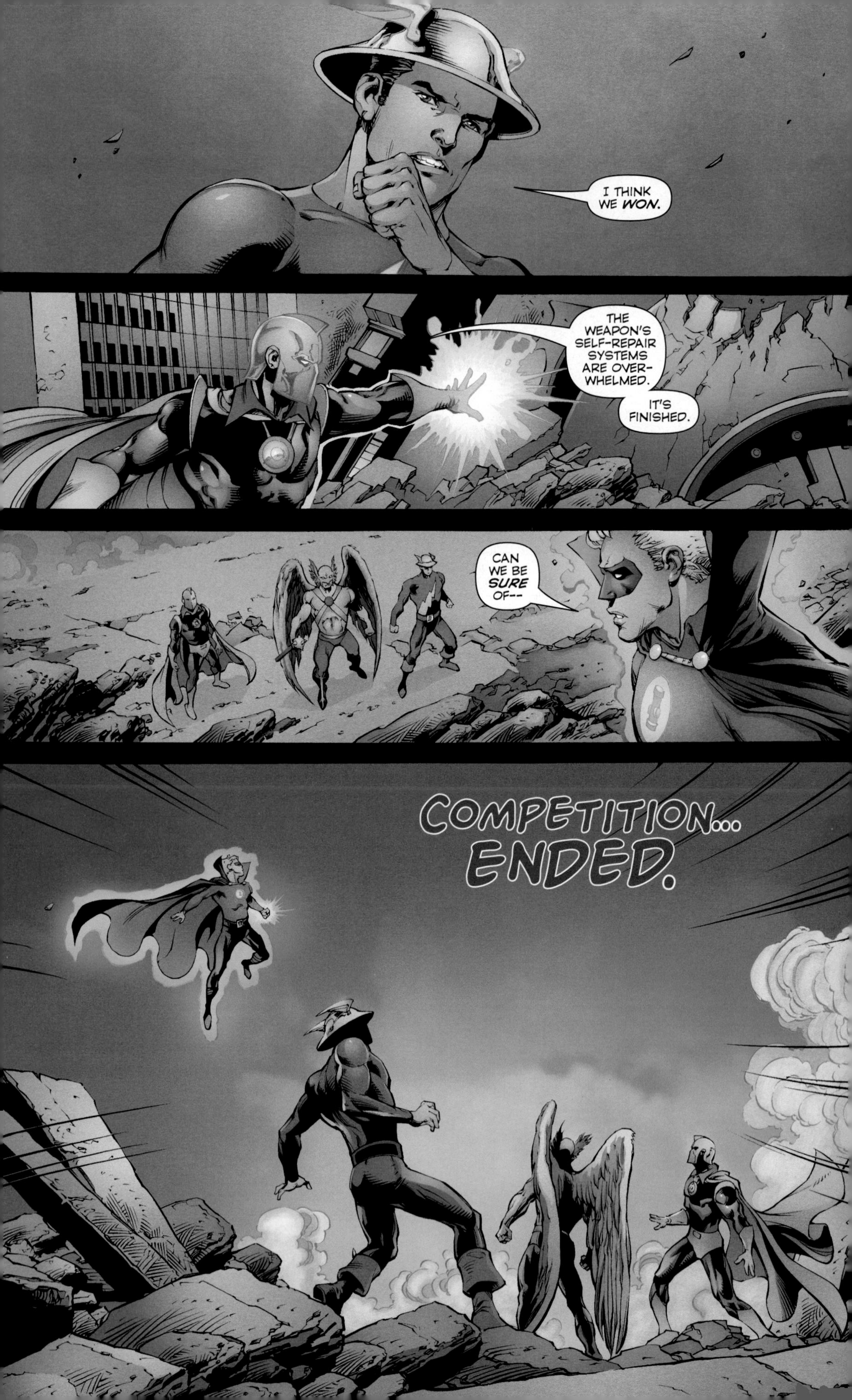

I THINK WE *WON*.
THE WEAPON'S SELF-REPAIR SYSTEMS ARE OVER-WHELMED.
IT'S FINISHED.
CAN WE BE *SURE* OF--
COMPETITION... ENDED.

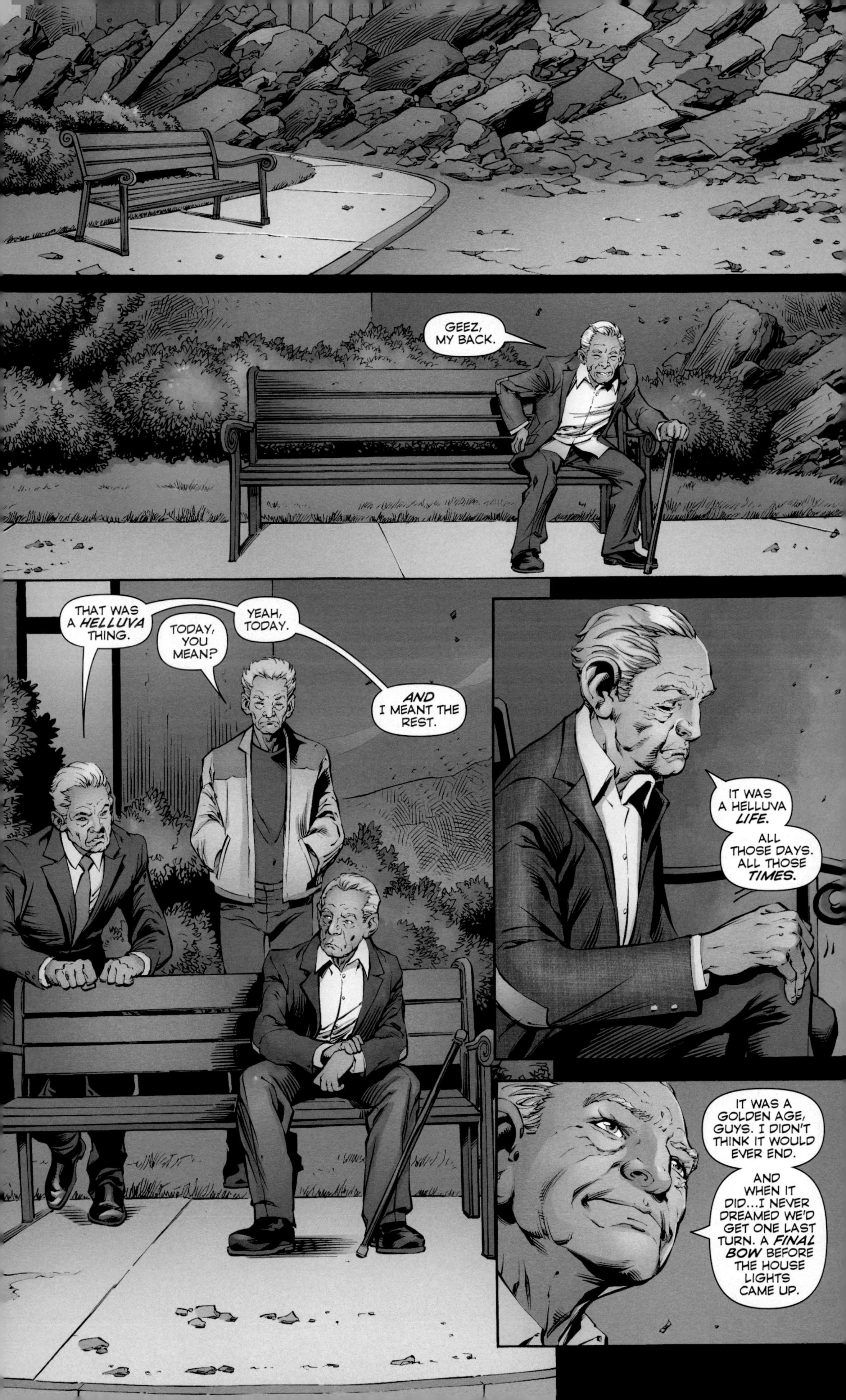
GEEZ, MY BACK.
THAT WAS A *HELLUVA* THING.
TODAY, YOU MEAN?
YEAH, TODAY.
AND I MEANT THE REST.
IT WAS A HELLUVA *LIFE*.
ALL THOSE DAYS. ALL THOSE *TIMES*.
IT WAS A GOLDEN AGE, GUYS. I DIDN'T THINK IT WOULD EVER END.
AND WHEN IT DID...I NEVER DREAMED WE'D GET ONE LAST TURN. A *FINAL BOW* BEFORE THE HOUSE LIGHTS CAME UP.

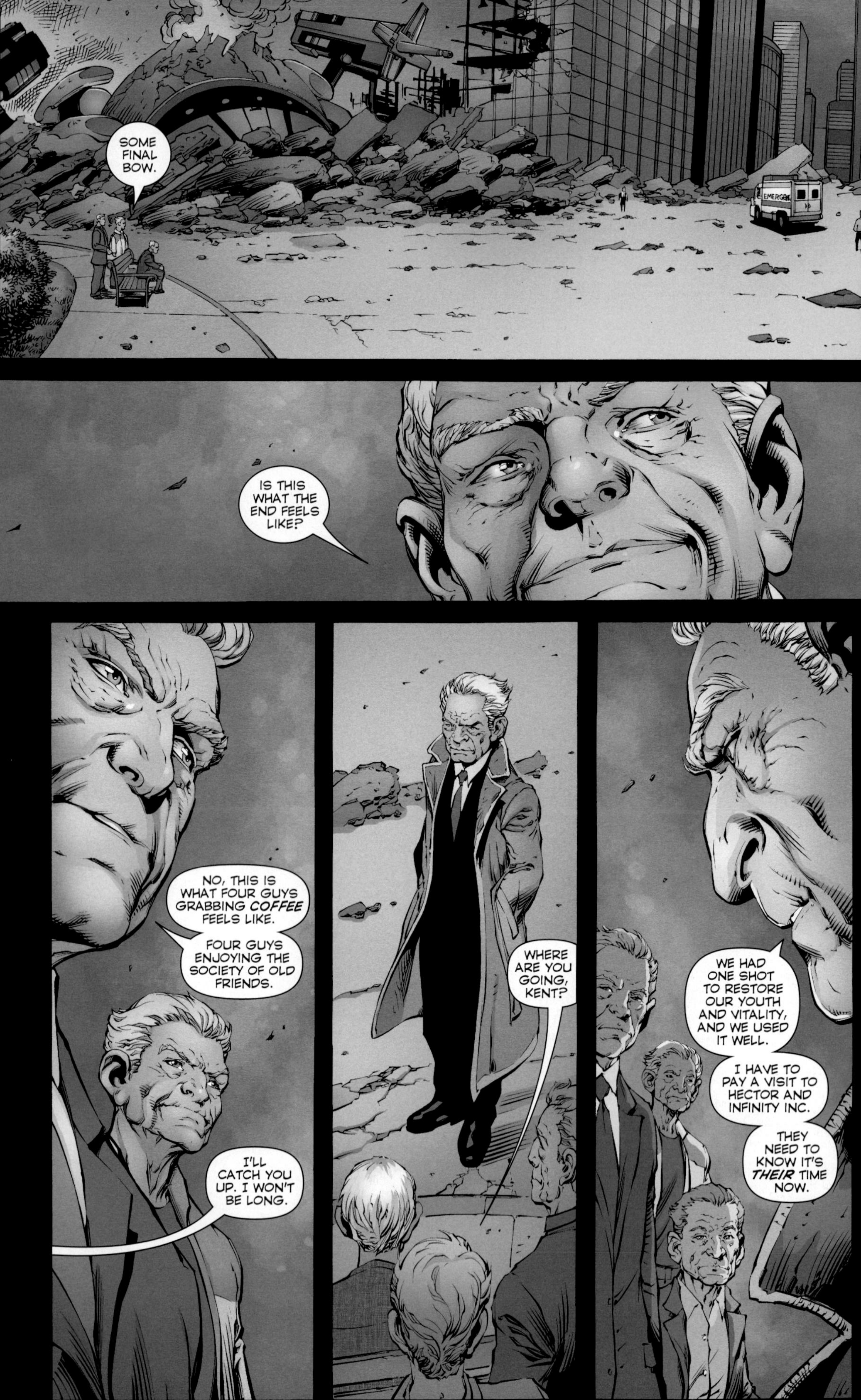
SOME FINAL BOW.
IS THIS WHAT THE END FEELS LIKE?
NO, THIS IS WHAT FOUR GUYS GRABBING *COFFEE* FEELS LIKE.
FOUR GUYS ENJOYING THE SOCIETY OF OLD FRIENDS.
I'LL CATCH YOU UP. I WON'T BE LONG.
WHERE ARE YOU GOING, KENT?
WE HAD ONE SHOT TO RESTORE OUR YOUTH AND VITALITY, AND WE USED IT WELL.
I HAVE TO PAY A VISIT TO HECTOR AND INFINITY INC.
THEY NEED TO KNOW IT'S *THEIR* TIME NOW.

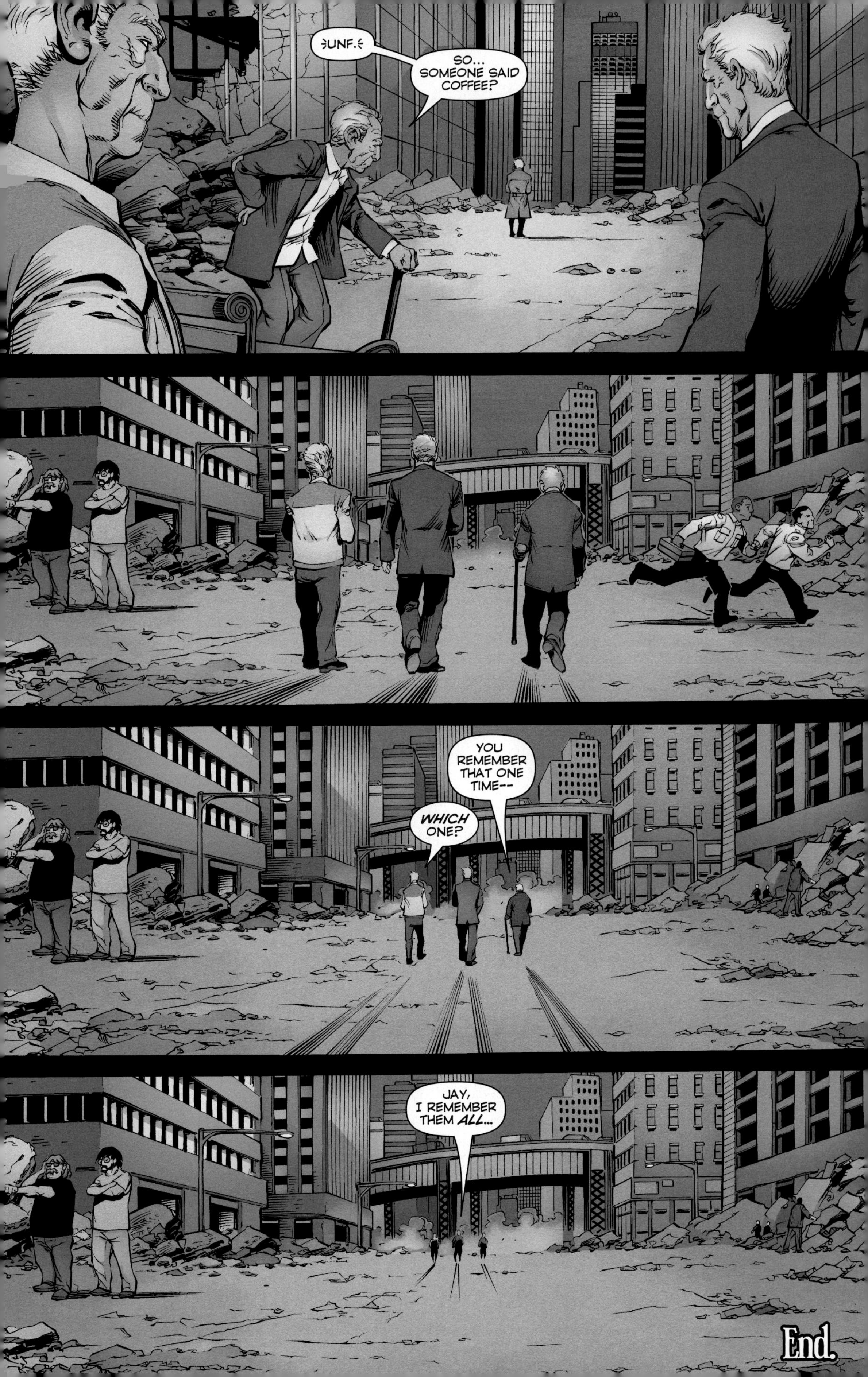
UNF.
SO... SOMEONE SAID COFFEE?
YOU REMEMBER THAT ONE TIME--
WHICH ONE?
JAY, I REMEMBER THEM ALL...
End.

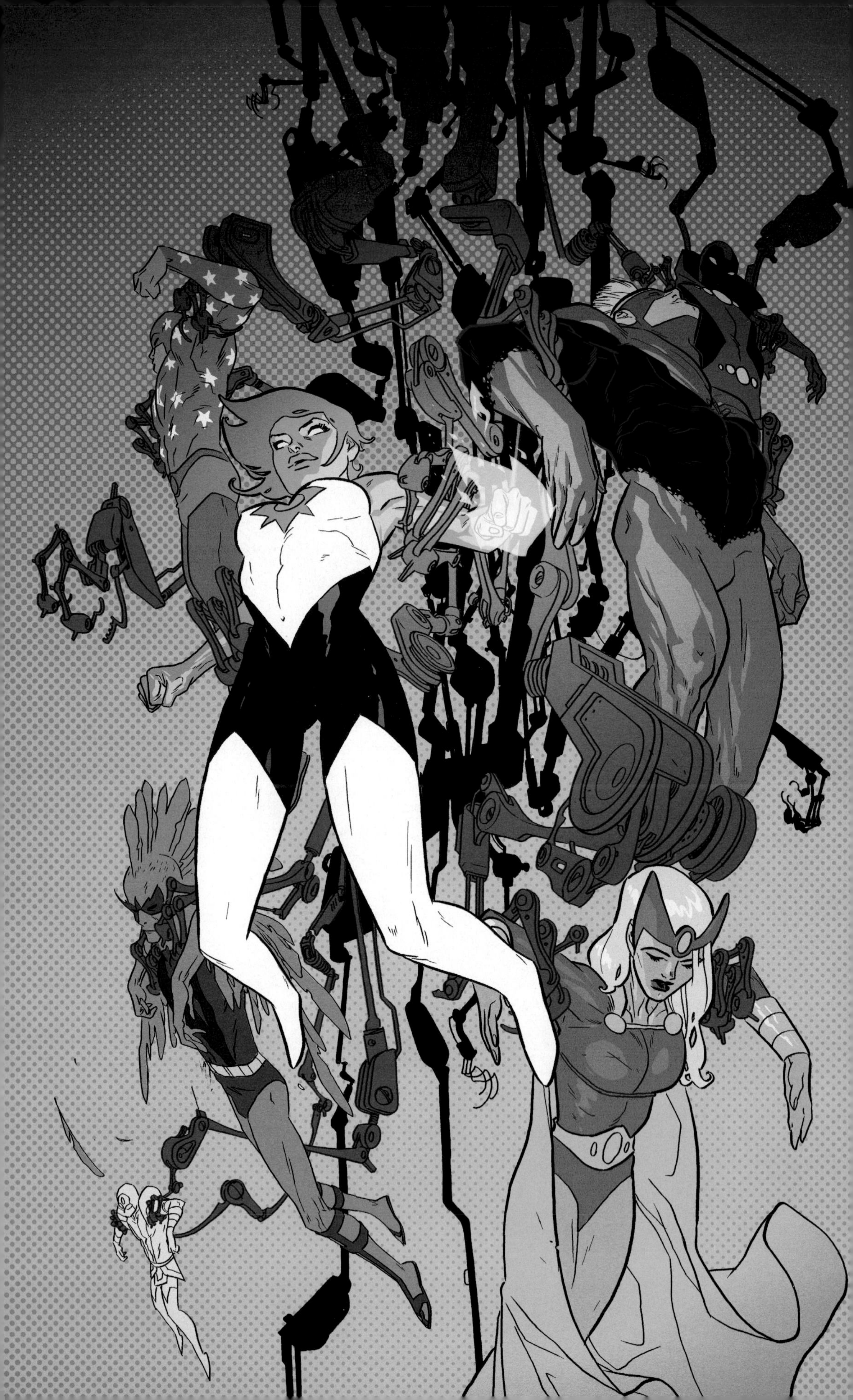

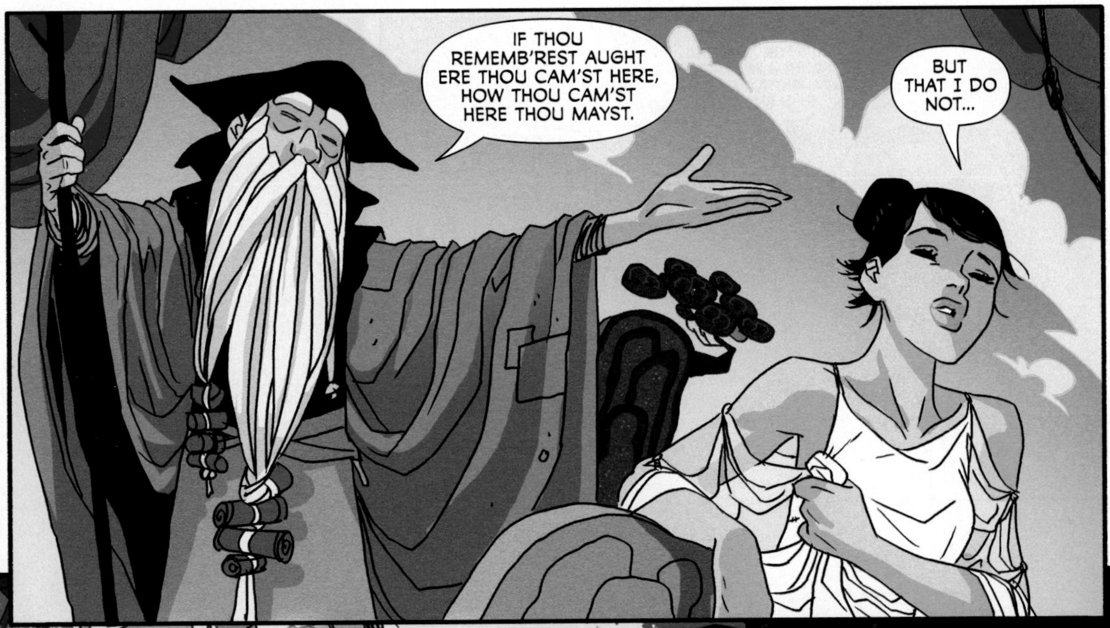
IF THOU REMEMB'REST AUGHT ERE THOU CAM'ST HERE, HOW THOU CAM'ST HERE THOU MAYST.
BUT THAT I DO NOT...

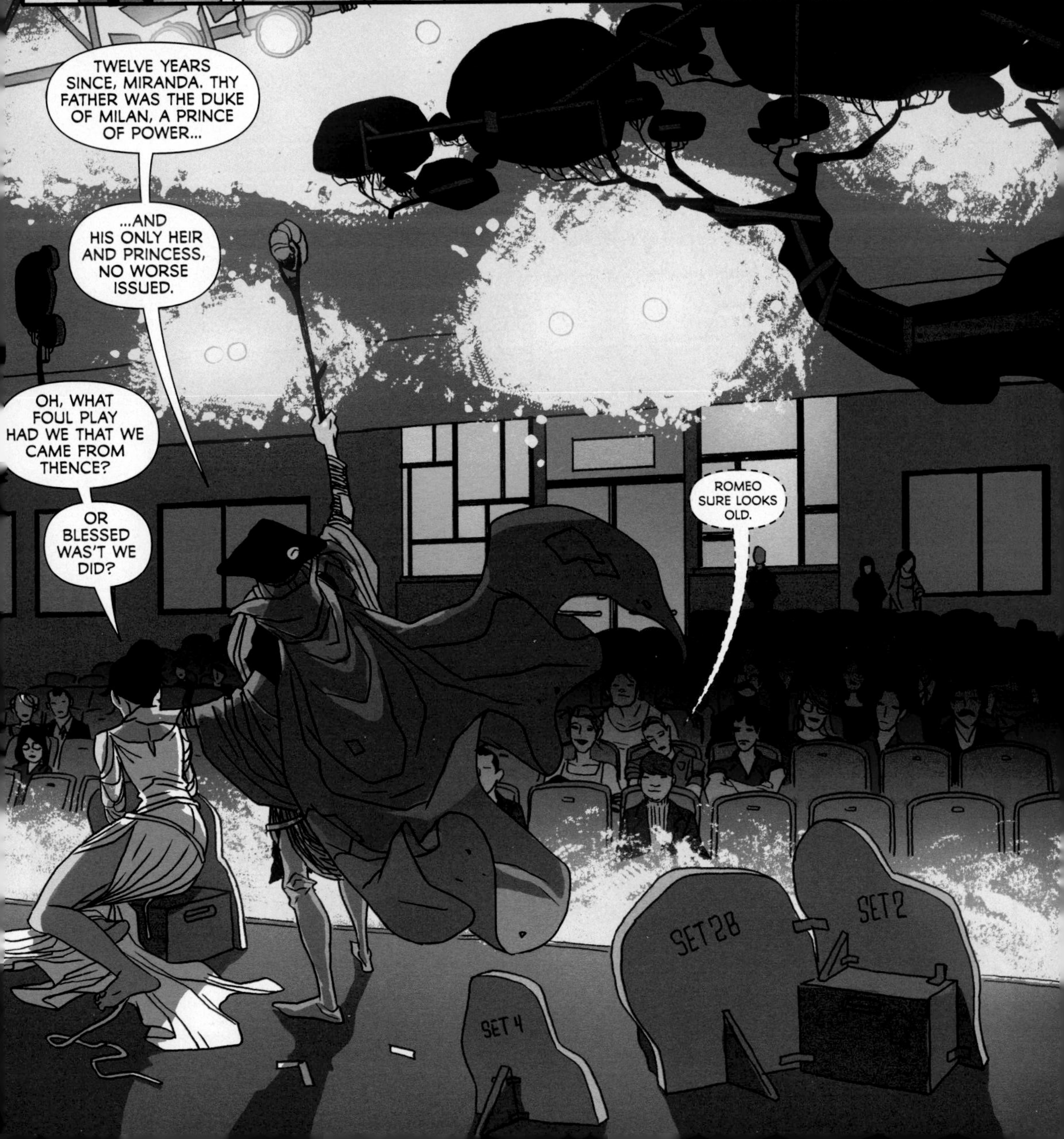
TWELVE YEARS SINCE, MIRANDA. THY FATHER WAS THE DUKE OF MILAN, A PRINCE OF POWER...
...AND HIS ONLY HEIR AND PRINCESS, NO WORSE ISSUED.
OH, WHAT FOUL PLAY HAD WE THAT WE CAME FROM THENCE?
OR BLESSED WAS'T WE DID?
ROMEO SURE LOOKS OLD.
SET 2B
SET 2
SET 4

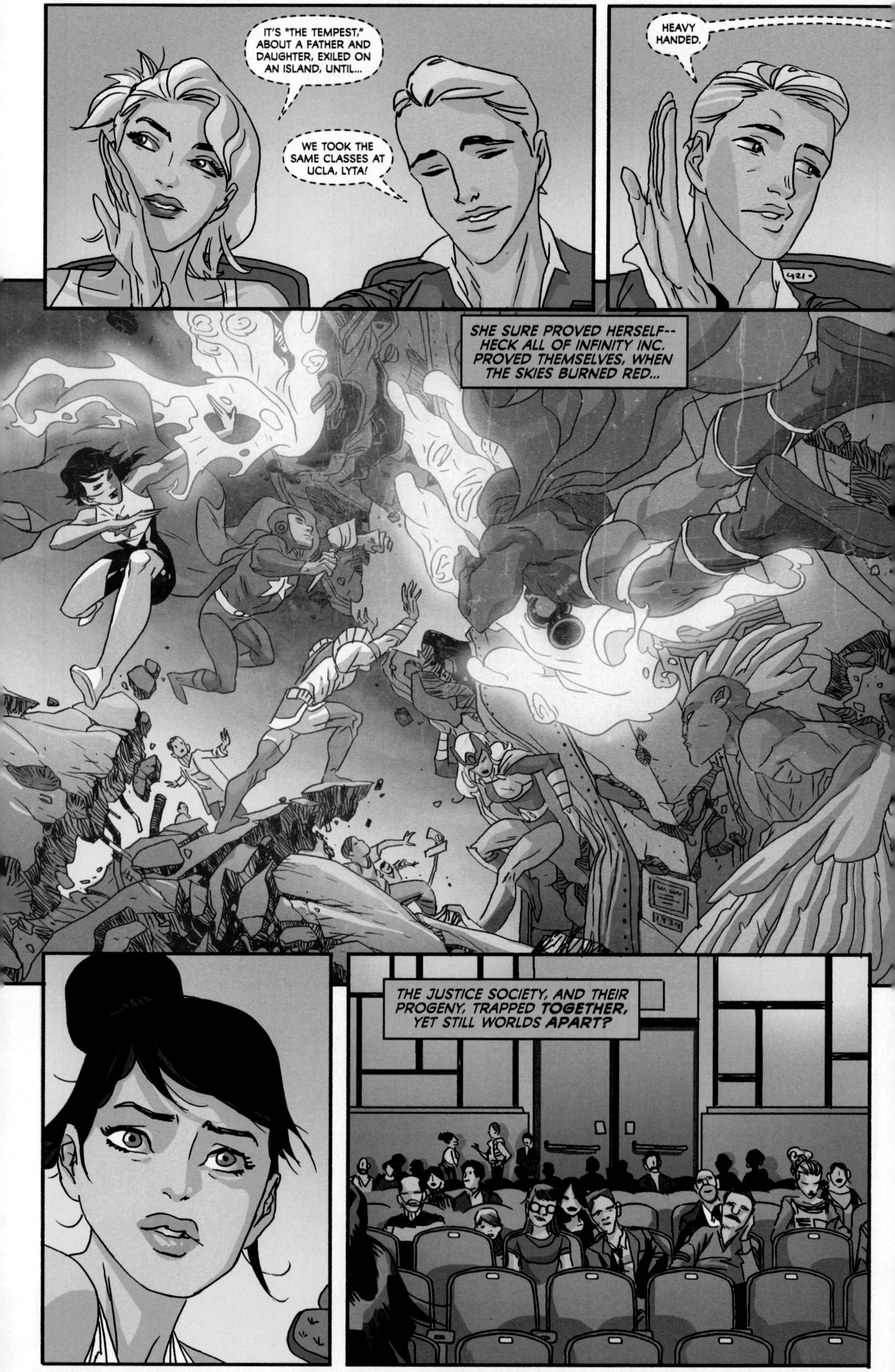
IT'S "THE TEMPEST," ABOUT A FATHER AND DAUGHTER, EXILED ON AN ISLAND, UNTIL...
WE TOOK THE SAME CLASSES AT UCLA, LYTA!
HEAVY HANDED.
SHE SURE PROVED HERSELF-- HECK ALL OF INFINITY INC. PROVED THEMSELVES, WHEN THE SKIES BURNED RED...
THE JUSTICE SOCIETY, AND THEIR PROGENY, TRAPPED TOGETHER, YET STILL WORLDS APART?

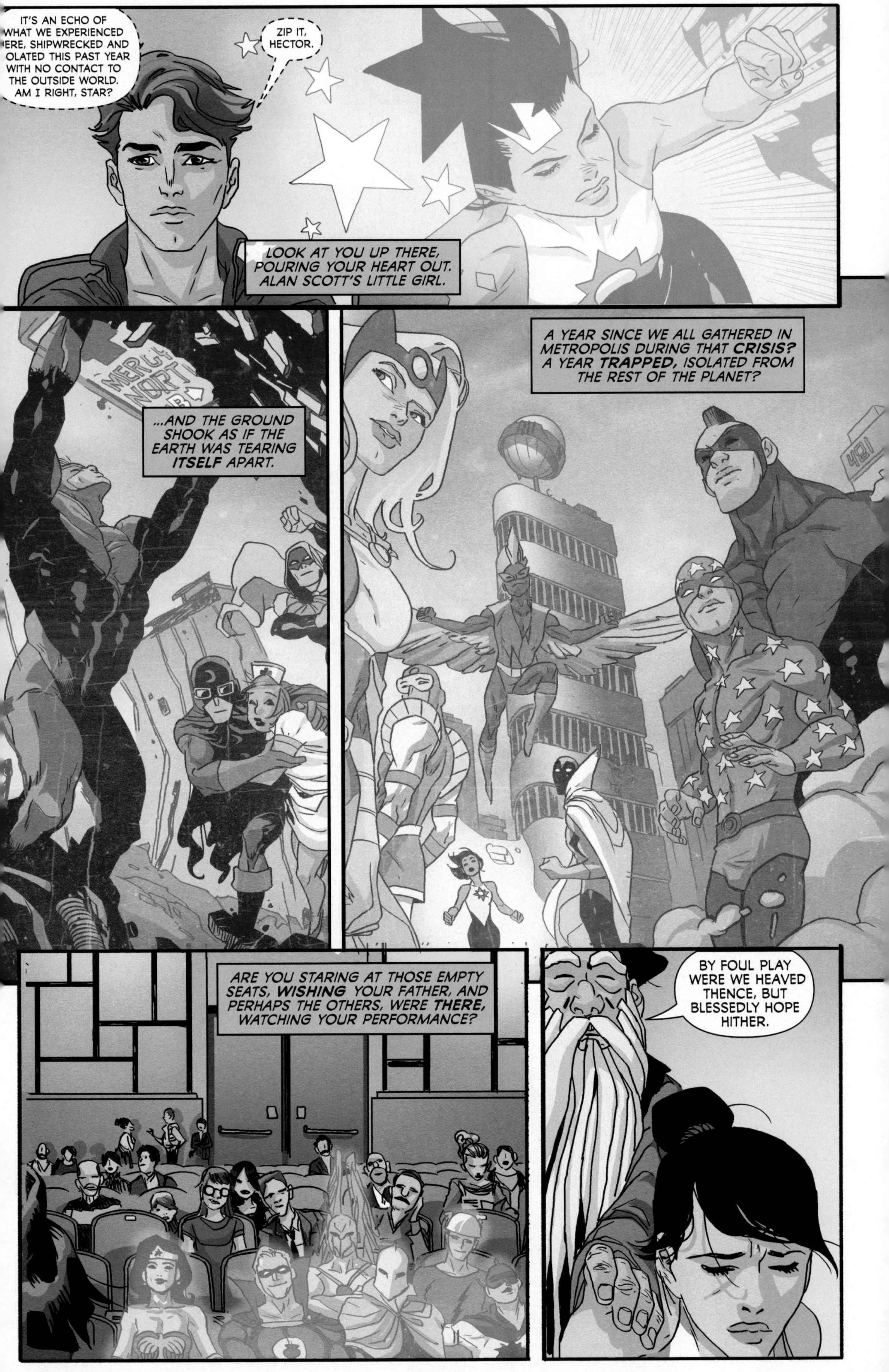
IT'S AN ECHO OF WHAT WE EXPERIENCED ERE, SHIPWRECKED AND OLATED THIS PAST YEAR WITH NO CONTACT TO THE OUTSIDE WORLD. AM I RIGHT, STAR?
ZIP IT, HECTOR.
LOOK AT YOU UP THERE, POURING YOUR HEART OUT. ALAN SCOTT'S LITTLE GIRL.
...AND THE GROUND SHOOK AS IF THE EARTH WAS TEARING ITSELF APART.
A YEAR SINCE WE ALL GATHERED IN METROPOLIS DURING THAT CRISIS? A YEAR TRAPPED, ISOLATED FROM THE REST OF THE PLANET?
ARE YOU STARING AT THOSE EMPTY SEATS, WISHING YOUR FATHER, AND PERHAPS THE OTHERS, WERE THERE, WATCHING YOUR PERFORMANCE?
BY FOUL PLAY WERE WE HEAVED THENCE, BUT BLESSEDLY HOPE HITHER.

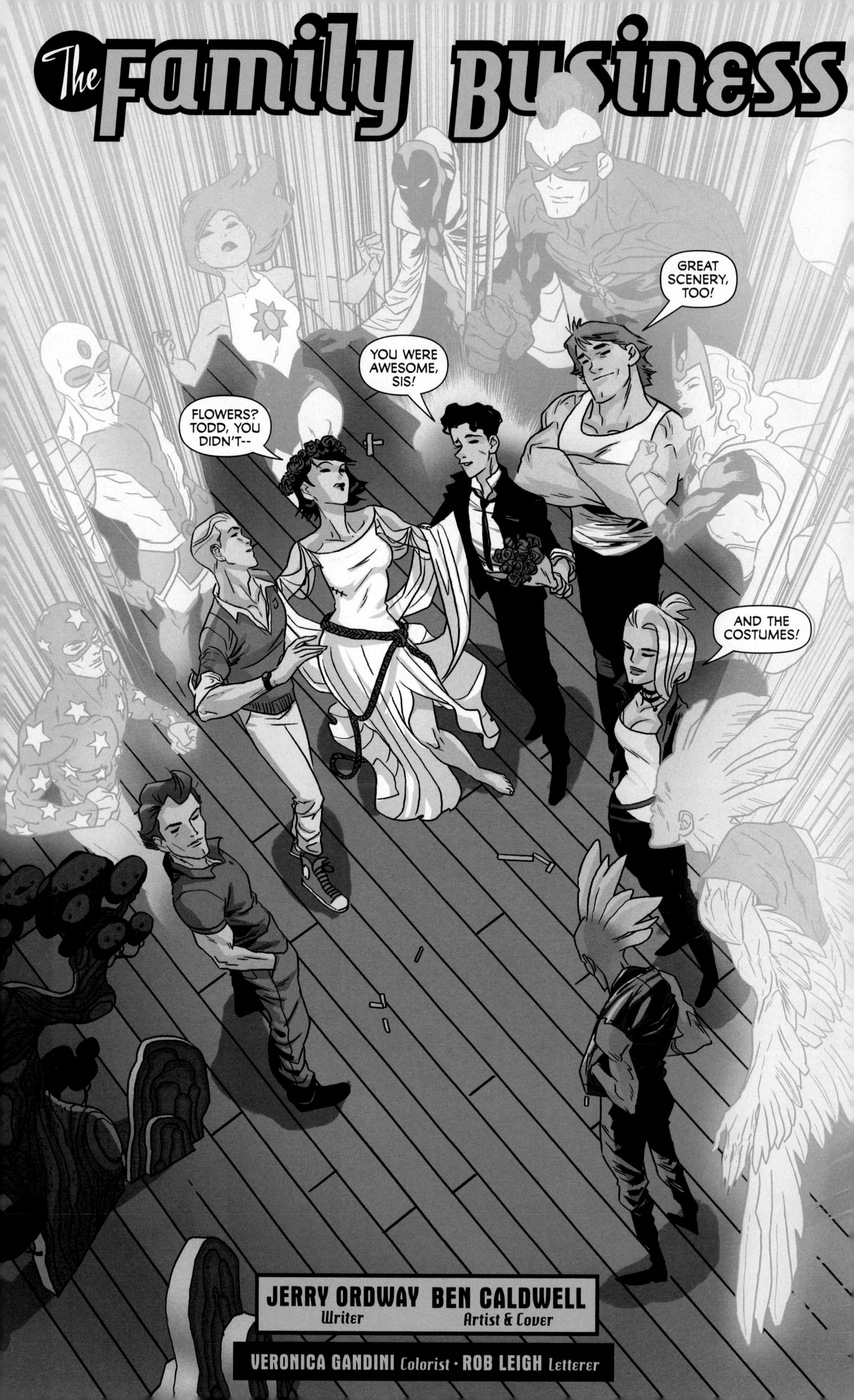
The Family Business
FLOWERS? TODD, YOU DIDN'T--
YOU WERE AWESOME, SIS!
GREAT SCENERY, TOO!
AND THE COSTUMES!
JERRY ORDWAY Writer
BEN CALDWELL Artist & Cover
VERONICA GANDINI Colorist • ROB LEIGH Letterer

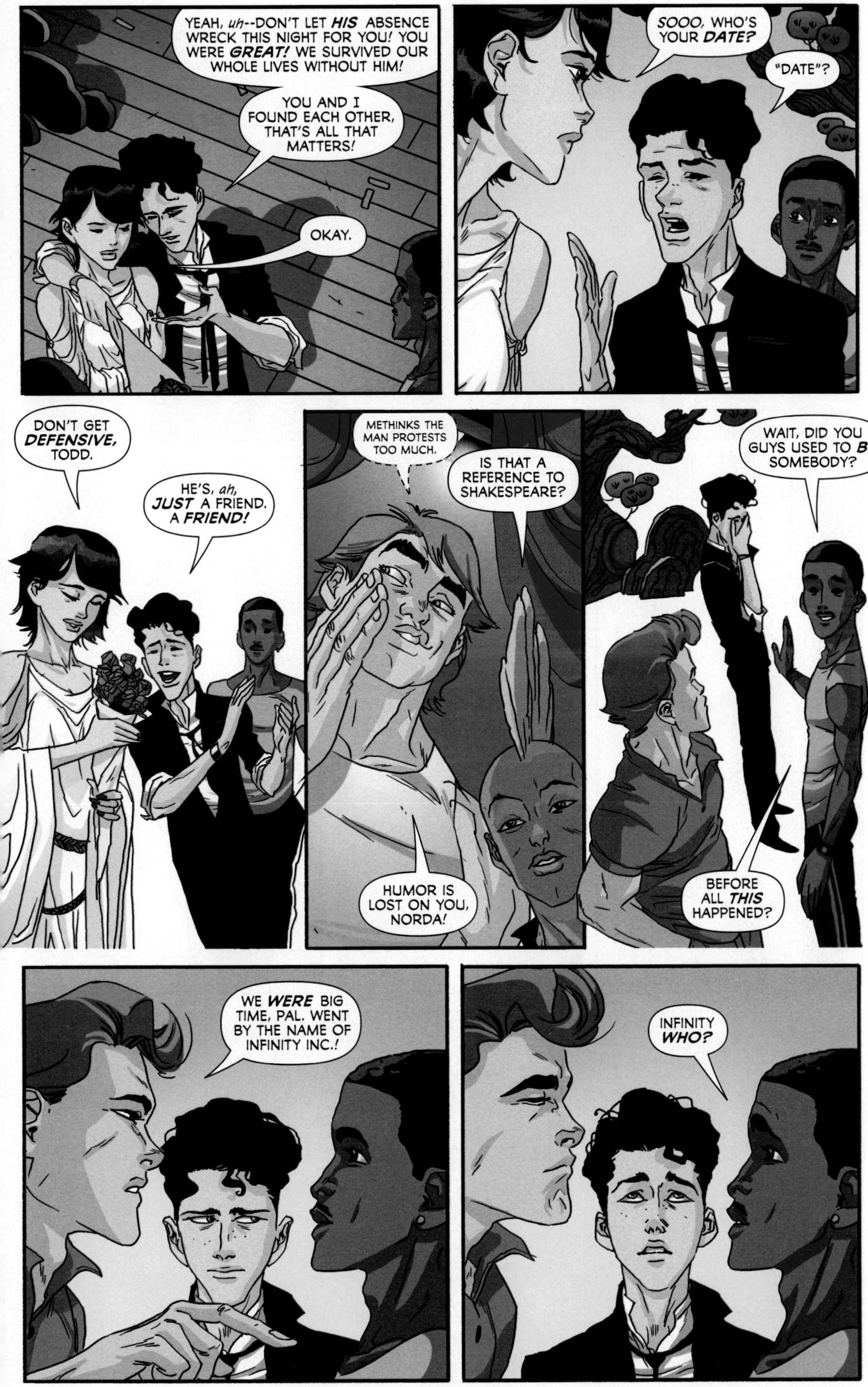
YEAH, *uh*--DON'T LET ***HIS*** ABSENCE WRECK THIS NIGHT FOR YOU! YOU WERE ***GREAT!*** WE SURVIVED OUR WHOLE LIVES WITHOUT HIM!
YOU AND I FOUND EACH OTHER, THAT'S ALL THAT MATTERS!
OKAY.
SOOO, WHO'S YOUR ***DATE?***
"DATE"?
DON'T GET ***DEFENSIVE,*** TODD.
HE'S, *ah,* ***JUST*** A FRIEND. A ***FRIEND!***
METHINKS THE MAN PROTESTS TOO MUCH.
IS THAT A REFERENCE TO SHAKESPEARE?
HUMOR IS LOST ON YOU, NORDA!
WAIT, DID YOU GUYS USED TO ***BE*** SOMEBODY?
BEFORE ALL ***THIS*** HAPPENED?
WE ***WERE*** BIG TIME, PAL. WENT BY THE NAME OF INFINITY INC.!
INFINITY ***WHO?***

PERHAPS WE SHOULD EXPLAIN *WHO* WE ARE?

WHY BOTHER?

CAN YOU *BELIEVE* THAT? NEVER HEARD OF *US?* WE SAVED MILWAUKEE! WE SAVED THE WHOLE JSA BEFORE THAT, FROM THE ULTRA-HUMANITE!

THE ULTRA-*WHO?*

SO, YOU GUYS WERE LIKE A *BAND?*

HA! *SOME*THING LIKE THAT.

YOU'RE A LAUGH RIOT, ALBERT!

DON'T BE SO TOUCHY, STAR. WE'RE BACK TO BEING REGULAR FOLK HERE.

AND YOU'RE *OKAY* WITH THAT?

WE WEREN'T A TEAM FOR VERY LONG. BESIDES, ALL THAT *ANY* OF US REALLY WANTED WAS TO BE IN THE JSA.

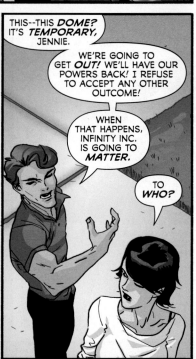

THIS--THIS *DOME?* IT'S *TEMPORARY,* JENNIE.

WE'RE GOING TO GET *OUT!* WE'LL HAVE OUR POWERS BACK! I REFUSE TO ACCEPT ANY OTHER OUTCOME!

WHEN THAT HAPPENS, INFINITY INC. IS GOING TO *MATTER.*

TO *WHO?*

THE JSA IS THE *PAST.* WE'RE THE *FUTURE!*

WAIT-- WHERE ARE YOU--?

THE JSA WASN'T THE ONLY *NO-SHOW* AT MY PLAY. YOUR NEPHEW? HENRY?

BRAINWAVE JUNIOR.

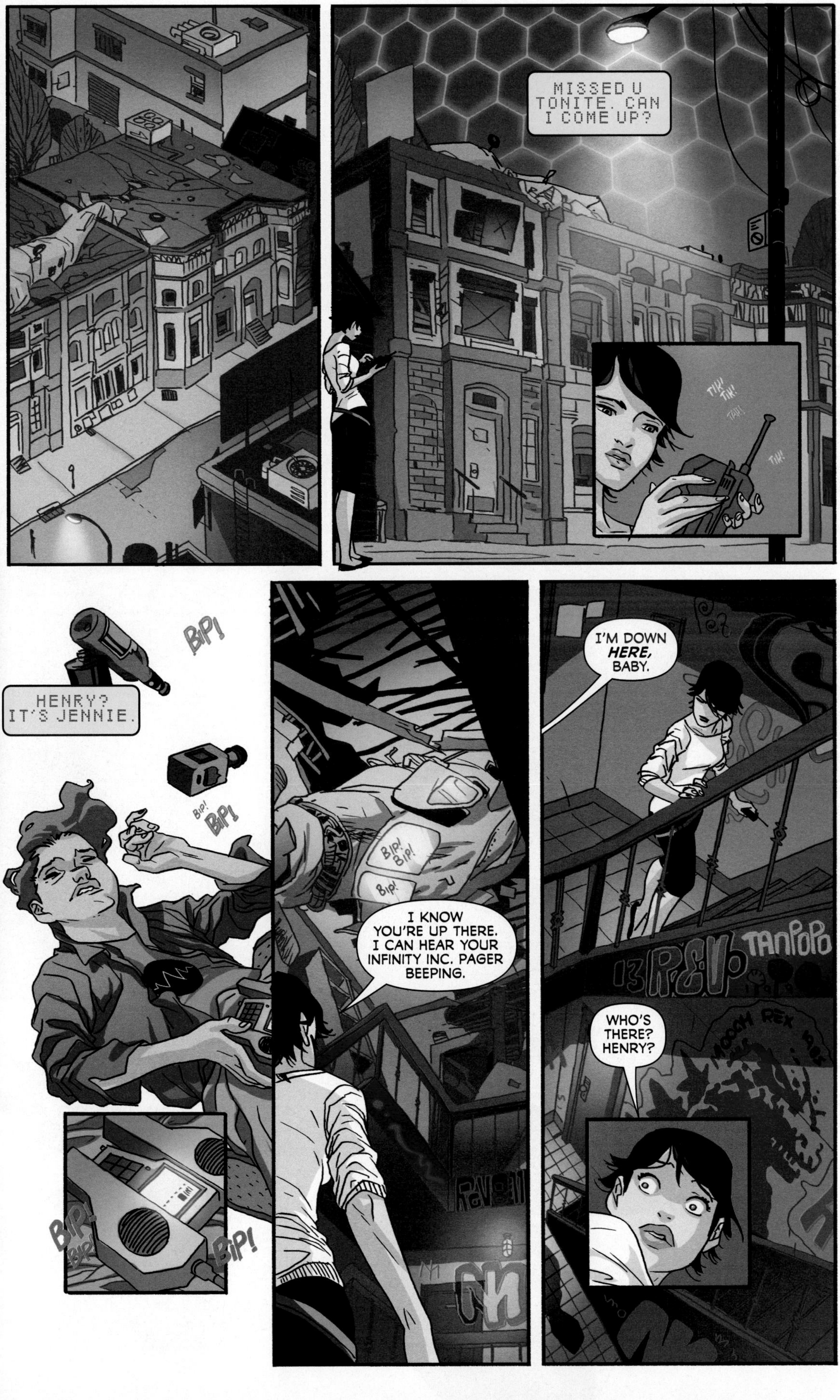
MISSED U TONITE. CAN I COME UP?
TIK! TIK!
TIK!
HENRY? IT'S JENNIE.
BIP!
BIP! BIP!
BIP! BIP!
BIP!
I KNOW YOU'RE UP THERE. I CAN HEAR YOUR INFINITY INC. PAGER BEEPING.
BIP! BIP!
BIP!
I'M DOWN *HERE,* BABY.
TANPOPO
WHO'S THERE? HENRY?

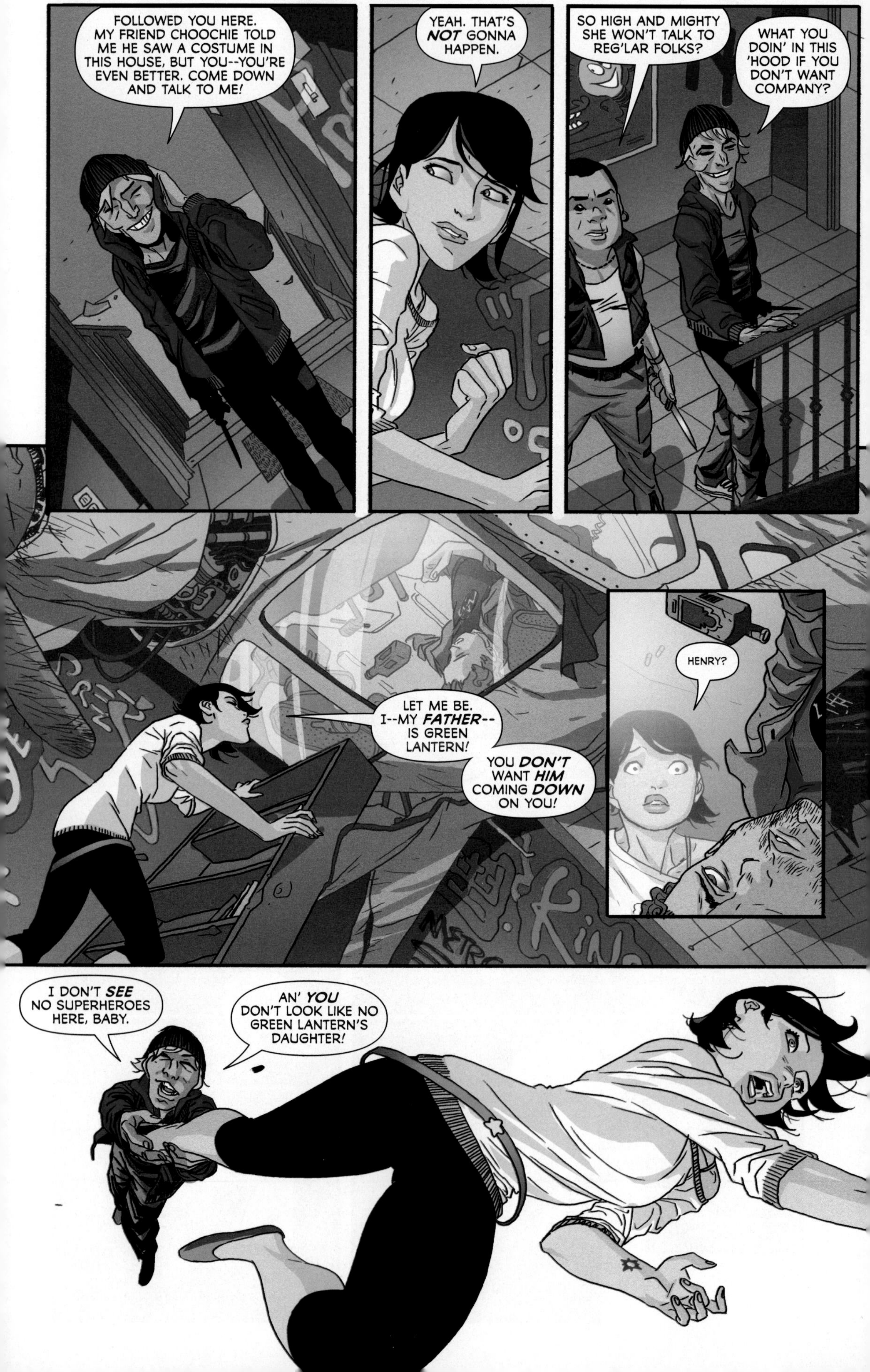
FOLLOWED YOU HERE. MY FRIEND CHOOCHIE TOLD ME HE SAW A COSTUME IN THIS HOUSE, BUT YOU--YOU'RE EVEN BETTER. COME DOWN AND TALK TO ME!
YEAH. THAT'S NOT GONNA HAPPEN.
SO HIGH AND MIGHTY SHE WON'T TALK TO REG'LAR FOLKS?
WHAT YOU DOIN' IN THIS 'HOOD IF YOU DON'T WANT COMPANY?
LET ME BE. I--MY FATHER-- IS GREEN LANTERN!
YOU DON'T WANT HIM COMING DOWN ON YOU!
HENRY?
I DON'T SEE NO SUPERHEROES HERE, BABY.
AN' YOU DON'T LOOK LIKE NO GREEN LANTERN'S DAUGHTER!

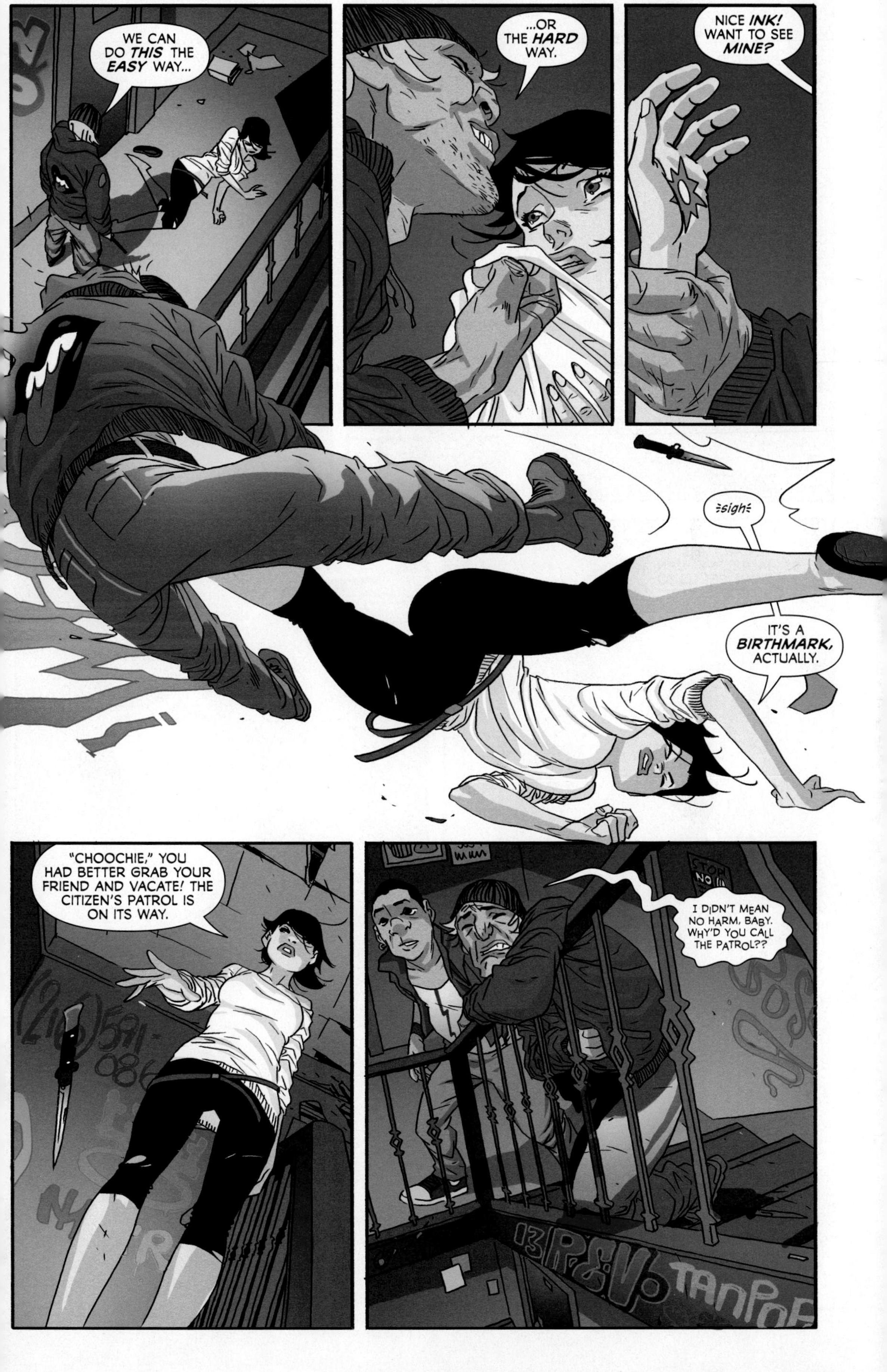
WE CAN DO THIS THE EASY WAY...
...OR THE HARD WAY.
NICE INK! WANT TO SEE MINE?
sigh
IT'S A BIRTHMARK, ACTUALLY.
"CHOOCHIE," YOU HAD BETTER GRAB YOUR FRIEND AND VACATE! THE CITIZEN'S PATROL IS ON ITS WAY.
I DIDN'T MEAN NO HARM, BABY. WHY'D YOU CALL THE PATROL??

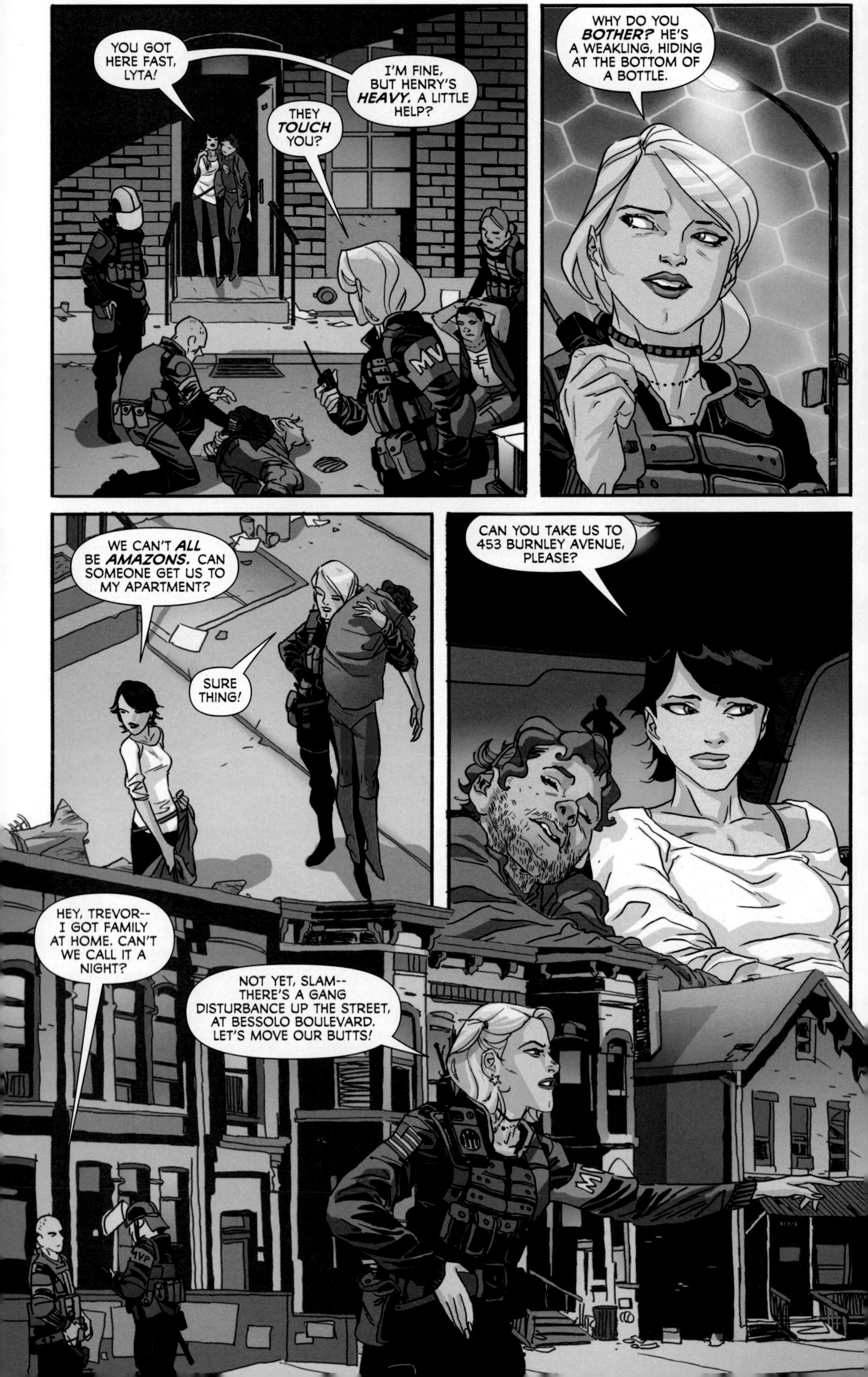
YOU GOT HERE FAST, LYTA!
I'M FINE, BUT HENRY'S HEAVY. A LITTLE HELP?
THEY TOUCH YOU?
WHY DO YOU BOTHER? HE'S A WEAKLING, HIDING AT THE BOTTOM OF A BOTTLE.
WE CAN'T ALL BE AMAZONS. CAN SOMEONE GET US TO MY APARTMENT?
SURE THING!
CAN YOU TAKE US TO 453 BURNLEY AVENUE, PLEASE?
HEY, TREVOR-- I GOT FAMILY AT HOME. CAN'T WE CALL IT A NIGHT?
NOT YET, SLAM-- THERE'S A GANG DISTURBANCE UP THE STREET, AT BESSOLO BOULEVARD. LET'S MOVE OUR BUTTS!

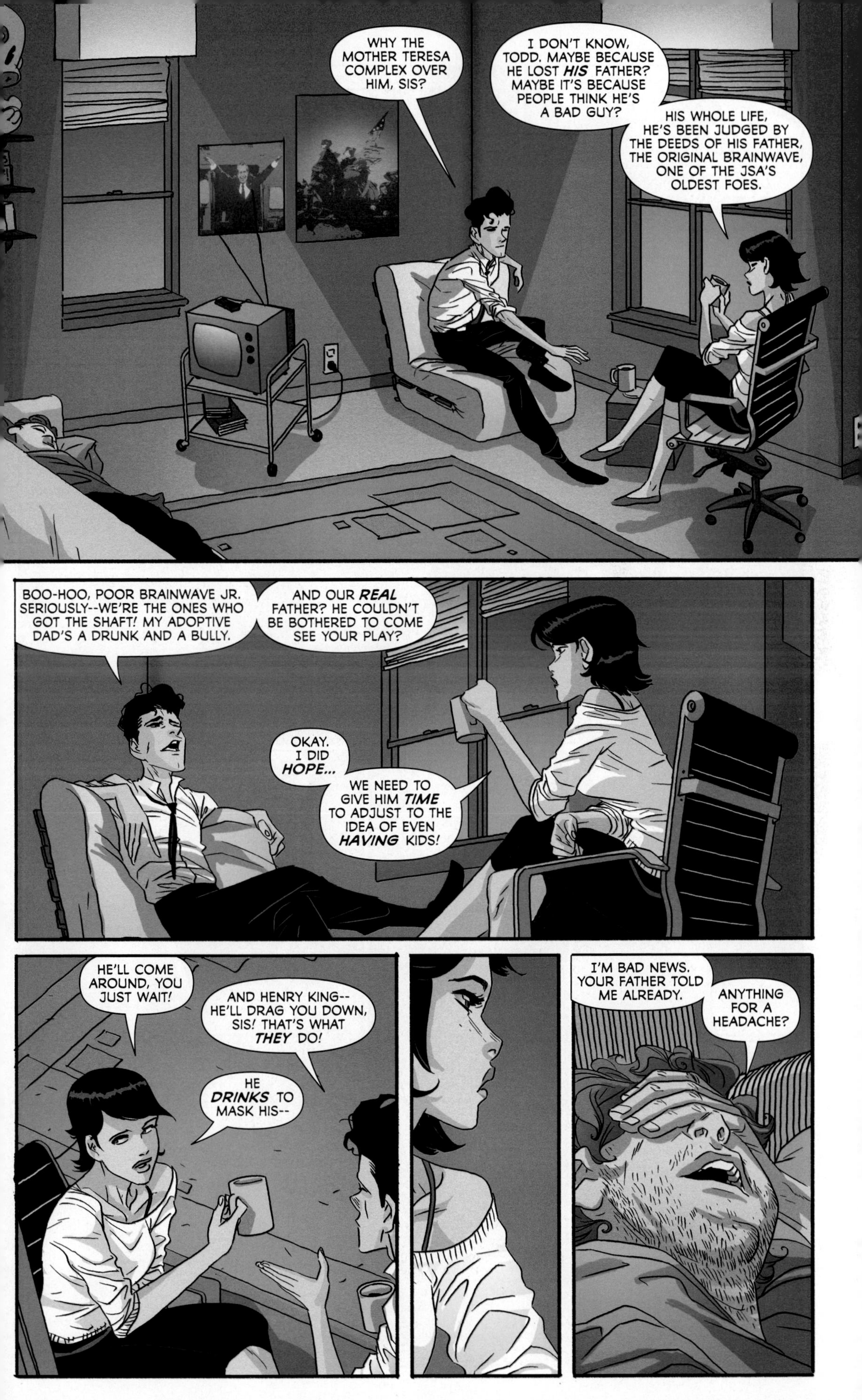
WHY THE MOTHER TERESA COMPLEX OVER HIM, SIS?
I DON'T KNOW, TODD. MAYBE BECAUSE HE LOST HIS FATHER? MAYBE IT'S BECAUSE PEOPLE THINK HE'S A BAD GUY?
HIS WHOLE LIFE, HE'S BEEN JUDGED BY THE DEEDS OF HIS FATHER, THE ORIGINAL BRAINWAVE, ONE OF THE JSA'S OLDEST FOES.
BOO-HOO, POOR BRAINWAVE JR. SERIOUSLY--WE'RE THE ONES WHO GOT THE SHAFT! MY ADOPTIVE DAD'S A DRUNK AND A BULLY.
AND OUR REAL FATHER? HE COULDN'T BE BOTHERED TO COME SEE YOUR PLAY?
OKAY. I DID HOPE...
WE NEED TO GIVE HIM TIME TO ADJUST TO THE IDEA OF EVEN HAVING KIDS!
HE'LL COME AROUND, YOU JUST WAIT!
AND HENRY KING-- HE'LL DRAG YOU DOWN, SIS! THAT'S WHAT THEY DO!
HE DRINKS TO MASK HIS--
I'M BAD NEWS. YOUR FATHER TOLD ME ALREADY.
ANYTHING FOR A HEADACHE?

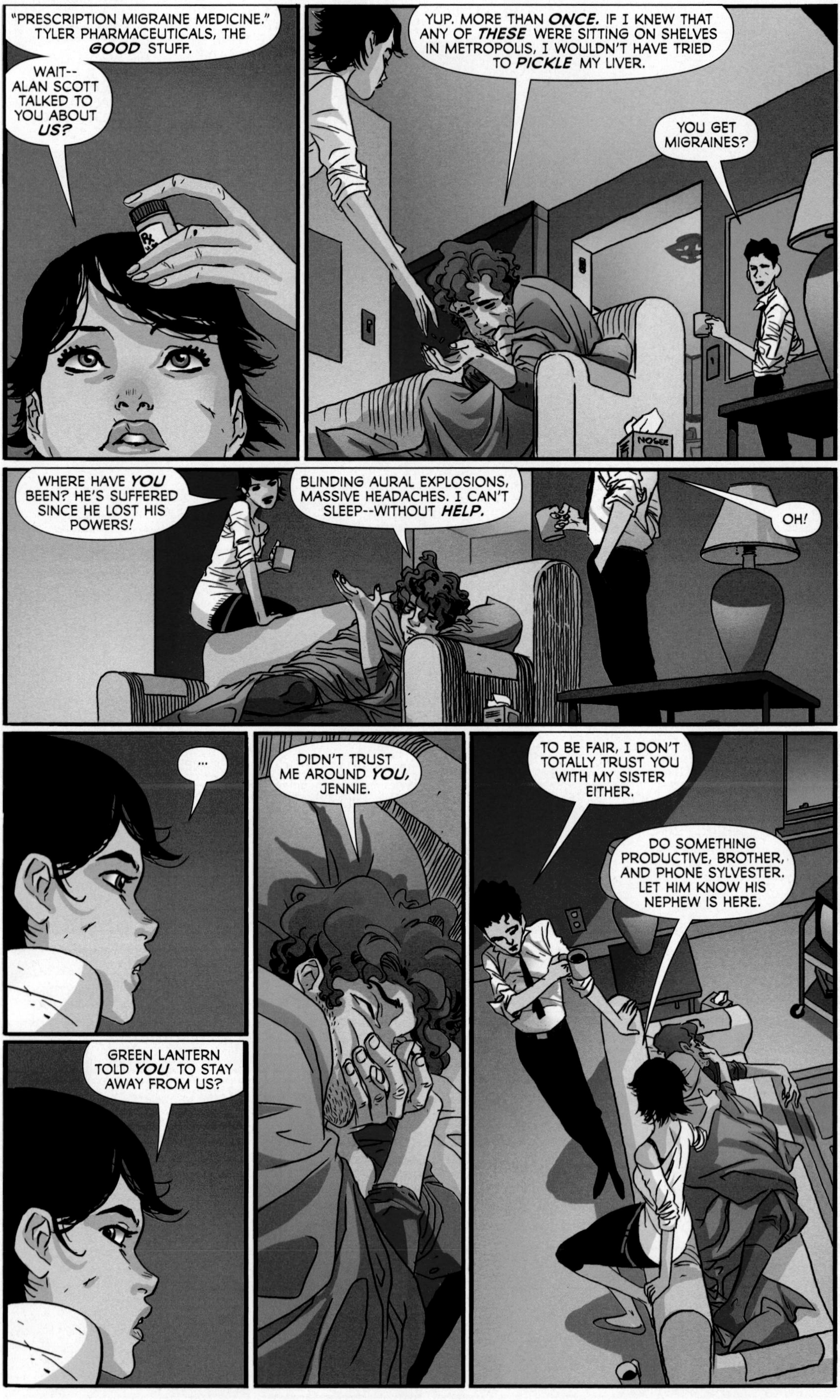
"PRESCRIPTION MIGRAINE MEDICINE." TYLER PHARMACEUTICALS, THE *GOOD* STUFF.
WAIT-- ALAN SCOTT TALKED TO YOU ABOUT *US?*
YUP. MORE THAN *ONCE.* IF I KNEW THAT ANY OF *THESE* WERE SITTING ON SHELVES IN METROPOLIS, I WOULDN'T HAVE TRIED TO *PICKLE* MY LIVER.
YOU GET MIGRAINES?
NOSEE
WHERE HAVE *YOU* BEEN? HE'S SUFFERED SINCE HE LOST HIS POWERS!
BLINDING AURAL EXPLOSIONS, MASSIVE HEADACHES. I CAN'T SLEEP--WITHOUT *HELP.*
OH!
...
GREEN LANTERN TOLD *YOU* TO STAY AWAY FROM US?
DIDN'T TRUST ME AROUND *YOU,* JENNIE.
TO BE FAIR, I DON'T TOTALLY TRUST YOU WITH MY SISTER EITHER.
DO SOMETHING PRODUCTIVE, BROTHER, AND PHONE SYLVESTER. LET HIM KNOW HIS NEPHEW IS HERE.

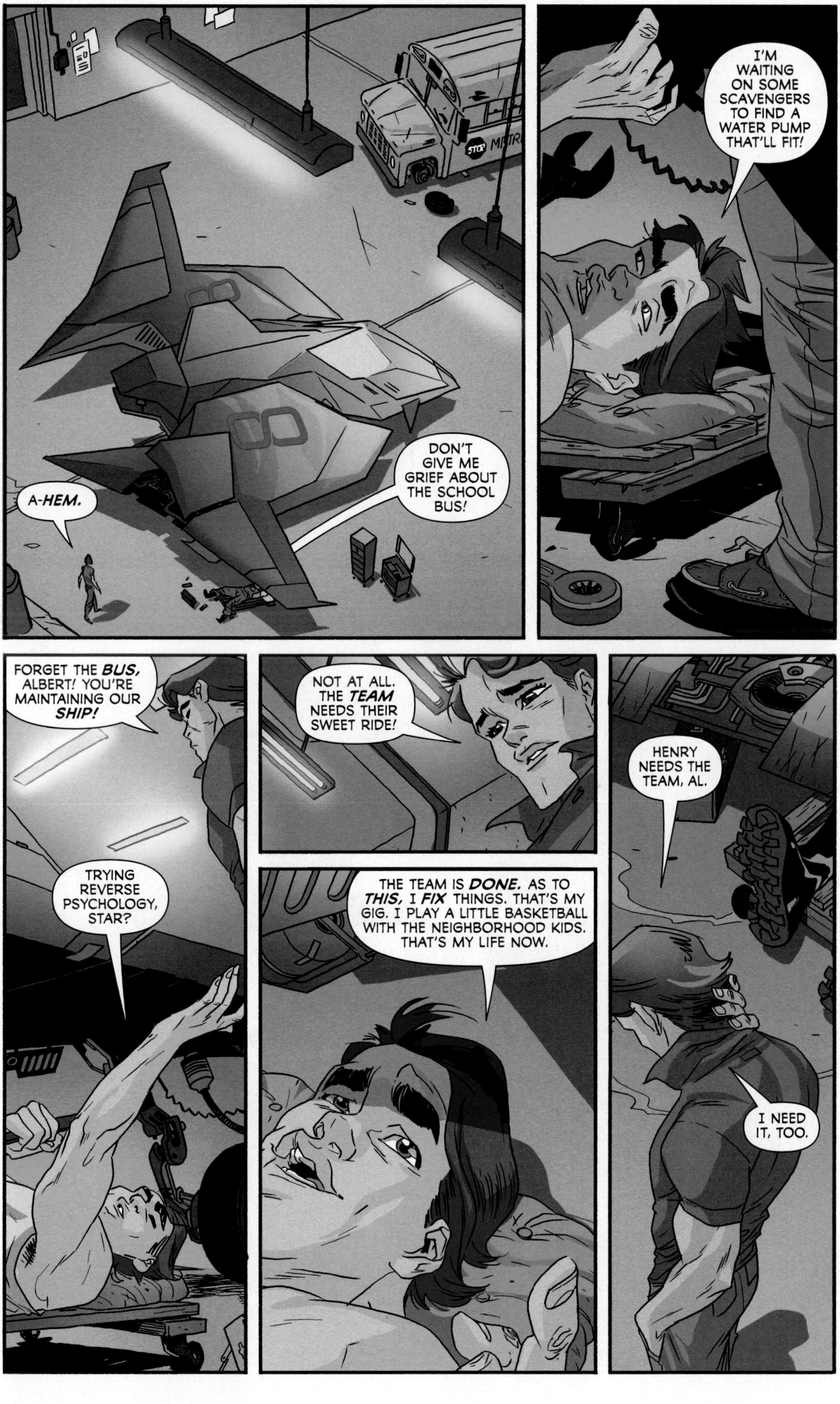
A-*HEM.*
DON'T GIVE ME GRIEF ABOUT THE SCHOOL BUS!
I'M WAITING ON SOME SCAVENGERS TO FIND A WATER PUMP THAT'LL FIT!
FORGET THE *BUS,* ALBERT! YOU'RE MAINTAINING OUR *SHIP!*
TRYING REVERSE PSYCHOLOGY, STAR?
NOT AT ALL. THE *TEAM* NEEDS THEIR SWEET RIDE!
THE TEAM IS *DONE.* AS TO *THIS,* I *FIX* THINGS. THAT'S MY GIG. I PLAY A LITTLE BASKETBALL WITH THE NEIGHBORHOOD KIDS. THAT'S MY LIFE NOW.
HENRY NEEDS THE TEAM, AL.
I NEED IT, TOO.

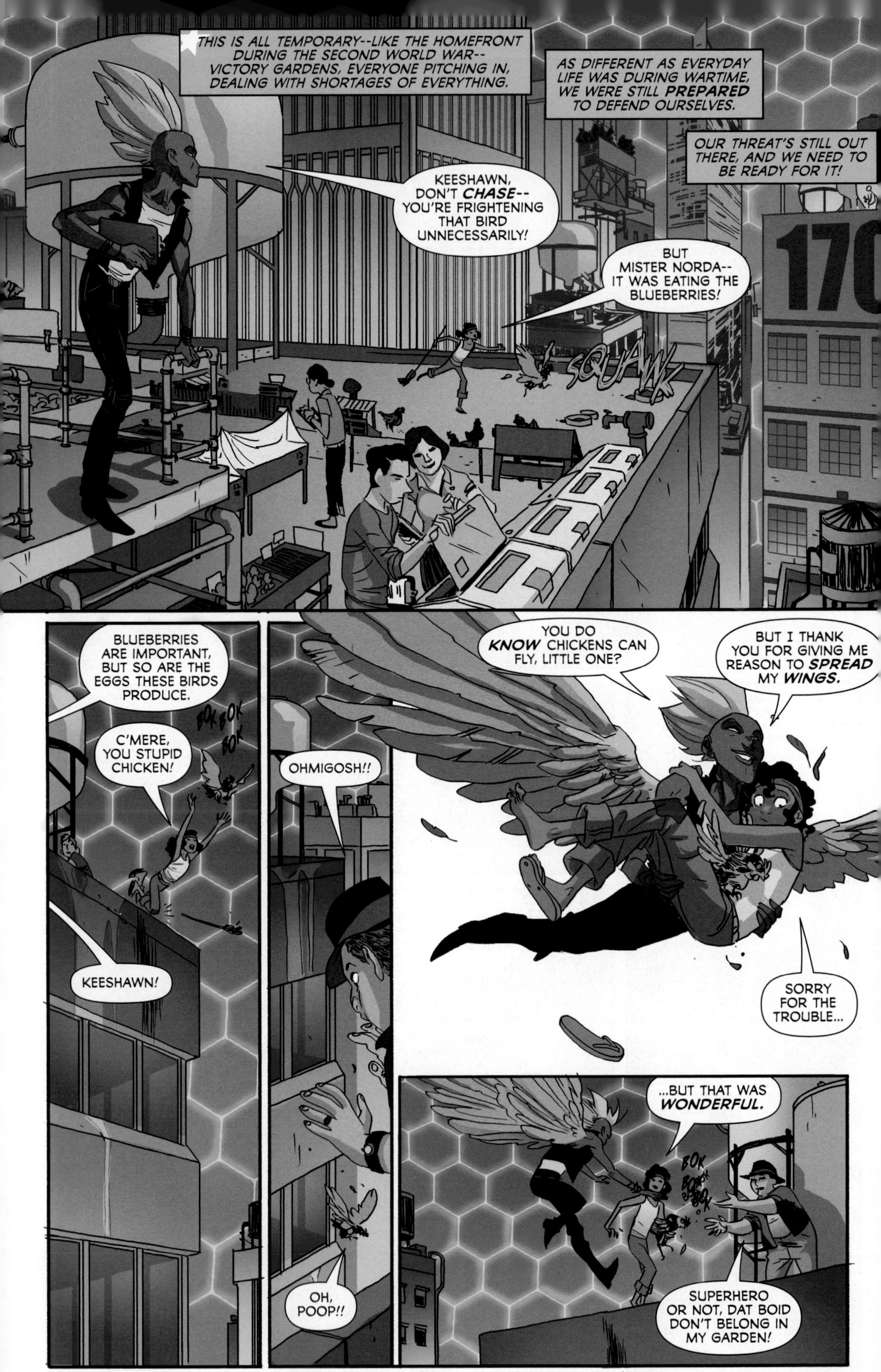
THIS IS ALL TEMPORARY--LIKE THE HOMEFRONT DURING THE SECOND WORLD WAR-- VICTORY GARDENS, EVERYONE PITCHING IN, DEALING WITH SHORTAGES OF EVERYTHING.
AS DIFFERENT AS EVERYDAY LIFE WAS DURING WARTIME, WE WERE STILL PREPARED TO DEFEND OURSELVES.
OUR THREAT'S STILL OUT THERE, AND WE NEED TO BE READY FOR IT!
KEESHAWN, DON'T CHASE-- YOU'RE FRIGHTENING THAT BIRD UNNECESSARILY!
BUT MISTER NORDA-- IT WAS EATING THE BLUEBERRIES!
SQUAWK
170
BLUEBERRIES ARE IMPORTANT, BUT SO ARE THE EGGS THESE BIRDS PRODUCE.
BOK BOK BOK
C'MERE, YOU STUPID CHICKEN!
KEESHAWN!
OHMIGOSH!!
OH, POOP!!
YOU DO KNOW CHICKENS CAN FLY, LITTLE ONE?
BUT I THANK YOU FOR GIVING ME REASON TO SPREAD MY WINGS.
SORRY FOR THE TROUBLE...
...BUT THAT WAS WONDERFUL.
SUPERHERO OR NOT, DAT BOID DON'T BELONG IN MY GARDEN!

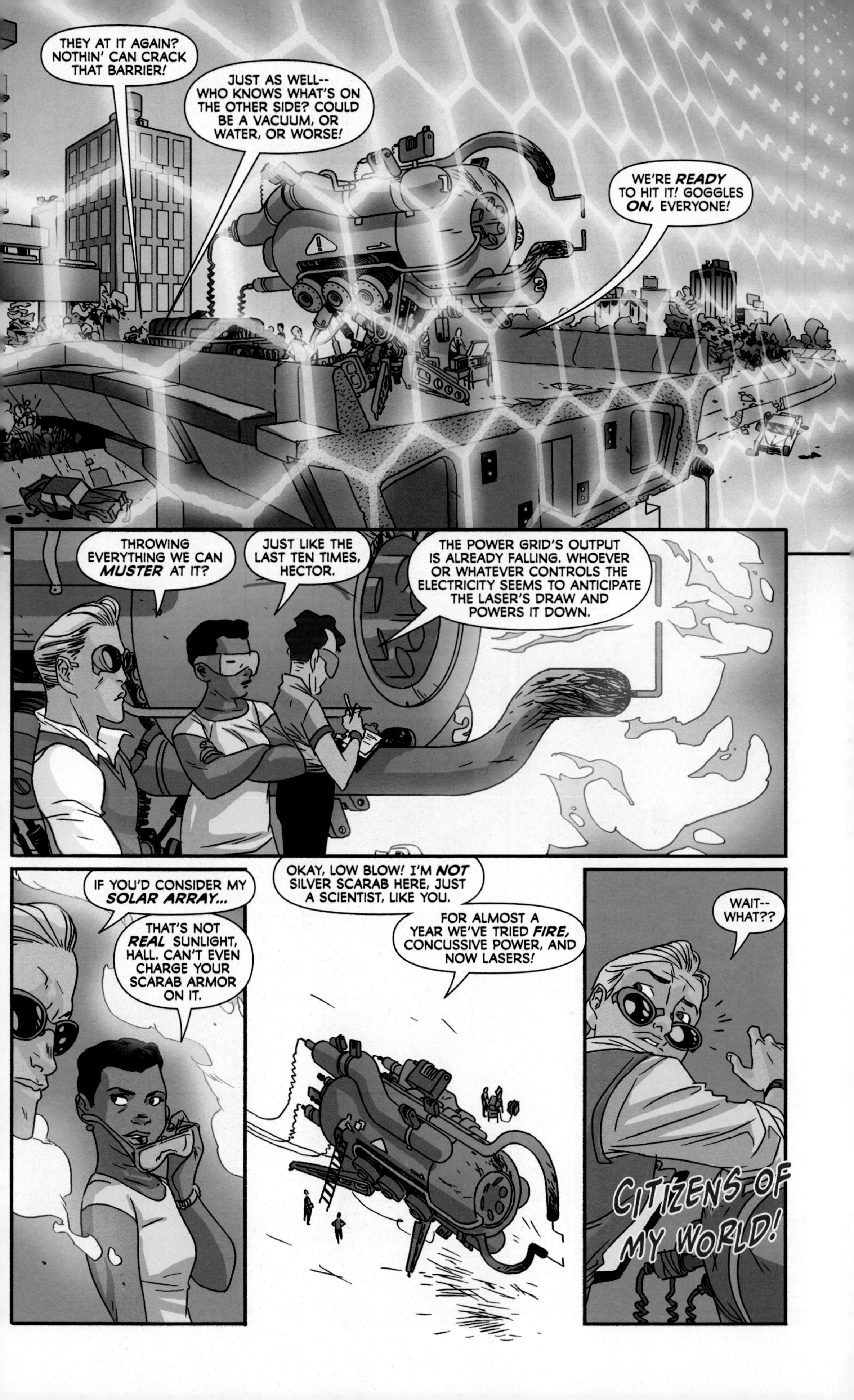
THEY AT IT AGAIN? NOTHIN' CAN CRACK THAT BARRIER!
JUST AS WELL-- WHO KNOWS WHAT'S ON THE OTHER SIDE? COULD BE A VACUUM, OR WATER, OR WORSE!
WE'RE READY TO HIT IT! GOGGLES ON, EVERYONE!
THROWING EVERYTHING WE CAN MUSTER AT IT?
JUST LIKE THE LAST TEN TIMES, HECTOR.
THE POWER GRID'S OUTPUT IS ALREADY FALLING. WHOEVER OR WHATEVER CONTROLS THE ELECTRICITY SEEMS TO ANTICIPATE THE LASER'S DRAW AND POWERS IT DOWN.
IF YOU'D CONSIDER MY SOLAR ARRAY...
THAT'S NOT REAL SUNLIGHT, HALL. CAN'T EVEN CHARGE YOUR SCARAB ARMOR ON IT.
OKAY, LOW BLOW! I'M NOT SILVER SCARAB HERE, JUST A SCIENTIST, LIKE YOU.
FOR ALMOST A YEAR WE'VE TRIED FIRE, CONCUSSIVE POWER, AND NOW LASERS!
WAIT-- WHAT??
CITIZENS OF MY WORLD!

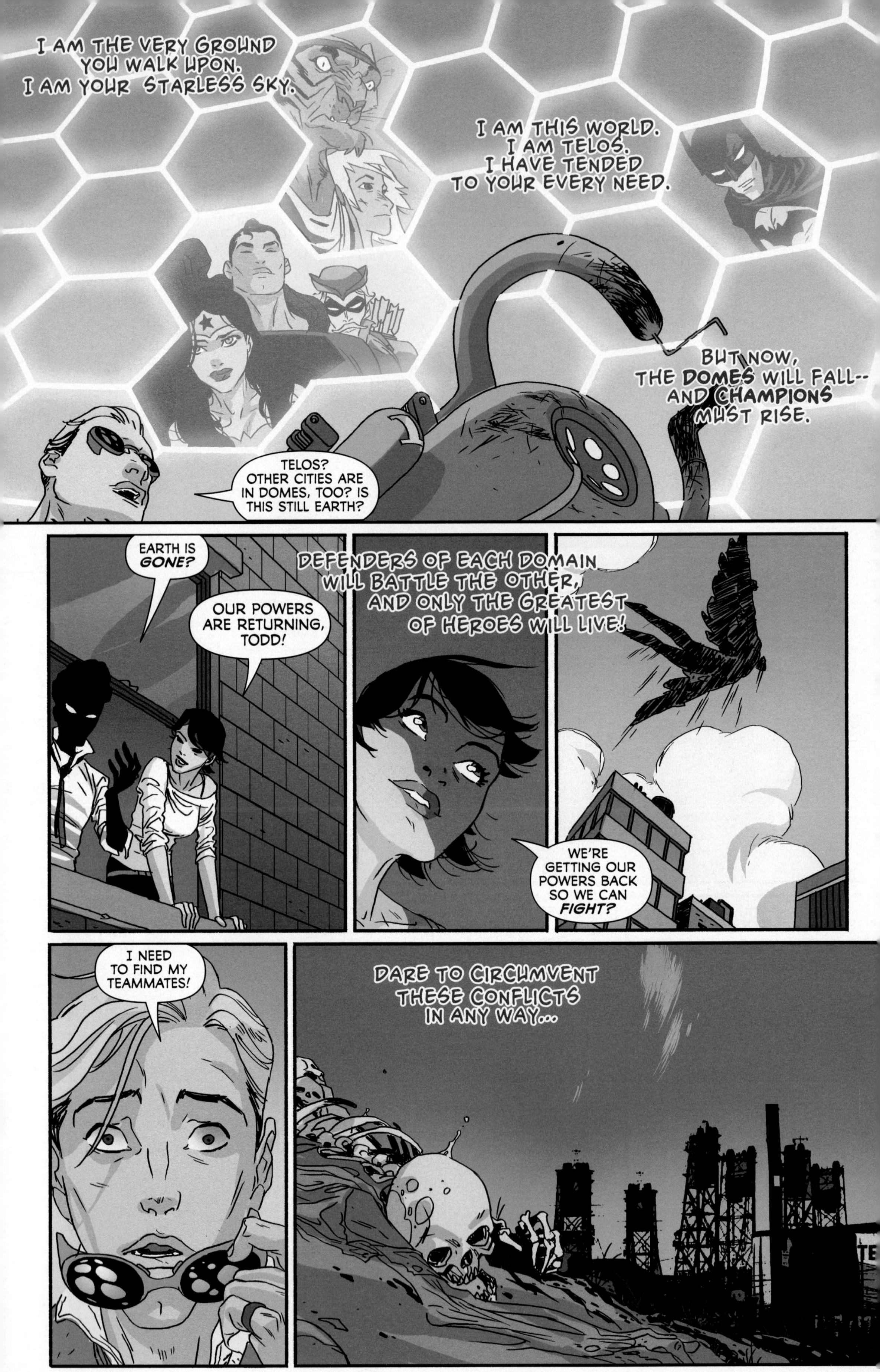

I AM THE VERY GROUND YOU WALK UPON. I AM YOUR STARLESS SKY.
I AM THIS WORLD. I AM TELOS. I HAVE TENDED TO YOUR EVERY NEED.
BUT NOW, THE DOMES WILL FALL-- AND CHAMPIONS MUST RISE.
TELOS? OTHER CITIES ARE IN DOMES, TOO? IS THIS STILL EARTH?
EARTH IS GONE?
OUR POWERS ARE RETURNING, TODD!
DEFENDERS OF EACH DOMAIN WILL BATTLE THE OTHER, AND ONLY THE GREATEST OF HEROES WILL LIVE!
WE'RE GETTING OUR POWERS BACK SO WE CAN FIGHT?
I NEED TO FIND MY TEAMMATES!
DARE TO CIRCUMVENT THESE CONFLICTS IN ANY WAY...

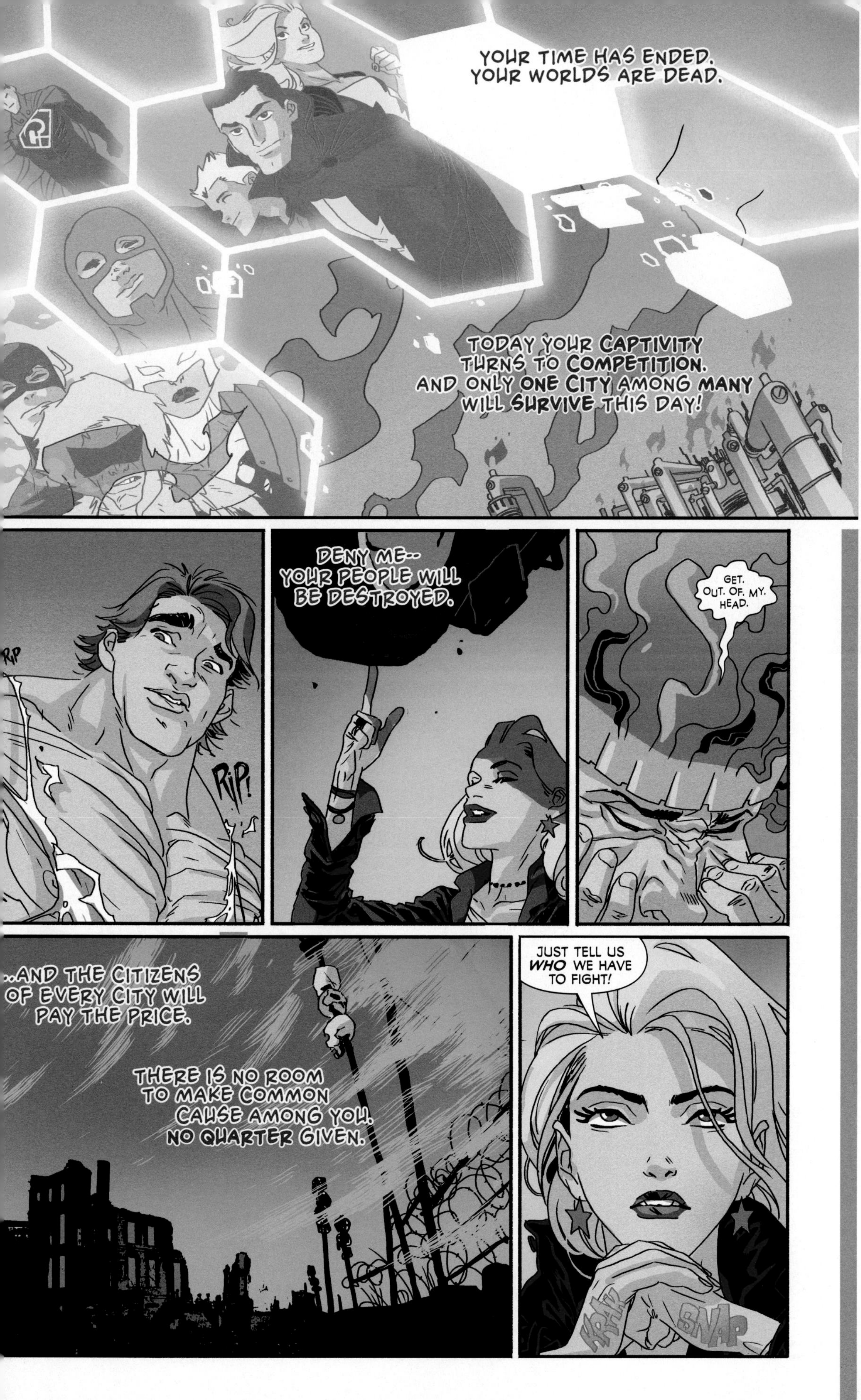
YOUR TIME HAS ENDED. YOUR WORLDS ARE DEAD.
TODAY YOUR CAPTIVITY TURNS TO COMPETITION. AND ONLY ONE CITY AMONG MANY WILL SURVIVE THIS DAY!
RIP
RIP!
DENY ME-- YOUR PEOPLE WILL BE DESTROYED.
GET. OUT. OF. MY. HEAD.
..AND THE CITIZENS OF EVERY CITY WILL PAY THE PRICE.
THERE IS NO ROOM TO MAKE COMMON CAUSE AMONG YOU. NO QUARTER GIVEN.
JUST TELL US *WHO* WE HAVE TO FIGHT!
KRAK
SNAP

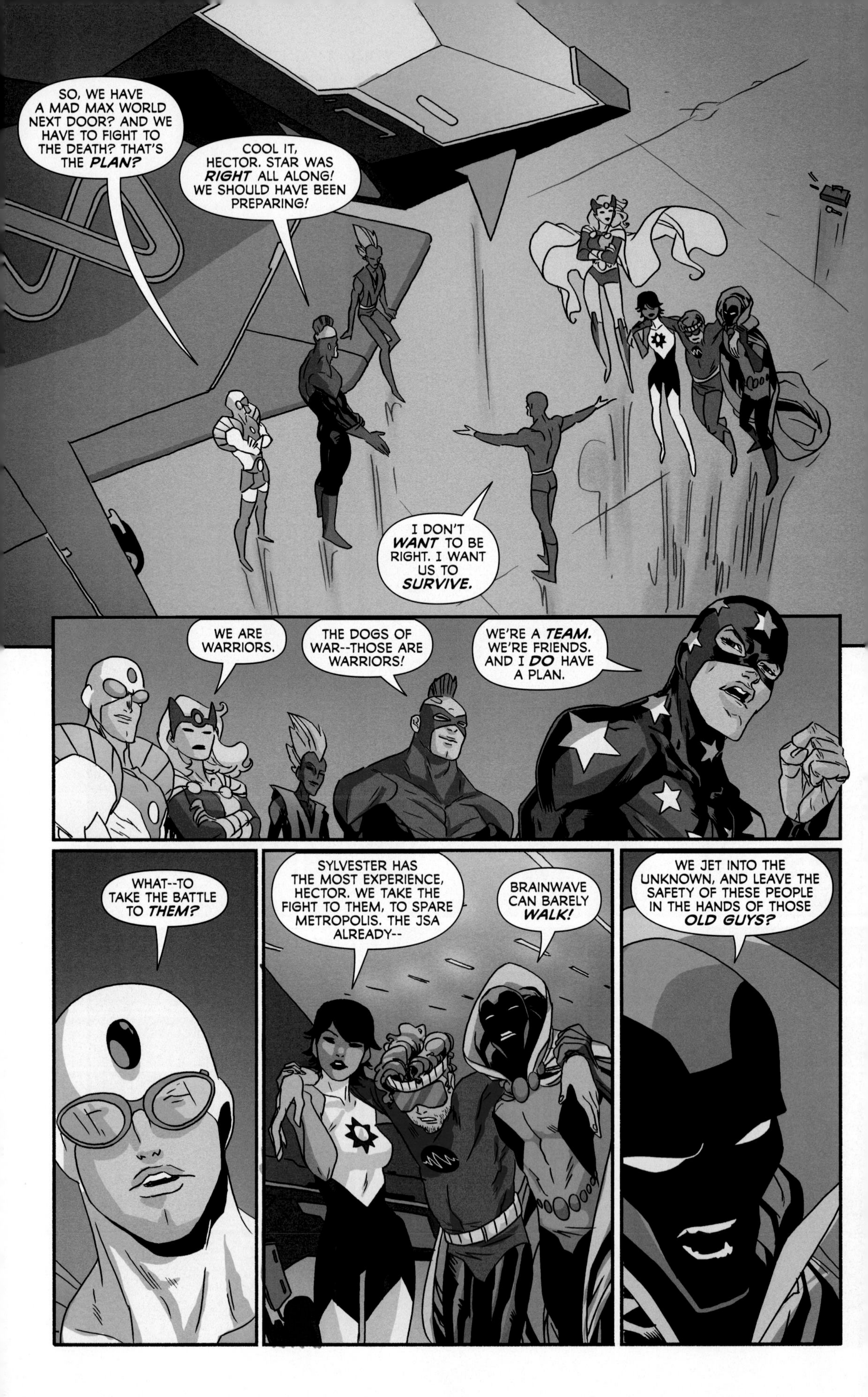
SO, WE HAVE A MAD MAX WORLD NEXT DOOR? AND WE HAVE TO FIGHT TO THE DEATH? THAT'S THE PLAN?
COOL IT, HECTOR. STAR WAS RIGHT ALL ALONG! WE SHOULD HAVE BEEN PREPARING!
I DON'T WANT TO BE RIGHT. I WANT US TO SURVIVE.
WE ARE WARRIORS.
THE DOGS OF WAR--THOSE ARE WARRIORS!
WE'RE A TEAM. WE'RE FRIENDS. AND I DO HAVE A PLAN.
WHAT--TO TAKE THE BATTLE TO THEM?
SYLVESTER HAS THE MOST EXPERIENCE, HECTOR. WE TAKE THE FIGHT TO THEM, TO SPARE METROPOLIS. THE JSA ALREADY--
BRAINWAVE CAN BARELY WALK!
WE JET INTO THE UNKNOWN, AND LEAVE THE SAFETY OF THESE PEOPLE IN THE HANDS OF THOSE OLD GUYS?

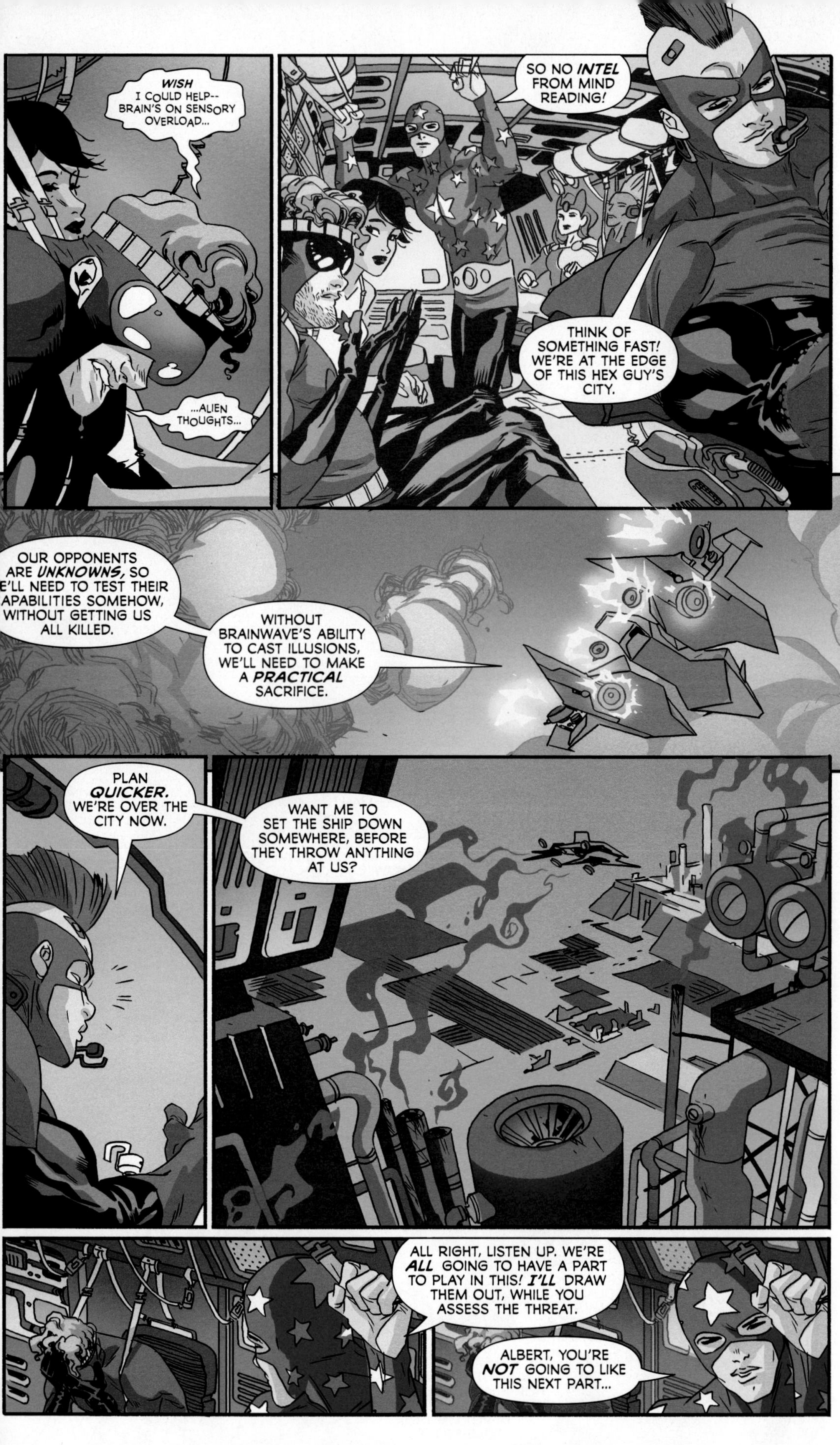
WISH I COULD HELP-- BRAIN'S ON SENSORY OVERLOAD...
...ALIEN THOUGHTS...
SO NO INTEL FROM MIND READING!
THINK OF SOMETHING FAST! WE'RE AT THE EDGE OF THIS HEX GUY'S CITY.
OUR OPPONENTS ARE UNKNOWNS, SO E'LL NEED TO TEST THEIR APABILITIES SOMEHOW, WITHOUT GETTING US ALL KILLED.
WITHOUT BRAINWAVE'S ABILITY TO CAST ILLUSIONS, WE'LL NEED TO MAKE A PRACTICAL SACRIFICE.
PLAN QUICKER. WE'RE OVER THE CITY NOW.
WANT ME TO SET THE SHIP DOWN SOMEWHERE, BEFORE THEY THROW ANYTHING AT US?
ALL RIGHT, LISTEN UP. WE'RE ALL GOING TO HAVE A PART TO PLAY IN THIS! I'LL DRAW THEM OUT, WHILE YOU ASSESS THE THREAT.
ALBERT, YOU'RE NOT GOING TO LIKE THIS NEXT PART...

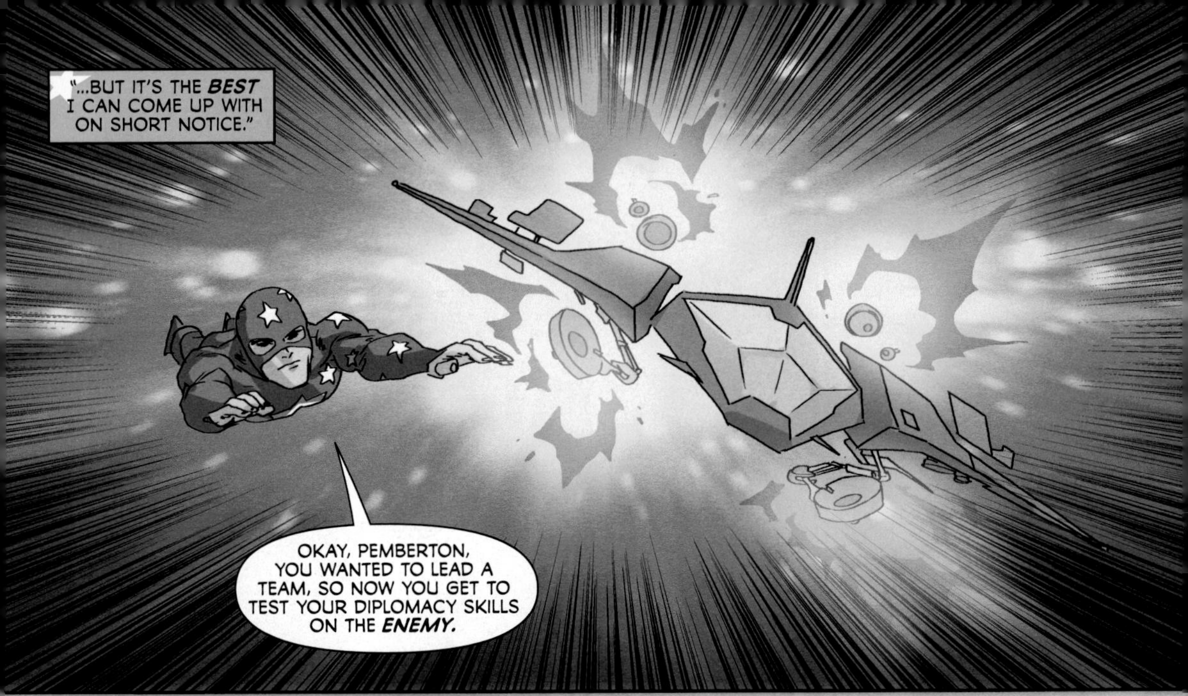
"...BUT IT'S THE BEST I CAN COME UP WITH ON SHORT NOTICE."
OKAY, PEMBERTON, YOU WANTED TO LEAD A TEAM, SO NOW YOU GET TO TEST YOUR DIPLOMACY SKILLS ON THE ENEMY.

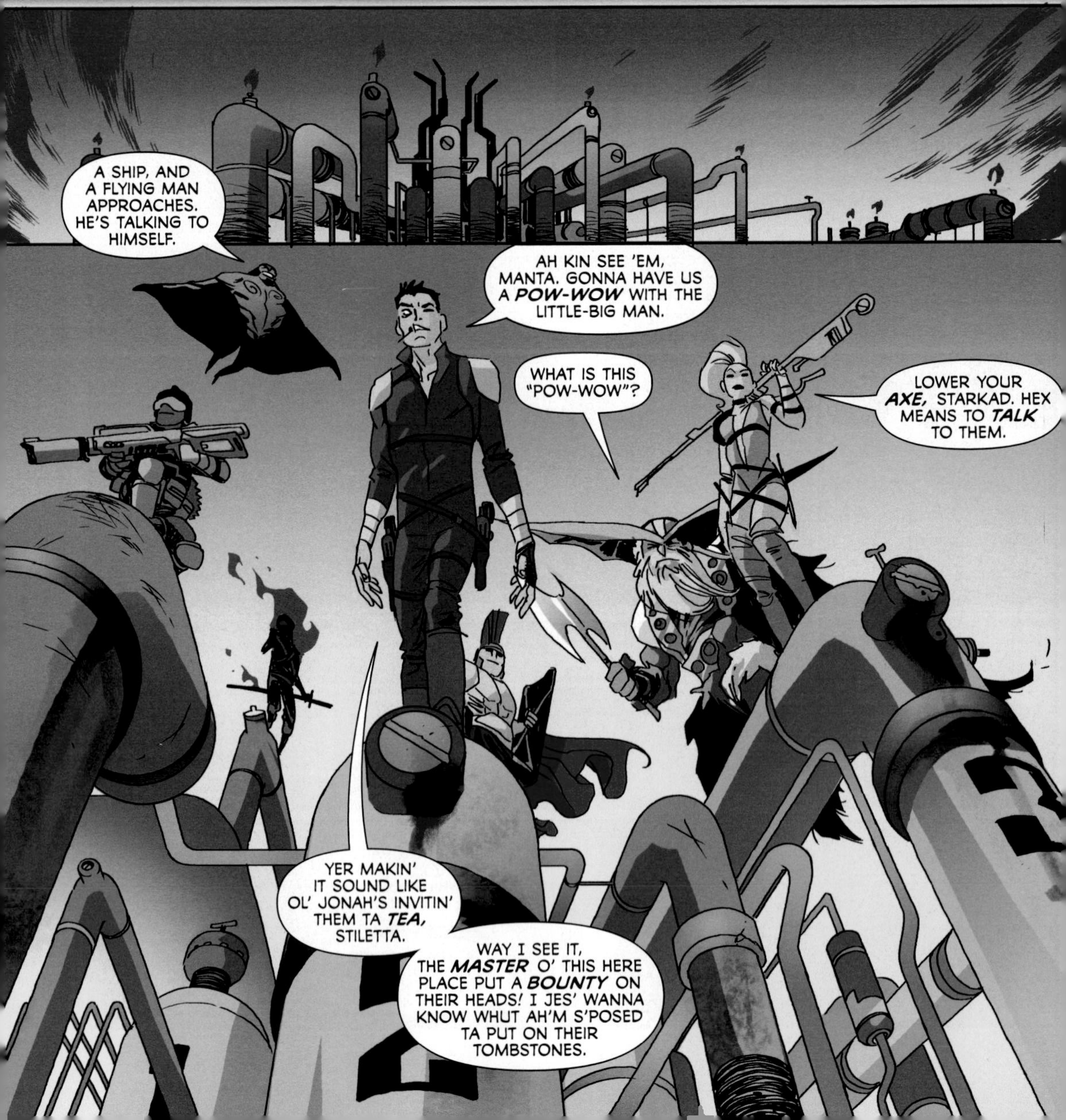
A SHIP, AND A FLYING MAN APPROACHES. HE'S TALKING TO HIMSELF.
AH KIN SEE 'EM, MANTA. GONNA HAVE US A POW-WOW WITH THE LITTLE-BIG MAN.
WHAT IS THIS "POW-WOW"?
LOWER YOUR AXE, STARKAD. HEX MEANS TO TALK TO THEM.
YER MAKIN' IT SOUND LIKE OL' JONAH'S INVITIN' THEM TA TEA, STILETTA.
WAY I SEE IT, THE MASTER O' THIS HERE PLACE PUT A BOUNTY ON THEIR HEADS! I JES' WANNA KNOW WHUT AH'M S'POSED TA PUT ON THEIR TOMBSTONES.

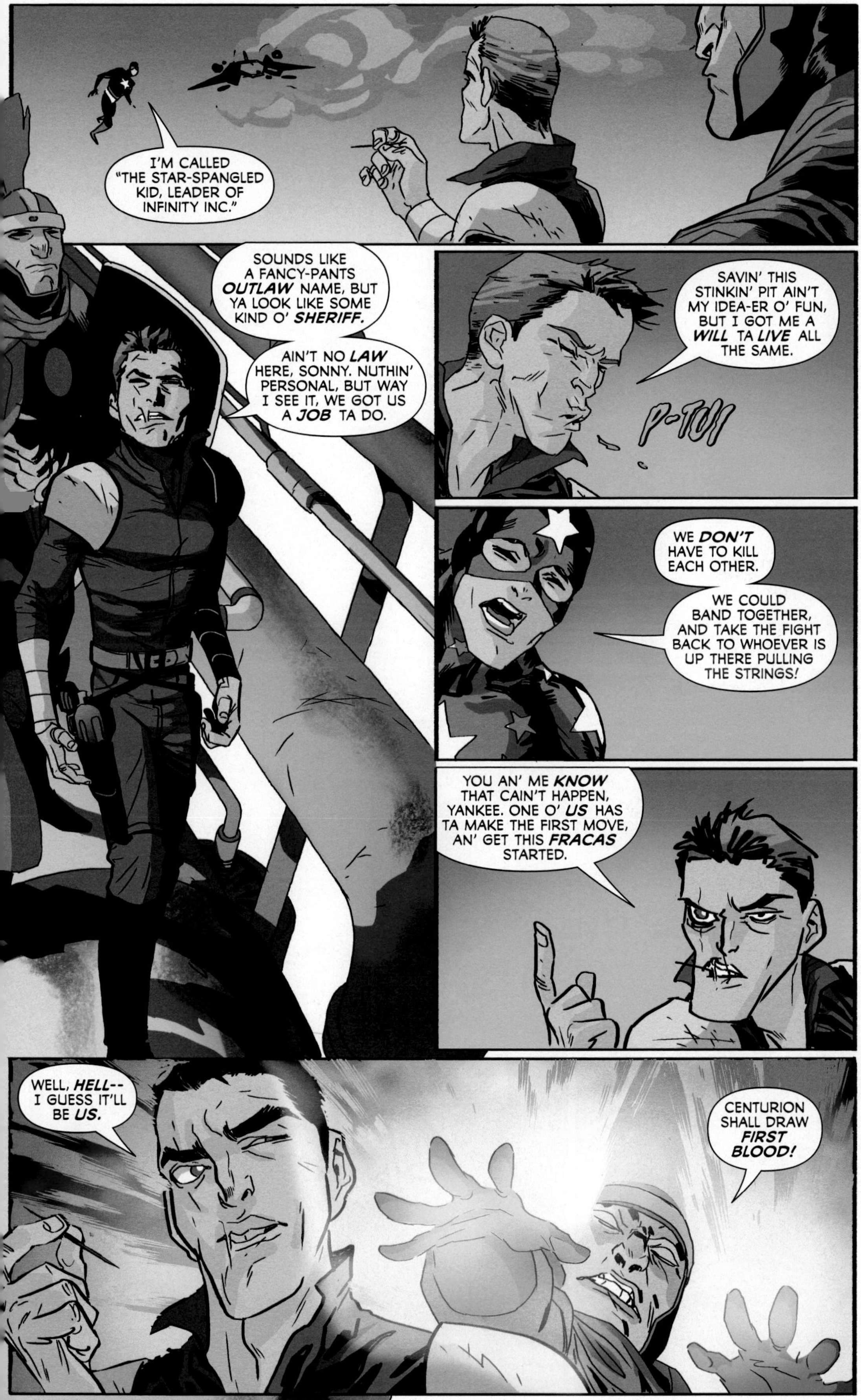

I'M CALLED "THE STAR-SPANGLED KID, LEADER OF INFINITY INC."
SOUNDS LIKE A FANCY-PANTS OUTLAW NAME, BUT YA LOOK LIKE SOME KIND O' SHERIFF.
AIN'T NO LAW HERE, SONNY. NUTHIN' PERSONAL, BUT WAY I SEE IT, WE GOT US A JOB TA DO.
SAVIN' THIS STINKIN' PIT AIN'T MY IDEA-ER O' FUN, BUT I GOT ME A WILL TA LIVE ALL THE SAME.
P-TOI
WE DON'T HAVE TO KILL EACH OTHER.
WE COULD BAND TOGETHER, AND TAKE THE FIGHT BACK TO WHOEVER IS UP THERE PULLING THE STRINGS!
YOU AN' ME KNOW THAT CAIN'T HAPPEN, YANKEE. ONE O' US HAS TA MAKE THE FIRST MOVE, AN' GET THIS FRACAS STARTED.
WELL, HELL-- I GUESS IT'LL BE US.
CENTURION SHALL DRAW FIRST BLOOD!

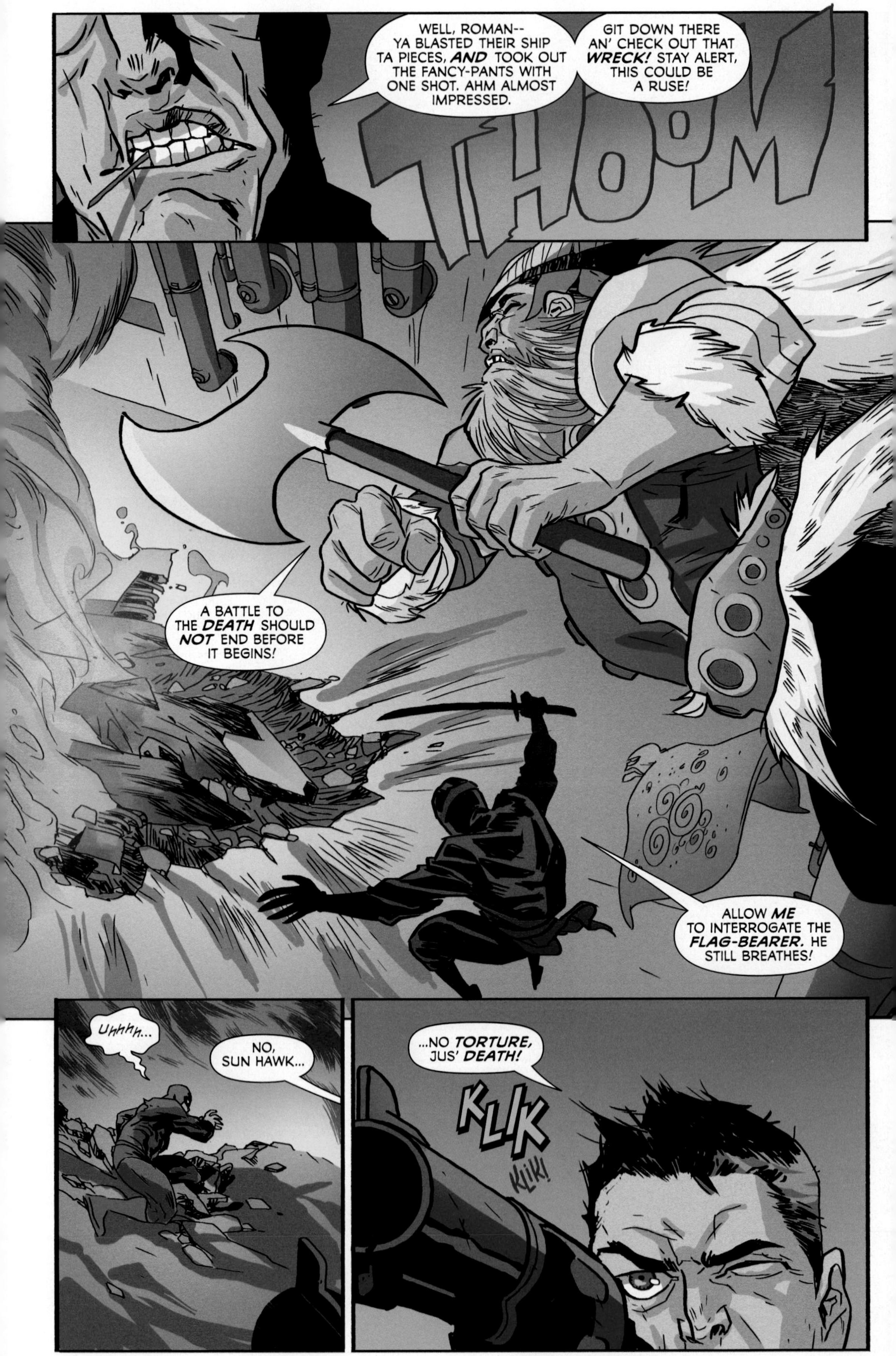
WELL, ROMAN-- YA BLASTED THEIR SHIP TA PIECES, AND TOOK OUT THE FANCY-PANTS WITH ONE SHOT. AHM ALMOST IMPRESSED.
GIT DOWN THERE AN' CHECK OUT THAT WRECK! STAY ALERT, THIS COULD BE A RUSE!
THOOM
A BATTLE TO THE DEATH SHOULD NOT END BEFORE IT BEGINS!
ALLOW ME TO INTERROGATE THE FLAG-BEARER. HE STILL BREATHES!
Uhhhh...
NO, SUN HAWK...
...NO TORTURE, JUS' DEATH!
KLIK
KLIK!

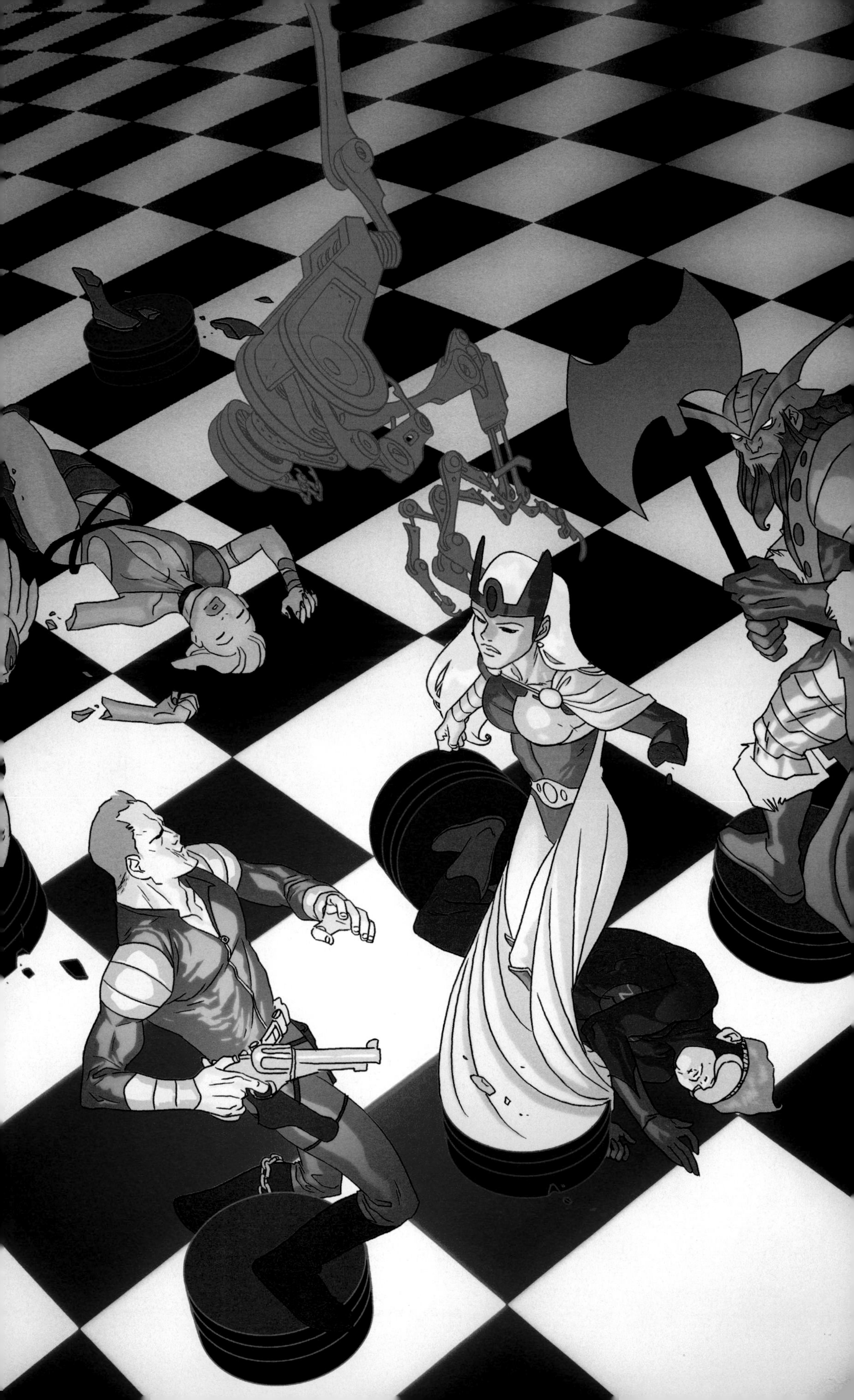

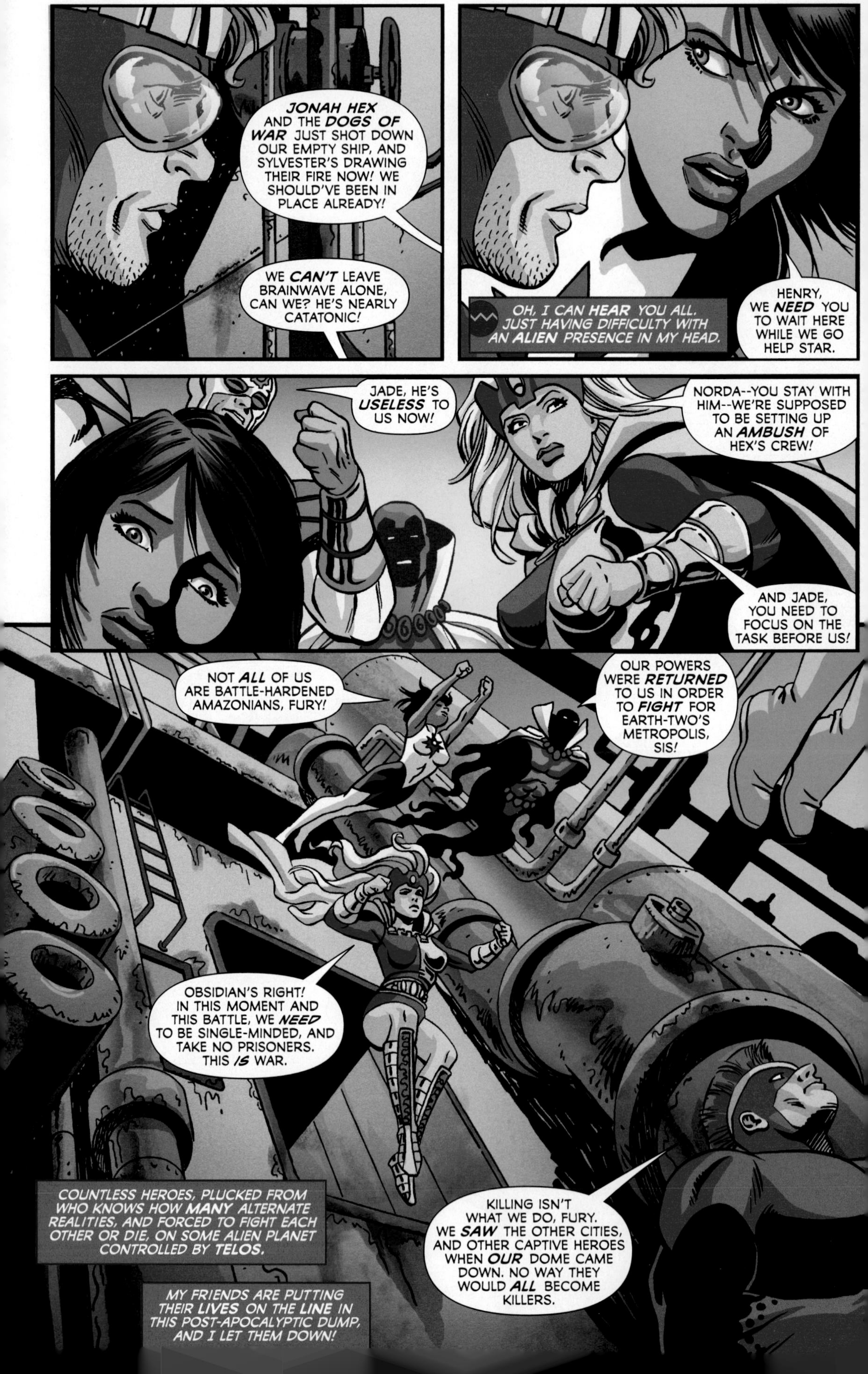
JONAH HEX AND THE DOGS OF WAR JUST SHOT DOWN OUR EMPTY SHIP, AND SYLVESTER'S DRAWING THEIR FIRE NOW! WE SHOULD'VE BEEN IN PLACE ALREADY!
WE CAN'T LEAVE BRAINWAVE ALONE, CAN WE? HE'S NEARLY CATATONIC!
OH, I CAN HEAR YOU ALL. JUST HAVING DIFFICULTY WITH AN ALIEN PRESENCE IN MY HEAD.
HENRY, WE NEED YOU TO WAIT HERE WHILE WE GO HELP STAR.
JADE, HE'S USELESS TO US NOW!
NORDA--YOU STAY WITH HIM--WE'RE SUPPOSED TO BE SETTING UP AN AMBUSH OF HEX'S CREW!
AND JADE, YOU NEED TO FOCUS ON THE TASK BEFORE US!
NOT ALL OF US ARE BATTLE-HARDENED AMAZONIANS, FURY!
OUR POWERS WERE RETURNED TO US IN ORDER TO FIGHT FOR EARTH-TWO'S METROPOLIS, SIS!
OBSIDIAN'S RIGHT! IN THIS MOMENT AND THIS BATTLE, WE NEED TO BE SINGLE-MINDED, AND TAKE NO PRISONERS. THIS IS WAR.
COUNTLESS HEROES, PLUCKED FROM WHO KNOWS HOW MANY ALTERNATE REALITIES, AND FORCED TO FIGHT EACH OTHER OR DIE, ON SOME ALIEN PLANET CONTROLLED BY TELOS.
MY FRIENDS ARE PUTTING THEIR LIVES ON THE LINE IN THIS POST-APOCALYPTIC DUMP, AND I LET THEM DOWN!
KILLING ISN'T WHAT WE DO, FURY. WE SAW THE OTHER CITIES, AND OTHER CAPTIVE HEROES WHEN OUR DOME CAME DOWN. NO WAY THEY WOULD ALL BECOME KILLERS.

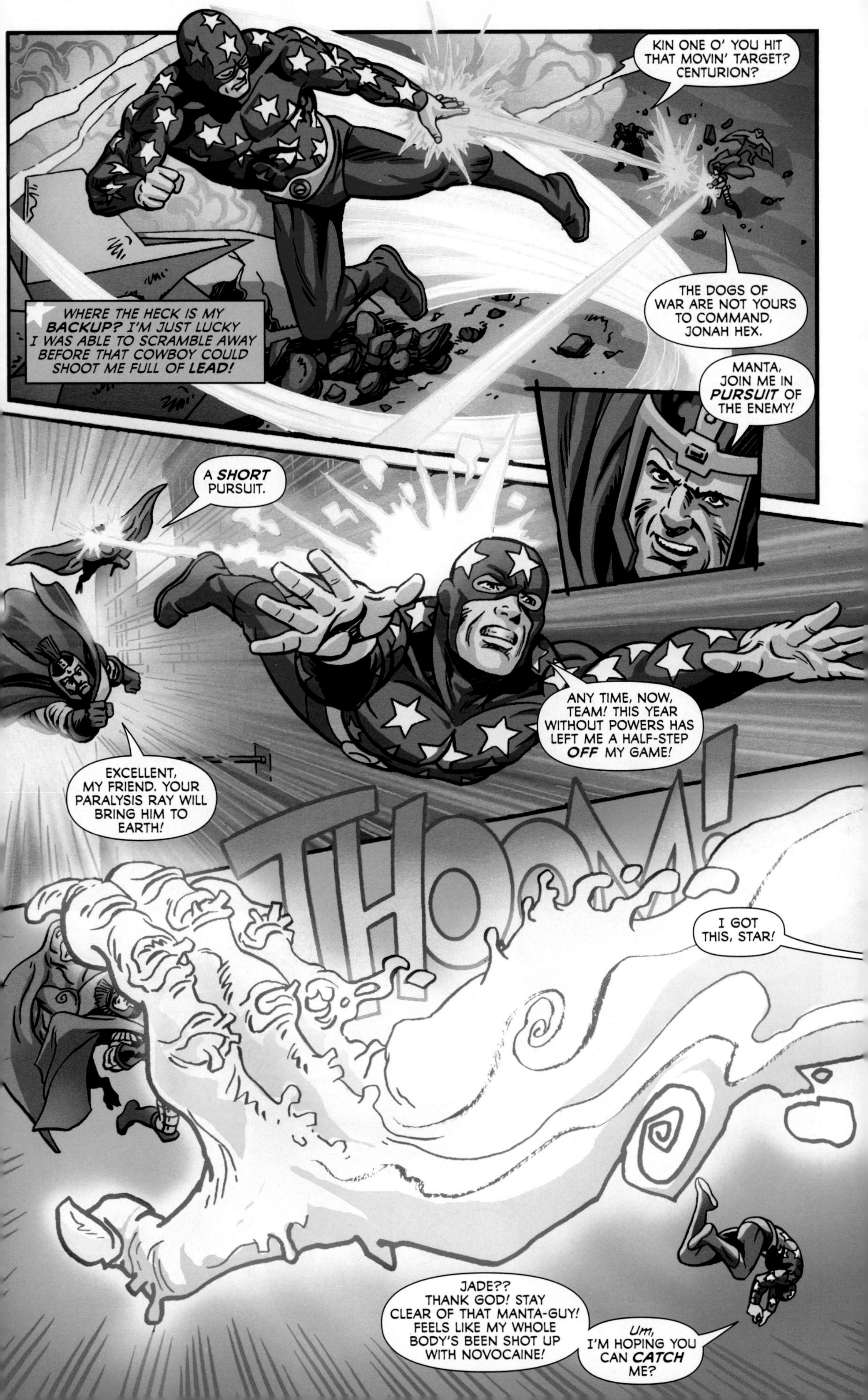
KIN ONE O' YOU HIT THAT MOVIN' TARGET? CENTURION?
WHERE THE HECK IS MY BACKUP? I'M JUST LUCKY I WAS ABLE TO SCRAMBLE AWAY BEFORE THAT COWBOY COULD SHOOT ME FULL OF LEAD!
THE DOGS OF WAR ARE NOT YOURS TO COMMAND, JONAH HEX.
MANTA, JOIN ME IN PURSUIT OF THE ENEMY!
A SHORT PURSUIT.
ANY TIME, NOW, TEAM! THIS YEAR WITHOUT POWERS HAS LEFT ME A HALF-STEP OFF MY GAME!
EXCELLENT, MY FRIEND. YOUR PARALYSIS RAY WILL BRING HIM TO EARTH!
THOOM!
I GOT THIS, STAR!
JADE?? THANK GOD! STAY CLEAR OF THAT MANTA-GUY! FEELS LIKE MY WHOLE BODY'S BEEN SHOT UP WITH NOVOCAINE!
Um, I'M HOPING YOU CAN CATCH ME?

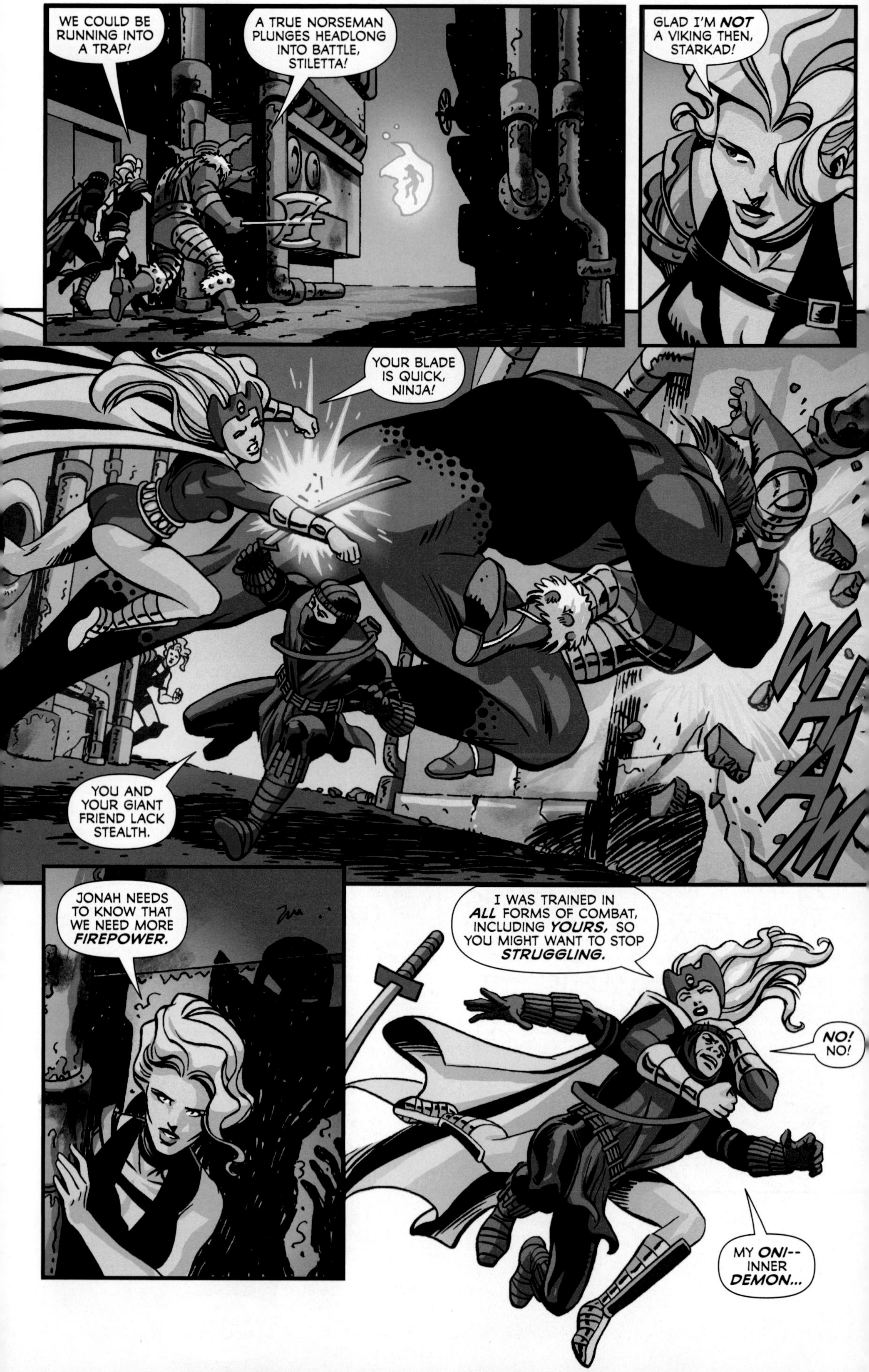
WE COULD BE RUNNING INTO A TRAP!
A TRUE NORSEMAN PLUNGES HEADLONG INTO BATTLE, STILETTA!
GLAD I'M **NOT** A VIKING THEN, STARKAD!
YOUR BLADE IS QUICK, NINJA!
YOU AND YOUR GIANT FRIEND LACK STEALTH.
WHAM
JONAH NEEDS TO KNOW THAT WE NEED MORE **FIREPOWER.**
I WAS TRAINED IN **ALL** FORMS OF COMBAT, INCLUDING **YOURS,** SO YOU MIGHT WANT TO STOP **STRUGGLING.**
NO! NO!
MY **ONI**-- INNER **DEMON...**

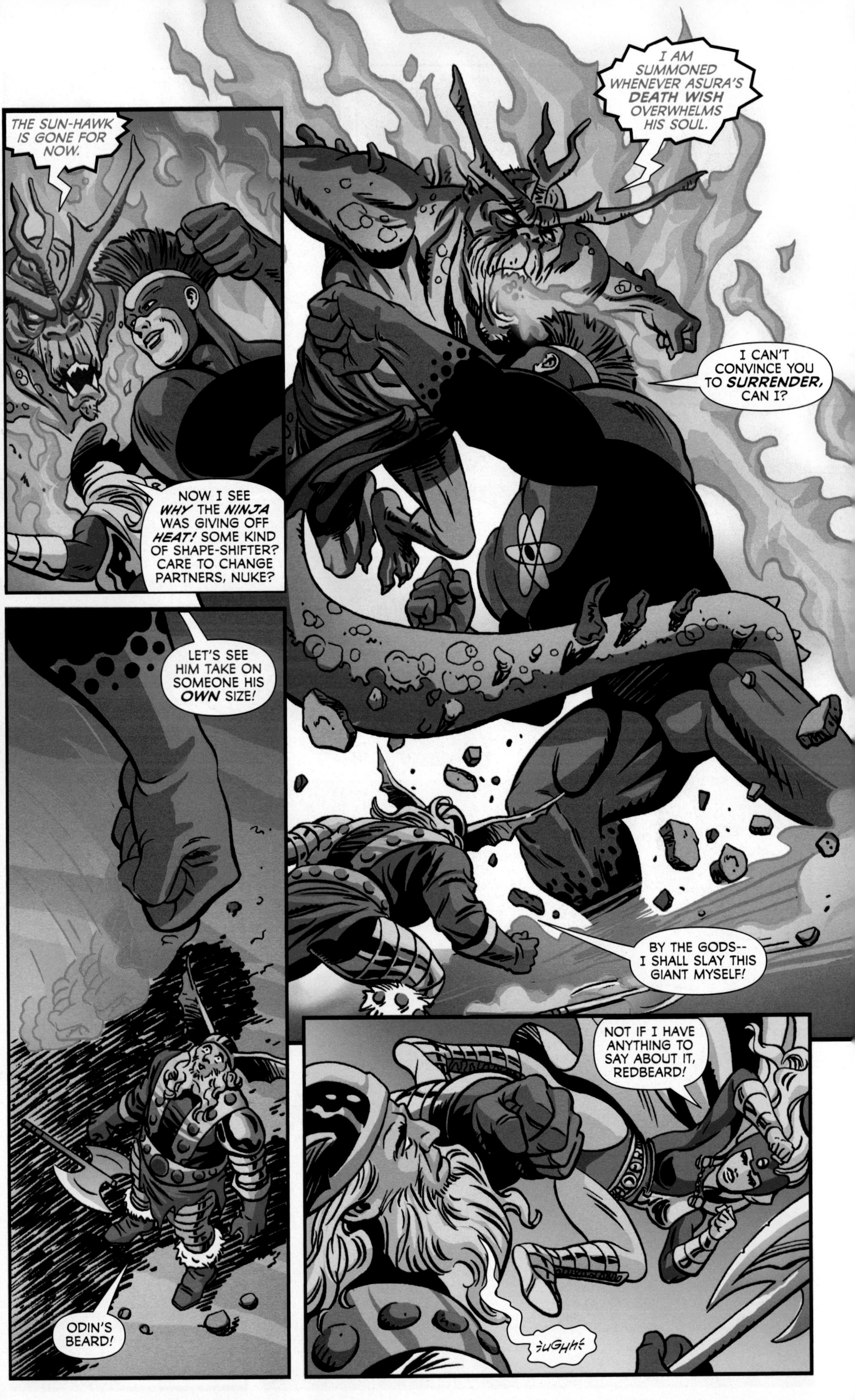
THE SUN-HAWK IS GONE FOR NOW.
I AM SUMMONED WHENEVER ASURA'S DEATH WISH OVERWHELMS HIS SOUL.
I CAN'T CONVINCE YOU TO SURRENDER, CAN I?
NOW I SEE WHY THE NINJA WAS GIVING OFF HEAT! SOME KIND OF SHAPE-SHIFTER? CARE TO CHANGE PARTNERS, NUKE?
LET'S SEE HIM TAKE ON SOMEONE HIS OWN SIZE!
BY THE GODS-- I SHALL SLAY THIS GIANT MYSELF!
ODIN'S BEARD!
NOT IF I HAVE ANYTHING TO SAY ABOUT IT, REDBEARD!
UGHH

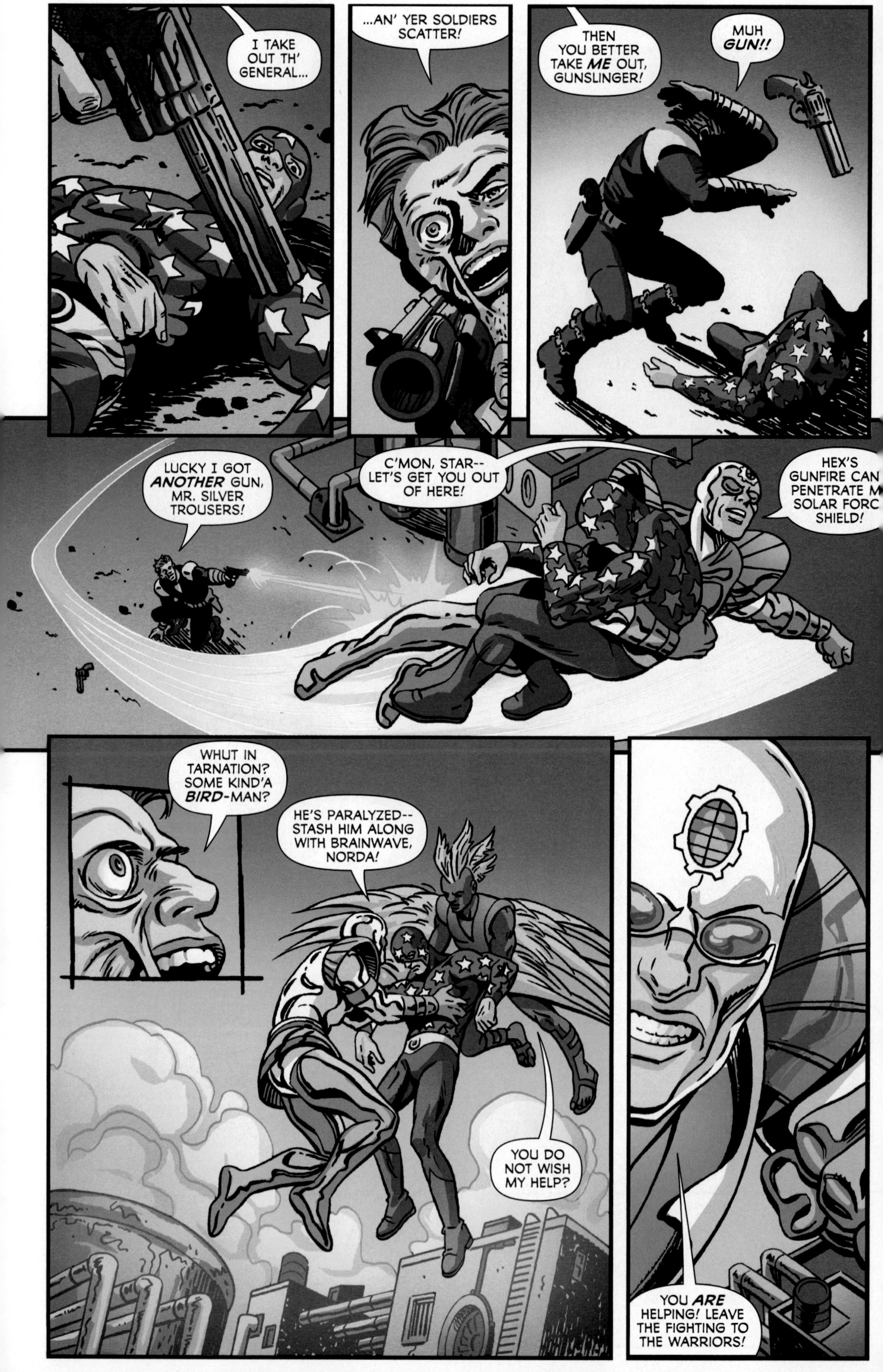
I TAKE OUT TH' GENERAL...
...AN' YER SOLDIERS SCATTER!
THEN YOU BETTER TAKE ME OUT, GUNSLINGER!
MUH GUN!!
LUCKY I GOT ANOTHER GUN, MR. SILVER TROUSERS!
C'MON, STAR-- LET'S GET YOU OUT OF HERE!
HEX'S GUNFIRE CAN PENETRATE M SOLAR FORC SHIELD!
WHUT IN TARNATION? SOME KIND'A BIRD-MAN?
HE'S PARALYZED-- STASH HIM ALONG WITH BRAINWAVE, NORDA!
YOU DO NOT WISH MY HELP?
YOU ARE HELPING! LEAVE THE FIGHTING TO THE WARRIORS!

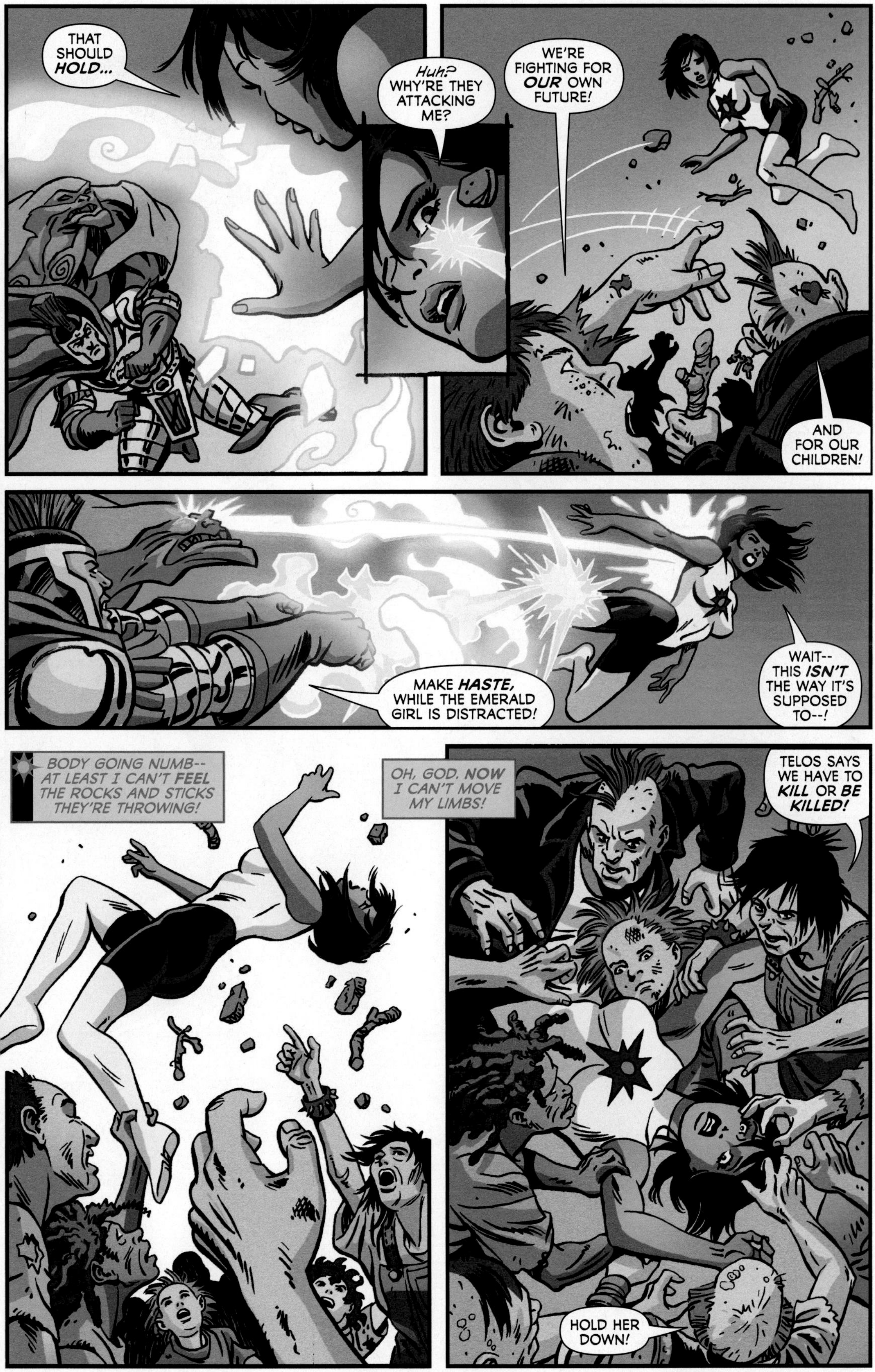
THAT SHOULD HOLD...
Huh? WHY'RE THEY ATTACKING ME?
WE'RE FIGHTING FOR OUR OWN FUTURE!
AND FOR OUR CHILDREN!
MAKE HASTE, WHILE THE EMERALD GIRL IS DISTRACTED!
WAIT-- THIS ISN'T THE WAY IT'S SUPPOSED TO--!
BODY GOING NUMB-- AT LEAST I CAN'T FEEL THE ROCKS AND STICKS THEY'RE THROWING!
OH, GOD. NOW I CAN'T MOVE MY LIMBS!
TELOS SAYS WE HAVE TO KILL OR BE KILLED!
HOLD HER DOWN!

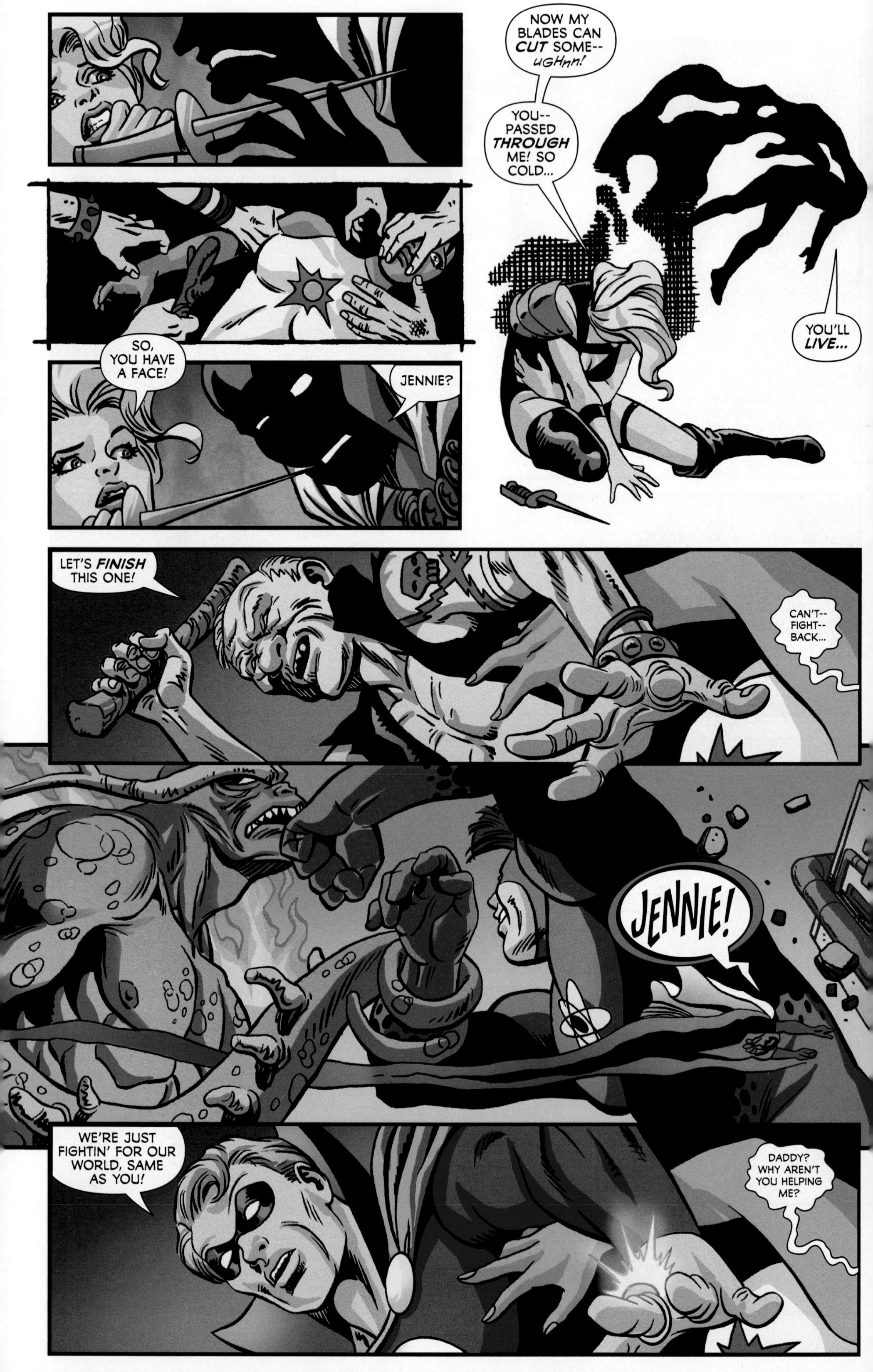
NOW MY BLADES CAN CUT SOME-- uGHnn!
YOU-- PASSED THROUGH ME! SO COLD...
YOU'LL LIVE...
SO, YOU HAVE A FACE!
JENNIE?
LET'S FINISH THIS ONE!
CAN'T-- FIGHT-- BACK...
JENNIE!
WE'RE JUST FIGHTIN' FOR OUR WORLD, SAME AS YOU!
DADDY? WHY AREN'T YOU HELPING ME?

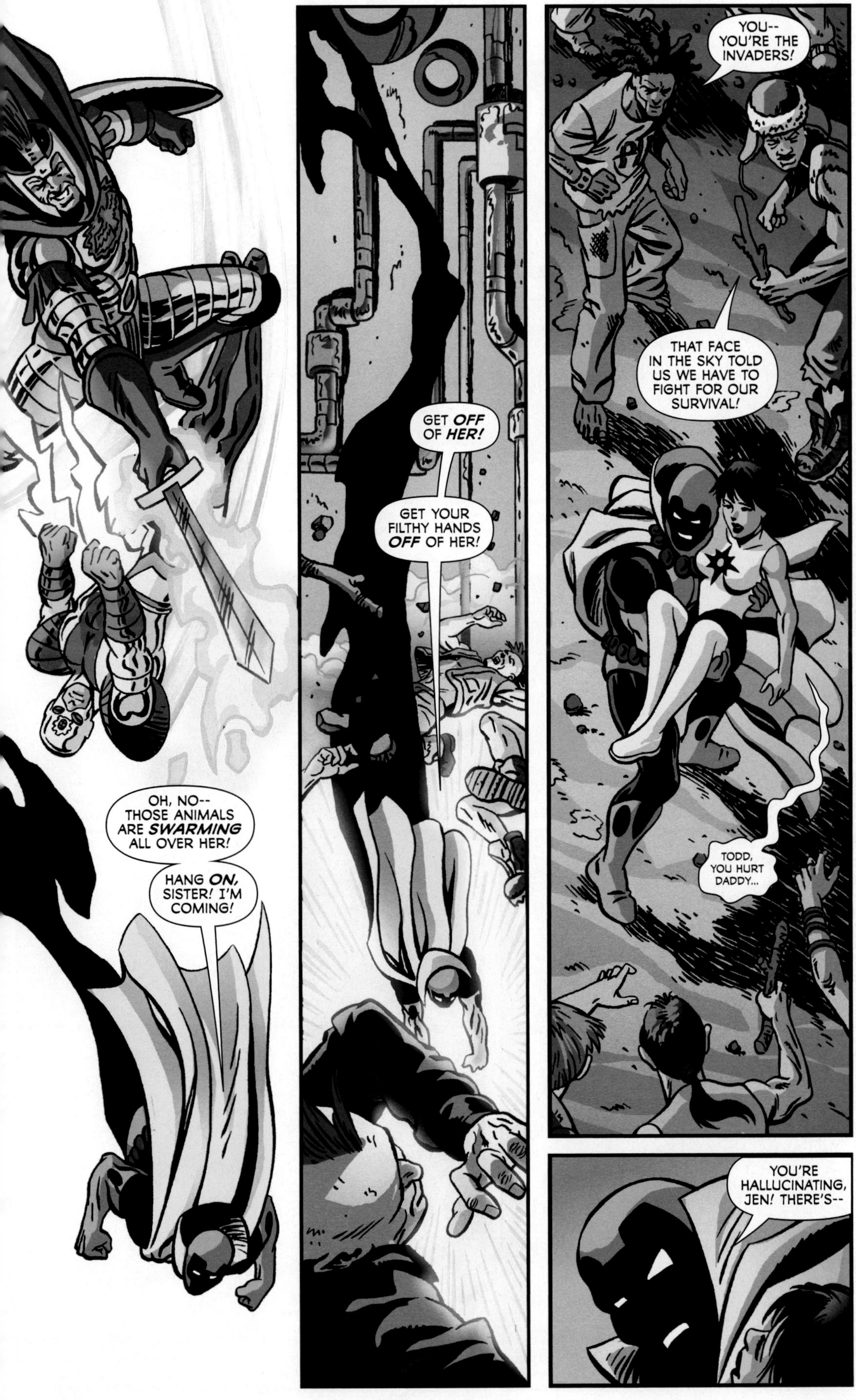
OH, NO-- THOSE ANIMALS ARE SWARMING ALL OVER HER!
HANG ON, SISTER! I'M COMING!
GET OFF OF HER!
GET YOUR FILTHY HANDS OFF OF HER!
YOU-- YOU'RE THE INVADERS!
THAT FACE IN THE SKY TOLD US WE HAVE TO FIGHT FOR OUR SURVIVAL!
TODD, YOU HURT DADDY...
YOU'RE HALLUCINATING, JEN! THERE'S--

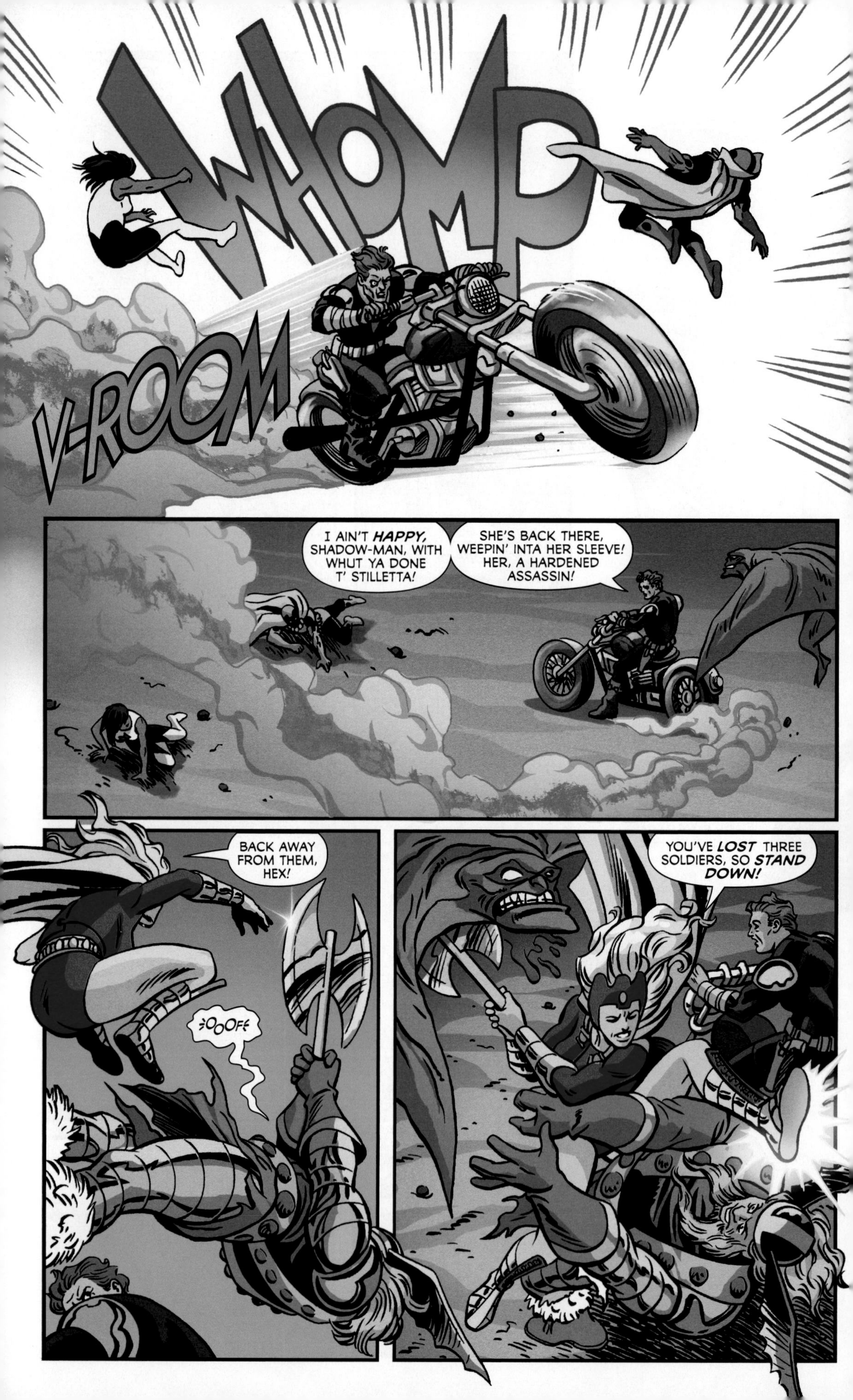
WHOMP
V-ROOM
I AIN'T *HAPPY,* SHADOW-MAN, WITH WHUT YA DONE T' STILLETTA!
SHE'S BACK THERE, WEEPIN' INTA HER SLEEVE! HER, A HARDENED ASSASSIN!
BACK AWAY FROM THEM, HEX!
OOOF
YOU'VE *LOST* THREE SOLDIERS, SO *STAND DOWN!*

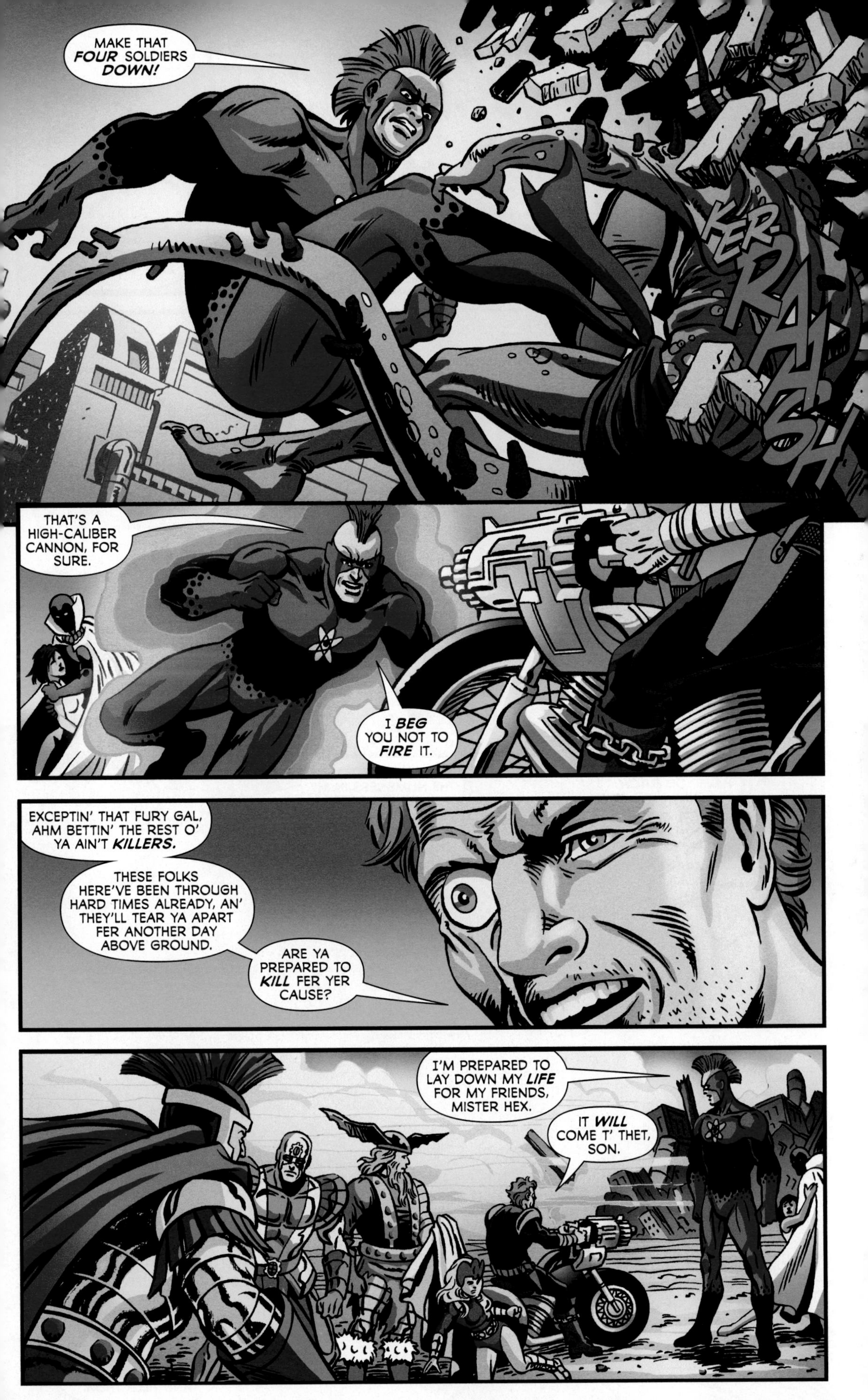
MAKE THAT FOUR SOLDIERS DOWN!
KER RA SH
THAT'S A HIGH-CALIBER CANNON, FOR SURE.
I BEG YOU NOT TO FIRE IT.
EXCEPTIN' THAT FURY GAL, AHM BETTIN' THE REST O' YA AIN'T KILLERS.
THESE FOLKS HERE'VE BEEN THROUGH HARD TIMES ALREADY, AN' THEY'LL TEAR YA APART FER ANOTHER DAY ABOVE GROUND.
ARE YA PREPARED TO KILL FER YER CAUSE?
I'M PREPARED TO LAY DOWN MY LIFE FOR MY FRIENDS, MISTER HEX.
IT WILL COME T' THET, SON.

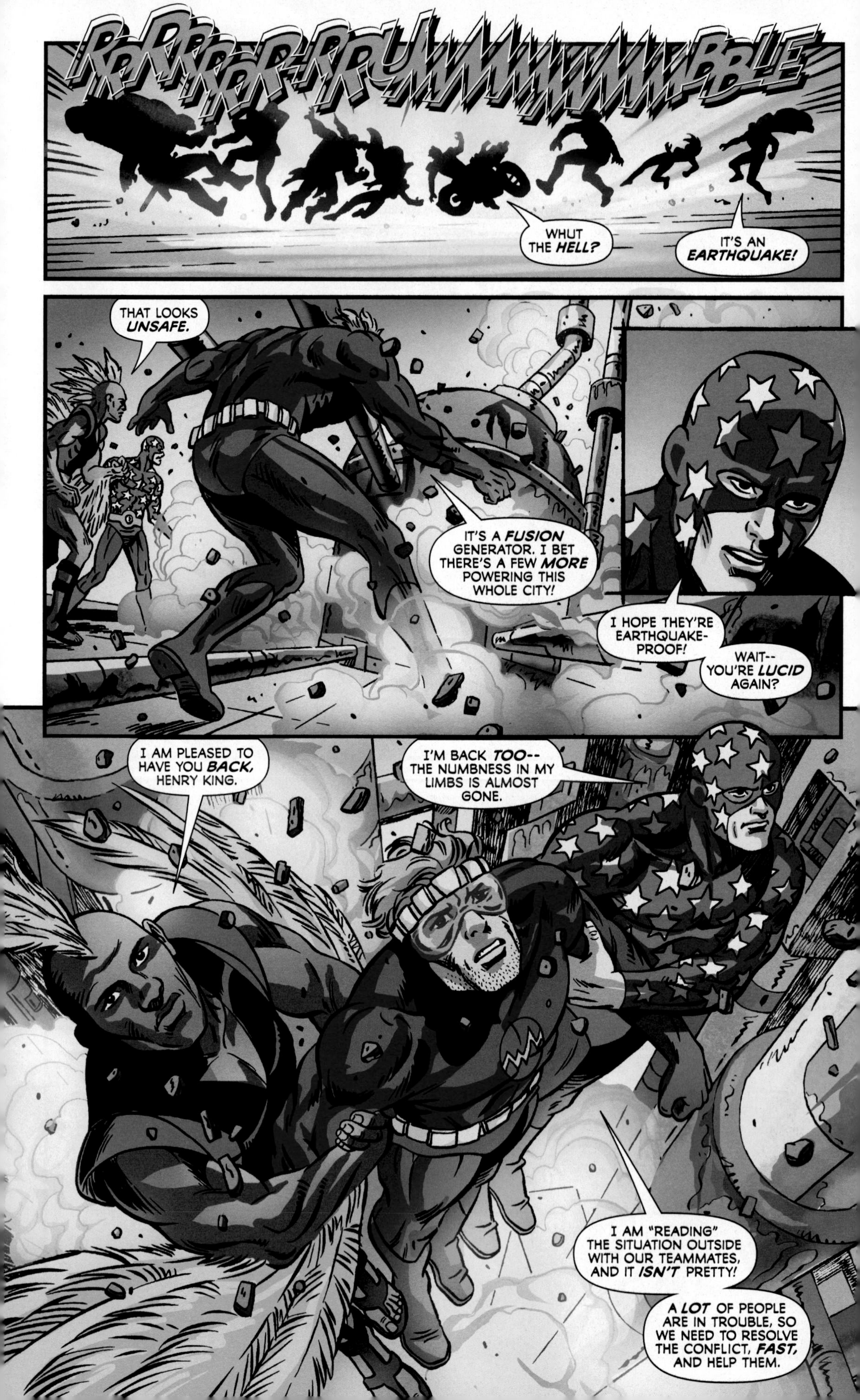
RRRRRRR-RRRUMMMMMMMMBBLE
WHUT THE HELL?
IT'S AN EARTHQUAKE!
THAT LOOKS UNSAFE.
IT'S A FUSION GENERATOR. I BET THERE'S A FEW MORE POWERING THIS WHOLE CITY!
I HOPE THEY'RE EARTHQUAKE-PROOF!
WAIT-- YOU'RE LUCID AGAIN?
I AM PLEASED TO HAVE YOU BACK, HENRY KING.
I'M BACK TOO-- THE NUMBNESS IN MY LIMBS IS ALMOST GONE.
I AM "READING" THE SITUATION OUTSIDE WITH OUR TEAMMATES, AND IT ISN'T PRETTY!
A LOT OF PEOPLE ARE IN TROUBLE, SO WE NEED TO RESOLVE THE CONFLICT, FAST, AND HELP THEM.

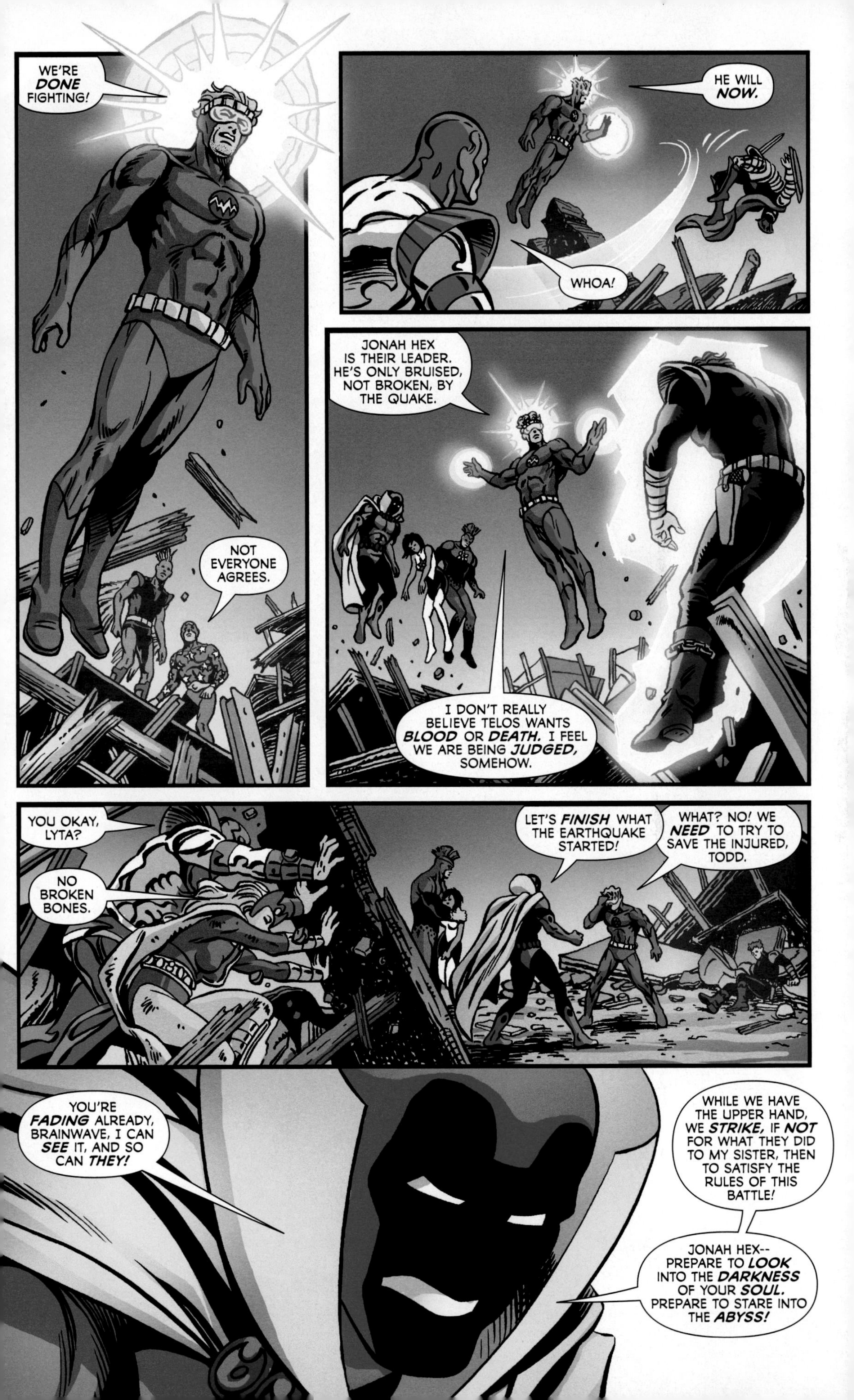
WE'RE *DONE* FIGHTING!
HE WILL *NOW.*
WHOA!
NOT EVERYONE AGREES.
JONAH HEX IS THEIR LEADER. HE'S ONLY BRUISED, NOT BROKEN, BY THE QUAKE.
I DON'T REALLY BELIEVE TELOS WANTS *BLOOD* OR *DEATH.* I FEEL WE ARE BEING *JUDGED,* SOMEHOW.
YOU OKAY, LYTA?
NO BROKEN BONES.
LET'S *FINISH* WHAT THE EARTHQUAKE STARTED!
WHAT? NO! WE *NEED* TO TRY TO SAVE THE INJURED, TODD.
YOU'RE *FADING* ALREADY, BRAINWAVE, I CAN *SEE* IT, AND SO CAN *THEY!*
WHILE WE HAVE THE UPPER HAND, WE *STRIKE,* IF *NOT* FOR WHAT THEY DID TO MY SISTER, THEN TO SATISFY THE RULES OF THIS BATTLE!
JONAH HEX-- PREPARE TO *LOOK* INTO THE *DARKNESS* OF YOUR *SOUL.* PREPARE TO STARE INTO THE *ABYSS!*

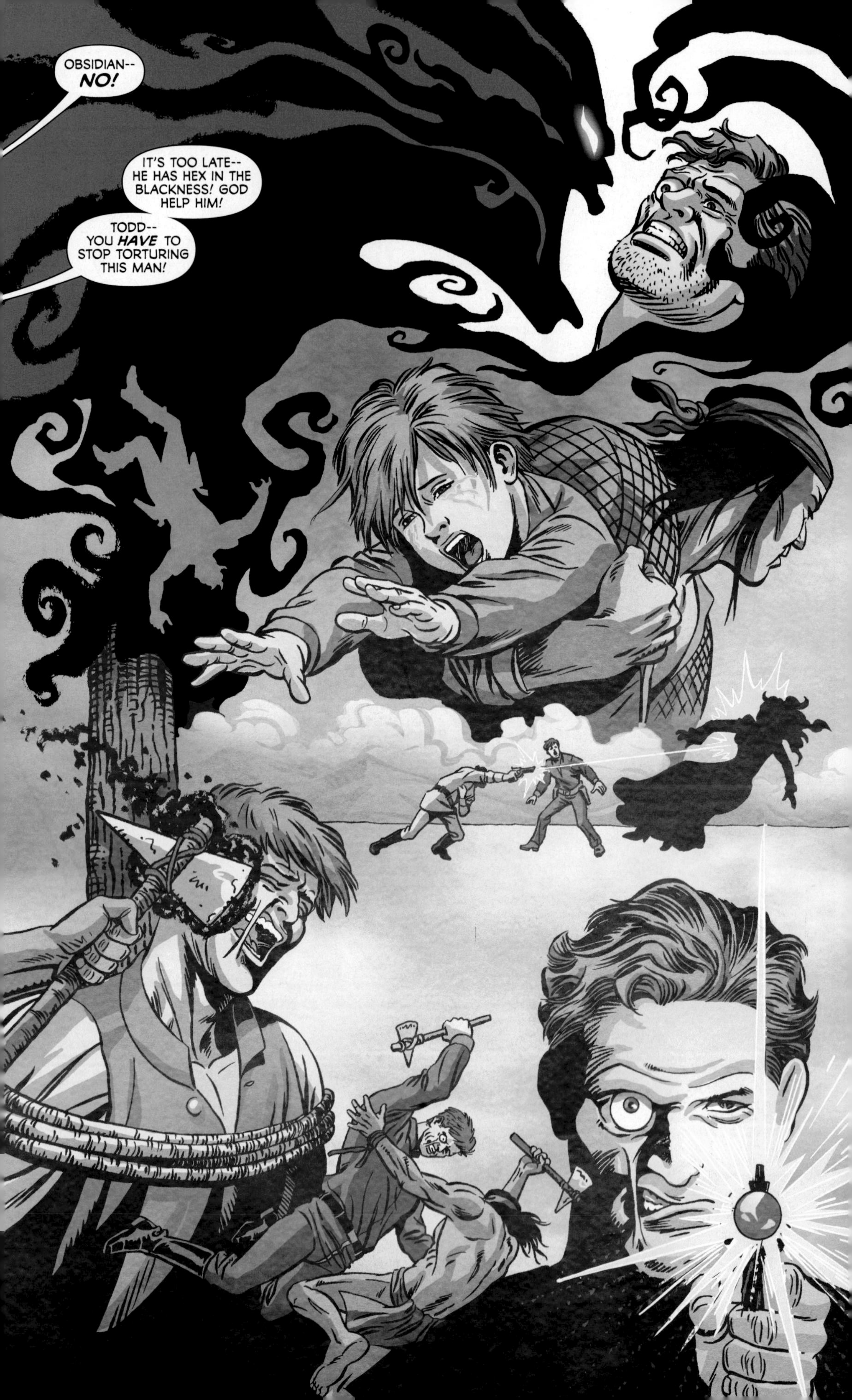
OBSIDIAN-- NO!
IT'S TOO LATE-- HE HAS HEX IN THE BLACKNESS! GOD HELP HIM!
TODD-- YOU HAVE TO STOP TORTURING THIS MAN!

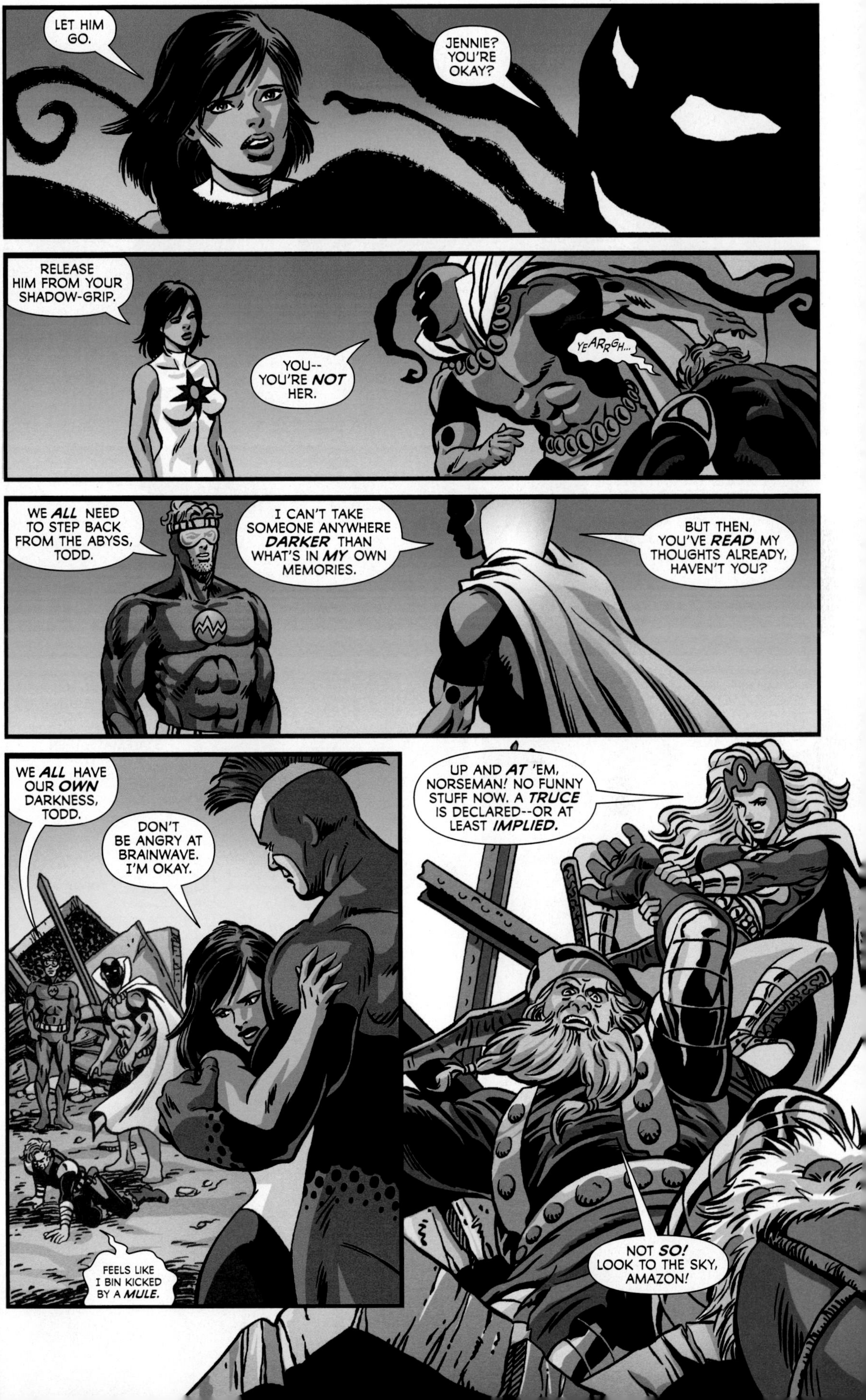
LET HIM GO.
JENNIE? YOU'RE OKAY?
RELEASE HIM FROM YOUR SHADOW-GRIP.
YOU-- YOU'RE NOT HER.
YEARRGH...
WE ALL NEED TO STEP BACK FROM THE ABYSS, TODD.
I CAN'T TAKE SOMEONE ANYWHERE DARKER THAN WHAT'S IN MY OWN MEMORIES.
BUT THEN, YOU'VE READ MY THOUGHTS ALREADY, HAVEN'T YOU?
WE ALL HAVE OUR OWN DARKNESS, TODD.
DON'T BE ANGRY AT BRAINWAVE. I'M OKAY.
FEELS LIKE I BIN KICKED BY A MULE.
UP AND AT 'EM, NORSEMAN! NO FUNNY STUFF NOW. A TRUCE IS DECLARED--OR AT LEAST IMPLIED.
NOT SO! LOOK TO THE SKY, AMAZON!

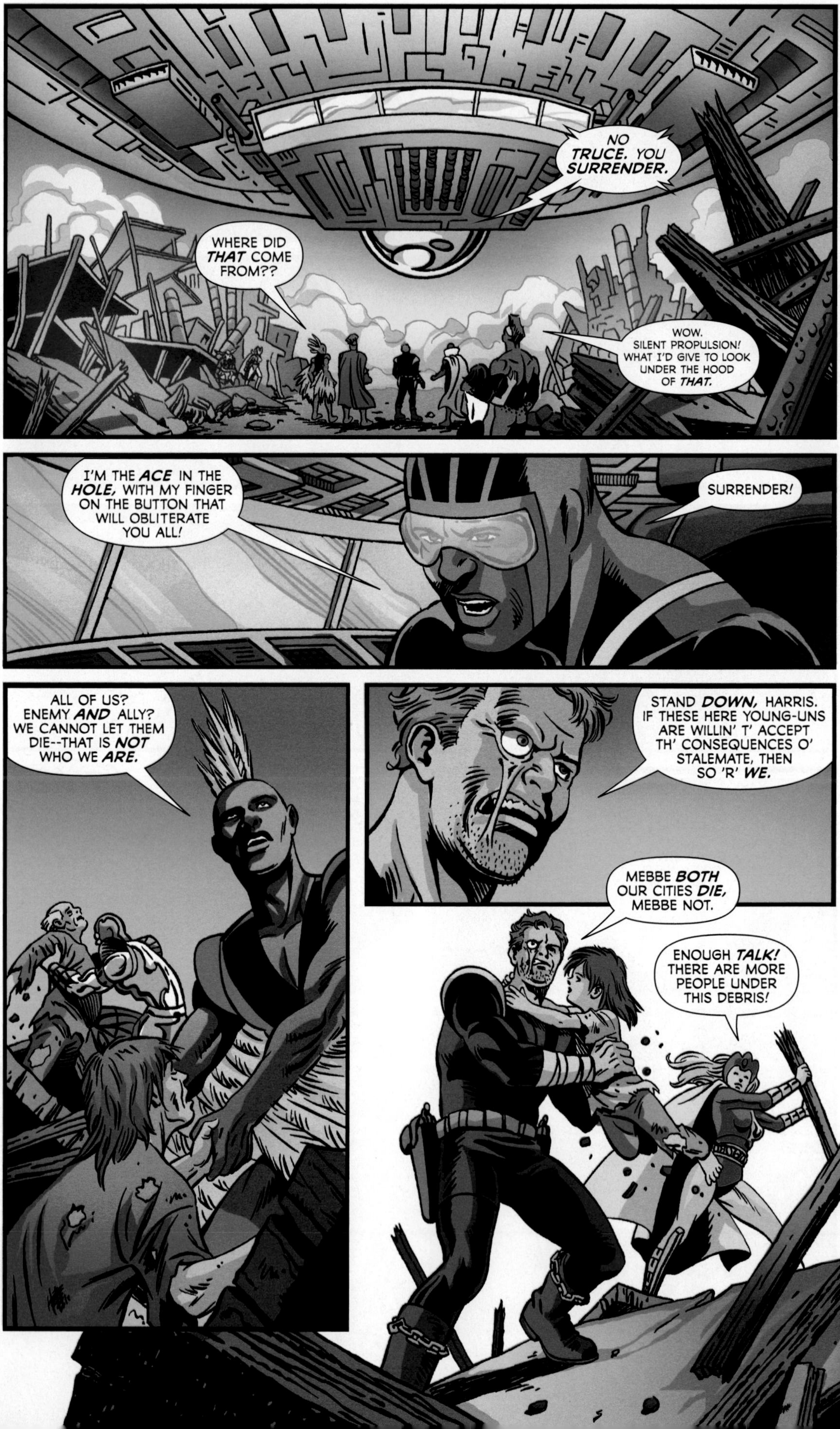
NO TRUCE. YOU SURRENDER.
WHERE DID THAT COME FROM??
WOW. SILENT PROPULSION! WHAT I'D GIVE TO LOOK UNDER THE HOOD OF THAT.
I'M THE ACE IN THE HOLE, WITH MY FINGER ON THE BUTTON THAT WILL OBLITERATE YOU ALL!
SURRENDER!
ALL OF US? ENEMY AND ALLY? WE CANNOT LET THEM DIE--THAT IS NOT WHO WE ARE.
STAND DOWN, HARRIS. IF THESE HERE YOUNG-UNS ARE WILLIN' T' ACCEPT TH' CONSEQUENCES O' STALEMATE, THEN SO 'R' WE.
MEBBE BOTH OUR CITIES DIE, MEBBE NOT.
ENOUGH TALK! THERE ARE MORE PEOPLE UNDER THIS DEBRIS!

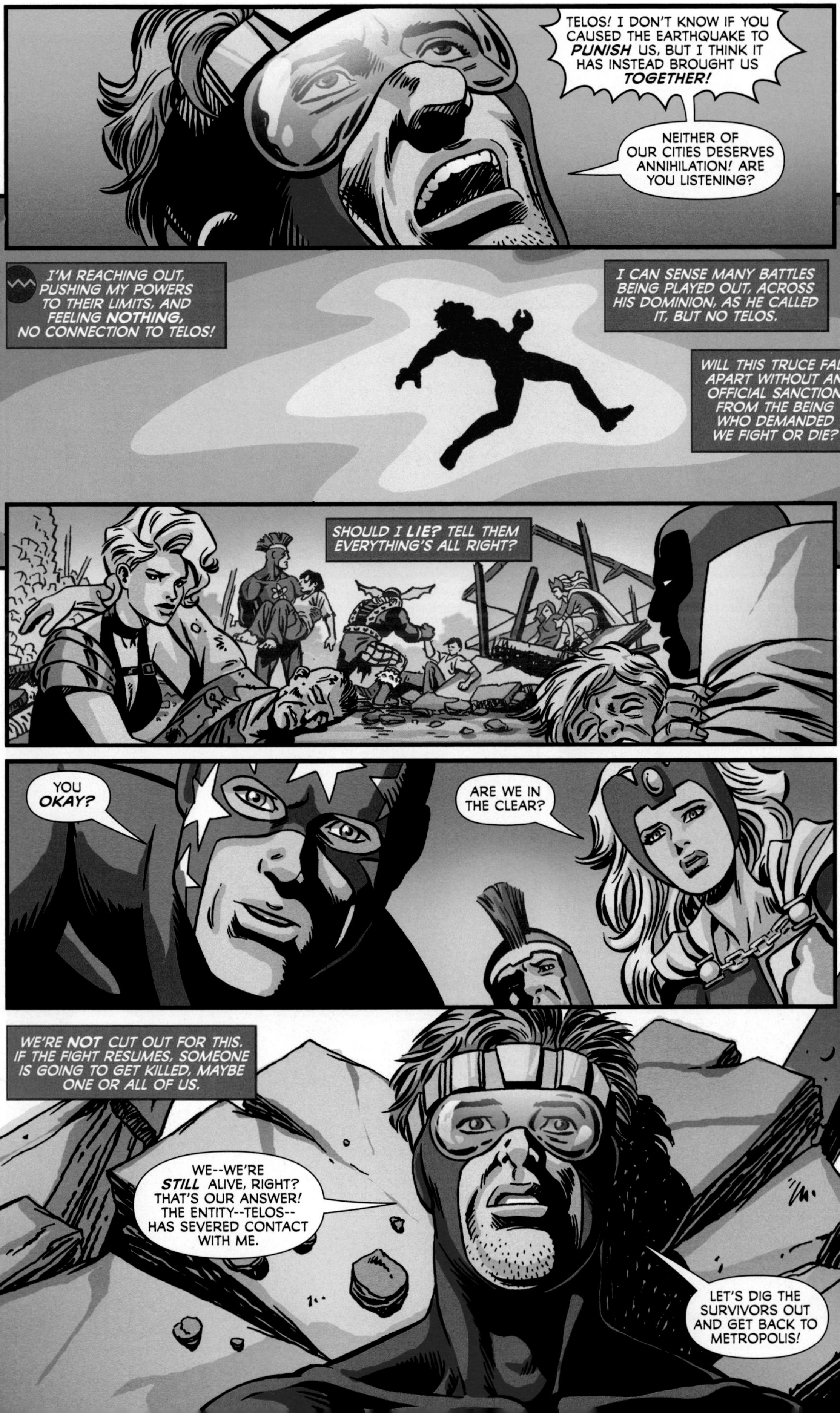
TELOS! I DON'T KNOW IF YOU CAUSED THE EARTHQUAKE TO PUNISH US, BUT I THINK IT HAS INSTEAD BROUGHT US TOGETHER!
NEITHER OF OUR CITIES DESERVES ANNIHILATION! ARE YOU LISTENING?
I'M REACHING OUT, PUSHING MY POWERS TO THEIR LIMITS, AND FEELING NOTHING, NO CONNECTION TO TELOS!
I CAN SENSE MANY BATTLES BEING PLAYED OUT, ACROSS HIS DOMINION, AS HE CALLED IT, BUT NO TELOS.
WILL THIS TRUCE FALL APART WITHOUT AN OFFICIAL SANCTION FROM THE BEING WHO DEMANDED WE FIGHT OR DIE?
SHOULD I LIE? TELL THEM EVERYTHING'S ALL RIGHT?
YOU OKAY?
ARE WE IN THE CLEAR?
WE'RE NOT CUT OUT FOR THIS. IF THE FIGHT RESUMES, SOMEONE IS GOING TO GET KILLED, MAYBE ONE OR ALL OF US.
WE--WE'RE STILL ALIVE, RIGHT? THAT'S OUR ANSWER! THE ENTITY--TELOS--HAS SEVERED CONTACT WITH ME.
LET'S DIG THE SURVIVORS OUT AND GET BACK TO METROPOLIS!

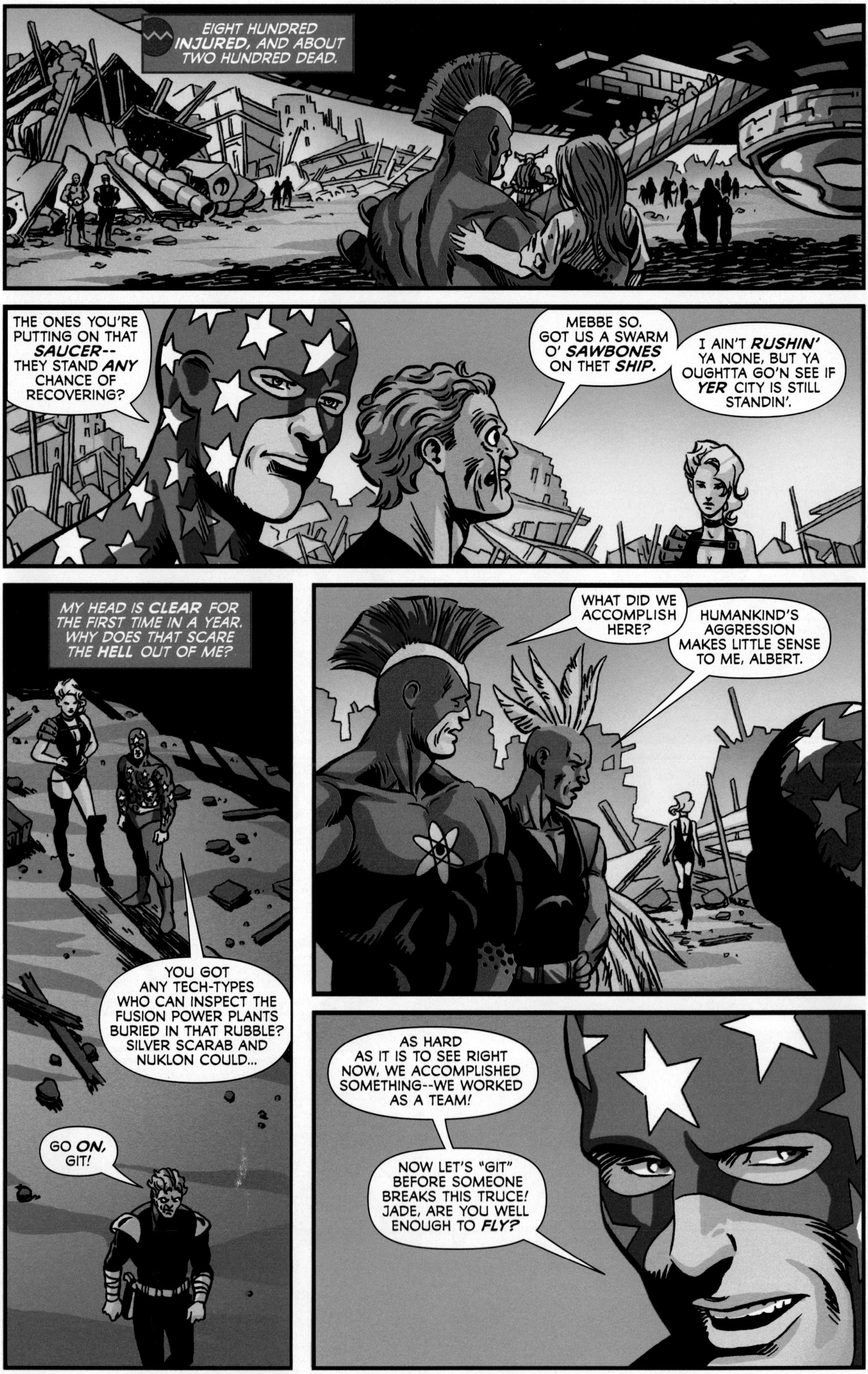
EIGHT HUNDRED INJURED, AND ABOUT TWO HUNDRED DEAD.
THE ONES YOU'RE PUTTING ON THAT SAUCER-- THEY STAND ANY CHANCE OF RECOVERING?
MEBBE SO. GOT US A SWARM O' SAWBONES ON THET SHIP.
I AIN'T RUSHIN' YA NONE, BUT YA OUGHTTA GO'N SEE IF YER CITY IS STILL STANDIN'.
MY HEAD IS CLEAR FOR THE FIRST TIME IN A YEAR. WHY DOES THAT SCARE THE HELL OUT OF ME?
YOU GOT ANY TECH-TYPES WHO CAN INSPECT THE FUSION POWER PLANTS BURIED IN THAT RUBBLE? SILVER SCARAB AND NUKLON COULD...
GO ON, GIT!
WHAT DID WE ACCOMPLISH HERE?
HUMANKIND'S AGGRESSION MAKES LITTLE SENSE TO ME, ALBERT.
AS HARD AS IT IS TO SEE RIGHT NOW, WE ACCOMPLISHED SOMETHING--WE WORKED AS A TEAM!
NOW LET'S "GIT" BEFORE SOMEONE BREAKS THIS TRUCE! JADE, ARE YOU WELL ENOUGH TO FLY?

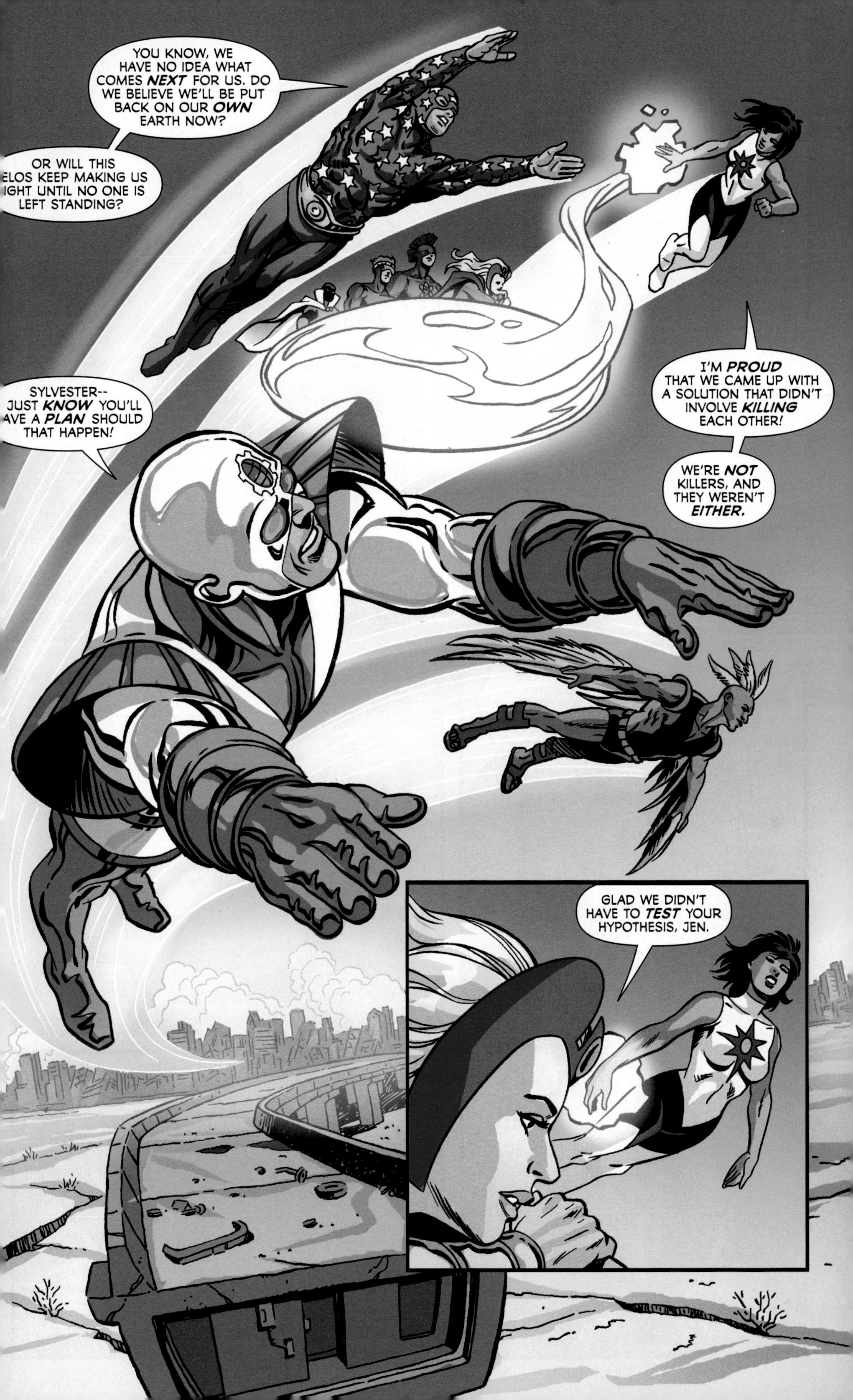

YOU KNOW, WE HAVE NO IDEA WHAT COMES ***NEXT*** FOR US. DO WE BELIEVE WE'LL BE PUT BACK ON OUR ***OWN*** EARTH NOW?
OR WILL THIS ELOS KEEP MAKING US IGHT UNTIL NO ONE IS LEFT STANDING?
SYLVESTER-- JUST ***KNOW*** YOU'LL AVE A ***PLAN*** SHOULD THAT HAPPEN!
I'M ***PROUD*** THAT WE CAME UP WITH A SOLUTION THAT DIDN'T INVOLVE ***KILLING*** EACH OTHER!
WE'RE ***NOT*** KILLERS, AND THEY WEREN'T ***EITHER.***
GLAD WE DIDN'T HAVE TO ***TEST*** YOUR HYPOTHESIS, JEN.

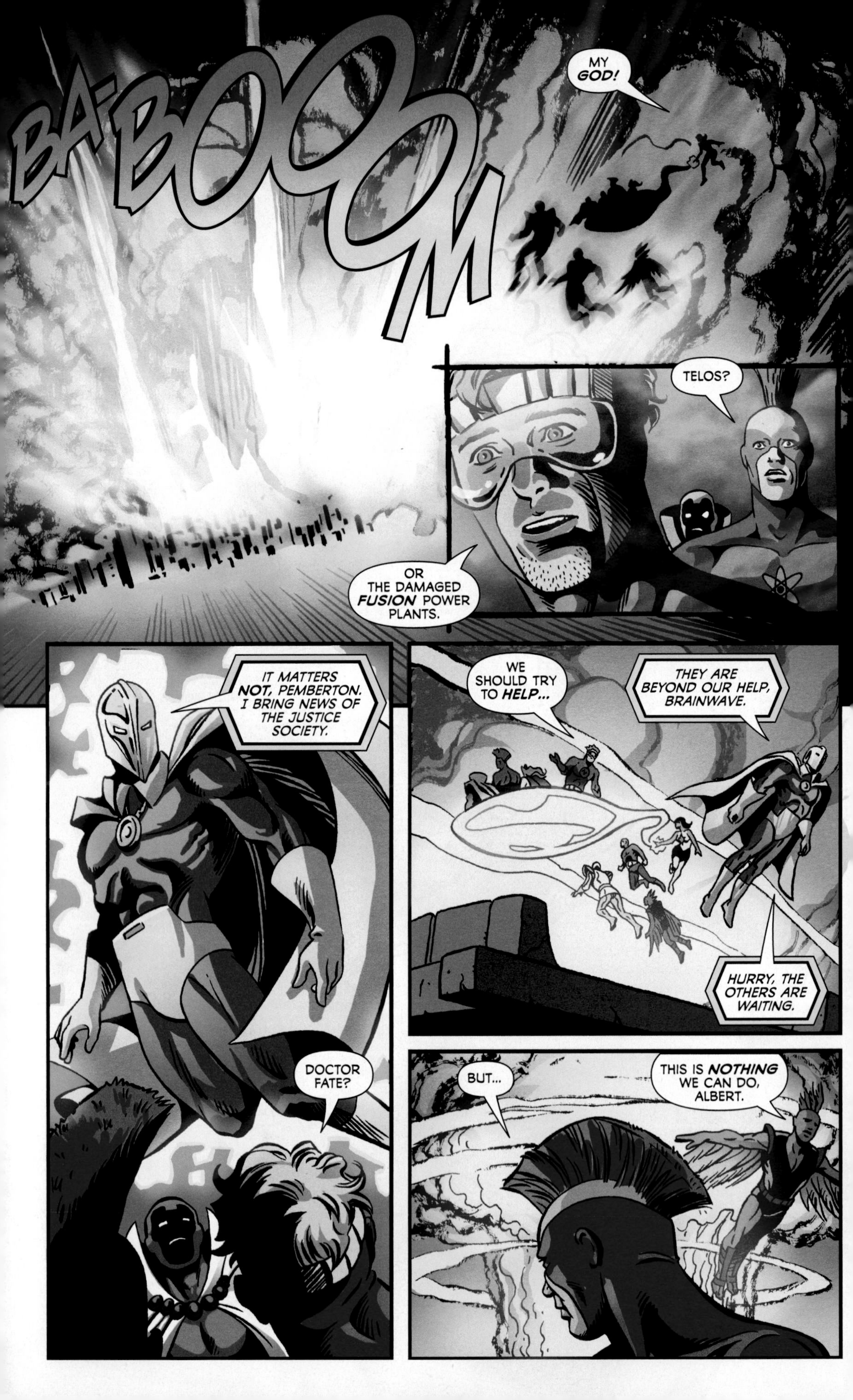
BA-BOOOM
MY GOD!
TELOS?
OR THE DAMAGED FUSION POWER PLANTS.
IT MATTERS NOT, PEMBERTON. I BRING NEWS OF THE JUSTICE SOCIETY.
DOCTOR FATE?
WE SHOULD TRY TO HELP...
THEY ARE BEYOND OUR HELP, BRAINWAVE.
HURRY, THE OTHERS ARE WAITING.
BUT...
THIS IS NOTHING WE CAN DO, ALBERT.

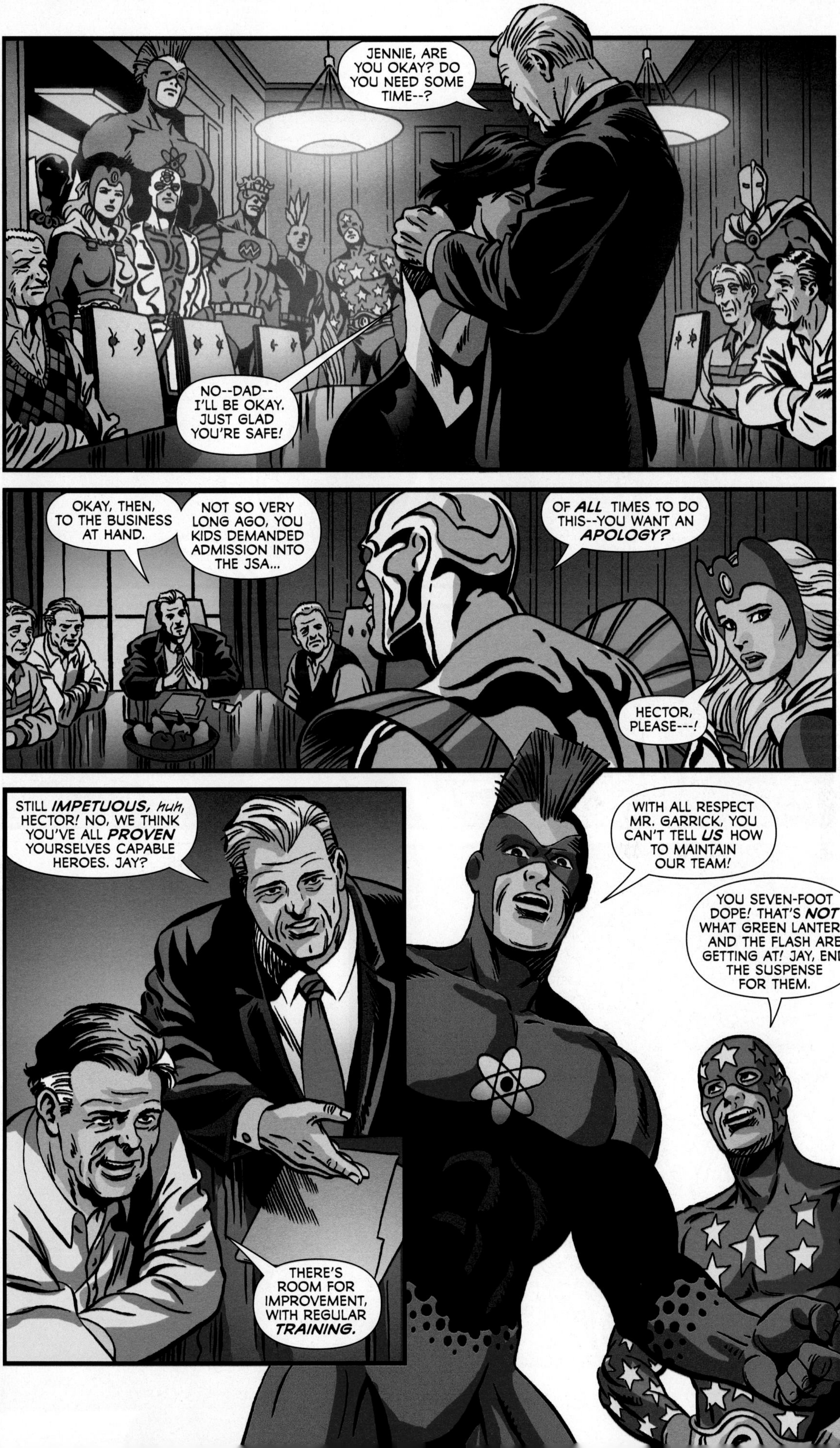
JENNIE, ARE YOU OKAY? DO YOU NEED SOME TIME--?
NO--DAD-- I'LL BE OKAY. JUST GLAD YOU'RE SAFE!
OKAY, THEN, TO THE BUSINESS AT HAND.
NOT SO VERY LONG AGO, YOU KIDS DEMANDED ADMISSION INTO THE JSA...
OF ALL TIMES TO DO THIS--YOU WANT AN APOLOGY?
HECTOR, PLEASE---!
STILL IMPETUOUS, huh, HECTOR! NO, WE THINK YOU'VE ALL PROVEN YOURSELVES CAPABLE HEROES. JAY?
THERE'S ROOM FOR IMPROVEMENT, WITH REGULAR TRAINING.
WITH ALL RESPECT MR. GARRICK, YOU CAN'T TELL US HOW TO MAINTAIN OUR TEAM!
YOU SEVEN-FOOT DOPE! THAT'S NOT WHAT GREEN LANTERN AND THE FLASH ARE GETTING AT! JAY, END THE SUSPENSE FOR THEM.

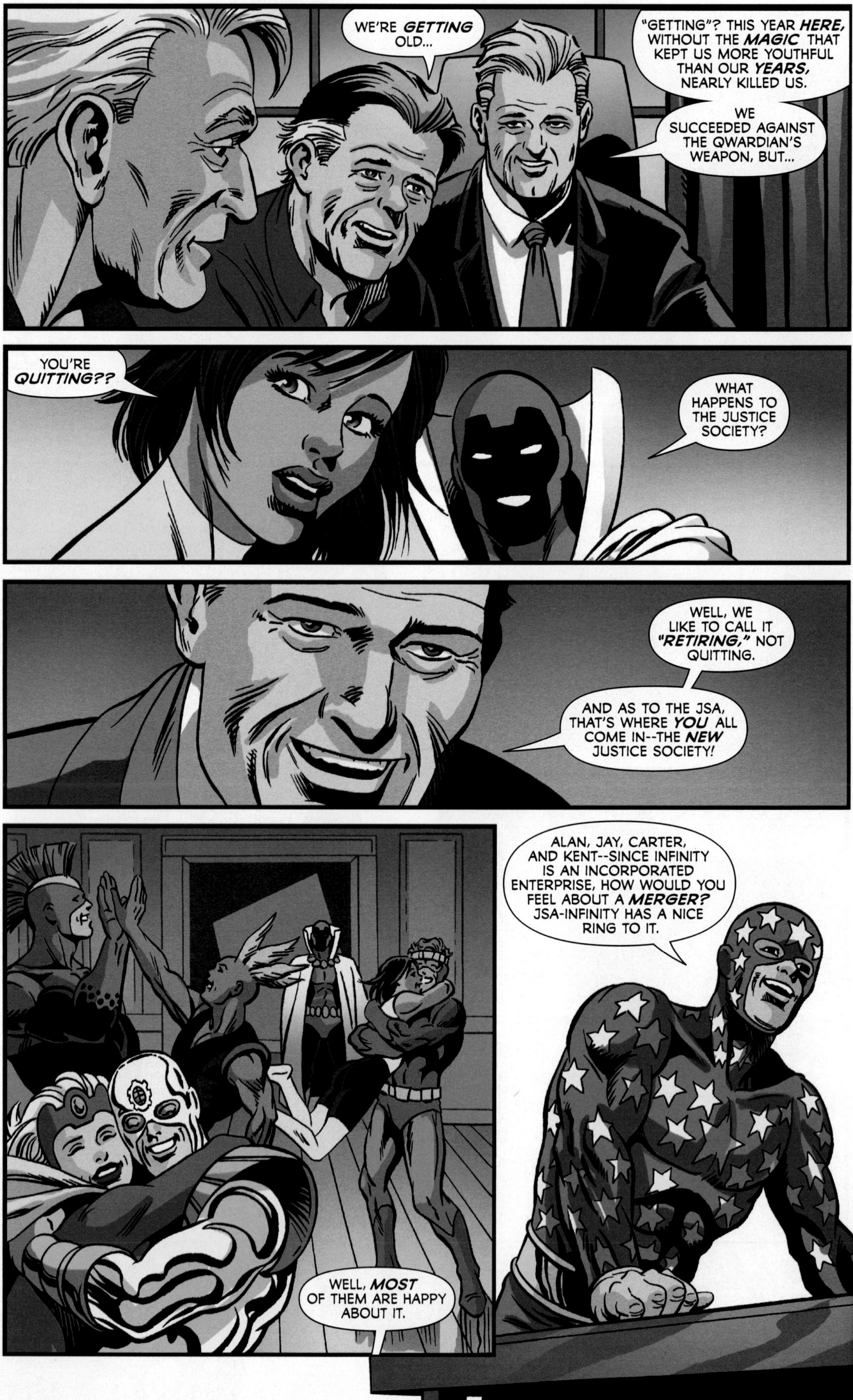
WE'RE GETTING OLD...
"GETTING"? THIS YEAR HERE, WITHOUT THE MAGIC THAT KEPT US MORE YOUTHFUL THAN OUR YEARS, NEARLY KILLED US.
WE SUCCEEDED AGAINST THE QWARDIAN'S WEAPON, BUT...
YOU'RE QUITTING??
WHAT HAPPENS TO THE JUSTICE SOCIETY?
WELL, WE LIKE TO CALL IT "RETIRING," NOT QUITTING.
AND AS TO THE JSA, THAT'S WHERE YOU ALL COME IN--THE NEW JUSTICE SOCIETY!
ALAN, JAY, CARTER, AND KENT--SINCE INFINITY IS AN INCORPORATED ENTERPRISE, HOW WOULD YOU FEEL ABOUT A MERGER? JSA-INFINITY HAS A NICE RING TO IT.
WELL, MOST OF THEM ARE HAPPY ABOUT IT.

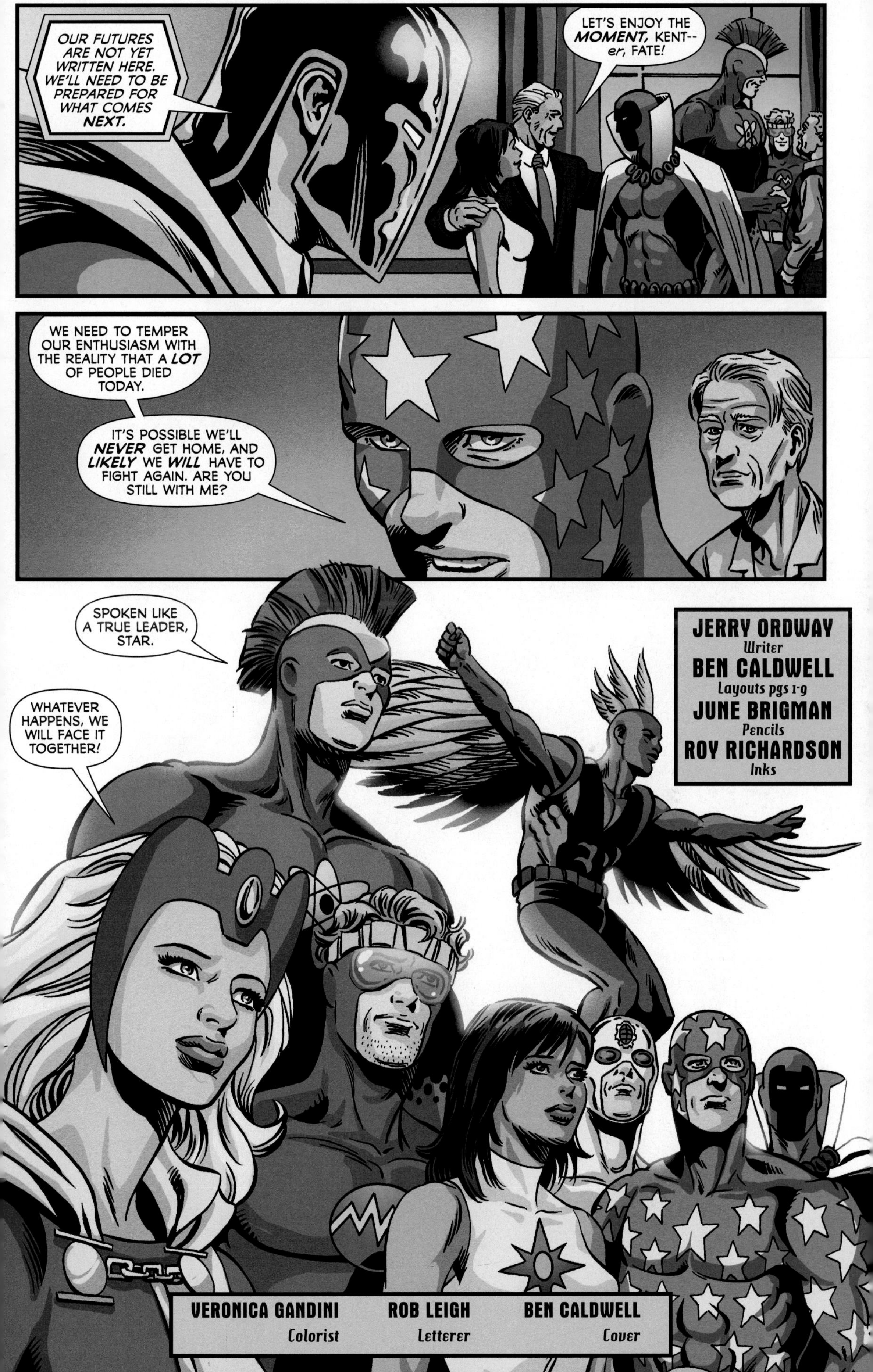
OUR FUTURES ARE NOT YET WRITTEN HERE. WE'LL NEED TO BE PREPARED FOR WHAT COMES NEXT.
LET'S ENJOY THE MOMENT, KENT-- er, FATE!
WE NEED TO TEMPER OUR ENTHUSIASM WITH THE REALITY THAT A LOT OF PEOPLE DIED TODAY.
IT'S POSSIBLE WE'LL NEVER GET HOME, AND LIKELY WE WILL HAVE TO FIGHT AGAIN. ARE YOU STILL WITH ME?
SPOKEN LIKE A TRUE LEADER, STAR.
WHATEVER HAPPENS, WE WILL FACE IT TOGETHER!
JERRY ORDWAY
Writer
BEN CALDWELL
Layouts pgs 1-9
JUNE BRIGMAN
Pencils
ROY RICHARDSON
Inks
VERONICA GANDINI
Colorist
ROB LEIGH
Letterer
BEN CALDWELL
Cover

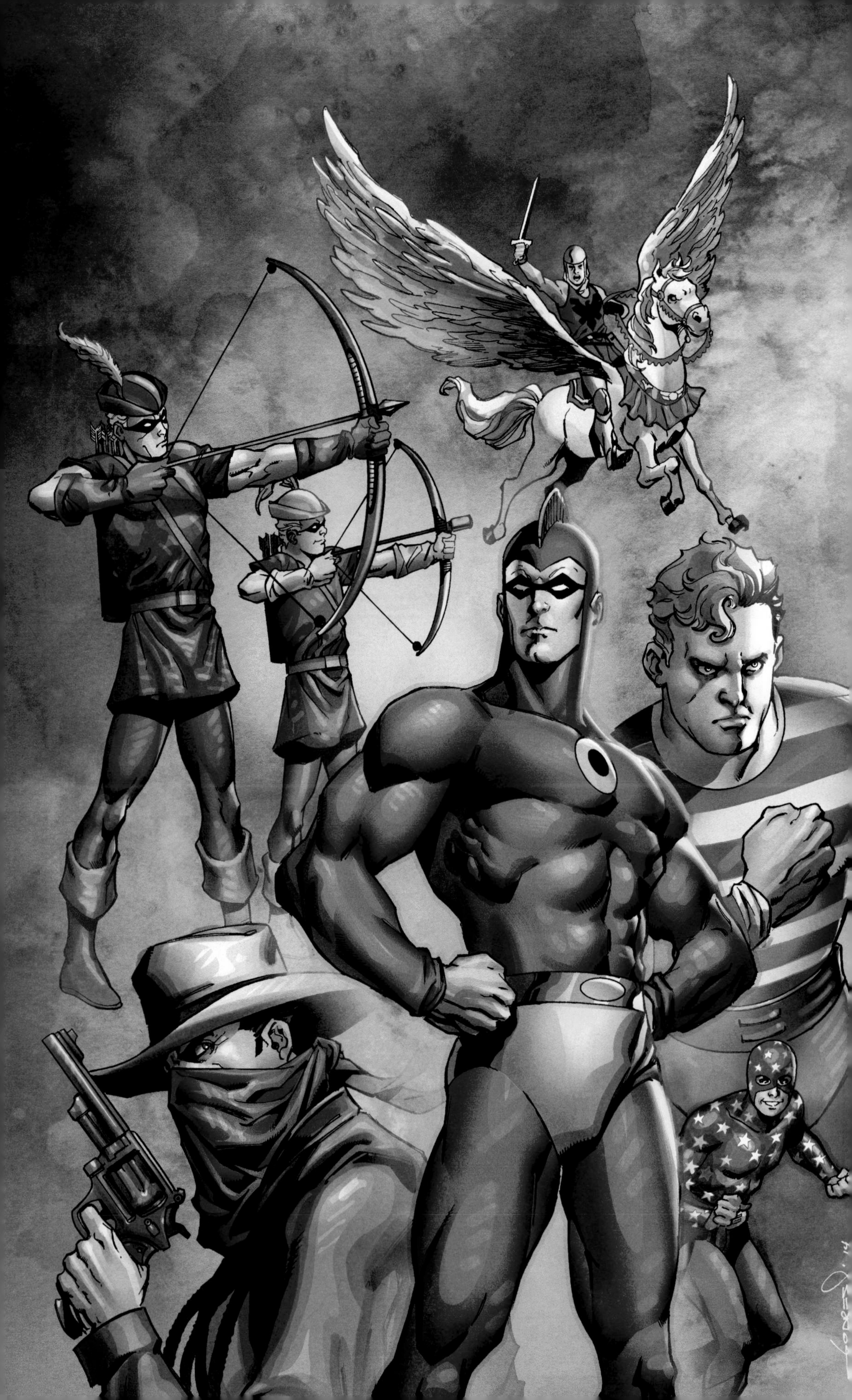

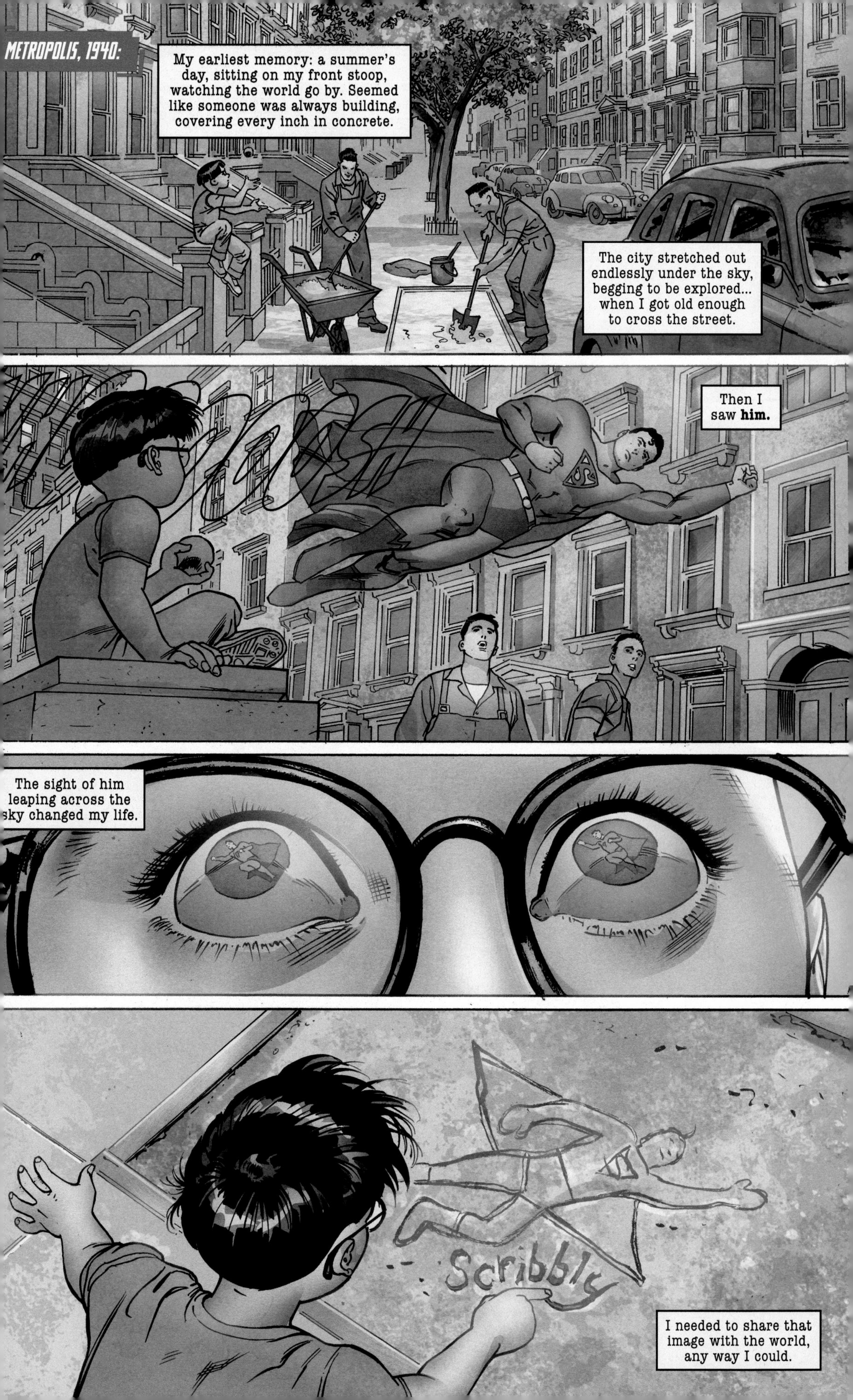
METROPOLIS, 1940:
My earliest memory: a summer's day, sitting on my front stoop, watching the world go by. Seemed like someone was always building, covering every inch in concrete.
The city stretched out endlessly under the sky, begging to be explored... when I got old enough to cross the street.
Then I saw **him.**
The sight of him leaping across the sky changed my life.
Scribbly
I needed to share that image with the world, any way I could.

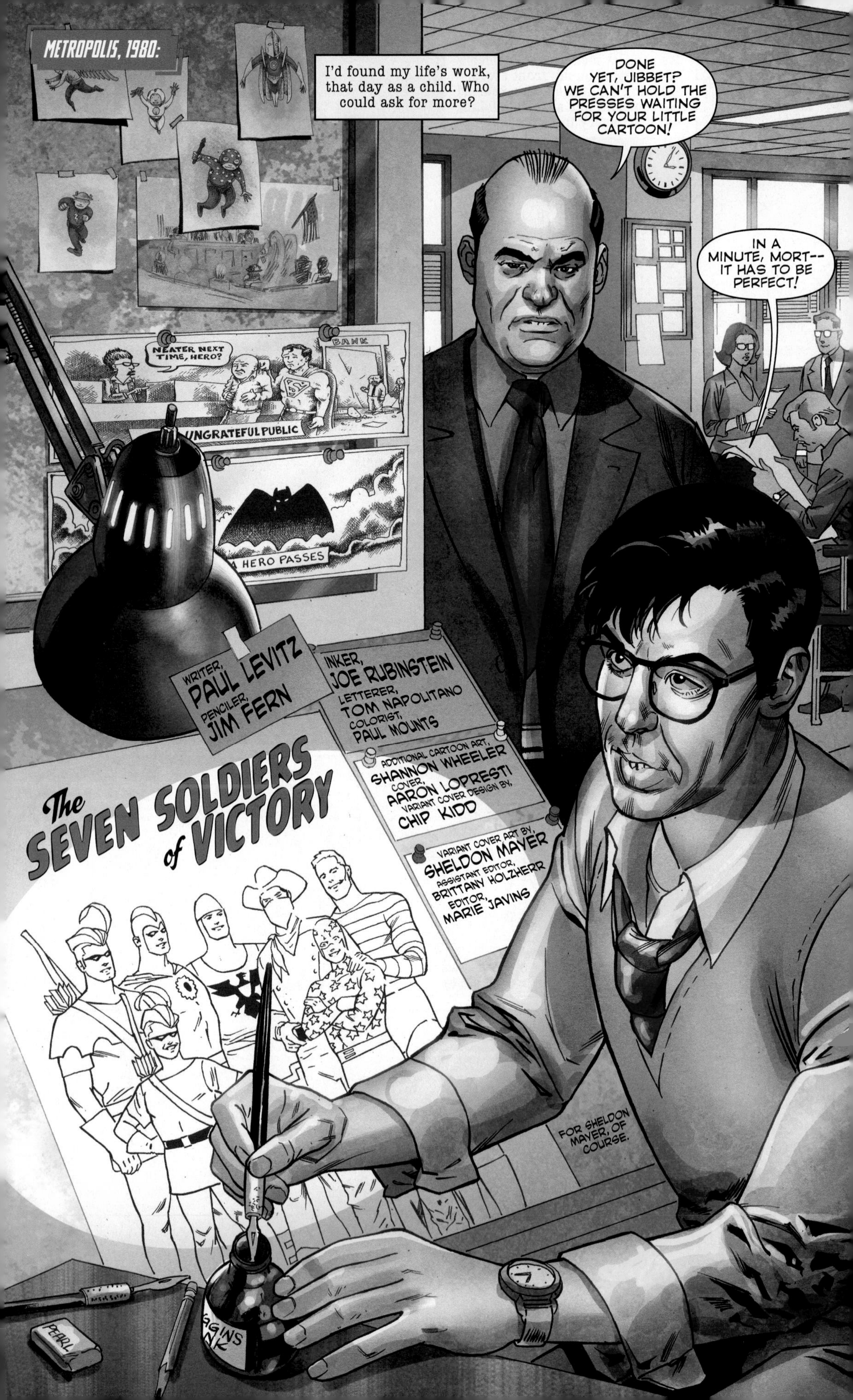
METROPOLIS, 1980:
I'd found my life's work, that day as a child. Who could ask for more?
DONE YET, JIBBET? WE CAN'T HOLD THE PRESSES WAITING FOR YOUR LITTLE CARTOON!
IN A MINUTE, MORT-- IT HAS TO BE PERFECT!
NEATER NEXT TIME, HERO?
BANK
UNGRATEFUL PUBLIC
A HERO PASSES
WRITER, PAUL LEVITZ
PENCILER, JIM FERN
INKER, JOE RUBINSTEIN
LETTERER, TOM NAPOLITANO
COLORIST, PAUL MOUNTS
ADDITIONAL CARTOON ART, SHANNON WHEELER
COVER, AARON LOPRESTI
VARIANT COVER DESIGN BY, CHIP KIDD
VARIANT COVER ART BY, SHELDON MAYER
ASSISTANT EDITOR, BRITTANY HOLZHERR
EDITOR, MARIE JAVINS
The SEVEN SOLDIERS of VICTORY
FOR SHELDON MAYER, OF COURSE.
PEARL

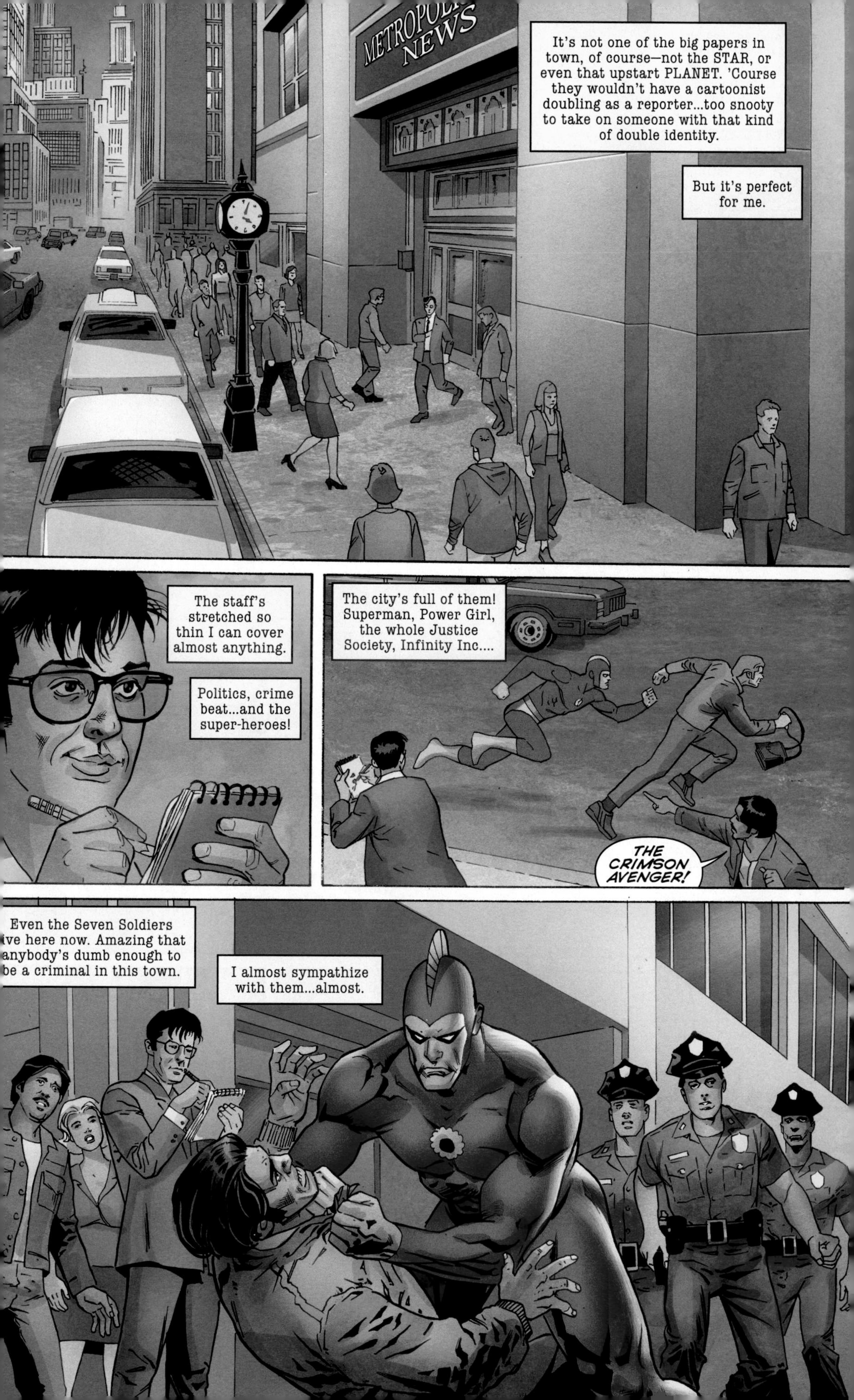
METROPOLIS NEWS
It's not one of the big papers in town, of course—not the STAR, or even that upstart PLANET. 'Course they wouldn't have a cartoonist doubling as a reporter...too snooty to take on someone with that kind of double identity.
But it's perfect for me.
The staff's stretched so thin I can cover almost anything.
Politics, crime beat...and the super-heroes!
The city's full of them! Superman, Power Girl, the whole Justice Society, Infinity Inc....
THE CRIMSON AVENGER!
Even the Seven Soldiers live here now. Amazing that anybody's dumb enough to be a criminal in this town.
I almost sympathize with them...almost.

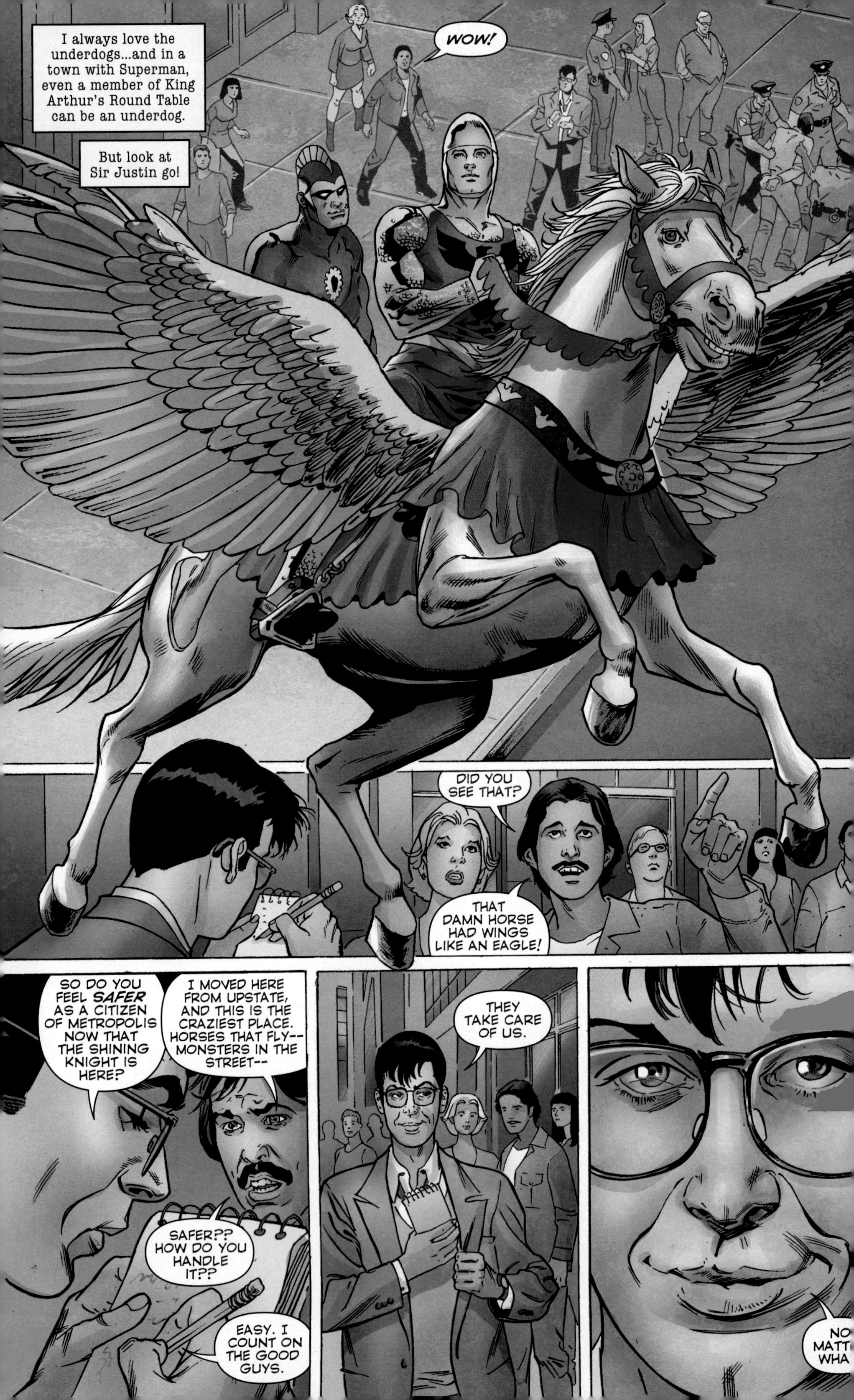
I always love the underdogs...and in a town with Superman, even a member of King Arthur's Round Table can be an underdog.
WOW!
But look at Sir Justin go!
DID YOU SEE THAT?
THAT DAMN HORSE HAD WINGS LIKE AN EAGLE!
SO DO YOU FEEL SAFER AS A CITIZEN OF METROPOLIS NOW THAT THE SHINING KNIGHT IS HERE?
I MOVED HERE FROM UPSTATE, AND THIS IS THE CRAZIEST PLACE. HORSES THAT FLY-- MONSTERS IN THE STREET--
SAFER?? HOW DO YOU HANDLE IT??
EASY. I COUNT ON THE GOOD GUYS.
THEY TAKE CARE OF US.

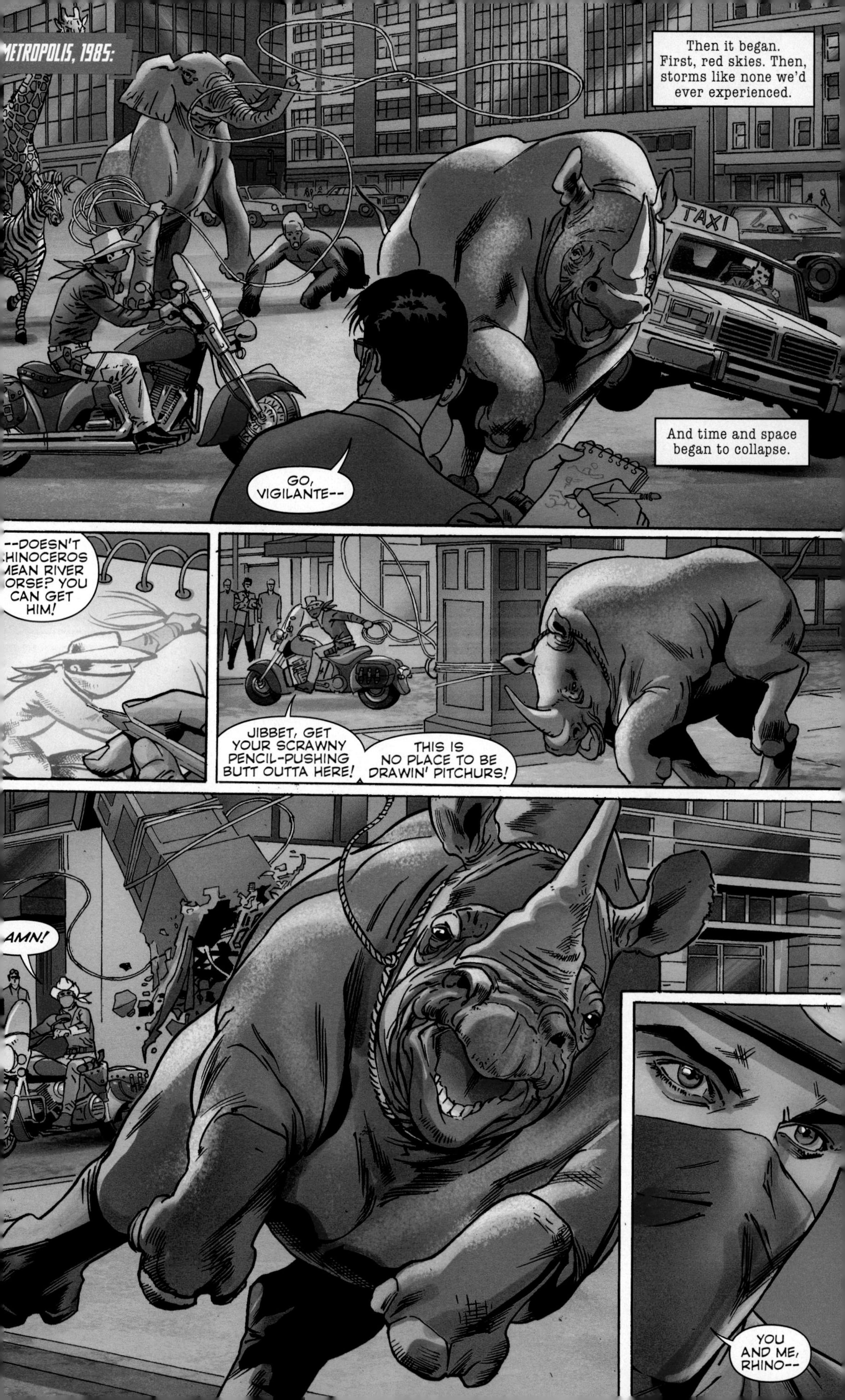
METROPOLIS, 1985:
Then it began. First, red skies. Then, storms like none we'd ever experienced.
And time and space began to collapse.
GO, VIGILANTE--
--DOESN'T RHINOCEROS MEAN RIVER HORSE? YOU CAN GET HIM!
JIBBET, GET YOUR SCRAWNY PENCIL-PUSHING BUTT OUTTA HERE!
THIS IS NO PLACE TO BE DRAWIN' PITCHURS!
AMN!
YOU AND ME, RHINO--

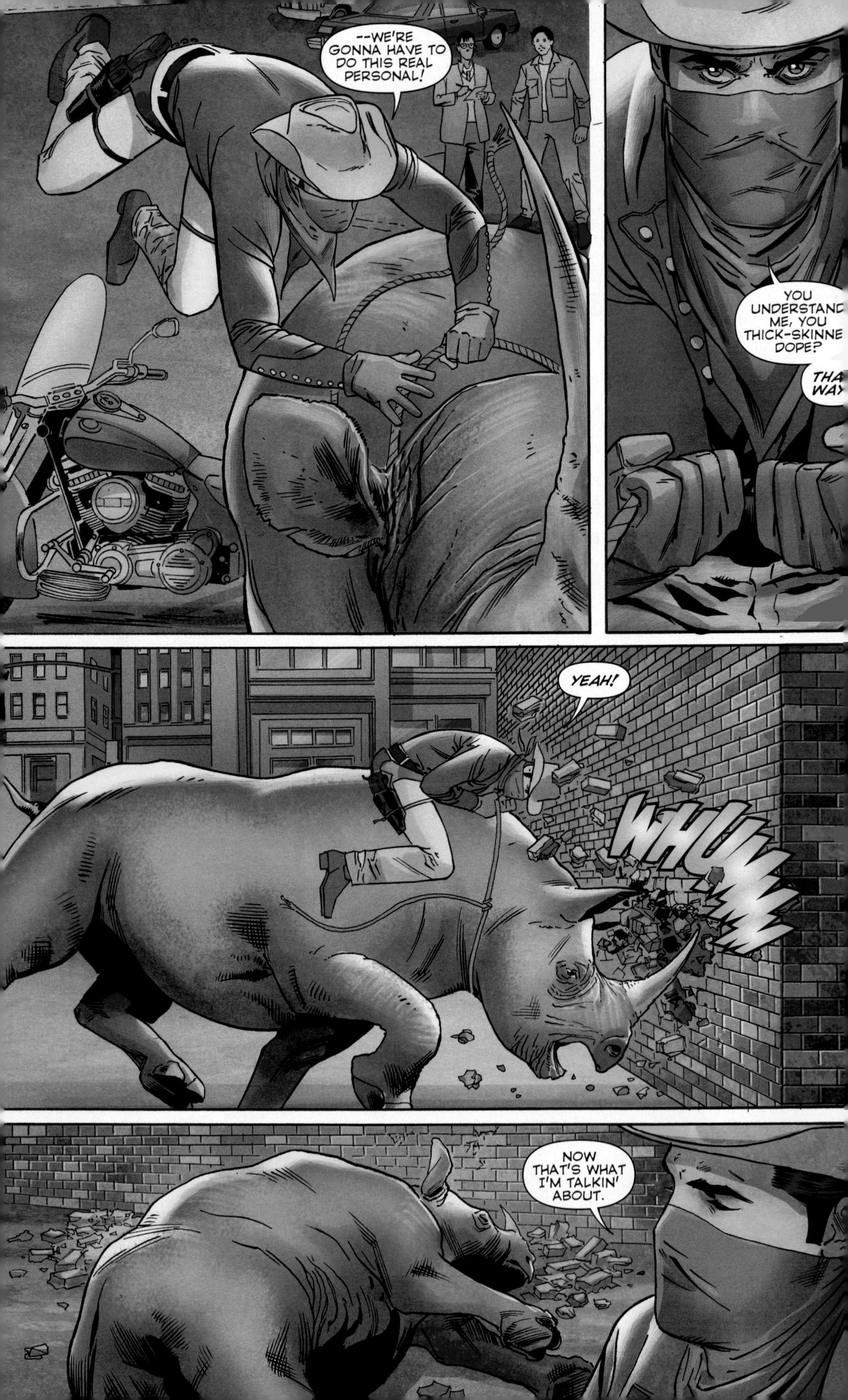
--WE'RE GONNA HAVE TO DO THIS REAL PERSONAL!
YOU UNDERSTAND ME, YOU THICK-SKINNE DOPE?
THA WAY
YEAH!
WHUMM
NOW THAT'S WHAT I'M TALKIN' ABOUT.

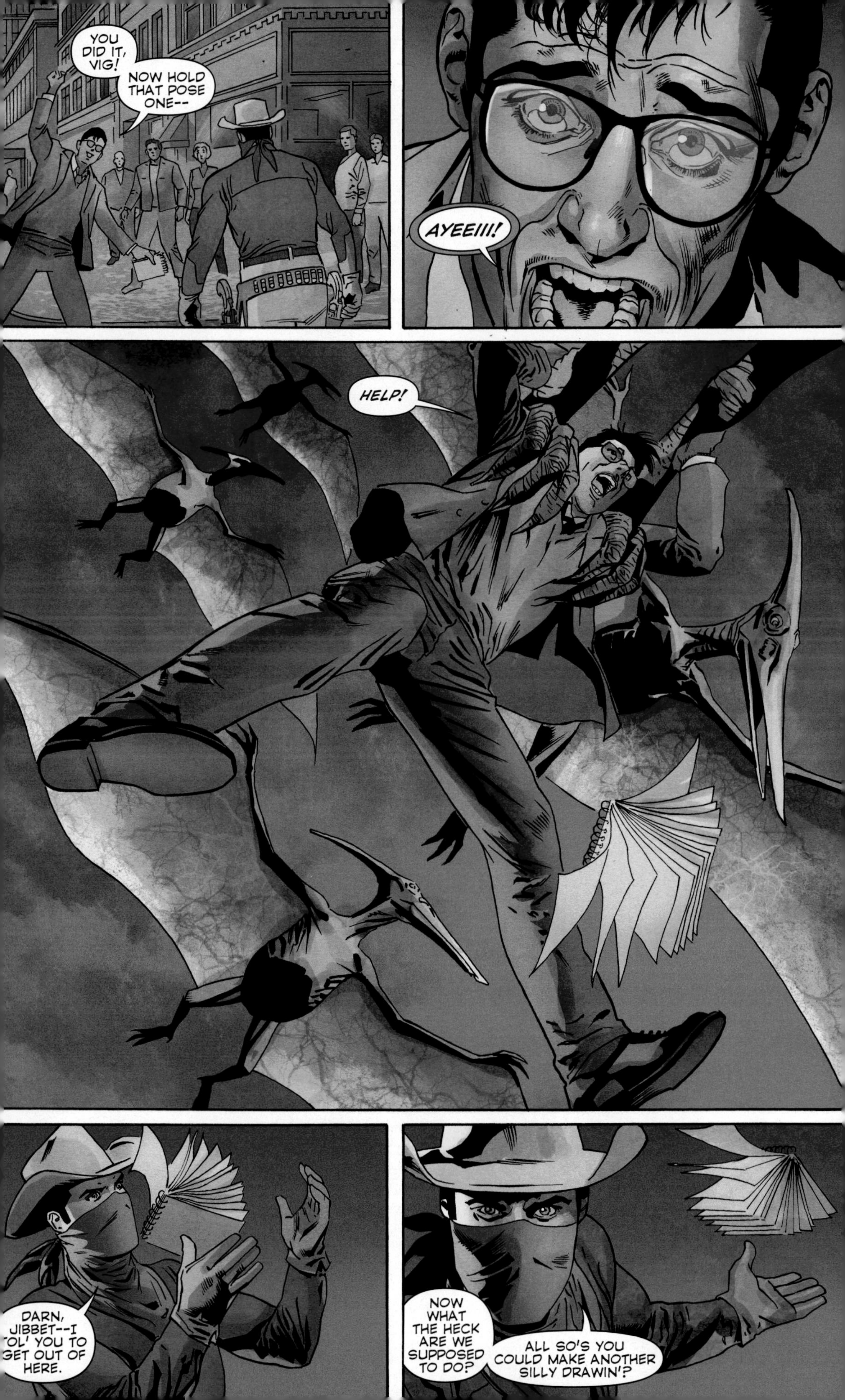
YOU DID IT, VIG!
NOW HOLD THAT POSE ONE--
AYEEIII!
HELP!
DARN, JIBBET--I TOL' YOU TO GET OUT OF HERE.
NOW WHAT THE HECK ARE WE SUPPOSED TO DO?
ALL SO'S YOU COULD MAKE ANOTHER SILLY DRAWIN'?

SPEEDY AND I WILL GET HIM, VIG!

HAVE A NET ARROW READY, SPEEDY--THIS VOLLEY SHOULD SHAKE HIM LOOSE!

THOOOM THOOOM THOOOM

My ears hurt, and I was shaking all over-- scariest moment of my life, up 'til then.

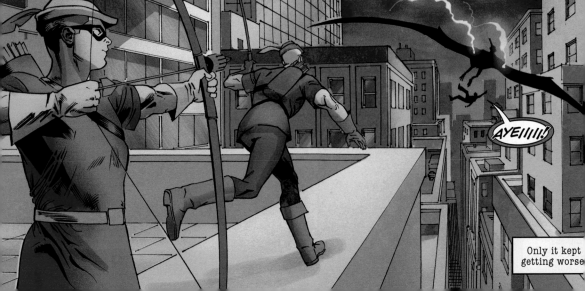

AYEIIIII!!

Only it kept getting worse

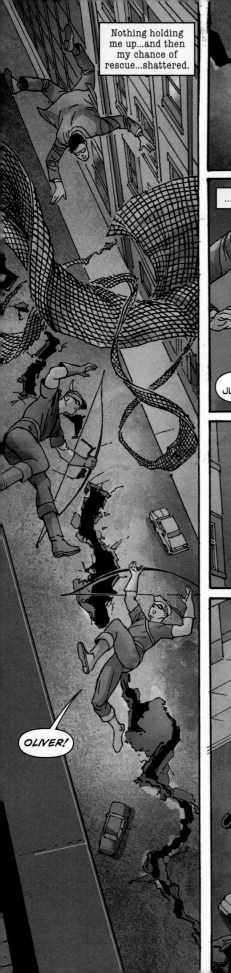

Nothing holding me up...and then my chance of rescue...shattered.

OLIVER!

Metropolis isn't supposed to **have** earthquakes.

But then, we don't usually have pterodactyls and red skies, either. I had picked some improbable ways to die...

...or not.

HO, SCRIBE-- IN DANGER *AGAIN??*

SIR JUSTIN!

GREEN ARROW-- SPEEDY--SAVE THEM, TOO!

COMMONERS AND THE INNOCENT FIRST, JIBBET, THEN MAY A KNIGHT LOOK TO HIS COMRADES...

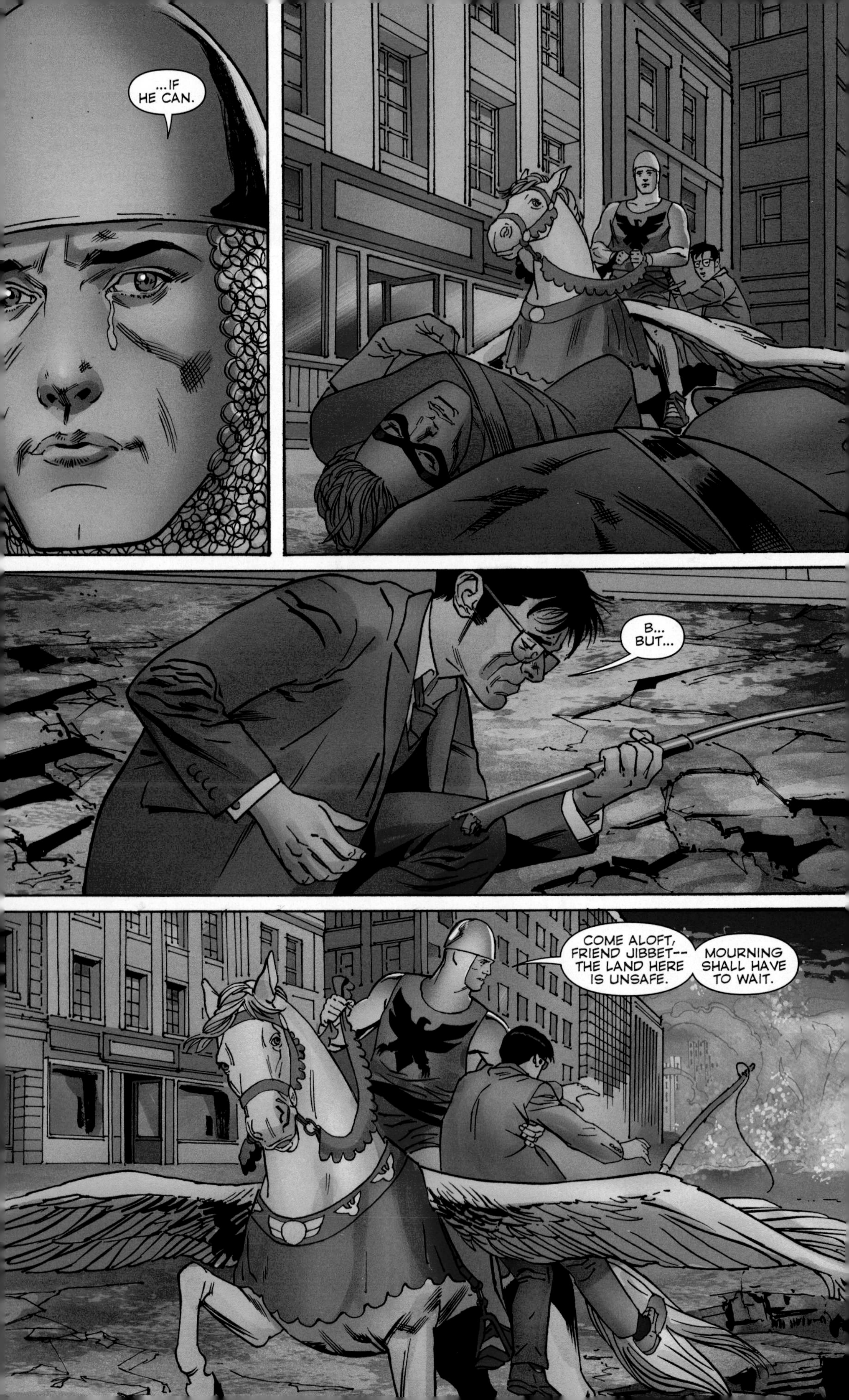
...IF
HE CAN.
B...
BUT...
COME ALOFT, FRIEND JIBBET--THE LAND HERE IS UNSAFE.
MOURNING SHALL HAVE TO WAIT.

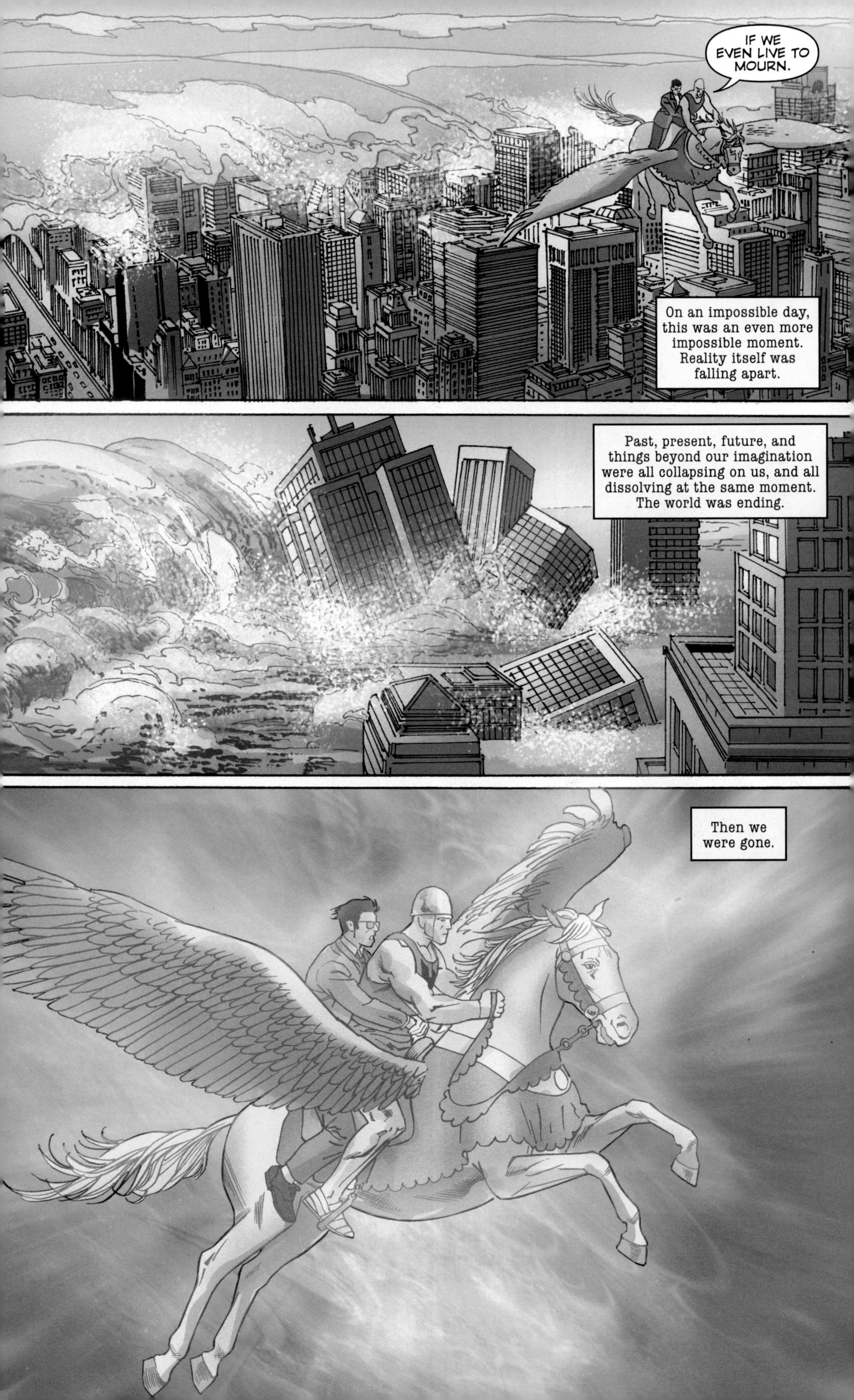
IF WE EVEN LIVE TO MOURN.
On an impossible day, this was an even more impossible moment. Reality itself was falling apart.
Past, present, future, and things beyond our imagination were all collapsing on us, and all dissolving at the same moment. The world was ending.
Then we were gone.

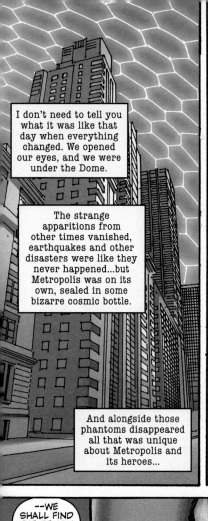

I don't need to tell you what it was like that day when everything changed. We opened our eyes, and we were under the Dome.

The strange apparitions from other times vanished, earthquakes and other disasters were like they never happened...but Metropolis was on its own, sealed in some bizarre cosmic bottle.

And alongside those phantoms disappeared all that was unique about Metropolis and its heroes...

BY MERLIN'S BEARD!

WHUMP

...with, I may add, a thud.

WHAT CURSE IS THIS, THAT OUR ENCHANTMENT FADES! VICTORY--BE STRONG, MY STEED--

HORSELEGS

--WE SHALL FIND THE DEMON THAT HAS DONE--

--AND RENDER JUST--

NO!!

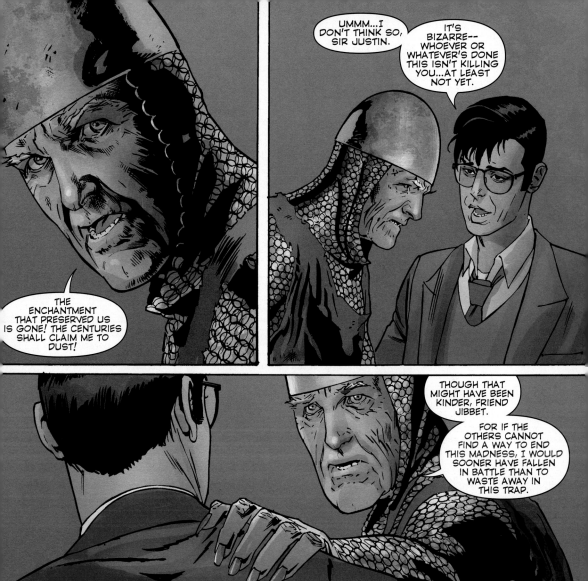

UMMM...I DON'T THINK SO, SIR JUSTIN.

IT'S BIZARRE-- WHOEVER OR WHATEVER'S DONE THIS ISN'T KILLING YOU...AT LEAST NOT YET.

THE ENCHANTMENT THAT PRESERVED US IS GONE! THE CENTURIES SHALL CLAIM ME TO DUST!

THOUGH THAT MIGHT HAVE BEEN KINDER, FRIEND JIBBET.

FOR IF THE OTHERS CANNOT FIND A WAY TO END THIS MADNESS, I WOULD SOONER HAVE FALLEN IN BATTLE THAN TO WASTE AWAY IN THIS TRAP.

I SEE NONE OF MY COMRADES IN THE SKY, STRIKING AT THE STRANGE FORCES THAT HAVE IMPRISONED US. HAVE WE BEEN SAVED? OR MERELY BROUGHT FROM ONE FORM OF DOOM TO ANOTHER?

IT'S BEYOND WEIRD, BUT IT CAN'T LAST...METROPOLIS CAN'T FEED ITSELF FOR A WEEK WITHOUT FOOD BEING BROUGHT IN, OR WATER FROM THE RESERVOIRS.

AND DOESN'T MOST OF OUR ELECTRICITY COME FROM THE NUCLEAR PLANTS UPSTATE?

At first, we thought time was running out. The big guns knew their powers were suddenly gone, but it didn't stop them from desperately trying to break us free.

Pointless.

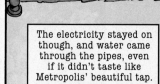

The electricity stayed on though, and water came through the pipes, even if it didn't taste like Metropolis' beautiful tap.

Life Support Inexplicably Working

l resources are continuing to be provided to th Mayor Gaines announced at today's press con e determined that drinking water is safe, and in warehouses are natural, even though the r ovision is not."

r investigations by other branches of the city tration indicate that most survival needs can for the short term. Arrangements to increase se in the new city limits are being developed,

What the Keepers (as we began calling them) didn't provide, we tried to manage. Heroes like the Star-Spangled Kid's sidekick, Stripesy, dug in—even fixing air conditioning units, so they could filter the Dome smell out.

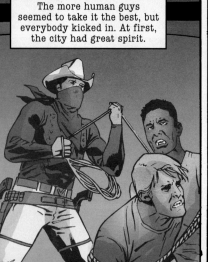

The more human guys seemed to take it the best, but everybody kicked in. At first, the city had great spirit.

It got tired fast. No news of the rest of the planet—cousins, parents, children living in different cities.

Hell, even libraries got popular again. There was no entertainment we didn't make ourselves. Hollywood was beyond the Dome, if it still existed.

If anything still existed

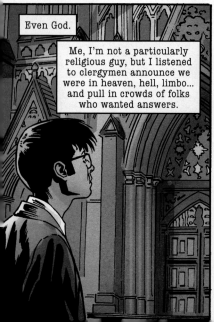

Even God.

Me, I'm not a particularly religious guy, but I listened to clergymen announce we were in heaven, hell, limbo... and pull in crowds of folks who wanted answers.

I watched the waters flowing, and wondered what was on the other side...

...and let other guys try to swim their way out, tunnel their way under...or adjust themselves to our captivity.

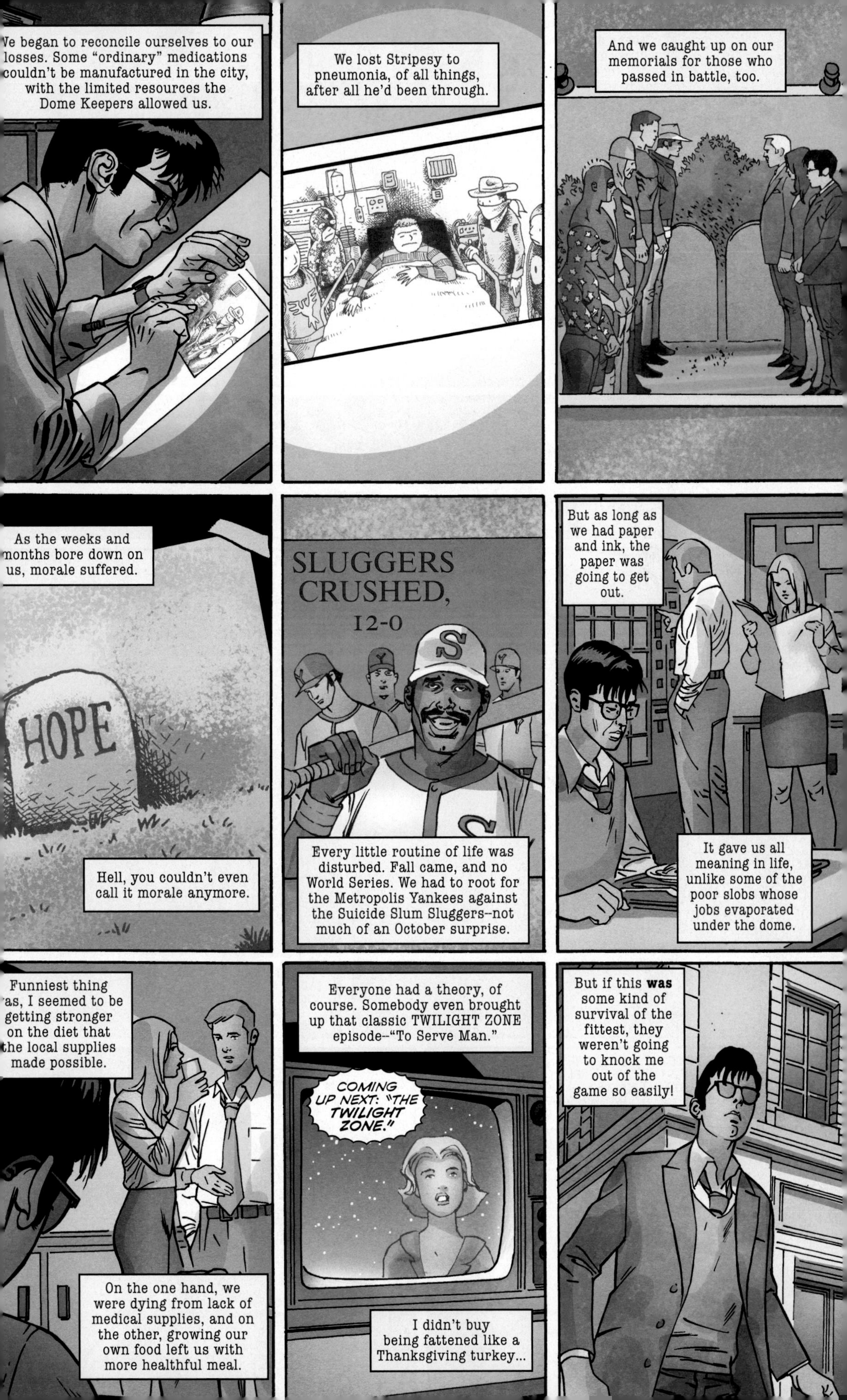

Ve began to reconcile ourselves to our losses. Some "ordinary" medications couldn't be manufactured in the city, with the limited resources the Dome Keepers allowed us.
We lost Stripesy to pneumonia, of all things, after all he'd been through.
And we caught up on our memorials for those who passed in battle, too.
As the weeks and nonths bore down on us, morale suffered.
HOPE
Hell, you couldn't even call it morale anymore.
SLUGGERS CRUSHED, 12-0
Every little routine of life was disturbed. Fall came, and no World Series. We had to root for the Metropolis Yankees against the Suicide Slum Sluggers--not much of an October surprise.
But as long as we had paper and ink, the paper was going to get out.
It gave us all meaning in life, unlike some of the poor slobs whose jobs evaporated under the dome.
Funniest thing 'as, I seemed to be getting stronger on the diet that the local supplies made possible.
On the one hand, we were dying from lack of medical supplies, and on the other, growing our own food left us with more healthful meal.
Everyone had a theory, of course. Somebody even brought up that classic TWILIGHT ZONE episode--"To Serve Man."
COMING UP NEXT: "THE TWILIGHT ZONE."
I didn't buy being fattened like a Thanksgiving turkey...
But if this **was** some kind of survival of the fittest, they weren't going to knock me out of the game so easily!

Every day, I was going out with my sketchbook, getting a fresh cartoon ready to buck up the city!

Lots of people had given up their jobs as meaningless, but not me.

My old art teacher taught me that cartoons created laughter, and laughter was the best medicine...

...at least for some.

HEY, VICTORY--GOT SOMETHING FOR YOU HERE, SOMEWHERE...

HARD TO GET THE SUGAR CUBES YOU LOVE, BUT HOW ABOUT SOMETHING NUTRITIOUS?

MAYBE THE DOME WANTS YOU IN SHAPE, TOO.

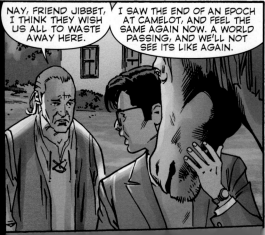

NAY, FRIEND JIBBET, I THINK THEY WISH US ALL TO WASTE AWAY HERE.

I SAW THE END OF AN EPOCH AT CAMELOT, AND FEEL THE SAME AGAIN NOW. A WORLD PASSING, AND WE'LL NOT SEE ITS LIKE AGAIN.

THE HEROES OF YOUR TIME HAVE ALL FADED, AND EVE THOSE WHO STILL STRUGGLE HAVE NO HOPE.

IT HAS BEEN TOO MANY MONTHS, MEASURED AS THEIR SHORT LIVES ARE TALLIED.

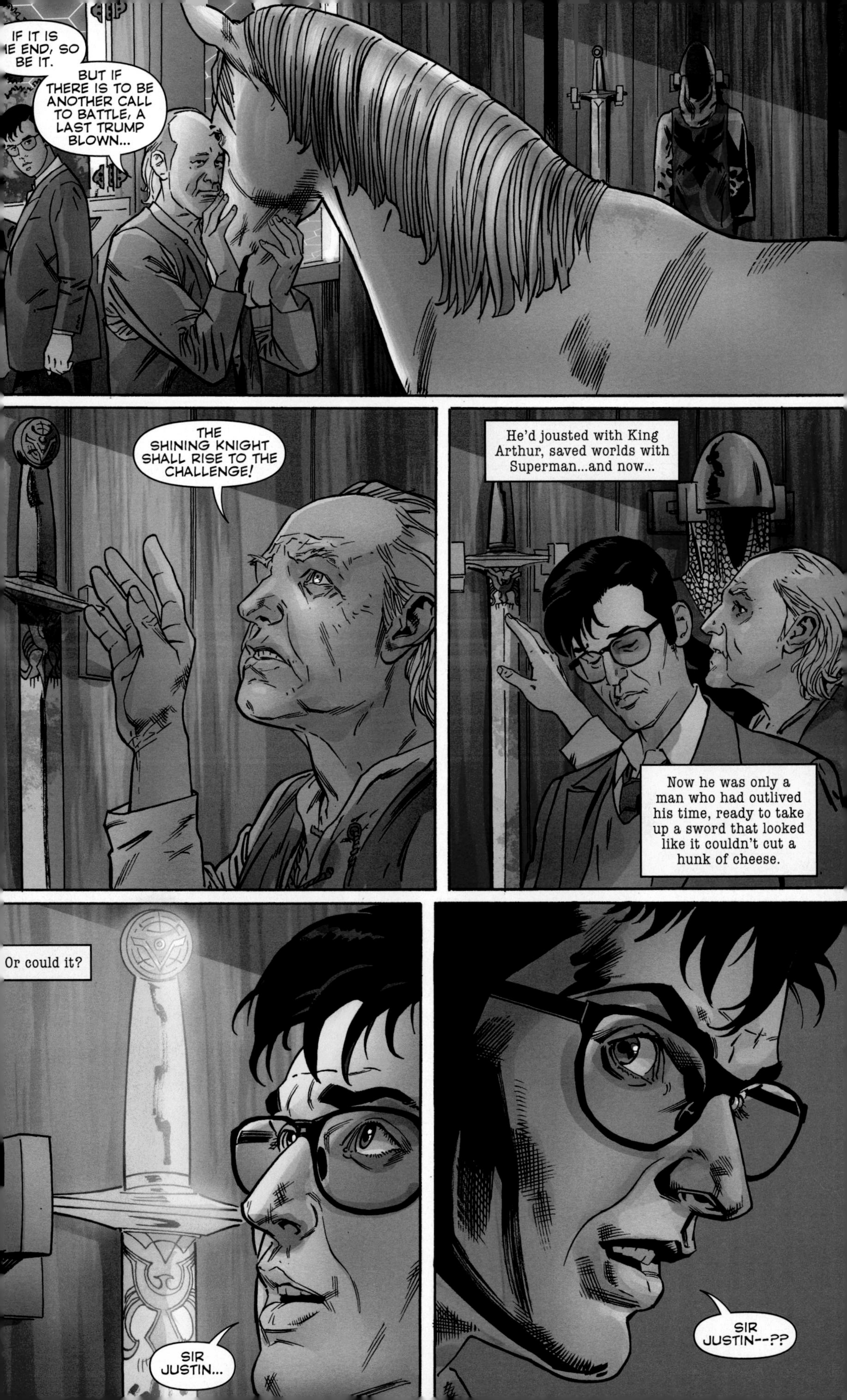
IF IT IS
IE END, SO BE IT.
BUT IF THERE IS TO BE ANOTHER CALL TO BATTLE, A LAST TRUMP BLOWN...
THE SHINING KNIGHT SHALL RISE TO THE CHALLENGE!
He'd jousted with King Arthur, saved worlds with Superman...and now...
Now he was only a man who had outlived his time, ready to take up a sword that looked like it couldn't cut a hunk of cheese.
Or could it?
SIR JUSTIN...
SIR JUSTIN--??

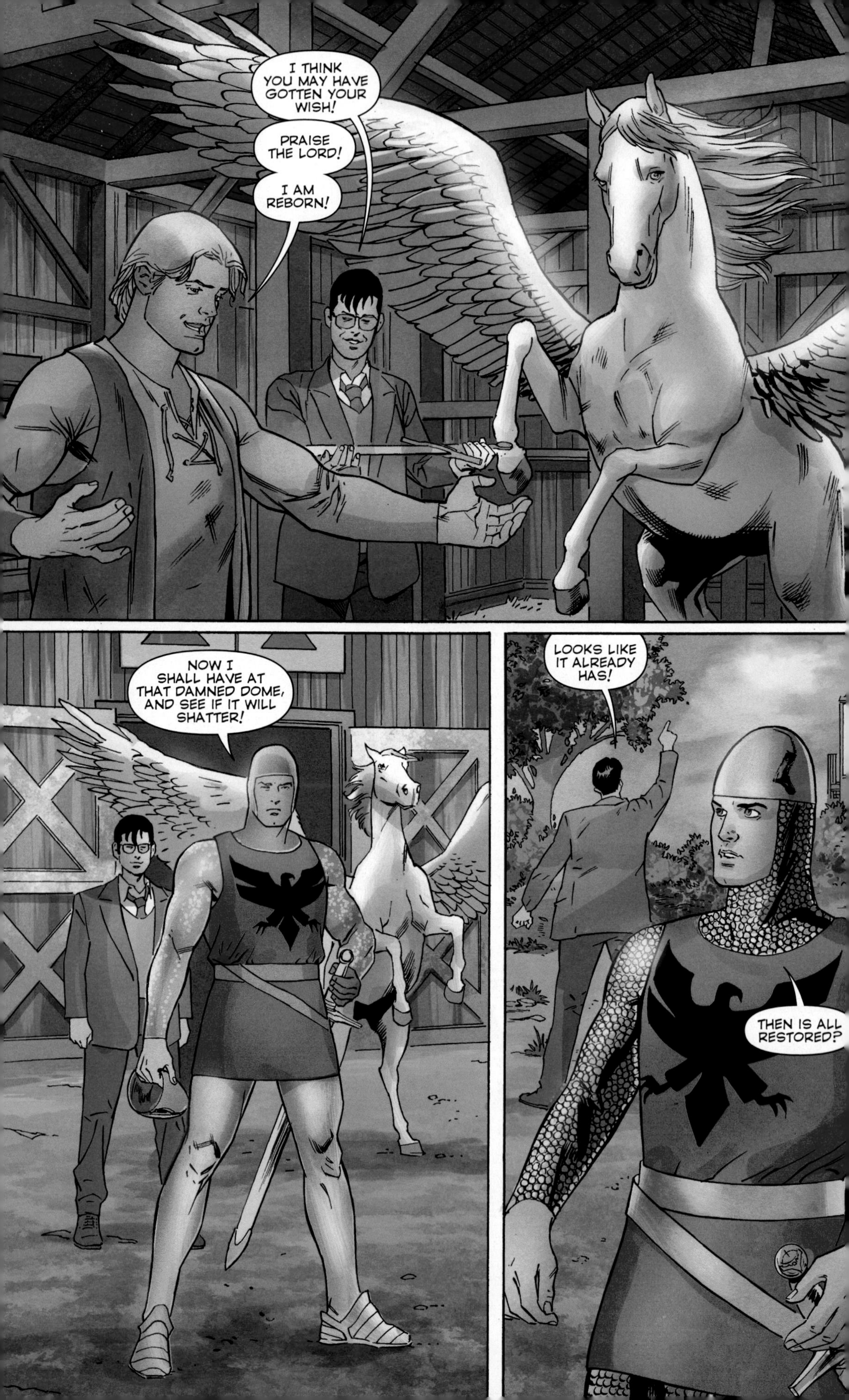
I THINK YOU MAY HAVE GOTTEN YOUR WISH!
PRAISE THE LORD!
I AM REBORN!
NOW I SHALL HAVE AT THAT DAMNED DOME, AND SEE IF IT WILL SHATTER!
LOOKS LIKE IT ALREADY HAS!
THEN IS ALL RESTORED?

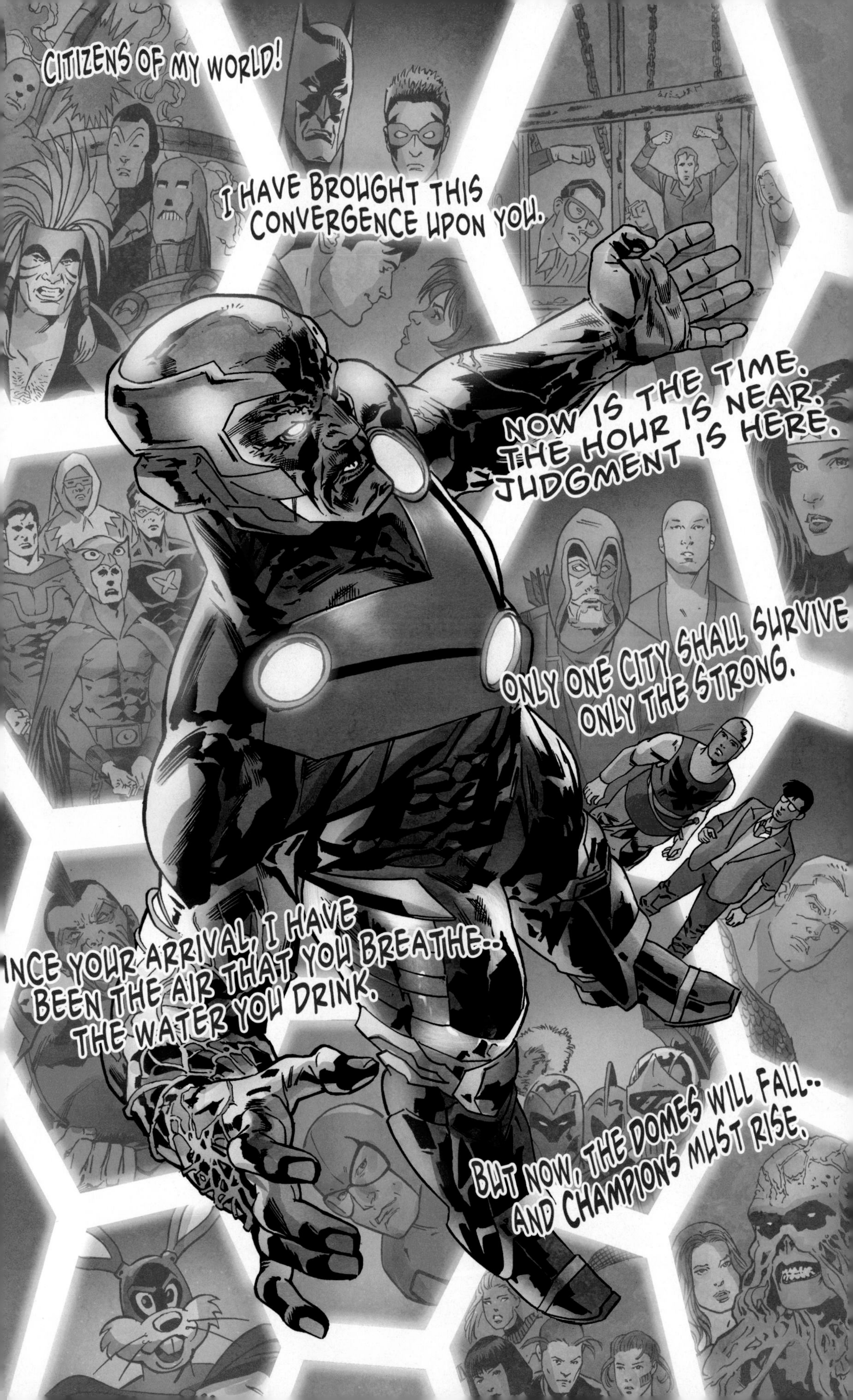
CITIZENS OF MY WORLD!
I HAVE BROUGHT THIS CONVERGENCE UPON YOU.
NOW IS THE TIME. THE HOUR IS NEAR. JUDGMENT IS HERE.
ONLY ONE CITY SHALL SURVIVE ONLY THE STRONG.
INCE YOUR ARRIVAL, I HAVE BEEN THE AIR THAT YOU BREATHE.. THE WATER YOU DRINK.
BUT NOW, THE DOMES WILL FALL.. AND CHAMPIONS MUST RISE.

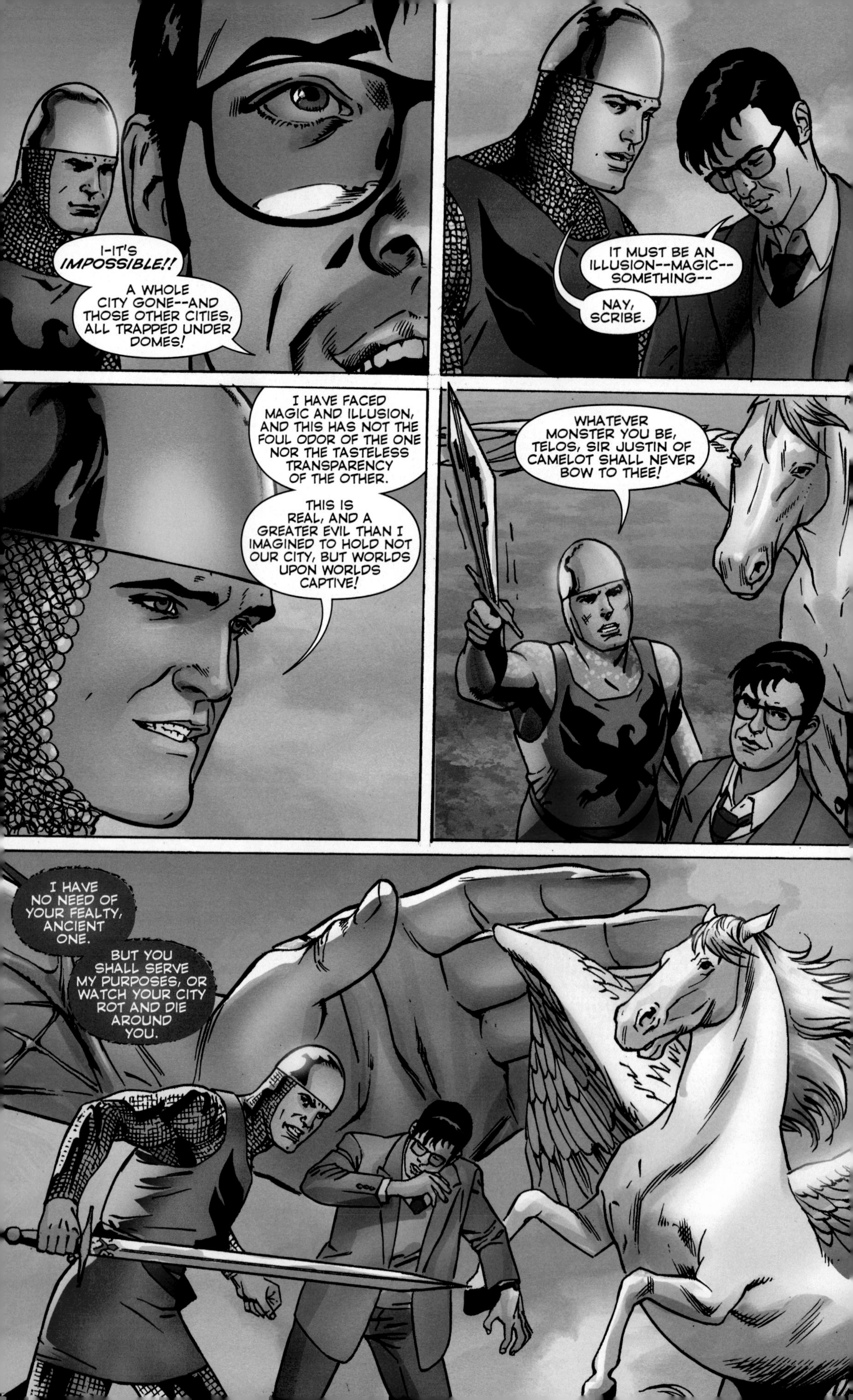
I-IT'S *IMPOSSIBLE!!*
A WHOLE CITY GONE--AND THOSE OTHER CITIES, ALL TRAPPED UNDER DOMES!
IT MUST BE AN ILLUSION--MAGIC--SOMETHING--
NAY, SCRIBE.
I HAVE FACED MAGIC AND ILLUSION, AND THIS HAS NOT THE FOUL ODOR OF THE ONE NOR THE TASTELESS TRANSPARENCY OF THE OTHER.
THIS IS REAL, AND A GREATER EVIL THAN I IMAGINED TO HOLD NOT OUR CITY, BUT WORLDS UPON WORLDS CAPTIVE!
WHATEVER MONSTER YOU BE, TELOS, SIR JUSTIN OF CAMELOT SHALL NEVER BOW TO THEE!
I HAVE NO NEED OF YOUR FEALTY, ANCIENT ONE.
BUT YOU SHALL SERVE MY PURPOSES, OR WATCH YOUR CITY ROT AND DIE AROUND YOU.

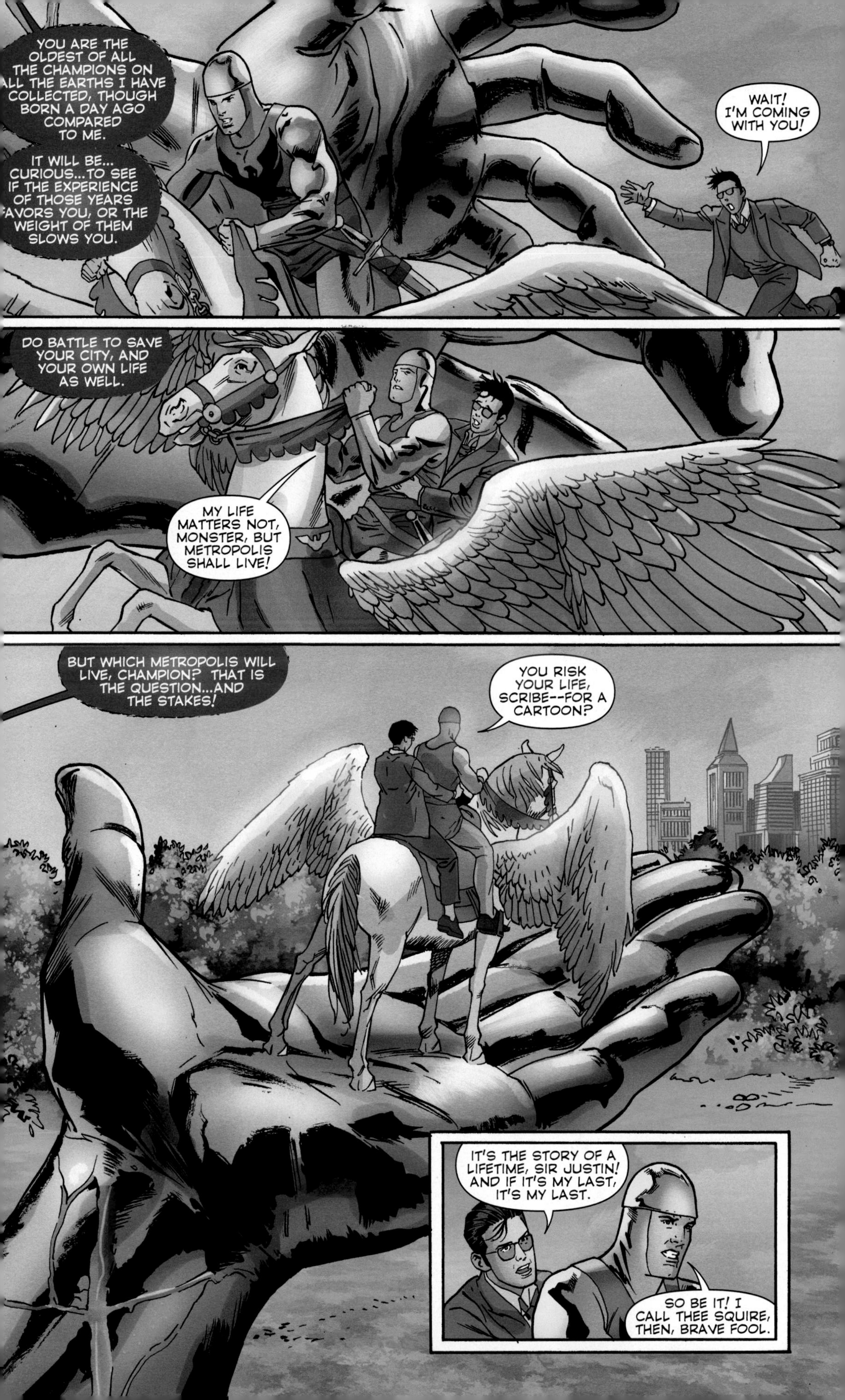
YOU ARE THE OLDEST OF ALL THE CHAMPIONS ON ALL THE EARTHS I HAVE COLLECTED, THOUGH BORN A DAY AGO COMPARED TO ME.
IT WILL BE... CURIOUS...TO SEE IF THE EXPERIENCE OF THOSE YEARS FAVORS YOU, OR THE WEIGHT OF THEM SLOWS YOU.
WAIT! I'M COMING WITH YOU!
DO BATTLE TO SAVE YOUR CITY, AND YOUR OWN LIFE AS WELL.
MY LIFE MATTERS NOT, MONSTER, BUT METROPOLIS SHALL LIVE!
BUT WHICH METROPOLIS WILL LIVE, CHAMPION? THAT IS THE QUESTION...AND THE STAKES!
YOU RISK YOUR LIFE, SCRIBE--FOR A CARTOON?
IT'S THE STORY OF A LIFETIME, SIR JUSTIN! AND IF IT'S MY LAST, IT'S MY LAST.
SO BE IT! I CALL THEE SQUIRE, THEN, BRAVE FOOL.

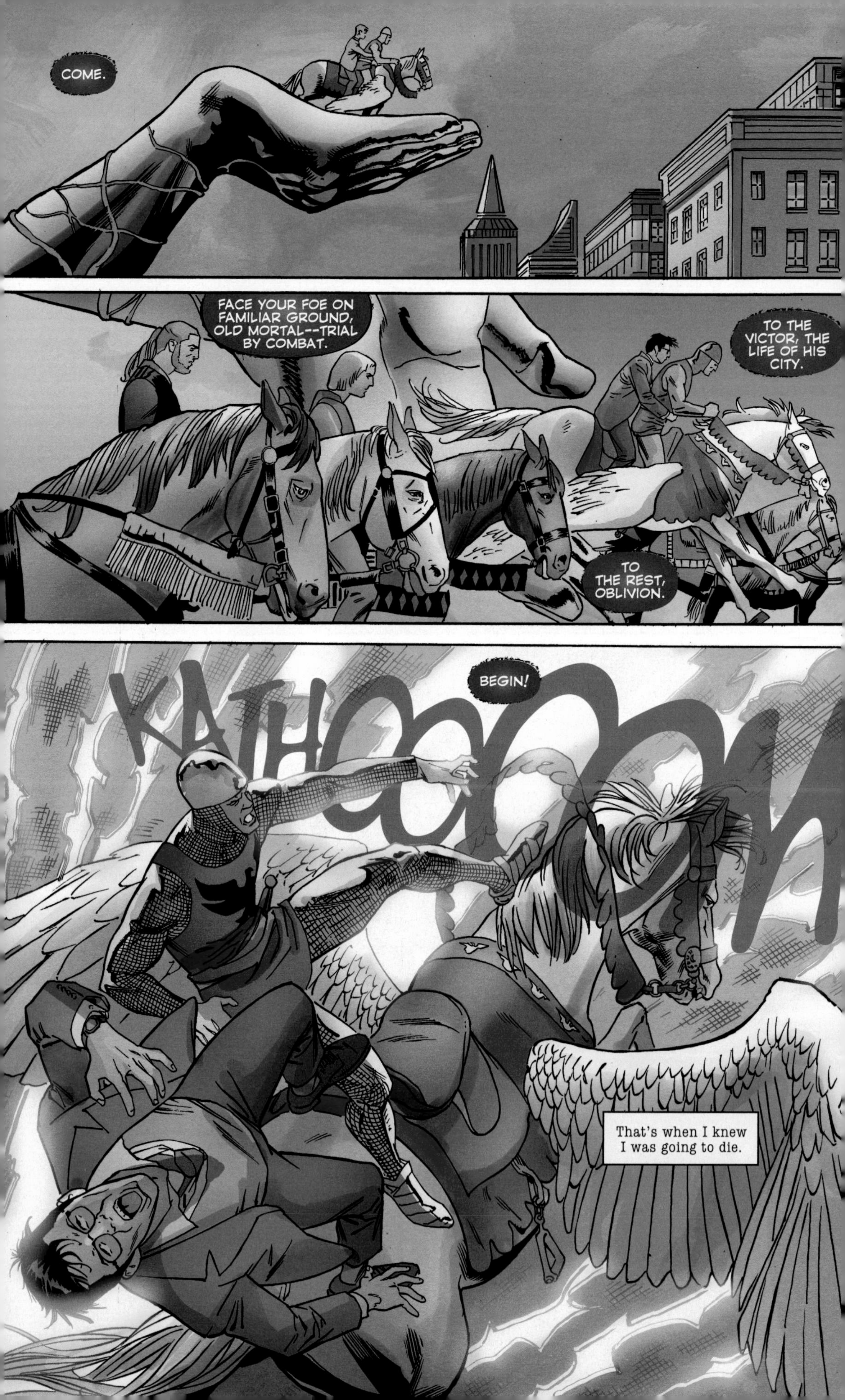
COME.
FACE YOUR FOE ON FAMILIAR GROUND, OLD MORTAL--TRIAL BY COMBAT.
TO THE VICTOR, THE LIFE OF HIS CITY.
TO THE REST, OBLIVION.
BEGIN!
KATHOOOOM
That's when I knew I was going to die.

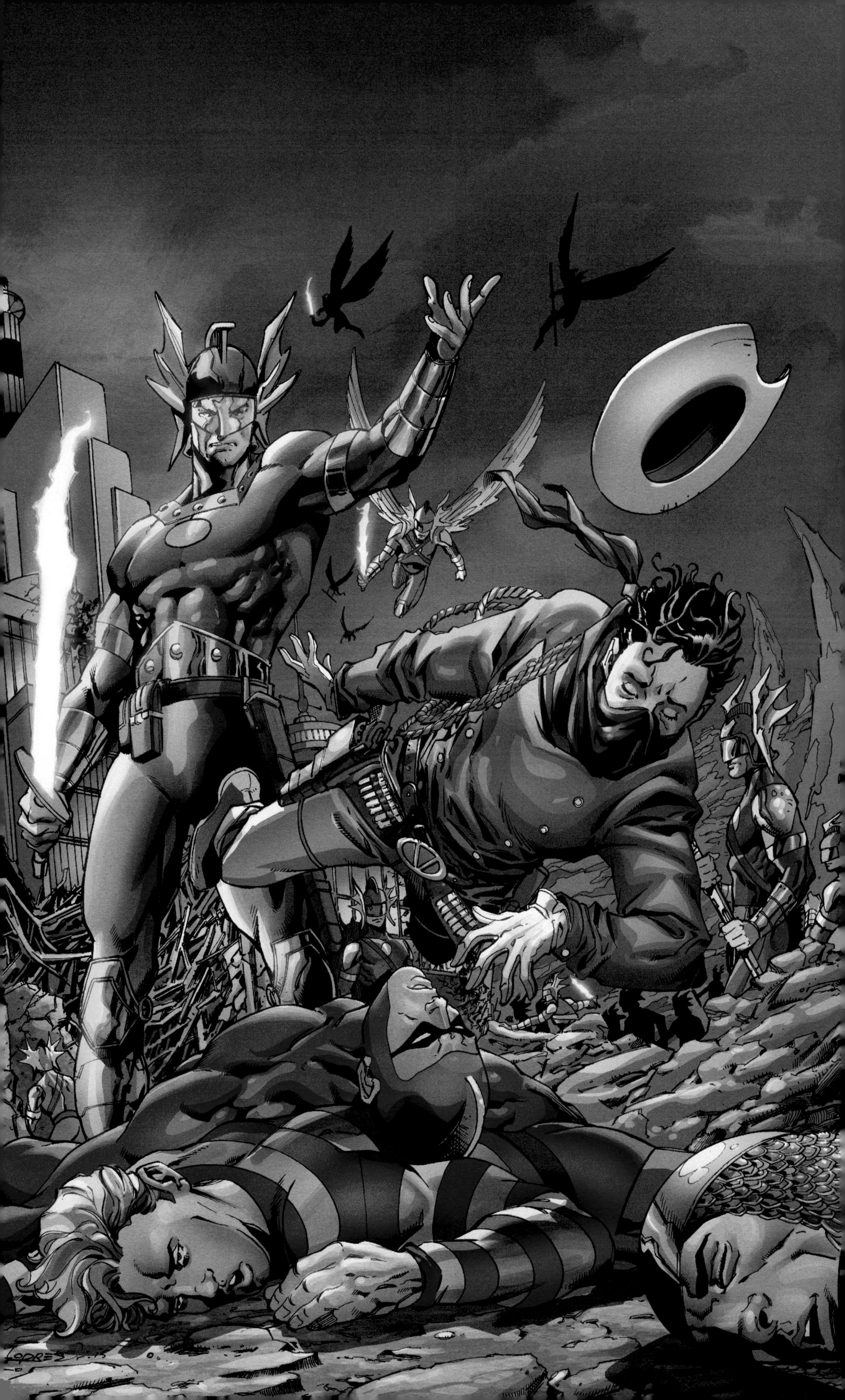

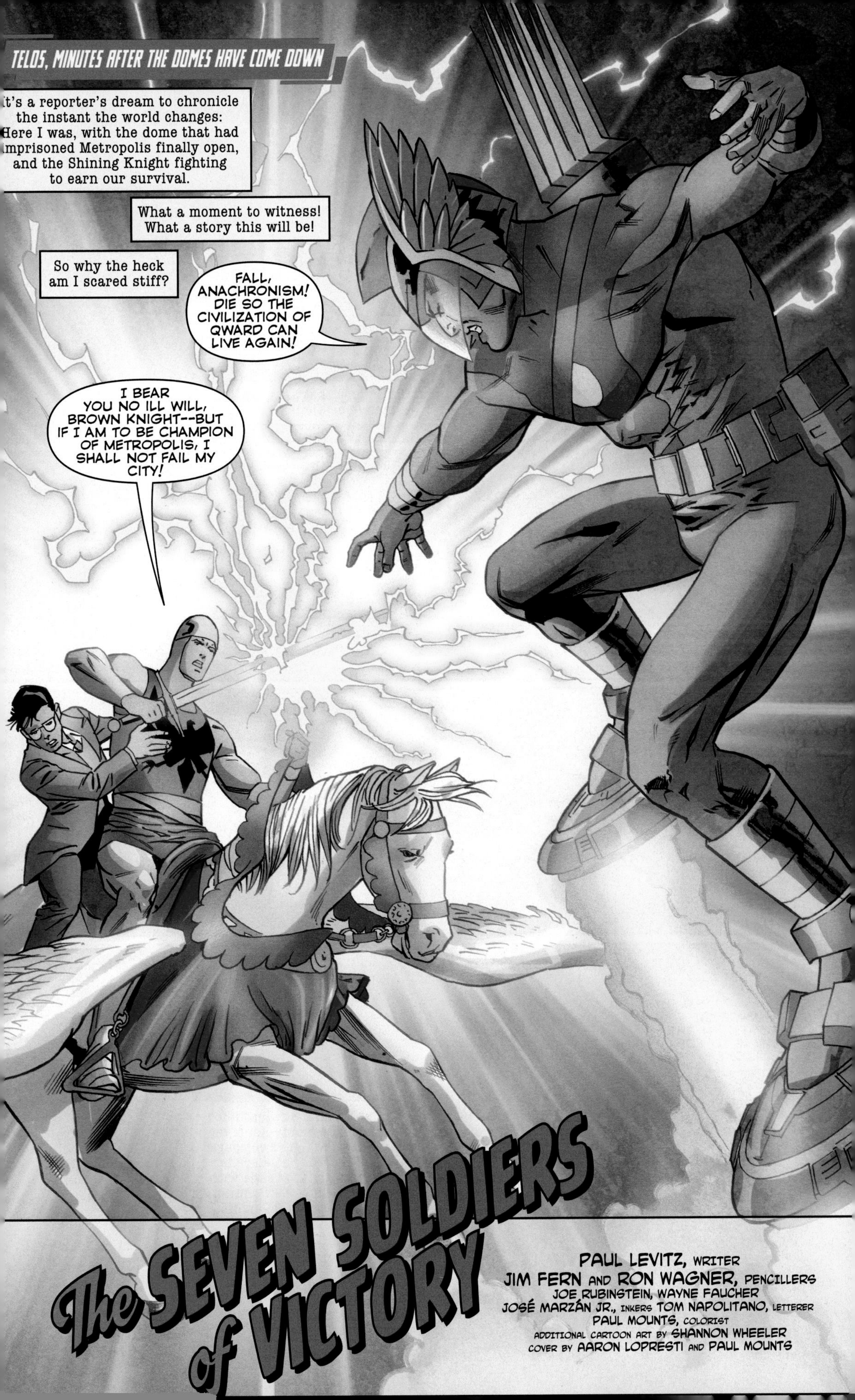
TELOS, MINUTES AFTER THE DOMES HAVE COME DOWN
It's a reporter's dream to chronicle the instant the world changes: Here I was, with the dome that had imprisoned Metropolis finally open, and the Shining Knight fighting to earn our survival.
What a moment to witness! What a story this will be!
So why the heck am I scared stiff?
FALL, ANACHRONISM! DIE SO THE CIVILIZATION OF QWARD CAN LIVE AGAIN!
I BEAR YOU NO ILL WILL, BROWN KNIGHT--BUT IF I AM TO BE CHAMPION OF METROPOLIS, I SHALL NOT FAIL MY CITY!
The SEVEN SOLDIERS of VICTORY
PAUL LEVITZ, WRITER
JIM FERN AND RON WAGNER, PENCILLERS
JOE RUBINSTEIN, WAYNE FAUCHER
JOSÉ MARZÁN JR., INKERS TOM NAPOLITANO, LETTERER
PAUL MOUNTS, COLORIST
ADDITIONAL CARTOON ART BY SHANNON WHEELER
COVER BY AARON LOPRESTI AND PAUL MOUNTS

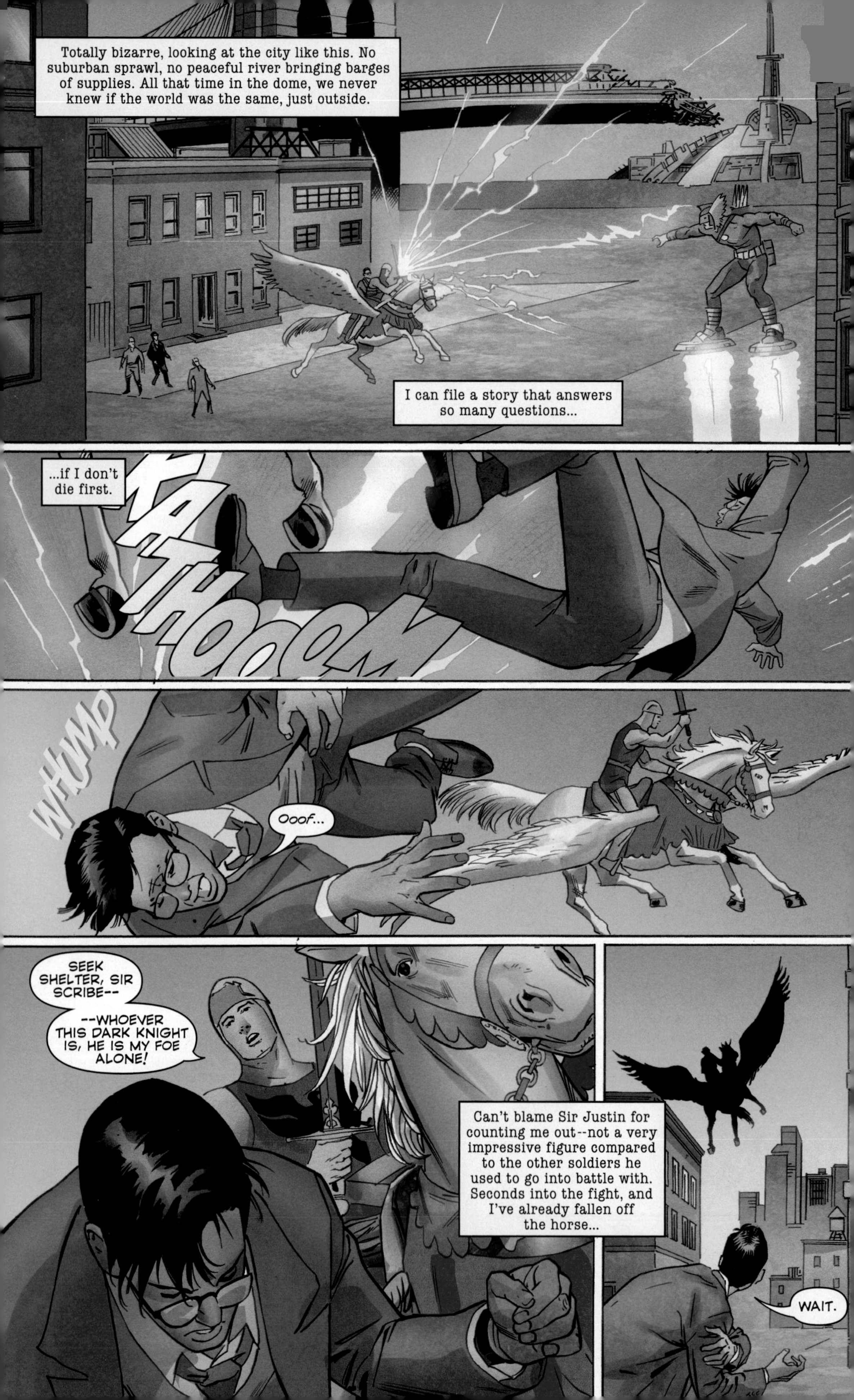
Totally bizarre, looking at the city like this. No suburban sprawl, no peaceful river bringing barges of supplies. All that time in the dome, we never knew if the world was the same, just outside.
I can file a story that answers so many questions...
...if I don't die first.
KATHOOOM
WHUMP
Ooof...
SEEK SHELTER, SIR SCRIBE--
--WHOEVER THIS DARK KNIGHT IS, HE IS MY FOE ALONE!
Can't blame Sir Justin for counting me out--not a very impressive figure compared to the other soldiers he used to go into battle with. Seconds into the fight, and I've already fallen off the horse...
WAIT.

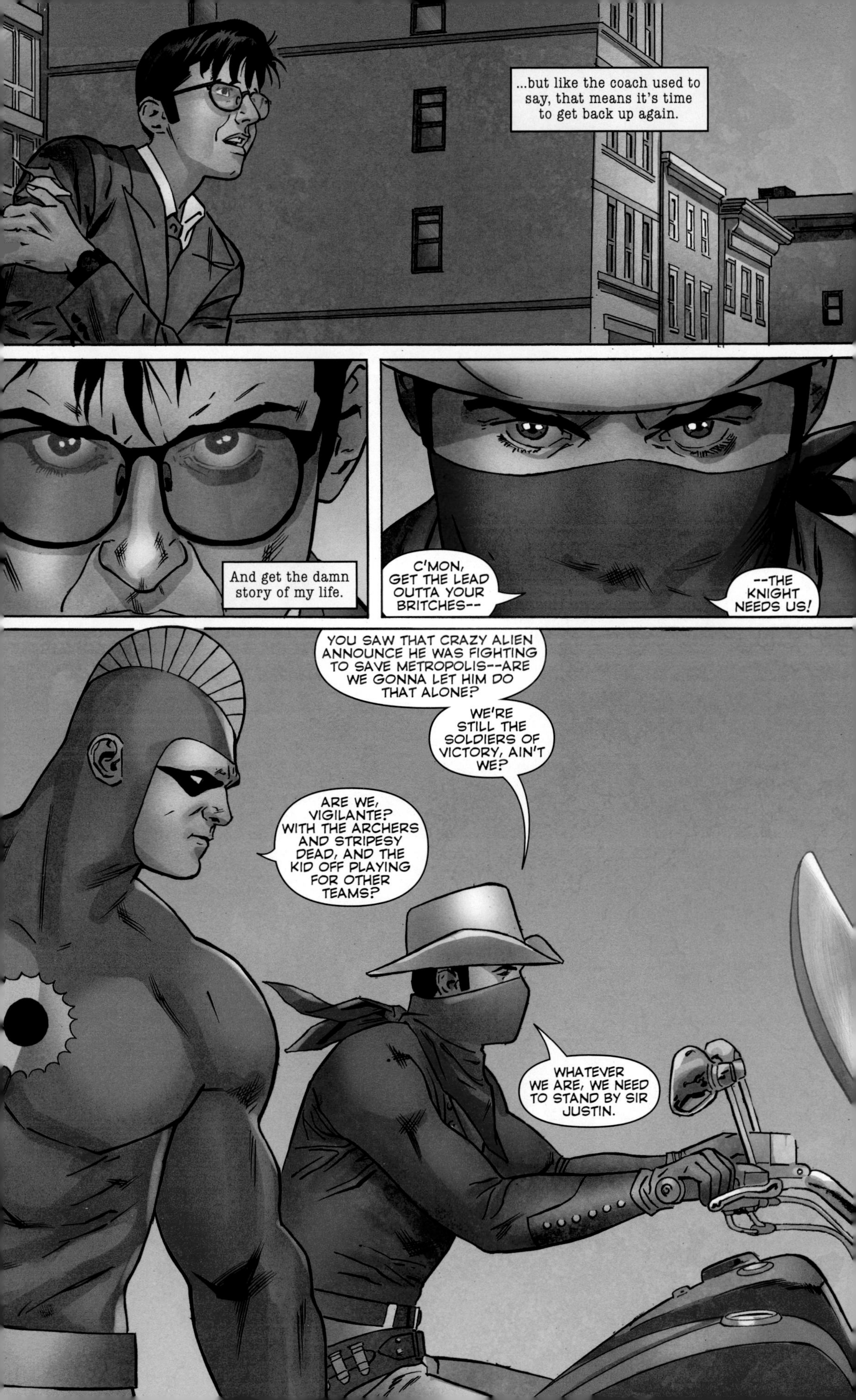
...but like the coach used to say, that means it's time to get back up again.
And get the damn story of my life.
C'MON, GET THE LEAD OUTTA YOUR BRITCHES--
--THE KNIGHT NEEDS US!
YOU SAW THAT CRAZY ALIEN ANNOUNCE HE WAS FIGHTING TO SAVE METROPOLIS--ARE WE GONNA LET HIM DO THAT ALONE?
WE'RE STILL THE SOLDIERS OF VICTORY, AIN'T WE?
ARE WE, VIGILANTE? WITH THE ARCHERS AND STRIPESY DEAD, AND THE KID OFF PLAYING FOR OTHER TEAMS?
WHATEVER WE ARE, WE NEED TO STAND BY SIR JUSTIN.

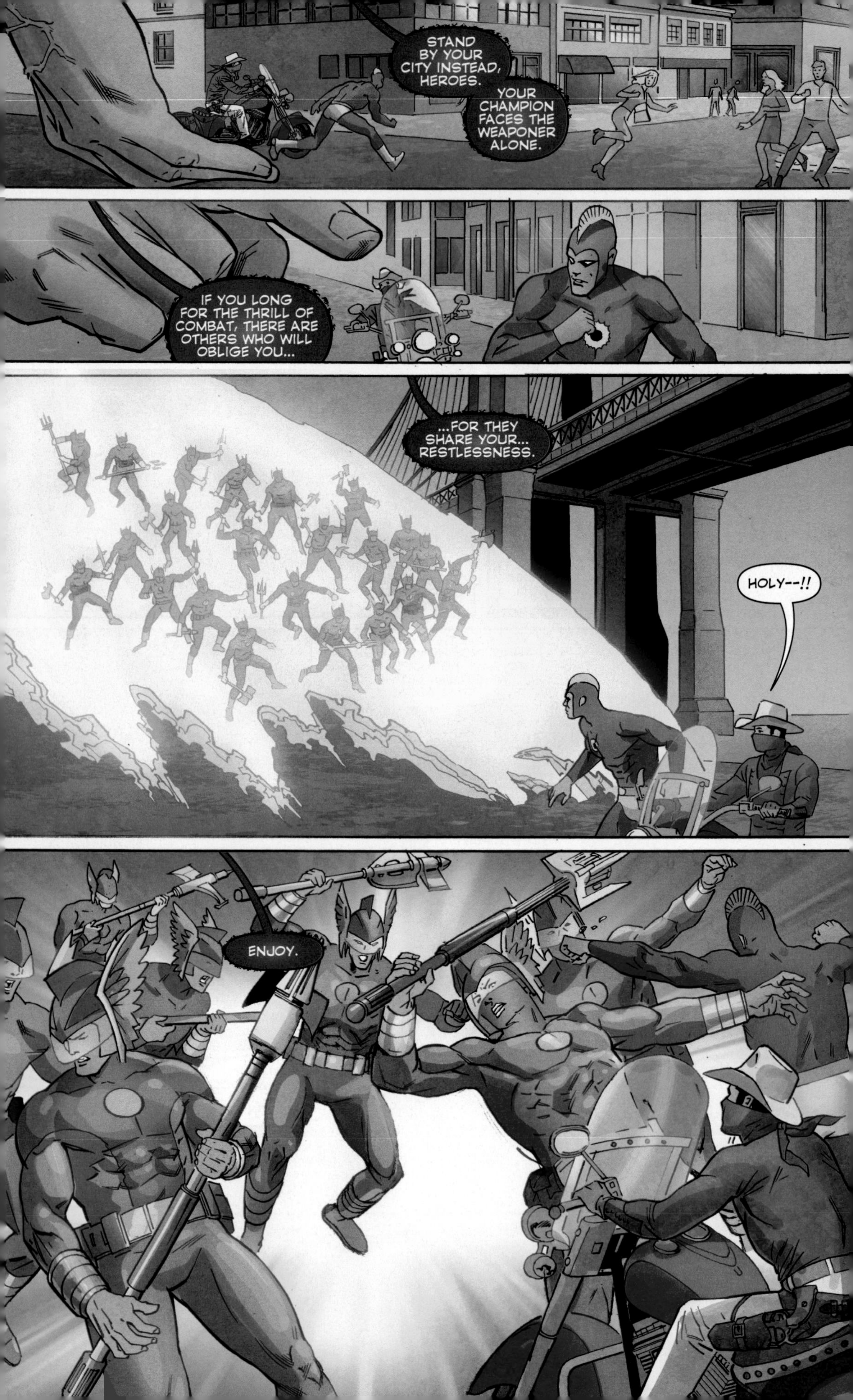
STAND BY YOUR CITY INSTEAD, HEROES.
YOUR CHAMPION FACES THE WEAPONER ALONE.
IF YOU LONG FOR THE THRILL OF COMBAT, THERE ARE OTHERS WHO WILL OBLIGE YOU...
...FOR THEY SHARE YOUR... RESTLESSNESS.
HOLY--!!
ENJOY.

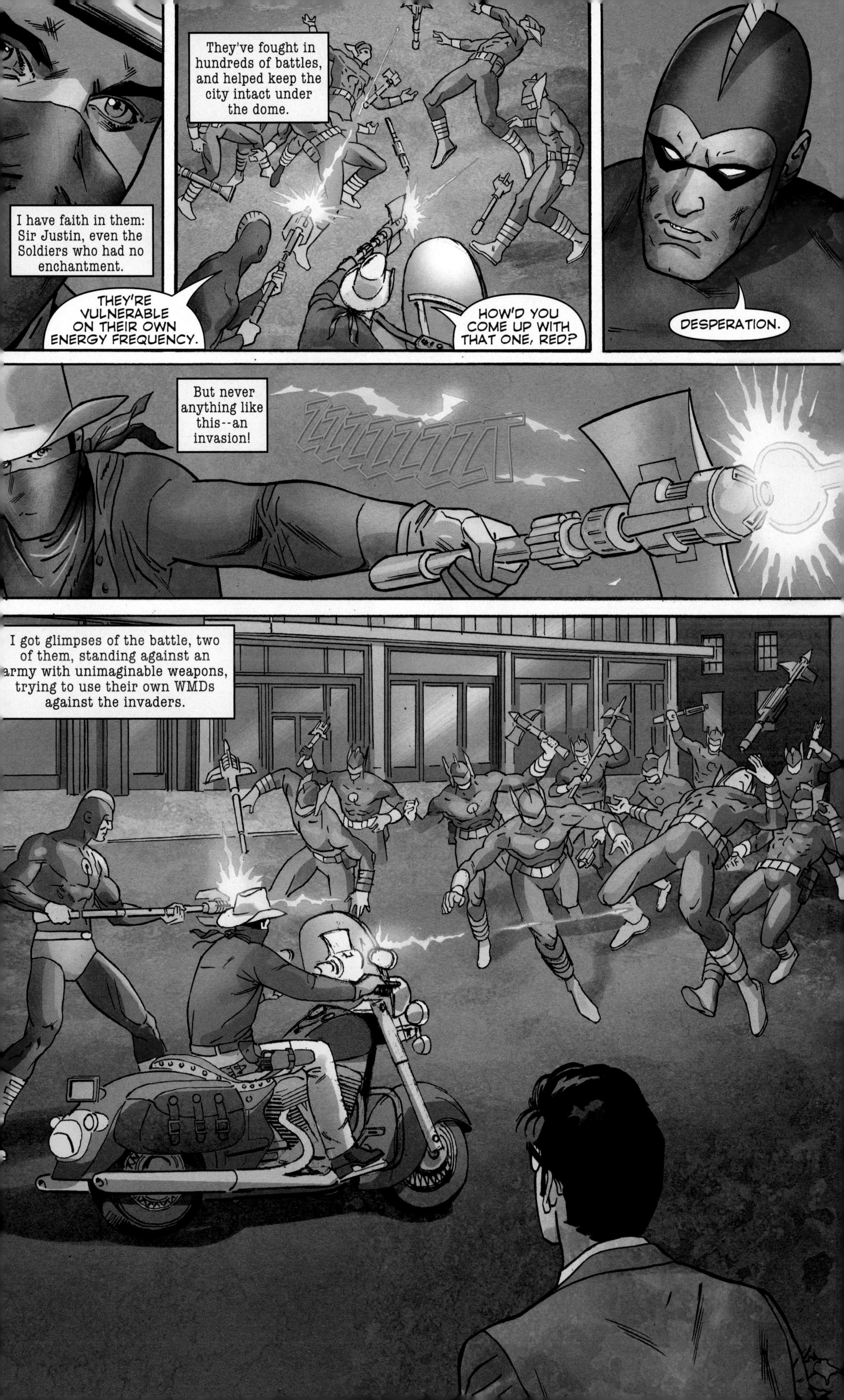

I have faith in them: Sir Justin, even the Soldiers who had no enchantment.
They've fought in hundreds of battles, and helped keep the city intact under the dome.
THEY'RE VULNERABLE ON THEIR OWN ENERGY FREQUENCY.
HOW'D YOU COME UP WITH THAT ONE, RED?
DESPERATION.
But never anything like this--an invasion!
I got glimpses of the battle, two of them, standing against an army with unimaginable weapons, trying to use their own WMDs against the invaders.

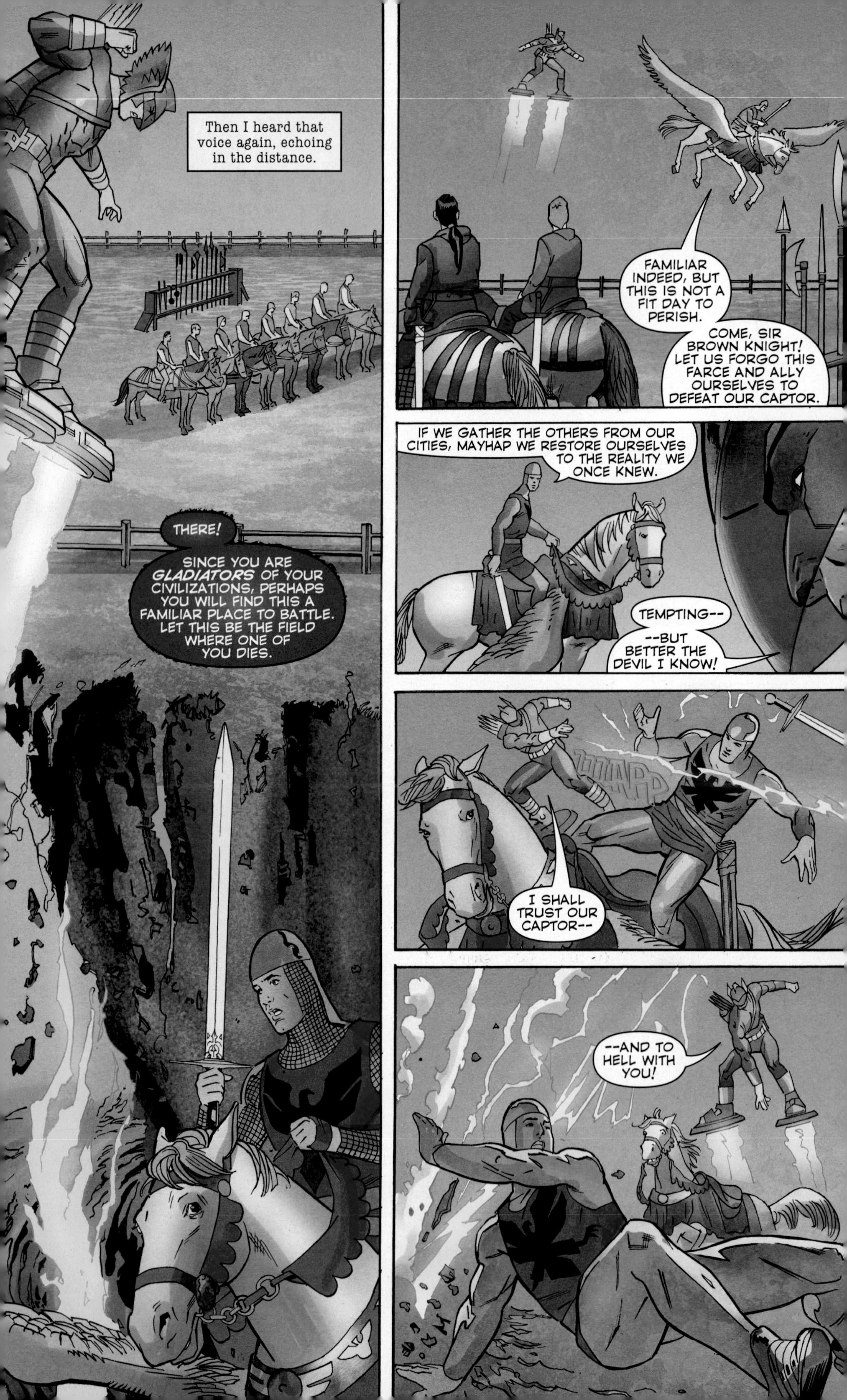
Then I heard that voice again, echoing in the distance.
THERE!
SINCE YOU ARE GLADIATORS OF YOUR CIVILIZATIONS, PERHAPS YOU WILL FIND THIS A FAMILIAR PLACE TO BATTLE. LET THIS BE THE FIELD WHERE ONE OF YOU DIES.
FAMILIAR INDEED, BUT THIS IS NOT A FIT DAY TO PERISH.
COME, SIR BROWN KNIGHT! LET US FORGO THIS FARCE AND ALLY OURSELVES TO DEFEAT OUR CAPTOR.
IF WE GATHER THE OTHERS FROM OUR CITIES, MAYHAP WE RESTORE OURSELVES TO THE REALITY WE ONCE KNEW.
TEMPTING--
--BUT BETTER THE DEVIL I KNOW!
I SHALL TRUST OUR CAPTOR--
--AND TO HELL WITH YOU!

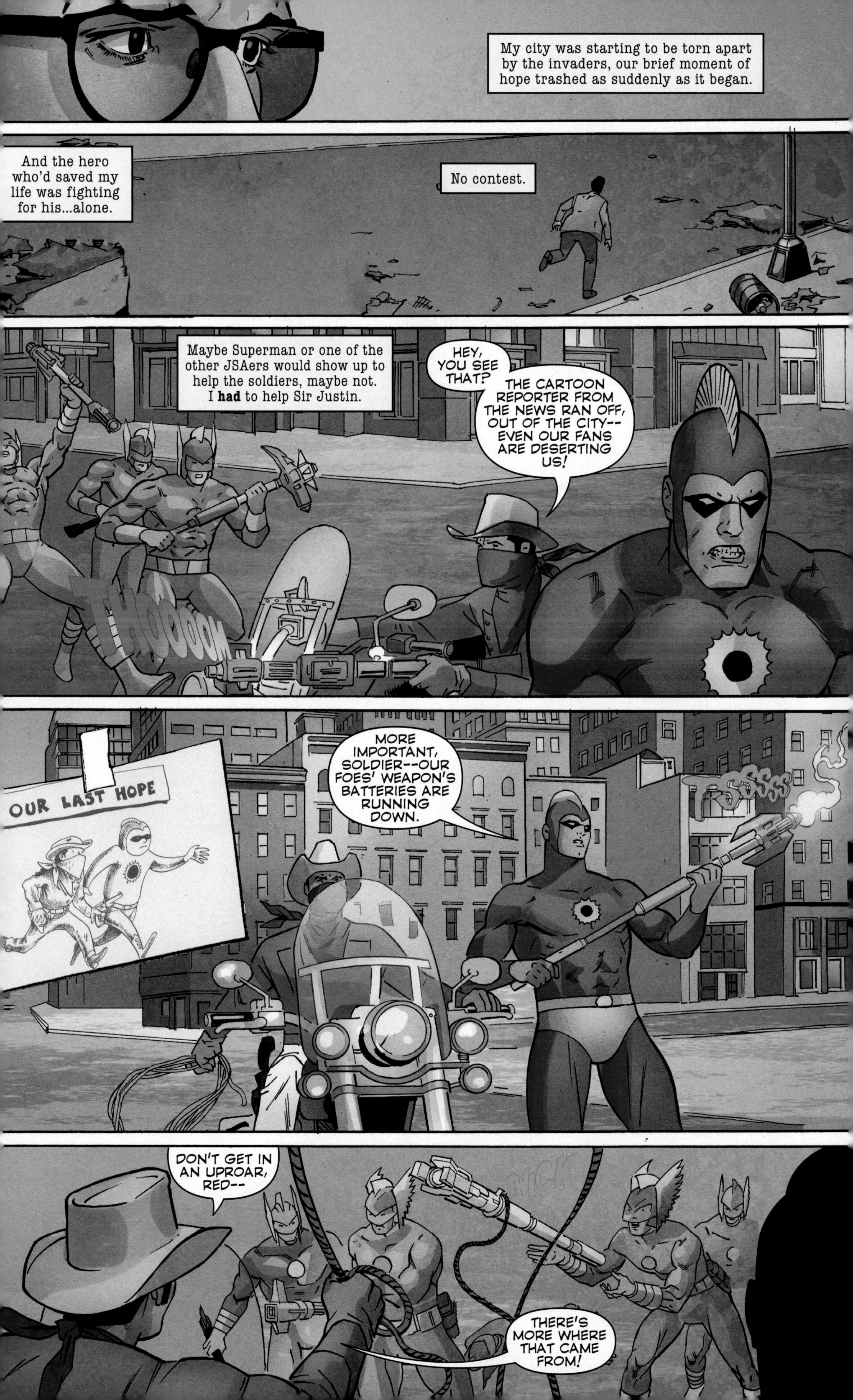

My city was starting to be torn apart by the invaders, our brief moment of hope trashed as suddenly as it began.
And the hero who'd saved my life was fighting for his...alone.
No contest.
Maybe Superman or one of the other JSAers would show up to help the soldiers, maybe not. I **had** to help Sir Justin.
HEY, YOU SEE THAT?
THE CARTOON REPORTER FROM THE NEWS RAN OFF, OUT OF THE CITY-- EVEN OUR FANS ARE DESERTING US!
THOOOOM
OUR LAST HOPE
MORE IMPORTANT, SOLDIER--OUR FOES' WEAPON'S BATTERIES ARE RUNNING DOWN.
DON'T GET IN AN UPROAR, RED--
THERE'S MORE WHERE THAT CAME FROM!

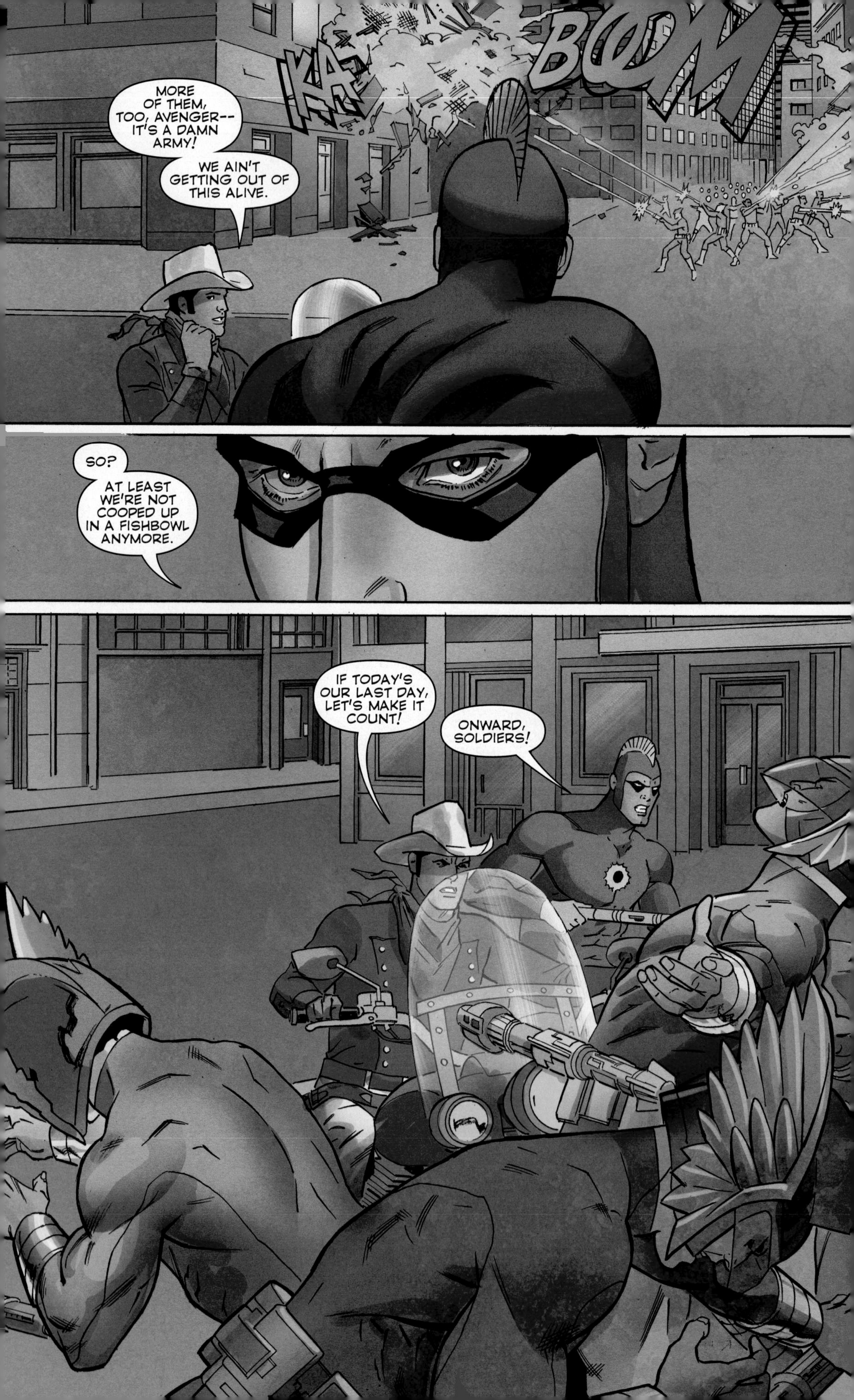
KA-BOOM
MORE OF THEM, TOO, AVENGER-- IT'S A DAMN ARMY!
WE AIN'T GETTING OUT OF THIS ALIVE.
SO?
AT LEAST WE'RE NOT COOPED UP IN A FISHBOWL ANYMORE.
IF TODAY'S OUR LAST DAY, LET'S MAKE IT COUNT!
ONWARD, SOLDIERS!

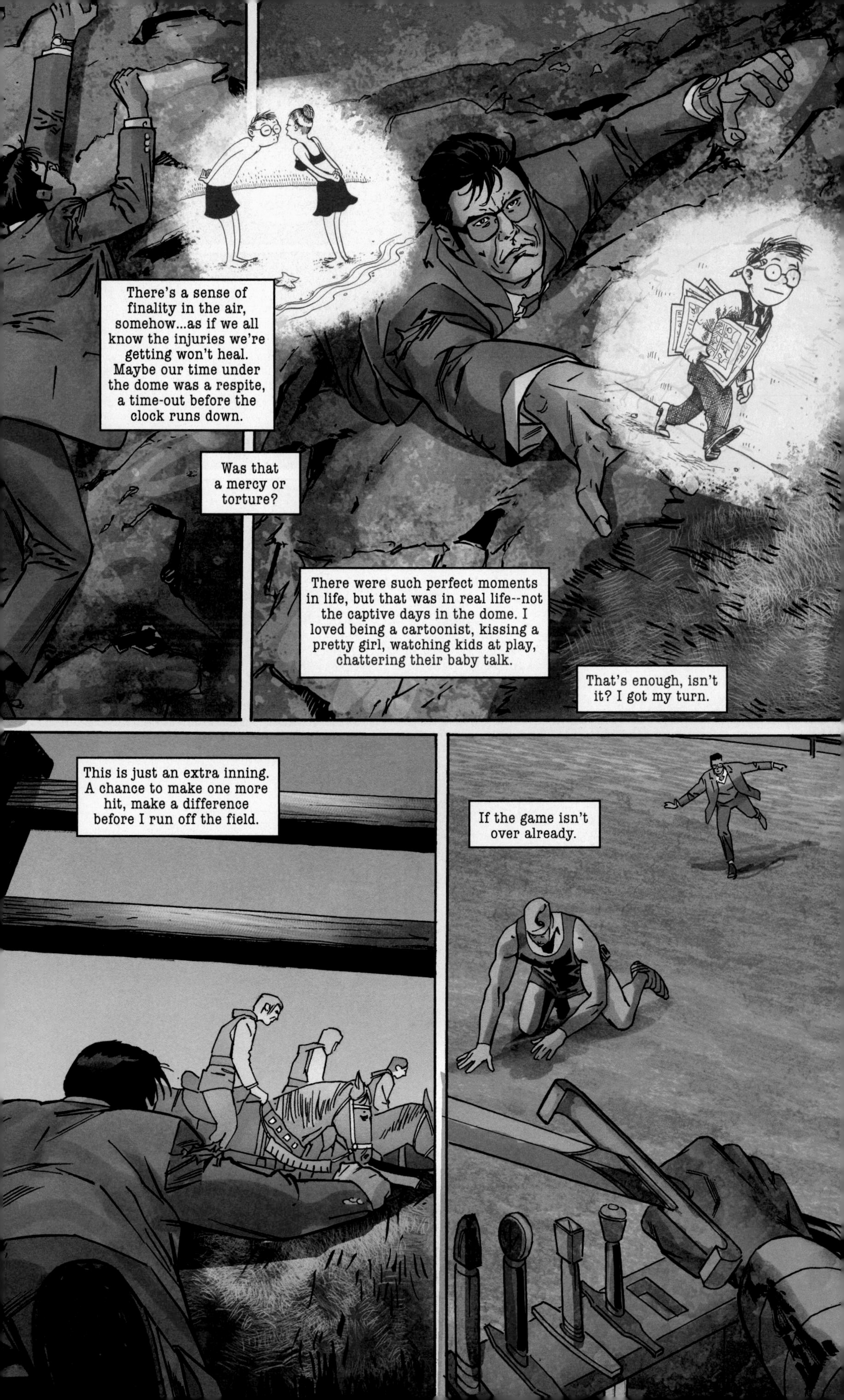
There's a sense of finality in the air, somehow...as if we all know the injuries we're getting won't heal. Maybe our time under the dome was a respite, a time-out before the clock runs down.
Was that a mercy or torture?
There were such perfect moments in life, but that was in real life--not the captive days in the dome. I loved being a cartoonist, kissing a pretty girl, watching kids at play, chattering their baby talk.
That's enough, isn't it? I got my turn.
This is just an extra inning. A chance to make one more hit, make a difference before I run off the field.
If the game isn't over already.

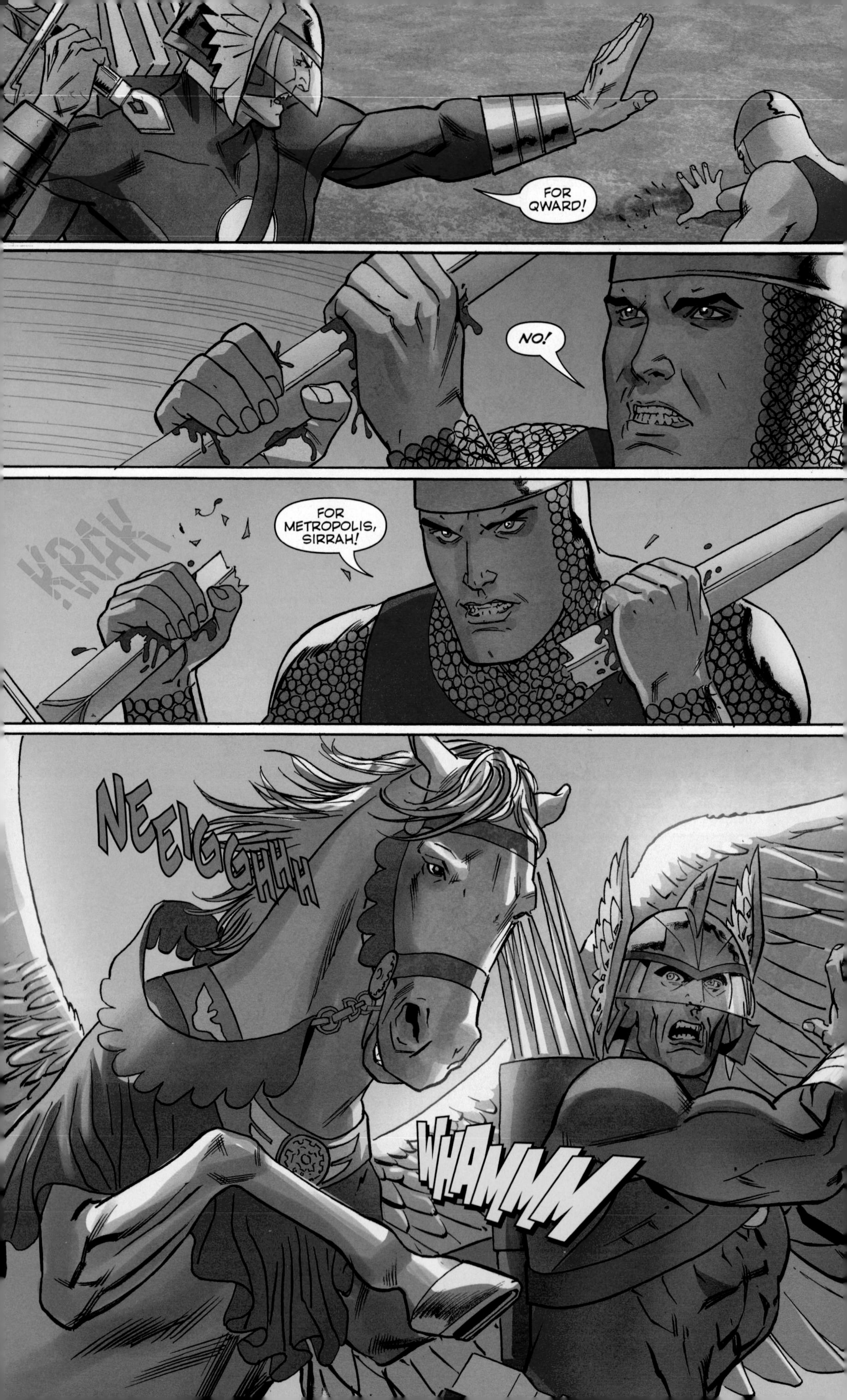
FOR QWARD!
NO!
KRAK
FOR METROPOLIS, SIRRAH!
NEEIGGHHH
WHAMMMM

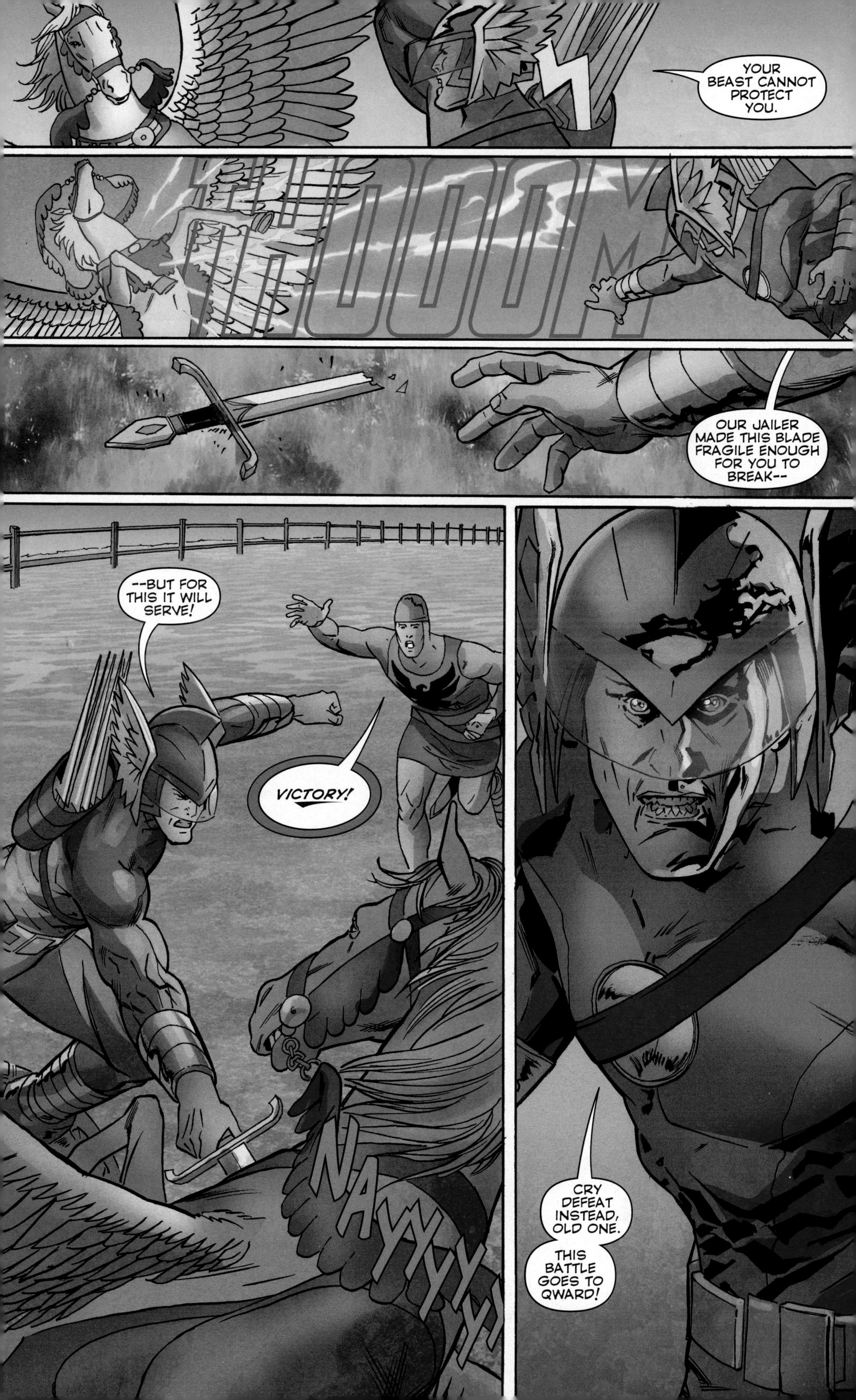
YOUR BEAST CANNOT PROTECT YOU.
THOOOOM
OUR JAILER MADE THIS BLADE FRAGILE ENOUGH FOR YOU TO BREAK--
--BUT FOR THIS IT WILL SERVE!
VICTORY!
NAYYYYY
CRY DEFEAT INSTEAD, OLD ONE.
THIS BATTLE GOES TO QWARD!

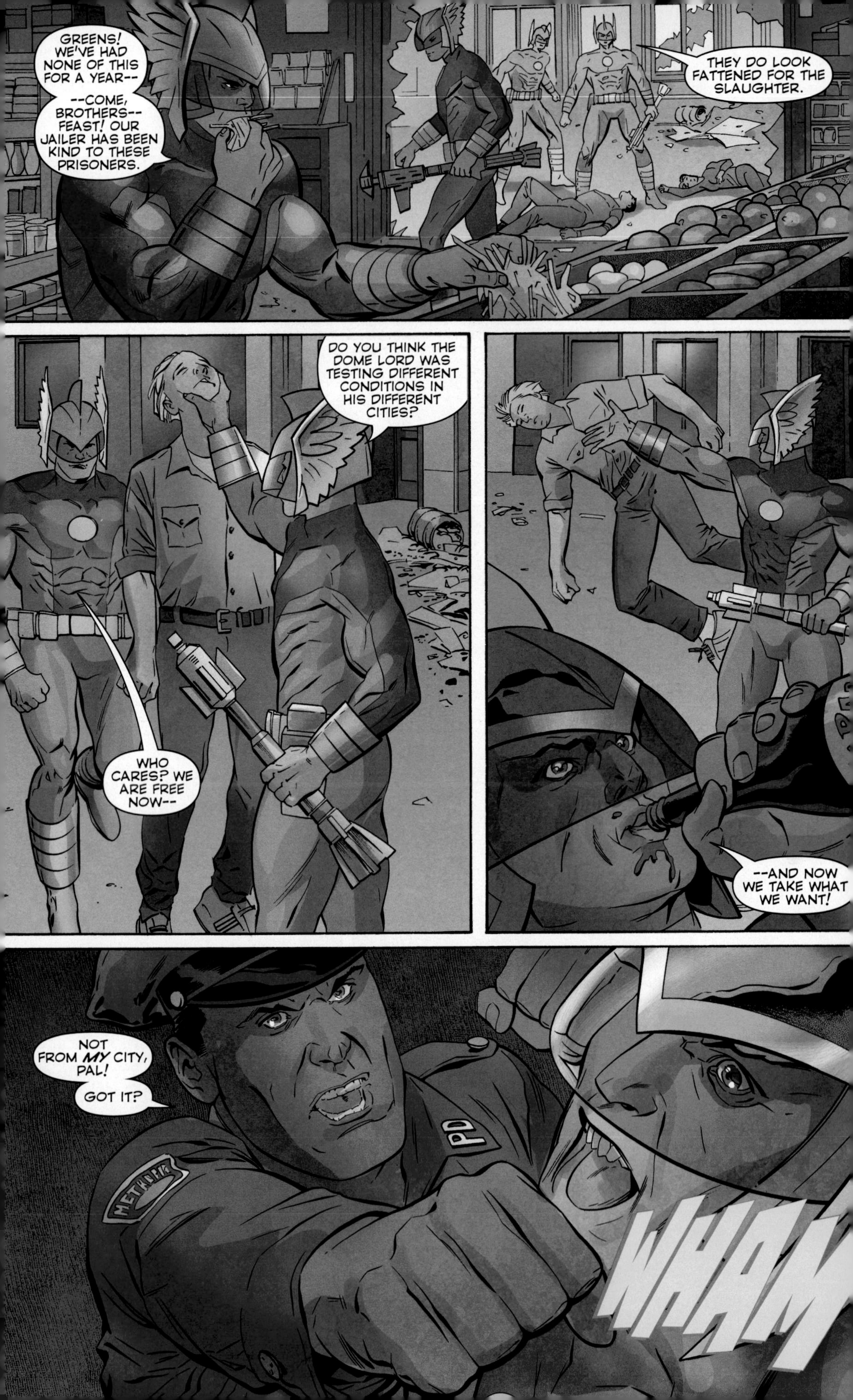
GREENS! WE'VE HAD NONE OF THIS FOR A YEAR--
--COME, BROTHERS-- FEAST! OUR JAILER HAS BEEN KIND TO THESE PRISONERS.
THEY DO LOOK FATTENED FOR THE SLAUGHTER.
DO YOU THINK THE DOME LORD WAS TESTING DIFFERENT CONDITIONS IN HIS DIFFERENT CITIES?
WHO CARES? WE ARE FREE NOW--
--AND NOW WE TAKE WHAT WE WANT!
NOT FROM MY CITY, PAL!
GOT IT?
PD
METROPOLIS
WHAM

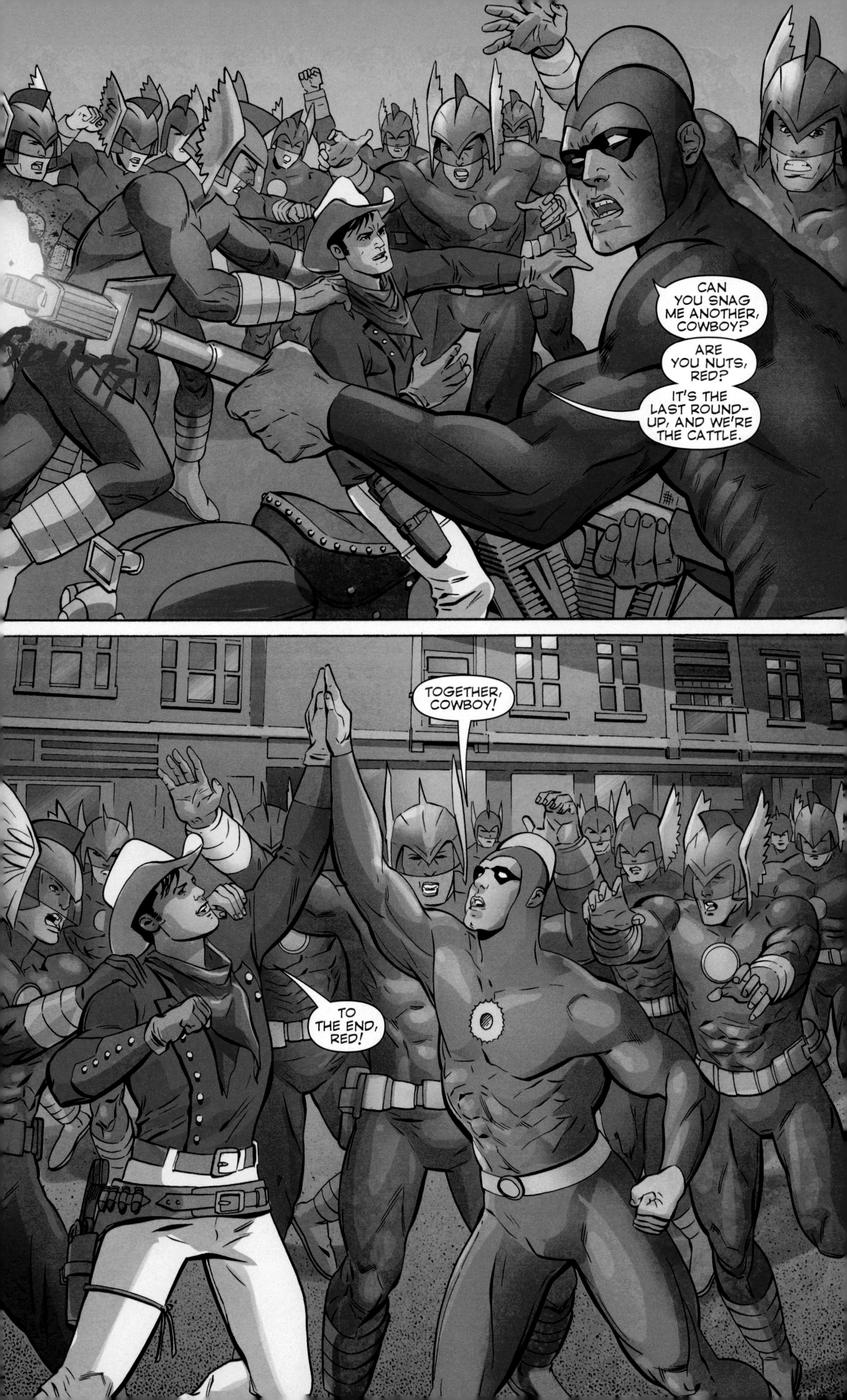
CAN YOU SNAG ME ANOTHER, COWBOY?
ARE YOU NUTS, RED?
IT'S THE LAST ROUND-UP, AND WE'RE THE CATTLE.
TOGETHER, COWBOY!
TO THE END, RED!

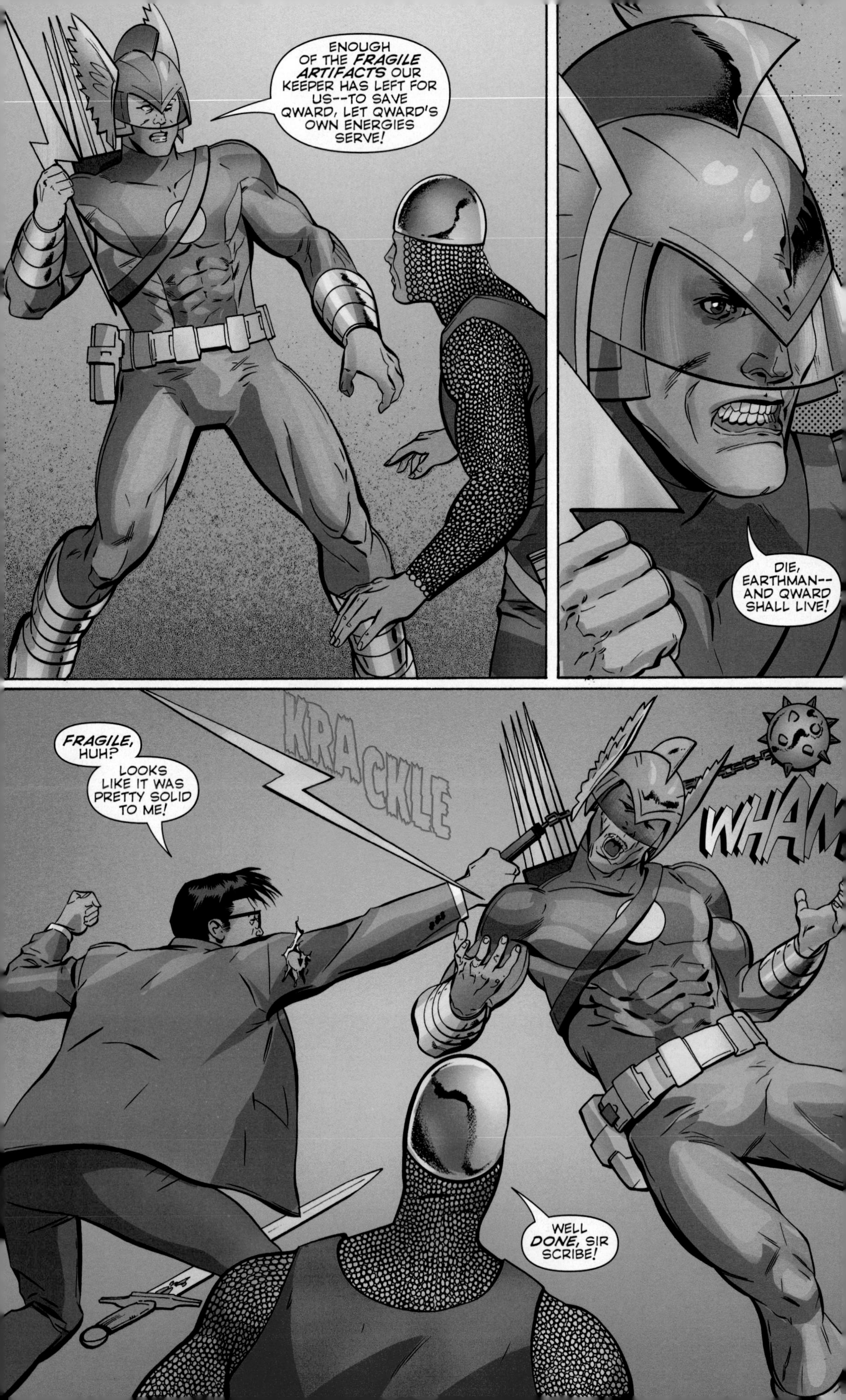

ENOUGH OF THE *FRAGILE ARTIFACTS* OUR KEEPER HAS LEFT FOR US--TO SAVE QWARD, LET QWARD'S OWN ENERGIES SERVE!
DIE, EARTHMAN--AND QWARD SHALL LIVE!
FRAGILE, HUH? LOOKS LIKE IT WAS PRETTY SOLID TO ME!
KRACKLE
WHAM
WELL *DONE,* SIR SCRIBE!

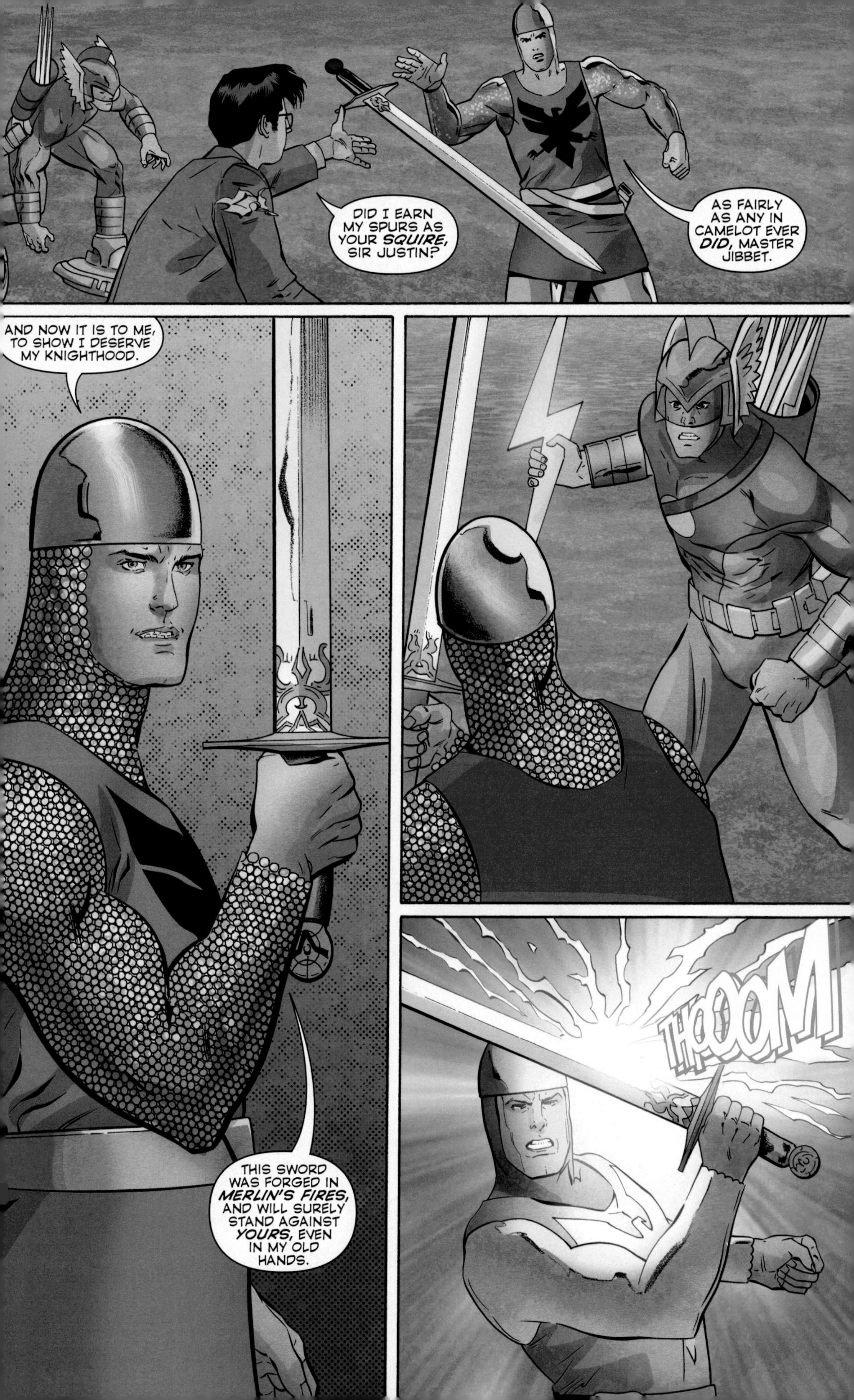
DID I EARN MY SPURS AS YOUR SQUIRE, SIR JUSTIN?
AS FAIRLY AS ANY IN CAMELOT EVER DID, MASTER JIBBET.
AND NOW IT IS TO ME, TO SHOW I DESERVE MY KNIGHTHOOD.
THIS SWORD WAS FORGED IN MERLIN'S FIRES, AND WILL SURELY STAND AGAINST YOURS, EVEN IN MY OLD HANDS.
THOOOM

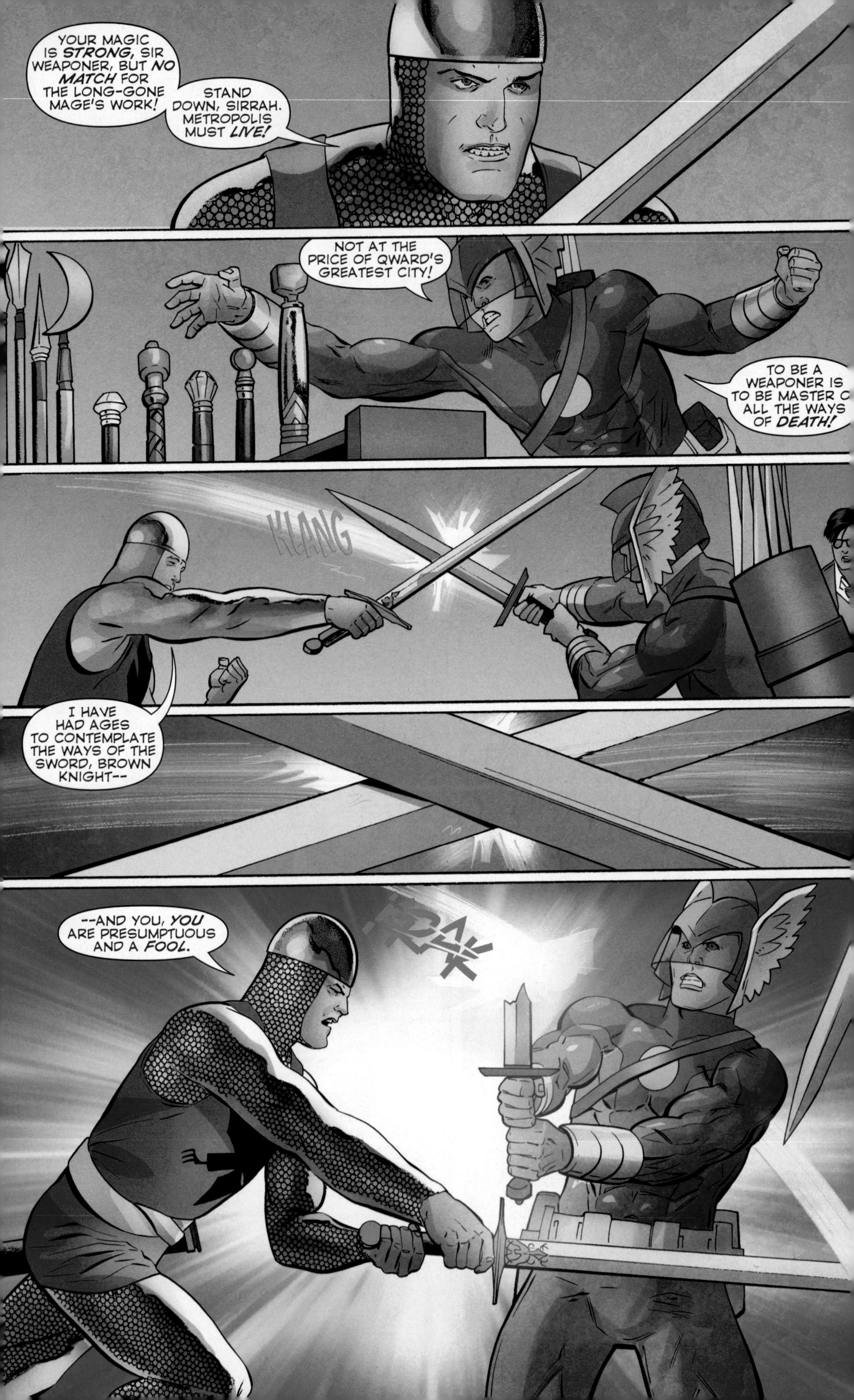
YOUR MAGIC IS STRONG, SIR WEAPONER, BUT NO MATCH FOR THE LONG-GONE MAGE'S WORK!
STAND DOWN, SIRRAH. METROPOLIS MUST LIVE!
NOT AT THE PRICE OF QWARD'S GREATEST CITY!
TO BE A WEAPONER IS TO BE MASTER ALL THE WAYS OF DEATH!
KLANG
I HAVE HAD AGES TO CONTEMPLATE THE WAYS OF THE SWORD, BROWN KNIGHT--
--AND YOU, YOU ARE PRESUMPTUOUS AND A FOOL.

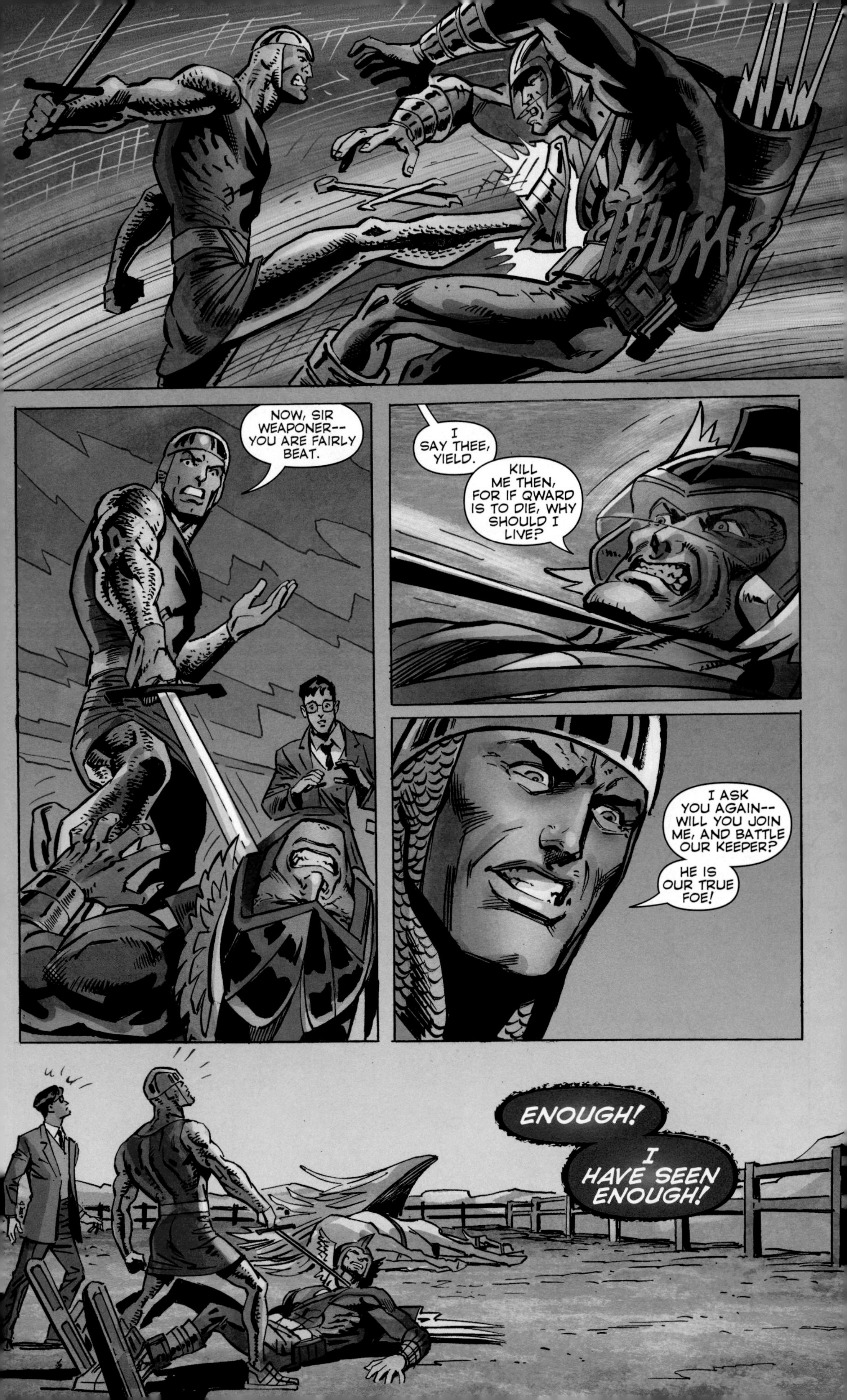
THUMP
NOW, SIR WEAPONER-- YOU ARE FAIRLY BEAT.
I SAY THEE, YIELD.
KILL ME THEN, FOR IF QWARD IS TO DIE, WHY SHOULD I LIVE?
I ASK YOU AGAIN-- WILL YOU JOIN ME, AND BATTLE OUR KEEPER?
HE IS OUR TRUE FOE!
ENOUGH!
I HAVE SEEN ENOUGH!

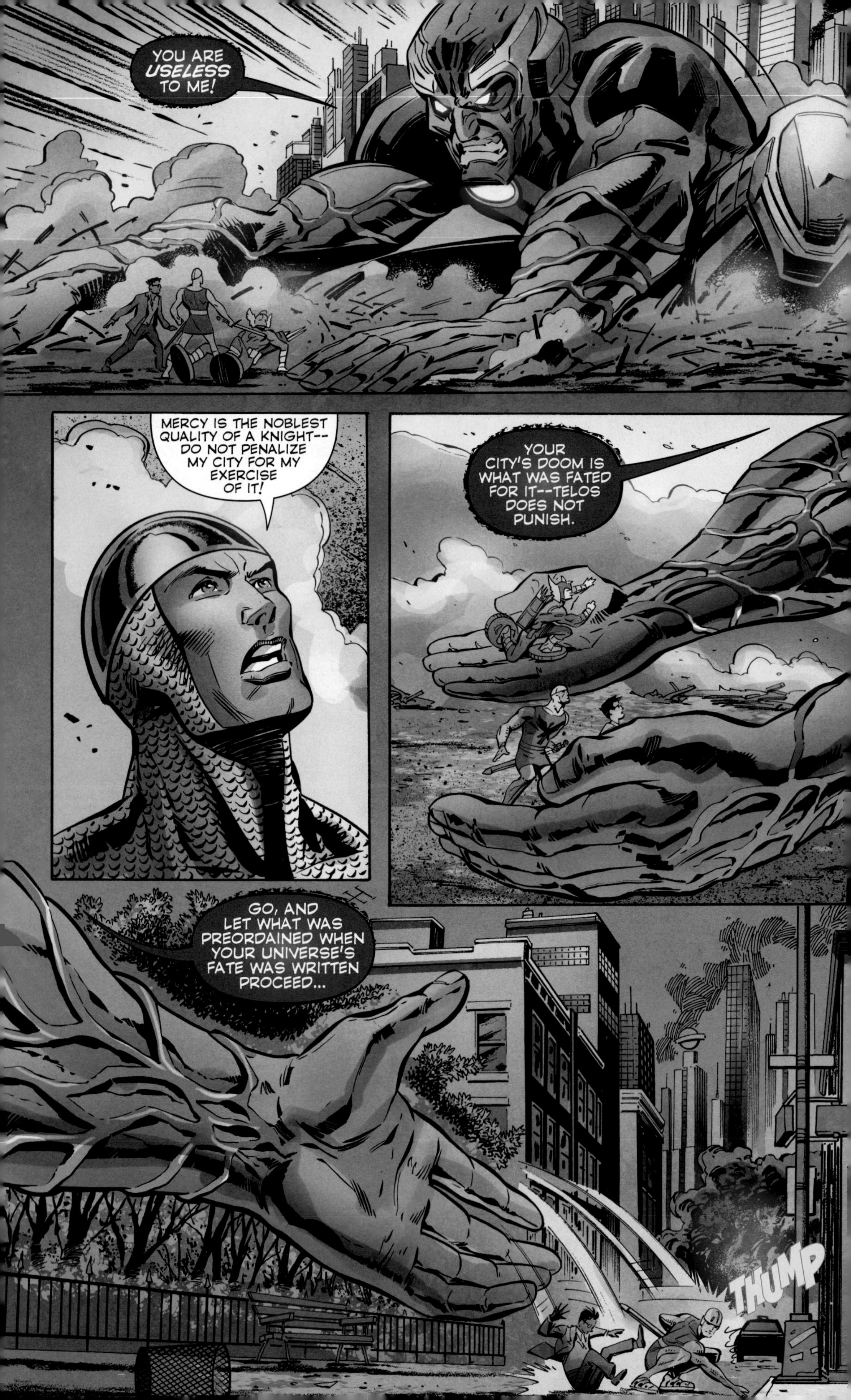
YOU ARE USELESS TO ME!
MERCY IS THE NOBLEST QUALITY OF A KNIGHT-- DO NOT PENALIZE MY CITY FOR MY EXERCISE OF IT!
YOUR CITY'S DOOM IS WHAT WAS FATED FOR IT--TELOS DOES NOT PUNISH.
GO, AND LET WHAT WAS PREORDAINED WHEN YOUR UNIVERSE'S FATE WAS WRITTEN PROCEED...
THUMP

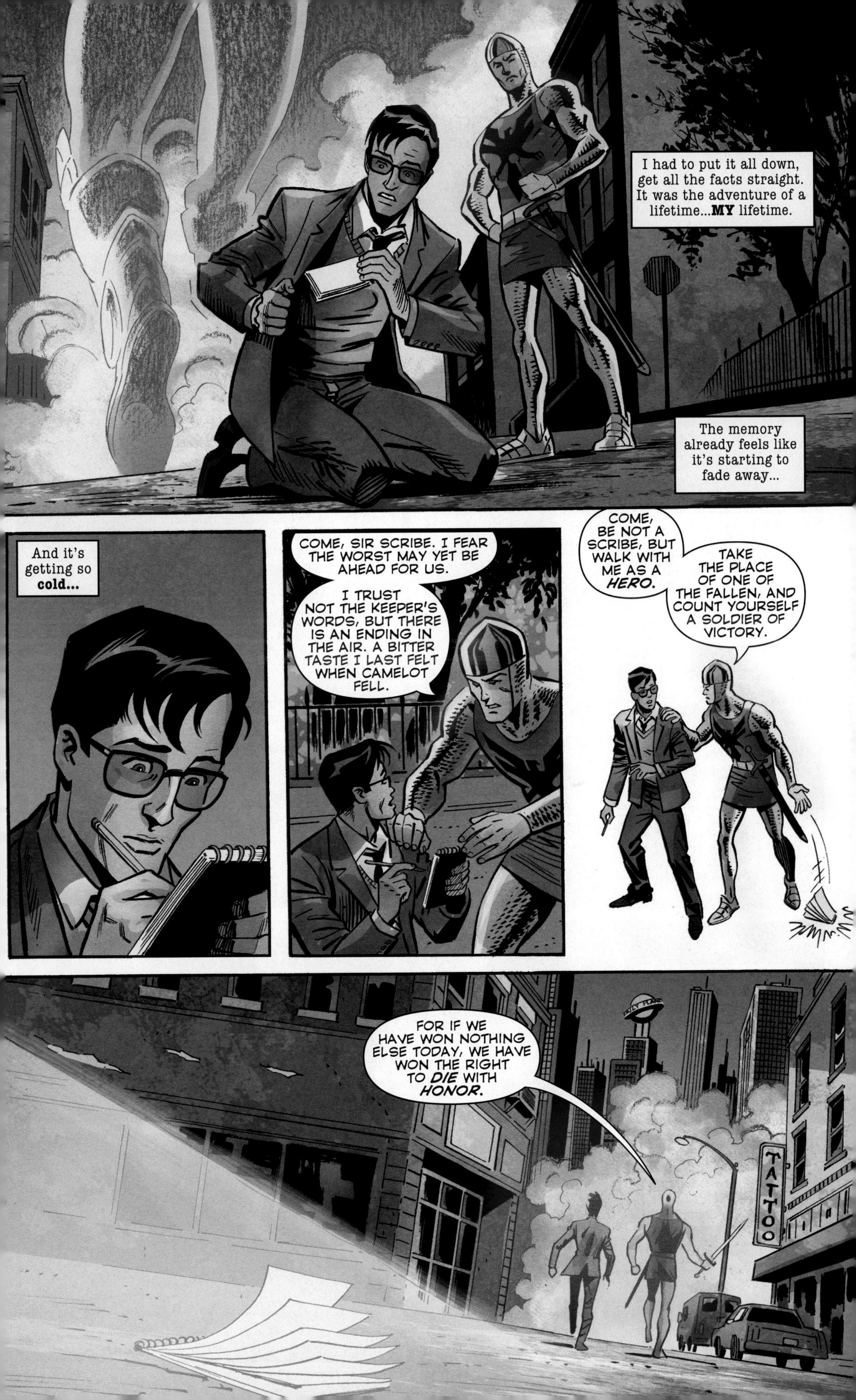
I had to put it all down, get all the facts straight. It was the adventure of a lifetime...MY lifetime.
The memory already feels like it's starting to fade away...
And it's getting so cold...
COME, SIR SCRIBE. I FEAR THE WORST MAY YET BE AHEAD FOR US.
I TRUST NOT THE KEEPER'S WORDS, BUT THERE IS AN ENDING IN THE AIR. A BITTER TASTE I LAST FELT WHEN CAMELOT FELL.
COME, BE NOT A SCRIBE, BUT WALK WITH ME AS A HERO.
TAKE THE PLACE OF ONE OF THE FALLEN, AND COUNT YOURSELF A SOLDIER OF VICTORY.
FOR IF WE HAVE WON NOTHING ELSE TODAY, WE HAVE WON THE RIGHT TO DIE WITH HONOR.
TATTOO

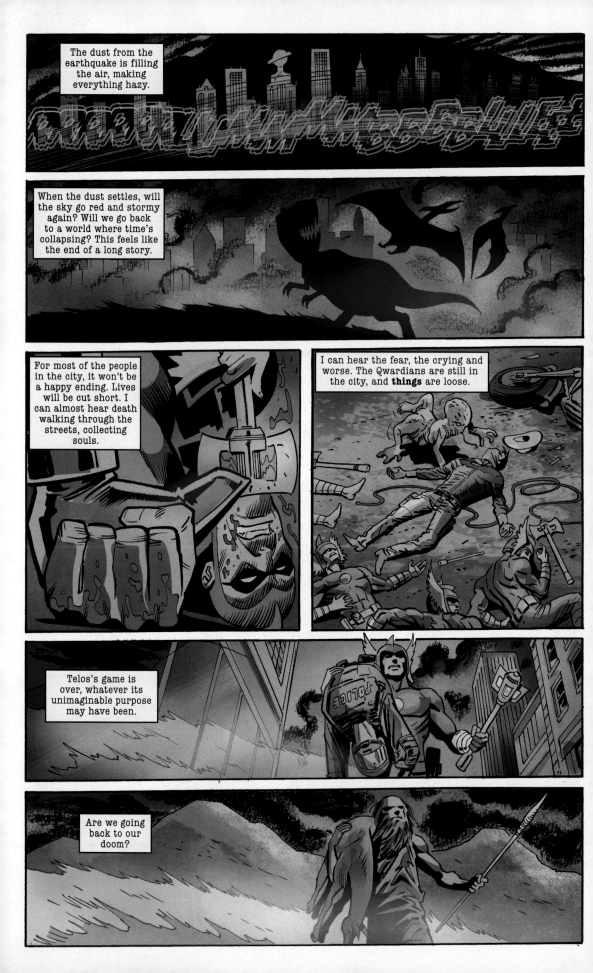

The dust from the earthquake is filling the air, making everything hazy.

When the dust settles, will the sky go red and stormy again? Will we go back to a world where time's collapsing? This feels like the end of a long story.

For most of the people in the city, it won't be a happy ending. Lives will be cut short. I can almost hear death walking through the streets, collecting souls.

I can hear the fear, the crying and worse. The Qwardians are still in the city, and **things** are loose.

Telos's game is over, whatever its unimaginable purpose may have been.

Are we going back to our doom?

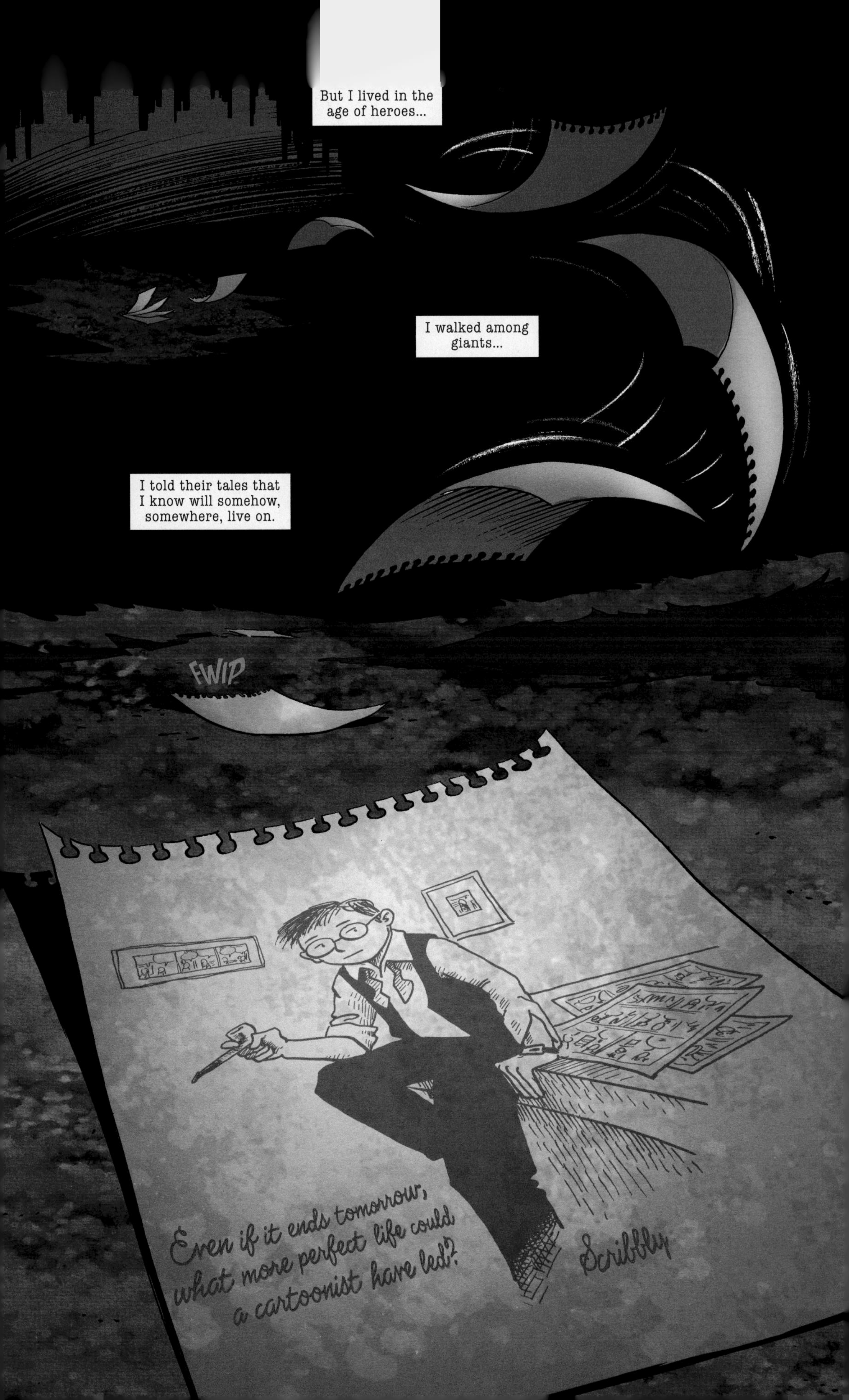

But I lived in the age of heroes...
I walked among giants...
I told their tales that I know will somehow, somewhere, live on.
FWIP
Even if it ends tomorrow, what more perfect life could a cartoonist have led?
Scribbly

Just like her cousin Kal-L, Kara Zor-L was rocketed away from Krypton just as the planet exploded. But her ship took a different route than Kal-L's. She slowly aged while in suspended animation. When she finally landed on Earth, she met her now middle-aged cousin, who had an entire career as Superman while she traveled through space. Eager to step out from her cousin's shadow and be her own person, Kara adopted the superhero persona of Power Girl.

Action Comics

THIRTY SECONDS AGO SHE CAME CRASHING THROUGH THE CEILING OF CENTRAL ELECTRONICS, INTERRUPTING A ROBBERY IN PROGRESS!
SSZZZZLL
AND IF YOU THINK SHE LOOKS EXCITING NOW, JUST HANG ON... THE BEST IS YET TO COME!
BLAM

DON'T YOU UNDERSTAND? THIS GAME IS FUTILE!
DURING THE YEARS OF MY IMPRISONMENT, I TRAINED MY MIND TO REACH LEVELS OF POWER YOU CAN NEVER COMPREHEND.
WITH MY MIND ALONE, I CAN TOSS YOU LIKE LEAVES IN A WIND.
WITH MY MIND ALONE, I CAN DO ANYTHING--

The villain Brainwave showed he could send Power Girl flying with just a thought. Power Girl foiled his plan to hurl Earth into the sun with the aid of the Super Squad. By pushing Brainwave's satellite toward the sun, Power Girl melted all his advanced technology. It was an impressive debut for the young heroine.

DON'T PATRONIZE ME, COUSIN! AND DON'T GIVE ME ANY MORE ORDERS, EITHER! I'M ON MY OWN NOW!
SO YOU ARE ...BUT YOU CAN STILL LISTEN TO MY ADVICE, CAN'T YOU?
NOT ANY MORE--I CAN'T-- AND I WON'T!

Power Girl wasn't too pleased to have her cousin around. But after a mission to rescue Hawkgirl from the monster Zanadu, Superman decided to step back and give Power Girl his spot on the Justice Society of America.

I SWEAR, P.G.--ONLY YOU WOULD HAVE THE GALL TO TELL THE FASTEST MAN ON EARTH-TWO TO "HURRY UP"!
IT'S NOT "GALL", FLASH-- IT'S DETERMINATION!

Only Power Girl would have the nerve to give a veteran hero like the Flash a hard time, as she did when the Justice Society teamed up with the Justice League and the Legion of Super-Heroes from Earth-One to fight Mordru.

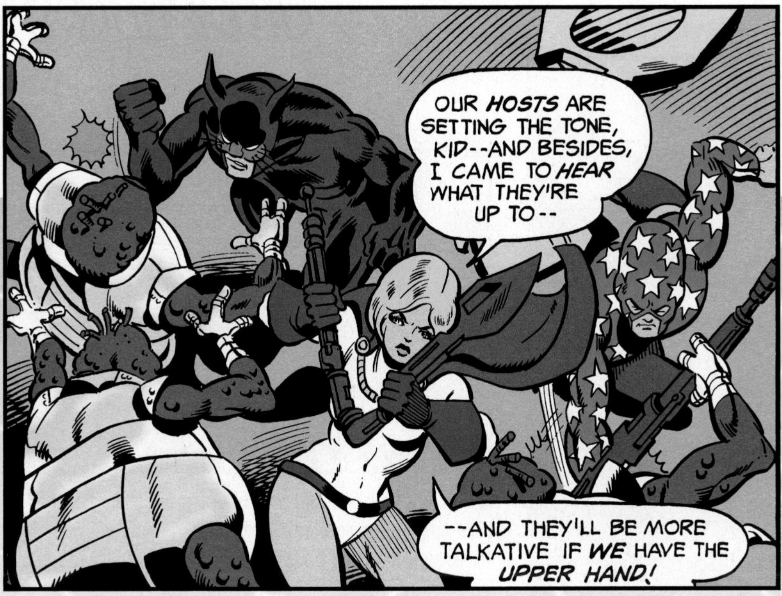
OUR *HOSTS* ARE SETTING THE TONE, KID--AND BESIDES, I CAME TO *HEAR* WHAT THEY'RE UP TO--
--AND THEY'LL BE MORE TALKATIVE IF *WE* HAVE THE *UPPER HAND!*

Power Girl learned an important lesson after she led members of the Justice Society down to the center of the earth where they encountered the Underlord and his minions. Acting impulsively and refusing to be a team player, she nearly got the Star-Spangled Kid killed.

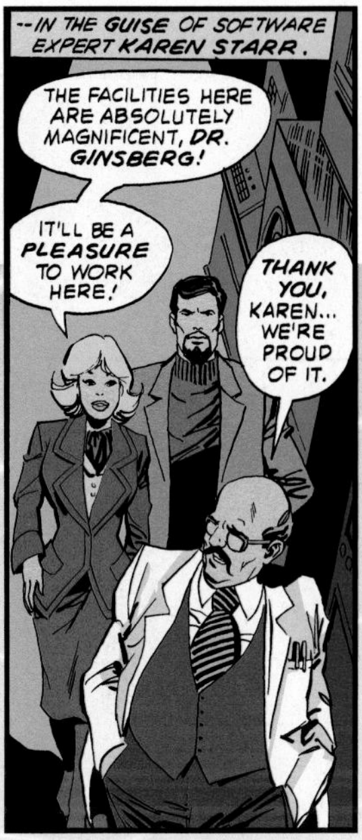
--IN THE *GUISE* OF SOFTWARE EXPERT *KAREN STARR*.
THE FACILITIES HERE ARE ABSOLUTELY MAGNIFICENT, *DR. GINSBERG!*
IT'LL BE A *PLEASURE* TO WORK HERE!
THANK YOU, KAREN... WE'RE PROUD OF IT.

With the help of reporter Andrew Vinson, Power Girl established a secret identity: Karen Starr, a software expert, and took a job at Ultimate Computer Corporation in Gotham City.

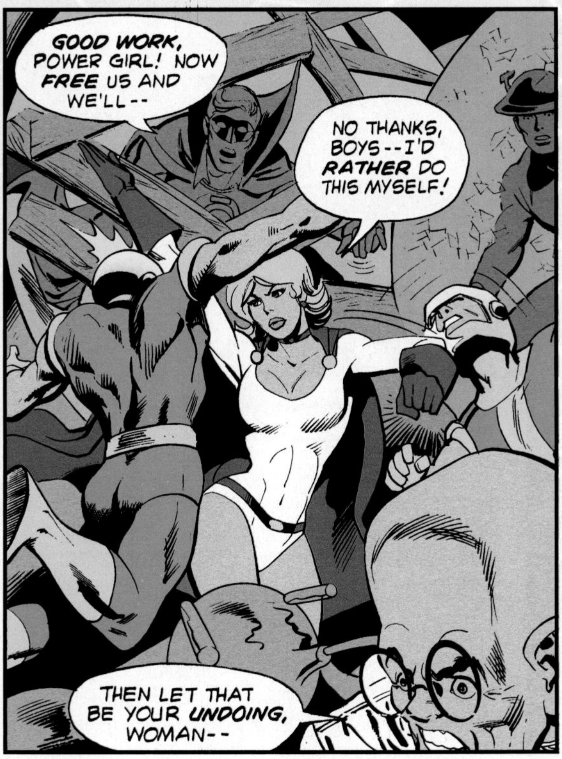
GOOD WORK, POWER GIRL! NOW *FREE* US AND WE'LL--
NO THANKS, BOYS--I'D *RATHER* DO THIS MYSELF!
THEN LET THAT BE YOUR *UNDOING,* WOMAN--

Wanting revenge against the Justice Society, Brainwave went after the cities in which each teammate lived, starting with Keystone City. He abducted the entire city and placed it in limbo, in addition to capturing both Green Lantern and the Flash. Power Girl used her strength against Brainwave's men, and then her computer smarts to get Keystone restored.

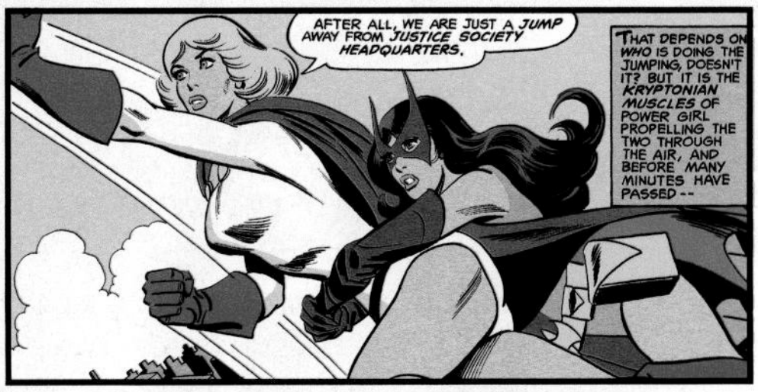
AFTER ALL, WE ARE JUST A *JUMP* AWAY FROM *JUSTICE SOCIETY HEADQUARTERS.*
THAT DEPENDS ON *WHO* IS DOING THE JUMPING, DOESN'T IT? BUT IT IS THE *KRYPTONIAN MUSCLES* OF POWER GIRL PROPELLING THE TWO THROUGH THE AIR, AND BEFORE MANY MINUTES HAVE PASSED--

When the Huntress (Helena Kyle) arrived on the scene, she and Power Girl hit it off right away. This friendship had some advantages for Huntress, such as easy transportation when summoned to a Justice Society meeting.

Detective Comics

On Earth-Two, Dick Grayson grew up to become a prominent attorney and diplomat, although that didn't keep him from moonlighting as Robin. With a new costume reminiscent of his mentor's, he even joined the Justice Society of America.

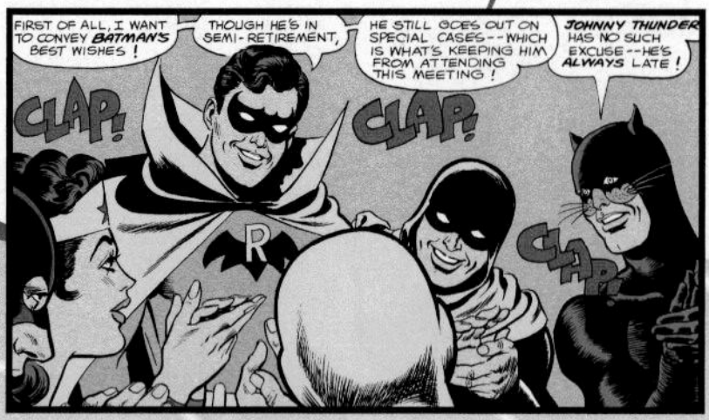
FIRST OF ALL, I WANT TO CONVEY BATMAN'S BEST WISHES!
THOUGH HE'S IN SEMI-RETIREMENT,
HE STILL GOES OUT ON SPECIAL CASES--WHICH IS WHAT'S KEEPING HIM FROM ATTENDING THIS MEETING!
JOHNNY THUNDER HAS NO SUCH EXCUSE--HE'S ALWAYS LATE!
CLAP!
CLAP!
CLAP!

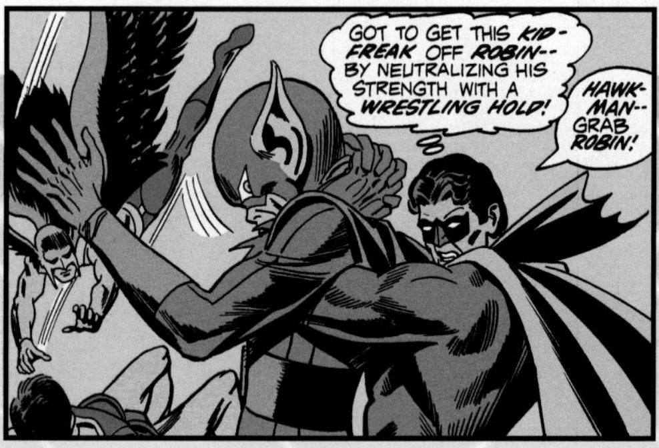
GOT TO GET THIS KID-FREAK OFF ROBIN--BY NEUTRALIZING HIS STRENGTH WITH A WRESTLING HOLD!
HAWK-MAN--GRAB ROBIN!

Robin's time with the Justice Society led to a few interesting team-ups, including one with his counterpart from Earth-One. The younger Robin had his costume shredded in a fight with the alien A-Rym. Fortunately, the Earth-Two Robin had a spare outfit.

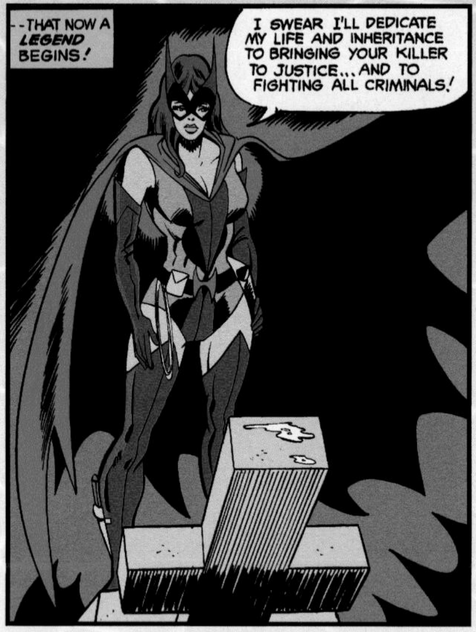
--THAT NOW A LEGEND BEGINS!
I SWEAR I'LL DEDICATE MY LIFE AND INHERITANCE TO BRINGING YOUR KILLER TO JUSTICE... AND TO FIGHTING ALL CRIMINALS!

Selina Kyle was blackmailed into one final heist as Catwoman. The robbery went awry, and Selina was killed. At Selina's grave, Helena Wayne vowed to avenge her mother's death as the Huntress.

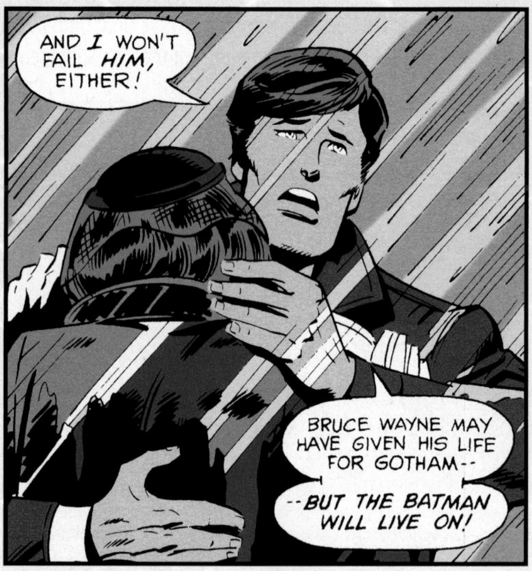
AND I WON'T FAIL HIM, EITHER!
BRUCE WAYNE MAY HAVE GIVEN HIS LIFE FOR GOTHAM--
--BUT THE BATMAN WILL LIVE ON!

After Batman died stopping Bill Jensen—who was mad with magical powers—from destroying Gotham City, Dick Grayson expressed a desire to take over as the Dark Knight. Helena Wayne said neither of them could do it. His legend would live on, but there could be no other Batman. The pair would carry on as Robin and Huntress.

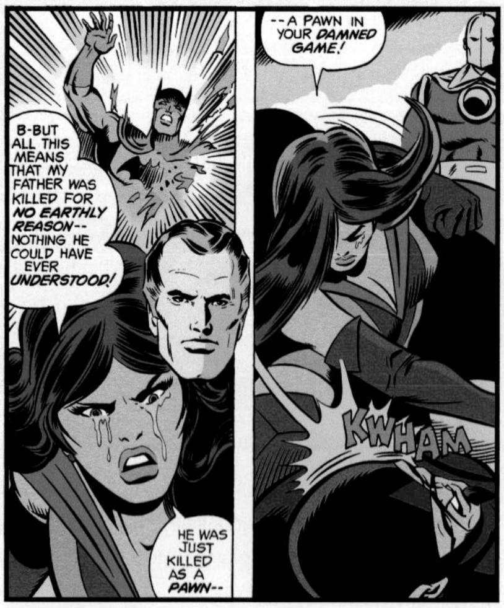
B-BUT ALL THIS MEANS THAT MY FATHER WAS KILLED FOR NO EARTHLY REASON--NOTHING HE COULD HAVE EVER UNDERSTOOD!
HE WAS JUST KILLED AS A PAWN--
--A PAWN IN YOUR DAMNED GAME!
KWHAM

The Justice Society discovered that the magic used by Bill Jensen to kill Batman was supplied by sorcerer Frederic Vaux. Vaux's next act was to wipe the all memory of super heroes from the world. With the aid of Doctor Fate, Huntress defeated Vaux. The encounter gave Doctor Fate the idea of removing knowledge that Bruce Wayne was Batman, thereby giving Huntress and Robin secret identities again.

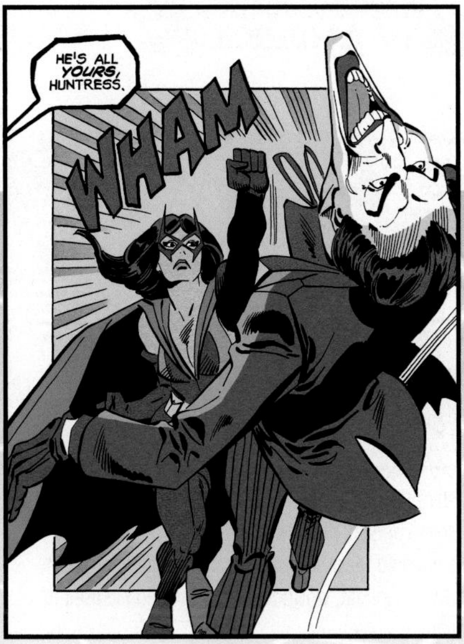
HE'S ALL YOURS, HUNTRESS.
WHAM

Dick Grayson donned Batman's cowl once, after the Joker came back in town. The lunatic refused to believe Batman was really dead and wanted to draw him out. While Grayson appeared as an apparition of Batman in the distance, Huntress delivered a delivered a finishing blow against the clown.

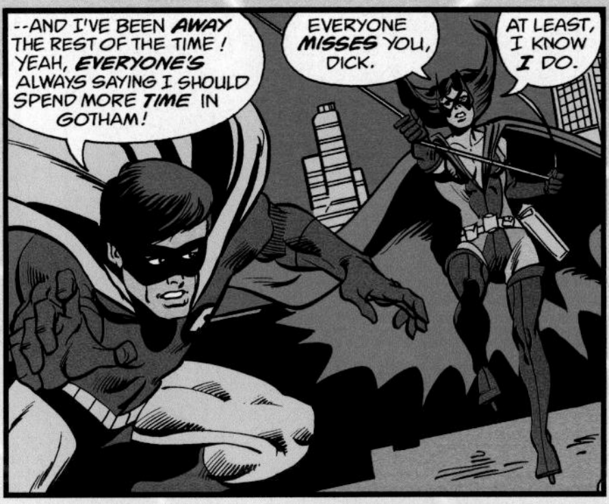
--AND I'VE BEEN AWAY THE REST OF THE TIME! YEAH, EVERYONE'S ALWAYS SAYING I SHOULD SPEND MORE TIME IN GOTHAM!
EVERYONE MISSES YOU, DICK.
AT LEAST, I KNOW I DO.

Despite their time in the Justice Society, Robin and Huntress never actually had a chance to patrol Gotham City together until after Batman was dead. But just as they started to grow closer over a case, Robin took off on another globe-trotting diplomatic journey.

While gone from Earth-Two, the Batman of Earth-One provided solace to both Huntress and Robin when traveling across the Multiverse brought them together.

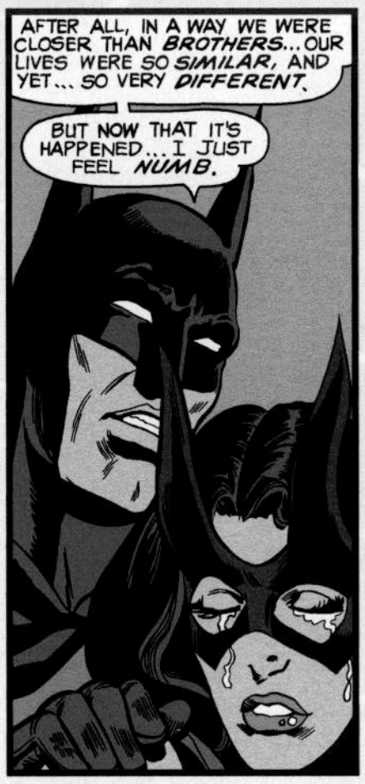
AFTER ALL, IN A WAY WE WERE CLOSER THAN BROTHERS... OUR LIVES WERE SO SIMILAR, AND YET... SO VERY DIFFERENT.
BUT NOW THAT IT'S HAPPENED... I JUST FEEL NUMB.

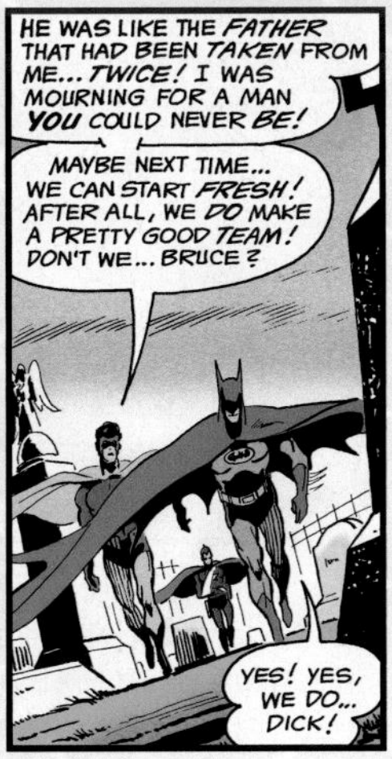
HE WAS LIKE THE FATHER THAT HAD BEEN TAKEN FROM ME... TWICE! I WAS MOURNING FOR A MAN YOU COULD NEVER BE!
MAYBE NEXT TIME... WE CAN START FRESH! AFTER ALL, WE DO MAKE A PRETTY GOOD TEAM! DON'T WE... BRUCE?
YES! YES, WE DO... DICK!

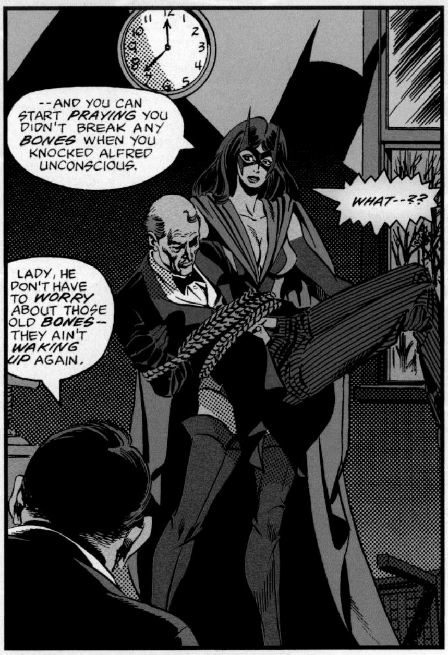
--AND YOU CAN START PRAYING YOU DIDN'T BREAK ANY BONES WHEN YOU KNOCKED ALFRED UNCONSCIOUS.
WHAT--??
LADY, HE DON'T HAVE TO WORRY ABOUT THOSE OLD BONES--THEY AIN'T WAKING UP AGAIN.

Huntress wasn't about to give up on Alfred after he was poisoned. The doctor said he couldn't save him, but Huntress insisted on going to the hospital's lab to find an antidote just as her father would have done.

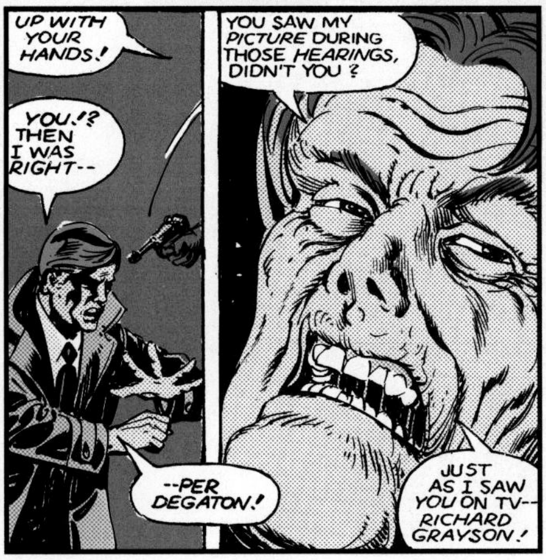
UP WITH YOUR HANDS!
YOU!? THEN I WAS RIGHT--
--PER DEGATON!
YOU SAW MY PICTURE DURING THOSE HEARINGS, DIDN'T YOU?
JUST AS I SAW YOU ON TV--RICHARD GRAYSON!

The Justice Society was called before a congressional committee and accused of treason based on a diary allegedly written by Batman. Dick Grayson was tasked with pursuing the allegations, putting him in opposition to the team. Through his investigation, he discovered the diary had been coded by Batman to alert the Justice Society to Per Degaton's latest time-travel plot. Dick's years of working with the world's greatest detective had paid off.

The Justice Society of America
—heroes of World War II—disbanded
in the 1950s instead of revealing their
identities to the Combined Congressional
Un-American Activities Committee. But two
decades later, when their old villains
began to resurface and new, younger heroes
appeared on the scene, the team
was reborn.

JUSTICE SOCIETY OF AMERICA

PERHAPS NOW WE'LL HAVE SOME ANSWERS. THIS STRANGER BARGED IN HERE AND ATTACKED US...
I WANT TO KNOW WHY.
AND I'D LIKE TO KNOW WHERE HE GAINED THAT STRANGE POWER--
NOT TA MENTION WHO HE IS UNDER THAT METAL MASK.

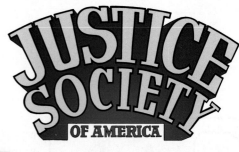

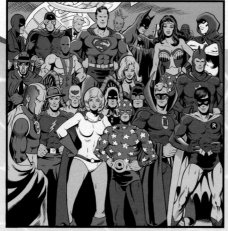

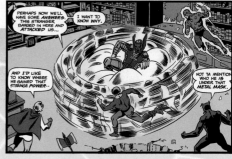

The Flash ran circles around Vulcan, an astronaut who was turned into a berserk monster by an alien attempting to save his doomed space shuttle. Vulcan had one flaw: super-sensitivity to sunlight, which the Star-Spangled Kid used to destroy him.

--AND BY THE SHOUTS OF THE MAN ONCE KNOWN AS THE DARKNIGHT DETECTIVE, AS WELL...
COUNT ON IT, FATE--AND NEXT TIME YOU'LL WALK AWAY--IN HANDCUFFS!
IF IT'S THE LAST THING I DO, I'M GOING TO TEACH YOU THAT YOU'RE NOT ABOVE THE LAW!

Brainwashed by the Psycho-Pirate, Commissioner Bruce Wayne began a vendetta to have the Justice Society arrested. Power Girl was gravely injured in the fight, but eventually Doctor Fate undid the Psycho-Pirate's work.

THEN, IN ONE SOUL-SHATTERING SECOND, JENSEN'S HATE CONSUMES HIM WITH A FIRE NOT SEEN ON THIS EARTH SINCE CREATION...
...AND THE BATMAN DIES WITH HIM!
OH MY GOD--NOOOOOO!

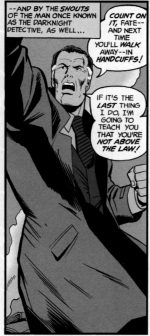

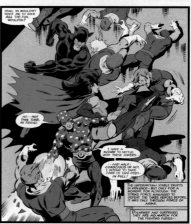

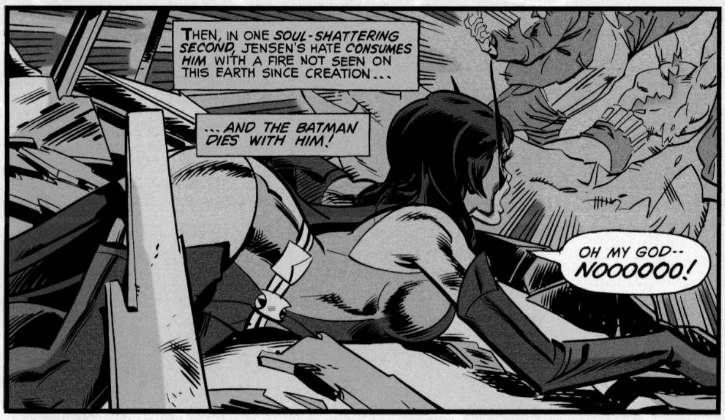

Bruce Wayne had retired as Batman after his wife Selina Kyle was killed , but he donned the mantle again to help the Justice Society against Bill Jensen, a thief who hated Wayne and was now imbued with magical powers. The magic consumed Jensen and Batman, killing them both. Wayne's daughter, the Huntress, was pinned under rubble from the fight and was unable to help her father.

YEAH, YA WOULDN'T WANT ME TO HAVE ALL THE FUN, WOULDYA?
NO--NOT THIS TIME, MY FRIEND.
I HAVE A SCORE TO SETTLE WITH THESE JOKERS--
--AND HALF-CONSCIOUS OR NOT, I INTEND TO TAKE CARE OF THAT DEBT--IN FULL!
THE UNDERGROUND STABLE ERUPTS IN VIOLENCE--BUT ONLY FOR A MOMENT. FOR ALTHOUGH THE STRIKE FORCE MANAGED TO DEFEAT THE THREE HEROES BEFORE, IT WAS ONLY THROUGH FORCE OF ARMS.
DISARMED AND SURPRISED, THEY ARE NO MATCH FOR THE FIGHTING FURIES--

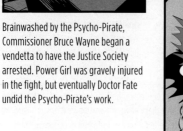

Nearly all members of the Justice Society were busy when Star-Spangled Kid was abducted and held for ransom by the Strike Force, leaving just Wildcat and the rookie Huntress to rescue him. The Strike Force was no match for the heroes.

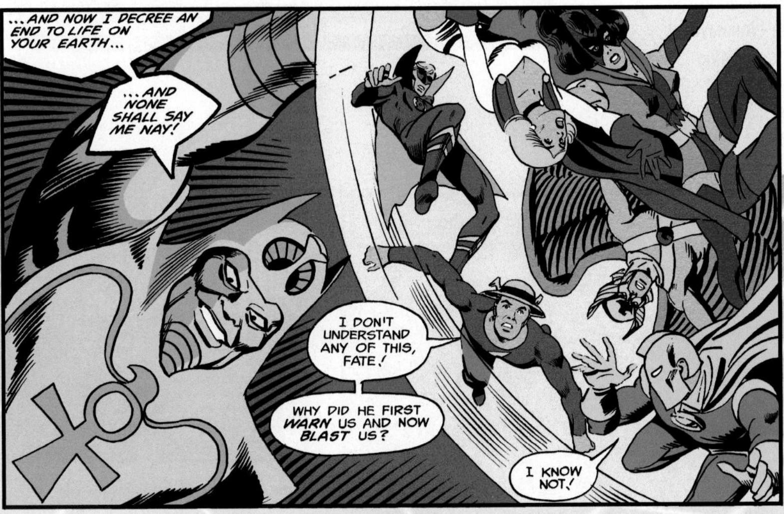
...AND NOW I DECREE AN END TO LIFE ON YOUR EARTH...
...AND NONE SHALL SAY ME NAY!
I DON'T UNDERSTAND ANY OF THIS, FATE!
WHY DID HE FIRST WARN US AND NOW BLAST US?
I KNOW NOT!

An ancient being known as the Master Summoner threatened to end all life on earth within an hour unless the Justice Society could figure out a way to stop him. Fighting only gave him the opportunity to siphon the team's powers to expedite the world's end. Dr. Fate deduced the only way to stop him was not to fight at all. The team did nothing for the remaining minutes, and the Master Summoner's window passed. He faded away to await another millennium to try again.

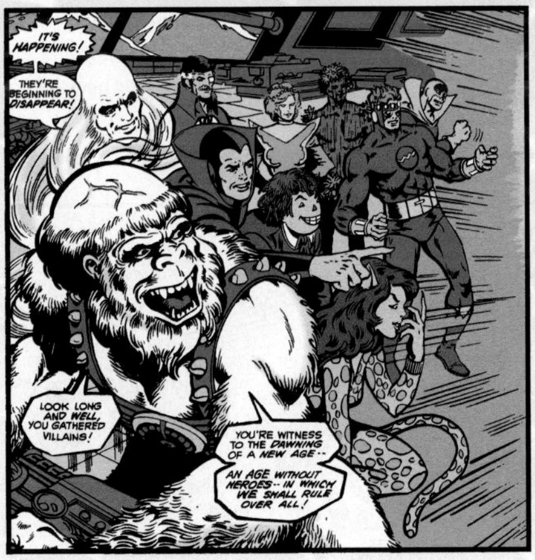
IT'S HAPPENING!
THEY'RE BEGINNING TO DISAPPEAR!
LOOK LONG AND WELL, YOU GATHERED VILLAINS!
YOU'RE WITNESS TO THE DAWNING OF A NEW AGE--
AN AGE WITHOUT HEROES-- IN WHICH WE SHALL RULE OVER ALL!

The Secret Society of Super-Villains, comprised of villains from both Earth-One and Earth-Two, plotted to exile their enemies into a limbo outside the universe. This attack coincided with the Justice Society's annual reunion with the Justice League of Earth-One. The defeated foes found themselves stuck in the limbo they had planned for the heroes.

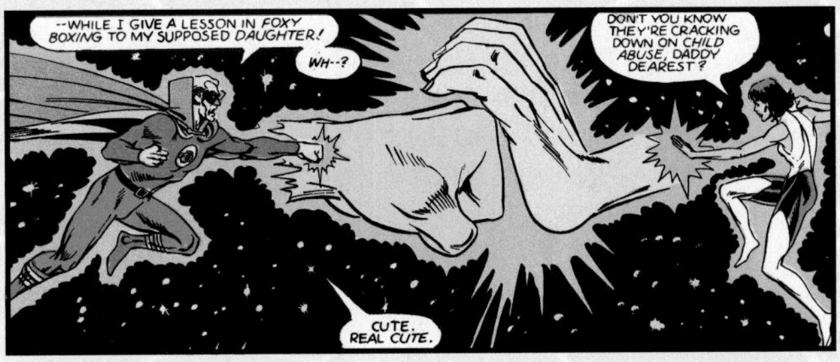
--WHILE I GIVE A LESSON IN FOXY BOXING TO MY SUPPOSED DAUGHTER!
WH--?
DON'T YOU KNOW THEY'RE CRACKING DOWN ON CHILD ABUSE, DADDY DEAREST?
CUTE. REAL CUTE.

Green Lantern was shocked to learn he had two full-grown children, Jade and Obsidian. The news couldn't have come at a worse time—Green Lantern and other Justice Society members were in a crazed state due to the Ultra-Humanite.

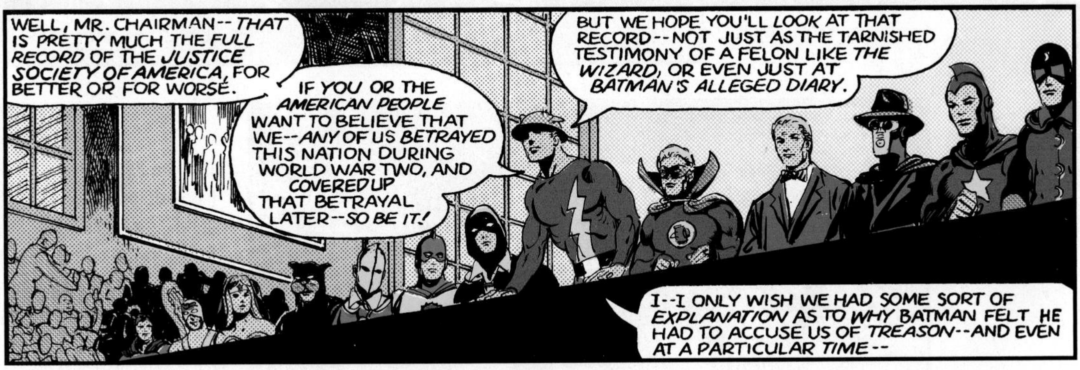
WELL, MR. CHAIRMAN-- THAT IS PRETTY MUCH THE FULL RECORD OF THE JUSTICE SOCIETY OF AMERICA, FOR BETTER OR FOR WORSE.
IF YOU OR THE AMERICAN PEOPLE WANT TO BELIEVE THAT WE-- ANY OF US BETRAYED THIS NATION DURING WORLD WAR TWO, AND COVERED UP THAT BETRAYAL LATER-- SO BE IT!
BUT WE HOPE YOU'LL LOOK AT THAT RECORD-- NOT JUST AS THE TARNISHED TESTIMONY OF A FELON LIKE THE WIZARD, OR EVEN JUST AT BATMAN'S ALLEGED DIARY.
I--I ONLY WISH WE HAD SOME SORT OF EXPLANATION AS TO WHY BATMAN FELT HE HAD TO ACCUSE US OF TREASON--AND EVEN AT A PARTICULAR TIME--

Their reputation already tarnished because of the Ultra-Humanite, the Justice Society took another hit when a bogus diary—allegedly written by Batman—accused the team of working with the Nazis during World War II. They were called before a congressional committee to address these accusations of treason. The Flash gave an impassioned speech that helped sway the committee.

Four costumed youths burst in on a Justice Society of America meeting on Christmas Eve: the Silver Scarab (Hector Hall, son of Hawkman and Hawkwoman); Fury (Lyta Trevor, daughter of Wonder Woman); Nuklon (Albert Rothstein, godson of the Atom); and Northwind (Norda Cantrell, godson of Hawkman). It was put to a vote, and they were denied membership. Just as the group was leaving, Jade (Jennie-Lynn Hayden) and Obsidian (Todd Rice) arrived, claiming to be Green Lantern's children, much to his surprise.

INFINITY INC.

...SO WHAT SAY YOU VOTE TO ADD FOUR NEW MEMBERS--
--LIKE RIGHT NOW!?
WHO IN BLAZES--?
GENERATIONS!
I THINK I KNOW-- AND I SURE WISH I DIDN'T!
WHOEVER THEY ARE, THEY'RE SUITED UP LIKE SOME NEW VERSION OF THE JUNIOR JUSTICE SOCIETY!--
--BUT MOST OF THEM LOOK BARELY OLD ENOUGH TO VOTE!
GREAT HERA! I CAN PRACTICALLY GUARANTEE THAT AT LEAST ONE OF THEM CAN.
WHAT IS THIS?? WE DIDN'T INTERRUPT OUR HOLIDAYS FOR THIS SPECIAL MEETING--JUST TO HAVE EVERY COSTUMED TOM, DICK, AND HARRIET BARGE IN.
CHECK! THIS IS THE JSA--NOT THE TOWN HALL MEETING OF THE AIR!
PRESENTING THE FIRST EPIC ADVENTURE OF
INFINITY INC.
AS CREATED BY:
ROY THOMAS WRITER/EDITOR
JERRY ORDWAY PENCILLER/CO-DESIGNER
MIKE MACHLAN INKER
DANN THOMAS CO-PLOTTER · ANTHONY TOLLIN COLORIST · JOHN COSTANZA LETTERER
"The world is yours for a season. It would be tragic if you realized too late, as so many others do, there's only one thing in the world worth having--and that is youth."
--Oscar Wilde, as paraphrased in the film "The Picture of Dorian Gray"

HOW'S THIS: I WAS GOING TO TELL THE JSA TONIGHT THAT I'M FORMING MY OWN SUPER-HERO GROUP, EFFECTIVE IMMEDIATELY.
--AND I'M INVITING ALL NINE OF YOU TO JOIN!
IT'S EVEN GOT A NAME ALREADY-- INFINITY, INC.--
18

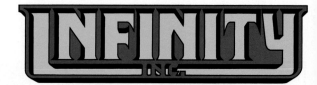

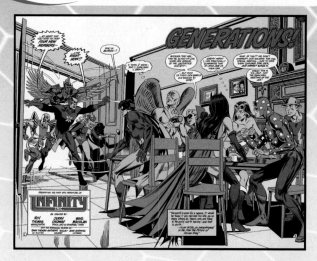

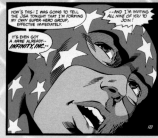

After joining up with the group and bringing along Brainwave Jr.—son of the Justice Society's notorious enemy—the Star-Spangled Kid made a bold declaration: They would start a new team—Infinity, Inc.

The same night the team formed, two Ultra-Humanites from different eras drew the Silver Scarab, Fury, Nuklon, Northwind, Jade, and Obsidian into the past. Brainwave Jr. followed after them. The Justice Society of the 1940s was reluctant to believe Brainwave Jr.'s story, but agreed to help Infinity, Inc. and prevent the Ultra-Humanite from altering history.

NO TIME, ATOM! THAT SCRIBBLED NOTE YOU SHOWED US REVEALS THAT ULTRA'S ASSAULT ON THE CAPITAL MUST BE NEARLY UNDER WAY BY NOW.
WE MUST STOP IT--OR ELSE, UNBELIEVABLE AS IT SEEMS, THE COURSE OF HISTORY ITSELF MAY WELL BE ALTERED-- FOREVER!
SAY, WE MAKE A PRETTY GOOD TRANSPORT TEAM, JADE.
I'M AFRAID FLATTERY WON'T GET ANY INFO OUT OF ME, GREEN LANTERN.
SO MANY QUESTIONS! BUT THEY'LL JUST HAVE TO WAIT.
NEXT STOP-- WASHINGTON, D.C.!

MOM, TOO--JUST LIKE ALL THE REST! ALL THE TIMES WE QUARRELED--AND ALL OF A SUDDEN, I CAN'T EVEN REMEMBER A SINGLE REASON WHY.
DON'T TORTURE YOURSELF LIKE THIS, LYTA.

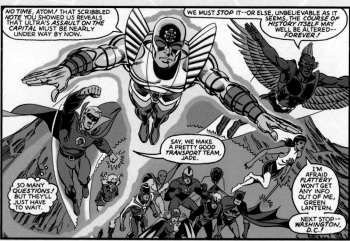

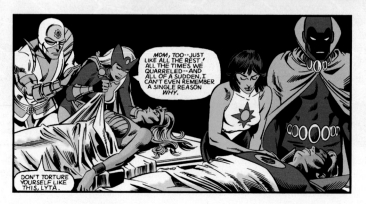

The Ultra-Humanite's misdeeds continued, drowning multiple Justice Society members in Koehaha, also known as the Stream of Ruthlessness. Jade and Obsidian felt robbed of their chance to find out if Green Lantern was really their father.

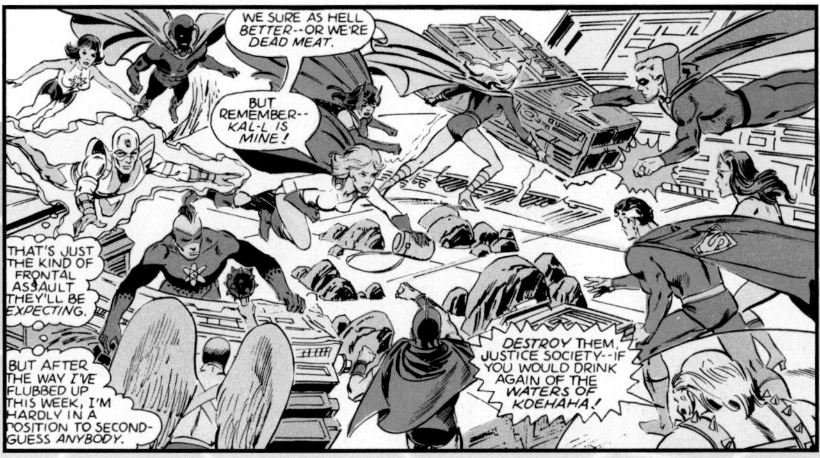
WE SURE AS HELL BETTER--OR WE'RE DEAD MEAT.
BUT REMEMBER-- KAL-L IS MINE!
THAT'S JUST THE KIND OF FRONTAL ASSAULT THEY'LL BE EXPECTING.
BUT AFTER THE WAY I'VE FLUBBED UP THIS WEEK, I'M HARDLY IN A POSITION TO SECOND-GUESS ANYBODY.
DESTROY THEM, JUSTICE SOCIETY--IF YOU WOULD DRINK AGAIN OF THE WATERS OF KOEHAHA!

The dead heroes returned to life, as Ultra-Humanite planned, now under the influence of the Stream of Ruthlessness. Children were pitted against their parents, but the young heroes were subdued in the end.

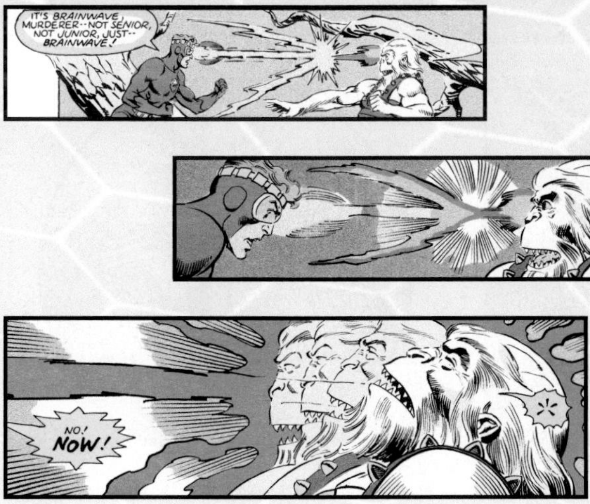
IT'S BRAINWAVE, MURDERER--NOT SENIOR, NOT JUNIOR, JUST-- BRAINWAVE!
NO! NOW!

Brainwave Jr. struck the final blow against the Ultra-Humanite, reducing his mental abilities to that of the ape whose body he inhabited. The battle cost Brainwave Jr. the life of his father.

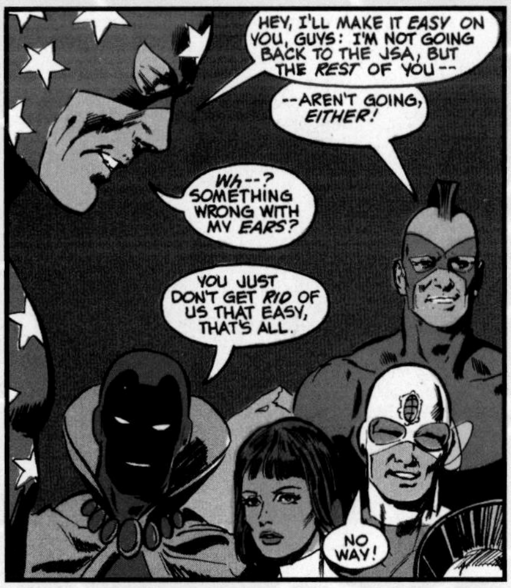
HEY, I'LL MAKE IT EASY ON YOU, GUYS: I'M NOT GOING BACK TO THE JSA, BUT THE REST OF YOU--
--AREN'T GOING, EITHER!
Wh--? SOMETHING WRONG WITH MY EARS?
YOU JUST DON'T GET RID OF US THAT EASY, THAT'S ALL.
NO WAY!

After rescuing the Justice Society, the members of Infinity, Inc. were offered the membership they first wanted, but the young heroes had something else in mind.

The team held a memorable press conference. Power Girl, Huntress, and Brainwave Jr. opted to step down, but the rest of the team made the controversial decision to unmask and reveal their secret identities to the public. And Silver Scarab and Fury announced their engagement. It all culminated in a fight against Harlequin, who crashed the event.

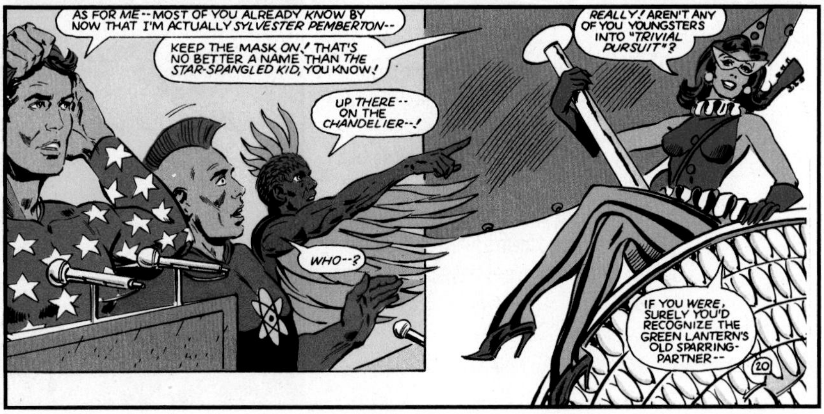
AS FOR ME--MOST OF YOU ALREADY KNOW BY NOW THAT I'M ACTUALLY SYLVESTER PEMBERTON--
KEEP THE MASK ON! THAT'S NO BETTER A NAME THAN THE STAR-SPANGLED KID, YOU KNOW!
REALLY! AREN'T ANY OF YOU YOUNGSTERS INTO "TRIVIAL PURSUIT"?
UP THERE-- ON THE CHANDELIER--!
WHO--?
IF YOU WERE, SURELY YOU'D RECOGNIZE THE GREEN LANTERN'S OLD SPARRING-PARTNER--
20

WORLD'S FINEST
COMICS

The Seven Soldiers of Victory formed under the most unlikely of circumstances. The evil mastermind known as the Hand recruited five criminals to carry out five perfect crimes and then challenged their foes to stop them. This loosely assembled team included the Shining Knight, the Crimson Avenger, the Vigilante, Green Arrow with his sidekick Speedy, and the Star-Spangled Kid with his sidekick Stripesy. They defeated the Hand and his associates, and decided they worked well together. They vowed to band together again whenever necessary.

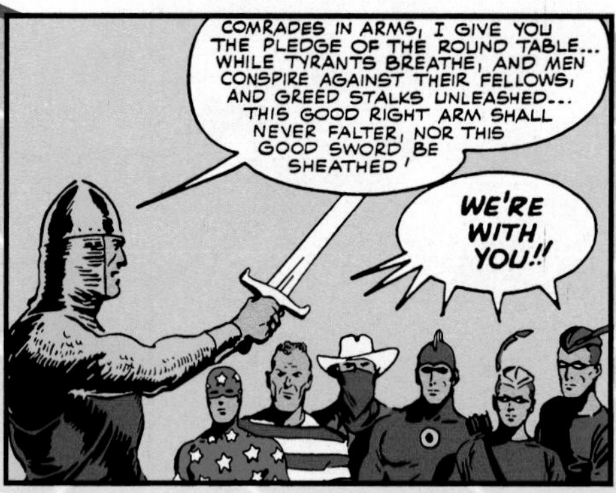
COMRADES IN ARMS, I GIVE YOU THE PLEDGE OF THE ROUND TABLE... WHILE TYRANTS BREATHE, AND MEN CONSPIRE AGAINST THEIR FELLOWS, AND GREED STALKS UNLEASHED... THIS GOOD RIGHT ARM SHALL NEVER FALTER, NOR THIS GOOD SWORD BE SHEATHED!
WE'RE WITH YOU!!

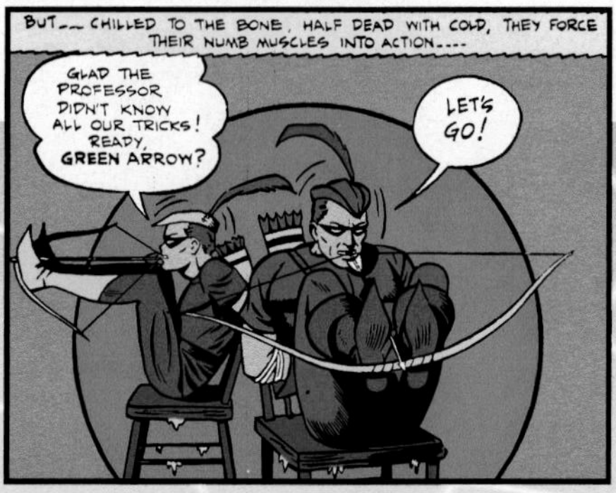
BUT... CHILLED TO THE BONE, HALF DEAD WITH COLD, THEY FORCE THEIR NUMB MUSCLES INTO ACTION....
GLAD THE PROFESSOR DIDN'T KNOW ALL OUR TRICKS! READY, GREEN ARROW?
LET'S GO!

Green Arrow and Speedy proved their archery skills weren't limited to the use of their arms after Professor Merlin tied them to chairs and left to freeze to death in a room at fifty below zero. The pair successfully escaped and stopped Merlin from robbing a gold mine.

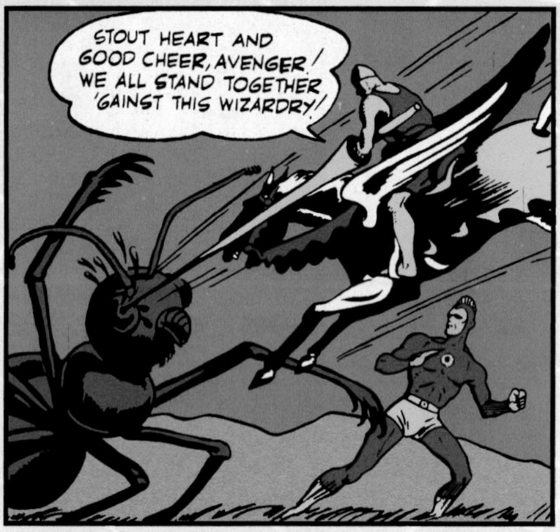
STOUT HEART AND GOOD CHEER, AVENGER! WE ALL STAND TOGETHER 'GAINST THIS WIZARDRY!

The evil Black Star acquired five rare elements that he used to create a black light enlarging ray. Attempting to storm his stronghold, the Seven Soldiers faced ants, spiders, sparrows, and even rabbits turned into monstrous giants.

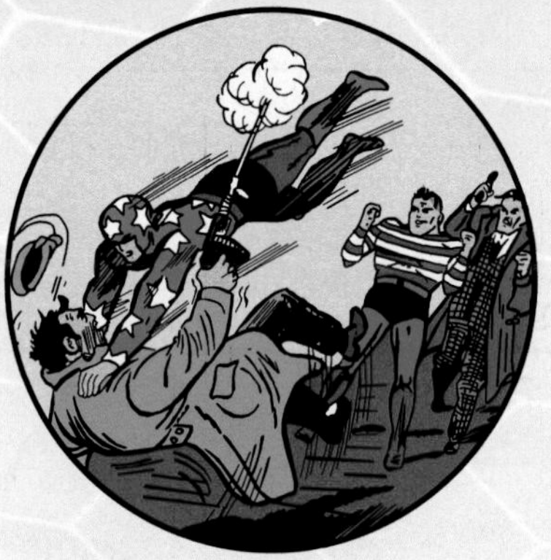

In a reversal of the usual dynamic, the teenaged Star-Spangled Kid called the shots while the adult Stripesy served as the sidekick.

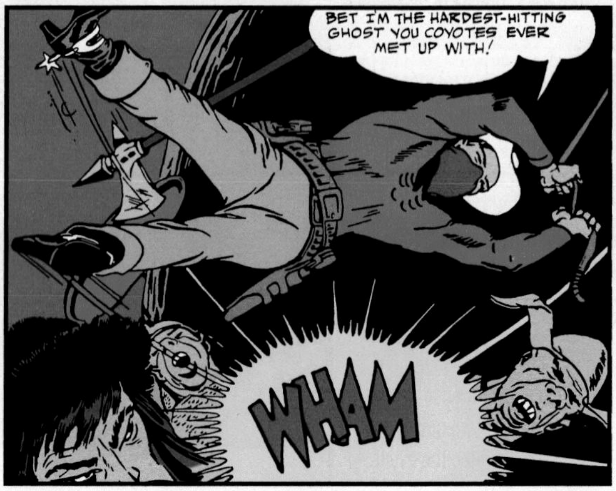
BET I'M THE HARDEST-HITTING GHOST YOU COYOTES EVER MET UP WITH!
WHAM

The Vigilante swooped in on Attila the Hun and his soldiers, who had been brought to the present by mad scientist Dr. Doome, along with Napoleon, Alexander the Great, Nero, and Genghis Khan. Dr. Doome promised them a future in which they could rule as kings, but the Seven Soldiers foiled his plans.

CONVERGENCE

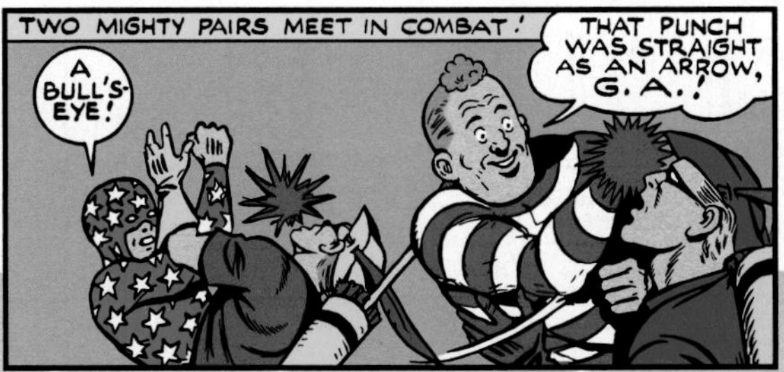
TWO MIGHTY PAIRS MEET IN COMBAT!
A BULL'S-EYE!
THAT PUNCH WAS STRAIGHT AS AN ARROW, G.A.!

Teammates were turned into enemies on a quest to find a billion-dollar gold treasure due to the trickery of a rival treasure-seeker. Each thought the other was trying to kill him. After discovering they'd been deceived, the team worked together to find the treasure, which they donated to the U.S. war effort.

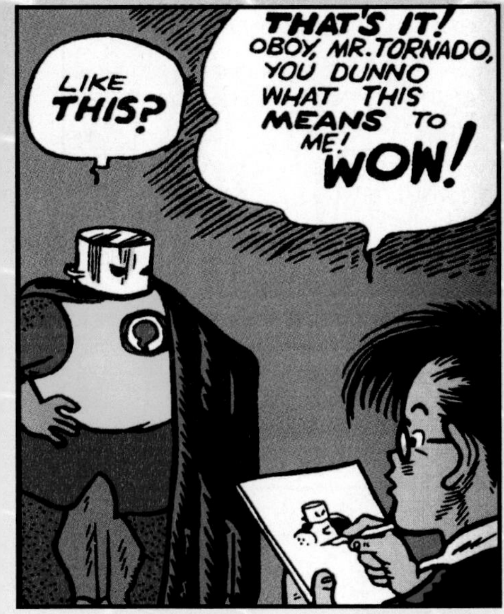
LIKE THIS?
THAT'S IT! OBOY, MR. TORNADO, YOU DUNNO WHAT THIS MEANS TO ME! WOW!

Decades after the Seven Soldiers were long gone and forgotten, Oracle told the Justice Society and Justice League what had happened to the team. In a battle against the Nebula-Man, the Seven Soldiers were scattered throughout time and all memory of their existence wiped from the world's minds. In order to stop the Iron Hand from destroying Earth-Two, Oracle tasked the Justice Society and Justice League to find the Seven Soldiers.

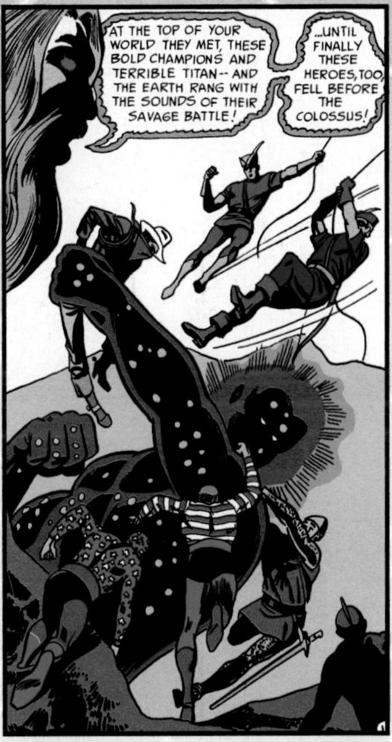
AT THE TOP OF YOUR WORLD THEY MET, THESE BOLD CHAMPIONS AND TERRIBLE TITAN-- AND THE EARTH RANG WITH THE SOUNDS OF THEIR SAVAGE BATTLE!
...UNTIL FINALLY THESE HEROES, TOO, FELL BEFORE THE COLOSSUS!

Shortly before the Seven Soldiers debuted, a young aspiring cartoonist named Scribbly Jibbet had his big career break, drawing mysterious new hero Red Tornado for the local newspaper. Unbeknownst to him, the Red Tornado was his neighbor Abigail "Ma" Hunkel.

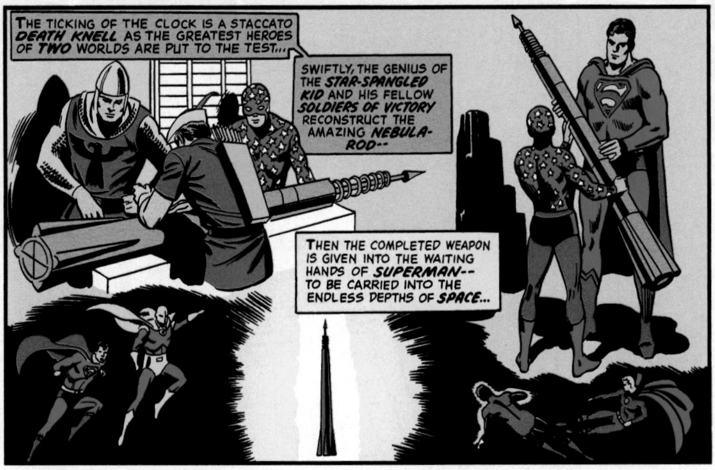
THE TICKING OF THE CLOCK IS A STACCATO DEATH KNELL AS THE GREATEST HEROES OF TWO WORLDS ARE PUT TO THE TEST...
SWIFTLY, THE GENIUS OF THE STAR-SPANGLED KID AND HIS FELLOW SOLDIERS OF VICTORY RECONSTRUCT THE AMAZING NEBULA-ROD--
THEN THE COMPLETED WEAPON IS GIVEN INTO THE WAITING HANDS OF SUPERMAN-- TO BE CARRIED INTO THE ENDLESS DEPTHS OF SPACE...

Reunited in the present day, the Seven Soldiers quickly assembled a Nebula-Rod, the device needed to disarm the Iron Hand's world-threatening weapon. Whoever wielded the Nebula-Rod would die in the process. While members of the team debated who would go, the android Red Tornado slipped away with the Nebula-Rod to do what needed to be done.

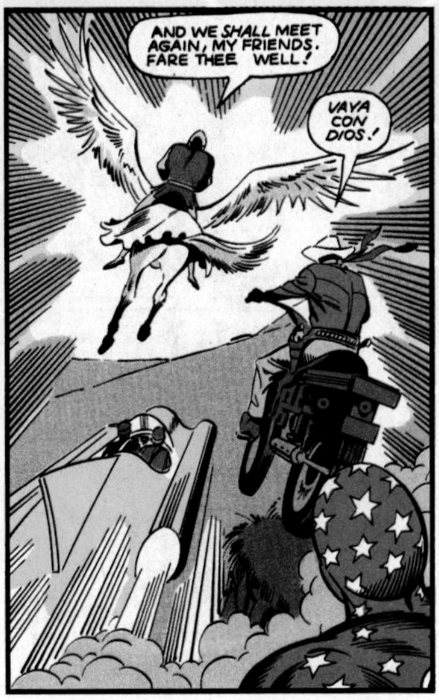
AND WE SHALL MEET AGAIN, MY FRIENDS. FARE THEE WELL!
VAYA CON DIOS!

The Seven Soldiers of Victory disbanded soon after. Each of them set out to become acclimated to a world greatly changed in the years since they were lost in time.

CONVERGENCE: JUSTICE SOCIETY OF AMERICA #1

LAYOUTS BY TOM DERENICK

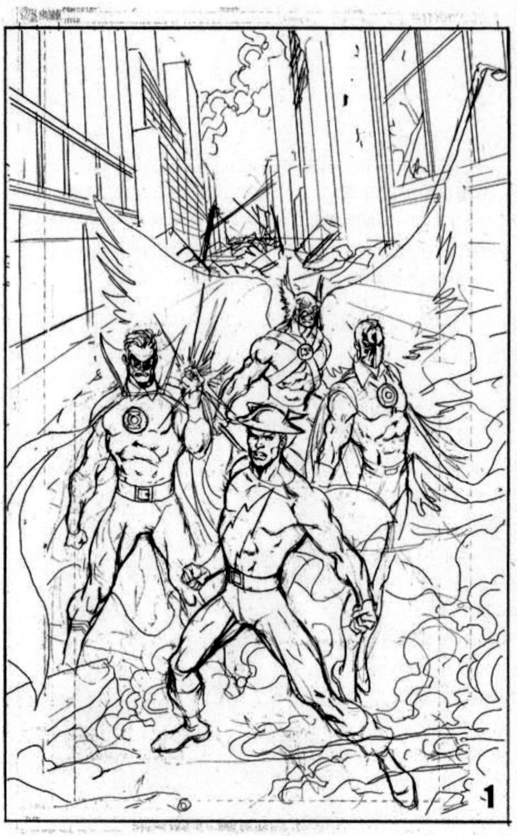

1

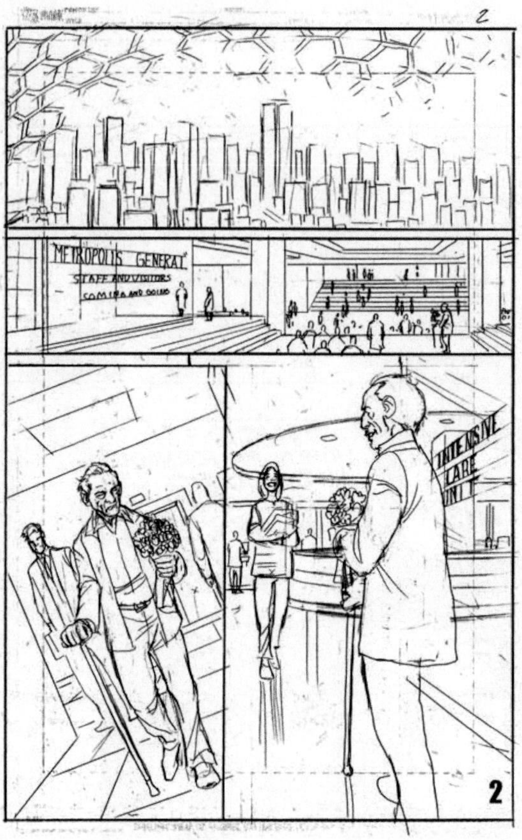
METROPOLIS GENERAL
STAFF AND VISITORS
INTENSIVE CARE UNIT

2

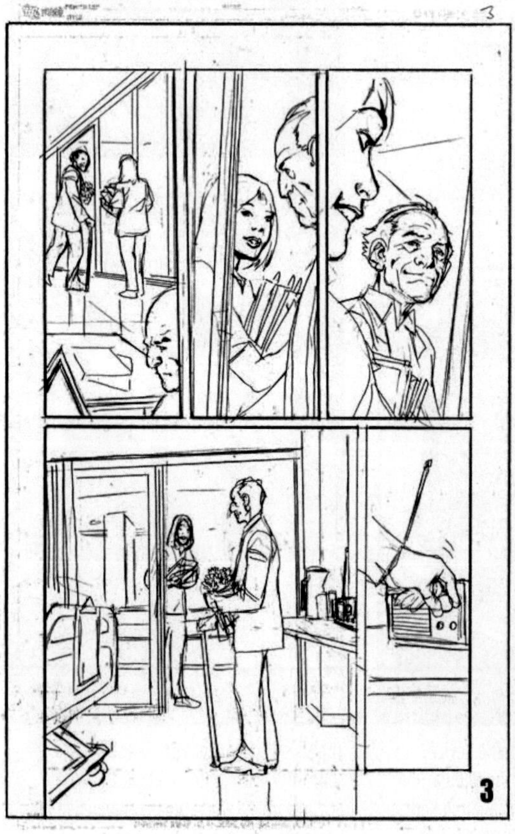

3

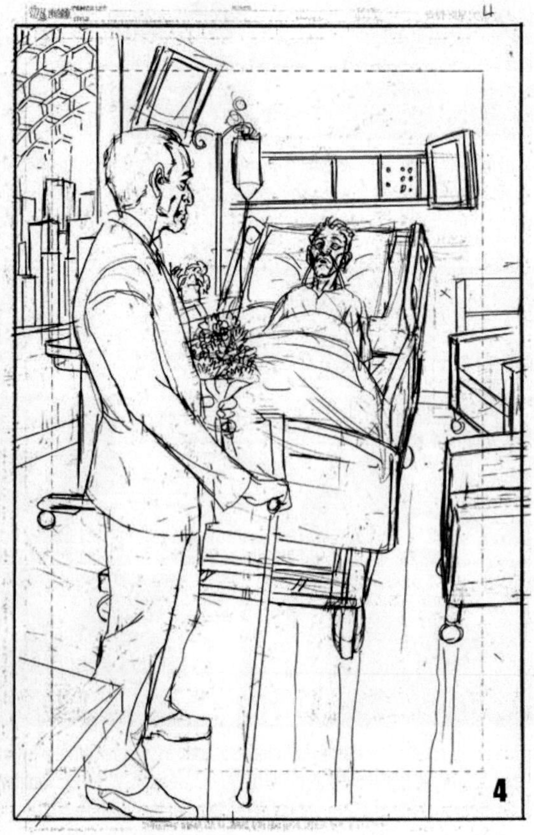

4

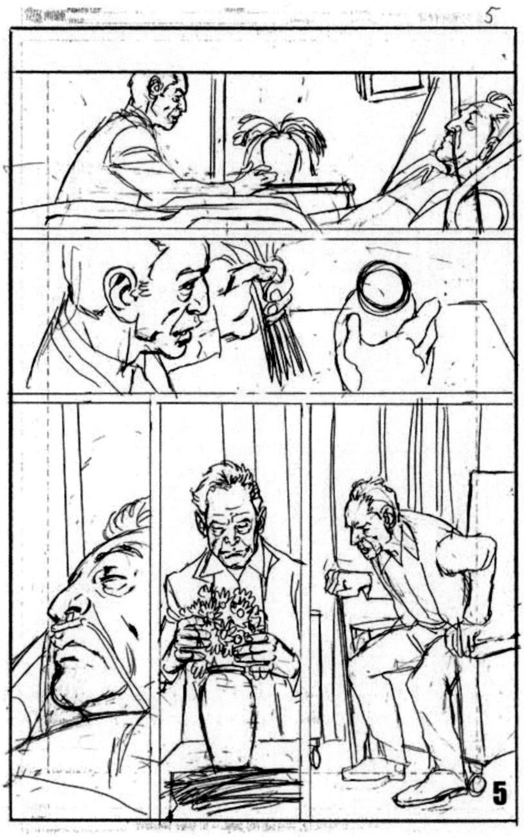
5

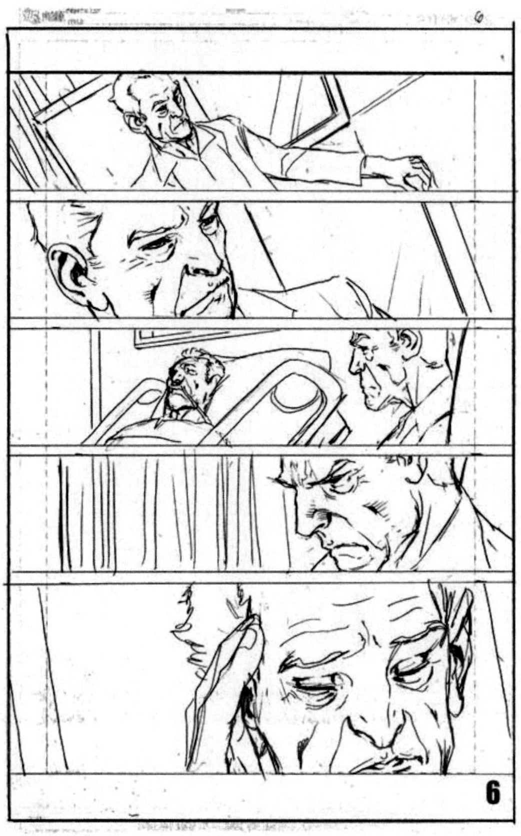
6

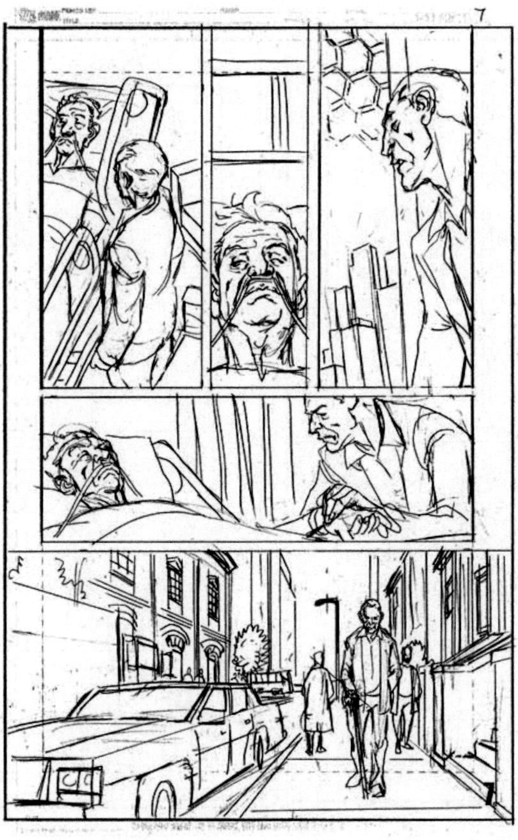
7

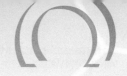

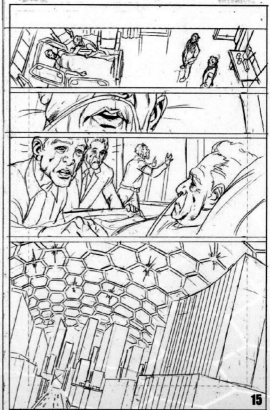

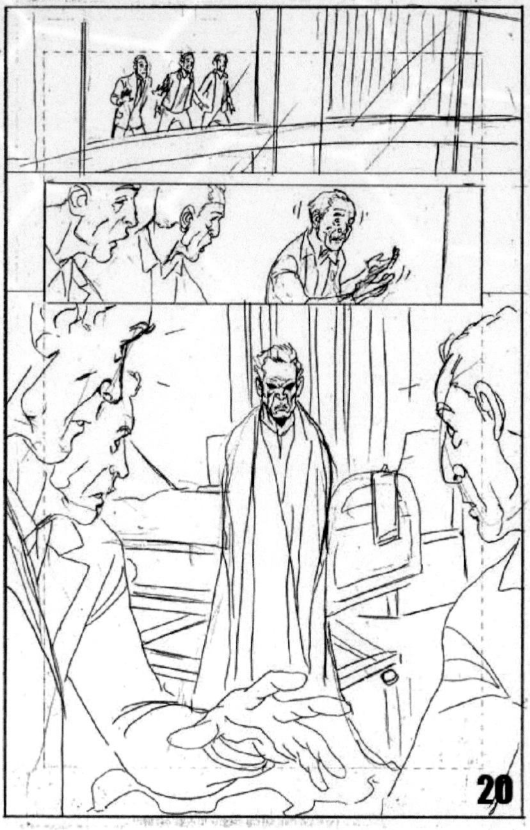
20

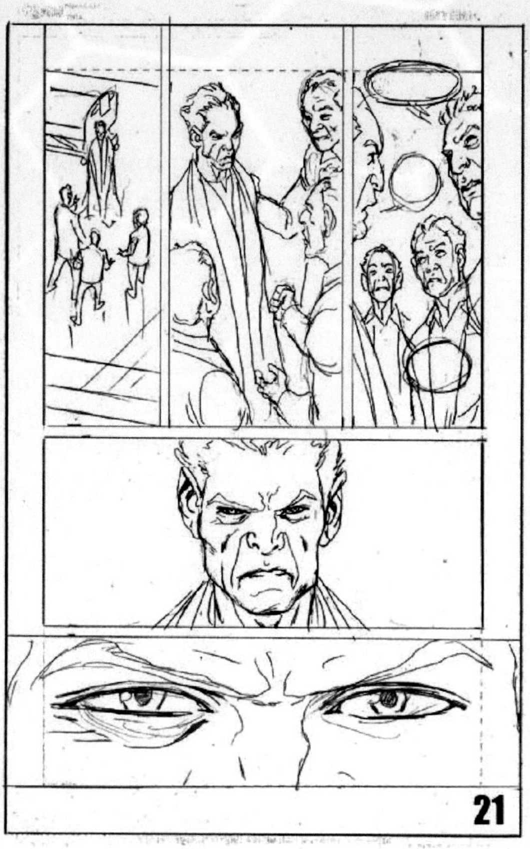
21

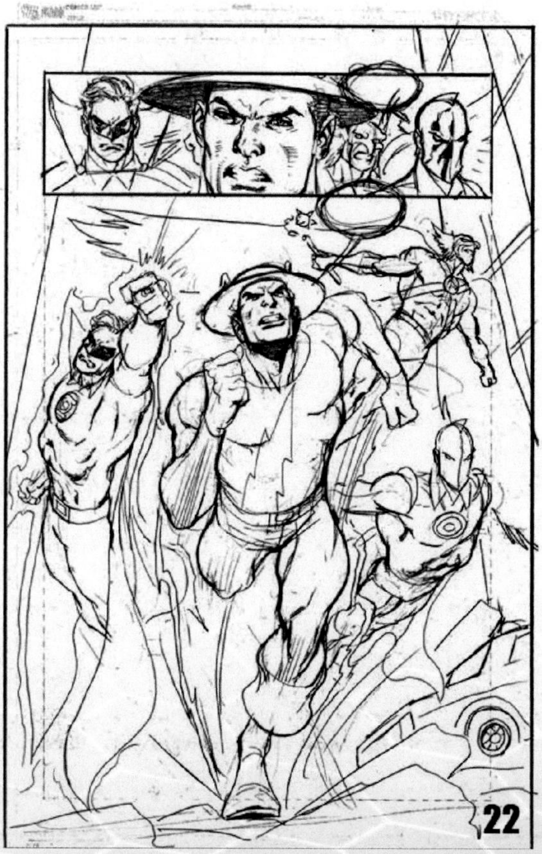
22

CONVERGENCE: INFINITY INC.
COVER SKETCHES BY BEN CALDWELL

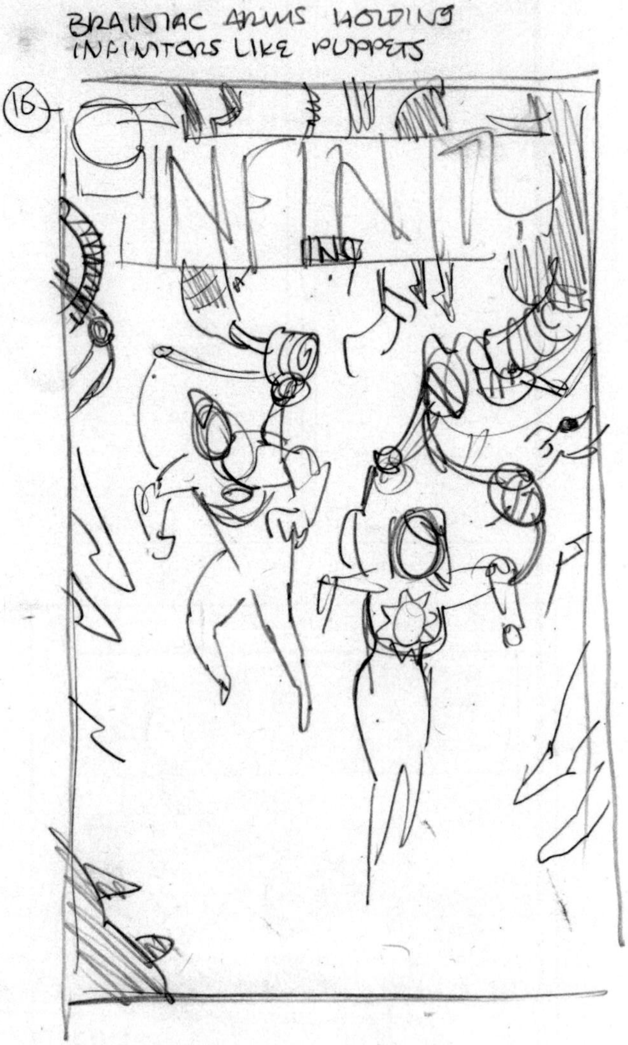
BRAINIAC ARMS HOLDING
INFINITORS LIKE PUPPETS
16
INFINITY
INC

INFINITORS AND HEXES IN CHESS BATTLE

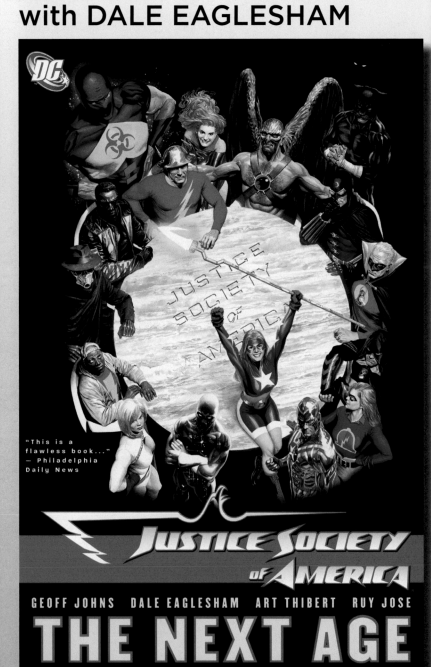

"This is your go-to book."—ENTERTAINMENT WEEKLY

"DETECTIVE COMICS is head-spinningly spectacular from top to bottom."—MTV GEEK

START AT THE BEGINNING!

BATMAN: DETECTIVE COMICS VOLUME 1: FACES OF DEATH

BATMAN: DETECTIVE COMICS VOL. 2: SCARE TACTICS

BATMAN: DETECTIVE COMICS VOL. 3: EMPEROR PENGUIN

THE JOKER: DEATH OF THE FAMILY

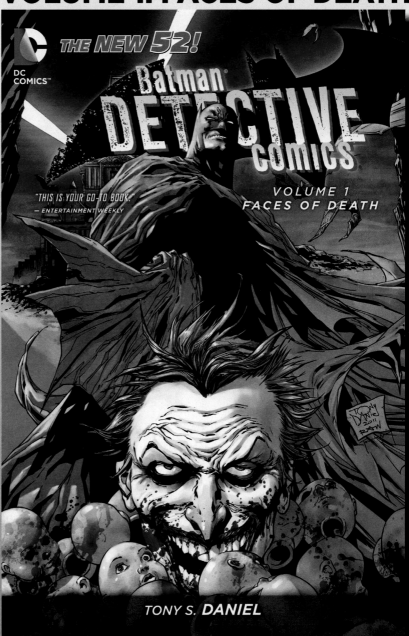

TONY S. **DANIEL**

"ACTION COMICS has successfully carved it
own territory and continued exploring Morrison'
familiar themes about heroism and ideas."—IGN

"Casts the character in a new light, opens up fresh storytell
ing possibilities, and pushes it all forward with dynamic Rag
Morales art. I loved it."—THE ONION/AV CLUB

START AT THE BEGINNING!

SUPERMAN: ACTION COMICS VOLUME 1:
SUPERMAN AND THE MEN OF STEEL

**SUPERMAN:
ACTION COMICS
VOL. 2: BULLETPROOF**

with GRANT
MORRISON and RAGS
MORALES

**SUPERMAN: ACTION
COMICS VOL. 3: AT
THE END OF DAYS**

with GRANT
MORRISON and RAGS
MORALES

**SUPERBOY VOL. 1:
INCUBATION**

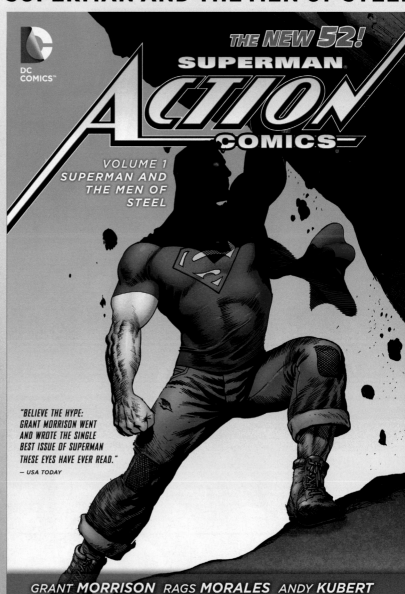